EDUCATIONAL RESEARCH

COMPETENCIES FOR ANALYSIS AND APPLICATION

FIFTH EDITION

Research is a creative and scholarly endeavor . . .

FIFTH EDITION

EDUCATIONAL RESEARCH
COMPETENCIES FOR ANALYSIS AND APPLICATION

L. R. GAY
Florida International University

Merrill
an imprint of Prentice Hall

Upper Saddle River, New Jersey   Columbus, Ohio

Library of Congress Cataloging-in-Publication Data
Gay, L. R.
    Educational research : competencies for analysis and application /
L. R. Gay. — 5th ed.
        p.   cm.
    Includes bibliographical references and index.
    ISBN 0-02-340814-6
    1. Education—Research.   I. Title.
LB1028.G37   1996
370'.78—dc20   95-16730
                                                                                       CIP

Cover Image: P. Degginger/H. Armstrong Roberts
Editor: Kevin M. Davis
Developmental Editor: Carol S. Sykes
Production Editor: Julie Anderson Tober
Production, Design, and Photo Coordination: Proof Positive/Farrowlyne Associates, Inc.
Cover Design: Brian Deep
Production Manager: Patricia A. Tonneman
Illustrations: Proof Positive/Farrowlyne Associates, Inc.

This book was set in Garamond Light by Proof Positive/Farrowlyne Associates, Inc. and
was printed and bound by R.R. Donnelly & Sons Company. The cover was printed by
Phoenix Color Corp.

© 1996 by Prentice-Hall, Inc.
A Simon & Schuster Company
Upper Saddle River, New Jersey 07458

Earlier editions © 1992 by Macmillan Publishing Company; © 1987, 1981, 1976 by Merrill
Publishing Company.

Printed in the United States of America

10 9 8 7 6 5 4

ISBN: 0-02-340814-6

Prentice-Hall International (UK) Limited, *London*
Prentice-Hall of Australia Pty. Limited, *Sydney*
Prentice-Hall of Canada, Inc., *Toronto*
Prentice-Hall Hispanoamericana, S. A., *Mexico*
Prentice-Hall of India Private Limited, *New Delhi*
Prentice-Hall of Japan, Inc., *Tokyo*
Simon & Schuster Asia Pte. Ltd., *Singapore*
Editora Prentice-Hall do Brasil, Ltda., *Rio de Janeiro*

TO DOTTIE. . .

P R E F A C E

PHILOSOPHY AND PURPOSE

This text is designed primarily for use in the introductory course in educational research that is a basic requirement for many graduate degrees. Since the topic coverage is relatively comprehensive, however, this book may be easily adapted for use in either a senior-level undergraduate course or a more advanced graduate-level course.

The philosophy that guided the development of the current and previous editions of this text was the conviction that an introductory research course should be skill oriented, rather than knowledge oriented, and application oriented, rather than theory oriented. Thus the purpose of this book is *not* to have students become familiar with research, understand research, or acquire a body of knowledge, per se. The purpose of this book is *not* to mystify students with theoretical and statistical jargon. The purpose of this book is *not* to have students acquire in-depth understanding of theory. The purpose of this book *is* to aid students in the acquisition of the skills and knowledge required of a competent consumer and producer of educational research, primarily the former; the emphasis is not on what the student knows, but rather on what the student can do with what he or she knows. It is recognized that being a "good" researcher involves more than the acquisition of skills and knowledge; in any field, significant research is usually produced by persons who through experience have acquired insights, intuitions, and strategies related to the research process. Research of any worth, however, is rarely conducted in the absence of basic research skills and knowledge. Further, a basic assumption of this text is that there is considerable overlap in the competencies required of a competent consumer of research and a competent producer of research, and that a person is in a much better position to evaluate the work of others after she or he has performed the major tasks involved in the research process.

■ ORGANIZATION AND STRATEGY

The overall strategy of the text is to promote attainment of a degree of expertise in research through the acquisition of knowledge and by involvement in the research process.

Organization

Part One discuss the scientific method and its application in education, and the major characteristics of the various types of research, in terms of purpose and method. In Part Two, each student selects and delineates a research problem of interest that has relevance to his or her professional area. In Part Two, and in succeeding Parts, the student then simulates the procedures that would be followed in conducting a study designed to investigate the problem; each Part develops a specific skill or set of skills required for the execution of a research study. Specifically, the student reviews and analyzes related literature and formulates hypotheses (Part Two), develops a research plan (Part Three), selects and defines samples (Part Four), evaluates and selects measuring instruments (Part Five), selects an experimental design and delineates experimental procedures (Part Six), statistically analyzes data (Part Seven), and prepares a research report (Part Eight). In Part Nine the student applies the skills and knowledge acquired in Parts One through Eight and evaluates a research report.

Strategy

This book represents more than just a textbook to be incorporated into a course; it is actually a total instructional system that includes stated objectives, or competencies, instruction, and procedures for evaluation of each competency. The instructional strategy of the system emphasizes demonstration of skills and individualization within structure. The format for each Part is essentially the same. Following a brief introduction, each task to be performed is described. Tasks require students to demonstrate that they can perform particular research functions. Since each student works with a different problem, each student demonstrates the competency required by a task as it applies to her or his problem. With the exception of Part One, each Part is directed toward the attainment of one task, and the text discussion of chapters within each Part relates to that task. Each chapter begins with a list of chapter objectives which entail knowledge and skills that facilitate students' ability to perform a related task. In many instances objectives may be evaluated either as written exercises submitted by students or by tests, whichever the instructor prefers. For some objectives the first option is clearly preferable. Text discussion is intended to be as simple and straightforward as possible. Whenever feasible, procedures are presented as a series of steps and concepts are explained in terms of illustrative examples. In a number of cases, relatively complex topics or topics beyond the scope of the text are presented at a very elementary level and students are directed to other sources for additional, in-depth discussion. There is also a degree of intentional repetition; a number of concepts are discussed in different contexts and from different perspectives. Also, at the risk of eliciting more than a few groans, an *attempt* has been made to sprinkle the text with touches of humor. Each chapter includes a detailed, often lengthy, summary with headings and subheadings directly paralleling those in the chapter. The summaries are designed to facilitate both review and location of related text discussion. Finally, each Part concludes with suggested criteria for elevation of the task, and an example of the task produced by a former introductory educational research student.

To the degree possible with a textbook, e.g., with respect to tables, figures, references, and student examples of tasks, this text reflects the guidelines of the *Publication Manual of the American Psychological Association*.

■ MAJOR REVISIONS

Like the fourth edition, the fifth edition reflects a combination of both unsolicited and solicited input. Positive feedback suggested aspects of the text and supplementary materials that should *not* be changed, the writing style for example. Every effort, however, was made to incorporate suggestions, even if made by only a few persons. For example, several users requested a table for determining sample size for survey research. I am indebted to everyone who took the time to send a letter or complete a feedback form.

Content changes reflect the inclusion of new topics, the expansion of existing topics, or the clarification of existing topics. A number of new tables, figures, and photos have been added, and references and examples have been updated to reflect current research trends. While all Parts have been revised to some degree, some of the highlights are described below.

Part One

Part One has been revised to reflect the inclusion of qualitative research as a major type of research. For example, types of research have been classified as representing either a qualitative approach (i.e., historical research and qualitative research) or a quantitative approach (i.e., descriptive research, correlational research, causal-comparative research, and experimental research).

Part Two

Two new tables have been added; one of them contains basic instructions for doing an ERIC CD-ROM search, and the other provides examples of various types of references in fourth edition APA format.

Part Four

A table has been added which indicates the sample size needed for survey research, given a population of a given size, in order for a sample to be representative.

Part Five

Discussion has been revised to reflect publication of the *Eleventh Mental Measurements Yearbook*.

Part Six

A chapter on qualitative research has been added; it includes a table which presents the major characteristics which differentiate qualitative and quantitative research.

Also, at the end of the chapter for each type of research, an article representing that type of research is presented with accompanying brief commentary.

Part Seven

The chapter on using the computer has been deleted and a condensed, more generic version of the information has been included in the chapter on preanalysis considerations. Also, related STATPAK printouts have been included following presentation of the computational procedures for the various statistics.

Part Eight

A figure has been added which illustrates some basic, fourth edition APA guidelines for preparing a student paper.

Part Nine

Method-specific evaluation criteria (questions) for qualitative research have been added.

Supplements

The student guide has been updated to include more recent journal articles and student examples. Test items have been added to the instructor's manual to reflect text additions and expansions, in particular, questions related to qualitative research.

■ SUPPLEMENTARY MATERIALS

A student guide, an instructor's manual, and statistical software are available for use with this text. For each Part in the text there is a corresponding Part in the student guide and instructor's manual.

Student Guide

The *Student Guide* contains examples, exercises, and suggested responses. Part One contains reprints of a number of journal articles representing each of the types of research discussed in the text (e.g., correlational research). In consonance with Part One in the text, students are asked to analyze each article in terms of study components (e.g., the problem) and types of research. In Parts Two through Eight, examples of tasks based on work submitted by previous students are presented, as well as a number of self-test exercises. Whenever feasible, exercises are application oriented; given independent and dependent variables, for example, the student is asked to write the corresponding hypotheses. Part Nine presents a journal article reprint and a detailed form for evaluating the research reported.

Instructor's Manual

The *Instructor's Manual* contains suggestions and test items. General suggestions are given regarding evaluation of tasks and chapter objectives, and specific suggestions regarding instructional strategies are given for each Part. Suggestions are based on personal experience teaching the course, feedback from text users, and research. In addition, over 500 test items are presented representing a variety of item types, primarily multiple-choice.

Statistical Software

STATPAK is available in PC-compatible, IBM, and Macintosh versions. STATPAK is menu-driven and extremely user-friendly. It computes all of the statistics which are calculated in the text and shows students the intermediate stages as well as the final answers.

■ SPECIAL ACKNOWLEDGMENTS

Words cannot express my immense appreciation for Sara Jane Calderin's assistance in the preparation of this edition. Without her conscientiousness, caring, and creativity, my task would have been exponentially more difficult. Thank you, Jane.

I also sincerely thank everyone who provided input for the development of this edition, including the following reviewers: John E. Bonfadini, George Mason University; J. Kent Davis, Purdue University; Ayres D'Costa, The Ohio State University; Jo D. Gallagher, Florida International University; Paul J. Staskey, Northern Arizona University; and Kenneth W. Wunderlich, University of Texas at San Antonio.

But especially, I thank John Bonfadini; Steven Brown, Northeastern Illinois University; Jo Gallagher; and Daryle Morgan, Texas A & M University, for taking the time to generously share their thoughts and/or their work. Jo, thank you *very* much.

Finally, at the risk of sounding effusive, I wholeheartedly thank my Merrill editors, Kevin Davis and Carol Sykes, and Lynn Metzger, editorial assistant. They were *always* responsive, supportive, and caring. Kevin, I think you know that without your support this edition could not have been completed in this decade.

L. R. Gay

BRIEF CONTENTS

CONTENTS

PART EIGHT

Research Reports   **537**

TABLES AND FIGURES

▦ TABLES

■ FIGURES

EDUCATIONAL RESEARCH
COMPETENCIES FOR ANALYSIS AND APPLICATION

FIFTH EDITION

PART ONE

Introduction

If you are taking a research course because it is required in your program of studies, raise your right hand. If you are taking a research course because it seemed like it would be a real fun elective, raise your left hand. When you have stopped laughing, read on. No, you are not the innocent victim of one or more sadists. There are several very legitimate reasons why decision makers believe your research course is an essential component of your education.

First, educational research findings significantly contribute to both educational theory and educational practice. The effectiveness of behavior modification techniques, for example, has repeatedly been demonstrated. It is important that you, as a professional, know how to access, understand, and evaluate such findings.

Second, you are constantly exposed to research findings, whether you seek them out or not, which are presented in professional publications and, increasingly, by the media. Reasons for lack of adequate student achievement and proposed remedies, for example, are recurrent themes. As a professional, you have a responsibility to be able to distinguish between legitimate claims and conclusions and ill-founded ones.

And third, believe it or not, research courses are a fruitful source of future researchers. A number of the author's students have become sufficiently intrigued with the research process to pursue further education and careers in the field. In fact, the author of this text was once a high school math teacher who decided to obtain a master's degree in math education. The first course required in the program was the dreaded research course. The rest, as they say, is history. A major advantage of a career in research is the wide variety of employment opportunities available. As the membership of the American Educational Research Association reflects, educational researchers work in such diverse settings as colleges and universities, research and development centers, federal and state agencies, public and private school systems, and business and industry.

It is recognized that for most of you educational research is probably a relatively unfamiliar discipline. Therefore, in order to meaningfully learn about and perform components of the research process, it is first necessary for you to develop a cognitive structure into which such experiences can be integrated.

Therefore, the goal of Part One is for you to acquire an understanding of research process and strategy which will facilitate acquisition of specific research knowledge and skills. In succeeding parts, specific components of the research process will be systematically studied and executed. After you have read Part One, you should be able to perform the following tasks.

■ TASK 1-A

Given a reprint of a research study, identify and briefly state:

(a) the problem (purpose of the study),
(b) the procedures,
(c) the method of analysis, and
(d) the major conclusions.

(See Performance Criteria, pp. 24).

■ TASK 1-B

Given reprints of three research studies, classify each as historical, qualitative, descriptive, correlational, causal-comparative, or experimental research and list the characteristics of each study which support the classification chosen.

(See Performance Criteria, pp. 24–25).

CHAPTER 1

"Despite a popular stereotype that depicts researchers as spectacled, stoop-shouldered, elderly gentlemen who endlessly add chemicals to test tubes, every day thousands of men and women of all ages, shapes, and sizes conduct educational research in a wide variety of settings (p. 7)."

Introduction to Educational Research

OBJECTIVES

After reading Chapter 1, you should be able to:

1. List and briefly describe the major steps involved in conducting a research study.

2. Select one article from a recent issue of *The Journal of Educational Research* and one from a research journal in your professional area. For each article, identify and state (or photocopy, identify, and underline):
   (a) the problem,
   (b) the procedures,
   (c) the method of analysis, and
   (d) the major conclusion.
   (Note: 1962 is not recent!)

3. Briefly define and state the major characteristics of each of the six types of research, i.e., historical, qualitative, descriptive, correlational, causal-comparative, and experimental.

4. For each of the six types of research, briefly describe three possible research studies.

   Example:
   Experimental—A study to determine the effect of peer tutoring on the computational skill of third graders.

THE SCIENTIFIC METHOD

The goal of all scientific endeavors is to explain, predict, and/or control phenomena. This goal is based on the assumption that all behaviors and events are

5

orderly and that they are effects which have discoverable causes. Progress toward this goal involves acquisition of knowledge and the development and testing of theories. The existence of a viable theory greatly facilitates scientific progress by simultaneously explaining many phenomena. Compared to other sources of knowledge, such as experience, authority, inductive reasoning, and deductive reasoning, application of the scientific method is undoubtedly the most efficient and reliable. Some of the problems associated with experience and authority as sources of knowledge are graphically illustrated by a story told about Aristotle. According to the story, one day Aristotle caught a fly and carefully counted and recounted the legs. He then announced that flies have five legs. No one questioned the word of Aristotle. For years his finding was uncritically accepted. Of course, the fly that Aristotle caught just happened to be missing a leg! Whether or not you believe the story, it does illustrate the limitations of relying on personal experience and authority as sources of knowledge.

Both inductive and deductive reasoning are also of limited value when used exclusively. Inductive reasoning involves formulation of generalizations based on observation of a limited number of specific events.

> **Example:** Every research textbook examined contains a
> chapter on sampling.
> Therefore, all research textbooks contain a
> chapter on sampling.

Deductive reasoning involves essentially the reverse process, arriving at specific conclusions based on generalizations.

> **Example:** All research textbooks contain a chapter on
> sampling.
> This book is a research text.
> Therefore, this book contains a chapter on
> sampling. (Does it?)

Although neither approach is entirely satisfactory, when used together as integral components of the scientific method, they are very effective. Basically, the scientific method involves induction of hypotheses based on observation, deduction of implications of the hypotheses, testing of the implications, and confirmation or disconfirmation of the hypotheses.

The scientific method is a very orderly process entailing a number of sequential steps: recognition and definition of the problem; formulation of hypotheses; collection of data; analysis of data; and statement of conclusions regarding confirmation or disconfirmation of the hypotheses. These steps can be applied informally in the solution of everyday problems such as the most efficient route to take from home to work or school, the best time to go to the drive-in window at the bank, or the best kind of microcomputer to purchase. The more formal application of the scientific method to the solution of problems is what research is all about.

■ APPLICATION OF THE SCIENTIFIC METHOD IN EDUCATION

Research is the formal, systematic application of the scientific method to the study of problems; educational research is the formal, systematic application of the scientific method to the study of educational problems. The goal of educational research follows from the goal of all science, namely, to explain, predict, and/or control educational phenomena. The major difference between educational research and other scientific research is the nature of the phenomena studied. It is considerably more difficult to explain, predict, and control situations involving human beings, by far the most complex of all organisms. There are so many variables, known and unknown, operating in any educational environment that it is extremely difficult to generalize or replicate findings. The kinds of rigid controls that can be established and maintained in a biochemistry laboratory are virtually impossible in an educational setting. Observation is also more difficult in educational research. Observers may be subjective in recording behaviors, and persons observed may behave atypically just because they are being observed; chemical reactions tend to be oblivious to the fact that they are being observed! Precise measurement is also considerably more difficult in educational research. Most measurement must be indirect; there are no instruments comparable to a barometer for measuring intelligence, achievement, or attitude. Note that the purpose of research is *not* to make a case in favor of a belief—that is what position papers are for—or to prove a point.

Perhaps it is precisely the difficulty and complexity of educational research that makes it such a challenging and exciting field. Despite a popular stereotype that depicts researchers as spectacled, stoop-shouldered, elderly gentlemen who endlessly add chemicals to test tubes, every day thousands of men and women of all ages, shapes, and sizes conduct educational research in a wide variety of settings. Every year many millions of dollars are spent in the quest for knowledge related to the teaching-learning process. Educational research has contributed many findings concerning principles of behavior, learning, and retention. In addition, significant contributions have been made related to curriculum, instruction, instructional materials, design, measurement, and analysis. Both the quantity and quality of research are increasing. This is partly because of better trained researchers. In fact, a great many graduate education programs, in such diverse areas as physical education, art education, and English education, require a course in research for all students.

The steps involved in conducting research should look familiar since they directly parallel those of the scientific method:

1. *Selection and definition of a problem.* A problem is a hypothesis or question of interest to education which can be tested or answered through the collection and analysis of data.
2. *Execution of research procedures.* The procedures reflect all the activities involved in collecting data related to the problem, e.g., how data were collected and from whom. The design of the study dictates to a great extent the specific procedures involved in the study.
3. *Analysis of data.* Data analysis usually involves application of one or more statistical techniques; data are analyzed in a way that permits the researcher to test the research hypothesis or answer the research question. For some studies, data analysis involves verbal synthesis of narrative data; these studies typically share resulting insights and/or generate hypotheses.
4. *Drawing and stating conclusions.* The conclusions are based on the results of data analysis. They should be stated in terms of the original hypothesis or question. Conclusions should indicate, for example, whether the research hypothesis was supported or not. For studies involving verbal synthesis, conclusions are much more tentative.

This text focuses on studies which collect numerical data in order to test hypotheses. Such studies are referred to as quantitative. Studies which collect narrative data in order to gain insights or generate hypotheses are referred to as qualitative. These concepts will be discussed shortly. As you read on, keep in mind that the discussion is quantitative-oriented, and does not necessarily apply to qualitative studies.

In a quantitative research report, such as a published article in a journal, the above steps (1–4) should be readily evident if the report is well written. The problem will generally be presented in statements which begin with phrases like "the purpose of this study was to . . ." and "it was hypothesized that. . . ." The procedures section of a report may be quite lengthy and detailed, but there are certain major steps which can be identified, such as the number and characteristics of the subjects (the sample), a description of the measuring instruments including when they were administered (e.g., whether there was a pretest) and a description of treatment groups, if appropriate. Data analysis techniques are usually easy to identify; they will generally be presented in statements which include phrases like "data were analyzed using . . ." or "a . . . was used to analyze the data." Conclusions are usually labeled as such. While many conclusions may be presented, at least one of them should relate directly to the original hypothesis or question. Statements such as "it was concluded that more research is needed in this area" are fine but certainly do not represent *the* major conclusion of the study. More research is *always* needed!

Research studies can be classified in a number of ways. Two major ways are to classify by degree of applicability and generalizability to educational settings (basic versus applied research) and to classify by general and specific approach to inquiry (qualitative versus quantitative research and related subtypes). Approach to inquiry refers to the overall strategy followed in collecting and analyzing data; this strategy is referred to as the research design. For a given general approach there are a number of different ways in which subtypes can be classified. The classification scheme used in this text identifies six distinct types, or kinds, of research: historical, qualitative, descriptive, correlational, causal-comparative, and experimental.

■ BASIC VERSUS APPLIED RESEARCH

It is difficult to discuss basic and applied research separately, as they are really on a continuum. Classification of a given study along this continuum is based primarily on the degree to which findings have direct educational application and the degree to which they are generalizable to other educational situations. Both of these criteria are a function of the research control exercised during the execution of the study. Basic research, either directly or indirectly, involves the development of theory; applied research is concerned with the application of theory to the solution of problems.

There is disagreement among educators and researchers concerning toward which end of the basic-applied continuum research should be directed. In its purest form, basic research is conducted solely for the purpose of theory development and refinement. It is not concerned with practical applicability and most closely resembles the laboratory conditions and controls usually associated with scientific research. Applied research, as the name implies, is conducted for the purpose of applying, or testing, theory and evaluating its usefulness in solving educational problems. Rightly or wrongly, most educational research studies would be classified at the applied end of the continuum; they are more concerned with "what" works best than with "why." Basic research is concerned with establishing general principles of learning; applied research is concerned with their utility in educational settings. For example, much basic research has been conducted with animals to determine principles of reinforcement and their effect on learning. Applied research has tested these principles to determine their effectiveness in improving learning (e.g., programmed microcomputer instruction) and behavior (e.g., behavior modification). Some studies, those located in the middle of the continuum, try to integrate both approaches by conducting controlled research in special or simulated classrooms, using school children, and involving school-relevant topics and materials. Both types of research are necessary. Basic research provides the theory that produces the implications for solving educational problems; applied research provides data to support theory, guide theory revision, or suggest development of new theory.

At the "most" applied end of the continuum there are several kinds of research worthy of special note: evaluation research, research and development (R & D), and action research. Evaluation research involves decision making regarding the relative worth of two or more alternative decisions; research and development is directed at the development of products that can be used in the schools; and action research is concerned with immediate solutions to real problems.

Evaluation Research

Evaluation is the systematic process of collecting and analyzing data in order to make decisions. Evaluation involves questions such as the following:

1. Is this special program worth what it costs?
2. Is the new, experimental reading curriculum better than the former curriculum?
3. Should Fenster be placed in a program for the gifted?

Answers to these questions require the collection and analysis of data and interpretation of that data with respect to one or more criteria. While generally the more objective the criteria and data the better, some degree of subjectivity is unavoidable since how people *feel* is often an important variable. For example, whether a new, experimental curriculum is "better" depends on the criteria for success. One obvious criterion would be student achievement. Other criteria might include student attitudes and teacher attitudes. Examination of test scores might reveal that students averaged 2 points higher with the new curriculum. Objectively, and strictly speaking, the new curriculum was "better" with respect to student achievement. School administrators, however, may have decided that an achievement difference of at least 10 points would be necessary in order to justify the time, effort, and cost required to change over to the new curriculum. Further, teachers may have expressed the opinion that the new curriculum is burdensome, overly restrictive, and does not allow for any creativity in teaching. Similarly, determining whether Fenster meets the criteria for admittance to the program for the gifted (e.g., has a specific IQ score and grade point average) would be an objective process; setting the criteria themselves would be more subjective, as would teacher input.

Deciding whether a special program is "worth" what it costs is even more complex and typically involves serious value judgments. If a special program cost a school system $100,000 per school year but reduced school vandalism by the amount of $150,000, there would not be much disagreement concerning whether the program was worth what it cost. But what if a program cost $100,000 per school year and reduced the ninth-grade dropout rate by 5%? How much is an education worth? How much is it worth to have a child increasing his or her knowledge instead of roaming the streets or attempting to enter an already crowded job market? Opinion on this issue varies greatly. The philosophy of the current school board would probably determine whether or not the program continued.

Notice that in none of the examples was the purpose of the evaluation to determine whether something was "good," or worthwhile, as opposed to "bad," or worthless, per se. That is not the function of evaluation. The purpose of evaluation is to select an alternative in order to make a decision. There may be only two alternatives (e.g., continue the program or not, adopt the new curriculum or keep the current one) or there may be several alternatives (e.g., many textbooks may be available for adoption).

A major point of disagreement among researchers is the issue of whether evaluation is a type of research or a separate discipline. A related issue is whether evaluations should be based on research designs, particularly when group comparisons are involved such as: Does curriculum A lead to higher achievement than curriculum B? Some argue that educational research and educational evaluation have distinctly different purposes, that research seeks control while evaluation assesses what is, and that the natural settings characteristic of evaluation essentially preclude that control. In reality, however, there is a fine line between research and evaluation, and an evaluation may very easily utilize a research design. Both research and evaluation involve decision making and both involve steps which parallel those of the scientific method. Further, many research studies are conducted in natural, real-world settings and are subject to the same control problems involved in many evaluations. Thus, while the issue has not yet been resolved, the case seems stronger for classifying evaluation as a type of research whose purpose is to facilitate decision making.

Research and Development (R & D)

The major purpose of R & D efforts is not to formulate or test theory but to develop effective products for use in schools. Products produced by R & D efforts include: teacher-training materials, learning materials, sets of behavioral objectives, media materials, and management systems. R & D efforts are generally quite extensive in terms of objectives, personnel, and time to completion. Products are developed to meet specific needs and according to detailed specifications. Once completed, products are field-tested and revised until a prespecified level of effectiveness is achieved. Although the R & D cycle is an expensive one, it does result in quality products designed to meet educational needs. School personnel who are the consumers of R & D endeavors may for the first time really see the value of educational research.

Action Research

The purpose of action research is to solve practical problems through the application of the scientific method. It is concerned with a local problem and is conducted in a local setting. It is not concerned with whether the results are generalizable to any other setting and is not characterized by the same kind of control evident in other categories of research. The primary goal of action research is the solution of a given problem, not contribution to science. Whether the research is conducted in one classroom or in many classrooms, the teacher is very much a part of the process. The more research training the teachers involved have had, the more likely it is that the research will produce valid, if not generalizable, results.

The value of action research is confined primarily to those conducting it. Despite its shortcomings, it does represent a scientific approach to problem solving that is considerably better than change based on the alleged effectiveness of untried procedures, and infinitely better than no change at all. It is a means by which concerned school personnel can attempt to improve the educational process, at least within their environment. Of course, the value of action research to true scientific progress is limited. True progress requires the development of sound theories having implications for many classrooms, not just one or two. One sound theory that includes 10 principles of learning may eliminate the need for hundreds of would-be action research studies. Given the current status of educational theory, however, action research provides immediate answers to problems that cannot wait for theoretical solutions.

APPROACHES TO INQUIRY: QUALITATIVE VERSUS QUANTITATIVE

Although there is sometimes a degree of overlap, most research studies represent a readily identifiable approach, or strategy. All studies have certain procedures in common, such as data collection and analysis. Beyond these, however, specific procedures are to a high degree determined by the specific type of research involved. Each type is designed to answer a different kind of question. Knowledge of the various types, and the procedures involved in each, is important both for consumers and conductors of research. Even using type and related kind of question as a criterion, there are several different ways in which research studies can be classified, for example, experimental versus nonexperimental, or historical versus descriptive versus experimental. However, these alternatives tend to lump together studies entailing distinctly different research strategies. A classification scheme that appears to be the most efficient, in that it minimizes categories and maximizes differentiation, places all research studies into one of six categories representing two overall approaches to inquiry: 1) historical, 2) qualitative (qualitative approaches), 3) descriptive, 4) correlational, 5) causal-comparative, or 6) experimental (quantitative approaches). The purpose of the following explanations is to provide you with an overview so that you will at least be able to read a research report and, based on its procedures, determine which of the six types it represents. This competency is one which will aid you in reviewing the literature for the problem which you select in Part Two. Each type will be discussed further in Part Six.

The word "versus" in the above heading is not used in the oppositional sense but in the compare/contrast sense. The terms "qualitative" and "quantitative" are used not so much because they involve mutually exclusive, unique research strategies and methodologies, but rather because they conveniently differentiate one from the other. Depending upon the nature of the question or problem to be investigated, either a qualitative *or* quantitative approach will generally be more appropriate, although both may be utilized in the same study. While this text focuses primarily on quantitative approaches, qualitative approaches are discussed in Part Six in order to give you a sense as to how they differ; other texts focus primarily on qualitative approaches.

Qualitative approaches involve the collection of extensive *narrative* data in order to gain insights into phenomena of interest; data analysis includes the coding of the data and production of a verbal synthesis. Quantitative approaches involve the collection of *numerical* data in order to explain, predict, and/or control phenomena of interest; data analysis is mainly statistical. Thus, qualitative and quantitative approaches represent complementary components of the scientific method; qualitative approaches involve primarily induction while quantitative approaches involve primarily deduction. If hypotheses are involved, a qualitative study is much more likely to *generate* them whereas a quantitative study is much more likely to *test* them. At a very basic level, while qualitative researchers agree that there is no such thing as value-free inquiry, quantitative researchers try to be totally objective, i.e., value-free. At a more operational level, qualitative approaches are more holistic and process-oriented, whereas quantitative approaches are more focused and outcome-oriented. Qualitative researchers typically study many variables intensely over an extended period of time in order to find out the way things are (or were), how and why they came to be that way, and what it all means. The fact that they study only one or a few "units" (e.g., classrooms) allows them to do this. Quantitative researchers, conversely, typically concentrate on one or a small number of variables in order to describe current conditions or to investigate relationships, including cause-effect relationships. Because they are more concerned with the generalizability of their findings than with the meaning of those findings, quantitative researchers typically collect data from as many subjects (e.g., geometry students) as feasible. Thus, for example, while a qualitative researcher might study in-depth one or a small number of mentoring relationships over a 2-year period, a quantitative researcher might compare the self-esteem of two groups of otherwise equivalent students, one mentored and one nonmentored.

A very real difference between qualitative approaches and quantitative approaches is the degree of intervention and control involved. Qualitative researchers do not want to intervene or to control anything; they want to study phenomena as they are (or were), in natural settings. Quantitative researchers, on the other hand, often "intervene" and attempt to control as many variables as possible. Researchers representing the two approaches, therefore, definitely prefer different methodologies and data collection strategies.

Qualitative Approaches

Qualitative approaches can be applied to the study of past events or current events. When applied to past events, the process is referred to as historical research; when applied to current events, it is referred to as qualitative research. As the term has come to be commonly used, qualitative research is conducted to promote greater understanding of not just the way things *are,* but also *why.* Thus, qualitative research may or may not utilize historical methods in order to gain a better perspective. Granted, the terminology may be a bit confusing at first. Just keep in mind that the term "qualitative *approach*" is broader in scope than either historical research or qualitative research.

Historical Research

Historical research involves studying, understanding, and explaining past events. The purpose of historical research is to arrive at conclusions concerning causes, effects, or trends of past occurrences that may help to explain present events and anticipate future events. While historical studies are less frequently conducted than other types, there are certain educational problems and issues (such as grading policies) that can be better understood in light of past experience.

Historical research studies do not typically gather data by administering instruments to individuals. They must seek out data that are already available. Sources of data are referred to as primary or secondary. Primary sources constitute firsthand knowledge, such as eyewitness reports and original documents; secondary sources constitute secondhand information, such as a description of an event by other than an eyewitness. If you interview someone who witnessed an accident, that someone is a primary source; if you interview that someone's husband or wife, who did not witness the accident but heard an account of what happened from his or her spouse, that person is a secondary source. Primary sources are admittedly harder to acquire (it would be quite a feat to find an eyewitness to the Boston Tea Party!) but are generally more accurate and to be preferred. A major problem with much historical research is an excess of secondary sources.

Evaluation of historical data involves external criticism and internal criticism. External criticism assesses the authenticity of the data; internal criticism evaluates their worth. The worth of the data, the degree to which data are accurate and reliable and do indeed support the hypothesis, is judgmental and sometimes a matter of opinion. For example, a researcher investigating trends in classroom discipline might utilize a letter, allegedly written by Albert Einstein, containing an expression of concern regarding the amount of physical punishment in the schools. The results of external criticism might verify that the letter was indeed written by Albert Einstein. Internal criticism would be involved with whether he could be considered a reliable source concerning educational practices of the day. As another example, in his book *Chariots of the Gods?* Erich Von Däniken hypothesizes that thousands of years ago our ancestors were visited by intelligent beings from other worlds who, among other things, presented early humanity with advanced technology.[1] Von Däniken points to such remains as cave drawings, ancient maps, and relics of advanced, early civilizations as evidence in support of his theory. In general, authenticity of his evidence is without question; it is his interpretation of its meaning which is debatable. A cave drawing of a strange being, which is an ancient astronaut to Von Däniken, may be seen as simply an imaginary god to an archaeologist. In any event, his work represents a fascinating example of historical research.

The following are examples of typical historical research studies:

1. Factors leading to the development and growth of cooperative learning.
2. Effects of decisions of the United States Supreme Court on American education.
3. Trends in reading instruction, 1940–1995.

Qualitative Research

Qualitative research (often referred to in education as ethnographic research) involves intensive data collection, that is, the collection of extensive narrative data on many variables over an extended period of time, in a naturalistic setting. The rationale behind the use of qualitative research is that behavior occurs in a context and a more complete understanding of the behavior requires understanding of the context in which it occurs, e.g., a school. Thus, qualitative researchers are not just concerned with describing the way things are, but also with gaining insights into how things got to be the way they are, how people *feel* about the way things are, what they *believe*, what *meanings* they attach to various activities, and so forth.

In order to achieve the objective of holistic, in-depth understanding, qualitative researchers utilize a variety of methods and data collection strategies, and qualitative research is often characterized as being "multimethod." The most common

---

[1]Von Däniken, E. (1972). *Chariots of the Gods?* New York: Bantam Books.

strategy used, however, is participant observation, usually supplemented by collection of relevant documents and extensive, informal interviewing; participant observation basically involves the researcher immersing herself or himself in the setting of interest, observing as much as possible, and taking extensive, detailed notes. *What* is observed is typically a single "unit" (or a small number of units). A unit may be (as examples) a school, a program, a classroom, an administrator, a teacher, or a student. Thus, most qualitative research efforts represent case studies, i.e., indepth investigations of one unit. Since qualitative studies typically involve collection of an enormous amount of information, analyzing data is quite a challenging task which involves coding of data and production of a coherent verbal synthesis.

The following are examples of typical qualitative research studies:

1. A case study of parental involvement at a magnet school.
2. A multicase study of students who excel despite nonfacilitating environments.
3. Teacher as researcher: Improving students' writing skills.

Quantitative Approaches

Quantitative approaches (the main focus of this text) are applied in order to describe current conditions or to investigate relationships, including cause-effect relationships. Studies designed to describe current conditions are referred to as descriptive research. This terminology may be confusing at first since qualitative studies definitely *describe;* however, the term has traditionally been used to characterize studies which describe *numerically,* e.g., questionnaire studies. Studies which investigate the relationship between two or more quantifiable variables are referred to as correlational research, and those which investigate cause-effect relationships are called causal-comparative *or* experimental research, depending on whether the relationship is studied after the fact or in a controlled environment.

Descriptive Research

Descriptive research involves collecting data in order to test hypotheses or answer questions concerning the current status of the subject of the study. A descriptive study determines and reports the way things are. One common type of descriptive research involves assessing attitudes or opinions toward individuals, organizations, events, or procedures; pre-election political polls and market research surveys are examples of this type of descriptive research. Descriptive data are typically collected through a questionnaire survey, an interview, or observation.

Descriptive research sounds very simple; there is considerably more to it, however, than just asking questions and reporting answers. Since one is generally asking questions that have not been asked before, instruments usually have to be developed for specific studies; instrument development requires time and skill. A major problem further complicating descriptive research is lack of response—failure of subjects to return questionnaires or attend scheduled interviews. If the response rate is low, valid conclusions cannot be drawn. For example, suppose you are doing a study to determine attitudes of principals toward research. You send a questionnaire to 100 principals and ask the question, "Do you usually cooperate if asked to participate in a research study?" Suppose 40 principals respond and they *all* answer "yes." Could you then conclude that principals cooperate? No! Even though all those who responded said "yes," those 60 who did not respond may never cooperate with research efforts. After all, they did not cooperate with you! Observational research also involves complexities that are not readily apparent. Observers must be trained and forms must be developed so that data will be collected objectively and reliably.

The following are examples of typical questions investigated by descriptive research studies:

1. *How do second-grade teachers spend their time?* Second-grade teachers would be observed for a period of time and results would probably be presented as percentages, e.g., 60% of their time is spent lecturing, 20% asking or answering questions, 10% administering discipline, and 10% performing administrative duties, such as collecting milk money.
2. *How will citizens of Yortown vote in the next presidential election?* A survey of citizens of Yortown would be taken (questionnaire or interview), and results would probably be presented as percentages, e.g., 70% indicated they will vote for Peter Pure, 20% for George Graft, and 10% are undecided.
3. *How do parents feel about a 12-month school year?* Parents would be surveyed and results would probably be presented in terms of the percentages for, against, or undecided.

Correlational Research

Correlational research attempts to determine whether, and to what degree, a relationship exists between two or more quantifiable variables.[2] The purpose of a correlational study may be to establish relationship (or lack of it) or to use relationships in making predictions. Relationship studies typically study a number of variables believed to be related to a major, complex variable, such as achievement. Variables found not to be highly related are eliminated from further consideration; variables that are highly related may suggest causal-comparative or experimental studies to determine if the relationships are causal. For example, the fact that there is a relationship between self-concept and achievement does not imply that self-concept "causes" achievement or that achievement "causes" self-concept. Such a relationship only indicates that students with higher self-concepts have higher levels of achievement and students with lower self-concepts have lower levels of achievement. From the fact that two variables are highly related, one cannot conclude that one is the cause of the other; there may be a third factor which "causes" both of the related variables. For example, suppose it were determined that there is a high degree of relationship between number of years of schooling and income at age 40 (two quantifiable variables). The temptation might be to conclude that if you stay in school longer you will make more money; this conclusion would not necessarily be justified. There might be a third variable, such as motivation, which "causes" people to stay in school *and* do well in their jobs. The important point to remember is that correlational research never establishes a cause-effect relationship, only a relationship.

Regardless of whether a relationship is a cause-effect relationship, the existence of a high relationship permits prediction. For example, high school grades and college grades are highly related; students who have high GPAs in high school tend to

---

[2]A variable is a concept that can assume any one of a range of values. Examples of variables include height, weight, income, achievement, intelligence, and motivation. Got the idea?

have high GPAs in college, and students who have low GPAs in high school tend to have low GPAs in college. Therefore, high school GPAs can be, and are, used to predict GPA in college. The degree of relationship between two variables is generally expressed as a correlation coefficient, which is a number between .00 and 1.00. Two variables that are not related will produce a coefficient near .00; two variables that are highly related will produce a coefficient near 1.00.[3] Since very few relationships are perfect, prediction is rarely perfect. However, for many decisions, predictions based on known relationships are very useful.

The following are examples of typical correlational studies:

1. *The relationship between intelligence and self-esteem.* Scores on an intelligence test and on a measure of self-esteem would be acquired from each member of a given group. The two sets of scores would be correlated and the resulting coefficient would indicate the degree of relationship.
2. *The relationship between anxiety and achievement.* Scores on an anxiety scale and on an achievement test would be acquired from each member of a group. The two sets of scores would be correlated and the resulting coefficient would indicate the degree of relationship.
3. *Use of an aptitude test to predict success in an algebra course.* Scores on an algebra aptitude test would be correlated with ultimate success in algebra as measured by final exam scores, for example. If the resulting coefficient were high, the aptitude test would be considered a good predictor.

Causal-Comparative and Experimental Research

While causal-comparative and experimental research represent distinctly different methods, they can best be understood through comparison and contrast. Both attempt to establish cause-effect relationships; both involve group comparisons. The major difference between them is that in experimental research the alleged "cause" is manipulated, and in causal-comparative research it is not. In experimental research, the alleged "cause," the activity or characteristic believed to make a difference, is referred to as a treatment; the more general term for "cause" is independent variable. The difference, or "effect," which is determined to occur or not occur is referred to as the dependent variable. Dependent on what? Dependent on the independent variable. Thus, a study which investigates a cause-effect relationship investigates the effect of an independent variable on a dependent variable.

In an experimental study the researcher manipulates at least one independent variable and observes the effect on one or more dependent variables. In other words, the researcher determines "who gets what," which group of subjects will get which treatment; the groups are generally referred to as experimental and control groups. Manipulation of the independent variable is the one single characteristic that differentiates experimental research from other methods. Ideally, in experimental research the groups to be studied are randomly formed before the experiment, a procedure not involved in the other methods of research. The essence of experimentation is control. The researcher strives to insure that the experiences of the groups are as equal as possible on all important variables except, of course, the independent variable. If, at the end of some period of time, groups differ in per-

[3]Two variables can be inversely related. When this occurs the coefficient is a negative number, and a high relationship is near −1.00. A negative relationship occurs when two variables are related in such a way that a high score on one is accompanied by a low score on the other, and vice versa. This will be discussed further in Chapter 9.

formance on the dependent variable, the difference can be attributed to the independent variable. Because of the direct manipulation and control of variables, experimental research is the only type of research that can truly establish cause-effect relationships.

The following are examples of typical experimental studies:

1. *The comparative effectiveness of personalized instruction versus traditional instruction on computational skill.* The independent variable, or cause, is type of instruction (personalized versus traditional); the dependent variable, or effect, is computational skill. Two groups, (preferably randomly formed) would be exposed to essentially the same experiences, except for method of instruction. After some period of time, their computational skill would be compared.

2. *The effect of self-paced instruction on self-concept.* The independent variable, or cause, is pacing (self-pacing versus teacher pacing); the dependent variable, or effect, is self-concept. Two groups (preferably randomly formed) would be exposed to essentially the same experiences, except for the pacing of instruction. After some period of time, their self-concepts would be compared.

3. *The effect of positive reinforcement on attitude toward school.* The independent variable, or cause, is type of reinforcement (e.g., positive versus negative, or positive versus none); the dependent variable, or effect, is attitude toward school. Two groups (preferably randomly formed) would be exposed to essentially the same experiences, except for they type of reinforcement received. After some period of time, their attitudes toward school would be compared.

In a causal-comparative study (note, the word is "causal," not "casual") the independent variable, or "cause," is not manipulated; it has already occurred. Independent variables in causal-comparative studies are variables which cannot be manipulated (e.g., sex, male-female), should not be manipulated (e.g., prenatal care), or simply are not manipulated, but could be (e.g., method of instruction). In causal-comparative research, groups are also compared on some dependent variable; these groups, however, are different on some variable before the study begins. Perhaps one group possesses a characteristic and one does not, or perhaps each group is a member of a different socioeconomic level. In any event, the difference between the groups (the independent variable) is not, was not, or could not be determined by the researcher. Further, since the independent variable has already occurred, the same kinds of controls cannot be exercised as in an experimental study. Due to the lack of manipulation and control, cause-effect relationships established are at best tenuous and tentative. On the positive side, causal-comparative studies are less expensive and take much less time to conduct. Further, apparent cause-effect relationships may lead to experimental studies designed to confirm or disconfirm the findings. Also, there are a number of important variables which simply cannot be manipulated. Studies designed to investigate the effects of a broken home, intelligence, or sex on achievement must be causal-comparative, as none of these variables can be manipulated. The following are examples of typical causal-comparative studies:

1. *The effect of preschool attendance on social maturity at the end of the first grade.* The independent variable, or cause, is preschool attendance (students attended preschool or they did not); the dependent variable, or effect, is social maturity at the end of the first grade. Two groups of first

graders would be identified—one group who had attended preschool and one group who had not. The social maturity of the two groups would be compared.

2. *The effect of having a working mother on school absenteeism.* The independent variable, or cause, is the employment status of the mother (the mother works or does not work); the dependent variable, or effect, is absenteeism, or number of days absent. Two groups of students would be identified—one group who had working mothers and one group who did not. The absenteeism of the two groups would be compared.

3. *The effect of sex on algebra achievement.* The independent variable, or cause, is sex (male versus female); the dependent variable, or effect, is algebra achievement. The achievement of males would be compared to the achievement of females.

Guidelines for Classification

Which of the six types is most appropriate for a given study depends upon the way in which the problem is defined. The same general problem can often be investigated using several of the types. Research in a given area is often sequential; preliminary descriptive and/or correlational studies may be conducted followed by causal-comparative and/or experimental studies, if such seem warranted. As an example, let us look at anxiety and achievement. The following studies might be conducted:

1. Descriptive: A survey of teachers to determine how and to what degree they believe anxiety affects achievement.
2. Correlational: A study to determine the relationship between scores on an anxiety scale and scores on an achievement measure.
3. Causal-comparative: A study to compare the achievement of a group of students classified as high-anxious and a group classified as low-anxious.
4. Experimental: A study to compare the achievement of two groups—one group taught in an anxiety-producing environment and one group taught in an anxiety-reducing environment.[4]

A related qualitative study might be a case study of an SAT prep course, with observed/reported signs of anxiety being a major variable.

When analyzing a study in order to determine the specific type of research represented, one strategy is to ask yourself a series of questions. First, does the study represent a qualitative or a quantitative approach? If the answer is qualitative, it should be easy to differentiate between historical and qualitative studies. If the answer is quantitative, was the researcher attempting to establish a cause-effect relationship? If yes, the research is either causal-comparative or experimental. The next question is, Was the alleged cause, or independent variable, manipulated by the researcher? Did the researcher control who got what and what they got? If yes, the research is experimental; if no, the research is causal-comparative. If the answer to the very first question is no, the next question should be, Was the researcher

---

[4]There are generally considered to be two types of anxiety—trait anxiety and state anxiety. Trait anxiety is a personality characteristic that cannot be manipulated (Study 3). State anxiety is a temporary condition that can be manipulated, i.e., heightened or lessened (Study 4). In an anxiety-producing environment, for example, the teacher would constantly emphasize the importance of doing well on all tests.

attempting to establish a relationship or use a relationship for prediction? If yes, the research is correlational. If no, the research is descriptive (see Figure 1.1). The following examples should further clarify the differences among the types:

1. *Teacher attitudes toward unions.* Probably descriptive. The study is determining the current attitudes of teachers. Data are probably collected through use of a questionnaire or an interview.
2. *Effect of socioeconomic status (SES) on self-concept.* Probably causal-comparative. The effect of SES on self-concept is being investigated. The independent variable, socioeconomic status, cannot be manipulated.
3. *Comparison of large-group versus small-group instruction on achievement.* Probably experimental. The effect of size of group on achievement is being investigated. The independent variable, group size, can be manipulated by the researcher.
4. *The nature of student interactions during learning on a shared microcomputer.* Probably qualitative. How students relate to each other in a given learning environment is being studied. Data are probably collected primarily using participant observation.
5. *Prediction of success in graduate school based on Graduate Record Examination (GRE) scores.* Probably correlational. A cause-effect relationship is not involved, but a relationship is involved, namely the relationship between GRE scores and success in graduate school (e.g., GPA).
6. *Participation of women in higher education, 1890–1990.* Probably historical. The study is investigating a trend, probably increased participation by women.

Of course, one cannot usually identify type simply by reading the title of a research report. However, by reading the report, looking for identifying characteris-

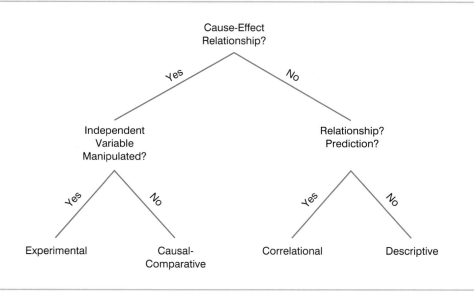

Figure 1.1. Decision diagram for determining the type of research represented by a particular quantitative study.

tics, and asking appropriate questions, you should have no trouble classifying most studies. Classifying a study by type is the first step in both conducting and reviewing a study, since each type entails different specific procedures and analyses.

■ SUMMARY/CHAPTER 1
THE SCIENTIFIC METHOD

1. The goal of all scientific endeavors is to explain, predict, and/or control phenomena.
2. Compared to other sources of knowledge, such as experience, authority, inductive reasoning, and deductive reasoning, application of the scientific method is undoubtedly the most efficient and reliable.
3. Basically, the scientific method involves induction of hypotheses based on observations, deduction of implications, and confirmation or disconfirmation of the hypotheses.

APPLICATION OF THE SCIENTIFIC METHOD IN EDUCATION

4. Research is the formal, systematic application of the scientific method to the study of problems; educational research is the formal, systematic application of the scientific method to the study of educational problems.
5. The major difference between educational research and other scientific research is the nature of the phenomena studied. It is considerably more difficult to explain, predict, and control situations involving human beings, by far the most complex of all organisms.

BASIC VERSUS APPLIED RESEARCH

6. Classification of a given study along this continuum is based primarily on the degree to which findings have direct educational application and the degree to which they are generalizable. Both of these criteria are a function of the research control exercised during the execution of the study.
7. In its purest form, basic research is conducted solely for the purpose of theory development and refinement.
8. Applied research, as the name implies, is conducted for the purpose of applying, or testing, theory and evaluating its usefulness in solving educational problems.

Evaluation Research

9. The purpose of evaluation research is to facilitate decision making regarding the relative worth of two or more alternative actions.

Research and Development (R & D)

10. The major purpose of R & D efforts is not to formulate or test theory but to develop effective products for use in the schools.

Action Research

11. The purpose of action research is to solve practical problems through the application of the scientific method.

APPROACHES TO INQUIRY: QUALITATIVE VERSUS QUANTITATIVE

12. While there is sometimes a degree of overlap, most research studies represent a readily identifiable approach, or strategy.
13. All studies have certain procedures in common, such as data collection and analysis; beyond these, specific procedures are to a high degree determined by the specific type of research involved.
14. The terms "qualitative" and "quantitative" are used not so much because they involve mutually exclusive, unique research strategies and methodologies, but rather because they conveniently differentiate one from the other.
15. Qualitative approaches involve the collection of extensive *narrative* data in order to gain insights into phenomena of interest; quantitative approaches involve the collection of *numerical* data in order to explain, predict, and/or control phenomena of interest.
16. Qualitative researchers typically study many variables intensely over an extensive period of time in order to find out the way things are (or were), how and why they came to be that way, and what it all means.
17. Quantitative researchers, conversely, typically concentrate on one or a small number of variables in order to describe current conditions or to investigate relationships, including cause-effect relationships.
18. Qualitative researchers do not want to intervene or to control anything; quantitative researchers often "intervene" and attempt to control as many variables as possible.
19. Researchers representing the two approaches definitely prefer different methodologies and data collection strategies.

Qualitative Approaches

20. Qualitative approaches can be applied to the study of past events (historical research) or current events (qualitative research).
21. The term "qualitative *approach*" is broader in scope than either historical research or qualitative research.

Historical Research

22. Historical research involves studying, understanding, and explaining past events.
23. The purpose of historical research is to arrive at conclusions concerning causes, effects, or trends of past occurrences that may help to explain present events and anticipate future events.
24. Primary sources of data constitute firsthand knowledge; secondary sources constitute secondhand information.
25. External criticism assesses the authenticity of the data; internal criticism evaluates their worth.

Qualitative Research

26. Qualitative research (often referred to in education as ethnographic research) involves intensive data collection, that is, collection of extensive narrative data on many variables over an extended period of time, in a naturalistic setting.

27. Qualitative researchers are not just concerned with describing the way things are, but also with gaining insights into how things got to be the way they are, how people *feel* about the way things are, what they *believe,* what *meanings* they attach to various activities, and so forth.

28. In order to achieve the objective of holistic, in-depth understanding, qualitative researchers utilize a variety of methods and data collection strategies, and qualitative research is often characterized as being "multimethod."

29. The most common data collection strategy used, however, is participant observation, usually supplemented by collection of relevant documents and extensive, informal interviewing.

30. Most qualitative research efforts represent case studies, i.e., in-depth investigations of one unit.

Quantitative Approaches

31. Quantitative studies designed to describe (numerically) current conditions are referred to as descriptive research.

32. Studies which investigate the relationship between two or more quantifiable variables are referred to as correlational research.

33. Those studies which investigate cause-effect relationships are called causal-comparative *or* experimental research, depending on whether the relationship is studied after the fact or in a controlled environment.

Descriptive Research

34. Descriptive research involves collecting data in order to test hypotheses or answer questions concerning the status of the subject of the study.

35. Descriptive data are typically collected through a questionnaire survey, an interview, or observation.

36. Since one is generally asking questions that have not been asked before, instruments usually have to be developed for specific studies.

37. A major problem further complicating descriptive research is lack of response—failure of subjects to return questionnaires or attend scheduled interviews.

Correlational Research

38. Correlational research attempts to determine whether, and to what degree, a relationship exists between two or more quantifiable variables.

39. The purpose of a correlational study may be to establish a relationship (or lack of it) or to use relationships in making predictions.

40. From the fact that two variables are highly related, one cannot conclude that one is the cause of the other; there may be a third factor which "causes" both of the related variables.

41. Regardless of whether a relationship is a cause-effect relationship, the existence of a high relationship permits prediction.

42. The degree of relationship between two variables is generally expressed as a correlation coefficient, which is a number between .00 and 1.00.

Causal-Comparative and Experimental Research

43. The activity or characteristic believed to make a difference is referred to as the "cause" or treatment, and more generally as the independent variable.
44. The difference, or "effect," which is determined to occur or not occur is referred to as the dependent variable.
45. In an experimental study the researcher manipulates at least one independent variable and observes the effect on one or more dependent variables.
46. Ideally, in experimental research the groups to be studied are randomly formed before the experiment, a procedure not involved in the other methods of research.
47. The essence of experimentation is control.
48. Only experimental research can truly establish cause-effect relationships.
49. In a causal-comparative study the independent variable, or "cause," is not manipulated; it has already occurred.
50. In causal-comparative research, the difference between the groups (the independent variable) is not, was not, or could not be determined by the researcher.
51. Due to the lack of manipulation and control, cause-effect relationships established through causal-comparative research are at best tenuous and tentative.

Guidelines for Classification

52. Which of the six types is most appropriate for a given study depends upon the way in which the problem is defined. The same general problem can often be investigated using several of the types.
53. When analyzing a study in order to determine the specific type of research represented, one strategy is to ask yourself a series of questions; first, Does the study represent a qualitative or a quantitative approach?
54. If the study is qualitative, it should be easy to differentiate between historical and qualitative studies.
55. If the study is quantitative, Was the researcher attempting to establish a cause-effect relationship? Was the alleged cause, or independent variable, manipulated by the researcher? Was the researcher attempting to establish a relationship or use a relationship for prediction?

TASK 1 PERFORMANCE CRITERIA

Task 1-A

If the study that you are given was quantitative and designed to investigate one major problem, one sentence should be sufficient to describe the problem. If several problems were investigated, one sentence per problem should be sufficient.

Six sentences or less will adequately describe the major procedures of most studies. Do not copy the procedures section of the study or describe each and every step. Briefly describe the subjects, instrument(s), and major steps.

As with the problem, one or two sentences will usually be sufficient to state the major analyses. You are not expected to understand the analyses, only identify them. By the time you get to Part Seven you will be at least somewhat desensitized and will not be unnerved by terms like *t* test and analysis of variance.

The major conclusions that you identify and state (one or two sentences should be sufficient) should directly relate to the original problem or problems. Remember, statements like "more research is needed in this area" do not represent major conclusions.

If the study you are given was qualitative, one sentence should be sufficient to describe the general focus. One or two sentences should be sufficient to describe the major data collection strategies, and one or two sentences should also be sufficient to describe the general conclusion.

Task 1-B

The characteristics of the study which you describe should be characteristics which are unique to the specific type of research represented by the study. The following are illustrative examples of responses you might give for studies representing each of the types of research.

1. The study was historical *because* changes in the public schools' legal responsibilities regarding disabled students during the past 50 years was investigated.
2. The study was qualitative *because* participant observation and interviewing were used in a case study of a model alternate-to-suspension program.
3. This study was descriptive *because* a questionnaire was used in order to determine how social studies teachers feel about global education.
4. This study was correlational *because* the predictive validity of a new scholastic aptitude test was investigated.
5. This study was causal-comparative *because* a cause-effect relationship was investigated but the independent variable was not manipulated; the researcher could not and did not determine "who got what," that is, which subjects were members of single-parent families and which were members of two-parent families.
6. This study was experimental *because* subjects were randomly assigned to treatments and the independent variable (cause) was manipulated; the researcher determined "who got what," that is, which subjects received conflict resolution training and which subjects received individual counseling.

On the following pages a research report is reprinted. Following the report, spaces are provided for listing the components required by Task 1-A and for classifying the research by specific type as specified by Task 1-B. As a self-test, after you have studied Part One, see if you can correctly identify the components and type. If your responses differ greatly from the Suggested Responses in Appendix D, study the article again until you see why you were in error.

Additional examples for these and subsequent tasks are included in the *Student Guide* which accompanies this text.

Motivational Effects on Test Scores of Elementary Students

STEVEN M. BROWN
Northeastern Illinois University

HERBERT J. WALBERG
University of Illinois at Chicago

ABSTRACT   A total of 406 heterogeneously grouped students in Grades 3, 4, 6, 7, and 8 in three K through 8 Chicago public schools were assigned randomly to two conditions, ordinary standardized-test instructions (control) and special instructions, to do as well as possible for themselves, their parents, and their teachers (experimental). On average, students given special instructions did significantly better ($p < .01$) than the control students did on the criterion measure, the mathematics section of the commonly used Iowa Test of Basic Skills. The three schools differed significantly in achievement ($p < .05$), but girls and boys and grade levels did not differ measurably. The motivational effect was constant across grade levels and boys and girls, but differed significantly ($p < .05$) across schools. The average effect was moderately large, .303 standard deviations, which implies that the special instructions raise the typical student's scores from the 50th to the 62nd percentile.

Parents, educators, business people, politicians, and the general public are greatly concerned about U.S. students' poor performance on international comparisons of achievement. Policy makers are planning additional international, state, district, and school comparisons to measure progress in solving the national crisis. Some members of those same groups have also grown concerned about the effects of students' high or low motivational states on how well they score on tests.

One commonly expressed apprehension is that some students worry unduly about tests and suffer debilitating anxiety (Hill, 1980). Another concern is that too much testing causes students to care little about how well they do, especially on standardized tests that have no bearing on their grades. Either case might lead to poorer scores than students would attain under ideal motivational states; such effects might explain, in part, the poor performance of U.S. students relative to those in other countries or in relation to what may be required for college and vocational success.

Experts and practicing educators have expressed a variety of conflicting opinions about motivational effects on learning and test scores (Association for Supervision and Curriculum Development, 1991, p. 7). Given the importance of testing policies, there is surprisingly little research on the topic. The purpose of the present study is to determine the effect of experimentally manipulated motivational conditions on elementary students' mathematical scores.

As conceived in this study, the term *motivation* refers to the commonsense meaning of the term, that is, students' propensity to engage in full, serious, and sustained effort on academic tests. As it has been measured in many previous studies, motivation refers to students' reported efforts to succeed or to excel on academic tasks. It is often associated with self-concept or self-regard in a successful student or test taker. A quantitative synthesis of the correlational studies of motivation and school learning showed that nearly all correlations were positive and averaged about .30 (Uguroglu & Walberg, 1979).

Previous Research

The National Assessment Governing Board (NAGB, 1990) recently characterized the National Assessment of Educational Progress (NAEP) as follows:

> . . . as a survey exam which by law cannot be reported for individual students and schools. NAEP may not be taken seriously enough by students to enlist their best efforts. Because it is given with no incentives for good performance and no opportunity for prior study, NAEP may understate achievement (NAGB, p. 17).

To investigate such questions, NAEP is adding items to ask students how hard they tried in responding to future achievement tests.

Motivation questions can be raised about nearly all standardized commercial tests, as well as state-constructed achievement tests. The content of those tests is often unrelated to specific topics that students have been recently studying; and their performance on such tests ordinarily does not affect their grades, college, or job prospects. Many students know they will not see how well they have done.

Address correspondence to Steven M. Brown, 924 South Austin, Apt. 2, Oak Park, IL 60304.

Brown, S. M., & Walberg, H. J. (1993). Motivational effects on test scores of elementary students. *The Journal of Educational Research, 86*, 133–136. Reprinted with the permission of the Helen Dwight Reid Educational Foundation. Published by Heldref Publications, 1319 Eighteenth St., N. W., Washington, DC 20036-1802. Copyright © 1993.

Some students admit deficient motivation, but surveys show reasonably favorable attitudes toward tests by most students. Paris, Lawton, and Turner (1991), for example, surveyed 250 students in Grades 4, 7, and 10 about the Michigan Educational Assessment Program. They found that most students reported that they tried hard, thought they did well, felt the test was not difficult or confusing, and saw little or no cheating. However, Karmos and Karmos's (1984) survey of 360 sixth- through ninth-grade student attitudes toward tests showed that 47% thought they were a waste of time, 22% saw no good reason to try to do well, and 21% did not try very hard.

Kellaghan, Madaus, and Arisian (1982) found various small fractions of a sixth-grade Irish sample disaffected by standardized tests, even though they are uncommon in Ireland. When asked about their experience with standardized tests, 29% reported feeling nervous, 19%, unconfident; 16%, bored; and 15% uninterested. Twenty-nine percent reported that they did not care whether they took the tests, and 16% said they did not enjoy the experience.

Paris, Lawton, and Turner (1991) speculated that standardized tests may lead both bright and dull students to do poorly: Bright students may feel heightened parental, peer, or self-imposed expectations to do well on tests, which makes them anxious. Slower, disadvantaged students may do poorly, then rationalize that school and tests are unimportant and, consequently, expend less effort preparing for and completing tests. Either case might lead to a self-reinforcing spiral of decelerating achievement.

Surveys, however, cannot establish causality. Poor motivation may cause poor achievement, or vice versa, or both may be caused by other factors such as deficiencies in ability, parental support of academic work, or teaching. To show an independent effect of motivation on achievement requires an experiment, that is, a randomized assignment of students to conditions of eliciting different degrees of motivation. Such was the purpose of our study.

Method

Sample

The subjects for the study included students from three K through 8 public schools in Chicago. The student populations of the schools are generally lower-middle, working class, mostly Hispanic and African-American. Two normal heterogeneous classes within the schools were sampled from Grades 3, 4, 6, 7, and 8; because of exigencies, we did not sample Grade 5 classes.

Instrument

We chose Form 7 of the Mathematics Concepts subtest of the Iowa Basic Skills (ITBS) 1978 edition, Levels 9–14, because it is a commonly used, highly reliable test. An earlier-than-contemporary edition was used so it would not interfere with current testing programs. In a review of the 1978 ITBS, Nitko (1985) judged that the reliability of its subtests is generally higher than .85 and that it contains content generally representative of school curriculum in Grades 3 though 9. "The ITBS," he concluded, "is an excellent basic skills battery measuring global skills that are likely to be highly related to the long-term goals of elementary schools" (p. 723).

Procedure

Pairs of classes at each grade level from each school were randomly chosen to participate. Classes were selected for experimental and control conditions by a flip of a coin.

The first author (Brown) met with all participating teachers in each school to explain the instructions from the ITBS test manual (see Appendix A). Then, the experimental teachers were retained for the following further instructions:

> We are conducting a research study to determine the effects of telling students that the test they are going to take is very important. It is extremely important that you read the brief script I have for you today EXACTLY as it is written to your students.

The following script was provided:

> It is really important that you do as WELL as you can on this test. The test score you receive will let others see just how well I am doing in teaching you math this year.
> Your scores will be compared to students in other grades here at this school, as well as to those in other schools in Chicago.
> That is why it is extremely important to do the VERY BEST that you can. Do it for YOURSELF, YOUR PARENTS, and ME.
> (Now read the instructions for the test.)

Following the administration of the test, teachers and the first author asked students for their reactions to the script that was read to them.

Analysis

An analysis of variance was run to test the effects of the experimental and normal conditions; the differences among the three schools and five grades; between boys and girls; and the interactions among the factors.

Results

The analysis of variance showed a highly significant effect of experimental condition ($F = 10.59$, $p < .01$), a significant effect of school ($F = 3.35$, $p < .05$), and an interaction between condition and school ($F = 5.01$, $p < .05$). No other effects, including grade level, were significant. The means and standard deviations of selected factors are shown in Table 1.

Task 1 Example (*continued*)

Table 1.—Normal Curve Equivalent Means and Standard Deviations

Grade	Condition	M	SD
3	Control	32.77	19.57
	Experimental	42.55*	16.59
4	Control	33.07	13.93
	Experimental	39.42*	13.12
6	Control	40.84	17.77
	Experimental	39.64	14.66
7	Control	43.21	16.07
	Experimental	41.21	16.48
8	Control	31.12	14.06
	Experimental	44.66**	15.94

*$p < .01$; **$p < .001$.

The mean normal curve equivalent test score of the 214 students in the experimental group was 41.37 ($SD = 15.41$), and the mean of the control group was 36.25 ($SD = 16.89$). The motivational effect is moderately large, .303 standard deviations, which implies that the special instructions raised the typical student's scores from the 50th to the 62nd percentile. The special instructions are comparable to the effects of better (though not the best) instructional practices over conventional classroom instruction (Walberg, 1986). If American students' average achievement in mathematics and science could be raised that much, it would be more comparable to that of students in other economically advanced countries.

The motivational effect was the same for boys and girls and constant across grade levels, but it differed among schools. Figure 1 shows a very large effect at School A, a large effect at School C, and the control group somewhat higher than the experimental group at School B.

Only 62 students (15% of the total sample) were tested at School B, which may account for the lack of effect in this school. At any rate, although the overall effect is moderately large and constant across grade levels and for boys and girls, the size of the effect varies from school to school. Such differences may depend on test-taking attitudes of teachers and students in the schools, motivational and cultural differences in the student populations, variations in conditions of administration, and other factors.

Several comments made by students and teachers during debriefing sessions illuminate the statistical findings. Student Comments 1, 2, and 3 illustrate students' motivation to do well to please their parents and teachers. Teacher Comments 1 and 2 also confirm the reasons for the effect. The last student and teacher comment, however, illustrate motivational states and conditions that diminish or vitiate the effect. When students are unthoughtful or when teachers keep constant pressures on for testing, special instructions may have little effect.

Conclusion

The results show that motivation can make a substantial difference in test scores. Students asked to try especially hard did considerably better than those who were given the usual standardized test instructions. The special conditions raised the typical student's score .303 standard deviation units, corresponding to a 12 percentile-point gain from the 50th to the 62nd percentile. Although the effect was the same for boys and girls and for students in different grade levels, it varied in magnitude among the three schools.

The results suggest that standardized commercial and state-constructed tests that have no bearing on students' grades may be underestimating U.S. students' real knowledge, understanding, skills, and other aspects of achievement. To the extent that motivation varies from school to school, moreover, achievement levels of some schools are considerably more underestimated than in others. Such motivational differences would tend to diminish the validity of comparisons of schools and districts.

We would be heartened to conclude that U.S. students' poor performance on achievement relative to students in other countries is attributable to the test-motivation effect. That conclusion is overly optimistic, however, because the effect may also operate to a greater or lesser extent in other countries. Further research is obviously in order.

The motivation effect might be reduced in several ways. Highly motivating instructions could be given to all students. The content of school lessons and standardized tests could be brought into closer correspondence, making the tests more plausible to students, and perhaps justifying their use in grading. Some students, moreover, may be unmotivated because they never see the results. Providing timely, specific, and useful feedback to stu-

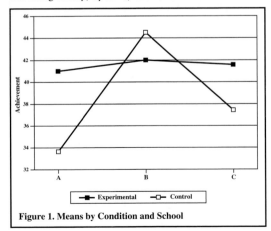

Figure 1. Means by Condition and School

dents, parents, and teachers on how well they have done might lead students to try harder.

APPENDIX A

Directions for Administering the Mathematics Concepts Subtest of the Iowa Test of Basic Skills (1979)

Now we are ready for the first mathematics test. Open your test booklets to page 73. (Pause) Find the section of your answer sheet for Test M-1: Mathematics Concepts. (Pause) Read the directions on page 73 silently while I read them aloud.

This is a test of how well you understand the number system and the terms and operations used in mathematics. Four answers are given for each exercise, but only one of the answers is right. You are to choose the one answer that you think is better than the others. Then, on the answer sheet, find the row of the answer numbered the same as the exercise. Fill in the answer space for the best answer.

Do not make any marks on the test booklet. Use your scratch paper for figuring. You will have 25 minutes for this test. If you finish early, recheck your work. Don't look at the other tests in the booklet. If you have questions, raise your hand, and I will help you after the others have begun. Now find your place to begin. (Pause)

Does everyone have the correct place? (Pause) Ready, BEGIN.

APPENDIX B

Selected Anecdotal Comments

Students

1. Third-Grade Girl: My teacher always tells us to get good scores on tests. I wanted to make her happy and my parents happy.

2. Fourth-Grade Boy: I think I did well. My teacher works hard with us. I also want my school to be the best.

3. Eighth-Grade Boy: I wanted to do really well for my teacher. She does a great job, and I didn't want to let her down.

4. Seventh-Grade Girl: I just took the test, and really didn't think much about the instructions she gave.

Teachers

1. I don't know what the results will show but my gut feeling is that students in the experimental groups will do better. I think it's probably because of motivational reasons.

2. The script gives me a feeling of *family*. I think if we told students just how much we want them to do well, and that it will not only benefit themselves but the whole school, they will probably do better.

3. I think all the students (control and experimental) will probably do equally well, because we always stress how important the tests are.

REFERENCES

Association for Supervision and Curriculum Development (1991). *Update, 33*(1), 1–8.

Hill, K. T. (1980). Motivation, evaluation, and testing policy. In L. J. Fyans, Jr. (Ed.), *Achievement motivation: Recent trends in theory and research.* New York, NY: Plenum Press.

Iowa Test of Basic Skills normal curve equivalent norms (1978). Boston, MA: Houghton Mifflin.

Karmos, A. H., & Karmos, J. S. (1984, July). Attitudes toward standardized achievement tests and their relation to achievement test performance. *Measurement and Evaluation in Counseling and Development, 12*, 56–66.

Kelleghan, T., Madaus, G. F., & Arisian, P. M. (1982). *The effects of standardized testing.* Boston, MA: Kluwer-Nijhoff.

National Assessment Governing Board (1991). Issues for the 1994–1996 NAEP. Washington, DC: Author.

Nitco, A. J. (1985). Review of the Iowa Test of Basic Skills. In James V. Mitchell (Ed.), *The ninth mental measurements yearbook.* Lincoln, NE: Buros Institute.

Paris, S. G., Lawton, T. A., & Turner, J. C. (1991). Reforming achievement testing to promote students' learning. In C. Collins & Mangieri (Eds.), *Learning in and out of school.* Hillsdale, NJ: Lawrence Erlbaum Associates.

Uguroglu, M. E., & Walberg, H. J. (1979). Motivation and achievement: A quantitative synthesis. *American Educational Research Journal, 16*, 375–390.

Walberg, H. J. (1986). Synthesis of research on teaching. In M. C. Wittrock (Ed.), *Handbook of research on teaching.* New York, NY: Macmillan.

■ MOTIVATIONAL EFFECTS ON TEST SCORES OF ELEMENTARY STUDENTS

Self-Test for Task 1-A

The Problem

_____

_____

_____

_____

The Procedures

_____

_____

_____

_____

_____

_____

_____

The Method of Analysis

_____

_____

_____

The Major Conclusion(s)

_____

_____

_____

Self-Test for Task 1-B

Type

_____

Reasons

_____

_____

_____

_____

_____

_____

PART TWO

Research Problems

Selection and definition of a research problem is a refinement process that begins with the identification of a problem area and terminates with one or more testable hypotheses or answerable questions. The refinement process is based primarily upon a thorough review and critical analysis of related literature. Once a problem area is identified and a specific problem within it selected, a tentative hypothesis is formulated; this tentative hypothesis guides the literature review, which in turn forms the basis for the final statement of the research hypothesis. Selection and definition of a problem is a very important component of the research process and entails much time and thought. The statement of the problem, the review of related literature, and the statement of the hypothesis comprise the introduction section of both research plans and research reports on completed research. The only difference may be the tense in which the introduction is written; research plans are usually written in the future tense ("Subjects *will* be selected . . ."), but research reports are always written in the past tense ("Subjects *were* selected . . .").

The problem which you ultimately select in this part is the problem which you will work with in succeeding parts. Therefore, it is important that you select a problem which is (1) relevant to your area of study (e.g., English education) and (2) of particular interest to you. Also, since you will be responsible for a literature search, it will be to your benefit to select a manageable, well-defined problem. For example, "the use of homework in mathematics instruction" is not manageable and well-defined; "the effect of daily homework assignments on the examination grades of ninth-grade algebra students" *is* manageable and well-defined.

The goal of Part Two is for you to acquire the ability to identify and define a meaningful problem, conduct an adequate review of related literature, and state the problem in terms of a testable hypothesis. After you have read Part Two, you should be able to perform the task described on the next page.

■ TASK 2

Write an introduction for a research plan. This will include a statement of the specific problem to be investigated in the study, a statement concerning the significance of the problem, a review of related literature, and a testable hypothesis. Include definitions of terms where appropriate.

(See Performance Criteria, p. 74)

"Some graduate students spend many anxiety-ridden days and sleepless nights worrying about where they are going to 'find' the problem they need for their thesis or dissertation (p. 36)."

Selection and Definition of a Problem

After reading Chapter 2, you should be able to:

1. Make a list of at least three educational problems for which you would be interested in conducting a research study.

2. Select one of the problems and identify 10 to 15 complete references which directly relate to the selected problem. The sources of the references should include as many of the following as possible:
   (a) *Education Index*
   (b) *Readers' Guide to Periodical Literature*
   (c) *Dissertation Abstracts International*
   (d) *Psychological Abstracts*
   (e) Educational Resources Information Center (ERIC)
       (1) *Resources in Education (RIE)*—ED numbers
       (2) *Current Index to Journals in Education (CIJE)*—EJ numbers
   (f) *Review of Educational Research* (the journal)

   While a number of references may be identified through several sources, you need to learn how to use all of them.

3. Read and abstract the references you have listed.

4. Formulate a testable hypothesis for your problem.

Note. These objectives will form the basis for Task 2.

■ SELECTION AND STATEMENT

After a problem area of interest is identified, a specific problem is selected for investigation. Theory and experience are two major sources of problems. A good problem has a number of identifiable characteristics. A good statement of a problem also conforms to a set of important criteria.

Selection

For beginning researchers, selection of a problem is the most difficult step in the research process. Some graduate students spend many anxiety-ridden days and sleepless nights worrying about where they are going to "find" the problem they need for their thesis or dissertation. To the poor student it seems as if every problem she or he identifies is dismissed by her or his advisor as being trivial or "already done." The problem is not a lack of problems; there is almost an unlimited supply of problems which need researching. The problem is a lack of familiarity with the literature on the student's part. Learning how and where to locate problems, and systematically attacking this phase of the research process, is much better for one's mental health than worrying oneself into an anxiety attack!

The first step in selecting a problem is to identify a general problem area that is related to your area of expertise and of particular interest to you. Examples of problem areas might be structured programs for preschoolers, use of manipulatives for elementary mathematics, discipline approaches for disruptive junior high school students, the use of paraprofessionals in the elementary school, the whole language approach to reading, and the use of reviews to increase retention. Since you will be doing a great deal of reading in the area you select, and devoting many hours to the planning and execution of the ultimate study, choosing a topic of interest which will increase your knowledge and understanding of your particular professional area makes good sense.

The next step is to narrow down the general problem area to a specific, researchable problem. A problem that is too general can only cause you grief. In the first place, the scope of the review of related literature that you must inevitably conduct will be unnecessarily increased, possibly resulting in many more hours being spent in the library. This will in turn complicate organization of the results of the review and subsequent hypothesis development. Even more important than the practicalities, a problem that is too general tends to result in a study which is too general, includes too many variables, and produces results that are too difficult to interpret. Conversely, a well-defined manageable problem results in a well-defined, manageable study. One major way to narrow your problem is to read sources giving overviews or summaries of the current status of research in your area; references such as the *Review of Educational Research* and the *Encyclopedia of Educational Research* may be very helpful.[1] In narrowing the problem area you should select an aspect of the general problem area that is related to your area of expertise. For example, the general problem area "the use of reviews to increase retention" could generate many specific problems such as "the comparative effectiveness of immediate versus delayed review on the retention of geometric concepts" and "the effect of review games on the retention of vocabulary words by second graders." In your efforts to sufficiently delineate a problem, however, be care-

---

[1]American Educational Research Association. (1931 to date). *Review of educational research*. Washington, DC: Author, *and* Alkin, M. C. (Ed.). (1992). *Encyclopedia of educational research* (6th ed.). New York: Macmillan.

ful not to get carried away; a problem that is too narrow is just a bad as a problem that is too broad. A study such as "the effectiveness of pre-class reminders in reducing instances of pencil sharpening during class time" would probably contribute little, if anything, to the science of education!

Selecting a good problem is well worth the time and effort. As mentioned previously, there is no shortage of significant problems that need to be researched; there is really no excuse for selecting a trite problem. Besides, it is generally to your advantage to select a worthwhile problem; you will certainly get a great deal more "out of it" professionally and academically. If the subsequent study is well conducted and reported, besides making a contribution to knowledge, publication in a professional journal is also a probable consequence. The potential personal benefits to be derived from publication include increased professional status and job opportunities, not to mention tremendous self-satisfaction.

Sources

You may be asking yourself, "So where do I find one of those numerous significant problems that need researching?" While there are several major sources of problems, the most meaningful ones are generally those derived from theory. There are many educationally relevant theories, such as theories of learning and behavior, from which problems can be drawn. The fact that a theory *is* a theory and *not* a body of facts means that it contains generalizations and hypothesized principles which must be subjected to rigorous scientific investigation. Problems derived from a theoretical problem area are not only preferable in terms of contribution to true scientific progress in education, they also facilitate the formulation of hypotheses based on sound rationale; these hypotheses in turn facilitate ultimate interpretation of study results. The results of a study based on a theoretical problem contribute to their related theory by confirming or disconfirming some aspect of the theory and also by suggesting additional studies that need to be done.

To be perfectly honest, however, selection of a problem based on theory may be a bit "heavy" for many beginning researchers. There are a great number of problems that need researching that are not theoretical in nature. An obvious source of such problems is the researcher's personal experiences. Most educational researchers come from the teaching profession. It is hard to imagine a teacher who has never had a hunch concerning a better way to do something (a way to increase learning or improve behavior, for example) or been a consumer of a program or materials whose effectiveness was untested. This is not to say that a hunch based on experience will never lead to a theoretical problem, it is just more probable that the problem will result in a very applied research study.

As mentioned previously, the literature is also a good source of problems. In addition to overviews and summaries, which are more helpful in narrowing down a problem area, specific studies often indicate "next-step" studies which need to be conducted. The suggested "next-step" may involve a logical extension of the described study or simply replication of the study in a different setting in order to establish the generalizability of its findings. For example, a study investigating the effectiveness of microcomputer-assisted instruction in elementary arithmetic might suggest the need for similar studies in other curriculum areas. It is generally not a good idea, however, to simply replicate a study as it was originally conducted; there is much to be learned from developing and executing your own study. Replication of certain studies, however, is highly desirable, especially those whose results conflict with previous research or disconfirm some aspect of an established theory.

Characteristics

Since a research problem by definition involves an issue in need of investigation, it follows that a basic characteristic of a research problem is that it is "researchable." A "researchable" problem is one that can be investigated through the collection and analysis of data. Problems dealing with philosophical or ethical issues are not researchable. Research can assess how people "feel" about such issues but research cannot resolve them. Whether or not there is reward and punishment in the here-after may be an important problem to many people but it is not researchable; there is no way to resolve it through the collection and analysis of data (at least at the present time!). Similarly, in education there are a number of issues that make great topics for debates (such as "should prayer be allowed in the schools?") but are not researchable problems.

A major characteristic of a good problem is that it has theoretical or practical significance. Of course the most significant problems are those derived from theory; even if the problem is nontheoretical, however, its solution should contribute in some way to improvement of the educational process. If the typical reaction to your problem is "who cares?" it probably is not of sufficient significance to warrant a study!

A third major characteristic of a good problem is that it is a good problem *for you*. The fact that you have chosen a problem of interest to you, in an area in which you have expertise, is not sufficient. It must be a problem that you can adequately investigate given (1) your current level of research skill, (2) available resources, and (3) time and other restrictions. The availability of appropriate subjects and measuring instruments, for example, is an important consideration. As a beginning researcher, you more than likely have access to one or more faculty advisors who can help you to assess the feasibility of your problem.

Statement

A well-written statement of a problem generally indicates the variables of interest to the researcher and the specific relationship between those variables which is to be investigated, and, ideally, the type of subjects involved, i.e., gifted learning-disabled fourth graders.[2] A well-written problem statement also defines all relevant variables, either directly or operationally; operational definitions define concepts in terms of operations, or processes. An example of a problem statement might be: "The problem to be investigated in this study is (or "the purpose of this study is to investigate") the effect of positive reinforcement on the quality of 10th graders' English compositions." The variables to be defined are "positive reinforcement" and "quality of English compositions." Positive reinforcement might be defined in terms of positive written comments on compositions such as "good thought" and "much better." The quality of the compositions might be defined in terms of such factors as number of complete sentences and number of words spelled incorrectly. In this example, the relationship to be investigated between the variables is cause-effect; the purpose of

---

[2]Certain descriptive studies simply state their problems in the form of questions to be answered. However, most meaningful descriptive studies are also concerned with relationships between variables. For example, a descriptive study concerned with voting patterns of various types of voters on a school bond issue would be preferable to a mere polling of voters.

the study is to see if positive reinforcement (the cause) influences the quality of compositions (the effect). Other possible problem statements might read:

> "The problem to be investigated in this study is . . .
> . . . secondary teachers' attitudes toward required inservice activities."
> . . . the relationship between school entrance age and reading comprehension skills of primary-level students."
> . . . the effect of wearing required school uniforms on the self-esteem of disadvantaged sixth-grade students."
> . . . the effect of periodic home visits on the recidivism rate of juvenile offenders."

A statement of the problem is invariably the first component of the introduction section of both a research plan and a research report on a completed study. Since the problem statement gives direction to the rest of the plan or report, it should be stated as soon as possible. The statement of the problem should be accompanied by a presentation of the background of the problem, including a justification for the study in terms of the significance of the problem. Background of the problem means information required for an understanding of the problem. The problem should be justified in terms of its contribution to educational theory or practice. For example, an introduction might begin with a problem statement such as "the purpose of this study is to compare the effectiveness of salaried paraprofessionals and parent volunteers with respect to the reading achievement of first-grade children." This statement might be followed by a discussion concerning (1) the role of paraprofessionals, (2) increased utilization of paraprofessionals by schools, (3) the expense involved, and (4) the search for alternatives, such as parent volunteers. The significance of the problem would be that if parent volunteers are equally effective, their use can be substituted for salaried paraprofessionals at great savings. Any educational practice that might increase achievement at no additional cost is certainly worthy of investigation!

After a problem has been carefully selected, delineated, and clearly stated, the researcher is ready to attack the review of related literature. The researcher typically has a tentative hypothesis that guides the review. In the above example, the tentative hypothesis would be that parent volunteers are equally effective as salaried paraprofessionals. It is not unlikely that the tentative hypothesis will be modified, even changed radically, as a result of the review. It does, however, give direction to the literature search, and narrows its scope to include only relevant topics.

■ REVIEW OF RELATED LITERATURE

Having happily found a suitable problem, the beginning researcher is usually "raring to go." Too often the review of related literature is seen as a necessary evil to be completed as fast as possible so that one can get on with the study. This feeling is due to a lack of understanding concerning the purpose and importance of the review, and to a feeling of uneasiness on the part of students who are not too sure exactly how to go about it. The review of related literature, however, is as important as any other component of the research process, and it can be conducted quite painlessly if it is approached in an orderly manner. Some researchers even find the process quite enjoyable!

Definition, Purpose, and Scope

The review of related literature involves the systematic identification, location, and analysis of documents containing information related to the research problem. These documents include periodicals, abstracts, reviews, books, and other research reports. The review has several important functions which make it well worth the time and effort. The major purpose of reviewing the literature is to determine what has already been done that relates to your problem. This knowledge not only avoids unintentional duplication, but it also provides the understandings and insights necessary for the development of a logical framework into which your problem fits. In other words, the review tells the researcher what has been done and what needs to be done. Studies that have been done will provide the rationale for your research hypothesis; indications of what needs to be done will form the basis for the justification for your study.

Another important function of the literature review is that it points out research strategies and specific procedures and measuring instruments that have and have not been found to be productive in investigating your problem. This information will help you to avoid other researchers' mistakes and to profit from their experiences. It may suggest approaches and procedures previously not considered. For example, suppose your problem involved the comparative effectiveness of experiment-based versus traditional instruction on the achievement of eighth-grade physical science students. The review of literature might reveal 10 related studies already conducted which have found no differences in achievement. Several of the studies, however, might suggest that experiment-based instruction may be more effective for certain kinds of students than others. Thus, you might reformulate your problem to involve the comparative effectiveness of experiment-based versus traditional instruction on the achievement of *low-aptitude* eighth-grade physical science students.

Being familiar with previous research also facilitates interpretation of the results of your study. The results can be discussed in terms of whether they agree with, and support, previous findings or not; if the results contradict previous findings, differences between your study and the others can be described, providing a rationale for the discrepancy. If your results are consistent with other findings, your report should include suggestions for the "next step"; if they are not consistent, your report should include suggestions for studies that will resolve the conflict.

Beginning researchers seem to have difficulty in determining how broad their literature review should be. They understand that all literature directly related to their problem should be reviewed; they just don't know when to quit! They have trouble determining which articles are "related enough" to their problem to be included. Unfortunately, there is no statistical formula that can be applied; the decisions must be based on judgment. These judgments become easier as one acquires experience; there are some general guidelines, however, which can assist the beginner. First, avoid the temptation to include everything you find; bigger does not mean better. A smaller, well-organized review is definitely to be preferred to a review containing many studies that are more or less related to the problem. Second, heavily researched areas usually provide enough references directly related to a specific problem to eliminate the need for relying on less related studies. For example, the role of feedback in learning has been extensively researched for both animals and human beings, for verbal learning and nonverbal learning, and for a variety of different learning tasks. If you were concerned with the relationship between frequency of feedback and chemistry achievement, you would probably not have to review, for example, feedback studies related to animal learning. Third, and conversely, new or little-researched problem areas usually require review of any study related in some meaningful way to the problem in order to develop a logical framework for the study and a sound rationale for the research hypothesis. For example, a study concerned with the effectiveness of the use of metal detectors for reducing incidents of injury-resulting violence would probably include in its literature search any study involving approaches to violence reduction. Five years from now there will probably be enough research on metal detectors to permit a much more narrowly focused literature review.

A common misconception among beginning researchers is the idea that the worth of their problem is a function of the amount of literature available on the topic. This is not the case. There are many new, important areas of research for which there is comparatively little available literature; use of metal detectors is one such area. The very lack of such research increases the worth of the study. On the other hand, the fact that 1,000 studies have already been done in a given problem area does not mean there is no further need for research in that area. Such an area will generally be very well developed with additional needed research readily identifiable. Such an area is anxiety theory, which is concerned with the relationships between anxiety and learning.

Preparation

Since it will be a second home to you, at least for a while, you should become completely familiar with the library before beginning your review. Time spent initially will save time in the long run. You should find out what references are available and where they are located. You should also be familiar with services offered by the library as well as the rules and regulations regarding the use of library materials. Since most of the references you will be seeking will be located in educational journals, you should spend extra time getting well acquainted with the various periodicals.

Many libraries provide written and/or video guides detailing what the library has to offer and the procedures for utilizing references and services. While many references are standard and can be found in most libraries, some sources, such as the ERIC microfiche collection, are not necessarily available. Also, significant library-related technological advances have been made in the last few years, and libraries vary greatly in their ability to capitalize on increasingly available options. Your library, for example, may or may not have an on-line computer search or CD-ROM access capability. Services also vary from library to library. One important service that is offered by most libraries is the interlibrary loan. This service permits you to obtain references not available in your library but available in another library. The small fee usually charged is generally happily paid by the researcher who "needs" a locally unavailable reference. Many libraries offer guided tours of the facilities; such tours are generally scheduled for groups. While librarians are usually very willing to help individuals, you should learn to use the library; the librarian may not be as cheerful the ninth time you approach as he or she was the first time!

Having formulated your problem, and acquainted yourself with the library, there is one more thing you need to do before you go marching merrily off into the library—make a list of key words to guide your literature search. Most of the sources you will consult will have alphabetical subject indexes to help you locate specific references. You will look in these indexes under the key words you have selected. For example, if your problem concerns the effect of interactive multimedia on the achievement of 10th-grade biology students, the logical key words would be *interactive multimedia* and *biology.* You will also need to think of alternative words under which your topic might be listed. For example, references related to the above problem might be found using the key words *multimedia or interactive videodiscs* rather than *interactive multimedia* (as is the case with the *Education Index*). Usually, the key words will be obvious; sometimes you may have to play detective. Some years ago a student of mine was interested in the effect of artificial turf on knee injuries in football. He looked under every key word he could think of, such as *surface, playing surface, turf,* and *artificial turf.* He could find nothing. Since we both knew that studies had been done, he kept trying. When he finally did find a reference it was listed under, of all things, *lawns*! Identifying key words is usually not such a big deal. In looking in initial sources you may identify additional key words that will help you in succeeding sources. However, giving some thought initially to possible key words should facilitate an efficient beginning to a task that requires organization. After you have identified your key words, you will finally be ready to begin to consult appropriate sources.

Sources

There are usually many sources of literature that might be related to a given problem. In general, however, there are a number of major sources commonly used by educational researchers. Some of these sources are primary sources and some are secondary; as with historical research, primary sources are definitely preferable. In historical research, a primary source is an eyewitness or an original document or relic; in the literature, a primary source is a description of a study written by the person who conducted it. A secondary source in the literature is generally a much briefer description of a study written by someone other than the original researcher. The *Review of Educational Research,* for example, summarizes many research studies conducted on a given topic. Since secondary sources usually give complete bibliographic information on references cited, they direct the researcher to relevant primary sources. You should not be satisfied with only the information contained in secondary sources; the corresponding primary sources will be considerably more detailed and will give you information "straight from the horse's mouth," as they say.

The number of individual references that could be consulted for a given problem is staggering; fortunately there are indexes, abstracts, and other retrieval mechanisms, such as computer searches, that facilitate identification of relevant references. In this section we will discuss the ones most often used in educational research; you should check the library for sources in your area of specialization. Following the discussion of the various sources, computer-assisted literature searches will be described.

Education Index

The *Education Index* is a major source of educational periodicals.[3] Educational periodicals (as other periodicals) typically are published at regular intervals (monthly or bimonthly, for example) and include such things as reports of research efforts, reviews of related research, and opinion articles on contemporary educational issues. The term *periodical* includes professional journals as well as yearbooks, bul-

---

[3]*Education index.* (1929 to date). New York: H. W. Wilson.

letins, and other educational reports. The *Education Index* lists bibliographical information on references appearing in literally hundreds of educational periodicals. The *Education Index* is used much the same way as any other index; entries are listed alphabetically under subject, author, and title headings. Since the procedure for using the *Index* is similar to the procedure followed for other indexes, it will be described in detail:

1. Start with the most recent issue of the *Index* and look under the key words you have already identified, *interactive multimedia,* for example.
2. Under the key words you will find a list of references presented alphabetically by title, or you will be directed to other key words. For example, if you looked under *Interactive multimedia* in the 1994 *Index* (volume 65, number 7), you would be directed to "See Multimedia." Under the indicated heading you would find the following entries (among others):

   > The application of multimedia CD-ROMs in schools.
   > L. Perzylo. bibl *Br J Educ Technol* v24 p191–7 S '93

   > Grow your own multimedia: tips for selecting
   > authoring software programs. K. S. Forney. il
   > por *Community Coll J* v64 p38–42 O/N '93

   > The multimedia difference. C. W. Day. il *Am Sch
   > Univ* v66 p26 O '93

3. Decide whether each reference is related to your problem or not. For example, assume your problem was concerned with the effect of interactive multimedia on the achievement of 10th-grade biology students. The first entry above, dealing with the application of CD-ROMs in schools, probably would be related. The second entry, which involves selecting software for making your own multimedia, would probably not be related. The third entry might or might not be related.
4. If the reference is probably related, or might be related, copy the complete reference.
5. If you are not familiar with abbreviations used by the *Index,* look in the front of the volume. Where you have written the reference, replace each abbreviation with the complete term. In the entry from the *Index* concerned with the application of CD-ROMs, for example, *Br J Educ Technol* is the abbreviation for the *British Journal of Educational Technology,* and S is the abbreviation for Summer.
6. Repeat steps 1 to 5 for previous issues of the *Index.*
7. Locate each of the references on the library shelves.

The *Education Index* is similar in purpose to *Current Index to Journals in Education* (CIJE), which will be discussed later.[4] When CIJE is available, the *Education Index* is less useful in that since it does not contain abstracts, time is often wasted locating "might be related" references which turn out not to be related. On the other hand, the *Education Index* provides wider journal coverage and, since CIJE was not available prior to 1969, the *Education Index* is the best source of educational periodicals published from 1929 to 1969. There are also a number of indexes similar to the *Education Index* available for specific fields such as business education.

---

[4]*Current index to journals in education.* (1969 to date). Phoenix: Oryx Press.

Readers' Guide to Periodical Literature

Readers' Guide to Periodical Literature is an index very similar in format to the *Education Index*.[5] Instead of professional publications, however, it indexes articles in close to 200 widely read magazines. Articles located through the *Guide* will generally be nontechnical, opinion-type references. These can be very useful, however, particularly in documenting the significance of your problem. For example, many articles have been written in popular magazines expressing concern on the part of the American public over the inability of many children to read adequately. *Readers' Guide* lists entries alphabetically by subject and author, and the procedures for its use are essentially the same as for using the *Education Index*. In addition to *Readers' Guide*, there are several other sources of popular literature, such as *Social Sciences Index, Humanities Index,* and *The New York Times Index*.[6]

Dissertation Abstracts International

Dissertation Abstracts International contains abstracts of doctoral dissertations conducted at hundreds of academic institutions.[7] Abstracts are summaries, usually brief; *Dissertation Abstracts International* summarizes the main components of dissertation studies. The advantage of having an abstract is that it usually allows you to classify all references as related to your problem or not related, and greatly reduces time spent looking up unrelated references with fuzzy titles. *Dissertation Abstracts International* classifies entries by subject, author, and institution. It is divided into two parts: Part A covers the humanities and social sciences, and Part B covers the sciences and engineering. Since Part A includes education, and Part B includes psychology, you will often have to check both sections. The procedure for using the *Abstracts* is similar to the procedure for using the *Education Index;* the major difference is that once a related dissertation title is located, the next step is not to locate the dissertation but to locate an abstract of the dissertation using the entry number given with the reference. For example, if the entry number were 27/03B/3720, the abstract would be located in volume 27, issue number 3B, page number 3720. If after reading an abstract you wish to obtain a copy of the complete dissertation, check and see if it is available in your library. If not, it can be obtained from University Microfilms International on microfilm for a small fee or in hardcopy for a larger fee. Complete and specific directions for ordering by phone or mail are given in the front of each *Dissertation Abstracts* volume. University Microfilms International also provides a computer retrieval service called DATRIX. By filling out a request form available at most libraries and indicating appropriate key words, you can receive a bibliography of related dissertations for a nominal fee.

Related dissertations may also be identified through the subject index of the *Comprehensive Dissertation Index*.[8] This index is indeed comprehensive, providing bibliographical data on hundreds of thousands of dissertations completed from 1861 to the present. Appropriate information for locating corresponding abstracts in

---

[5]*Readers' guide to periodical literature*. (1900 to date). New York: H. W. Wilson.

[6]*Social sciences index*. (1974 to date). New York: H. W. Wilson; *Humanities index*. (1974 to date). New York: H. W. Wilson; and *The New York Times index*. (1913 to date). New York: The New York Times Co.

[7]*Dissertation abstracts international*. (1969 to date). Ann Arbor, MI: University Microfilms International. (Prior to 1969, the title was *Dissertation abstracts*.)

[8]*Comprehensive dissertation index*. (1861 to date). Ann Arbor, MI: University Microfilms International.

Dissertation Abstracts International is also given for dissertations for which abstracts are available.

Psychological Abstracts

Psychological Abstracts presents summaries of completed psychological research studies.[9] Each issue contains 12 sections corresponding to 12 areas of psychology. The sections on developmental psychology and educational psychology are generally the most useful to educational researchers. The December issue contains an annual cumulative author index and subject index. In addition, cumulative subject indexes and cumulative author indexes, which cover approximately 30 years, are available.

The first step in using *Psychological Abstracts* is to identify the terms which *Psychological Abstracts* uses to index references. The *Thesaurus of Psychological Index Terms,* available in most libraries, is a compilation of the key words used in indexing *Psychological Abstracts* documents.[10] The *Thesaurus* indicates the various terms under which a given topic is indexed. If, for example, your research problem concerned the effect of interactive multimedia on the achievement of 10th-grade biology students, you would find that interactive multimedia is not a descriptor used by the *Thesaurus.* You would have to try other descriptors such as instructional media.

The procedure for using *Psychological Abstracts* is similar to the procedure for the *Education Index.* The major difference is that the *Psychological Abstracts* index does not give bibliographic information; for a given topic, abstract numbers of related references are given. This number is located in *Psychological Abstracts,* which provides the complete reference as well as an abstract of the reference. If the abstract indicates that the study is related to the problem of interest, the original reference can then be located. In addition to the key words identified for a given problem, the word *bibliography* should also be checked. A bibliography related to your problem may exist which might lead you to important references that might otherwise be missed.

How fruitful *Psychological Abstracts* will be for you will depend upon the nature of your problem. If it is a nontheoretical problem, such as the previously mentioned study concerned with in-class pencil-sharpening behavior, you probably will not find anything in *Psychological Abstracts.* If the problem does relate to some theory, such as a study on the effects of positive reinforcement, you more than likely will find useful references. In such cases, both *Psychological Abstracts* and the educational indexes should be checked to make sure you do not miss anything.

Another source of similar information is the *Annual Review of Psychology;* it includes reviews of psychological research that are often of relevance to educational research.[11] There are also a number of journals of abstracts for specific areas such as child development, educational administration, exceptional child education, and language teaching.

Educational Resources Information Center (ERIC)

Established in the mid-sixties by the United States Office of Education, ERIC is a national information system currently supported and operated by the National

---

[9]American Psychological Association. (1927 to date). *Psychological abstracts.* Washington, DC: Author.

[10]American Psychological Association. (1994). *Thesaurus of psychological index terms* (7th ed.). Washington, DC: Author.

[11]*Annual review of psychology.* (1950 to date). Palo Alto, CA: Annual Reviews.

Institute of Education (NIE). Its primary purpose is to collect and disseminate reports of current educational research, evaluation, and development activities. Many educators are not fully aware of the range of services offered by the ERIC network. Although there is some overlap in the references included in ERIC, The *Education Index,* and *Psychological Abstracts,* ERIC contains abstracts for many additional references. Research reports that would not typically be included in other sources (such as papers presented at professional meetings and studies conducted in school districts) are indexed and abstracted by ERIC. Another factor in favor of ERIC is the comparatively short time interval between collection of a document and its dissemination. Documents become part of ERIC much more quickly than if they are published by a professional journal. Thus for very current topics, ERIC is often a source of data not available through other sources. Manuscripts submitted for possible inclusion in the ERIC system undergo a review process similar to that associated with professional journals.

ERIC comprises a central office and a number of clearinghouses, each devoted to a different area (such as assessment and evaluation, disabilities and gifted education, information and technology, teaching and teacher education, and urban education). Each clearinghouse collects, abstracts, stores, and disseminates documents specific to its area of specialization. Disseminated documents include information analysis products (books, monographs, and other publications), fact sheets, computer search reprints, and information bulletins.

Two major ERIC publications are *Resources in Education* (RIE) and *Current Index to Journals in Education* (CIJE).[12] Since they both use a common format, if you learn how to use one of them you know how to use the other. The first step in using ERIC resources is to become familiar with the terms which ERIC uses to index references. As with the thesaurus for *Psychological Abstracts,* the *Thesaurus of ERIC Descriptors,* also available in most libraries, is a compilation of the key words used in indexing ERIC documents.[13] The ERIC *Thesaurus* indicates the various terms under which a given topic is indexed. If, for example, your research problem concerned the effect of interactive multimedia on the achievement of 10th-grade biology students, you would find that *interactive multimedia* is not a descriptor in the ERIC system, but *Multimedia Instruction* is. Each issue of RIE and CIJE includes new additions to the pool of descriptors. After you have identified appropriate descriptors, the next logical step is to consult RIE.

RIE. RIE is published monthly, and semiannual indexes are available. RIE indexes over 1,000 documents per issue and for many entries provides an abstract prepared by one of the clearinghouses. If the title of an article sufficiently conveys its content, an abstract is not included; otherwise an abstract is included. Entries are indexed by subject, author, institution, and accession number. Using the accession numbers given in each index, abstracts are located in the Document Resumés section. For example, in the 1993 July-December semiannual index of RIE in the subject index under *Multimedia Instruction,* the following entry is listed (among others):

> Introduction to Multimedia in Instruction. An IAT
> Technology Primer
>
> ED 354 877

This entry appears to be related to our problem. Using the accession number, ED 354 877, more complete information can be located in the Document Resumés sec-

---

[12]National Institute of Education. (1966 to date). *Resources in education.* Washington, DC: Author. See also footnote 4.

[13]Houston, J. E. (Ed.). (1990). *Thesaurus of ERIC descriptors* (12th ed.). Phoenix: Oryx Press.

tion. This information includes the author's name, the publication date, the cost of obtaining the complete document in microfiche and hard copy, descriptors under which this entry is listed, and an abstract of the contents. Since most libraries have the ERIC document collection in microfiche form, it is usually not necessary to order documents, although instructions are given for doing so. Note that the ED prefix indicates that this reference is *not* a journal article; it is an *educational document*.

The next step in using ERIC is to consult the monthly and semiannual indexes of CIJE.

CIJE. CIJE, mentioned previously as an improvement on the *Education Index,* indexes articles in the educational periodical literature. It covers close to 800 education and education-related publications, and includes close to 1,500 documents per issue. As with RIE, CIJE is published monthly and semiannual indexes are available. The procedure for using CIJE is very similar to the procedure for using RIE. Using the same descriptors, relevant entries are identified in one of the indexes. Using the accession numbers, additional information is located in the Main Entry section. As with RIE, if the title of an article sufficiently conveys its content, an abstract is not included; otherwise an abstract is included. The addition of abstracts when needed makes CIJE more useful than the *Education Index* for those years for which it is available. Although CIJE was first published in 1969, abstracts were not included until 1970. After reading the abstract, the entire article may be read by consulting the appropriate journal. As an example, in the June, 1994, subject index (volume 26, number 6), under the descriptor *Multimedia Instruction,* the following entry is listed (among others);

> Interactive Multimedia Research Questions: Results from the
> Delphi Study. *Journal of Special Education Technology;*
> v12 n2 p107–17 fall 1993
>
> EJ 477 678

This entry tells us that in volume 12, issue number 2, of the publication *Journal of Special Education Technology,* we will find an article entitled "Interactive Multimedia Research Questions: Results from the Delphi Study." If we wish to know more about the contents of the article, we can use the accession number, EJ 477 678, to locate the abstract and other information in the Main Entry section. Note that the prefix EJ indicates that this reference appears in an *educational journal*.

Obtaining ERIC Documents and Information. In addition to those already mentioned, a number of other services are provided by ERIC. For example, the various clearinghouses prepare and disseminate annotated bibliographies in their particular area of specialization. Also, a variety of curriculum guides, teachers' guides, and instructional materials can be obtained from clearinghouses. You should ask your librarian for an up-to-date listing of the clearinghouses and their addresses.

As mentioned, all ERIC documents are available in hardcopy and/or microfiche. Hardcopy is more convenient but microfiche is considerably less expensive. Most libraries have the complete ERIC microfiche collection and microfiche readers. If they are not available, you can order any document directly by calling 1-800-443-ERIC.

If you would like more information on searching, obtaining, or submitting ERIC documents, read *All About ERIC*.[14] If your library does not have a copy, or if you need additional assistance, call 1-800-LET-ERIC (1-800-538-3742).

---

[14] Educational Resources Information Center. (1994). *All about ERIC*. Washington, DC: U.S. Department of Education.

Review of Educational Research

The RER, mentioned previously, reviews and briefly summarizes a number of related studies on given topics. For example, volume 63 contains reviews of research on word processing and writing instruction,[15] assessing cognitive skills,[16] and giftedness and self-concept.[17] Although the RER is a secondary source, each article concludes with an extensive bibliography. By reading the review article, and using the bibliography, you can easily identify important primary sources. To use the RER, simply check the table of contents of each issue. If a listed review is relevant to your problem, read the review and note specific studies of interest. Finally, use the bibliography to obtain the complete reference on the selected studies. Up until 1970, the RER was concerned with a limited number of general problem areas; however, the RER now accepts unsolicited reviews on a wide variety of topics.

Books

It is hard to imagine a graduate student who has never used the library card catalog to find books related to a given problem. However, without the data it would not be very "researchy" to say that there is no such graduate student, thus the inclusion of this discussion. Briefly, the card catalog alphabetically indexes (by author, subject, and title) all publications contained in the library, with the exception of the periodicals. Not infrequently, a comprehensive description of research in a given field will be compiled and published in book form. If such a book exists for your problem, it can be an invaluable reference.

Although libraries may maintain their card catalogs, many have converted to a computer-based catalog system such as LUIS (Library User Information Service) which alphabetically indexes (by author, title, and subject) all the entries in the card catalog. In addition to the usual information, such as the call number, some of these systems provide other useful information such as whether a given book is on the shelf or checked out, and when it is supposed to be returned. Using such a system is quite easy once you get the hang of it and become familiar with its little idiosyncrasies. (For example, the cursor may need to be *exactly* two spaces to the right of the "arrow" in order to type in an entry—computers are very picky!)

Encyclopedias may also be useful, especially those in specialized areas such as educational research. General encyclopedias contain articles on a wide range of topics written by experts. Encyclopedias in specialized areas contain more detailed discussions on a restricted number of topics. A good example is the *Encyclopedia of Educational Research,* which contains critical reviews and summaries on a number of educational topics.[18] Like the RER, the *Encyclopedia* is a secondary source which also follows each article with an extensive bibliography helpful in identifying pertinent sources. Two additional encyclopedias you might find useful are *The Encyclopedia of Human Development and Education: Theory, Research, and Studies,*[19] and *The*

---

[15] Bangert-Drowns, R. L. (1993). The word processor as an instructional tool: A meta-analysis of word processing in writing instruction. *Review of Educational Research, 63,* 69–93.

[16] Royer, J. M., Cisero, C. A., & Carlo, M. S. (1993). Techniques and procedures for assessing cognitive skills. *Review of Educational Research, 63,* 201–243.

[17] Hoge, R. D., & Renzulli, J. S. (1993). Exploring the link between giftedness and self-concept. *Review of Educational Research, 63,* 449–465.

[18] See footnote 1.

[19] Thomas, R. M. (Ed.). (1990). *The encyclopedia of human development and education: Theory, research, and studies.* New York: Pergamon.

International Encyclopedia of Education: Research and Studies.[20] The *Handbook of Research on Teaching* is also a valuable resource for certain topics.[21]

Computer Searches

With relatively little effort, you can use a computer to identify related references for you. Searching that would take you days and days to do, a computer can do in a matter of minutes. No, a computer won't do your review of related literature for you, but it will help a lot: It will search databases such as the ERIC system and provide you with a list of references and, if provided by the database, abstracts.

Hundreds of databases are available through a number of information retrieval systems. The H. W. Wilson retrieval system, for example, contains 27 databases, including the *Education Index* and *Readers' Guide to Periodical Literature,* representing more than one-half million articles from nearly 4,000 periodicals. In contrast, the DIALOG system provides access to close to 150 different databases, including ERIC, and is the largest system of its type. Virtually all retrieval systems include ERIC: It is the bibliographic database most widely used in education. ERIC searches can be obtained at hundreds of locations across the United States (and around the world). Many universities also provide computer searches of the ERIC system, and a number of them access at least one major information retrieval system such as DIALOG, BRS, or SilverPlatter. You can find out about the services at your library by inquiring at the reference desk about the availability of online and CD-ROM searches.

Types of Computer Searches

Computer searches can be done online or by using CD-ROM. An online search is performed at a computer terminal which is directly connected via telephone lines to a central database system. A CD-ROM search involves using software onto which database information has been transferred. All of the sources of related literature which were discussed previously can be accessed using online and CD-ROM searches and can be downloaded onto diskette. Depending on the retrieval system being used, various support services are available to help you, e.g., manuals, training seminars, and toll-free search assistance numbers.

Online Searches.   Online computer searches are made possible by the fact that various databases are available on computer tapes. Information retrieval systems provide institutions with access to the tapes in their system; some institutions have some tapes themselves. Two major vendors of online retrieval services are BRS (Bibliographic Retrieval Services Information Technologies) and DIALOG (Dialog Information Services). While specifics for their utilization differ, both contain the *Dissertation Abstracts International, Psychological Abstracts* (PsycINFO) and ERIC databases (among others). The *Education Index* and *Readers' Guide to Periodical Literature* databases are available from the WILSONLINE online retrieval system (H. W. Wilson). Databases are updated frequently and can be accessed by virtually all types of computer terminals. It is even possible to do online searches in your

---

[20]Husén, T., & Postlethwaite, T. N. (Eds.). (1994). *The international encyclopedia of education: Research and studies.* New York: Pergamon.

[21]Wittrock, M. C. (Ed.). (1986). *Handbook of research on teaching* (3rd ed.). New York: Macmillan.

own home using your personal microcomputer and a modem (telephone hook-up). There is at least one software program, EndNote, which allows you to download (transfer to diskette) references, abstracts, and articles and then puts your reference list into proper American Psychological Association format (WOW!).[22]

CD-ROM Searches.   CD-ROM searches are becoming increasingly available at university libraries. If your library does not now provide this resource, chances are it soon will. CD-ROM refers to a compact disc that "plays" visual information instead of music. In the case of a literature search, the information which is stored on, and played by, the CD is the contents of one or more databases. Such CDs are very efficient; the entire ERIC collection can fit on as few as two CDs. A CD is "read" by a laser player and the contents are displayed on a computer screen (neat, huh?). ROM stands for "read-only memory," which basically means that you can read the contents of the CD, you can interact with the contents, and you can even print the contents; but you can't change the contents.

Two major vendors of CD-ROM versions of databases are DIALOG and SilverPlatter. Both provide the ERIC databases (DIALOG OnDisc ERIC and SilverPlatter ERIC), and SilverPlatter also provides the *Psychological Abstracts* database (PsychLit). Both vendors include the related thesaurus on each CD: Thus, for example, DIALOG OnDisc ERIC has the ERIC *Thesaurus* as an index option. The *Education Index* and *Readers' Guide to Periodical Literature* databases are available from the WILSONDISC CD-ROM retrieval system, and the *Dissertation Abstracts International* database is provided by University Microfilms International (Dissertation Abstracts Ondisc). CDs are typically updated quarterly; an advantage of using DIALOG OnDisc ERIC is that it allows users to transfer to DIALOG online in order to search the most recent entries in the ERIC databases, a feature which will probably become a standard feature of CD-ROM systems.

With few exceptions, search locations such as university libraries have CDs and hardware sufficient to accommodate only one user at a time; you must typically sign up to use the CDs for a limited period of time, usually 20 to 30 minutes. Of course, you may come back another time, or use them longer if no one is signed up for the time slot after you, but you are limited in your access. On the plus side, you get your printout immediately. Increased flexibility comes from your ability to "play" with various key words to see what you'll get using them, and to review references and abstracts prior to printing them. You might find out, for example, that the key words Multimedia Instruction and Secondary Education will yield 4 references, but Multimedia Instruction and Science Education will yield 22. After you have selected the best combination of descriptors for your purpose, you can then select the print option and take the output with you. Unlike online searches (which also permit the above), there is usually no cost involved because search locations pay a set yearly fee for CD-ROMS. If a CD-ROM is used frequently, the actual cost per search will be minimal.

Learning how to do a CD-ROM search involves becoming familiar with the options and commands involved with the system you wish to use. Clearly, it would not be feasible to explain in this text how to use all of the CD-ROM systems available. Table 2.1, however, which reproduces a portion of a document titled *Basic Instruction for Using ERIC on CD—Easy Menu Searching,* should give you the general idea.[23] It describes the procedure for using DIALOG OnDisc ERIC.

---

[22]Niles & Associates. (1988). EndNote [Computer program]. Emeryville, CA: Author.

[23]Dunbar, M., & Beary, M. (1994). *Basic instructions for using ERIC on CD—Easy menu searching.* Unpublished document, Library Services, Florida International University, Miami, FL.

The Computer Search Process

Learning how to do a computer search is not difficult: Learning how to do an efficient search that meets your needs requires practice and experience. While you are getting the hang of it, feel free to seek help from reference (or information) desk personnel; they are typically very nice and they do not make you feel like you have the IQ of an ice-cube tray. At first, you may have lots of little questions: How do I

Table 2.1

Basic Instructions for Using ERIC on CD: An Example of a Procedure for Doing a CD-ROM Search

Executing Your Search:

1. Press the F3 key—then press the y key to clear the previous search.
2. If you see the "Select Search Mode" menu in the middle of the screen, go to step 3 now. If you see the "Select Main Activity" menu in the middle of the screen, use the up and down arrow keys to move the highlight bar to "Quit Easy Menu Mode" and then press the enter key.
3. You should now see the "Select Search Mode" menu in the middle of the screen. Use the up and down arrow keys to move the highlight bar to "Easy Menu" and then press the enter key.
4. You should now see the "Select a File" menu. Use the up and down arrow keys to move the highlight bar to the file you want to search (8393=1983 to 1993; 6682=1966 to 1982) and then press the enter key.
5. You should now see the "Select Main Activity" menu in the middle of the screen. Make sure the option "Begin a new search" is highlighted. Press the enter key to begin your search.
6. You should now see the "Search Options" menu in the middle of the screen. Use the up and down arrows to choose either the "Word/Phrase Index" or the "ERIC Subject Headings" option (or another option if you are now ready to modify your search). The differences between those two choices are:

   In general, it is preferable to choose the "ERIC Subject Headings" option. In this case the computer will search only the subject headings area of each item on the ERIC disc you are searching. Each item indexed in ERIC is read by an education specialist who then chooses those descriptors (subject headings) from the **Thesaurus of ERIC Descriptors** which best describe the article (or unpublished document). Therefore, you can take advantage of the specialist's knowledge and will be more likely to retrieve items most relevant to your topic.

   Occasionally, a topic may not have an appropriate ERIC descriptor in the **Thesaurus. . . .** In this case using the "Word/Phrase Index" option would be your best choice. If you choose the "Word/Phrase Index" the computer will search in the title, the summary, and the subject headings for your word(s). However, before you decide there is no ERIC descriptor for your topic you should: think of synonyms for your topic and then look them up in the alphabetical part of the **Thesaurus . . .** (which starts on p. 1); look up your topic in the rotated part of the **Thesaurus . . .** (which starts on p. 291); or, break your topic down into smaller concepts and then look up each concept in the **Thesaurus. . . .** For more information on using the **Thesaurus . . .** read "Thesaurus Construction and Format" on pp. xxi–xxv of the **Thesaurus.**

Table 2.1 (*continued*)

7. When the screen says "type the first few characters of your search term" you should type each keyword or subject heading (ONE AT A TIME). When the keyword you want is highlighted, press the enter key to select the ERIC documents or articles which include that term. (If there are any related terms you can press the F2 key when your keyword is highlighted; then choose any related terms in which you are interested.) NOTE that the word "SEARCHING" will appear at the top of the screen in the area where you typed your keyword. When the blinking word "SEARCHING" disappears, the term you have selected will be starred, meaning that it has been searched and selected. If you have synonyms or related terms, repeat step **7**. If you do not have synonyms or related terms, this segment of your search is completed; proceed to step **8**.

8. Press the F10 key. A statement of the number of sources which include your keyword (or ERIC subject heading) will appear on the screen. At this point you may want to narrow or expand your search. If so, highlight the menu option "Modify the Current Search" and press the enter key. To narrow your search, highlight the menu option "Limit with Additional Terms" and press the enter key. To expand your search, highlight the menu option "Include Alternate Terms" and press the enter key. Whether you want to limit or expand your search, you can now repeat steps **6–8**.

9. When you have the desired number of sources, highlight the menu option "Display, Print, or Transfer" and press the enter key. Look at the "Display Format" options menu. Generally, you want the complete record. First time users may want to select the option "Complete Record Tagged." A list of definitions for these "TAGS" is on page 7 of this handout.

10. Move the highlight bar to the desired display format and then press the enter key. You may now view the results of your search. If you wish, you may mark each record you want to keep by pressing the F7 key and then the enter key (while the record you want is on the screen). Use the pgdn key to move from one record to the next.

    Remember, your appointment is for 30 minutes. You should not spend all of that time reading and displaying your search results or you won't have any time left to print them out. You should read the first 4 or 5 records to be sure you're getting the results you want—if so, proceed to the next step.

11. Printing: AFTER you have displayed your search results, you may then print your search results or transfer them to a formatted disk. To print your results, press the F8 key. Now highlight the option you want, e.g., "Print Current Record Only" or "Print All Records" or "Print Marked Records" and press the enter key. The records will be printed in the format you chose in step **9**, above.

insert the CD? How do I highlight my choice? And so forth. But, after a few sessions, you will know enough to "play the game," and will be able to concentrate on improving your search strategies. Regardless of how you do your search, it is to your advantage to plan your search strategy very carefully. Hundreds of more or less related abstracts take a long time to read and analyze.

The steps involved in conducting a computer search, be it an on-line search or a CD-ROM search, are very similar to those involved in a manual search, to a point:

1. State your problem.

2. Identify your key words.

3. Select the databases you wish to search.

4. Specify your search strategy.

As discussed earlier, your problem statement suggests obvious key words. Additional, or more useful, key words are identified by checking descriptors found in the thesauruses (thesauri, if you prefer!). Usually, the resident search analyst is available to assist you in identifying appropriate descriptors. Normally, if they are available, the databases you select represent the same sources you would otherwise be checking manually, e.g., CIJE. The last step, specifying your search strategy, is the tricky one.

The ideal search strategy is one that gets you just the right number of references, all related to your problem in a meaningful way, and does not prevent you from locating one or more significant references. A search may be classified as *narrow* or *broad*. If a search is narrow, it is likely that all identified references will be related to your problem; if it is too narrow, you may not get enough references or you may miss some important ones. If you find that your search strategy was too narrow, you broaden it. If a search is broad, it is likely that you will not miss any significant references, although you may get some that are not really related to your problem. If your search is too broad, you will have many references that are not relevant, and you will waste time. If you find that your search strategy was too broad, you narrow it. How narrow or broad your initial strategy should be depends on factors such as the purpose for which the search is being conducted and the amount of material available on your topic. If you only need a relatively small number of references and/or if much has been published which is directly related to your problem, a narrow search will be appropriate. If, on the other hand, you need a relatively large number of references and/or very little has been published which is directly related to your problem, a broad search will be appropriate. If you do not have a sense of what is available, your best strategy is to start narrow and broaden as necessary. You might find, for example, that there are very few references related to the effect of interactive multimedia on the achievement of 10th-grade biology students. You could broaden your search by including, for example, all sciences or all secondary students.

There are three basic ways to narrow or broaden a search. One way is by decreasing or increasing the years searched: A search which covers the years 1990 to the present will be more narrow than a search which covers 1985 to the present. A second way is by changing, adding, or deleting key words or concepts, as the above example illustrates. Some CD-ROM systems, the DIALOG OnDisc ERIC Easy Menu Search, for example, allow you to broaden your search by simply adding additional terms for each concept. A third way is through the use of the *and* and *or* connectors.

Most search systems use Boolean logic (whoa!), which involves the use of the *and* and *or* connectors. Put simply, using *and* narrows a search; using *or* broadens a search. Let's say you have two key words, which we will refer to as A and B. If you indicate that you are only interested in references that relate to A *and* B, you are saying that you only want references that refer to *both* concepts. If you indicate that you will take references related to A *or* B, you are saying you will take references that relate to *either* concept. This basic principle is illustrated in Figure 2.1 (Remember Venn diagrams?). Thus, for example, a recent CD-ROM search indicated that there were 603 references for Multimedia Instruction, 14,845 for Science Education, but only 22 for Multimedia Instruction *and* Science Education.

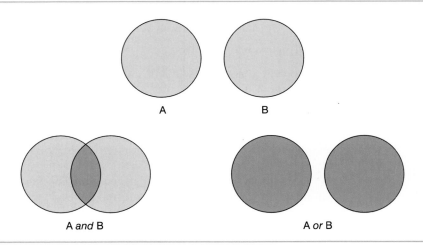

Figure 2.1. An illustration of *and* and *or* connector logic.

By using various combinations of the *and* and *or* connectors, you can vary your search strategy as needed. For example, it was found that the combination Multimedia Instruction *and* Biology *and* Secondary Education yielded zero references (too narrow, for sure!). The ERIC *Thesaurus* indicated that 1) a related term (RT) for Multimedia Instruction is Educational Technology, 2) a related term for Science Education is Science Curriculum, and 3) a related term for Secondary Education is Secondary School Curriculum, and a broader term (BT) is Elementary Secondary Education. Thus, one strategy which was used for a search was as follows:

Multimedia Instruction *or* Educational Technology	*and*	Science Education *or* Science Curriculum	*and*	Secondary Education *or* Secondary School Curriculum *or* Elementary Secondary Education

This strategy broadened the search because it broadened the definition of each concept. Thus the following citation (abridged) was retrieved (among others):

```
EJ 467761
Computer Center.
Kramer, David W.
American Biology Teacher, v53 n2 p122–25 Feb 1991
Target Audience: Teachers; Practitioners
   Discusses the use of videodisk technology to teach biology. Presents videodisk
selection criteria for biology teachers, lists 13 biology videodisks and their
suppliers, and lists videodisks offered with biology textbooks. (MDH)
   Descriptors: Audiovisual Aids; *Biology; Computer Assisted Instruction;
Educational Technology; Educational Television; *Instructional Material
Evaluation; Media Selection; Science Education; *Science Instruction; Secondary
Education; *Teaching Methods; *Videodisks
   Identifiers: *Video Technology
```

This citation is clearly related to the problem of interest. It was retrieved because the strategy used allowed for citations which involved Educational Technology, Science Education, and Secondary Education, not just Multimedia Instruction. Note that Educational Technology is listed as a descriptor in the above citation. Several experimental studies involving the same descriptors were also retrieved.

Another strategy which was used was to delete the second concept; thus, the resulting strategy was as follows:

| Multimedia Instruction *or* Educational Technology | *and* | Secondary Education *or* Secondary School Curriculum *or* Elementary Secondary Education |

This strategy broadened the search because it allowed for relevant references related to all curriculum areas. The following citation (abridged) was retrieved (among others):

```
EJ 478541
A Technophile Looks at Technology, Education, and Art.
Munoz, Zina C.
Art Education, v46 n6 p48–49 Nov 1993
Target Audience: Teachers; Administrators; Practitioners
   Asserts that introducing educational technology into the K–12 curriculum is a
major trend. Presents a set of questions that educators should answer as they
increase the use of technology in the classroom. Maintains educators need to
resist the temptation to use technology to replace important educational activi-
ties rather than to enhance them.
   Descriptors: *Art Education; Computer Software; *Computer Uses in Education;
Curriculum Development; *Educational Change; Educational Objectives; *Educational
Technology; Elementary Secondary Education; Ethical Instruction; *Visual Arts
```

By deleting the curriculum area (science) concept, we retrieved a citation dealing with use of educational technology *in art education*. (Note the descriptors.) Given the original problem statement, whether this citation was included in your review of the literature would depend on how many citations you had which were *more* related, and the purpose for which the search was being conducted. Given the purpose of completing Task 2, for example, it probably would not be included, since there are a number of references specifically related to science. It should be noted that since the main variable of interest was multimedia instruction, all of the search strategies used included that concept. Got the idea?

The end result of your search will be a printout containing references and abstracts, such as those shown above. After you have reviewed the printout and eliminated entries which are not of sufficient relevance, the next step is to locate each original source, e.g., the complete journal article, and abstract it.

Abstracting

After you have identified the primary references related to your problem, using the appropriate indexes, abstracts, and reviews, you are ready to move on to the next phase of a review of related literature—abstracting the references. Basically, this involves locating, reviewing, summarizing, and classifying your references. Students sometimes ask why it is necessary to read and abstract original, complete articles (or reports, or whatever), if they already have perfectly good abstracts. There are two basic reasons. First, provided abstracts are not necessarily "perfectly good." They may not be totally accurate summaries of the articles' contents, and often just enough information is given to permit you to make a tentative decision concerning relevance to your problem. And, second, there is a great deal of important information that can only be obtained by reading the complete article. (You'll see.)

Since the references you identified in each source are listed in reverse chronological order, starting with the most recent, the abstracting process will be conducted in the same order. The main advantage to beginning with the latest references on a given problem is that in terms of research strategy the most recent research is likely to have profited from previous research. Also, recent references may contain references to preceding studies you may not have identified. For each reference, a suggested procedure for abstracting is as follows:

1. If the article has an abstract or a summary, which most do, read it to determine the article's relevancy to your problem.
2. Skim the entire article, making mental note of the main points of the study.
3. Write the complete bibliographic reference, including the library call number if it is a book. If you know that your final report must follow a particular style, put your bibliographic reference in that form. If not, use the format of the American Psychological Association (APA).[24] The APA format is becoming increasingly popular, primarily because it eliminates the need for formal footnotes. Table 2.2 gives illustrative examples of references in APA format. It should be noted that, if you simply examine examples of references in the APA manual, it *appears* as if the basic format has changed from that presented in the previous (third) edition, in that the first line is indented as opposed to the second and succeeding lines. The format, however, has *not* changed. As section 4.18 *References* indicates, *final copy* always involves indentation of the second and succeeding lines. Examples given in the APA manual reflect the format which should be used *if a paper is being submitted for publication* since the typesetting system will convert references to the format shown in Table 2.2. While this may seem confusing, the intent was to facilitate the work of authors using word processors. For a journal article, the APA bibliographic reference would be:

> Snurd, B. J. (1995). The use of white versus yellow chalk in the teaching of advanced calculus. Journal of Useless Findings, 11, 1–99.

In the above example, 1995 refers to the date of publication, *11* to the volume, and 1–99 to the page numbers. If this reference were cited in a paper (perhaps written by Senator Proxmire and concerning funding for useless research), then its description would be followed by (Snurd, 1995), and no other footnote (beyond the bibliographic reference) would be required. If, however, the citation were a direct quote, the appropriate page number would need to be included, e.g., (Snurd, 1995, p.45).

---

[24]American Psychological Association. (1994). *Publication manual of the American Psychological Association* (4th ed.). Washington, DC: Author.

Table 2.2

Examples of References in APA Format

Journal Article[a]

Kneedler, P. E. (1993). California adopts multimedia science program.
    Technological Horizons in Education Journal, 20(7), 73–76.

Magazine Article

Corcoran, E. (1989, July). Show and tell: Hypermedia turns information into a
    multisensory event. Scientific American, 261, 72, 74.

Dissertation[b]

Chagas, I. (1993). Teachers as innovators: A case study of implementing the
    interactive videodisc in a middle school science program. Dissertation
    Abstracts International, 53, 4268A. (University Microfilms No. DA9311115)

ERIC – RIE Document[c]

Helms, C. W., & Helms, D. R. (1992, June). Multimedia in education (Report No.
    IR-016-090). Proceedings of the 25th Summer Conference of the Association
    of Small Computer Users in Education, North Myrtle Beach, SC. (ERIC
    Document Reproduction Service No. ED 357 732)

Note. As discussed in the text, indentation of the second and succeeding lines of each reference reflects the format required for *final copy* of a paper. The indentation system used for examples in the APA manual reflects *submission for publication* format.

[a] This format applies to all journal articles identified through *Education Index, Readers' Guide to Periodical Literature, Psychological Abstracts, Current Index to Journals in Education (CIJE)*, or the *Review of Educational Research (RER)*.

[b] This format is for a dissertation obtained on university microfilm.

[c] Depending upon the type of document, e.g., paper presented, this format will vary somewhat. Consult an APA manual.

Whatever format you use, be certain the reference you copy is accurate; you never know when you might have to go back and get additional information from an article. Besides, even if you do not have to find it again, it is very unscholarly to have an incorrect reference in a research report. Also, if you are using index cards, put only one reference on each card. The purpose of using index cards is that they allow easy sorting and facilitate organization of the articles prior to writing the review of the literature. An alternative strategy is to use a laptop computer for note taking. If you use this option, you still need to record correct and complete reference information. Many students prefer to photocopy articles, a strategy to be discussed shortly.

4. Classify and code the article according to some system and place the code on the same index card, or on the photocopy, in a conspicuous place, such as the upper right- or left-hand corner. If you are a laptop computer user, create a code that can be easily accessed when you want the computer to sort your notes into the categories you devise. For example, if your problem was concerned with salaried paraprofessionals versus parent volunteers (discussed earlier), you might use a three-part coding system to describe each article; the code might indicate whether the study was

concerned with the use of paraprofessionals, parent volunteers, or both (PP versus PV versus B), whether is was an opinion article or a study (O versus S), and the degree of its relevance to your study (say 1, 2, or 3, with 3 meaning very relevant). Thus, PV/O/3 might be a code for an article describing the potential benefits to be derived from using parent volunteers. Any coding system that makes sense to you, given your problem, will facilitate your task later when you have to sort, organize, analyze, synthesize, and write your review of the literature.

5. Abstract, or summarize, the reference. As neatly as you can (*you're* going to have to read them later!), write the essential points of the reference. If it is an opinion article write the main points of the author's position, for example, "Jones believes parent volunteers should be used because . . ." and list the "becauses." If it is a study, write the same kind of information you wrote for Task 1-A, Chapter 1: the problem, the procedures (including the sample and instruments), and the major conclusions. Make special note of any particularly interesting or unique aspect of the study, such as a new measuring instrument that was utilized. Double-check the reference to make sure you have not omitted any pertinent information. If the abstract provided at the beginning of the article contains all the essential information (and that is a big *if*), by all means use it.

6. Indicate any thoughts that come to your mind, such as points on which you disagree (make an *X,* for example) or components which you do not understand (put a ? next to them). For example, if an author stated that he or she had used a double-blind procedure, and you were unfamiliar with that technique, you could indicate that with a ?. Later, you can seek out a knowledgeable person, such as your advisor, and quickly identify points on which you need clarification or explanation.

7. Indicate any statements that are direct quotations or personal reactions: Plagiarism (intentional or not) is an absolute no-no, with the direst of consequences. If you do not put quotation marks around direct quotations on your index card, for example, you may not remember later which statements are, and which are not, direct quotations. Also, jot down the exact page number of the quotation in case you use the quotation later in your paper. Incidentally, direct quotations should be kept to minimum in your research plan and report; both should be in your words, not other researchers'. Occasionally, however, a direct quotation may be quite appropriate.

As mentioned, an alternative strategy to taking notes on index cards is to photocopy references whenever feasible. (You wouldn't want to copy a book, and if you did, you would probably get nasty treatment from those behind you in the copy machine line!) If you copy the articles, you can take them home with you and make your notes in the comfort of your home. The advantages of this approach are reduced time in the library and elimination of the possibility that you might have to go back and find a reference because you inadvertently left something out of your notes. Be sure, however, that you record all needed reference information (the volume number, for example) on your photocopy; not all journals list everything you need on each page (or even on the first page). Another alternative, for the truly technological among us, is to use a portable hand-held scanner (with the same caveat concerning reference information). The main disadvantage of photocopying documents is the cost; photocopies cost a lot more than 4" x 6" index cards. Many researchers, however, feel that this approach is well worth it in terms of convenience. Probably some sort of compromise make sense, such as using index cards for minor references and photocopying the articles that apply very directly to your study, provide lots of information, or use very complicated procedures.

Whichever approach you use, guard your notes with your life. When you have completed your reviewing task, those notes will represent many hours of work. Students have been known to be literally in tears because they left their notes "on the bus" or "on a table in the cafeteria." Beyond being sympathetic, your instructor can do little more than to tell you to start over (ouch!). Also, when the research report is completed, the index cards can be filed (photocopies can be placed in notebooks), and saved for future reference and future studies (nobody can do just one!).

Analyzing, Organizing, and Reporting

For beginning researchers, the hardest part about writing the review of related literature is thinking about how hard it is going to be to write the review of related literature. More time is spent worrying about doing it than actually doing it. If you have efficiently abstracted the literature related to your problem, and if you approach the task in an equally systematic manner, then analyzing, organizing, and reporting it will be relatively painless. First, to get warmed up, read quickly through your notes. This will first of all refresh your memory and also you will more than likely identify some references which no longer seem sufficiently related. Do not force references into your review that do not really "fit"; the review forms the background and rationale for your hypothesis and should only contain references that serve this purpose. It may hurt a little to discard references representing work on your part, but your review will be better for it. The following guidelines and suggestions are based on experience acquired the hard way and should be helpful to you:

1. Make an outline. Don't groan; your eighth-grade teacher was right about the virtues of an outline. For those of you who are working on computers, there are several software programs that can help you outline. In addition, the word processing program you are using may have an outlining program as one of its features. However you do it, the time and thought you put into the outline will save you time in the long run and will increase your probability of having an organized review. The outline does not have to be excessively detailed. First, identify the main topics and the order in which they should be presented. For example, the outline I formatted for this chapter started out as three main headings—Selection and Statement, Review of Related Literature, and Formulation and Statement of a Hypothesis. As another example, the outline of the review for the problem concerned with the effectiveness of salaried paraprofessionals versus parent volunteers might begin with the headings Literature on Salaried Paraprofessionals, Literature on Parent Volunteers, and Literature Comparing the Two. The next step is to differentiate each major heading into logical subheadings. In my outline, for example, Review of Related Literature was subdivided into the following:

   Review of Related Literature
   　　Definition, Purpose, and Scope
   　　Preparation
   　　Sources
   　　Computer Searches
   　　Abstracting
   　　Analyzing, Organizing, and Reporting

The need for further differentiation will be determined by your problem; the more complex it is, the more subheadings will be required. When you have completed your outline you will invariably see topics that need rearranging. It is much easier, however, to reorganize an outline than it is to reorganize a document written in paragraph form.

2. Analyze each reference in terms of your outline; in other words, determine under which subheading each one fits. Then sort your references into appropriate piles. If you end up with one or more references without a home, there are three logical possibilities: (1) there is something wrong with your outline; (2) they do not belong in your review, and should be discarded; or (3) they do not belong in your review but do belong somewhere else in your introduction. For example, a reference concerned with the problem of school vandalism might state that school vandalism costs American taxpayers X thousands of dollars per year. Such a reference would belong in the significance section of the statement of the problem if the specific problem to be investigated were concerned with several alternative methods of reducing school vandalism. Opinion articles, or reports of descriptive research, will more often be useful in the problem statement portion of an introduction, whereas formal studies will almost always be included in the review of related literature portion.

3. Take all the references identified for a given subheading and analyze the relationships or differences between them. If three references say essentially the same thing, there is no need to describe each one; it is much better to make one summary statement followed by three references. For example:

> Several studies have found white chalk to be more effective
> than yellow chalk in the teaching of advanced mathematics
> (Snurd, 1995; Trivia, 1991; Ziggy, 1984).

Do not present your references as a series of abstracts or annotations (Jones found X, Smith found Y, and Brown found Z). Your task is to organize and summarize the references in a meaningful way. Do not ignore studies which are contradictory to most other studies or to your personal bias. Analyze and evaluate contradictory studies and try to determine a possible explanation. For example:

> Contrary to these studies is the work of Rottenstudee
> (1990), who found yellow chalk to be more effective than
> white chalk in the teaching of trigonometry. However, the
> size of the treatment groups (two students per group) and
> the duration of the study (one class period) may have seriously affected the results.

4. The review should flow in such a way that the references least related to the problem are discussed first, and the most related references discussed last, just prior to the statement of the hypothesis. Think in terms of a big V. At the bottom of the V is your hypothesis; directly above your hypothesis are the studies most directly related to it, and so forth. For example, if your hypothesis stated that white chalk would be more effective than yellow chalk in teaching biology to 10th graders, immediately preceding it would be the studies indicating the effectiveness of white chalk in the teaching of mathematics. Preceding those studies might be studies indicating that students prefer to read white chalk. At the top of the V (the begin-

ning of the review), several references might be cited, written by well-known educators, expressing the belief that variables such as chalkboard color and color of chalk are important ones in the learning process, too often overlooked. These might be followed by similar references indicating that these variables might be even more critical in technical areas such as mathematics that entail a lot of chalkboard usage, and so forth. The idea is to organize and present your literature in such a way that it leads logically to a tentative, testable conclusion, namely your hypothesis. If your problem has more than one major aspect, you may have two Vs or one V that logically leads to two tentative, testable conclusions.

5. The review should conclude with a brief summary of the literature and its implications. How lengthy this summary needs to be depends upon the length of the review. It should be detailed enough to clearly show the logic chain you have followed in arriving at your implications and tentative conclusion.

Having systematically developed and presented your rationale, you will now be ready to state your hypothesis.

■ FORMULATION AND STATEMENT OF A HYPOTHESIS

Before you review the related literature, you have a tentative hypothesis which guides your search. Following the review, and preceding the actual execution of the study, the hypothesis is refined and finalized.

Definition and Purpose

A hypothesis is a tentative explanation for certain behaviors, phenomena, or events that have occurred or will occur. A hypothesis states the researcher's expectations concerning the relationship between the variables in the research problem; a hypothesis is the most specific statement of a problem. It states what the researcher thinks the outcome of the study will be. The researcher does not then set out to "prove" his or her hypothesis, but rather collects data that either support the hypothesis or do not support it; research studies do not "prove" anything. Hypotheses are essential to all quantitative research studies with the possible exception of some descriptive studies whose purpose is to answer certain specific questions.

The hypothesis is formulated following the review of related literature and prior to the execution of the study. It logically follows the review since it is based on the implications of previous research. The related literature leads one to expect a certain relationship. For example, studies finding white chalk to be more effective than yellow chalk in teaching mathematics would lead a researcher to expect it to be more effective in teaching physics, if there were not other findings to the contrary. Hypotheses precede the study proper because the entire study is determined by the hypothesis. Every aspect of the research is affected by the hypothesis, including subjects (samples), measuring instruments, design, procedures, data analysis techniques, and conclusions. Although all hypotheses are based on previous knowledge and aimed at extending knowledge, they are not all of equal worth. There are a number of criteria that can be, and should be, applied to a given hypothesis to determine its value.

Characteristics

By now it should be clear that a hypothesis should be based on a sound rationale. It should follow from previous research and lead to future research; its confirmation or disconfirmation should contribute to educational theory or practice. Therefore, a major characteristic of a good hypothesis is that it is consistent with previous research. The chances of your being a Christopher Columbus of educational research who is going to show that something believed to be "square" is really "round" are slim! Of course, in areas of research where there are conflicting results, you will not be able to be consistent with all of them, but your hypothesis should follow from the rule, not the exception.

The previously stated definition of a hypothesis indicated that it is a tentative explanation for the occurrence of certain behaviors, phenomena, or events. A good hypothesis provides a reasonable explanation. If your telephone is out of order, you might hypothesize that it is because there are butterflies sitting on your telephone wires; such a hypothesis would not be a reasonable explanation. A reasonable hypothesis might be that you forgot to pay your bill, or that a repair crew is working outside. In a research study, a hypothesis suggesting that children with freckles pay attention longer than children without freckles would not be a reasonable explanation for attention behavior. On the other hand, a hypothesis suggesting that children who have a good breakfast pay attention longer would be.

A good hypothesis states as clearly and concisely as possible the expected relationship (or difference) between two variables and defines those variables in operational, measurable terms. A simply but clearly stated hypothesis makes it easier for consumers to understand, simplifies its testing, and facilitates formulation of conclusions following data analysis. The relationship expressed between two variables may or may not be a causal one. For example, the variables anxiety and math achievement might be hypothesized to be significantly related (there is a significant correlation between anxiety and math achievement), or it might be hypothesized that on low-difficulty math problems high-anxiety students perform better than low-anxiety students. The above example also illustrates the need for operational definitions. What is a low-difficulty math problem? What is a high-anxiety student? What does it mean to perform better? In this example, "high-anxiety student" might be defined as any student whose score on the A-State scale of the State-Trait Anxiety Inventory is in the upper 30% of the distribution of student scores.[25] The dependent variable in a hypothesis will often be operationally defined in terms of scores on a given test. For example "better achievement" might be defined in terms of higher scores on the California Achievement Test Battery. If the appropriate terms can be operationally defined within the actual hypothesis statement without making it unwieldy, this should be done. If not, the hypothesis statement should be stated and the appropriate terms defined immediately following it. Of course if all necessary terms have already been defined, either within or immediately following the problem statement, there is no need to repeat the definitions in the statement of the hypothesis. The general rule of thumb is to define terms the first time they are used.

A well-stated and defined hypothesis must be (and will be if well-formulated and stated) testable. It should be possible to support or not support the hypothesis by collecting and analyzing data. It would not be possible to test a hypothesis that indicated that some students behave better than others because some have an invisible little angel on their right shoulder and some have an invisible little devil on

---

[25]Spielberger, C. D., Gorsuch, R. L., & Lushene, R. E. (1983). *Manual for the State-Trait Inventory: Form Y*. Palo Alto, CA: Mind Garden.

their left shoulder. There would be no way to collect data to support or not support the hypothesis. In addition to being testable, a good hypothesis should normally be testable within some reasonable period of time. For example, the hypothesis that requiring first-grade students to brush their teeth after lunch every day will result in fewer people with false teeth at age 60 would obviously take a very long time to test. The researcher would very likely be long gone before the study was completed, not to mention the negligible educational significance of the hypothesis! A more manageable hypothesis with the same theme might be that requiring first-grade children to brush their teeth after lunch every day will result in fewer cavities at the end of the first grade.

Types of Hypotheses

Hypotheses can be classified in terms of how they are derived (inductive versus deductive hypotheses) or how they are stated (declarative versus null hypotheses). An inductive hypothesis is a generalization based on observation. Certain variables are noted to be related in a number of situations and a tentative explanation, or hypothesis, formulated. Deductive hypotheses derived from theory contribute to the science of education by providing evidence that supports, expands, or contradicts a given theory and by suggesting future studies. For example, in a study conducted in 1966, Ausubel found no significant differences in retention between groups receiving a review one day after learning versus seven days after learning.[26] Ausubel suggested that the position of the review did not have a significant effect because early and late reviews each contribute to retention in a different way; an early review consolidates material, while a delayed review promotes relearning of forgotten material. In a subsequent study, this author hypothesized that if Ausubel was correct, then two reviews, one early and one delayed, will be more effective than either two early reviews or two delayed reviews. The results generally supported this hypothesis.[27] In deriving a hypothesis from a theory, you should be sure that your V does not have any holes in it (you remember the big V!). In other words, your hypothesis should be a logical implication of previous efforts, not an inferential leap.

A research hypothesis states an expected relationship or difference between two variables, in other words, what relationship the researcher expects to verify through the collection and analysis of data. Research, or declarative, hypotheses are nondirectional or directional. A nondirectional hypothesis simply indicates that a relationship or difference exists; a directional hypothesis indicates the nature of the relationship or difference. For example, a nondirectional hypothesis might state:

> There is a significant difference in the achievement of 10th-grade biology students who are instructed using interactive multimedia and those who receive regular instruction only.

The corresponding directional hypothesis might state:

> Tenth-grade biology students who are instructed using interactive multimedia achieve at a higher level than those who receive regular instruction only.

---

[26] Ausubel, D. P. (1966). Early versus delayed review in meaningful learning. *Psychology in the Schools, 3,* 195–198.

[27] Gay, L. R. (1973). Temporal position of reviews and its effect on the retention of mathematical rules. *Journal of Educational Psychology, 74,* 171–182.

A directional hypothesis should not be stated if you have any reason to believe that the results may occur in the opposite direction. Nondirectional and directional hypotheses involve different types of statistical tests of significance; a nondirectional hypothesis usually requires a two-tailed test of significance and a directional hypothesis a one-tailed test.[28]

A null hypothesis states that there is no relationship (or difference) between variables, and that any relationship found will be a chance relationship, not a true one. For example, a null hypothesis might state:

> There is no difference in the achievement level of 10th-grade biology students who are instructed using interactive multimedia and those who receive regular instruction.

While a research hypothesis may be a null hypothesis, this is not very often the case. The disadvantage of null hypotheses is that they rarely express the researcher's true expectations regarding the results of a study, expectations based on literature, insights, and logic. One approach is to state a research hypothesis, analyze your data assuming a null hypothesis, and then make inferences concerning your research hypothesis based on your testing of a null hypothesis. Given that few studies are really designed to verify the nonexistence of a relationship, it seems logical that most studies should be based on a nonnull research hypothesis.

Stating the Hypothesis

As previously discussed, a good hypothesis is stated clearly and concisely, expresses the relationship between two variables, and defines those variables in operational measurable terms. A general paradigm, or model, for stating hypotheses for experimental studies which you may find useful is as follows:

> Ss who get X do better on Y than
> Ss who do not get X (or get some other X)

If this model appears to be an oversimplification, it is because it is, and it may not always be appropriate. However, this model should help you to understand the nature of a hypothesis statement. Further, this model, or a variation of it, will be applicable in a surprising number of situations. In the model,

> Ss = the subjects,
> X = the treatment, the independent variable (IV), and
> Y = the observed outcome, the dependent variable (DV).

Study the following problem statement and see if you can identify the Ss, X, and Y:

> The purpose of this study is to investigate the effectiveness of senior mentors with respect to the absenteeism of low-achieving 10th graders.

In this example,

> Ss = low-achieving 10th graders,
> X = presence or absence of a senior mentor (IV), and
> Y = absenteeism (days absent or, stated positively, days present) (DV).

---

[28]These will be discussed further in Part Seven.

A review of the literature might indicate that mentors have been found to be effective in a variety of contexts. Therefore, the resulting hypothesis might read:

> Low-achieving 10th graders (Ss) who have a senior mentor (X) have less absenteeism (Y) than low-achieving 10th graders who do not.

As another example, suppose your problem statement was as follows:

> The purpose of the proposed research is to investigate the effectiveness of the use of conflict resolution techniques in reducing aggressive behaviors of high school students in an alternative educational setting.

For this problem statement,

> Ss = high school students in an alternative educational setting,
> X = type of discipline intervention (conflict resolution techniques versus traditional) (IV), and
> Y = instances of aggressive behaviors (DV).

The related hypothesis might read:

> High school students in an alternative educational setting which uses conflict resolution techniques exhibit fewer instances of aggressive behaviors than high school students in an alternative setting which does not.

Got the idea? Let's try one more.

Problem Statement:

> The problem to be investigated in this study is the effectiveness of token reinforcement, in the form of free time contingent on the completion of practice work sheets, with respect to the math computation skills of ninth-grade general math students.

> Ss = ninth-grade general math students,
> X = token reinforcement in the form of free time contingent on the completion of practice work sheets, and
> Y = math computation skills

Hypothesis:

> Ninth-grade general math students, who receive token reinforcement in the form of free time contingent on the completion of practice work sheets, have greater math computation skills than ninth-grade general math students who do not receive token reinforcement for completed work sheets.

Of course, in all of the above examples there are terms which would need to be defined, e.g., "aggressive behaviors."

For a null hypothesis, the paradigm is:

> There is no difference on Y between Ss who get X and Ss who do not get X (or get some other X).

See if you can write the null hypothesis for the following problem statement:

> The purpose of this study is to assess the impact of formal versus informal preschool reading instruction on reading comprehension at the end of the first grade.

Testing the Hypothesis

Hypothesis testing is really what scientific research is all about. In order to test a hypothesis, the researcher determines the sample, measuring instruments, design, and procedure that will enable her or him to collect the necessary data. Collected data are then analyzed in a manner that permits the researcher to determine the validity of the hypothesis. Analysis of collected data does not result in a hypothesis being proven or not proven, only supported or not supported. The results of a study only indicate whether a hypothesis was "true" for the particular subjects involved in the study. Many beginning researchers have the misconception that if their hypothesis is not supported by their data, then their study is a failure, and conversely, if it is supported then their study is a success. Neither of these beliefs is true. It is just as important, for example, to know what variables are *not* related as it is to know what variables *are* related. If a hypothesis is not supported, a valuable contribution may be made in the form of a revision of some aspect of a theory; such revision will generate new or revised hypotheses. Thus, hypothesis testing contributes to the science of education primarily by expanding, refining, or revising theory.

■ SUMMARY/CHAPTER 2
SELECTION AND STATEMENT
Selection

1. The first step in selecting a problem is to identify a general problem area that is related to your area of expertise and of particular interest to you.
2. The next step is to narrow down the general problem area to a specific, researchable problem.

Sources

3. The most meaningful problems are generally derived from theory.
4. A major source of nontheoretical problems is the researcher's personal experiences.
5. The literature is also a good source of problems; in addition to overviews and summaries, specific studies often indicate "next-step" studies which need to be conducted.
6. It is generally not a good idea to simply replicate a study as it was originally conducted; there is much to be learned from developing and executing your own study.

Characteristics

7. A basic characteristic of a research problem is that it is "researchable," that is, can be investigated through the collection and analysis of data.

8. A good problem has theoretical or practical significance; its solution should contribute in some way to improvement of the educational process.
9. A good problem must be a good problem *for you.* It must be a problem that you can adequately investigate given (1) your current level of research skill, (2) available resources, and (3) time and other restrictions.

Statement

10. A well-written statement of a problem generally indicates the variables of interest to the researcher, the specific relationship between those variables which is to be investigated and, ideally, the type of subjects involved.
11. A well-written problem statement also defines all relevant variables, either directly or operationally; operational definitions define concepts in terms of operations, or processes.
12. Since the problem statement gives direction to the rest of the plan or report, it should be stated as soon as possible.
13. The statement of the problem should be accompanied by a presentation of the background of the problem, including a justification for the study in terms of the significance of the problem.

REVIEW OF RELATED LITERATURE

Definition, Purpose, and Scope

14. The review of related literature involves the systematic identification, location, and analysis of documents containing information related to the research problem.
15. The major purpose of reviewing the literature is to determine what has already been done that relates to your problem.
16. Another important function of the literature review is that it points out research strategies and specific procedures and measuring instruments that have and have not been found to be productive in investigating your problem.
17. Being familiar with previous research also facilitates interpretation of the results of the study.
18. A smaller, well-organized review is definitely to be preferred to a review containing many studies that are more or less related to the problem.
19. Heavily researched areas usually provide enough references directly related to a specific problem to eliminate the need for relying on less related studies.
20. New or little-researched problem areas usually require review of any study related in some meaningful way to the problem in order to develop a logical framework for the study and a sound rationale for the research hypothesis.
21. A common misconception among beginning researchers is the idea that the worth of their problem is a function of the amount of literature available on the topic.

Preparation

22. Time spent initially will save time in the long run; you should find out what references are available and where they are located, especially the periodicals.

23. You should also be familiar with services offered by the library as well as the rules and regulations.
24. Many libraries provide written and/or video guides detailing what the library has to offer and the procedures for utilizing references and services.
25. One important service offered by most libraries is the interlibrary loan.
26. Before beginning the review, make a list of key words related to your problem to guide your literature search.

Sources

27. A primary source is a description of a study written by the person who conducted it; a secondary source is generally a much briefer description of a study written by someone other than the original researcher.
28. You should not be satisfied with only the information contained in secondary sources; the corresponding primary sources will be considerably more detailed and may be more accurate.
29. The number of individual references that could be consulted for a given problem is staggering; fortunately, there are indexes, abstracts, and other retrieval mechanisms that facilitate identification of relevant references.

Education Index

30. The *Education Index* lists bibliographic information on references appearing in literally hundreds of educational periodicals.
31. The *Education Index* is used much the same way as any other index; entries are listed alphabetically under subject, author, and title headings.
32. The procedure for using the *Education Index* is as follows: Start with the most recent issue and look under your key words; under the key words you will find a list of references presented alphabetically by title; decide whether each reference is related to your problem or not; if the reference is related, copy the complete reference; look up unfamiliar abbreviations in the front of the volume; repeat these steps for previous issues; locate each of the references.
33. The *Education Index* is the best source of educational periodicals published from 1929 to 1969.

Readers' Guide to Periodical Literature

34. *Readers' Guide* is an index, very similar in format to the *Education Index,* which indexes articles in widely read magazines.
35. *Readers' Guide* lists entries alphabetically by subject and author, and the procedures for its use are essentially the same as for using the *Education Index.*

Dissertation Abstracts International

36. *Dissertation Abstracts International* contains abstracts (usually brief summaries) of doctoral dissertations conducted at hundreds of academic institutions.
37. The procedure for using the *Abstracts* is similar to the procedure for using the *Education Index* with the exception that the reference also gives an entry number with which one locates an abstract.

Psychological Abstracts

38. *Psychological Abstracts* presents summaries of completed psychological research studies.
39. The *Thesaurus of Psychological Index Terms* is a compilation of the key words used in indexing *Psychological Abstracts* documents.
40. The procedure for using *Psychological Abstracts* is similar to the procedure for using the *Education Index;* the major difference is that the *Abstracts* index gives numbers that are used to locate both references and accompanying abstracts.
41. In addition to the key words identified for a given problem, the word *bibliography* should also be checked.
42. *Psychological Abstracts* will be more useful for theoretical problems.

Educational Resources Information Center (ERIC)

43. The primary purpose of ERIC is to collect and disseminate reports of current educational research, evaluation, and development activities.
44. Research reports that would not typically be included in other sources are indexed and abstracted by ERIC.
45. The comparatively short time interval between collection of a document and its dissemination results in sources of data for very current issues being available that are not available through other sources.
46. ERIC comprises a central office and a number of clearinghouses, each devoted to a different area, which collect, store, and disseminate documents specific to their area of specialization.
47. The *Thesaurus of ERIC Descriptors* is a compilation of the key words used in indexing ERIC documents.

RIE

48. A major ERIC publication is *Resources in Education* (RIE), which indexes over 1,000 documents per issue and for many entries provides an abstract.
49. RIE entries are indexed by subject, author, institution, and accession number. Using accession numbers, abstracts are located in the Document Resumés section.

CIJE

50. Another major ERIC publication, Current Index to Journals in Education (CIJE), indexes articles in the periodical literature and covers close to 800 education and education-related publications.
51. The procedure for using CIJE is very similar to the procedure for using RIE. Using the accession numbers, additional information is located in the Main Entry section.
52. The addition of abstracts when needed makes CIJE more useful than the *Education Index* for those years for which it is available.

Obtaining ERIC Documents and Information

53. ERIC provides a number of additional services such as the preparation and dissemination of annotated bibliographies in various areas of specialization.
54. All ERIC documents are available in hardcopy and/or microfiche, which is less expensive.

Review of Educational Research (RER)

55. The RER reviews and briefly summarizes a number of related studies on given topics.
56. The RER is a secondary source; each article concludes with an extensive bibliography which facilitates location of important primary sources.

Books

57. The card catalog alphabetically indexes (by author, subject, and title) all publications contained in the library, with the exception of the periodicals.
58. Many libraries have converted to a computer-based catalog which alphabetically indexes (by author, title, and subject) all the entries in the card catalog.
59. Encyclopedias in special areas contain detailed discussions, written by experts, on a restricted number of topics. The *Encyclopedia of Educational Research*, for example, contains critical reviews and summaries on a number of educational topics.

Computer Searches

60. With relatively little effort, you can use a computer to identify related references for you.
61. A computer search checks databases such as the ERIC system and provides you with a list of references and, if provided by the database, abstracts.
62. ERIC is the bibliographic database most widely used in education; ERIC searches can be obtained at hundreds of locations, including universities.

Types of Computer Searches

63. Computer searches may be done online or by using CD-ROM.
64. An online search is performed at a computer terminal which is directly connected via telephone lines to a central database system.
65. A CD-ROM search involves using software onto which database information has been transferred.

Online Searches

66. Online computer searches are made possible by the fact that various databases are available on computer tapes.
67. Information retrieval systems provide institutions with access to the tapes in their system; some institutions have some tapes themselves.
68 Two major vendors of online retrieval services are BRS and DIALOG.

CD-ROM Searches

69. CD-ROM refers to a compact disc that "plays" visual information; in the case of a literature search, the information which is stored on, and played by, the CD is the contents of one or more databases.
70. A CD is "read" by a laser player and the contents are displayed on a computer screen.
71. ROM stands for "read-only memory," which basically means that you can read, interact with, and print the contents, but you can't change the contents.
72. Two major vendors of CD-ROM versions of databases are DIALOG and SilverPlatter.

The Computer Search Process

73. The steps involved in conducting a computer search, be it an online search or a CD-ROM search, are very similar to those involved in a manual search, to a point; state your problem, identify your key words, select the databases you wish to search, and specify your search strategy.

74. The ideal search strategy is one that gets you just the right number of references, all related to your problem in a meaningful way, and does not prevent you from locating one or more significant references.

75. If a search is narrow, it is likely that all references identified will be related to your problem; if it is too narrow, you may not get enough references or you may miss some important ones.

76. If a search is broad, it is likely that you will not miss any significant references, although you may get some that are not really related to your problem; if your search is too broad, you will have many references that are not relevant, and you will waste time and perhaps money.

77. How narrow or broad your initial strategy should be depends on factors such as the purpose for which the search is being conducted and the amount of material available on your topic.

78. If you do not have a sense of what is available, your best strategy is to start narrow and broaden as necessary.

79. There are three basic ways to narrow or broaden a search; by decreasing or increasing the years searched, by changing, adding, or deleting key words or concepts, and by using the *and* and *or* connectors.

80. Using *and* narrows a search; using *or* broadens a search.

81. By using various combinations of the *and* and *or* connectors, you can vary your search strategy as needed.

Abstracting

82. Abstracting references involves locating, reviewing, summarizing, and classifying your references.

83. The main advantage of beginning with the latest references on a given problem is that in terms of strategy, the most recent research is likely to have profited from previous research; also, references may contain references to preceding studies you may not have identified.

84. A suggested procedure for abstracting is as follows: if available, read the article abstract or summary first to determine the relevancy of the article to your problem; skim the entire article, making mental note of main points; write the complete bibliographic reference, using either a required format or the APA format; classify and code the article according to some system; abstract or summarize the reference; write down any thoughts that come to your mind concerning the reference; and identify direct quotations.

85. An alternate strategy to taking notes on index cards is to photocopy references whenever feasible; another alternative is to use a hand-held scanner.

86. Save your notes for future reference and future studies.

Analyzing, Organizing, and Reporting

87. All notes should be reread; this will first of all refresh your memory and also you will more than likely identify some references which no longer seem sufficiently related.

88. The following guidelines should be helpful: make an outline; analyze each reference in terms of your outline and sort your references into appropriate piles; take all the references identified for a given subheading and analyze the relationships and differences between them (do not present your references as a series of abstracts or annotations); the review should flow in such a way that the references least related to the problem are discussed first, and the most related references are discussed last, just prior to the statement of the hypothesis (think in terms of a big V); the review should conclude with a brief summary of the literature and its implications.

FORMULATION AND STATEMENT OF A HYPOTHESIS

Definition and Purpose

89. A hypothesis is a tentative explanation for certain behaviors, phenomena, or events that have occurred or will occur.
90. The researcher does not set out to "prove" his or her hypothesis but rather collects data that either support the hypothesis or do not support it.
91. The hypothesis is formulated following the review of related literature and prior to the execution of the study. The hypothesis logically follows the review and it is based on the implications of previous research; it precedes the study proper because the entire study is determined by the hypothesis (including subjects, instruments, design, procedures, analysis, and conclusions).

Characteristics

92. A major characteristic of a good hypothesis is that it is consistent with previous research.
93. A good hypothesis is a tentative, reasonable explanation for the occurrence of certain behaviors, phenomena, or events.
94. A good hypothesis states as clearly and concisely as possible the expected relationship (or difference) between two variables and defines those variables in operational, measurable terms.
95. A well-stated and defined hypothesis must be testable.

Types of Hypotheses

96. An inductive hypothesis is a generalization based on observation.
97. Deductive hypotheses derived from theory contribute to the science of education by providing evidence that supports, expands, or contradicts a given theory.
98. A research hypothesis states the expected relationship (or difference) between two variables, in other words, what relationship the researcher expects to verify through the collection and analysis of data.
99. A nondirectional hypothesis simply indicates that a relationship or difference exists; a directional hypothesis indicates the nature of the relationship or difference.

100. A null hypothesis states that there will be no relationship (or difference) between variables, and that any relationship found will be a chance relationship, not a true one.

Stating the Hypothesis

101. A general paradigm, or model, for stating hypotheses for experimental studies is as follows:

> Ss who get X do better on Y than
> Ss who do not get X (or get some other X)

102. In the model, Ss are the subjects, X is the treatment (independent variable), and Y is the observed outcome (dependent variable).

Testing the Hypothesis

103. In order to test a hypothesis, the researcher determines the sample, measuring instruments, design, and procedure that will enable him or her to collect the necessary data; collected data are then analyzed in a manner that permits the researcher to determine the validity of the hypothesis.

104. It is just as important to know what variables are *not* related as it is to know what variables *are* related.

Task 2 Performance Criteria

The introduction which you develop for Task 2 will be the first part of the research report required for Task 8. Therefore, it may save you some revision time later if, when appropriate, statements are expressed in the past tense ("it was hypothesized," for example).

Your introduction should include the following subheadings and contain the following types of information:

INTRODUCTION (Background and significance of the problem)

Statement of the Problem (Problem statement and necessary definitions)

Review of Related Literature (Don't forget the big V)

Statement of the Hypothesis(es)

As a guideline, three typed pages will generally be a sufficient length for Task 2. Of course for a *real* study you would review not just 10 to 15 references but all relevant references and the introduction would be correspondingly longer.

Because of feedback from your instructor on Objective 4, and insight gained through developing your review of related literature, the hypothesis you state in Task 2 may very well be somewhat different from the one you stated for Objective 4.

One final note. The hypothesis you formulate now will influence all further tasks, i.e., who will be your subjects, what they will do, and so forth. In this connection, the following is an informal observation based on the behavior of thousands of students, not a research-based finding. All beginning research students fall some place on a continuum of realism. At one extreme are the Cecil B. DeMille students who want to design a study involving a cast of thousands, over an extended period of time, and so forth. At the other extreme are the Mr. Magoo students who will not even consider a procedure unless they know *for sure* they could actually execute it in their work setting, with their students or clients, and so forth. Since you do not have to actually execute the study you design, feel free to operate in the manner most comfortable for you. Keep in mind, however, that there is a middle ground between DeMille and Magoo.

On the following pages an example is presented which illustrates the format and content of an introduction which meets the criteria described above (see the following Task 2 example). This task example (and task examples for succeeding parts), with few modifications, represents the task as submitted by a former student in an introductory educational research course—Sara Jane Calderin, Florida International University. While an example from published research could have been used, the example given more accurately reflects the performance which is expected of you at your current level of expertise.

Additional examples for this and subsequent tasks are included in the *Student Guide* which accompanies this text.

1

Effect of Interactive Multimedia on the Achievement of
10th-Grade Biology Students

Introduction

One of the major concerns of educators and parents
alike, is the decline in student achievement(as measured by
standardized tests). An area of particular concern is science
education where the high-level thinking skills and problem
solving techniques so necessary for success in our
technological society need to be developed (Smith & Westhoff,
1992).

Research is constantly providing new proven methods for
educators to use and technology has developed all kinds of
tools ideally suited to the classroom. One such tool is
interactive multimedia (IMM). IMM provides teachers with an
extensive amount of data in a number of different formats
including text, sound, and video making it possible to appeal
to the different learning styles of the students and to offer
a variety of material for students to analyze (Howson & Davis,
1992).

When teachers use IMM students become highly motivated
which results in improved class attendance and more completed
assignments (O'Connor, 1993). Students also become actively
involved in their own learning, encouraging comprehension
rather than mere memorization of facts (Kneedler, 1993;
Reeves, 1992).

Statement of the Problem

The purpose of this study was to investigate the effect
of interactive multimedia on the achievement of 10th-grade
biology students. Interactive multimedia was defined as "a
computerized database that allows users to access information

2

in multiple forms, including text, graphics, video and audio"
(Reeves, 1992, p. 47).

Review of Related Literature

Due to modern technology, students receive more
information from visual sources than they do from the written
word and yet in school the majority of information is still
transmitted through textbooks. While textbooks cover a wide
range of topics superficially, IMM provides in depth
information on essential topics in a format that students find
interesting (Kneedler, 1993). Smith and Westhoff (1992) note
that when student interest is sparked curiosity levels are
increased and students are motivated to ask questions. The
interactive nature of multimedia allows the students to seek
out their own answers and by so doing they become owners of
the concept involved. Ownership translates into comprehension
(Howson & Davis, 1992).

Many science concepts are learnt through observation of
experiments. Using multimedia students can participate in a
variety of experiments which are either too expensive, too
lengthy or too dangerous to carry out in the laboratory
(Howson & Davies, 1992; Leonard, 1989; Louie, Sweat, Gresham &
Smith, 1991). While observing the experiments the students can
discuss what is happening and ask questions. At the touch of a
button teachers are able to replay any part of the procedings
and they also have random access to related information which
can be used to completely illustrate the answer to the
question (Howson & Davies, 1992). By answering students
questions in this detailed way the content will become more
relevant to the needs of the student (Smith & Westhoff, 1992).
When knowledge is relevant students are able to use it to
solve problems and in so doing develop higher-level thinking

3

skills (Helm & Helm, 1992; Sherwood, Kinzer, Bransford, & Franks, 1987).

A major challenge of science education is to provide students with large amounts of information that will encourage them to be analytical (Howson & Davis, 1992; Sherwood et al., 1987). IMM offers electronic access to extensive information allowing students to organize, evaluate and use it in the solution of problems (Smith & Wilson, 1993). When information is introduced as an aid to problem solving it becomes a tool with which to solve other problems, rather than a series of solitary, disconnected facts (Sherwood et al., 1987).

Although critics complain that IMM is entertainment and students do not learn from it (Corcoran, 1989), research has shown that student learning does improve when IMM is used in the classroom (Sherwood et al., 1987; Sherwood & Others, 1990). A 1987 study by Sherwood et al., for example, showed that seventh and eighth grade science students receiving instruction enhanced with IMM had better retention of that information, and O'Connor (1993) found that the use of IMM in high school mathematics and science increased the focus on students' problem solving and critical thinking skills.

Statement of the Hypothesis

The quality and quantity of software available for science classes has dramatically improved during the past decade. Although some research has been carried out on the effects of IMM on student achievement in science, due to promising updates in the technology involved, further study is warranted. Therefore, it was hypothesized that 10th-grade biology students whose teachers use IMM as part of their instructional technique will exhibit significantly higher achievement than 10th-grade biology students whose teachers do not use IMM.

4

References

Corcoran, E. (1989, July). Show and Tell: Hypermedia turns
    information into a multisensory event. <u>Scientific American,
    261,</u> 72, 74.

Helms, C. W., & Helms, D. R. (1992, June). <u>Multimedia in
    education</u> (Report No. IR-016-090). Proceedings of the 25th
    Summer Conference of the Association of Small Computer
    Users in Education. North Myrtle Beach, SC. (ERIC Document
    Reproduction Service No. ED 357 732)

Howson, B. A., & Davis, H. (1992). Enhancing comprehension
    with videodiscs. <u>Media and Methods, 28</u>(3), 12-14.

Kneedler, P. E. (1993). California adopts multimedia science
    program. <u>Technological Horizons in Education Journal,
    20</u>(7), 73-76.

Lehmann, I. J. (1990). Review of National Proficiency Survey
    Series. In J. J. Kramer & J. C. Conoley (Eds.), <u>The
    eleventh mental measurements yearbook</u> (pp. 595-599).
    Lincoln: University of Nebraska, Buros Institute of Mental
    Measurement.

Leonard, W. H. (1989). A comparison of student reaction to
    biology instruction by interactive videodisc or
    conventional laboratory. <u>Journal of Research in Science
    Teaching, 26,</u> 95-104.

Louie, R., Sweat, S., Gresham, R., & Smith, L. (1991).
    Interactive Video: Disseminating vital science and math
    information. <u>Media and Methods, 27</u>(5), 22-23.

O'Connor, J. E. (1993, April). <u>Evaluating the effects of
    collaborative efforts to improve mathematics and science
    curricula</u> (Report No. TM-019-862). Paper presented at the
    Annual Meeting of the American Educational Research
    Association, Atlanta, GA. (ERIC Document Reproduction
    Service No. ED 357 083)

Task 2 Example (*continued*)

5

Reeves, T. C. (1992). Evaluating interactive multimedia.
Educational Technology, 32(5), 47-52.

Sherwood, R. D., Kinzer, C. K., Bransford, J. D., & Franks,
J. J. (1987). Some benefits of creating macro-contexts for
science instruction: Initial findings. _Journal of Research
in Science Teaching, 24,_ 417-435.

Sherwood, R. D., & Others. (1990, April). _An evaluative study
of level one videodisc based chemistry program_ (Report No.
SE-051-513). Paper presented at a Poster Session at the
63rd. Annual Meeting of the National Association for
Research in Science Teaching, Atlanta, GA. (ERIC Document
Reproduction Service No. ED 320 772)

Smith, E. E., & Westhoff, G. M. (1992). The Taliesin project:
Multidisciplinary education and multimedia. _Educational
Technology, 32._ 15-23.

Smith, M. K., & Wilson, C. (1993, March). _Integration of
student learning strategies via technology_ (Report No.
IR-016-035). Proceedings of the Fourth Annual Conference of
Technology and Teacher Education. San Diego, CA. (ERIC
Document Reproduction Service No: ED 355 937)

PART THREE

Research Plans

Development of a research plan is a critical step in conducting research. Having formulated specific hypotheses, it is necessary to carefully delineate the method and procedure to be followed in testing them. Occasionally it will become apparent in formulating a plan that the proposed study is not feasible in its present form. That decision is best made *before* you have expended considerable time and energy on a study which cannot be adequately executed. While very few research plans are executed exactly as planned, the existence of a plan permits the researcher to assess the overall impact of any changes on the study as a whole.

You, of course, are not yet in a position to develop a complete plan. A research plan, for example, generally states the statistical technique which will be used to analyze the data; this ensures that data will be collected which are analyzable. By now, however, you have read enough research reports to be aware of some of the possibilities. It will be interesting for you to compare the plan you develop now with the research report you will develop in Chapter 16 after you have acquired competencies related to the research process.

The goal of Part Three is for you to understand the importance of developing a research plan and become familiar with the components of such a plan. After you have read Part Three, you should be able to perform the following task.

■ TASK 3

For the hypothesis you have formulated, develop the remaining components of a research plan for a study you would conduct in order to test your hypothesis. Include the following:

    Method
        Subjects
        Instruments
        Design
        Procedure
    Data Analysis
    Time Schedule

Note: Assumptions, limitations, and definitions should be included where appropriate.

(See Performance Criteria, p. 106).

"Having a research plan permits it to be carefully scrutinized by yourself and by others" and "allows others not only to identify problems but also to make suggestions as to how the study might be improved (p. 100)."

Preparation and Evaluation
of a Research Plan

OBJECTIVES

After reading Chapter 3, you should be able to:

1. Briefly describe three ethical considerations involved in conducting and reporting educational research.

2. Briefly describe two major pieces of legislation affecting educational research.

3. Briefly describe each of the components of a research plan.

4. Briefly describe two major ways in which a research plan can be evaluated.

■ DEFINITION AND PURPOSE

A research plan is a detailed description of a proposed study designed to investigate a given problem. It includes justification for the hypothesis to be tested, a detailed presentation of the research steps that will be followed in collecting and analyzing required data, and a projected time schedule for each major step. A research plan may be relatively brief and informal, such as the one which you will develop for Task 3, or very lengthy and formal, such as the proposals which are submitted to governmental and private funding agencies. Graduate schools typically require that a proposal, or prospectus, be submitted for approval prior to the execution of a thesis or dissertation study.

   The research plan must be completed before a study is begun. Playing it by ear is all right for piano playing, but not for conducting research. After you have completed the review of related literature and formulated your hypothesis, you are ready to develop the rest of the plan. Since your study will be designed to test a hypothesis, it must be developed first. The nature of your hypothesis will determine to a high degree the sample group, measuring instruments, design, procedures, and statistical techniques used in your study. A research plan serves several important purposes. First, it makes you think; it forces you to think through every aspect of the study. The very process of getting it down on paper usually makes you think of something you might otherwise have overlooked. A second purpose of a written plan is that it facilitates evaluation of the proposed study, by you and by others. Sometimes great ideas do not look so great after all when they are written down. Also, certain problems may become apparent or some aspect may be seen to be infeasible. Having a written plan also allows others to not only identify flaws but also to make suggestions as to ways the study might be improved. This is as true for "old hands" as it is for beginning researchers. A third major purpose of a research plan is that it provides a guide for conducting the study. Detailed procedures need only be thought through once and then followed, not remembered. Also, if something unexpected occurs that alters some phase of the study, the overall impact on the rest of the study can be assessed. For example, suppose you ordered 60 copies of a test which was to be administered on May 1. If on April 15, you received a letter saying that due to a shortage of available tests your order could not be filled until May 15, your study might be seriously affected. At the very least it would be delayed several weeks. Reworking of the time schedule in your research plan might indicate that given your deadlines you could not afford to wait. Therefore, you might decide to use an alternate measuring instrument.

A well-thought-out plan saves time, reduces the probability of costly mistakes, and generally results in higher quality research. If your study is a disaster because of poor planning, *you* lose. The research plan is not really written for your advisor's or major professor's benefit, it is written for yours. If something goes wrong, which could have been avoided with a little foresight, you may have to redo the whole study, at worst, or somehow salvage the remnants of a less-than ideal study, at best.

Murphy's law states approximately that "if anything can go wrong, it will." Gay's law states that "if anything can go wrong, it will—unless you make sure that it doesn't!" Most of the minor tragedies that occur during studies could have been avoided with proper planning, good coordination, and careful monitoring. Part of good planning is anticipation. Do not wait until something happens before you figure out how to deal with it. Try to anticipate potential problems that might arise and then do what you can to prevent them. Plan your strategies for dealing with them if they do occur. For example, you might anticipate resistance on the part of some principals to giving you permission to use their students as subjects in your study. To deal with this contingency you should work up the best sales pitch possible. Do not ask, "Hey, can I use your kids for my study?" Instead, tell them how wonderful the study is and how it will benefit their students or their schools. If there is still opposition, you might tell them how enthusiastic central administration is about the study. Got the idea?

You may tend to get frustrated at times because you cannot do everything the way you would like to because of real or bureaucratic constraints. Don't let such obstacles exasperate you. Just relax and do your best. On the positive side, a sound plan critiqued by others is likely to result in a sound study conducted with a minimum of grief. You cannot guarantee that your study will be executed exactly as planned, but you can guarantee that things will go as smoothly as possible.

■ GENERAL CONSIDERATIONS

In planning the actual procedures of your study, there are a number of factors you should consider. Two of these factors, the ethics of conducting research and legal restrictions, are relevant to all research studies. Any potential subject in your study, for example, has the right to refuse to be involved *and* the right to stop being involved at any time. A third factor to consider is strategies for achieving and maintaining necessary cooperation, from school personnel, for example. A fourth factor is the need for training if others will be assisting you in conducting your study. Your research plan may not specifically address any of these factors, but the plan's chances of being properly executed will be increased if you are aware of them.

The Ethics of Research

There are ethical considerations involved in all research studies. Ethical concerns are, of course, more acute in experimental studies which, by definition, "manipulate" and "control" subjects. The ends do not justify the means, and perhaps the foremost rule of ethics is that subjects should not be harmed in any way (physically or mentally) in the name of science. If an experiment involves any risk to subjects, they should be completely informed concerning the nature of the risk, and permission for participation in the experiment should be acquired in writing from the subjects themselves, or from persons legally responsible for the subjects if they are not of age. The researcher should take every precaution and make every effort to minimize potential risk to subjects. Even if there is no risk to subjects, they should be completely informed concerning the nature of the study. Frequently, for control purposes, subjects are not aware of their participation in a study or, if aware, do not know the exact nature of the experiment. Such subjects should be debriefed, or informed, as soon as the study is completed. If school children are involved, it is also a good idea to inform parents, before the study is conducted if possible, concerning the purpose and procedures of the study. This may be done in writing or a presentation may be made to a parents' organization.

The subject's right to privacy is also an important consideration. Collecting information on subjects or observing them without their knowledge or without appropriate permission is not ethical. Furthermore, any information or data which are collected, either from or about a subject, should be strictly confidential, especially if it is at all personal. Individual scores should never be reported, or made public, even for an innocuous measure such as an arithmetic test. It is usually sufficient to present data in terms of group statistics; if individual scores, or raw data, need to be presented, they should be coded and should not be associated with subjects' names or other identifying information. Access to the data should be limited to persons directly involved in conducting the research.

Probably the most definitive source of ethical guidelines for researchers is *Ethical Principles in the Conduct of Research with Human Participants,* which was prepared for, and published by, the American Psychological Association (APA).[1] In the APA publication (which is currently being revised), these principles are preceded by a statement to the effect that research should be conducted ". . . with respect and concern for the dignity and welfare of the people who participate and with cognizance of federal and state regulations and professional standards governing the conduct of research with human participants." As the above suggests, the bottom-line objective of all principles, standards, and laws relating to the ethics of research with human participants is "respect and concern for the dignity and welfare of the people who participate." Fair enough.

---

[1]Committee for the Protection of Human Participants in Research. (1982). *Ethical principles in the conduct of research with human participants.* Washington, DC: American Psychological Association. An updated version of these principles should be available by 1997.

Above all, the researcher must have personal integrity. The reader of a research report must be able to believe that what the researcher says happened, really happened; otherwise it is all for nothing. Falsifying data in order to make findings agree with a hypothesis is unprofessional, unethical, and unforgivable.

Legal Restrictions

The year 1974 marked the beginning of an era in which ethical standards are increasingly being given the force of law. The need for legal restrictions is graphically illustrated by a study on the effects of group pressure which was conducted some years ago.[2] The purpose of the study was to answer the question "Can a group induce a person to deliver punishment of increasing severity to a protesting individual?" Basically, the study involved one person (A) testing another person (B) on a paired-associate learning task. Person A was instructed to administer an electric shock to person B each time person B gave an incorrect response. In the experimental group, each A subject was pressured by two confederates (persons working with the experimenter but pretending to be part of the experiment) to progressively increase voltage levels for succeeding wrong answers given by the corresponding B subject. In the control group, each A subject made independent, unpressured decisions concerning voltage levels throughout the experiment.

For both groups, B subjects were also confederates; in other words, no one actually got shocked, but A subjects did not know this. Prerecorded tapes provided pain responses from B subjects which ranged from mild protests at lower voltage levels to agonized screams at higher levels. The results were very clear: the two pressuring confederates strongly influenced the level of shock administered to B subject confederates. In the experimental group, mean (average) shock levels steadily increased as the experiment progressed, whereas mean shock levels remained relatively stable in the control group. It is more than likely that at least some of the subjects in the experimental group suffered mental stress for some time following the experiment, even though they were told that they had not really hurt anyone. The point was that they knew what they were capable of, regardless of what they had actually done.[3]

The major provisions of legislation passed to date have been designed to protect subjects who participate in research and to ensure the confidentiality of students' records. Although provisions may seem to be overly restrictive at times, the intent of the legislation is clearly worthy. Two major pieces of legislation affecting educational research are the National Research Act of 1974 and the Family Educational Rights and Privacy Act of 1974, more commonly referred to as the Buckley Amendment. The National Research Act requires that proposed research activities involving human subjects be reviewed and approved by an authorized group in an institution, prior to the execution of the research, to ensure protection of the subjects. Protection of subjects is broadly defined and requires that subjects not be harmed in any way (physically or mentally) and that they participate only if they freely agree to do so (informed consent). If subjects are not of age, informed consent must be given by parents or legal guardians.

---

[2] Milgram, S. (1964). Group pressure and action against a person. *Journal of Abnormal and Social Psychology, 69,* 137–143.

[3] For a complete description of Milgram's work, see Milgram, S. (1975). *Obedience to authority: An experimental view.* New York: Harper & Row.

Most colleges and universities either have such a review group or assign the review function to an already constituted group such as a university research committee. Typically, the researcher submits a proposal to the chair of the review group, who in turn distributes copies to all the members. They in turn review the proposal in terms of proposed treatment of subjects. If there is any question as to whether subjects might be harmed in *any way,* the researcher is usually asked to meet with the review group to answer questions and to clarify proposed procedures. In rare cases the researcher is asked to rewrite the questionable or unclear areas in the research plan. When the review group is satisfied that the subjects will not be placed at risk (or that potential risk is minimal compared to the potential benefits of the study), the committee members sign the appropriate approval forms. Members' signatures on the approval forms signify that the proposal is acceptable with respect to subject protection and that the actual execution of the research will be periodically reviewed to insure that subjects are being properly treated. For complete information on the provisions of the National Research Act, write to the National Commission for the Protection of Human Subjects, 5333 Westbard Avenue, Bethesda, MD 20016.

The Buckley Amendment basically protects the privacy of the educational records of students. Among its provisions is the specification that data that actually identify the students may not usually be made available unless written permission is acquired from the students (if of age), parents, or legal guardians. The consent must indicate what data may be disclosed, for what purposes, and to whom. There are exceptions in terms of who is bound by the written consent provision. In most cases, however, the researcher does not need to identify individual data as the interest is in group results. Data can easily be coded in such a way that relevant information such as group membership is identifiable but the identity of individual students is not. For complete information on the provisions of the Buckley Amendment, write to the Family Educational Rights and Privacy Office, 200 Independence Avenue, S.W., Washington, DC 20201.[4]

Figure 3.1 presents a cover letter written by a principal in support of a doctoral student's proposed study. Note that the student secured not only the principal's permission, but also his strong support and cooperation, by sharing the potential benefits of the study to the principal's students. Figure 3.2 presents the parental consent form which accompanied the cover letter. It addresses many of the ethical and legal concerns discussed in this chapter.

Cooperation

Very rarely is it possible to conduct educational research without the cooperation of a number of people, typically school personnel. The first step in acquiring the needed cooperation is to follow required procedures. Typically, approval for the proposed research must be granted by the superintendent or some other high-level administrator, the associate superintendent for instruction, for example. The approval process usually involves the completion of one or more forms on which the nature of the research and the specific request being made of the school system are described, and a meeting with the approval-granting administrator.

---

[4] For additional guidelines concerning the legal restrictions of research activities, see Michael, J. A., & Weinberger, J. A. (1977). Federal restrictions on educational research: Protection for research participants. *Educational Researcher, 6* (1), 3–7; and Weinberger, J. A., & Michael, J. A. (1976). Federal restrictions on educational research. *Educational Researcher, 5* (11), 3–8.

THE SCHOOL BOARD OF BROWARD COUNTY, FLORIDA

The Nation's Largest Fully Accredited School System

BETHUNE ELEMENTARY
PERFORMING ARTS SCHOOL
Linda H. Arnold, Principal
2400 Meade Street
Hollywood, Florida 33020
(305) 926-0860

Robert D. Parks
Chairperson

Diana Wasserman
Vice Chairperson

Karen Dickerhoof
Donald J. Samuels
Eileen S. Schwartz
Toni J. Siskin
Neil Sterling

Virgil L. Morgan
Superintendent

January 23, 1990

Dear Parent/Guardian:

Country Isles Elementary School has been chosen to participate in a research study. Our school was selected out of the entire county as a result of our outstanding students and computer program. All third and fifth grade students will be able to participate. The results of this study will enable our teachers and parents to discover and understand the learning styles of our students. This knowledge will enable teachers and parents to provide special instruction and materials to improve student learning. It will also provide valuable information for the future development of effective professional computer software.

This study will take place from January 25 to March 30, 1990. It will be conducted by Mr. Joel Levine, a recognized and experienced computer educator. He has been Director of Computer Education at Barry University for six years. During that time he has participated in many projects in Dade and Broward Counties, which involved teacher training, computer curriculum development and computer assisted instruction implementation.

I have reviewed this research study and feel that it is a very worthwhile endeavor for our students and school. Please review the information on the following page in order to make a decision concerning parental consent for your child to participate in this study.

Sincerely,

Thos. J. Bardash

Thomas J. Bardash
Principal

Equal Opportunity Employer, Using Affirmative Action Guidelines

Figure 3.1.   Principal's cover letter of support for a proposed research study.

PARENTAL CONSENT FORM

The information provided on this form and the accompanying cover letter is presented to you in order to fulfill legal and ethical requirements for Florida International University (institution sponsoring this doctoral dissertation study) and the Department of Health and Human Services (HHS) regulations for the Protection of Human Research Subjects (45 CFR 46, as amended on January 26, 1983). The wording used in this form is utilized for all types of studies and should not be misinterpreted for this particular study.

The dissertation committee at Florida International University and the Research Review Committee of Broward County Public Schools have both given approval to conduct this study, "The Relationships Between the Modality Preferences of Elementary Students and Selected Instructional Styles of CAI as They Affect Verbal Learning of Facts." The purpose of this study is to determine the effect on achievement scores when the identified learning styles (visual, audio, tactile/kinesthetic) of elementary students in grade 3 and 5 are matched or mismatched to the instructional methods of specifically selected computer assisted instruction (CAI).

Your child will be involved in this study by way of the following:

1. Pretest on animal facts.
2. Posttest on animal facts.
3. Test on learning styles.
4. Interaction with computer-assisted instruction (CAI-software on the computer)—visual, audio, tactile CAI matching the student's own learning style.

All of these activities should not take more than two hours per student. There are no foreseeable risks to the students involved. In addition, the parent or researcher may remove the student from the study at any time with just cause. Specific information about individual students will be kept <u>strictly confidential</u> and will be obtainable from the school principal if desired. The results that are published publicly will not reference any individual students since the study will only analyze relationships among groups of data.

The purpose of this form is to allow your child to participate in the study, and to allow the researcher to use the information already available at the school or information obtained from the actual study, in order to analyze the outcomes of the study. Parental consent for this research study is strictly voluntary without undue influence or penalty. The parent signature below also assumes that the child understands and agrees to participate cooperatively.

If you have additional questions regarding the study, the rights of subjects, or potential problems, please call the principal, Mr. Tom Bardash or the researcher, Mr. Joel Levine (Director/Assistant Professor of Computer Education, Barry University, 463-1360).

_____

Student's Name

_____   _____

Signature of Parent/Guardian   Date

Figure 3.2.   Parental consent form for a proposed research study.

Approval may also be required from the principal or principals whose schools will be involved. Even if such approval is not required it should be sought, both out of courtesy and for the sake of a smoothly executed study.

The key to gaining approval and cooperation is good planning. The key to good planning is a well-designed, carefully thought-out study. Administrators who are hesitant or hostile about people doing research in their schools have probably had a bad experience. They don't want anyone else running around their schools disrupting classes and administering useless, poorly constructed questionnaires. Unfortunately, there are instances in which improperly trained, though well-intended, persons go into a school and become a source of bad feelings regarding research. It is up to you to convince school personnel that what you are proposing is of value, that your study is carefully designed, and that you will work with teachers to minimize inconvenience.

Achieving full cooperation, and not just approval on paper, requires that you invest as much time as is necessary to discuss your study with the principal, the teachers, and perhaps even parents. These groups have varying levels of knowledge and understanding regarding the research process. Their concerns will focus mainly on the perceived value of the study, its potential affective impact, and the actual logistics of carrying it out. The principal, for example, will probably be more concerned with whether you are collecting any data that might be viewed as objectionable by the community than with the specific design you will be using. All groups will be interested in what you might be able to do *for them*. Potential benefits to be derived by the students, teachers, or principal as a result of your study should be explained fully. Your study, for example, might involve special instructional materials which are to be shared with the teachers and left with them after the study has ended. Even if all parties are favorably impressed, however, the spirit of cooperation will quickly dwindle if your study will involve considerable extra work on their part or will inconvenience them in any major way. Thus if changes can be made in the planned study to better accommodate their normal routine, they should be made *unless* the study will suffer as a consequence. No change should be made solely for the sake of compromise without considering its impact on the study as a whole.

Clearly, human relations is an important factor in conducting research in applied settings. That you should be your usual charming self goes without saying. But you should keep in mind that you are dealing with sincere, concerned educators who may not have your level of research expertise. Therefore, you must make a special effort to discuss your study in plain English (it is possible!) and to never give the impression that you are talking down to them. Also, your task is not over once the study begins. The feelings of involved persons must be monitored and responded to throughout the duration of the study if the initial level of cooperation is to be maintained.

Training Research Assistants

In addition to determining *what* will be done, it must also be decided *who* will do it. Anyone who is going to assist you in any way in actually conducting your study, whether a colleague or a teacher, should be considered a research assistant. Regardless of who they are, or what role they will play, all assistants should participate in some type of orientation that explains the nature of the study and the part they will play in it. They should understand exactly *what* they are going to do and *how* they are to do it. Their responsibilities should be described in writing and, if necessary, they should receive training related to their assigned task and be given opportunities for supervised practice. Simulations, in which assistants go through the entire task (e.g., conducting an interview) with each other or with you, are an especially effective training strategy.

Before any data are actually collected, anyone involved in any way with data collection procedures should become thoroughly familiar with all relevant restrictions, legal or otherwise, related to the collection, storing, and sharing of obtained information. All necessary permissions from participants, school administrators, federal agencies, and the like should be obtained *in writing*. And finally, all data collection activities should be carefully and systematically monitored to ensure that correct procedures are being followed.

■ COMPONENTS

Although they may go by other names, research plans typically include an introduction, a method section, a description of proposed data analyses, and a time schedule. Each component will be discussed in detail, but basically the format for a typical research plan is as follows:

Introduction
>   Statement of the Problem
>   Review of Related Literature
>   Statement of the Hypothesis

Method
>   Subjects
>   Instruments
>   Design
>   Procedure

Data Analysis

Time Schedule

Budget (if appropriate)

Other headings may also be included, as needed. For example, if special materials are being developed for the study, or special equipment is being used (such as computer terminals), then headings such as Materials or Apparatus might be included under Method and before Design.

Introduction

If you have completed Task 2, you are very familiar with the content of the introduction: a statement of the problem, a review of related literature, and a statement of the hypothesis.

Statement of the Problem

Since the problem sets the stage for the rest of the plan, it should be stated as early as possible. The statement should be accompanied by a description of the background of the problem and a rationale for its significance.

Review of Related Literature

The review of related literature should present the least related references first and the most related references last, just prior to the statement of the hypothesis (do not forget the big V). The literature review should lead logically to a tentative, testable conclusion, your hypothesis. The review should conclude with a brief summary of the literature and its implications.

Statement of the Hypothesis

Each hypothesis should represent a reasonable explanation for some behavior, phenomenon, or event. It should clearly and concisely state the expected relationship (or difference) between the variables in your study, and should define those variables in operational, measurable terms. Finally, each hypothesis should be clearly testable within some reasonable period of time. Be certain that all terms in the introduction are either common-usage terms or are operationally defined. The persons reading your plan (and especially persons reading your final report, of which this introduction will be a part) may not be as familiar with your terminology as you are.

Method

The specific method of research your study represents will affect the format and content of your method section. The method section for an experimental study, for example, typically includes a description of the experimental design, whereas a descriptive study may combine the design and procedure sections into one. In general, however, the method section includes a description of the subjects, measuring instruments, design, and procedure.

Subjects

The description of subjects should clearly define the population, the larger group, from which the sample will be selected. The description should indicate the size and major characteristics of the population. In other words, where are the subjects for your study going to come from? What are they like? How many do you have to choose from? For example, a description of subjects might include the following:

> Subjects will be selected from a population of 157 students
> enrolled in an algebra I course at a large urban high school
> in Miami, Florida. The population is tricultural, being com-
> posed primarily of Caucasian non-Hispanic students,
> African-American students, and Hispanic students from a
> variety of Latin American backgrounds. . . .

The procedural technique for selecting the sample or samples to be included in the study may be described here but usually is described in the procedure section of the plan.

Instruments

Since measurement in education is primarily indirect (there is no yardstick for achievement), the measuring instrument you select or develop really represents an operational definition of whatever construct you are trying to measure. For example, intelligence may be defined to be scores on the Wechsler Intelligence Scale for Children. Therefore, it is important to provide a rationale for the selection of the instrument to be used as well as a description of the instrument. Validity and reliability data should also be presented; the degree to which the instrument for collecting data is invalid is directly related to the degree to which the study is invalid. If you are going to develop your own instrument, you should describe how the instrument will be developed, what it will measure, and how you plan to evaluate its validity and reliability before its utilization in the actual study. For example, a description of the instrument might include the following:

> The Stanford Achievement Test: Arithmetic Test (level 7.0–9.9) will be utilized as the data-gathering instrument. Split-half reliability coefficients are reported to range from .86 to .93 and reviewers are in agreement concerning its high content validity. . . .

Of course, if more than one instrument is to be used, which is not uncommon, each should be described separately, and in detail. You are probably not yet able to identify and describe the instrument you would use in your study. Therefore, in Task 3, you should describe the *kind* of instrument which would be used.[5] This section may include a description of when each instrument will be administered and for what purpose (for example, as a pretest), but such a description is usually included in the procedure section. In writing this section of a research plan, a researcher may discover that an appropriate instrument for collecting data to test the hypothesis is not available. If this occurs, a decision needs to be made, probably either to alter the hypothesis and change the dependent variable (you remember *Y!*) or to develop an instrument. Again, it is better to be made aware of the unavailability of an appropriate instrument *before* a study has begun than *during* its execution.

Materials/Apparatus

As mentioned previously, if special materials (such as booklets, training manuals, or computer programs) are going to be developed, they should be described in some detail in the research plan. Also, if special apparatus (such as computer terminals) are going to be used, they also should be described. If biofeedback equipment were going to be utilized, for example, the description might include the following:

> Biofeedback training will be provided using the Holdthatthot instrument; this equipment records heart rate, galvanic skin response (GSR), and skin temperature. . . .

Design

The description of the design indicates the basic structure of the study. The nature of the hypothesis, the variables involved, and the constraints of the "real world"— all contribute to the design to be used. For example, if the hypothesis involved comparing the effectiveness of high-impact versus low-impact aerobic exercises with respect to exercise-related injuries, the study would involve comparing the number

---

[5] Task 5 will require you to select and describe a particular instrument of the kind which you describe here.

of injuries occurring in two groups during some period of time, one group performing high-impact exercises and one group performing low-impact exercises. Therefore, a design involving two groups would be needed. The "real world" might determine whether those groups could be randomly formed or whether existing groups would have to be used; these two alternatives dictate distinctly different designs. The nature of the variables also may affect the design. If the dependent variable involves measurement of attitudes, for example, use of a design involving a pretest may be precluded. Administration of a pretest of attitudes may alert students to what is coming, to what the study is all about—the "I know what you're up to" phenomenon. Subjects may then react differently to a treatment intended to change attitudes, for example, than they would have had they not been pretested. Thus, the design typically indicates the number of groups to be included in the study, whether the groups will be randomly formed, and whether there will be a pretest. Other factors may also be discussed, such as particular arrangements of groups and time intervals between components of the design. For example, in the study by the author previously described (Gay, 1973), the design section indicated that "the design for both experiments followed that used by Peterson et al. (1935) and Sones and Stroud (1940) in that the interval between learning and retention testing was equated for all groups."[6] This entire discussion, it should be pointed out, is appropriate primarily for experimental studies. The choice of designs is greatly reduced for a causal-comparative study, for example. Research plans and reports for studies involving the other methods of research typically do not include a separate design section.

There are a number of basic designs to select from as well as an almost endless number of variations on those designs which can be used. While the design can become very complex, especially if multiple independent and/or dependent variables are involved, such complex designs are really sophisticated variations of the basic designs. By the time you develop Task 6, you will be familiar with the basic designs and will be able to identify them by name and apply them to your study. In developing Task 3, you will not have this knowledge. You should be able, however, to describe the kinds of information which a given design conveys. In other words, you should be able to indicate the number and arrangement of groups, whether they will be randomly formed groups or existing groups, and whether there will be a pretest.

Procedure

The procedure section describes all the steps that will be followed in conducting the study, from beginning to end, in the order in which they will occur, in other words, how the design selected for testing the hypothesis will be operationalized. The procedure section typically begins with a description of the technique to be used in selecting the sample, or samples, for the study. A description might be as follows:

> In the summer of 1995, prior to the assignment of students
> to classes, a list of all students scheduled to take general
> math I in the fall (approximately 150 students) will be
> obtained. Using this list, 60 students will be randomly
> selected to participate in the study. These 60 students will
> then be randomly assigned to one of two general math I

---

[6]Peterson, H. A., Ellis, M., Toohill, N., & Kloess, P. (1935). Some measurements of the effects of reviews. *Journal of Educational Psychology, 26,* 65–72, and Sones, A. M., & Stroud, J. B. (1940). Review, with special reference to temporal position. *Journal of Educational Psychology, 31,* 665–676.

classes, one class to receive programmed instruction and
one to receive lecture-discussion instruction.

Occasionally an entire population is used and simply randomly assigned to two or
more groups. This situation might be described as follows:

> The entire eighth-grade population (approximately 200 stu-
> dents) will participate in the study. All students will be ran-
> domly assigned to one of six classes; three of those classes
> will randomly be designated as experimental classes, and
> three as control classes.

In both examples, the population would already have been described under
Subjects at the beginning of the Method section.

If the design includes a pretest, the procedure for its administration—when it
will be administered, and how—will usually be described next. Any other measure
to be administered at the beginning of the study will also be discussed; for example, in addition to a pretest on current skill in reading music, a general musical
achievement test might be administered in order to check for initial equivalence of
groups. For a study designed to investigate a new method for improving reading
comprehension, this portion of the procedure section might include a statement
such as the following:

> In September, on the day following the first day of school,
> the Magoo Test of Reading Comprehension, Form A, will be
> administered to all experimental and control groups.

In research plans which do not include a separate section for a description of the
instrument, relevant information concerning the measure will be presented here.

From this point on, the procedure section will describe exactly what is going
to occur in the study. In an experimental study, this will basically involve a description of how the groups will be the same and how they will be different. How they
will be different should be a function of the independent variable only; in other
words, major differences between groups should be intentional treatment differences. How they will be the same will be a function of control procedures. Since
the essence of experimentation is groups equivalent on all relevant variables except
the experimental variable, all procedures designed to insure equivalence should be
described; if two groups are equivalent to begin with, are treated the same for some
period of time except for the independent variable, and are different at the end on
some dependent variable, that difference can be attributed to the independent variable. Variables that typically need to be controlled include teacher skill and experience, materials, time on task, instructional environment, and testing conditions. For
example, if an experimental group was taught by Carmel Kandee (teacher-of-the-
year Mary Poppins type), and a control group was taught by Hester Hartless (char-
ter member of the Lizzie Borden fan club), then final differences between groups
might be attributable to teacher differences, not treatment differences. In order to
control for the teacher variable, you might have both groups taught by the same
teacher, or you might have several experimental groups and several control groups
and randomly assign teachers to groups. The following are examples of the kinds
of statements which typically appear in the procedure section:

> The curriculum for both groups will be the same. . . .
> All experimental and control classes will utilize the Miss
> Muffet Reading Series. . . .
> All eight teachers have more than five years of experience. . . .

> All students will meet for the same amount of time
> each day. . . .

The procedure section will generally conclude with a discussion concerning administration of the posttest similar to the discussion for the pretest. As an example:

> In June, on the next to the last day of school, the Magoo
> Test of Reading Comprehension, Form B, will be adminis-
> tered to all experimental and control groups.

The procedure section should also include any identified assumptions and limitations. An assumption is any important "fact" presumed to be true but not actually verified. For example, in a study involving reading instruction for preschool children it might be assumed that, given the population, none of the children had received reading instruction at home. Such assumptions are probabilistic in nature; the reader of the research plan (and ultimately the research report) can determine whether he or she is willing to "buy" the researcher's assumption. For example, if the population were preschool children in an upper-middle-class suburban area, the assumption just discussed would be questionable. A limitation is some aspect of the study that the researcher knows may negatively affect the results or generalizability of the results but over which he or she probably has no control. In other words, something is not as "good" as it should be but the researcher cannot do anything about it. Two common limitations are sample size and length of the study. A research plan might state, for example:

> Only one class of 30 students will be available for
> participation.
>
> OR
>
> While ideally subjects should be exposed to the experimen-
> tal treatment for a longer period of time in order to more
> accurately assess its effectiveness, permission has been
> granted to the researcher to be in the school for a maxi-
> mum of two weeks.

If such limitations are openly and honestly stated, the readers can judge for themselves how seriously the study may be affected.

Assumptions and limitations are generally stated within context; for example, a time limitation would be stated within the procedure section, probably at the same time administration of the posttest was discussed. Some colleges and universities require that assumptions and limitations be presented in a separate section. This forces the student to give some thought to where they occur in her or his study.

The procedure section should be as detailed as possible, and any new terms introduced should of course be defined. The key to writing this section is replicability. It should be precise to the point where someone else could read your plan and execute your study exactly as you intended it to be conducted. In fact, it should be detailed enough to permit *you* to execute it exactly as planned!

Data Analysis

The research plan must include a description of the statistical technique or techniques that will be used to analyze study data. For certain descriptive studies, data analysis may involve little more than simple tabulation and presentation of results. For most studies, however, one or more statistical methods will be required. Identification of appropriate analysis techniques is extremely important; very few situations cause as much "weeping and gnashing of teeth" as collecting data only to find that there is no appropriate analysis or that the analysis that is appropriate requires sophistication beyond the researcher's level of statistical competence. Once the data are collected, it is too late. Settling for a less appropriate technique in order to salvage the study is definitely a no-no, although this is done on occasion by poor planners. The hypothesis of the study determines the design, which in turn determines the statistical analysis; an inappropriate analysis, therefore, does not permit a valid test of the research hypothesis. Which available analysis technique should be selected depends on a number of factors, such as how the groups will be formed (for example, by random assignment, by matching, or by using existing groups), how many different treatment groups will be involved, how many independent variables will be involved, and the kind of data to be collected (interval data, for example, will require different techniques than ordinal data). In a correlational study, similar factors will determine the appropriate correlational analysis.

If you do not understand any of the terms mentioned, do not worry about it; you are not supposed to, *yet!* They will be discussed in succeeding chapters. Although you probably are not familiar with any specific statistical analyses, you should be able to describe in your research plan the *kind* of analysis you would need. For example, you might say:

> An analysis will be used appropriate for comparing the achievement, on a test of reading comprehension, of two randomly formed groups of second-grade students.

By the time you get to Task 7, you *will* know exactly what you need (honest!).

Time Schedule

A realistic time schedule is equally important for both beginning researchers working on a thesis or dissertation and for experienced researchers working under the deadlines of a research grant or contract. It is an infrequent event when a researcher has as long as he or she pleases to conduct a study. The existence of deadlines typically necessitates careful budgeting of time. Basically, a time schedule includes a listing of major activities or phases of the proposed study and a corresponding expected completion time for each activity. Such a schedule in a research plan enables the researcher to assess the feasibility of conducting a study within existing time limitations. It also helps the researcher to stay on schedule during the execution of the study. In developing a time frame, do not make the mistake of "cutting it too thin" by allowing a minimum amount of time for each activity. Allow yourself enough time so that if an unforeseen minor delay occurs, you can still meet your final deadline. You should also plan to have as the completion date for your final activity a date sometime in advance of your actual deadline. Your schedule will not necessarily be a series of sequential steps such that one activity must be completed before another is begun. For example, while the study is being conducted, you may also be working on the first part of the research report.

A very useful approach for constructing a time schedule is to use what is called the Gantt chart method.[7] A Gantt chart lists the activities to be completed down the left-hand side of a page and the time to be covered by the entire project across the top of the page. A bar graph format is used to indicate the beginning and ending date for each activity. Such a chart permits the researcher to easily see the "big picture" and to identify concurrent activities (see Figure 3.3).

---

[7] Carlisle, H. M. (1979). *Management essentials: Concepts and applications.* Chicago: Science Research Associates.

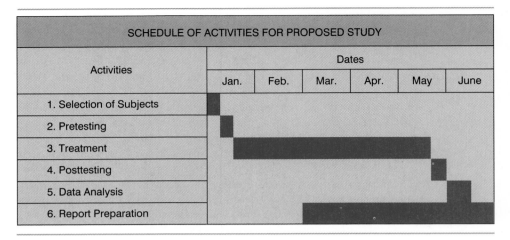

Figure 3.3. Hypothetical, simplified example of a Gantt chart for a proposed research study.

Budget

Formal research plans are referred to as proposals. Proposals are generally submitted to governmental or private funding agencies in the hope of receiving financial assistance for the execution of a study. Proposals almost always require the inclusion of a tentative budget. Depending upon the amount requested and the agency to which the proposal is submitted, items included in the budget will vary. With the exception of some very small grants, however, budgets typically include such items as personnel, clerical assistance, expenses (such as travel and postage), equipment, and overhead (see Figure 3.4). Assistance in developing budgets is usually available at most colleges and universities, provided either formally by a research office or informally by colleagues who have had experience in developing proposals.

▪ EVALUATION OF A RESEARCH PLAN

Evaluation of a research plan can involve both informal and formal procedures. Informally, it should be reviewed and critiqued; formally, it may be field-tested in a preliminary pilot study. Having a research plan permits it to be carefully scrutinized by yourself and by others. Rereading a plan several days after having written it often results in flaws or weaknesses suddenly being very evident. Having a written plan also allows others not only to identify problems but also to make suggestions as to how the study might be improved. A research plan should be reviewed by at least one skilled researcher and at least one expert in the study's area of investigation, for example, reading. There is no researcher, no matter how long she or he has been "in the business," whose plan cannot benefit from the insight of others.

Formal evaluation of a research plan involves a pilot study, which is sort of a dress rehearsal. In a pilot study the entire study is conducted, each and every procedure is followed, and the resulting data are analyzed—all according to the research plan. Beginning researchers gain valuable experience from conducting a pilot study; the quality of one's dissertation, for example, may be considerably improved as a result. Even a small-scale pilot study, based on a small number of subjects, can help

Budget	
Direct Costs	**Amount**
Personnel salaries	
Director (9 mos. at $40,000/yr.)	$30,000
Graduate assistance (9 mos. at $10,000/yr.)	7,500
Secretary (1/2 time for 9 mos. at $14,000/yr.)	5,250
Fringe benefits for director (31.5%)	9,450
	$52,200
Expenses	
Travel (60 on-site visits at $14/visit)	840
Instructional materials	1,200
Office supplies	600
Postage	600
Duplicating	800
Computer time	1,000
	$5,040
Subtotal: Direct costs	57,240
Overhead (48% of personnel salaries)	25,056
Total costs	$82,296

Figure 3.4. Hypothetical, simplified example of a budget for a proposed research study.

in refining procedures, such as instrument administration and scoring routines, and in trying out analysis techniques. The larger the scope of the pilot study, the more like the "real" study it is, the more likely it is that potential problems such as uncontrolled variables and inefficient data processing routines will be identified. The research plan will almost always be modified as a result of a pilot study, and in some cases it may be completely "overhauled." Besides time constraints, a major reason more large-scale pilot studies are not conducted is lack of available subjects. It is usually difficult enough to locate a sufficient number of subjects for the actual study, let alone a like number for a pilot study. Whenever feasible, however, a pilot study should be considered a very worthwhile use of your time.

■ SUMMARY/CHAPTER 3
DEFINITION AND PURPOSE

1. A research plan is a detailed description of a proposed study designed to investigate a given problem; it includes justification for the hypothesis to be tested, a detailed presentation of the research steps that will be

followed in collecting and analyzing required data, and a projected time schedule for each major step.

2. A research plan may be relatively brief and informal or very lengthy and formal, such as the proposals which are submitted to governmental and private funding agencies.

3. The research plan must be completed before a study is begun.

4. Since your study will be designed to test a hypothesis, it must be developed first; the nature of your hypothesis will determine to a high degree the sample group, measuring instruments, design, procedures, and statistical techniques used in your study.

5. The research plan makes you think; it forces you to think through every aspect of the study.

6. A written plan facilitates evaluation of the proposed study by you and by others.

7. A research plan provides a guide for conducting the study.

8. A well-thought-out plan saves time, reduces the probability of costly mistakes, and generally results in higher quality research.

9. Part of good planning is anticipation. Try to anticipate potential problems which might arise, do what you can to prevent them, and plan your strategies for dealing with them if they do occur.

GENERAL CONSIDERATIONS

The Ethics of Research

10. There are ethical considerations involved in all research studies. Ethical concerns are, of course, more acute in experimental studies which, by definition, "manipulate" and "control" subjects.

11. Perhaps the foremost rule of ethics is that subjects should not be harmed in any way (physically or mentally) in the name of science.

12. The subject's right to privacy is also an important consideration.

13. Probably the most definitive source of ethical guidelines for researchers is *Ethical Principles in the Conduct of Research with Human Participants,* which was prepared for, and is published by, the American Psychological Association (APA).

14. Above all, the researcher must have personal integrity.

Legal Restrictions

15. The major provisions of legislation passed to date have been designed to protect subjects who participate in research and to ensure the confidentiality of students' records.

16. The National Research Act of 1974 requires that proposed research activities involving human subjects be reviewed and approved by an authorized group in an institution, prior to the execution of the research, to ensure protection of the subjects.

17. The Family Educational Rights and Privacy Act of 1974, more commonly referred to as the Buckley Amendment, basically protects the privacy of the educational records of students.

18. Among the provisions of the Buckley Amendment is the specification that data that actually identify the students may not usually be made available unless written permission is acquired from the students (if of age), parents, or legal guardians.

Cooperation

19. The first step in acquiring needed cooperation is to follow required procedures.
20. The approval process usually involves the completion of one or more forms on which the nature of the research and the specific request being made of the school system are described and a meeting with the approval-granting administrator.
21. The key to gaining approval and cooperation is good planning. The key to good planning is a well-designed, carefully thought-out study.
22. Achieving full cooperation, and not just approval on paper, requires that you invest as much time as is necessary to discuss your study with the principal, the teachers, and perhaps even parents. Potential benefits to be derived by the students, teachers, or principal as a result of your study should be explained fully.
23. If changes can be made in the planned study to better accommodate the normal routine of participating personnel, these changes should be made *unless* the study will suffer as a consequence.
24. The feelings of involved persons must be monitored and responded to throughout the duration of the study if the initial level of cooperation is to be maintained.

Training Research Assistants

25. Regardless of who they are, or what role they will play, all assistants should participate in some type of orientation that explains the nature of the study and the part they will play in it.
26. Responsibilities should be described in writing and, if necessary, assistants should receive training related to their assigned task and be given opportunities for supervised practice.
27. Before any data are actually collected, anyone involved in any way with data collection procedures should become thoroughly familiar with all relevant restrictions, legal or otherwise, related to the collection, storing, and sharing of obtained information.

COMPONENTS

28. Although they may go by other names, research plans typically include an introduction, a method section, a description of proposed data analysis, a time schedule, and a budget, if appropriate.

Introduction

29. The introduction includes a statement of the problem, a review of related literature, and a statement of the hypothesis.

30. Be certain that all terms are either common-usage terms or are operationally defined.

Method

31. The specific method of research your study represents will affect the format and content of your method section.

Subjects

32. The description of subjects should clearly define the population, the larger group from which the sample will be selected.
33. The description should indicate the size and major characteristics of the population.

Instruments

34. Since measurement in education is primarily indirect, the measuring instrument you select or develop really represents an operational definition of whatever construct you are trying to measure.
35. It is important to provide a rationale for the selection of the instrument to be used as well as a description of the instrument.
36. If you are going to develop your own instrument, you should describe how the instrument will be developed, what it will measure, and how you plan to evaluate its validity and reliability.

Materials/Apparatus

37. If special materials (such as booklets, training manuals, or computer programs) are going to be developed, they should be described in some detail.
38. If special apparatus (such as computer terminals) are going to be utilized, they also should be described.

Design

39. The description of the design indicates the basic structure of the study.
40. The nature of the hypothesis, the variables involved, and the constraints of the "real world"—all contribute to the design to be used.
41. The design typically indicates the number of groups to be included in the study, whether the groups will be randomly formed, and whether there will be a pretest.
42. There are a number of basic designs to select from as well as an almost endless number of variations on those designs which can be used.

Procedure

43. The procedure section describes all the steps that will be followed in conducting the study, from beginning to end, in the order in which they will occur.

44. The procedure section typically begins with a description of the technique to be used in selecting the sample, or samples, for the study.
45. If the design includes a pretest, the procedure for its administration, when it will be administered, and how will usually be described next.
46. From this point on, the procedure section will describe exactly what is going to occur in the study. In an experimental study, this will basically involve a description of how the groups will be the same (control procedures) and how they will be different (the independent variable, or treatment).
47. The procedure section will generally conclude with a discussion concerning the administration of the posttest similar to the discussion for the pretest.
48. The procedure section should also include any identified assumptions and limitations. An assumption is any important "fact" presumed to be true but not actually verified; a limitation is some aspect of the study that the researcher knows may negatively affect the results or generalizability of the results, but over which he or she probably has no control.
49. The procedure section should be as detailed as possible and any new terms introduced should of course be defined; it should be precise to the point where someone else could read your plan and execute your study exactly as you intended it to be conducted.

Data Analysis

50. The research plan must include a description of the statistical technique or techniques that will be used to analyze study data.
51. The hypothesis of the study determines the design, which in turn determines the statistical analysis; an inappropriate analysis, therefore, does not permit a valid test of the research hypothesis.
52. Which available analysis technique should be selected depends on a number of factors, such as how the groups will be formed (for example, by random assignment, by matching, or by using existing groups), how many different treatment groups will be involved, how many independent variables will be involved, and the kind of data to be collected. (Interval data, for example, will require different techniques than ordinal data.) In a correlational study, similar factors will determine the appropriate correlational analysis.

Time Schedule

53. Basically, a time schedule includes a listing of major activities or phases of the proposed study and a corresponding expected completion time for each activity.
54. A very useful approach for constructing a time schedule is to use the Gantt chart method, which uses a bar graph format.

Budget

55. Formal research plans are referred to as proposals; they almost always require the inclusion of a tentative budget.
56. Budgets typically include such items as personnel, clerical assistance, expenses, equipment, and overhead.

EVALUATION OF A RESEARCH PLAN

57. Having a research plan permits it to be carefully scrutinized, by yourself and others.

58. Having a plan also allows others not only to identify problems but also to make suggestions as to how the study might be improved.

59. A research plan should be reviewed by at least one skilled researcher and at least one expert in the study's area of investigation, for example, reading.

60. Formal evaluation of a research plan involves a pilot study; in a pilot study the entire study is conducted, each and every procedure is followed, and the resulting data are analyzed—all according to the research plan.

61. Even a small-scale pilot study based on a small number of subjects can help in refining procedures, such as instrument administration and scoring routines, and in trying out analysis techniques.

62. The research plan will almost always be modified as a result of a pilot study, and in some cases it may be completely "overhauled."

TASK 3 PERFORMANCE CRITERIA

As repeatedly pointed out, you are not yet in a position to develop a sound research plan. You are not expected to. The purpose of Task 3 is to have you demonstrate the ability to develop a complete research plan. What is required is that your plan contain all the components of a research plan, not that those components be technically correct. For example, you must describe how you will select your subjects, but it is not necessary that your selection method be a valid one. Beginning with Chapter 4, you will learn the correct way to formulate each of the components. Feedback from your instructor concerning your research plan will alert you to specific sections of succeeding chapters.

On the following pages, an example is presented which illustrates the performance called for by Task 3. (See Task 3 example.) This example represents the task submitted by the same student whose task for Part Two was previously presented; consequently, the research plan matches the introduction. Keep in mind that since you do not yet possess the necessary level of expertise, the proposed activities described in your plan (and in the example presented) do not necessarily represent ideal research procedure. You should also be aware that research plans are usually more detailed. The example given, however, does represent what is expected of you at this point.

Additional examples for this and subsequent tasks are included in the *Student Guide* which accompanies this text.

1

Effect of Interactive Multimedia on the Achievement of
10th-Grade Biology Students

Method

Subjects

Subjects for this study will be 10th-grade biology students in an upper-middle class all-girl Catholic high school in Miami, Florida. Forty students will be randomly selected and randomly assinged to two groups.

Instrument

The effectiveness of interactive multimedia (IMM) will be determined by comparing the biology achievement of the two groups as measured by a standardized test, if there is an acceptable test available. Otherwise, one will be developed.

Design

There will be two randomly-formed groups of 20 students each. Students in both groups will be posttested in May using a test of biology achievement.

Procedure

At the beginning of the school year, 40 10th-grade biology students will be randomly selected from a population of approximately 200. Selected students will be randomly assigned to two groups, and one group will be randomly designated to be the experimental group. The same teacher will teach both classes.

During the school year, control group students will be taught biology using traditional lecture and discussion methods. The students in the experimental group will be taught using IMM. Both groups will cover the same subject matter and use the same text. The groups will recieve biology instruction for the same amount of time and in the same room,

2

but not at the same time as they will be taught by the same teacher.

Academic objectives will be the same for each class and all tests measuring achievement will be identical. Both classes will have the same homework reading assignments. In May, a biology achievement test will be administered to both classes at the same time.

Data Analysis

The posttest scores of the two groups will be compared using a t test.

Time Schedule

	August	September	...	April	May	June
Select Subjects	___					
Pretest	_____					
Execute Study		_____				
Posttest				____		
Analyze Data					_____	
Write Report			_____			

PART FOUR

Subjects

The purpose of selecting a sample is to gain information concerning a population. To use a former example, if you were interested in the effect of daily homework assignments on the examination grades of ninth-grade algebra students, it would not be possible for you to include *all* ninth-grade algebra students in the United States in your study. It would be necessary for you to select a sample. Since inferences concerning a population are made based on the behavior of a sample, it is imperative that the sample be representative and sufficiently large, and that care be taken to avoid possible sources of sampling error and bias.

The goal of Part Four is for you to understand the importance of selecting an adequate sample and be familiar with various sampling techniques. After you have read Part Four, you should be able to perform the following task.

■ TASK 4

Having selected a problem, and having formulated one or more testable hypotheses or answerable questions, describe a sample appropriate for evaluating your hypotheses or answering your questions. This description will include:

(a) a definition of the population from which the sample would be drawn;
(b) the procedural technique for selecting the sample and forming the groups;
(c) sample sizes; and
(d) possible sources of sampling bias.

(See Performance Criteria, p. 131)

" . . . every individual has the same probability of being selected and selection of one individual in no way affects selection of another individual (p. 114)."

Selection of a Sample

After reading Chapter 4, you should be able to:

1. Identify and define, or briefly describe, four sampling techniques.

2. Apply the procedures for using a table of random numbers to select a random sample.

3. Identify three variables on which you could stratify.

4. Apply the procedures for selecting a stratified sample.

5. Identify three possible clusters.

6. Apply the procedures involved in cluster sampling.

7. Apply the procedures for selecting a systematic sampling.

8. Identify minimum sample sizes required for descriptive, correlational, causal-comparative, and experimental studies.

9. Identify and briefly describe two major sources of sampling bias.

SAMPLING: DEFINITION AND PURPOSE

Sampling is the process of selecting a number of individuals for a study in such a way that the individuals represent the larger group from which they were selected. The individuals selected comprise a sample and the larger group is referred to as a population. The purpose of sampling is to gain information about a population; rarely is a study conducted that includes the total population of interest as subjects. In fact, not only is it generally not feasible to use the total group, it is also not necessary. If the group of interest is unmanageably large or geographically scattered, study of this group could result in considerable expenditure of time, money, and effort. Further, if a sample is well selected, research results based on it will be generalizable to the population. The degree to which the sample represents the population is the degree to which results for one are applicable to the other.

As an example, suppose the superintendent of a large school system wanted to find out how the 5,000 teachers in that system felt about teacher unions, whether they would join one, and for what reasons. If an interview were determined to be the best way to collect the desired data, it would take a very long time to interview each and every teacher; even if one interview only took 15 minutes, it would take a minimum of 1,250 hours, which is equivalent to 156 eight-hour days, or approximately 30 school weeks to collect the desired information. On the other hand, if 10%, or 500, of the teachers were interviewed, it would take only 125 hours, or approximately 3 weeks. Assuming that the superintendent needed the information "now, not next year," as the saying goes, the latter approach would definitely be preferable *if* the same information could be acquired. As it happens, the conclusions based on the interviews of the sample of teachers would in all probability be the same as the conclusions based on interviews of all the teachers *if* the sample were correctly selected. Just any 500 teachers would not do. Interviewing 500 elementary teachers, for example, would not be satisfactory. In the first place, there is a highly disproportionate number of female teachers at that level and males might feel differently about unions. In the second place, opinions of elementary teachers might not be the same as those of junior high teachers or senior high teachers. How about 500 teachers who were members of the National Education Association (NEA)? While they would probably be more representative of all 5,000 teachers than the elementary teachers, they still would not do. Teachers who are already members of one professional organization would probably be more likely to join another organization. Of course, it could also be argued that nonmembers of the NEA might be more likely to join a union since the approaches of the two organizations to certain problems would be distinctly different. In either case, however, it is reasonable to assume that the opinions toward unions of members and nonmembers of the NEA would be different. How then could it be done; how could a representative sample be selected?

Give up? Don't! As you will see shortly, there are several relatively simple procedures or sampling techniques which could be applied to select a very "nice" sample of teachers. These procedures would not guarantee a sample that was perfectly representative of the population, but they would definitely increase the odds. They would also correspondingly increase the degree of confidence that the superintendent could have regarding the generalizability of findings for the 500 teachers to all 5,000 teachers.

■ DEFINITION OF A POPULATION

Regardless of the technique to be used in selecting a sample, the first step in sampling is definition of the population. The population is the group of interest to the researcher, the group to which she or he would like the results of the study to be generalizable. The defined population has at least one characteristic that differentiates it from other groups. Examples of research populations include all 10th-grade students in the United States, all primary-level gifted children in Utah, and all first-grade culturally deprived students in Utopia County who have participated in preschool training. These examples illustrate two important points about populations. First, populations may be virtually any size and may cover almost any geographical area. Second, the group the researcher would really like to generalize to is rarely available. The population that the researcher would ideally like to generalize to is referred to as the *target population;* the population that the researcher can realistically select from is referred to as the *accessible,* or available, *population.* Thus, the definition of a population is generally a realistic choice, not an idealistic one.

As another example, suppose you wanted to investigate the problem discussed in Chapter 2, that is, the effect of interactive multimedia on the biology achievement of 10th-grade students. Ideally, your study would involve measurement of the biology achievement of all such students. Of course, this would not be very feasible. By the time the very last student was tested, he or she could well be in college! By now it may have occurred to you that the "obvious" solution would be to select a representative sample and test all the members of the sample. A little more thought will reveal that this procedure would also probably be highly impractical. Since the population would be located from coast to coast, even if all appropriate students could be identified, you would still require a staff of qualified researchers and a healthy bank account (which very few researchers have!) to adequately conduct the study. Clearly, your idealistic research plan would have to be brought into line with cold, hard reality. In the end, you would probably settle for a more manageable population, such as all defined students in a given school system, and you would select your sample from this group. By selecting from a more narrowly defined population you would be saving time and money but you would also be losing generalizability. Assuming you selected an adequate sample, the results of your study would be directly generalizable to all appropriate students in the school system, but not to all appropriate students in the United States. The degree to which the students in your school system, or population, were similar to students in other systems would be the degree to which your results would have implications for other settings.

The key is to define your population in sufficient detail so that others may determine how applicable your findings might be to their situation.

■ METHODS OF SELECTING A SAMPLE

Selection of a sample is a very important step in conducting a research study. The "goodness" of the sample determines the generalizability of the results. Since conducting a study generally requires a great deal of time and energy, nongeneralizable results are extremely wasteful; if all results were true only for the group on which they were based, educators could never benefit from anyone else's work and each and every study would have to be replicated an almost infinite number of times. Imagine how slow the progress of science would be if every scientist had to reconfirm Newton's laws!

As discussed previously, a "good" sample is one that is representative of the population from which it was selected. As we saw with our superintendent who needed to assess teachers' attitudes, selecting a representative sample is not a haphazard process. There are, however, several valid techniques for selecting a sample. While certain techniques are more appropriate for certain situations, each of the techniques does not give the same level of assurance concerning representativeness. However, as with populations, we sometimes have to compromise the ideal for the real, that is, what is feasible. This is true in many areas of scientific research, however, and is not a situation peculiar to educational research. Much medical research aimed at relieving human suffering, for example, must be conducted on lower forms of life such as rats; researchers in this field encounter similar problems to those faced by educational researchers with respect to the generalizability of their findings.

Regardless of the specific technique used, the steps in sampling are essentially the same: identification of the population, determination of required sample size, and selection of the sample. The degree to which the selected sample represents the population is the degree to which results are generalizable. There are four basic sampling techniques or procedures: random sampling, stratified sampling, cluster sampling, and systematic sampling. These are referred to as *probability sampling* techniques because it is possible for the researcher to specify the probability, or chance, that each member of a defined population has of being selected for the sample.

Random Sampling

Random sampling is the process of selecting a sample in such a way that all individuals in the defined population have an equal and independent chance of being selected for the sample. In other words, every individual has the same probability of being selected and selection of one individual in no way affects selection of another individual. You may recall in physical education class the teacher occasionally formed teams by having the class line up and count off by twos, one-two-one-two, and so on. With this method, you could never be on the same team as the person next to you. Selection was not independent; whether you were on one team or another was determined by where you were in line and the team for which the person next to you was selected. If selection of teams had been random, you would have had a 50-50 chance of being on either team regardless of which team the person next to you was on.

Random sampling is the best single way to obtain a representative sample. No technique, not even random sampling, *guarantees* a representative sample, but the probability is higher for this procedure than for any other. Differences between the sample and the population should be small and unsystematic. For example, you would not expect the exact same ratio of males and females in a sample as in a population; random sampling, however, assures that the ratio will be close and that the probability of having too many females is the same as the probability of having too many males. In any event, differences are a function of chance and are not the result of any conscious or unconscious bias on the part of the researcher.

Another point in favor of random sampling is that it is required by inferential statistics. This is very important since inferential statistics permit the researcher to make inferences about populations based on the behavior of samples. If samples are not randomly selected, then one of the major assumptions of inferential statistics is violated, and inferences are correspondingly tenuous.[1]

Steps in Random Sampling

In general, random sampling involves defining the population, identifying each member of the population, and selecting individuals for the sample on a completely

---

[1]In Part Seven, you will learn how to select and apply several commonly used inferential statistics. By the way, don't you dare groan and say you're no good at anything mathematical! You will be amazed at how easy statistics really is!

chance basis. One way to do this is to write each individual's name on a separate slip of paper, place all the slips in a hat or other container, shake the container, and select slips from the container until the desired number of individuals is selected. This procedure is not exactly satisfactory, however; if a population had 1,000 members, for example, one would need a relatively large hat! A much more satisfactory approach is to use a table of random numbers. In essence, a table of random numbers selects the sample for you, each member being selected on a purely random, or chance, basis. Such tables are included in the appendix of most statistics books and some educational research books; they usually consist of columns of five-digit numbers which have been randomly generated by a computer. (See Table A.1 in the Appendix.) Using a table of random numbers to select a sample involves the following specific steps:

1. Identify and define the population.
2. Determine the desired sample size.
3. List all members of the population.
4. Assign all individuals on the list a consecutive number from zero to the required number, for example, 000 to 249 or 00 to 89.
5. Select an arbitrary number in the table of random numbers. (Close your eyes and point!)
6. For the selected number, look at only the appropriate number of digits. For example, if a population has 800 members, you only need to use the last 3 digits of the number; if a population has 90 members, you only need to use the last 2 digits.
7. If the number corresponds to the number assigned to any of the individuals in the population, then that individual is in the sample. For example, if a population had 500 members and the number selected was 375, the individual assigned 375 would be in the sample; if a population had only 300 members, then 375 would be ignored.
8. Go to the next number in the column and repeat step 7.
9. Repeat step 8 until the desired number of individuals has been selected for the sample.

Once the sample has been selected, members may then be randomly *assigned* to two (or more) treatment groups (by randomly selecting half of the sample to be the experimental group, for example, or by flipping a coin) if an experimental study is being conducted.

Actually, the random selection process is not as complicated as the above explanation may have made it sound. The following example should make the procedure clear.

An Example of Random Sampling

It is now time to help our long-suffering superintendent who wants to select a sample of teachers so that their attitudes toward unions can be determined. We will apply each of the nine steps described above to the solution of this problem:

1. The population is all 5,000 teachers in the superintendent's school system.
2. The desired sample size is 10% of the 5,000 teachers, or 500 teachers.
3. The superintendent has supplied a directory which lists all teachers in the system.
4. Using the directory, the teachers are each assigned a number from 0000 to 4999.

5. A table of random numbers is entered at an arbitrarily selected number such as the one which is underlined.

    59058
    11859
    <u>53634</u>
    48708
    71710
    83942
    33278
    etc.

6. Since the population has 5,000 members, we only are concerned with the last four digits of the number, 3634.
7. There is a teacher assigned the number 3634; that teacher is therefore in the sample.
8. The next number in the column is 48708. The last four digits are 8708. Since there are only 5,000 teachers, there is no teacher assigned the number 8708. The number is therefore skipped.
9. Applying the above steps to the remaining numbers shown in the above column, teachers 1710, 3942, and 3278 are included. This procedure would be applied to numbers following 33278 in that column and succeeding columns until 500 teachers were selected.

At the completion of this process the superintendent would in all probability have a representative sample of all the teachers in the system. The 500 selected teachers could be expected to appropriately represent all relevent subgroups of teachers such as elementary teachers and male teachers. With random sampling, however, such representation of subgroups is probable but not guaranteed. The probable does not always occur. If you flip a quarter 100 times, the probable outcome is 50 heads and 50 tails. You may get 53 heads and 47 tails, or 45 heads and 55 tails, but most of the time you can expect to get close to a 50-50 split. (You may want to try this during your next study break!) Other outcomes are possible, however; they may be less probable but they are possible. In tossing a quarter 100 times, 85 heads and 15 tails is a possible, low-probability outcome. Similarly, it would be possible, although less probable, for the sample of teachers to be unrepresentative of the total group on one or more dimensions. For example, if 55% of the 5,000 teachers were female and 45% male, we would expect roughly the same percentages in the sample of 500. Just by chance, however, the sample might contain 30% females and 70% males.

If there were one or more variables which the superintendent believed might be highly related to attitudes toward unions, he might not be willing to leave accurate representation on those variables to chance. He might decide, for example, that teaching level (elementary, junior high, senior high) might be a significant variable and that elementary teachers might feel differently toward unions than junior high or senior high teachers. He would want to sample in such a way that appropriate representation on this variable would be guaranteed. In this case he would probably use stratified sampling rather than simple random sampling.

Stratified Sampling

Stratified sampling is the process of selecting a sample in such a way that identified subgroups in the population are represented in the sample in the same proportion that they exist in the population. It can also be used to select equal-sized samples from each of a number of subgroups if subgroup comparisons are desired. Proportional stratified sampling would be appropriate, for example, if you were going to take a survey prior to a national election in order to predict the probable winner. You would want your sample to represent the voting population. Therefore, you would want the same proportion of Democrats and Republicans, for example, in your sample as existed in the population. Other likely variables for proportional stratification might include race, sex, and socioeconomic status. On the other hand, equal-sized samples would be desired if you wanted to compare the performance of different subgroups.

Suppose, for example, that you were interested in comparing the performance of students of different IQ levels (say high, medium, and low) following two different methods of mathematics instruction. Simply randomly selecting a sample and assigning one-half of the sample to each of the methods would not (as you know!) guarantee equal representation of each of the IQ levels in each method. In fact, just by chance, one of the methods might not have any students from one of the levels. However, randomly selecting students from each level, and then assigning half of each selected group to each of the methods, would guarantee equal representation of each IQ level in each method. That is the purpose of stratified sampling, to *guarantee* desired representation of relevant subgroups.

Steps in Stratified Sampling

The steps in stratified sampling are very similar to those in random sampling *except* that selection is from subgroups in the population rather than the population as a whole. In other words, random sampling is done more than once; it is done for each subgroup. Stratified sampling involves the following steps:

1. Identify and define the population.
2. Determine desired sample size.
3. Identify the variable and subgroups (strata) for which you want to guarantee appropriate representation (either proportional or equal).
4. Classify all members of the population as members of one of the identified subgroups.
5. Randomly select (using a table of random numbers) an "appropriate" number of individuals from each of the subgroups, "appropriate" meaning either a proportional number of individuals or an equal number of individuals.

As with simple random sampling, once the samples from each of the subgroups have been randomly selected, each may be randomly assigned to two or more treatment groups. If we were interested in the comparative effectiveness of two methods of mathematics instruction for different levels of IQ, the steps in sampling might be as follows:

1. The population is all 300 eighth-grade students enrolled in general math at Central Junior High School.
2. The desired sample size is 45 students in each of the two methods.
3. The desired subgroups are three levels of IQ—high (over 115), average (85–115), and low (below 85).
4. Classification of the 300 students indicates that there are 45 high IQ students, 215 average IQ students, and 40 low IQ students.

5. Using a table of random numbers, 30 students are randomly selected from each of the IQ subgroups, that is, 30 high IQ, 30 average IQ, and 30 low IQ students.
6. The 30 students in each sample are randomly assigned to one of the two methods, that is 15 of each 30 are randomly assigned to one of the two methods. Therefore, each method contains 45 students—15 high IQ students, 15 average IQ students, and 15 low IQ students (see Figure 4.1).

As you may have guessed, stratification can be done on more than one variable. In the above example, we could have stratified on IQ and math aptitude. The following example, based on a familiar situation, should help to further clarify the process of stratified sampling.

An Example of Stratified Sampling

Let us suppose that our old friend the superintendent wanted to guarantee appropriate representation of teaching level in the sample of teachers. We will apply each of the five steps previously described for selecting a stratified sample:

1. The population is all 5,000 teachers in the superintendent's school system.
2. Desired sample size is 10% of the 5,000 teachers, or 500 teachers.

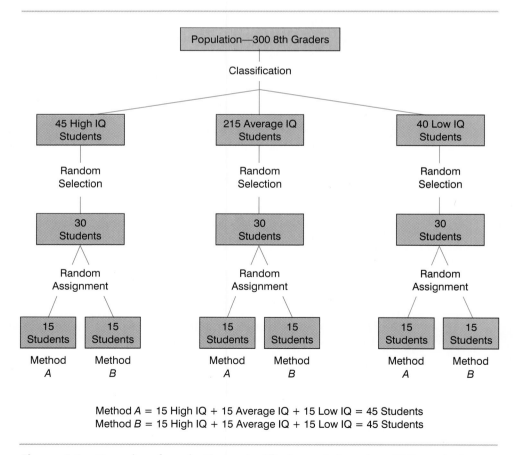

Method *A* = 15 High IQ + 15 Average IQ + 15 Low IQ = 45 Students
Method *B* = 15 High IQ + 15 Average IQ + 15 Low IQ = 45 Students

Figure 4.1. Procedure for selecting a stratified sample based on IQ for a study designed to compare two methods (*A* and *B*) of mathematics instruction.

3. The variable of interest is teaching level and there are three subgroups—elementary, junior high, and senior high.
4. We classify the teachers into the subgroups. Of the 5,000 teachers,
    65%, or 3,250, are elementary teachers;
    20%, or 1,000, are junior high teachers, and;
    15%, or 750, are senior high teachers.
5. We want 500 teachers. Since we want proportional representation,
    65% of the sample (325 teachers) should be elementary teachers,
    20% (100 teachers) should be junior high teachers, and
    15% (75 teachers) should be senior high teachers.
Therefore, using a table of random numbers,
    325 of the 3,250 elementary teachers are randomly selected
        (makes sense since we want a total sample of 10%!),
    100 of the 1,000 junior high teachers are selected, and
    75 of the 750 senior high teachers are selected.

At the completion of this process, the superintendent would have a sample of 500 teachers (325 + 100 + 75), or 10% of the 5,000, and each teaching level would be proportionally represented.

So far we have discovered two ways in which the superintendent could get a sample of teachers, random sampling and stratified sampling. Both of these techniques, however, would result in a sample scattered over the entire district. The interviewer would have to visit many, many schools; any one school might contain only one teacher in the sample.[2] In the event that the superintendent wanted the information quickly, a more expedient method of sampling would be needed. For the sake of convenience, cluster sampling might be used.

Cluster Sampling

Cluster sampling is sampling in which groups, not individuals, are randomly selected. All the members of selected groups have similar characteristics. Instead of randomly selecting fifth graders, for example, you could randomly select fifth-grade classrooms and use all the students in each classroom. Cluster sampling is more convenient when the population is very large or spread out over a wide geographic area. Sometimes it is the only feasible method of selecting a sample. It is not always possible, for example, to obtain or compile a list of all members of the population; thus, in such cases, it is not possible to use simple random sampling. Also, often researchers do not have the control over subjects that they would like. For example, if your population were 10th-grade biology students, it is very unlikely that you would obtain administrative approval to randomly select 10th-grade students and remove a few students from each of many classrooms for your study. You would have a much better chance of securing permission to use several intact classrooms.

Any location, within which we find an intact group of similar characteristics (population members) is a cluster. Examples of clusters include classrooms, schools, city blocks, hospitals, and department stores. Cluster sampling usually involves less time and less expense and is generally more convenient. Let us look at a few examples that illustrate this point. As the above example concerning 10th-grade biology students illustrated, it is easier to use all the students in several classrooms than several students in many classrooms. Similarly, in taking a survey, it is easier to use all the people in a limited number of city blocks than a few people in many city

---

[2] It is highly unlikely that teachers would be asked to come to the interviewer.

blocks. You should be able to apply this logic to the examples of clusters mentioned above. In each case you should see that cluster sampling would be easier (though not necessarily as good, as we shall see later!) than either random sampling or stratified sampling.

Steps in Cluster Sampling

The steps in cluster sampling are not very different from those involved in random sampling. The major difference, of course, is that random selection of groups (clusters) is involved, not individuals. Cluster sampling involves the following steps:

1. Identify and define the population.
2. Determine the desired sample size.
3. Identify and define a logical cluster.
4. List all clusters (or obtain a list) that comprise the population.
5. Estimate the average number of population members per cluster.
6. Determine the number of clusters needed by dividing the sample size by the estimated size of a cluster.
7. Randomly select the needed number of clusters (using a table of random numbers).
8. Include in your study all population members in each selected cluster.

Cluster sampling can be done in stages, involving selection of clusters within clusters. This process is called multistage sampling. For example, schools can be randomly selected and then classrooms within each selected school can be randomly selected.

One common misconception that seems to exist among beginning researchers is the belief that it is all right to randomly select only one cluster. It is not uncommon, for example, for a beginning researcher to define a population as all fifth graders in X County, a cluster as a school, and to indicate random selection of *a* school. However, these same "researchers" would not dream of randomly selecting one student! The principle is the same. Keeping in mind that a good sample is representative of the population from which it is selected, it is highly unlikely that one randomly selected student could ever be representative of an entire population. Similarly, it is unlikely that one randomly selected school could be representative of all schools in a population. Thus, one would normally have to select a number of clusters in order for the results of a study to be generalizable to the population. The following example should make the procedures involved in cluster sampling clear.

An Example of Cluster Sampling

Let us see how our superintendent would get a sample of teachers if cluster sampling were used. We will follow the steps previously listed:

1. The population is all 5,000 teachers in the superintendent's school system.
2. The desired sample size is 500.
3. A logical cluster is a school.
4. The superintendent has a list of all the schools in the district; there are 100 schools.
5. Although the schools vary in the number of teachers per school, there is an average of 50 teachers per school.

6. The number of clusters (schools) needed equals the desired sample size, 500, divided by the average size of a cluster, 50. Thus, the number of schools needed is 500 ÷ 50 = 10.
7. Therefore, 10 of the 100 schools are randomly selected.
8. All the teachers in each of the 10 schools are in the sample (10 schools, 50 teachers per school, equals the desired sample size).

Thus the interviewer could conduct interviews at 10 schools and interview many teachers at one time instead of traveling to a possible 100 schools.

The advantages of cluster sampling are evident. As with most things, however, nothing is all good. Cluster sampling has several drawbacks. For one thing, the chances are greater of selecting a sample that is not representative in some way of the population; the teachers in the above example are all from a limited number of schools, for example, not from a high percentage of the schools. Thus the possibility exists that the 10 schools selected are somehow different from the other 90 in the district (socioeconomic level of the students, racial composition, and so forth). One way to compensate for this problem is by selecting a larger sample, for example including more schools, thus increasing the likelihood that the schools selected adequately represent all the schools.

As another example, suppose our population were all fifth graders in 10 schools (each school having an average of 120 students in 4 classes of 30 students each), and we wanted a sample of 120 students. There are any number of ways we might select our sample. For example, we could: (*a*) randomly select one school and use all the fifth graders in that school, (*b*) randomly select 2 classes from each of 2 schools, or (*c*) randomly select 120 students from the 10 schools. In any of these ways we would wind up with 120 students, but our sample would probably not be equally "good" in each case. In case *a* we would have students from only one school. It is very likely that this school would be different from the other 9 in some significant way (e.g., socioeconomic level or racial composition). In case *b* we would be doing a little better, but we would still only have 2 of the 10 schools represented. Only in case *c* would we have a chance of selecting a sample containing students from all or most of the schools, and the classes within those schools. If random sampling were not feasible, selecting 2 classes from each of 2 schools would be preferable to selecting all the students in one school. Actually, if cluster sampling were used, it would be even better to select 1 class each from 4 of the schools. One way we could attempt to compensate for the loss of representativeness associated with cluster sampling would be to select more than 4 classes. As in most cases, however, the number of classes selected would be not just a matter of desirability but also of feasibility.

Another problem is that commonly used inferential statistics are not appropriate for analyzing data resulting from a study using cluster sampling. Such statistics generally require random sampling. Randomly assigning treatments to existing groups (clusters) is not enough; the groups must be randomly formed. The statistics that are available and appropriate for cluster samples are generally less sensitive to differences which may exist between groups. Thus, one should carefully weigh the advantages and disadvantages of cluster sampling before choosing this method of sampling.

There is one more type of sampling with which you should be familiar, systematic sampling. Although systematic sampling is not used very often, it is appropriate in certain situations and in some instances is the only feasible way to select a sample.

Systematic Sampling

Systematic sampling is sampling in which individuals are selected from a list by taking every Kth name. So what's a "Kth" name? That depends on what K is. If K = 4, selection involves taking every 4th name, if K = 10, every 10th name, and so forth. What K actually equals depends on the size of the list and the desired sample size. The major difference between systematic sampling and the other types of sampling so far discussed is the fact that all members of the population do not have an independent chance of being selected for the sample. Once the first name is selected, all the rest of the individuals to be included in the sample are automatically determined.

Even though choices are not independent, a systematic sample can be considered a random sample *if* the list of the population is randomly ordered. One or the other has to be random—either the selection process or the list. Since randomly ordered lists are rarely available, systematic sampling is rarely "as good" as random sampling. While some researchers argue this point, the major objection to systematic sampling of a nonrandom list is the possibility that certain subgroups of the population can be systematically excluded from the sample. The classic example usually given to support this contention is the statement that certain nationalities have distinctive last names that tend to group together under certain letters of the alphabet; when taking every Kth name, if K is at all large, it is possible that certain nationalities can be skipped over completely.

Steps in Systematic Sampling

Systematic sampling involves the following steps:

1. Identify and define the population.
2. Determine the desired sample size.
3. Obtain a list of the population.
4. Determine what K is equal to by dividing the size of the population by the desired sample size.
5. Start at some random place at the top of the population list.
6. Starting at that point, take every Kth name on the list until the desired sample size is reached.
7. If the end of the list is reached before the desired sample is reached, go back to the top of the list.

Now let us see how our superintendent would use systematic sampling.

An Example of Systematic Sampling

If our superintendent were to use systematic sampling, the process would be as follows:

1. The population is all 5,000 teachers in the superintendent's school system.
2. The desired sample size is 500.
3. The superintendent has supplied a directory which lists all teachers in the system in alphabetical order. The list is not randomly ordered, but it is the best available.
4. K is equal to the size of the population, 5,000, divided by the desired sample size, 500. Thus $K = (5,000 \div 500) = 10$.
5. Some random name at the top of the list of teachers is selected.

6. From that point, every following 10th name is automatically in the sample. For example, if the teacher selected in step 5 were the 3rd name on the list, then the sample would include the 13th name, the 23rd, the 33rd, the 43rd, and so forth.

In this case, due to the nonrandom nature of the list, the sample used would not be as likely to be representative as the samples resulting from application of the other techniques.

Conclusion

In most studies, simple, or stratified random, sampling will usually be the most appropriate sampling technique. Sometimes cluster sampling will be most expedient, and, in a few cases, systematic sampling will be appropriate. Depending upon the type of study, a sample may be used intact or may be randomly assigned to two or more treatments. A study will not necessarily use one of the four techniques discussed so far. It may not use any of them, if the entire population is used in the study, or it may use a combination of more than one. In addition to identification and definition of the population, determination of the desired sample size is a step common to all sampling techniques.

■ DETERMINATION OF SAMPLE SIZE

The question about sampling most frequently asked by beginning researchers is probably, "How do you know how large a sample should be?" And the answer is "large enough!" While the answer is not very comforting, the question is a difficult one. If the sample is too small, the results of the study may not be generalizable to the population. The results may hold only for the sample and may not be the same results that would have been obtained if the entire population had been used. Another way of looking at it is in terms of the hypothesis of the study. If the sample is not large enough, the wrong decision may be made concerning the validity of the hypothesis.

A sample which is too small can affect the generalizability of the study regardless of how well it is selected. Suppose, for example, the population were 300 first graders. If we randomly selected only one student, clearly that student could not represent all the students. Nor could 2, 3, or 4 students, even if randomly selected, adequately represent the population. On the other hand, we would all agree that a sample of 299, 298, or 297 students would represent the population. How about 10? Too small, you say. OK, how about 30? 75? 100? At what point does the sample size stop being "too small" and become "big enough"? That is a question without an easy answer. Knowing that the sample should be as large as possible helps some but still does not give any guidance as to what size sample is "big enough." In most cases, the researcher does not have access to many, many subjects. In fact, obtaining permission to involve students in a study, or finding adults willing to participate in a study, is generally not an easy task. Usually the problem is too few subjects rather than too many. In any event, there are some guidelines that can be applied in order to determine what size sample is "big enough."

In general, the minimum number of subjects believed to be acceptable for a study depends upon the type of research involved. For correlational, causal-comparative, and experimental research, some experts consider the magic "general guideline" to be 30. Thus, for correlational studies at least 30 subjects are needed to establish the existence or nonexistence of a relationship. For causal-comparative studies and many experimental studies, a minimum of 30 subjects per group is recommended. Experimental studies with tight experimental controls, however, may be valid with as few as 15 subjects per group.[3] Some authorities believe that 30 subjects per group should always be considered minimum. However, considering the difficulty involved in securing subjects, and the number of studies that are reported with fewer than 15 in a group, requiring 30 seems to be a little on the idealistic side. Further, while we would not be super confident about the results of a single study based on small samples, if a number of such studies obtained similar results, our confidence in the findings would generally be as high as, if not higher than, for a single study based on very large samples. There is a lot to be said for replication of findings.

Of course, the "minimums" discussed above are just that, minimums. If it is at all possible to use more subjects, you should do so. Using samples larger than the minimums is especially important in certain situations. For example, in an experimental study if the expected difference between groups is small, this difference might not "show up" if the samples are too small. Also, it should be noted that there are relatively precise statistical techniques which can be used to estimate required sample sizes for experimental studies; use of such techniques requires knowledge of certain facts about the population such as the difference expected between groups.[4] Also, there are computer programs available to assist you in estimating needed sample sizes.

For descriptive research, the corresponding general guideline is to sample 10 to 20% of the population. This guideline can be misleading, however, for several reasons. In reality, the appropriate sample size depends on a number of factors such as the specific type of descriptive research involved, the size of the population, and whether data will be analyzed for given subgroups. If, for example, you were going to interview (or observe) a sample of high school students who had been disciplined for bringing a weapon to school, then a 20% sample (say 20 out of 100) would probably be sufficient. If you were interested in questions such as why, how, and where the weapons were obtained, a sample of 20 would probably yield some valuable data. If, on the other hand, you wanted to do a questionnaire survey of teachers in the state of Florida (N = approximately 50,000), a sample of even 10% (5,000) would be excessive, not to mention expensive. In fact, a 1% sample would be more than adequate. Based on a formula originally developed by the United States Office of Education, Krejcie and Morgan generated the figures shown in Table 4.1.[5] For a given population size (N), Table 4.1 indicates the sample size (S) needed in order for the sample to be representative, assuming one is going to survey a random sample. While it is true that in certain respects Table 4.1 represents an oversimplified approach to determination of sample size, it does suggest some general "rules of thumb." As with other types of research, there are statistical techniques and related software available for determining sample size in a more precise way, given knowledge of relevant related variables. Table 4.1 does, however, suggest the following generalities:

---

[3]Roscoe, J. T. (1975). *Fundamental research statistics for the behavioral sciences* (2nd ed.). New York: Holt, Rinehart and Winston.

[4]For further discussion of these techniques, see Cohen, J. (1988). *Statistical power analysis for the behavioral sciences* (2nd ed.). Hillsdale, NJ: Lawrence Erlbaum.

[5]Krejcie, R. V., & Morgan, D. W. (1970). Determining sample size for research activities. *Educational and Psychological Measurement, 30,* 607–610.

Table 4.1

Sample Sizes (S) Required for Given Population Sizes (N)

N	S	N	S	N	S	N	S	N	S
10	10	100	80	280	162	800	260	2800	338
15	14	110	86	290	165	850	265	3000	341
20	19	120	92	300	169	900	269	3500	346
25	24	130	97	320	175	950	274	4000	351
30	28	140	103	340	181	1000	278	4500	354
35	32	150	108	360	186	1100	285	5000	357
40	36	160	113	380	191	1200	291	6000	361
45	40	170	118	400	196	1300	297	7000	364
50	44	180	123	420	201	1400	302	8000	367
55	48	190	127	440	205	1500	306	9000	368
60	52	200	132	460	210	1600	310	10000	370
65	56	210	136	480	214	1700	313	15000	375
70	59	220	140	500	217	1800	317	20000	377
75	63	230	144	550	226	1900	320	30000	379
80	66	240	148	600	234	2000	322	40000	380
85	70	250	152	650	242	2200	327	50000	381
90	73	260	155	700	248	2400	331	75000	382
95	76	270	159	750	254	2600	335	100000	384

Note. From R. V. Krejcie and D. W. Morgan, Determining sample size for research activities. *Educational and Psychological Measurement, 30,* 608. Copyright © 1970 by Sage Publications. Reprinted by permission of Sage Publications, Inc.

1. The larger the population size, the smaller the percentage of the population required to get a representative sample.
2. For smaller populations, say *N* = 100 or fewer, there is little point in sampling; survey the entire population.
3. If the population size is around 500 (give or take 100!), 50% should be sampled.
4. If the population size is around 1,500, 20% should be sampled.
5. Beyond a certain point (about *N* = 5,000), the population size is almost irrelevant and a sample size of 400 will be adequate.

Thus, the superintendent from our previous examples would be relatively safe with a sample of 400 teachers, but would be even more confident with a sample of 500. However, although larger samples are in general better than smaller samples, even very large samples can lead to erroneous conclusions. There are many sources of sampling bias that can affect a study, regardless of sample size.

■ Avoidance of Sampling Bias

Selecting samples using the very best technique does not guarantee that they will be representative of the population. Sampling *error*, beyond the control of the researcher, can exist. Of course no sample will have a composition precisely identical to that of the population. The sample may have, for example, fewer males proportionally, or a higher average IQ. If well selected and sufficiently large, however, the chances are that the sample will be highly similar on such variables. Occasionally, however, just by chance, a sample will differ significantly from the population on some major variable. Usually this will not make a significant difference. If there is a variable for which nonrepresentation might really affect the outcome of the study, the researcher should stratify on that variable rather than leaving all to chance.

Sampling *bias* is another story. Sampling bias does not result from random, chance differences between samples and populations. Sampling bias is systematic and is generally the fault of the researcher. If aware of sources of bias, a researcher can avoid bias if at all possible. The fact that size alone does not guarantee representativeness was graphically illustrated by the presidential election of 1936. The *Literary Digest* poll predicted that Roosevelt would be defeated by Landon. It based its prediction on a poll of several million people. Unfortunately for the *Literary Digest*, the prediction was wrong because it was based on a biased sample. The sample of people polled was selected primarily from automobile registration lists and telephone directories. In 1936, however, a sizable portion of the voting population did not own a car or have a telephone. Thus, the sample did not adequately represent the voting population. And guess what—people without cars and telephones voted anyway! Modern pollsters are more knowledgeable and take great care to insure that samples are representative of the voting population on relevant variables such as socioeconomic status.

A major source of bias is the use of *nonprobability sampling* techniques. When such techniques are used, it is not possible to specify the probability, or chance, that each member of a population has of being selected for the sample. In fact, it is usually difficult, if not impossible, to even describe the population from which a sample was drawn and to whom results can be generalized. These techniques, which include convenience sampling, judgment sampling, and quota sampling, are used mainly for reasons of cost and expediency. Of these sampling methods, convenience sampling is the most used in educational research, and is therefore the major source of sampling bias in educational research studies.

Convenience sampling, also referred to as accidental sampling and haphazard sampling, basically involves using as the sample whoever happens to be available. Two major examples of convenience sampling are the use of volunteers and the use of existing groups just because "they are there." Volunteers are bound to be different from nonvolunteers. For example, they may be more motivated in general or more interested in the particular study. Since a population is composed of volunteers and nonvolunteers, the results of a study based on volunteers are not generalizable to the entire population, only to other volunteers. Two examples should help to make this point clear. Suppose you send a questionnaire to 100 randomly selected people and ask the question, "How do you feel about questionnaires?" Suppose that 40 people respond and all 40 indicate that they love questionnaires. Should you then conclude that the group from which the sample was selected loves questionnaires? Certainly not. The 60 who did not respond may not have done so simply because they hate questionnaires!

As a second example, suppose you want to do a study on the effectiveness of study-habit training on the achievement of college freshmen. You ask for volunteers from the freshman classes and 80 students volunteer. Of course right off the bat they are not representative of all freshmen! For example, they may be students who are not doing well academically but wish that they were. In any event, suppose you then randomly assign the volunteers to 2 groups of 40, one group to receive study-habit training and one group to serve as a control. The experimental group is to receive study-habit training for 1 hour every day for 2 weeks, the control group is to do nothing special. Since they are all volunteers, the subjects feel free to drop out of the study. Members of the control group have no need to drop out since no demands are made on their time. Members of the experimental group, on the other hand, may drop out after one or more sessions, not wishing to "donate" any more of their time. Suppose at the end of the study, only 20 of the original 40 students in the training group remain while all 40 members of the control group remain. Suppose a comparison of their subsequent achievement indicates that the group which received training achieved significantly higher grades. Could you then conclude that the training was effective? Cer-tain-ly not! In essence, we would be comparing the achievement of those in the control group with those members of the experimental group who *chose to remain*. Thus, they might very well be more motivated to achieve, as a group, than the control group; the less motivated students dropped out of the study! It would be very difficult to determine how much of their achievement was due to the treatment (training) and how much was due to motivation.

The problem with using groups just because "they are there" is illustrated in the following example. Suppose you want to do a study on the effect of homework on the achievement of ninth-grade algebra students. You happen to have a friend who teaches two ninth-grade algebra classes. You ask your friend if you may conduct a study using those classes and your friend says yes. You then tell your friend to continue homework assignments in one class and to eliminate homework assignments in the other. At the end of the grading period the achievement of the two groups is compared and the homework group has achieved significantly more than the nonhomework group. Can you conclude that homework is effective? Not necessarily. In your study homework was effective for one class. Since the class was not selected from any larger group, you have no assurance that the class is representative of any other classes. Therefore, you have no assurance that your results are generalizable to any other ninth-grade algebra classes.

Judgment sampling, also referred to as purposive sampling, basically involves selecting a sample which is *believed* to be representative of a given population. In other words, the researcher uses expert judgment to select a representative sample. For example, a number of schools in a given system may be selected to obtain a representative cross section of all schools in the system. The problem, however, as Kalton (1983, p. 91) points out, is that in practice different researchers would likely disagree on what constitutes a "representative" sample and, in any case, a judgment sample is "subject to a risk of bias of unknown magnitude."[6]

Quota sampling is most often used in survey research involving interviews, usually when it is not possible to list all members of the population of interest. When quota sampling is involved, interviewers are given exact numbers, or quotas, of persons of varying characteristics who are to be interviewed, e.g., 35 working women with children under the age of 16 and 20 working women with no children under the age of 16. The most widely known survey of this type is probably the Gallup Poll. Obviously, when quota sampling is used, interviews are obtained from easily accessible individuals. Thus, people who are less accessible (more difficult to contact, more reluctant to participate, and so forth), are underrepresented.[7]

---

[6]Kalton, G. (1983). *Introduction to survey sampling*. Newbury Park, CA: Sage.

[7]See footnote 6. For further discussion of nonprobability sampling, see Badia, P., & Runyon, R. P. (1982). *Fundamentals of behavioral research*. Hightstown, NJ: McGraw-Hill.

As mentioned before, securing administrative approval to involve students in a study is not generally easy. Researchers often use whatever subjects they can get, whatever is most convenient for the administration. This may amount to a researcher receiving permission to use several classes of the administration's choice. Cooperating with the administration is of course advisable, but not at the expense of good research. If the study cannot be conducted properly, the researcher should try hard to convince the administration to allow the study to be conducted the "researcher's way." If this fails, the researcher should look elsewhere for subjects. If suitable subjects cannot be found or selected properly, the study probably should be temporarily abandoned. Conducting a study requires considerable time and energy. To expend such time and energy on a study with little generalizability is a waste of both.

The researcher should be aware of sources of sampling bias and do his or her best to avoid it. If this is not possible, the researcher must decide whether the bias is so severe that the results will be seriously affected. If a decision is made to continue with the study, with full awareness of the existing bias, such bias should be completely reported in the final research report. The consumers of the research findings may then decide for themselves how serious they believe the bias to be.

▪ SUMMARY/CHAPTER 4

SAMPLING: DEFINITION AND PURPOSE

1. Sampling is the process of selecting a number of individuals for a study in such a way that the individuals represent the larger group from which they were selected.
2. The purpose of sampling is to use a sample to gain information about a population.

DEFINITION OF A POPULATION

3. A population is the group to which a researcher would like the results of a study to be generalizable.
4. A defined population has at least one characteristic that differentiates it from other groups.
5. The population that the researcher would ideally like to generalize results to is referred to as the *target population;* the population that the researcher realistically selects from is referred to as the *accessible,* or available, *population.*

METHODS OF SELECTING A SAMPLE

6. Regardless of the specific technique used, the steps in sampling include identification of the population, determination of required sample size, and selection of the sample.
7. The degree to which the selected sample represents the population is the degree to which results are generalizable.
8. When a probability sampling technique is used, it is possible to specify the probability, or chance, that each member of a defined population has of being selected for the sample.

Random Sampling

9. Random sampling is the process of selecting a sample in such a way that all individuals in the defined population have an equal and independent chance of being selected for the sample.
10. Random sampling is the best single way to obtain a representative sample.
11. Random sampling involves defining the population, identifying each member of the population, and selecting individuals for the sample on a completely chance basis.
12. A random sample is generally selected using a table of random numbers.

Stratified Sampling

13. Stratified sampling is the process of selecting a sample in such a way that identified subgroups in the population are represented in the sample in the same proportion that they exist in the population.
14. Stratified sampling can also be used to select equal- sized samples from each of a number of subgroups if subgroup comparisons are desired.
15. The steps in stratified sampling are very similar to those in random sampling *except* that selection is from subgroups in the population rather than the population as a whole. In other words, random sampling is done more than once; it is done for each subgroup.

Cluster Sampling

16. Cluster sampling is sampling in which groups, not individuals, are randomly selected.
17. Any location within which we find an intact group of similar characteristics (population members) is a cluster.
18. The steps in cluster sampling are similar to those in random sampling except that the random selection of groups (clusters) is involved, not individuals.

Systematic Sampling

19. Systematic sampling is sampling in which individuals are selected from a list by taking every Kth name, where K equals the number of individuals on the list divided by the number of subjects desired for the sample.
20. Even though choices are not independent, a systematic sample can be considered a random sample *if* the list of the population is randomly ordered (a relatively infrequent event).

DETERMINATION OF SAMPLE SIZE

21. Samples should be as large as possible; in general, the larger the sample, the more representative it is likely to be, and the more generalizable the results of the study are likely to be.
22. Minimum, acceptable sample sizes depend on the type of research.
23. Even large samples can lead to erroneous conclusions if they are not well selected.

AVOIDANCE OF SAMPLING BIAS

24. Sampling bias does not result from random, chance differences between samples and populations; sampling bias is systematic and is generally the fault of the researcher.

25. A major source of bias is the use of nonprobability sampling techniques.

26. When nonprobability sampling techniques are used, it is not possible to specify the probability, or chance, that each member of a population has of being selected for the sample; it is usually difficult, if not impossible, to even describe the population from which a sample was drawn and to whom results can be generalized.

27. Convenience sampling, also referred to as accidental sampling or haphazard sampling, is the major source of bias in educational research studies; it basically involves using as the sample whoever happens to be available.

28. Two major examples of convenience sampling are the use of volunteers and the use of existing groups just because "they are there."

29. Judgment sampling, also referred to as purposive sampling, basically involves selecting a sample which is *believed* to be representative of a given population; in other words, the researcher uses expert judgment to select a "representative" sample.

30. Quota sampling, which is most often used in survey research using interviews, involves giving interviewers exact numbers, or quotas, of persons of varying characteristics who are to be interviewed.

31. You should not be talked into using a seriously biased sample for the sake of administrative convenience.

32. Any sampling bias present in a study should be fully described in the final research report.

TASK 4 PERFORMANCE CRITERIA

The definition of the population should describe its size and relevant characteristics (such as age, ability, and socioeconomic status).

The procedural technique for selecting subjects should be described in detail. For example, do not just say that stratified sampling will be used; indicate on what basis population members will be stratified and how (and how many) subjects will be selected from each subgroup. Also describe how selected subjects will be placed into treatment groups, by random assignment, for example. If the entire population will be used in the study, say so and simply describe how population members will be assigned to groups.

Include a summary statement that indicates resulting sample size for each group. For example:

> Thus there will be 2 groups of 30 subjects each; each group
> will include 15 subjects with above-average intelligence and
> 15 subjects with below-average intelligence.

Any identifiable source of sampling bias should also be discussed, small sample sizes, for example.

On the following page, an example is presented which illustrates the performance called for by Task 4. (See Task 4 example.) Again, this example represents the task submitted by the same student whose tasks for Parts Two and Three were previously presented. Consequently, the sampling plan represents a refinement of the one included in Task 3.

Additional examples for this and subsequent tasks are included in the *Student Guide* which accompanies this text.

1

Effect of Interactive Multimedia on the Achievement of
10th-Grade Biology Students

Subjects for this study will be selected from the
population of 10th-grade biology students at an upper-middle-
class all-girl Catholic high school in Miami, Florida. The
student population is multicultural, reflecting the diverse
ethnic groups which comprise Dade County. The student body is
composed of approximately 90% Hispanic students from a variety
of Latin American backgrounds, the major one being Cuban, 9%
Caucasian non-Hispanic students, and 1% African-American
students. The population is anticipated to contain
approximately 200 biology students.

Prior to the beginning of the school year, before
students have been scheduled, 60 students will be randomly
selected (using a table of random numbers) and randomly
assigned to 2 classes of 30 each; 30 is the normal class size.
One of the classes will be randomly chosen to receive IMM
instruction.

PART FIVE

Instruments

Whether you are testing hypotheses or seeking answers to questions, you must have a valid, reliable instrument for collecting your data. In most cases it is a matter of selecting the best instrument for your purpose from those that are available. Sometimes, however, you may have to develop your own instrument. Whichever is the case, you must administer an instrument that will yield precisely the data you wish to collect in a quantifiable form.

When selecting a test, there are a number of factors which must be considered; some of these are more crucial than others. The major point to remember, however, is that one does not identify *an* instrument appropriate for a study, but rather selects the *best* instrument available.

The goal of Part Five is for you to be able to select the best instrument for a given study from those instruments that are available and appropriate. After you have read Part Five, you should be able to perform the following task.

■ TASK 5

Having stated a problem, formulated one or more hypotheses or questions, and described a sample, describe three instruments appropriate for collection of data pertinent to the hypothesis or question. For each instrument selected, the description will include:

(a) the name, publisher, and cost;
(b) a description of the instrument;
(c) validity and reliability data;
(d) the type of subjects for whom the instrument is appropriate;
(e) instrument administration requirements;
(f) information regarding scoring and interpretation; and
(g) reviewers' overall impressions.

Based on these descriptions, indicate which test is most acceptable for your "study," and why.

(See Performance Criteria, p. 177)

"The Thematic Apperception Test presents the individual with a series of pictures; the respondent is then asked to tell a story about each picture (p. 158)."

Selection of Measuring Instruments

After reading Chapter 5, you should be able to:

Validity
1. Define or describe content validity.

2. Define or describe construct validity.

3. Define or describe concurrent validity.

4. Apply the procedures for determining concurrent validity by establishing relationship.

5. Define or describe predictive validity.

6. Apply the procedures for determining predictive validity.

Reliability
7. Define or describe reliability.

8. Apply the procedures for determining test-retest reliability.

9. Apply the procedures for determining equivalent-forms reliability.

10. Apply the procedures for determining split-half reliability.

11. Define or describe rationale equivalence reliability.

12. Explain the difference between interscorer and intrascorer reliability.

13. Define or describe standard error of measurement.

Types of Measuring Instruments

14. Describe the purpose of an achievement test; that is, describe what an achievement test measures.

15. Describe the purpose of each of the following types of nonprojective instruments:
    (a) personality inventories
    (b) attitude scales
    (c) tests of creativity
    (d) interest inventories

16. Describe the purpose of aptitude tests.

Selection of a Test

17. State the two most important guidelines, or rules, for test selection.

18. Identify and briefly describe three sources of test information.

19. List, in order of importance, the factors that should be considered in selecting one test from a number of alternatives.

Test Administration

20. List three guidelines for test administration.

■ PURPOSE AND PROCESS

All research studies involve data collection. Since all studies are designed to either test hypotheses or answer questions, they all require data with which to do so. Most studies use some sort of data collection instrument, often a published, standardized instrument. Actually, there are three major ways to collect data:

(1) administer a standardized instrument,
(2) administer a self-developed instrument, or
(3) record naturally available data (such as grade point averages and absenteeism rates).

For several good reasons, this chapter will be concerned only with the selection of published, standardized tests. Collection of available data, requiring a minimum of effort, sounds very attractive. There are not very many studies, however, for which this type of data is appropriate. Even when it is appropriate, that is, when it can be employed to test the intended hypothesis or answer the desired question, there are problems inherent in this type of data. For example, the same grade does not necessarily represent the same level of achievement, even in two different schools in the same system. Developing an instrument for a particular study also has several major drawbacks. The development of a "good" instrument requires considerable time, effort, *and* skill. Total time for execution of a study can be greatly increased if instrument development is involved. Also, training at least equivalent to a course in measurement is necessary in order to acquire the skills needed for good instrument development.[1]

---

[1] The nature of descriptive research often necessitates the development of instruments for particular studies. Guidelines for the development of certain types of instruments, such as questionnaires, will be presented in Chapter 8.

On the positive side, the time it takes to select an appropriate standardized instrument is invariably less than the time it takes to develop an instrument that measures the same thing. Further, standardized instruments are developed by experts who possess the necessary skills. From a research point of view, an additional advantage of using a standardized instrument is that results from different studies using the same instrument can be compared. Suppose, for example, that two separate studies were conducted to determine which method of teaching algebra results in higher final achievement, method A or method B. Suppose further that study 1 utilized a self-developed test of algebra achievement and study 2 used a standardized test of algebra achievement. Now if study 1 found no difference between methods A and B, but study 2 found method B to be superior, interpretation of these conflicting results would be difficult. It might be that the two tests were measuring different abilities, for example, application of formulas versus word-problem solving. It might also be that the test used in study 1 was inadequately constructed. In any event, it would be difficult to distinguish differences due to the teaching method and differences due to the test used. Finally, use of a standardized instrument facilitates replication of a study by an independent researcher.

There are thousands of standardized instruments available which yield a wide variety of data for a wide variety of purposes. Major areas for which numerous measuring instruments have been developed include achievement, personality, intelligence, and aptitude. Each of these can in turn be further divided into many subcategories. Personality instruments, for example, can be classified as nonprojective or projective; nonprojective instruments include measures of attitude and interest. Selection of an instrument for a particular research purpose involves identification and selection of the most appropriate one from among alternatives; a researcher does not find *an* instrument suited for his or her study but rather selects the *best* one of those that are available. The selection process involves determination of the most appropriate type of instrument, for example, reading comprehension, and then a comparative analysis of available tests of that type. Therefore, in order to intelligently select an instrument, a researcher must be familiar with the wide variety of types of instruments that exist and must also be knowledgeable concerning the criteria which should be applied in selecting one from among alternatives.

■ CHARACTERISTICS OF A STANDARDIZED TEST

As you may have noticed, the word "test" has thus far been carefully avoided. This is because "test" has a very narrow connotation for many people. A test is not necessarily a written set of questions to which an individual responds in order to determine whether he or she "passes." A more inclusive definition of a test is...a means of measuring the knowledge, skill, feeling, intelligence, or aptitude of an individual or group. Tests produce numerical scores that can be used to identify, classify, or evaluate test takers. In addition, there are a number of characteristics shared by standardized tests. While these characteristics are desirable *for all tests,* they are much more likely to be in evidence for a standardized test. Regardless of the type of test being sought, there are certain kinds of information that should be available about any standardized test. This information, or lack of it, forms the basis for test selection.

Standardized tests are typically developed by experts and are therefore well constructed. Individual test items are analyzed and revised until they meet given standards of quality. Directions for administering, scoring, and interpreting a standardized test are carefully specified. One resulting characteristic of a standardized test is referred to as objectivity. In essence, test objectivity means that an individual's score is the same, or essentially the same, regardless of who is doing the scoring. Another major characteristic of standardized tests is the existence of validity and reliability data. Validity is the most important quality of any test. Validity is concerned with what a test measures and for whom it is appropriate; reliability refers to the consistency with which a test measures whatever it measures. Because of their importance, these two concepts will be discussed in considerable detail later in this section.

Specification of conditions of administration is a very important characteristic of a standardized test. This insures that if directions are carefully followed, the test will always be administered the same way and will always yield the same kind of data. If directions are carefully spelled out, even a beginning researcher should be able to properly administer most tests. The directions usually include instructions to be read to the test takers; restrictions on time, if any; and guidelines concerning the amount and nature of communication permitted between the test administrator and the test takers. Last, but not least, standardized tests generally include directions for scoring and guidelines for interpretation of scores. Directions for scoring include specifications such as the criteria for acceptable responses, when such are appropriate, the number of points to be assigned to various responses, and the procedure for computing total scores. Guidelines for test score interpretation generally include a table of norms. Typically, a test is administered to a large number of appropriately defined individuals, and resulting test scores are analyzed. A table of norms presents raw scores and one or more equivalent transformations, such as corresponding percentile ranks, which facilitate interpretation of an individual's score with respect to the performance of the group. Since researchers generally work with raw scores, this type of information is generally of more value to other consumer groups such as public school personnel.

As stated previously, the most important characteristic of a standardized test, or any test for that matter, is validity. Validity is totally indispensable; there is no quality or virtue of a test that can compensate for inadequate validity.

Validity

The most simplistic definition of validity is that it is the degree to which a test measures what it is supposed to measure and, consequently, permits appropriate interpretation of scores. A common misconception is that a test is, or is not, valid. A test is not valid per se; it is valid for a particular purpose and for a particular group. The question is not "valid or invalid" but rather "valid for what and for whom?" A valid test of biology achievement is not very likely to be a valid personality test. It would be obvious to almost anyone looking at a test of biology achievement that the test did not measure any aspect of personality. It would probably not be quite as evident whether the test was a valid measure of biology facts or biology principles, if either. With respect to the "for whom" aspect of validity, a test which is a valid measure of vocabulary for high school students is certainly not a valid measure for second graders. Again, this would undoubtedly be self-evident to anyone examining a high school-level vocabulary test. It might not be as evident whether the test was valid for both ninth graders and seniors, if either. To further clarify the concept of valid "for what and for whom," let us apply the concept of validity to teaching. In general, a valid teacher is one who teaches whatever he or she is supposed to teach (or, if you prefer, whose students learn what they are supposed to learn!). But a teacher, no matter how outstanding, is not valid per se. A teacher is valid for a particular purpose, that is, a particular area of instruction, and a particular age or grade level. A valid kindergarten teacher is not very likely also to be a valid high school teacher, and a valid high school trigonometry teacher is not very likely also to be a valid high school physical education teacher. While the above analogy is admittedly loose, the concept it illustrates is important.

It is the "valid for whom" concern that makes the description of the norm group so important. Only to the degree that persons in the norm group are like the persons to whom we wish to administer the test can proper interpretation of results be made. Twenty-year-old achievement norms are not likely to be appropriate for students in the 1990s. The usefulness of norms based on a sample of 50,000 upper-middle-class high school students in the Midwest is certainly questionable if the test is to be administered to inner-city students in Boston. And so forth. Of course even an "ideal" norm group with a cast of thousands is not going to be *entirely* appropriate in any situation. There are just too many variables and student characteristics that might affect results. Thus care must always be taken in selecting a test and interpreting results. But if information concerning the norm group is insufficient or if the information given indicates any major way in which the norm group is inappropriate, then every effort must be made to locate a more suitable test. If none is available, then the shortcomings must be seriously considered when results are interpreted. Of course, appropriateness of the norm group is less of a concern for, say, an experimental study, in which two groups are compared using scores from the same test, than it is for other situations such as a school testing program.

Since tests are designed for a variety of purposes, and since validity can be evaluated only in terms of purpose, it is not surprising that there are several different types of validity: content, construct, concurrent, and predictive. Because of the different ways in which they are determined, they are classified as either logical or criterion-related validity. *Logical validity* includes content validity and is so named because validity is determined primarily through judgment. *Criterion-related*, or *empirical, validity* includes concurrent and predictive validity and is so named because in each case validity is determined by relating performance on a test to performance on another criterion. Criterion-related validity is determined in a more objective manner than content validity. Assessment of construct validity involves both judgment and external criteria. For any test it is important to seek evidence concerning the appropriate type of validity, given the intended purpose or purposes of the test.

Content Validity

Content validity is the degree to which a test measures an intended content area. Content validity requires both item validity and sampling validity. *Item validity* is concerned with whether the test items represent measurement in the intended content area, and *sampling validity* is concerned with how well the test samples the total content area. A test designed to measure knowledge of biology facts might have good item validity, because all the items do indeed deal with biology facts, but might have poor sampling validity, for example, if all the items deal only with vertebrates. A test with good content validity adequately samples the appropriate content area. This is important because we cannot possibly measure each and every aspect of a certain content area; the required test would be "humongously" long. And yet we do wish to make inferences about performance in the entire content area based on performance on the items included in the test. Such inferences are only possible if the test items adequately sample the domain of possible items. This sampling is of course easier for well-defined areas such as spelling than for fuzzier content areas such as social studies.

The term "face validity" is sometimes used in describing tests. While its meaning is somewhat ambiguous, basically *face validity* refers to the degree to which a test *appears* to measure what it purports to measure. While determining face validity is not a psychometrically sound way of estimating validity, the process is sometimes used as an initial screening procedure in test selection.

Content validity is of prime importance for achievement tests. A test score cannot accurately reflect a student's achievement if it does not measure what the student was supposed to learn. While this seems obvious, content validity has been a problem in a number of research studies. Many studies are designed to compare the effectiveness of two (or more) different ways of teaching the same thing. Effectiveness is often defined in terms of final achievement of the treatment groups as measured by a test. It is sometimes the case that the test used is more content valid for one of the groups than for the other. When this happens, final achievement differences may be at least partially attributable to the test used and not just to the teaching methods. This phenomenon frequently occurs when an "innovative" approach is compared to a traditional approach. The different approaches often emphasize different areas of content. A classic case is the early studies that compared the "new" math with the "old" math. These studies invariably found no achievement differences between students learning under the two approaches. The problem was that the "new" math was emphasizing concepts and principles while the achievement tests were emphasizing computational skill.[2] When tests were developed which contained an adequate sampling of items measuring concepts and principles, studies began to find that the two approaches to teaching math resulted in essentially equal computational ability, but that the "new" math resulted in better conceptual understanding. The moral of the story is—in a study which compares treatments and measures achievement, take care that the test measures what the students learned in the treatments, that is, be sure that the test is *valid for your study* and *for your subjects*.

Content validity is determined by expert judgment. There is no formula by which it can be computed and there is no way to express it quantitatively. Usually experts in the area covered by the test are asked to assess its content validity. These experts carefully review the process used in developing the test as well as the test itself and make a judgment concerning how well items represent the intended content area. This judgment is based on whether all subareas have been included, and in the correct proportions. In other words, a comparison is made between what ought to be included in the test, given its intended purpose, and what is actually included. When selecting a test for a research study, the researcher assumes the role of "expert" and determines whether the test is content valid for her or his study. The researcher compares what will be taught in the study with what is measured by the test.

Construct Validity

Construct validity is the degree to which a test measures an intended hypothetical construct. A construct is a nonobservable trait, such as intelligence, which explains behavior. You cannot see a construct, you can only observe its effect. In fact con-

---

[2]See, for example, Brown, K. E., & Abell, T. L. (1966). Research in the teaching of high school mathematics. *The Mathematics Teacher, 59,* 52–57.

structs were "invented" to explain behavior. We cannot prove they exist; we cannot perform brain surgery on a person and "see" his or her intelligence. Constructs, however, do an amazingly good job of explaining certain differences between individuals. For example, it was always observed that some students learn faster than others, learn more, and retain longer. To explain these differences, a theory of intelligence was developed, and it was hypothesized that there is something called intelligence which is related to learning and which everyone possesses to a greater or lesser degree. Tests were developed designed to measure how much of it a person has. As it happens, students whose scores indicate that they have a "lot" of it, that is , they have high IQs, tend to do better in school and other learning environments. Other constructs which have been hypothesized to exist, and for which tests have been developed, include anxiety, creativity, and curiosity.

Research studies that involve a construct, either as an independent or a dependent variable, are only valid to the extent that the measure of the construct involved is valid. Anxiety, for example, can be an independent or a dependent variable. A study might be designed to determine whether high-anxiety students perform better on difficult tasks than low-anxiety students. A test of anxiety would need to be administered to the students in the study in order to classify them as "high-anxiety" or "low-anxiety." Another study might be designed to determine whether microcomputer-assisted instruction results in lower anxiety among slow learners than traditional instruction. A test of anxiety would need to be administered to both groups at the conclusion of the study. In both cases, the validity of the findings would be a direct function of the validity of the anxiety test used. If the test did not really measure anxiety, conclusions based on a study that utilized it would be meaningless. When selecting a test of a given construct, the researcher must look for and critically evaluate evidence presented related to the construct validity of the instrument.

The process of validating a test of a construct is by no means an easy task. Basically, it involves testing hypotheses deduced from a theory concerning the construct. If, for example, a theory of anxiety hypothesized that high-anxiety persons will work longer on a problem than low-anxiety persons, then if persons who scored high on the test under consideration did indeed work longer on a subsequent task this would be evidence to support the construct validity of the test. Of course if the high-anxiety persons did not, as hypothesized, work longer, then it would not necessarily mean that the test did not measure anxiety; the hypotheses related to the behavior of high-anxiety persons might be incorrect. Generally, a number of independent studies are required to establish the credibility of a test of a construct.

Concurrent Validity

Concurrent validity is the degree to which the scores on a test are related to the scores on another, already established, test administered at the same time, or to some other valid criterion available at the same time. Often, a test is developed that claims to do the same job as some other tests, easier or faster. If this is shown to be the case, that is, the concurrent validity of the new test is established, in most cases the new test will be utilized instead of the other tests. A paper-and-pencil test that does the same job as a performance test, or a short test that measures the same behaviors as a longer test, would certainly be preferred, especially in a research study.

Concurrent validity is determined by establishing relationship or discrimination. The relationship method involves determining the relationship between scores on the test and scores on some other established test or criterion (e.g., GPA). In this case, the steps involved in determining concurrent validity are as follows:

1. Administer the new test to a defined group of individuals.
2. Administer a previously established, valid test (or acquire such scores if already available) to the same group, at the same time, or shortly thereafter.
3. Correlate the two sets of scores.
4. Evaluate the results.

The resulting number, or validity coefficient, indicates the concurrent validity of the new test; if the coefficient is high, the test has good concurrent validity. Suppose, for example, that Professor Jeenyus developed a group test of intelligence for children which took only five minutes to administer. If scores on this test did indeed correlate highly with scores on the Wechsler Intelligence Scale for Children (which must be administered to one child at a time and takes at least an hour), then Professor Jeenyus' test would definitely be preferable in a great many situations. The discrimination method of establishing concurrent validity involves determining whether test scores can be used to discriminate between persons who possess a certain characteristic and those who do not, or those who possess it to a greater degree. For example, a test of mental adjustment would have concurrent validity if scores resulting from it could be used to correctly classify institutionalized and non-institutionalized persons.

When selecting a test for a given research purpose, you will usually be seeking a test that measures what you wish in the most efficient manner. If you select a shorter or more convenient test that allegedly measures the desired behavior, be careful that concurrent validity has been established using a valid criterion.

Predictive Validity

Predictive validity is the degree to which a test can predict how well an individual will do in a future situation. An algebra aptitude test that has high predictive validity will fairly accurately predict which students will do well in algebra and which students will not. Predictive validity is extremely important for tests that are used to classify or select individuals. An example with which you are all too familiar is the use of Graduate Record Examination (GRE) scores to select students for admission to graduate school. Many graduate schools require a certain minimum score for admission, often 1,000, in the belief that students who achieve that score have a higher probability of succeeding in graduate school. The predictive validity of the GRE has been the subject of many research studies. Results seem to indicate that the GRE has higher predictive validity for certain areas of graduate study than for others. For example, while it appears to have satisfactory predictive validity for predicting success in graduate studies in English, its validity in predicting success in an art education program appears to be questionable. Also, in general, GRE Subject Tests for specific areas of graduate study tend to be better predictors of first-year GPA than the GRE General Test.[3] Another example that illustrates the critical importance of predictive validity is the use of tests to determine which students should be assigned to special education classes. The decision to remove a child from the

---

[3]Cohn, S. J. (1985). Review of Graduate Record Examinations—General Test. In J. V. Mitchell, Jr. (Ed.). *The ninth mental measurements yearbook* (pp. 622–624). Lincoln, NE: The University of Nebraska Press.

normal educational environment, and to place him or her in a special class, is a serious one. In this situation it is imperative that the decision be based on the results of valid measures.

As the GRE example illustrates, the predictive validity of a given instrument varies with a number of factors. The predictive validity of an instrument may vary depending upon such factors as the curriculum involved, textbooks used, and geographic location. The Mindboggling Algebra Aptitude Test, for example, may predict achievement better in courses using the Brainscrambling Algebra I text than in courses using other texts. Thus, if a test is to be used for prediction, it is important to compare the description of the manner in which it was validated with the situation in which it is to be used.

No test, of course, has perfect predictive validity. Therefore, predictions based on the scores of any test will be imperfect. However, predictions based on a combination of several test scores will invariably be more accurate than predictions based on the scores of any one test. Therefore, when important classification or selection decisions are to be made, they should be based on data from more than one indicator. For example, we can use high school grade point average (GPA) to predict college GPA at the end of the freshman year. We can also use scholastic aptitude score or rank in graduating class to predict college GPA. A prediction based on any two of the variables, however, will be more accurate than a prediction based on any one of them, and a prediction based on all three variables will be more accurate than a prediction based on any two of them. Similarly, with respect to the GRE, predictions of graduate GPA which are based on GRE scores *and* undergraduate GPA are more accurate than predictions based on GRE scores only or undergraduate GPA only.

The predictive validity of a test is determined by establishing the relationship between scores on the test and some measure of success in the situation of interest. The test used to predict success is referred to as the predictor, and the behavior predicted is referred to as the criterion. In establishing the predictive validity of a test, the first step is to identify and carefully define the criterion. The criterion selected must be a valid measure of the behavior to be predicted. For example, if we wished to establish the predictive validity of an algebra aptitude test, final examination scores at the completion of a course in algebra might be considered a valid criterion, but number of days absent during the course probably would not. As another example, if we were interested in establishing the predictive validity of a given test for predicting success in college, grade point average at the end of the first year would probably be considered a valid criterion, but number of extracurricular activities in which the student participated probably would not. A word of caution is in order related to the concept of base rate. Base rate is the proportion of individuals who can be expected to meet a given criterion. You should avoid trying to predict a criterion for which the base rate is very high or very low. For example, suppose we wished to establish the predictive validity of a test designed to predict who will graduate summa cum laude. Since a very, very small percentage of students do so, all we would have to do is predict that no one would and we would be correct in almost every case! A test could hardly do better and would therefore be of very limited value.

Once the criterion has been identified and defined, the procedure for determining predictive validity is as follows:

1. Administer the test, the predictor variable, to a group.
2. Wait until the behavior to be predicted, the criterion variable, occurs.

3. Obtain measures of the criterion *for the same group.*
4. Correlate the two sets of scores.
5. Evaluate the results.

The resulting number, or validity coefficient, indicates the predictive validity of the test; if the coefficient is high, the test has good predictive validity. For example, suppose we wished to determine the predictive validity of a physics aptitude test. First we would administer the test to a large group of potential physics students. Then we would wait until the students had completed a course in physics and would obtain a measure of their success, for example, final exam scores. The correlation between the two sets of scores would determine the predictive validity of the test; if the resulting correlation coefficient was high, the test would have high predictive validity.

As mentioned previously, often a combination of predictors is used to predict a criterion. In this case a prediction equation may be developed. A person's scores on each of a number of tests are inserted into the equation and her or his future performance is predicted. In this case the validity of the equation should be reestablished through cross-validation. Cross-validation involves administering the predictor tests to a different sample from the same population and developing a new equation. Of course, even if only one predictor test is involved, it is a good idea to determine predictive validity for more than just one sample of individuals. In other words, the predictive validity of a test should be reconfirmed.

You may have noticed (if you had a high score on the GRE!) that the procedures for determining concurrent validity and predictive validity are very similar. The major difference is in terms of when the criterion measure is administered. In establishing concurrent validity, it is administered at the same time as the predictor, or within a relatively short period of time; in establishing predictive validity, one usually has to wait for a much longer period of time to pass before criterion data can be collected. Occasionally, concurrent validity is substituted for predictive validity in order to save time and to eliminate the problems of keeping track of subjects. For example, we might administer a mechanical aptitude test to a group of mechanics and correlate scores on the test with some measure of their skill. The problem with this approach is that we would be dealing only with those who made it! Persons for whom the test would have predicted a low probability of success would not become mechanics. In other words, most of the persons in the sample would be persons for whom the test would have predicted success. Therefore, the resulting validity coefficient would probably be an underestimate of the predictive validity of the test.

In the discussion of both concurrent and predictive validity there was a statement to the effect that if the resulting coefficient is high, the test has good validity. You may have wondered, "How high is high?" The question of how high the coefficient must be in order to be considered "good" is not easy to answer. There is no magic number that a coefficient should reach. In general, it is a comparative matter. A coefficient of .50 might be acceptable if there is only one test available designed to predict a given criterion; on the other hand, a coefficient of .50 might be inadequate if there are other tests available with higher coefficients.

Closely related to the concept of validity is the concept of reliability, which deals with the question of score consistency.

Reliability

In everyday English, reliability means dependability, or trustworthiness. The term means essentially the same thing with respect to measurement. Basically, reliability is the degree to which a test consistently measures whatever it measures. The more reliable a test is, the more confidence we can have that the scores obtained from the administration of the test are essentially the same scores that would be obtained if the test were readministered. An unreliable test is essentially useless; if a test is unreliable, then scores for a given sample would be expected to be different every time the test was administered. If an intelligence test was unreliable, for example, then a student scoring an IQ of 120 today might score an IQ of 140 tomorrow, and a 95 the day after tomorrow. If the test was reliable, and if the student's IQ was 110, then we would not expect his or her score to fluctuate too greatly from testing to testing; a score of 105 would not be unusual, but a score of 145 would be very unlikely.

Reliability is expressed numerically, usually as a coefficient; a high coefficient indicates high reliability. If a test were perfectly reliable, the coefficient would be 1.00; this would mean that a student's score perfectly reflected her or his true status with respect to the variable being measured. However, alas and alack, no test is perfectly reliable. Scores are invariably affected by errors of measurement resulting from a variety of causes. High reliability indicates minimum error variance; if a test has high reliability, then the effect of errors of measurement has been reduced. Errors of measurement affect scores in a random fashion; some scores may be increased while others are decreased. Errors of measurement can be caused by characteristics of the test itself (ambiguous test items, for example, that some students just happen to interpret correctly), by conditions of administration (directions not properly followed, for example), by the current status of the persons taking the test (some may be tired, others unmotivated), or by a combination of any of the above. High reliability indicates that these sources of error have been eliminated as much as possible.

Errors of measurement that affect reliability are random errors; systematic or constant errors affect validity. If an achievement test was too difficult for a given group of students, all scores would be systematically lowered; the test would have low validity for that group (remember "valid for whom"). The test might, however, yield consistent scores, i.e., might be reliable; in other words, the scores might be systematically lowered in the same way every time. A given student whose "true" achievement score was 80 and who scored 60 on the test (invalidity) might score 60 every time he took the test (reliability). This illustrates an interesting relationship between validity and reliability: a valid test is always reliable but a reliable test is not necessarily valid. In other words, if a test is measuring what it is supposed to be measuring, it will be reliable and do so every time, but a reliable test can consistently measure the wrong thing and be invalid! Suppose a test that purported to measure social studies concepts really measured facts. It would not be a valid measure of concepts, but it could certainly measure the facts very consistently. To illustrate, suppose the reported reliability coefficient for a test were .24, which is definitely not good. Would this tell you anything about the validity? Yes, it would. It would tell you that the validity was not hot because, if it were, the reliability would be higher. What if the reported reliability coefficient were .92, which is definitely good. Would this tell you anything about the validity? H-m-m-m. The answer is— not really. It would only tell you that the validity *might be* good, because the reliability is good, but *not necessarily;* the test could be consistently measuring the wrong thing. Got it?

All this talk about error might lead you to believe that measurement in education is pretty sloppy and imprecise to say the least. Actually it's not as bad as it may sound. There are many tests that measure intended traits quite accurately. In fact, as Nunnally has pointed out, measurement in other areas of science often involves as much, if not more, random error.[4] To use his example, the measurement of blood pressure, a physiological trait, is far less reliable than most psychological measures. There are any number of "conditions of the moment" which may temporarily affect blood pressure—joy, anger, fear, and anxiety, to name a few. In fact, the very act of having their blood pressure taken raises some people's blood pressure. Thus, a person's blood pressure reading is also the result of a combination of "true" blood pressure and error.

Reliability is much easier to assess than validity. There are a number of different types of reliability; each is determined in a different manner and each deals with a different kind of consistency. Test-retest, equivalent-forms, and split-half reliability are all determined through correlation; rationale equivalence reliability is established by determining how each item on a test relates to all other items on the test and to the total test. Split-half reliability and rationale equivalence reliability are types of *internal consistency reliability* which, as the name implies, is based on the internal consistency of the test. Whereas test-retest reliability and equivalent-forms reliability require a group to take two tests (either the same test twice, or two forms of the same test), internal consistency reliability can be estimated based on one administration of a test to a group.

Test-Retest Reliability

Test-retest reliability is the degree to which scores are consistent over time. It indicates score variation that occurs from testing session to testing session as a result of errors of measurement. In other words, we are interested in evidence that the score a person obtains on a test at some moment in time is the same score, or close to the same score, that the person would get if the test were administered some other time. We want to know how consistently the test measures whatever it measures. This type of reliability is especially important for tests used as predictors, aptitude tests, for example. Such a test would not really be too helpful if it indicated a different aptitude level each time it was given.

Determination of test-retest reliability is appropriate when alternate (equivalent) forms of a test are not available, and when it is unlikely that persons taking the test the second time will remember responses made on the test the first time. Test takers are more likely to remember items from a test with a lot of history facts, for example, than from a test with algebra problems. The procedure for determining test-retest reliability is basically quite simple:

1. Administer the test to an appropriate group.
2. After some time has passed, say two weeks, administer the *same test* to the *same group*.
3. Correlate the two sets of scores.
4. Evaluate the results.

If the resulting coefficient, referred to as the *coefficient of stability,* is high, the test has good test-retest reliability. A major problem with this type of reliability is the difficulty of knowing how much time should elapse between the two testing sessions. If the interval is too short, the chances of students' remembering responses made on the test the first time are increased, and the estimate of reliability tends to be artificially high. If the interval is too long, students' ability to do well on the test may increase due to intervening learning or maturation, and the estimate of reliability tends to be artificially low.

---

[4]Nunnally, J. C. (1994). *Psychometric theory* (3rd ed.). New York: McGraw-Hill.

Thus, when test-retest information is given concerning a test, the time interval between testings should be given as well as the actual coefficient. Although it is difficult to say precisely what, in general, the ideal time interval should be, especially since it depends somewhat on the kind of test involved, less than a week will generally be too short. The problems associated with test-retest reliability are taken care of by equivalent-forms reliability.

Equivalent-Forms Reliability

Equivalent forms of a test are two tests that are identical in every way except for the actual items included. The two forms measure the same variable, have the same number of items, the same structure, the same difficulty level, and the same directions for administration, scoring, and interpretation. In fact, if the same group takes both tests, the average score as well as the degree of score variability should be essentially the same on both tests. Only the specific items are not the same, although they do measure the same traits, or objectives. In essence, we are selecting, or sampling, different items from the same behavior domain. We are interested in whether scores depend upon the particular set of items selected or whether performance on one set of items is generalizable to other sets. If items are well selected, and if each set adequately represents the domain of interest, the latter should be true.

Equivalent-forms reliability, also referred to as alternate-forms reliability, indicates score variation that occurs from form to form, and is appropriate when it is likely that test takers will recall responses made during the first session and, of course, when two different forms of a test are available. When alternate forms are available, it is important to know the equivalent-forms reliability; it is reassuring to know that a person's score will not be greatly affected by which form is administered. Also, sometimes in research studies two forms of a test are administered to the same group, one as a pretest and the other as a posttest. It is crucial, if the effects of the intervening activities are to be validly assessed, that the two tests be measuring essentially the same things.

The procedure for determining equivalent-forms reliability is very similar to that for determining test-retest reliability:

1. Administer one form of the test to an appropriate group.
2. At the same session, or shortly thereafter, administer the *second form* of the test to the *same group*.
3. Correlate the two sets of scores.
4. Evaluate the results.

If the resulting coefficient (referred to as the *coefficient of equivalence*) is high, the test has good equivalent-forms reliability. If the two forms of the test are administered at two different times (the best of all possible worlds!) the resulting coefficient is referred to as the *coefficient of stability and equivalence*. In essence this approach represents a combination of test-retest and equivalent-forms reliability and thus assesses stability of scores over time as well as the generalizability of the sets of items. Since more sources of measurement error are possible than with either method alone, the resulting coefficient is likely to be somewhat lower. Thus the coefficient of stability and equivalence represents a conservative estimate of reliability.

Equivalent-forms reliability is the most commonly used estimate of reliability for most tests used in research. The major problem involved with this method of estimating reliability is the difficulty of constructing two forms that are essentially equivalent. Lack of equivalence is a source of measurement error. Even though equivalent-forms reliability is considered to be a very good estimate of reliability, it is not always feasible to administer two different forms of the same test, or even the same test twice. Imagine telling your students that they had to take two final examinations! Imagine someone telling you to take the GRE or SAT twice! Fortunately, there are other methods of estimating reliability that require administering a test only once.

Split-Half Reliability

A common type of internal consistency reliability is referred to as *split-half reliability*. Since split-half reliability procedures require only one administration of a test, certain sources of errors of measurement are eliminated, such as differences in testing conditions, which can occur in establishing test-retest reliability. Split-half reliability is especially appropriate when a test is very long and/or when it would be difficult to administer either the same test at two different times or two different forms to a group.

The procedure for determining split-half reliability is as follows:

1. Administer the *total* test to *a* group.
2. Divide the test into two comparable halves, or subtests—the most common approach is to include all odd items in one half and all even items in the other half.
3. Compute each subject's score on the two halves—each subject will consequently have two scores, a score for the odd items and a score for the even items.
4. Correlate the two sets of scores.
5. Apply the Spearman-Brown correction formula.
6. Evaluate the results.

If the coefficient is high, the test has good split-half reliability. A number of logical and statistical methods can be used to divide a test in half, random selection of half of the items, for example. In reality, the odd-even strategy, however, is most often used. Actually, this approach works out rather well regardless of how a test is organized. Suppose, for example, a test is a 20-item power test and the items get progressively more difficult.[5] Items 1, 3, 5, 7, 9, 11, 13, 15, 17, and 19 as a group should be approximately as difficult as items 2, 4, 6, 8, 10, 12, 14, 16, 18, and 20. Items 1 and 2 will be easy, 3 and 4 will be more difficult, and so forth. Or, suppose a test is organized by topic so that items 1 to 10 deal with circles and items 11 to 20 deal with quadrilaterals. In this case the odd items will contain items on circles and quadrilaterals and so will the even items. Thus, regardless of how the test is organized, an odd-even split should produce essentially equivalent halves. In fact, what we are doing, in essence, is artificially creating two equivalent forms of a test and computing equivalent-forms reliability; the two equivalent forms just happen to be in the same test. Thus the label "internal consistency reliability."

Since longer tests tend to be more reliable, and since split-half reliability represents the reliability of a test only half as long as the actual test, a correction formula must be applied to the coefficient. The correction formula which is used is the

---

[5]A *power test* is one in which the items vary in difficulty, usually being arranged in order of increasing difficulty from very easy to very difficult. This is in contrast to a *speed test,* for which the time limit is fixed and the items, or tasks, are of low difficulty, and a *mastery test,* in which the items are of a low level of difficulty and the time limit is generous.

Spearman-Brown prophecy formula. For example, suppose the split-half reliability coefficient for a 50-item test were .80. The .80 would be based on the correlation between scores on 25 even items and 25 odd items and would therefore be an estimate of the reliability of a 25-item test, not a 50-item test. The Spearman-Brown formula would need to be applied to estimate the reliability (r) of the 50-item test. The formula is a very simple one, even for those of you who are not mathematically inclined:

$$r_{\text{total test}} = \frac{2r_{\text{split half}}}{1 + r_{\text{split half}}}$$

Applying the formula to our example:

$$r_{\text{total test}} = \frac{2(.80)}{1 + .80} = \frac{1.60}{1.80} = .89$$

Thus, the split-half estimate of .80 was corrected to an estimate of .89. One problem with the correction formula is that it tends to give a higher estimate of reliability than would be obtained using other procedures; in other words, the correction formula overcorrects.

Another approach to determining internal consistency is the method of rationale equivalence.

Rationale Equivalence Reliability

Rationale equivalence reliability is not established through correlation but rather estimates internal consistency by determining how all items on a test relate to all other items and to the total test. Rationale equivalence reliability is determined through application of one of the Kuder-Richardson formulas, usually formula 20 or 21 (KR-20 or KR-21). Application of a Kuder-Richardson formula results in an estimate of reliability that is essentially equivalent to the average of the split-half reliabilities computed for all possible halves. Formula 20 is a highly regarded method of assessing reliability, and formula 21 is an easy-to-apply approach which provides an estimate of the KR-20 reliability. Both formulas require that each item be scored dichotomously, i.e., correct or incorrect, 1 or 0. If items are scored such that different answers are worth different numbers of points, e.g., 0, 1, 2, or 3, then Cronbach's alpha (α), also referred to as coefficient alpha and Cronbach's coefficient alpha, can be used; Cronbach's alpha is the general formula of which the KR-20 formula is a special case.[6] Of course, most tests used in educational research are scored dichotomously. Use of formula 21 requires less time than any other method of estimating reliability. Its application also usually results in a more conservative estimate of reliability, especially if more than one trait is being measured.

The formula is as follows:

$$r_{\text{total test}} = \frac{(K)(SD^2) - \overline{X}(K - \overline{X})}{(SD^2)(K - 1)}$$

where

K = the number of items in the test
SD = the standard deviation of the scores
$\overline{X}$ = the mean of the scores

---

[6]Cronbach, L. J. (1951). Coefficient alpha and the internal structure of tests. *Psychometrika, 16,* 297–334.

In a later chapter you will learn how to compute the mean and standard deviation of a set of scores. For the moment, let it suffice to say that the mean ($\overline{X}$) is the average score on the test for the group that took it and the standard deviation (*SD*) is an indication of the amount of score variability, or how spread out the scores are. For example, assume that you have administered a 50-item test and have calculated the mean to be 40 ($\overline{X}$ = 40) and the standard deviation to be 4 (*SD* = 4). The reliability of the test (which in this example turns out to be not too hot!) would be calculated as follows:

$$r_{\text{total test}} = \frac{(50)(4^2) - 40(50 - 40)}{(4^2)(50 - 1)}$$

$$= \frac{(50)(16) - 40(10)}{(16)(49)} = \frac{800 - 400}{784} = \frac{400}{784} = .51$$

This formula should be more comprehensible to you after you have completed the task and objectives for Chapter 12, but even at this stage the ease of application of this formula should be evident.

Figure 5.1 summarizes the methods for estimating test reliability. One (1) test administration time indicates either that only one test is administered (split-half and KR-21 reliability) or that two tests are administered at essentially the same time (equivalent-forms reliability). Two (2) administration times indicates a time interval exists (say 2 weeks) between the two administrations (test-retest and stability and equivalence reliability). You should keep in mind when reviewing test information that while the size of the reliability coefficient is of prime importance, the method used to calculate it should also be considered.

Scorer/Rater Reliability

There are other situations for which reliability must be investigated. Such situations usually occur when the scoring of tests involves subjectivity, such as with essay tests, short-answer tests involving more than a one-word response, rating scales, and observation instruments. In such situations we are concerned with interjudge (interscorer, interrater, interobserver) reliability and/or intrajudge reliability. *Interjudge reliability* refers to the reliability of two (or more) independent scorers; *intrajudge reliability* refers to the reliability of the scoring of individual scorers. Scoring and rating are sources of errors of measurement, and it is important to estimate the consistency of scorers' assessments. Estimates of interjudge or intrajudge

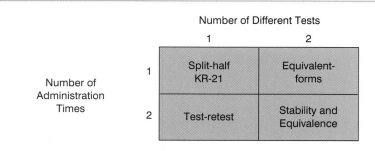

Figure 5.1. Summary of methods for estimating reliability.

reliability are usually obtained using correlational techniques, as has already been discussed, but can also be expressed simply as percent agreement. While such reliabilities are unfortunately usually not very good, a number of standardized instruments have been developed to the point where interjudge and intrajudge reliability appear to be relatively quite good. Validation studies involving the Flanders system for the observation of classroom verbal behavior, for example, have reported interrater and intrarater reliabilities ranging from the mid eighties (e.g., .85) to the low nineties.

Reliability Coefficients

What constitutes an acceptable level of reliability is to some degree determined by the type of test although, of course, a coefficient over .90 would be acceptable for any test. The question really is concerned with what constitutes a minimum level of acceptability. For achievement and aptitude tests, there is generally no good reason for selecting a test whose reliability is not at least .90. There are a number of achievement and aptitude tests available that report such reliabilities and it is therefore not usually necessary to settle for less. Personality measures do not typically report such high reliabilities (although certainly some do) and one would therefore be very satisfied with a reliability in the eighties and might even accept a reliability in the seventies. When tests are developed in new areas, one usually has to settle for lower reliability, at least initially. For example, tests which measure curiosity are a relatively recent addition to the testing field. One would not expect high reliabilities for these new tests at this stage of their development. If you are using a fairly new test, or using an established test with a group that is somewhat different than the test norm group, you should report reliability figures for your group; by doing so, you will verify that the test was reliable *for your group,* and you will provide valuable data for the test developers and for other researchers.

If a test is composed of several subtests, then the reliability of each subtest must be evaluated, not just the reliability of the total test. Since reliability is a function of test length, the reliability of a given subtest is typically lower than the total test reliability. Examination of subtest reliability is especially important if one or more of the subtests is going to be used in the research rather than the total test. You, as a researcher, should be a good consumer of test information. If a test manual states that "the total test reliability is .90, and all subtest reliabilities are satisfactory," you should immediately become suspicious. If subtest reliabilities are "satisfactory," the publisher will certainly want to tell you just how satisfactory they are. Most of the major, well-established tests report subtest reliabilities. Remember, test publishers are in the business of selling tests. If they omit pertinent information, it is your responsibility to be aware of such omissions and to request additional data.

Standard Error of Measurement

Reliability can also be expressed in terms of the *standard error of measurement.* This is a concept that you should be familiar with since such data are often reported for a test. Basically, the standard error of measurement is an estimate of how often you can expect errors of a given size. Thus, a small standard error of measurement indicates high reliability, and a large standard error of measurement indicates low reliability. If a test were perfectly reliable (which no test is), a person's obtained score would be his or her true score. As it is, an obtained score is an estimate of a true score. If you administered the same test over and over to the same group, the score of each individual would vary. How much variability would be present in individual scores would be a function of the test's reliability. The variability would be small for a highly reliable test (zero if the test were perfectly reliable) and large for a test with low reliability. If we could administer the test many times we could see how much variation actually occurred. Of course, realistically we can't do this; administering the same test twice to the same group is tough enough. Fortunately, it is possible to estimate this degree of variation (the standard error of measurement) using the data from the administration of a test once to a group. In other words, the standard error of measurement allows us to estimate how much difference there probably is between a person's obtained score and true score, the size of this difference being a function of the reliability of the test. We can estimate the standard error of measurement using the following simple formula:

$$SE_m = SD\sqrt{1 - r}$$

where

$$SE_m = \text{standard error of measurement}$$
$$SD = \text{the standard deviation of the test scores}$$
$$r = \text{the reliability coefficient}$$

For example, for a 25-item test we might calculate the standard deviation of a set of scores to be 5 ($SD = 5$) and the split-half reliability to be .84 ($r = .84$). In this case the standard error of measurement would be calculated as follows:

$$SE_m = SD\sqrt{1 - r} = 5\sqrt{1 - .84}$$
$$= 5\sqrt{.16}$$
$$= 5(.4)$$
$$= 2.0$$

As the above example illustrates, the size of the SE_m is a function of both the SD and r. Higher reliability is associated with a smaller SE_m and a smaller SD is associated with a smaller SE_m. If in the above example $r = .64$, would you expect SE_m to be larger or smaller? Right, larger, and in fact it would be 3.0. Also, if in the above example $SD = 10$, what would you expect to happen to SE_m? Right, it would be larger, 4.0 to be exact. While we prefer the SE_m to be small, indicating less error, it is impossible to say how small is "good." This is because SE_m is expressed in the same units as the test and how small is "small" is relative to the size of the test. Thus $SE_m = 5$ would be large for a 20-item test but small for a 200-item test. In our example, $SE_m = 2.0$ would be considered moderate.

To facilitate better interpretation of scores, some test publishers do not just present the SE_m for the total group but also give a separate SE_m for each of a number of identified subgroups.

■ TYPES OF TESTS

There are many different kinds of tests available and many different ways to classify them. The *Mental Measurements Yearbooks* are the major source of test information for educational researchers.[7] In addition to a number of curriculum areas such

[7]Kramer, J. J., & Conoley, J. C. (1992). *The eleventh mental measurements yearbook.* Lincoln, NE: The University of Nebraska Press (the latest in a series which began in 1938).

as English, Mathematics, and Reading, major headings in the *Yearbooks* include: Personality, Intelligence and Scholastic Aptitude, Speech and Hearing, and Vocations. Table 5.1 presents a complete listing of major classifications in *The Eleventh Mental Measurements Yearbook,* as well as the number and percentage of test entries related to each.

Achievement

Achievement tests measure the current status of individuals with respect to proficiency in given areas of knowledge or skill. Standardized achievement tests are carefully developed to include measurement of objectives common to many school systems. They measure knowledge of facts, concepts, and principles. An individual's level of achievement is compared to the norm, or average score, for his or her grade or age level. Standardized achievement tests are available for individual curriculum areas such as reading and mathematics, and also in the form of comprehensive batteries that measure achievement in a number of different areas. The Stanford Achievement Test, the Metropolitan Achievement Test, and the California Achievement Test Battery are examples of commonly used batteries. They include subtests which measure achievement in areas such as reading, math, spelling, social studies, science, and listening comprehension. Depending upon such factors as the number of achievement areas included, batteries take from one hour to several days to administer.

Table 5.1

Number and Percentage of Tests, by Major Classifications, in The Eleventh Mental Measurements Yearbook

Classification	Number	Percentage
Personality	135	28.3
Vocations	84	17.6
Developmental	33	6.9
English	32	6.7
Education	29	6.1
Miscellaneous	29	6.1
Achievement	22	4.6
Intelligence and Scholastic Aptitude	22	4.6
Reading	21	4.4
Speech and Hearing	20	4.2
Mathematics	14	2.9
Neuropsychological	14	2.9
Behavior Assessment	10	2.1
Sensory-Motor	6	1.3
Science	2	.4
Social Studies	2	.4
Fine Arts	1	.2
Multi-Aptitude Batteries	1	.2

Note. Behavior Assessment is a new category.

Many research studies are designed to compare the effectiveness of two or more curriculum approaches or methods of instruction. Effectiveness is usually defined in terms of pupil achievement at the end of the study. Sometimes, studies are designed to investigate various aspects of remedial instruction. In such studies diagnostic instruments are occasionally utilized. A diagnostic test is a type of achievement test yielding multiple scores for each area of achievement; these scores facilitate identification of specific areas of deficiency. The Stanford Diagnostic Reading Test is an example of a commonly used diagnostic instrument.

Personality

Tests of personality are designed to measure characteristics of individuals along a number of dimensions and to assess feelings and attitudes toward self, others, and a variety of other activities, institutions, and situations. They may well be the most used tests in educational research. Such tests come in many different varieties (performance versus paper and pencil, individual versus group, power versus speed), and there are tests to measure almost any aspect of personality you can think of. Although they can be classified many ways, a logical initial differentiation, the one used by the *Yearbooks*, is to categorize such tests as nonprojective or projective.

Nonprojective Tests

Most tests of character and personality are nonprojective, or self-report, measures; such tests ask an individual to respond to a series of questions or statements. Nonprojective tests are frequently used in descriptive studies (to describe, for example, the personality structure of various groups such as high school dropouts), correlational studies (to determine, for example, relationships between various personality traits and other variables such as achievement), and experimental studies (to investigate, for example, the comparative effectiveness of different instructional methods for different personality types).

Personality Inventories.   Personality inventories present lists of questions or statements describing behaviors characteristic of certain personality traits, and the individual is asked to indicate (yes, no, undecided) whether the statement describes him or her. Some inventories are presented as checklists; the individual simply checks items that characterize him or her. An individual's score is based on the number of responses characteristic of the trait being measured. An introvert, for example, would be expected to respond "yes" to the statement "Reading is one of my favorite pastimes" and "no" to the statement "I love large parties." Inventories may be specific and measure only one trait, such as introversion-extroversion, or may be general and measure a number of traits. Since general inventories measure more than one trait at the same time, they are typically relatively long and take at least an hour to complete.

General inventories frequently used in educational research studies include the following: Adjective Check List, California Psychological Inventory, Minnesota Multiphasic Personality Inventory, Mooney Problem Check List, Myers-Briggs Type Indicator, and the Sixteen Personality Factor Questionnaire. The Minnesota Multiphasic Personality Inventory alone has been utilized in hundreds of educational research studies.

One serious problem involved with the use of self-report inventories is the problem of accurate responses. Personality scores are only valid to the degree that the respondent is honest and selects responses that truly characterize him or her. A common phenomenon is the concept of a response set, or the tendency of an individual to continually respond in a given way. A common response set is the tendency of an individual to select the responses that he or she believes are the most socially acceptable. Whether response sets result from conscious or unconscious motivations, they can seriously distort an appraisal of the individual's personality structure. If a large proportion of a research sample is not responding honestly, results of the study may be essentially meaningless. Therefore, in studies utilizing such tests, every effort should be made to increase the likelihood that valid test results are obtained.

Attitude Scales.   Attitude scales attempt to determine what an individual believes, perceives, or feels. Attitudes can be measured toward self, others, and a variety of other activities, institutions, and situations. There are four basic types of scales used to measure attitudes: Likert scales, semantic differential scales, Thurstone scales, and Guttman scales. The first two are used more often, but you should at least be aware of the existence of the other two.

A *Likert scale* asks an individual to respond to a series of statements by indicating whether she or he strongly agrees (SA), agrees (A), is undecided (U), disagrees (D), or strongly disagrees (SD) with each statement.[8] Each response is associated with a point value, and an individual's score is determined by summing the point values for each statement. For example, the following point values might be assigned to responses to positive statements: SA = 5, A = 4, U = 3, D = 2, SD = 1. For negative statements, the point values would be reversed, that is, SA = 1, A = 2, and so on. An example of a positive statement might be "Short people are entitled to the same job opportunities as tall people." A high point value on a positively stated item would indicate a positive attitude and a high total score on the test would be indicative of a positive attitude. Recall that in the article at the end of Chapter 1, self-esteem was measured "by a widely used 10-item Likert scale."

A *semantic differential scale* asks an individual to give a quantitative rating to the subject of the attitude scale on a number of bipolar adjectives such as good-bad, friendly-unfriendly, positive-negative. The respondent indicates the point on the continuum between the extremes that represents her or his attitude. Based on their research, the original developers of this approach reported that most adjective pairs represent one of three dimensions which they labeled evaluation (e.g., good-bad), potency (e.g., strong-weak), and activity (e.g., active-passive).[9] For example, on a scale concerning attitudes toward property taxes, the following items might be included:

$$\text{Necessary} \;\underline{\quad}\;\underline{\quad}\;\underline{\quad}\;\underline{\quad}\;\underline{\quad}\;\underline{\quad}\;\underline{\quad}\; \text{Unnecessary}$$
$$\text{Fair} \;\underline{\quad}\;\underline{\quad}\;\underline{\quad}\;\underline{\quad}\;\underline{\quad}\;\underline{\quad}\;\underline{\quad}\; \text{Unfair}$$

In practice, however, these dimensions are frequently ignored and/or replaced by other dimensions thought to be more appropriate in a particular situation.

Each position on a continuum has an associated score value; by totaling score values for all items, it can be determined whether the respondent's attitude is positive or negative. Semantic differential scales usually have 5 to 7 intervals with a neutral attitude being assigned a score value of 0. For the above items, the score values would be as follows:

---

[8]Likert, R. (1932). A technique for the measurement of attitudes. *Archives of Psychology,* No. 140.

[9]Osgood, C. E., Suci, G. J., & Tannenbaum, P. H. (1957). *The measurement of meaning.* Urbana, IL: University of Illinois Press.

Necessary ——— ——— ——— ——— ——— ——— ——— Unnecessary
            3   2   1   0   −1 −2 −3

Fair ——— ——— ——— ——— ——— ——— ——— Unfair
            3   2   1   0   −1 −2 −3

A person who checked the first interval (i.e., 3) on both of these items would be indicating a very positive attitude toward property taxes (fat chance!).[10]

A *Thurstone scale* asks an individual to select from a list of statements that represent different points of view from those with which he or she is in agreement. Each item has an associated point value between 1 and 11; point values for each item are determined by averaging the values of the items assigned by a number of "judges." An individual's attitude score is the average point value of all the statements checked by that individual.[11] A *Guttman scale* also asks respondents to agree or disagree with a number of statements. A Guttman scale, however, attempts to determine whether an attitude is unidimensional; it is unidimensional if it produces a cumulative scale. In a cumulative scale, an individual who agrees with a given statement also agrees with all related preceding statements; for example, if you agree with statement 3, you also agree with statements 2 and 1.[12]

Measures of "attitude toward self" are referred to as measures of self-concept. Measures of self-concept are used in many educational research studies, especially studies designed to investigate: (1) the relationship between self-concept and other variables such as achievement; (2) the effects of self-concept on variables such as motivation; and (3) the effects of various curricula and teaching methods on self-concept.

Rating scales are also used to measure attitudes toward others. Such scales ask an individual to rate another individual on a number of behavioral dimensions. There are two basic types of such rating scales. One type is composed of items that ask an individual to rate another on a continuum (good to bad, excellent to poor). The second type asks the individual to rate another on a number of items by selecting the most appropriate response category (e.g., excellent, above average, average, below average, poor). Two problems associated with rating scales are referred to as the "halo effect" and the "generosity error." The halo effect is the tendency of a rater to let overall feelings toward a person affect responses to individual items. A principal might rate one of his or her better teachers high on variables not directly related to teaching, such as honesty, even if he or she has no real basis for judgment. The generosity error is the tendency of a rater to give the person being rated the benefit of the doubt whenever the rater does not have enough knowledge to make an objective rating. Both the halo effect and the generosity error can work in reverse, of course. When rating scales are involved in a study, every effort should be made to reduce these problems by giving appropriate instructions to the raters.

Attitude scales suffer from the same problems as personality inventories. The researcher can never be sure that the individual is expressing his or her true attitude rather than a "socially acceptable" attitude. Again, the validity of a study is directly related to the validity of the responses made by individuals in the sample.

---

[10]For further discussion of this approach, see Snider, J. G., & Osgood, C. E. (1969). *Semantic differential technique: A sourcebook.* Chicago: Aldine.

[11]Thurstone, L. L., & Chave, E. J. (1929). *The measurement of attitude.* Chicago: The University of Chicago Press.

[12]Guttman, L. (1950). The basis for scaleogram analysis. In S. Stouffer, et al. (Eds.). *Measurement and prediction.* Princeton, NJ: Princeton University Press.

Every effort should be made, therefore, to increase honesty of response by giving appropriate directions to those completing the instruments.

Creativity Tests. Tests of creativity are really tests designed to measure those personality characteristics that are related to creative behavior. One such trait is referred to as divergent thinking. Unlike convergent thinkers, who tend to look for *the* right answer, divergent thinkers tend to seek alternatives. J. P. Guilford, probably the most well-known researcher in this area, has developed a number of widely used tests of divergent thinking.[13] One such test asks the individual to list as many uses as he or she can think of for an ordinary brick. Think about it and list a few. If you listed uses such as build a school, build a house, build a library, etc., then you are not very creative; all of those uses are really the same, namely, you can use a brick to build something. Now, if you are creative, you listed different uses such as break a window, drown a rat, and hit a robber on the head.

Another test asks individuals to compose plot titles for brief stories. The titles are then rated for their originality. One of the stories concerns a missionary in Africa who is captured by cannibals. He is given a choice of being boiled alive or marrying a princess of the tribe. He chooses death. Take a few minutes and think of some possible titles. Perhaps you came up with a title like Missionary in Africa, The Cannibal and the Missionary, or Boiled in Africa. If you are especially clever, you may have come up with a title like Better Boil than Goil (my favorite!), A Mate Worse than Death, or He Left a Dish for a Pot. The more clever titles a person comes up with, the higher the score on originality, which is one aspect of divergent thinking.

Another well-known researcher in this area is E. P. Torrance. The Torrance Tests of Creativity include graphic, or pictorial, items as well as verbal items. Tests are scored in terms of four factors: fluency, flexibility, originality, and elaboration.[14] The Torrance tests involve tasks such as listing as many uses as possible for an object and coming up with titles for pictures.

Interest Inventories. An interest inventory asks an individual to indicate personal likes and dislikes, such as the kinds of activities he or she prefers to engage in. Responses are generally compared to known interest patterns. The most widely used type of interest measure is the vocational interest inventory. Such inventories typically ask the respondent to indicate preferences with respect to leisure time activities, such as hobbies. The respondent's pattern of interest is then compared to the patterns of interest typical of successful persons in various occupational fields. The individual can then be counseled as to the fields in which she or he is more likely to be happy and successful. Two frequently used inventories are the Strong-Campbell Interest Inventory, which measures interest in professional and business fields, and the Kuder Preference Record—Vocational, which measures interest in broad occupational areas such as mechanical, scientific, persuasive, and social science.

Projective Tests

Projective tests were developed in an attempt to eliminate some of the major problems inherent in the use of self-report measures, such as the tendency of some

[13]Guilford, J. P. (1967). *The nature of human intelligence.* New York: McGraw-Hill; *and* Guilford, J. P. (1959). Three faces of intellect. *American Psychologist, 14,* 469–479.

[14]Torrance, E. P. (1984). *Torrance Tests of Creative Thinking.* Bensenville, IL: Scholastic Testing Service.

respondents to give "socially acceptable" responses. The purposes of such tests are usually not obvious to respondents; the individual is typically asked to respond to ambiguous items. Since the purpose of the test is not clear, conscious dishonesty of response is reduced, and the respondent "projects" his or her true feelings. Projective tests are utilized mainly by clinical psychologists and very infrequently by educational researchers. This is due partly to their questionable validity and partly to the fact that administration, scoring, and interpretation of projective tests require very specialized training. However, if it is necessary to use a projective device in your research study, be sure to have it administered by qualified personnel.

The most commonly used projective technique is the method of association. This technique asks the respondent to react to a stimulus such as a picture, inkblot, or word. Word-association tests are probably the most well known of the association techniques (tell me the first thing that comes to your mind!). Two of the most commonly used association tests are the Rorschach Inkblot Test and the Thematic Apperception Test; thousands of studies utilizing the Rorschach test have been conducted. The Rorschach test presents the respondent with a series of inkblots, and the respondent is asked to tell what he or she sees. The Thematic Apperception Test presents the individual with a series of pictures; the respondent is then asked to tell a story about each picture.

Until recently, all projective tests were required to be administered individually. There have been some recent efforts, however, to develop group projective tests. One such test is the Holtzman Inkblot Technique, which is intended to measure the same variables as the Rorschach Inkblot Test. Group projective instruments, including the Holtzman, are still in relatively early stages of development. They do, however, offer great promise of becoming more objective projective devices.

Aptitude

Aptitude tests are measures of potential. They are used to predict how well someone is likely to perform in a future situation. Tests of general aptitude are variously referred to as scholastic aptitude tests, intelligence tests, and tests of general mental ability. Since intelligence tests have developed a bad reputation in recent years, the term "scholastic aptitude" has become more popular. The intents of all such tests, however, are basically the same. Aptitude tests are also available to predict a person's likely level of performance following some specific future instruction or training. Aptitude tests are available in the form of individual tests in specific areas, such as algebra, and in the form of batteries that measure aptitude in several related areas. Virtually all aptitude tests are standardized and are administered as part of a school testing program; the results are useful to teachers, counselors, and administrators.

General Aptitude

There are a variety of tests that fall into this category representing a variety of different definitions of general aptitude (or scholastic aptitude, or intelligence, or what have you). While the basic purpose of all such tests is to predict future academic performance, there is disagreement as to the factors that are being measured and are serving as the predictors. The term is variously defined to include variables such as abstract reasoning, problem solving, and verbal fluency. General aptitude tests typically ask the individual to perform a variety of verbal and nonverbal tasks that measure the individual's ability to apply knowledge and solve problems. Such tests generally yield three scores—an overall score, a verbal score, and a quantitative score—representing, for example, a total IQ, a verbal IQ, and a quantitative IQ. While general aptitude tests are intended to be measures of innate ability or potential, they appear actually to measure current ability; there is also some evidence to suggest that scores are to some degree affected by an individual's past and present environment. However, since they seem to do a reasonable job of predicting future academic success, and are in that sense measures of "potential," they are very useful to educators.

General aptitude tests may be group tests or individually administered tests. Each type has its relative advantages and disadvantages. Group tests are more convenient to administer, save considerable time, and provide an estimate of academic potential that is adequate for most educational research studies. Batteries are also available which comprise a number of tests suitable for different grade and age levels. Since tests in a battery are similarly structured, they permit the study of intellectual growth over time and comparisons among different levels. A commonly used group-administered battery is the California Test of Mental Maturity (CTMM). The CTMM has six levels and can be administered to all school-age children, college students, and adults. It includes 12 subtests representing five factors: logical reasoning, spatial relations, numerical reasoning, verbal concepts, and memory. The results include a language IQ, a nonlanguage IQ, and a total IQ. Although some of the subtests are not as good as they might be, overall the test is considered to be a respectable measure of potential. Another frequently administered group test is the Otis-Lennon Mental Ability Test, which also has six levels and is designed for school-age children in grades K—12. The Otis-Lennon Mental Ability Test measures four factors—verbal comprehension, verbal reasoning, figurative reasoning, and quantitative reasoning—and is also considered to be a respectable measure of potential.

A serious disadvantage of group tests is that they require a great deal of reading. Thus, students with poor reading ability are at a disadvantage and may receive scores reflecting, for example, an IQ level lower than their true level. Individual tests, on the other hand, require much less reading. Another advantage of individual tests is that since they are administered one-on-one, the examiner is aware of factors such as illness or anxiety that might be adversely affecting the individual's ability to respond. From a research point of view, the main disadvantage of individual tests is that they are more difficult to administer and score; trained personnel are required to administer them and to score them. However, if there is any reason to question the validity of group tests for a particular sample, very young children for example, an individual test should be used, even if this requires a reduction of sample size. Probably the most well known of the individually administered tests is the Stanford-Binet Intelligence Scale; it has been used extensively in research projects, and there is considerable data concerning its validity. More and more, however, the Wechsler scales are being utilized. While the Stanford-Binet is appropriate only for older adolescents and adults, Wechsler scales are available to measure the intelligence of persons from the age of 4 to adulthood: the Wechsler Preschool and Primary Scale of Intelligence (WPPSI)—ages 4–6 1/2; the Wechsler Intelligence Scale for Children-Revised (WISC-R)—ages 5–15; and the Wechsler Adult Intelligence Scale-Revised (WAIS-R)—older adolescents and adults. As an example, the WISC is a scholastic aptitude test which includes verbal tests (e.g., general information, vocabulary) and performance tests (e.g., picture completion, object assembly). While the Stanford-Binet yields one IQ score, the Wechsler scales also yield a number of subscores.

Specific Aptitude

As the term is generally used, specific aptitude tests attempt to predict the level of performance that can be expected of an individual following future instruction or training in a specific area or areas. Aptitude tests are available for a wide variety of academic and nonacademic areas such as mathematics and mechanical reasoning. As with tests of general aptitude, they are used by teachers, counselors, and administrators, and for the same reasons. They are also used as a basis for grouping, in math classes, for example. Specific aptitude tests are also frequently used in research studies. Their most common use in this regard is probably to equate groups that are going to be compared on achievement after receiving different treatments. If groups are different in aptitude to begin with, then final achievement differences might be attributable to this initial difference rather than to differences in treatment. Aptitude scores can be used to equate groups either by using stratified sampling or through a statistical procedure called analysis of covariance. While most aptitude tests are standardized, written tests, some are performance tests. The latter are appropriate when the students taking the tests have an English language difficulty, foreign students, for example.

Aptitude tests are available for a number of specific areas such as algebra, music, and mechanical ability. Multi-aptitude batteries, which measure aptitudes in several related areas, are available for the assessment of both academic and nonacademic aptitudes. Multi-aptitude batteries include a number of subtests that have been normed on the same group. The Sequential Tests of Educational Progress (STEP) battery, an academic aptitude battery, includes tests on reading, writing, mathematics, and science, among others. The Differential Aptitude Tests (DAT), on the other hand, include tests on space relations, mechanical reasoning, and clerical speed and accuracy, among others, and are designed to predict success in various job areas.

Readiness

Readiness, or prognostic, tests are sometimes classified as aptitude tests, sometimes as achievement tests. Aptitude does seem to be a more appropriate categorization, however, since a readiness test is administered prior to instruction or training in a specific area in order to determine whether and to what degree a student is ready for, or will profit from, instruction. Due to increased interest in the basic skills, reading readiness tests have been given more attention than other types. Reading readiness tests typically include measurement of variables such as auditory discrimination, visual discrimination, and motor ability. Readiness batteries have also been developed to assess readiness in a number of areas. The Metropolitan Readiness Test, for example, was designed to measure the degree to which students starting school have developed the skills and abilities that contribute to readiness for first-grade instruction in areas such as reading, arithmetic, and writing. Given the state of the art, the Metropolitan Readiness Test is considered to be a good test of its type.

■ SELECTION OF A TEST

The most important guidelines for test selection are the following related rules: *Do not,* repeat, do not stop with the first test you find that appears to measure what you want, say "Eureka, I have found it!" and blithely use it in your study! *Do* identify those tests that are appropriate for your study, compare them on relevant factors, and select the best one. If you are knowledgeable concerning the qualities a test should possess, and familiar with the various types of tests that are available (which you are of course by now!), then the selection of an instrument is a very orderly process. Assuming you have defined the specific purpose of your study and defined your population, the first step is to determine precisely what type of test you need. The next step is to identify and locate appropriate tests. Finally, you must do a comparative analysis of the tests and select *the best one*. In order to locate appropriate tests, you need to be familiar with sources of test information.

Sources of Test Information

A vast amount of test information is available to researchers, if they know where to look. Collectively, the various sources of information help the researcher to identify the possibilities, narrow the list of candidates, and make a final selection.

Mental Measurements Yearbooks

Once you have determined the type of test you need, for example, a test of reading comprehension for second graders, a logical place to start looking for tests is in the *Mental Measurements Yearbooks (MMYs)*.[15] Currently produced by the Buros Institute of Mental Measurements at the University of Nebraska, the *MMYs* have been published periodically since 1938, and represent the most comprehensive source of test information available to educational researchers. The *MMYs* were conceived by, and until relatively recently produced under the auspices of, Oscar Buros, who recognized the need for a source of comprehensive test information for both researchers and practitioners. *The Eleventh Mental Measurements Yearbook* is the latest publication in a series which includes the *MMYs, Tests in Print* (to be discussed shortly), and other related works such as *Vocational Tests and Reviews* (see Table 5.2). Currently, an *MMY* is published every few years (e.g., 1989, 1992), and a *Supplement* is published between major revisions (e.g., 1990, 1994).[16] The *MMYs* are expressly designed to assist test users in making informed selection decisions. The stated purposes of the *MMYs* are to provide: (1) factual information on all known new or revised tests in the English-speaking world; (2) objective test reviews written specifically for the *MMY*; and (3) comprehensive bibliographies, for specific tests, of related references from published literature. Each volume contains information on tests which have been published or revised since the previous *MMY*, or have generated 20 or more references since the last *MMY*.

As Mitchell, the editor of the *Ninth MMY*, suggests, getting maximum benefit from the *MMYs* requires becoming knowledgeable concerning their contents and the various ways of using them.[17] At the very least, you should familiarize yourself with the organization and with the indexes provided. The basic organization of the most recent *MMYs* is encyclopedic in that all the test descriptions and reviews are presented alphabetically by test title. Thus, if you are looking for a particular test, you can go right to it without using any index. Perhaps the most important thing you need to know in order to use the *MMYs* is that all the numbers given by the indexes are *test* numbers, not page numbers. For example, in the Classified Subject

---

[15]See footnote 7.

[16]Conoley, J. C., & Impara, J. C. (1994). *Supplement to the eleventh mental measurements yearbook.* Lincoln, NE: The University of Nebraska Press.

[17]Mitchell, J. V., Jr. (Ed.). (1985). *The ninth mental measurements yearbook.* Lincoln, NE: The University of Nebraska Press.

Table 5.2

Complete Listing of Mental Measurements Yearbooks, Tests in Print, *and Related Works*

Educational, Psychological, and Personality Tests of 1933 and 1934
Educational, Psychological, and Personality Tests of 1933, 1934, and 1935
Educational, Psychological, and Personality Tests of 1936
The Nineteen Thirty-Eight Mental Measurements Yearbook
The Nineteen Forty Mental Measurements Yearbook
The Third Mental Measurements Yearbook
The Fourth Mental Measurements Yearbook
The Fifth Mental Measurements Yearbook
Tests in Print
The Sixth Mental Measurements Yearbook
Reading Tests and Reviews
Personality Tests and Reviews
The Seventh Mental Measurements Yearbook
Tests in Print II
English Tests and Reviews
Foreign Language Tests and Reviews
Intelligence Tests and Reviews
Mathematics Tests and Reviews
Personality Tests and Reviews II
Reading Tests and Reviews II
Science Tests and Reviews
Social Studies Tests and Reviews
Vocational Tests and Reviews
The Eighth Mental Measurements Yearbook
Tests in Print III
The Ninth Mental Measurements Yearbook
Supplement to The Ninth Mental Measurements Yearbook
The Tenth Mental Measurements Yearbook
Supplement to The Tenth Mental Measurements Yearbook
The Eleventh Mental Measurements Yearbook
Supplement to The Eleventh Mental Measurements Yearbook
Tests in Print IV

Index, under Achievement, you will find the following entry (among others):

Iowa Tests of Basic Skills, Form J, grades K.1–1.5, K.8–1.9, 1.7–2.6, 2.5–3.5, 3, 4, 5, 6, 7, 8–9, see 184

The 184 means that the description of the Iowa Tests of Basic Skills is entry 184 in the main body of the volume; it does *not* mean that it is on page 184. Page numbers are used only for table of contents purposes.

The *MMY* provides six indexes. The Index of Titles is simply an alphabetical listing of test titles. The Index of Acronyms gives full titles for commonly used abbreviations. Not everyone who has heard of the MMPI, for example, knows that MMPI stands for Minnesota Multiphasic Personality Inventory. The Classified Subject Index lists tests alphabetically under each classification heading, e.g., Achievement. As previously illustrated, each entry also gives the population for which the test is intended. A feature new to the *Ninth MMY* is that, when appropriate, a test is listed under more than one classification. The Publishers Directory and Index gives the names and addresses of the publishers of all the tests included in the *MMY,* as well as a list of test numbers for each publisher. The Index of Names includes the names of test developers and test reviewers, as well as authors of related references. So, for example, if you heard that Professor Jeenyus had developed a new IQ test, but you did not know its name, you would look under Jeenyus; there you would be given test numbers for all tests developed by Professor Jeenyus which were included in the volume. Lastly, the Score Index, a recent addition to the *MMYs,* directs you to information concerning the scores obtained from tests in the *MMY*.

As mentioned previously, if you are looking for information on a particular test, you can find it easily because of the alphabetical organization of the most recent *MMYs*. If you have no specific test in mind, but know generally what kind of test you need, you may use the following procedure:

1. Go to the back of the *MMY* to the Classified Subject Index and find the appropriate classification (and subclassification, if appropriate), e.g., Personality.
2. Identify promising titles from among those listed and their corresponding entry numbers.
3. Using the entry numbers, locate the test descriptions in the Tests and Reviews section of the *MMY* (the main body of the volume).

Entries for new tests in the Tests and Reviews section typically include the following information: title; author (developer); publisher; cost; a brief description; a description of groups for whom the test is intended; norming information; validity and reliability data; whether the test is a group or individual test; time requirements; test references; and critical reviews by qualified reviewers. Among other things, the reviews generally cite any special requirements or problems involved in test administration, scoring, or interpretation.

MMYs published prior to the *Ninth MMY,* while differing organizationally from the latest editions, provide essentially the same information. Also, while your library may not yet have it, there is a CD-ROM version of the *Eleventh MMY*. (Coming attractions!)

Tests in Print

A very useful supplemental source of test information is *Tests in Print (TIP)*.[18] *TIP* is a comprehensive bibliography of all tests that have appeared in preceding *MMYs*. It also serves as a master index of tests which directs the reader to all original reviews that have appeared in the *MMYs* to date. The structure of *TIP* is very similar to that of the Classified Subject Index of the *MMYs,* but considerably more infor-

---

[18]Mitchell, J. V., Jr. (Ed.). (1983). *Tests in print III: An index to tests, test reviews, and the literature on specific tests*. Lincoln, NE: The University of Nebraska Press (the third in a series which began in 1961).

mation is given for each entry; for all commercially available tests, descriptions and references are given.

The criteria for inclusion of a test in *TIP* are very different from the criteria for inclusion in an *MMY*. As discussed previously, to be included in a new edition of the *MMYs*, a test must have been published or revised, or have generated 20 or more references, since publication of the last *MMY*. To be included in *TIP*, a test must simply be in print and available for purchase or use.

The main body of *TIP III*, the latest edition, is organized alphabetically, like the latest *MMYs*. *TIP* also provides an Index of Titles, a Classified Subject Index, a Publishers Directory and Index, and an Index of Names, all of which are utilized in the same way as they are used in the *MMYs*. Also, as with the *MMYs*, it is beneficial to familiarize yourself with the format and content of *TIP* before attempting to use it. And, if you are seeking a particular test, you can find it easily since entries are listed alphabetically. If not, the following procedure may be utilized:

1. Go to the Classified Subject Index and find the appropriate classification.
2. Identify promising titles from among those listed and their corresponding entry numbers.
3. Using the entry numbers, locate the test descriptions in the main body of the volume.
4. If you are referred to additional information in *MMYs*, as you often will be, go to the suggested *MMYs*.

Thus, *TIP* provides information on many more tests than the *MMYs*, but is less comprehensive in terms of information given for each test. Both *TIP* and the *MMYs* are virtually indispensible tools for educational researchers. As Mitchell, the editor of both *TIP III* and the *Ninth MMY*, has stated, the two publications are "interlocking volumes with extensive cross-referencing requiring their coordinated use as a system." At the time this text was being revised, a *Tests in Print IV* was scheduled to be available "in the near future." (Look for it at a library near you!)

PRO-ED Publications

A relatively new source of test information is the works of Keyser and Sweetland, currently published by PRO-ED. *Tests* provides information on over 3,000 tests intended for assessment in psychology, education, and business.[19] Although no reviews are included, complete information is given regarding test publishers so that you can call or write for additional information. In addition, tests appropriate for individuals with physical, visual, and hearing impairments are listed, as well as tests that are available in a variety of languages.

Test Critiques Compendium includes reviews of 60 "major" psychological and educational test instruments,[20] while the multivolumed *Test Critiques* contains reviews for more than 800 tests widely used in psychology, education, and business.[21] The reviews are quite extensive and provide the following information: a description of the test, administration, scoring, and interpretation information, valid-

---

[19]Keyser, D. J., & Sweetland, R. C. (Eds.). (1990). *Tests: A comprehensive reference for assessments in psychology, education, and business* (3rd ed.). Austin, TX: PRO-ED.

[20]Keyser, D. J., & Sweetland, R. C. (Eds.). (1987). *Test critiques compendium*. Austin, TX: PRO-ED.

[21]Keyser, D. J., & Sweetland, R. C. (Eds.). (1984–1994). *Test critiques* (Vols. I–X). Austin, TX: PRO-ED.

ity and reliability data, a critique of the test, and a list of related references. *Test Critiques* contains both subject and title indexes, and each volume provides a cumulative index.

ETS Test Collection

Sometimes you may be aware of a new test which sounds exactly like what you need but for which you can find no information. An excellent source of test information, especially for recently developed tests, is the ETS (Educational Testing Service) Test Collection. The ETS Collection is an extensive, ever-growing library containing, to date, over 15,000 tests. Like the *Mental Measurements Yearbooks,* its stated purpose is to make test information available to educational researchers and other interested professionals. In contrast to the *MMYs,* it includes unpublished as well as published tests, but provides much less information per test.

The Collection provides several publications and services. Probably the most valuable of these for researchers is the availability of annotated test bibliographies for a wide variety of testing areas. For each test included in a bibliography, the following information is given: title; author; publication date; target population; publisher or source; and an annotation describing the purpose of the instrument. There are currently over 200 annotated bibliographies available, representing eight major categories: achievement (e.g., reading readiness, psychology); aptitude (e.g., nonverbal aptitude, memory); attitudes and interests (e.g., attitudes toward curriculum, teacher attitudes); personality (e.g., leadership, stress); sensory-motor (e.g., auditory skills, motor skills); special populations (e.g., brain-damaged, juvenile delinquents); vocational/occupational (e.g., nurses, teacher assessment); and miscellaneous (e.g., culture-fair tests, moral development). The illustrative examples for each category just given indicate the scope of the Test Collection bibliographies.

The Collection publishes two sources of test-related information, one on an ongoing basis. Upon request, anyone may receive, at no charge, a pamphlet which gives the names, addresses, and telephone numbers of major U.S. publishers of standardized tests. Ten times a year it produces *News on Tests,* which includes announcements of new tests, citations of test reviews, new reference materials, and other, related items. Because of its frequency of publication, it provides more current information on tests than the *MMYs.* The ETS Collection also provides two services to test users, Tests in Microfiche and the Test Collection Database. Tests in Microfiche provides copies of tests which are not available commercially. Test microfiche purchasers are given permission to make copies for their own use. Test Collection Database makes the Test Collection library a publicly searchable database through Bibliographic Retrieval Services.

For further information and current prices, write ETS Test Collection, Princeton, NJ 08541. Also, check your library for the availability of Collection materials and services.

Professional Journals

There are a number of journals which regularly publish information of interest to test users. Since a number of these journals are American Psychological Association publications, *Psychological Abstracts* is a potential source of desired information. Using the monthly or annual index, you can quickly determine if the *Abstracts* contain any information on a given test. Journals of interest to test users include: *Journal of Applied Measurement; Journal of Consulting Psychology; Journal of*

Educational Measurement; Journal of Educational Psychology; Journal of Personnel Psychology; and *Educational and Psychological Measurement.* The *Journal of Educational Measurement,* for example, contains reviews of recently published tests.

Test Publishers and Distributors

After reading their descriptions and reviews, you will generally quickly eliminate many of the tests whose titles looked promising; some will not be appropriate for your sample, some will have inadequate validity and reliability data, and some will have one or more serious problems identified by reviewers. After you have narrowed the list of candidates, you will still usually require additional information. A good source of information on tests is publishers' test manuals. Manuals typically include: detailed validity and reliability data; a description of the population for whom the test is intended to be appropriate; a detailed description of norming procedures; conditions of administration; detailed scoring instructions; and requirements for score interpretation.

As mentioned previously, however, you must be a good consumer. Relevant data omitted from a manual are probably unfavorable to the test. Thus, if information on subtest reliabilities is missing, they probably are not very good; if they were, they would be reported! As the Romans used to say, CAVEAT EMPTOR.[22]

If no information can be found, or if available information is inadequate, you can generally obtain additional data by writing to the test developer, if known. Test developers will usually comply with such requests, especially if you agree to supply the results of your study in return.

Final selection of a test usually requires examination of the actual tests. A test which appears from all descriptions to be exactly what you need may have one or more problems detectable only by inspection of the test itself. The test may not be content valid *for your study;* for example, it may contain many items measuring content not covered by your treatment groups. An initial inspection copy of a test, as well as additional required copies if you select that test for your study, should be acquired from the test publisher if it is commercially available. For many tests, the publisher's name and address are given in the *Mental Measurements Yearbooks.* If not commercially available, tests may usually be obtained either in microfiche form from the ETS Test Collection or directly from the test developer.

Selecting From Alternatives

Eventually a decision must be reached. Once you have narrowed the number of candidates and acquired all relevant information, a comparative analysis of the tests must be made. While there are a number of factors to be considered, for example, validity data and cost, these factors are not of equal importance; the least expensive test is not necessarily the best test! This principle is graphically illustrated by an experience the author of this text had some years ago. A small school system had made improved reading skills of its elementary students its number one priority. At the beginning of the school year, a reading test was administered to all elementary students in the system and, based on the results, students were placed in appropriate classes; students with low scores, for example, were grouped together. The lowest scoring students were required to have an additional period of reading

---

[22]Let the buyer beware!

each day. It was not very long before teachers realized that something was amiss. A number of students in the highest reading groups, for example, apparently had very poor reading skills, while a number of students in the remedial groups could read quite well, and so forth. The author was asked to meet with school system personnel to discuss the situation. One of the first questions asked was "What test did you use to form the groups?" The author had never heard of the test named—let's call it the Bozo Test—which seemed unusual given constant exposure to available tests. As a result of a little homework, the Bozo Test was located in a *Mental Measurements Yearbook*. There was no information on validity or reliability, but there was a review; in essence, the reviewer stated that it was the worst instrument ever created, and that a person might just as well randomly assign students to groups as use the results of the Bozo. In a subsequent meeting with school personnel, the author diplomatically asked how the test had been identified and on what basis it had been selected. A book containing test information on a number of tests was produced and, sure enough, the Bozo Test was included. Under validity and reliability data it was clearly indicated that there was none. Perplexed, personnel were again asked on what basis the Bozo had been selected. And there, under administration requirements, was the answer—time to administer, five minutes. How efficient! The bottom line was that some very sincere, hard-working, bright professionals had wasted considerable time, energy, and money because of lack of knowledge concerning test selection criteria.

As you undoubtedly know by now, the most important factor to be considered in test selection is validity. Is one of the tests more appropriate for your sample? If you are interested in prediction, does one of the tests have a significantly higher validity coefficient? If content validity is of prime importance, are the items of one test based on the same textbook that will be used in your study? These are typical of the questions which might be raised. If after the validity comparison there are still several tests that seem appropriate, the next factor for consideration is reliability.

Assuming all coefficients were acceptable, you would presumably select the test with the highest reliability, but there are other considerations. A factor to be considered in relation to reliability, for example, is the length of the test and the time it takes to administer it. Shorter tests are, in general, to be preferred. A test that can be administered during one class period, for example, would be considerably more convenient than a 2-hour test; shorter tests are also preferable in terms of student fatigue and motivation. However, since reliability is related to length, a shorter test will tend to be less reliable. For example, for many tests a short form is also available; the reliability of the short form is invariably lower. Thus, if a long form and a short form of a test (or two different tests of different lengths) are both valid for your study, the questions to be considered are: How much shorter? How much less reliable? If one test takes half as long to administer and is only slightly less reliable, the shorter test is probably better. For example, suppose Test A (or Form A) has a KR-20 reliability of .94 and takes 90 minutes to administer, and Test B (or Form B) has a KR-20 reliability of .90 and takes 50 minutes to administer; which would you choose? Most probably Test B. If after comparing validity and reliability data, you still have more than one candidate, you should consider administration, scoring, and interpretation requirements.

By the time you get to this point, you have probably made a decision concerning whether you need an individually administered test. If not, and if there is no essential reason for using an individually administered test, now is the time to eliminate them from contention. Most of the time individually administered tests will not even be a consideration since they are used primarily for certain IQ and personality testing situations. However, when they are, you should keep in mind the potential disadvantages associated with their use; additional cost, additional time, the need for trained administrators, complicated scoring procedures, and the need for trained interpreters. Of course, if the nature of your subjects or the research variable of interest requires it, by all means use an individually administered test. In either case, you should consider the administration, scoring, and interpretation requirements. In addition to the time consideration mentioned previously, you should consider factors such as unusual administration conditions, difficult scoring procedures, and sophisticated interpretation. Are you qualified to execute the requirements of the test as specified? If not, can you afford to acquire the necessary personnel? If after all this soul-searching, by some miracle you still have more than one test in the running, by all means pick the cheapest one!

There are two additional considerations in test selection which have nothing to do with the psychometric qualities of a test. Both are related to the use of tests in schools. If you are planning to use school children in your study, you should check to see what tests they have already been administered. You would not want to administer a test with which subjects had familiarity. Second, you should be sensitive to the fact that some parents or administrators might object to a test which contains "touchy" items. Certain personality inventories, for example, ask questions related to the sexual behavior of the respondents. If there is any possibility that the test contains potentially objectionable items, either choose another test or acquire appropriate permissions before administering the test. There have been instances where researchers have been ordered to destroy (even burn!) test results. As the old saying goes, an ounce of prevention. . . .

Occasionally, hopefully not very often, you will find yourself in the position of not being able to locate a suitable test. The solution is *not* to use an inadequate test with the rationale, "Oh well, I'll do the best I can!" One logical solution is to develop your own test. Good test construction requires a variety of skills. As mentioned previously, training at least equivalent to a course in measurement is needed. If you do develop your own test, you must collect validation data; a self-developed test should not be utilized in a research study unless it has been pretested first with a group very similar to the group to be used in the actual study. In addition to collecting validity and reliability data, you will need to try out the administration and scoring procedures. In some cases, the results of pretesting will indicate the need for revisions and further pretesting. This procedure may also sometimes be followed for an existing test. You may find a test that seems very appropriate but for which certain relevant types of validation data are not available. In this case you may decide to try to validate this test with your population rather than develop a test "from scratch."

◼ TEST ADMINISTRATION

There are several general guidelines for test administration of which you should be aware. First, if testing is to be conducted in a school setting, arrangements should be made beforehand with the appropriate person, usually the principal. Consultation with the principal should result in agreement as to when the testing will take place, under what conditions, and with what assistance from school personnel. The principal can be very helpful in supplying such information as dates for which testing is inadvisable (e.g., assembly days and days immediately preceding or following holidays). Second, whether you are testing in the schools or elsewhere, you should do everything you can to insure ideal testing conditions; a comfortable, quiet environment is more conducive to subject cooperation. Also, if testing is to take place in more than one session, the conditions of the sessions should be as identical as possible. Third, follow the Scout motto and be prepared. Be thoroughly familiar with the administration procedures presented in the test manual and follow the directions precisely. If they are at all complicated, practice beforehand. Administer the test to some friends; if this is not feasible, stand in front of a mirror and give it to yourself!

As with everything in life, good planning and preparation usually pay off. If you have made all necessary arrangements, secured all necessary cooperation, and are completely familiar and comfortable with the administration procedures, the actual testing situation should go well. If some unforeseen catastrophe occurs during testing, such as an earthquake or a power failure, make careful note of the incident. If it is serious enough to invalidate the testing, you may have to try again another day with another group. If in your judgment the effects of the incident are not serious, at least relate its occurrence in your final research report. Despite the possibility of unforeseen tragedies, it is certain that the probability of all going well will be greatly increased if you adequately plan and prepare for the big day.

■ SUMMARY/CHAPTER 5

PURPOSE AND PROCESS

1. The time and skill it takes to select an appropriate standardized instrument are invariably less than the time and skill it takes to develop an instrument that measures the same thing.
2. There are thousands of standardized instruments available which yield a wide variety of data for a wide variety of purposes.
3. Selection of an instrument for a particular research purpose involves identification and selection of the most appropriate one from among alternatives.

CHARACTERISTICS OF A STANDARDIZED TEST

4. A test is a means of measuring the knowledge, skill, feeling, intelligence, or aptitude of an individual or group.
5. Test objectivity means that an individual's score is not affected by the person scoring the test.
6. Validity is the most important quality of any test. Validity is concerned with what a test measures and for whom it is appropriate; reliability refers to the consistency with which a test measures whatever it measures.
7. Specification of conditions of administration, directions for scoring, and guidelines for interpretation are important characteristics of standardized tests.
8. A table of norms presents raw scores and one or more equivalent transformations, such as corresponding percentile ranks.

Validity

9. Validity is the degree to which a test measures what it is supposed to measure and, consequently, permits appropriate interpretation of scores.

10. A test is not valid per se; it is valid for a particular purpose and for a particular group.

Content Validity

11. Content validity is the degree to which a test measures an intended content area.
12. Item validity is concerned with whether the test items represent measurement in the intended content area, and sampling validity is concerned with how well the test samples the total content area.
13. Content validity is of prime importance for achievement tests.
14. Content validity is determined by expert judgment.
15. When selecting a test for a research study the researcher assumes the role of "expert" and determines whether the test is content valid for her or his study.

Construct Validity

16. Construct validity is the degree to which a test measures an intended hypothetical construct.
17. A construct is a nonobservable trait, such as intelligence, which explains behavior.
18. Validating a test of a construct involves testing hypotheses deduced from a theory concerning the construct.

Concurrent Validity

19. Concurrent validity is the degree to which the scores on a test are related to the scores on another, already established test administered at the same time, or to some other valid criterion available at the same time.
20. The relationship method of determining concurrent validity involves determining the relationship between scores on the test and scores on some other established test or criterion.
21. The discrimination method of establishing concurrent validity involves determining whether test scores can be used to discriminate between persons who possess a certain characteristic and those who do not, or those who possess it to a greater degree.

Predictive Validity

22. Predictive validity is the degree to which a test can predict how well an individual will do in a future situation.
23. The predictive validity of a test is determined by establishing the relationship between scores on the test and some measure of success in the situation of interest.
24. The test that is used to predict success is referred to as the predictor, and the behavior that is predicted is referred to as the criterion.

Reliability

25. Reliability is the degree to which a test consistently measures whatever it measures.

26. Reliability is expressed numerically, usually as a coefficient; a high coefficient indicates high reliability.

Test-Retest Reliability

27. Test-retest reliability is the degree to which scores are consistent over time.
28. Test-retest reliability is established by determining the relationship between scores resulting from administering the same test, to the same group, on different occasions.

Equivalent-Forms Reliability

29. Equivalent forms of a test are two tests that are identical in every way except for the actual items included.
30. Equivalent-forms reliability is determined by establishing the relationship between scores resulting from administering two different forms of the same test, to the same group, at the same time.
31. Equivalent-forms reliability is the most commonly used estimate of reliability for most tests used in research.

Split-Half Reliability

32. Split-half reliability is determined by establishing the relationship between the scores on two equivalent halves of a test administered to a total group at one time.
33. Since longer tests tend to be more reliable, and since split-half reliability represents the reliability of a test only half as long as the actual test, a correction known as the Spearman-Brown prophecy formula must be applied to the coefficient.

Rationale Equivalence Reliability

34. Rationale equivalence reliability is not established through correlation but rather estimates internal consistency by determining how all items on a test relate to all other items and to the total test.
35. Rationale equivalence reliability is determined through application of the Kuder-Richardson formulas, usually formula 20 or 21 in educational research studies.
36. Cronbach's alpha is the general formula of which the KR-20 formula is a special case which requires that items be scored dichotomously, i.e., correct or incorrect.

Scorer/Rater Reliability

37. Interjudge reliability refers to the reliability of two (or more) independent scorers; intrajudge reliability refers to the reliability of the scoring of individual scorers.
38. Estimates of interjudge or intrajudge reliability are usually obtained using correlational techniques but can also be expressed simply as percent agreement.

Reliability Coefficients

39. What constitutes an acceptable level of reliability is to some degree determined by the type of test, although, of course, a coefficient over 90 would be acceptable for any test.
40. If a test is composed of several subtests, then the reliability of each subtest must be evaluated, not just the reliability of the total test.

Standard Error of Measurement

41. The standard error of measurement is an estimate of how often you can expect errors of a given size.
42. A small standard error of measurement indicates high reliability; a large standard error of measurement, low reliability.
43. The standard error of measurement allows us to estimate how much difference there probably is between a person's obtained score and true score, the size of this difference being a function of the reliability of the test.

TYPES OF TESTS

Achievement

44. Achievement tests measure the current status of individuals with respect to proficiency in given areas of knowledge or skill.
45. Standardized achievement tests are available for individual curriculum areas such as reading and mathematics, and also in the form of comprehensive batteries that measure achievement in several different areas.

Personality

46. Tests of personality are designed to measure characteristics of individuals along a number of dimensions and to assess feelings and attitudes toward self, others, and a variety of other activities, institutions, and situations.
47. They may well be the most used tests in educational research.

Nonprojective Tests

Personality Inventories

48. Personality inventories present lists of questions or statements describing behaviors characteristic of certain personality traits, and the individual is asked to indicate (yes, no, undecided) whether the statement describes her or him.
49. Personality inventories may be specific and measure only one trait, such as introversion-extroversion, or may be general and measure a number of traits.

Attitude Scales

50. Attitude scales attempt to determine what an individual believes, perceives, or feels.
51. Attitudes can be measured toward self, others, and a variety of other activities, institutions, or situations.

52. There are four basic types of scales used to measure attitudes: Likert scales, semantic differential scales, Thurstone scales, and Guttman scales.
53. Measures of "attitude toward self" are referred to as measures of self-concept.
54. Rating scales are also used to measure attitudes toward others.

Creativity Tests

55. Tests of creativity are really tests designed to measure those personality characteristics that are related to creative behavior.
56. One such trait is referred to as divergent thinking; unlike convergent thinkers, who tend to look for *the* right answer, divergent thinkers tend to seek alternatives.

Interest Inventories

57. An interest inventory asks an individual to indicate personal likes and dislikes, such as kinds of activities he or she likes to engage in.
58. Responses are generally compared to known interest patterns.
59. The most widely used type of interest measure is the vocational interest inventory.

Projective Tests

60. Projective tests were developed in an attempt to eliminate some of the major problems inherent in the use of self-report measures, such as the tendency of some respondents to give "socially acceptable" responses.
61. The purposes of such tests are usually not obvious to respondents; the individual is typically asked to respond to ambiguous items.
62. The most commonly used projective technique is the method of association; this technique asks the respondent to react to a stimulus such as a picture, inkblot, or word.

Aptitude

63. Aptitude tests are used to predict how well someone is likely to perform in a future situation.
64. Tests of general aptitude are variously referred to as scholastic aptitude tests, intelligence tests, and tests of general mental ability.

General Aptitude

65. General aptitude tests typically ask the individual to perform a variety of verbal and nonverbal tasks that measure the individual's ability to apply knowledge and solve problems.
66. While general aptitude tests are intended to be measures of innate ability or potential, they appear actually to measure current ability.
67. Since they seem to do a reasonable job of predicting future academic success, and are in that sense measures of "potential," they are very useful to educators.
68. Culture-fair tests attempt to exclude culturally related items, such as items which include words that might not be familiar to certain groups of individuals.

Specific Aptitude

69. Specific aptitude tests attempt to predict the level of performance that can be expected of an individual following future instruction or training in a specific area or areas.
70. Aptitude tests are available for a number of specific areas such as algebra, music, and mechanical ability.
71. Multi-aptitude batteries, which measure aptitudes in several related areas, are available for the assessment of both academic and nonacademic aptitudes.

Readiness

72. A readiness test is administered prior to instruction or training in a specific area in order to determine whether and to what degree a student is ready for, or will profit from, instruction.
73. Reading readiness tests typically include measurement of variables such as auditory discrimination, visual discrimination, and motor ability.

SELECTION OF A TEST

74. *Do not* use the first test you find that appears to measure what you want.
75. *Do* identify those tests that are appropriate for your study, compare them on relevant factors, and select the best one.

Sources of Test Information

Mental Measurements Yearbooks

76. The *Mental Measurements Yearbooks (MMYs)* represent the most comprehensive source of test information available to educational researchers.
77. The stated purposes of the latest *MMYs* are to provide: (1) factual information on all known new or revised tests; (2) objective test reviews; and (3) comprehensive bibliographies.
78. Perhaps the most important thing you need to know in order to use the *MMYs* is that all the numbers given by the indexes are test numbers, not page numbers.

Tests in Print

79. *Tests in Print (TIP)* is a comprehensive bibliography of all tests that have appeared in preceding *MMYs*.
80. *TIP* also serves as a master index of tests which directs the reader to all original reviews that have appeared in the *MMYs* to date.
81. *TIP* provides information on many more tests than the *MMYs*, but is less comprehensive in terms of information given for each test.

PRO-ED Publications

82. *Tests* provides information on over 3,000 tests intended for assessment in psychology, education, and business.

83. *Test Critiques Compendium* includes reviews of 60 "major" psychological and educational test instruments.
84. The multivolumed *Test Critiques* contains reviews for more than 800 tests widely used in psychology, education, and business.
85. Reviews are quite extensive and provide: a description of the test, administration, scoring, and interpretation information, validity and reliability data, a critique, and related references.

ETS Test Collection

86. The ETS Test Collection is an extensive, ever-growing library containing, to date, over 15,000 tests.
87. Like the *MMYs,* its stated purpose is to make test information available to researchers and other interested professionals.
88. In contrast to the *MMYs,* it includes unpublished tests, but provides much less information per test.
89. The Collection provides several publications and services; probably the most valuable of these for researchers is the availability of annotated test bibliographies for a wide variety of testing areas.

Professional Journals

90. There are a number of journals which regularly publish information of interest to test users, e.g., the *Journal of Educational Measurement.*
91. Since a number of these journals are American Psychological Association publications, *Psychological Abstracts* is a potential source of desired test information.

Test Publishers and Distributors

92. A good source of information on tests is publishers' test manuals.
93. If no information can be found, or if available information is inadequate, you can generally obtain additional data by writing to the test developer, if known.
94. Final selection of a test usually requires examination of the actual tests.

Selecting From Alternatives

95. Final selection of a test requires a comparative analysis of the alternatives.
96. The most important factor to be considered is validity.
97. The next factor for consideration is reliability.
98. Other important factors include administration, scoring, and interpretation requirements.
99. A self-developed test should not be utilized in a research study unless it has been pretested first with a group very similar to the group to be used in the actual study.

Test Administration

100. If testing is to be conducted in a school setting, arrangements should be made beforehand with the appropriate person, usually the principal.

101. Every effort should be made to insure ideal testing conditions.
102. Be thoroughly familiar with the administration procedures presented in the test manual and follow the directions precisely.

TASK 5 PERFORMANCE CRITERIA

All the information required for each test will be found in the *Mental Measurements Yearbooks*. Following the description of the three tests, you should present a comparative analysis of the tests which forms a rationale for your selection of the "most acceptable" test for your study. As an example, you might indicate that all three tests have similar reliability coefficients reported but that one of the tests is more appropriate for your subjects.

On the following pages, an example is presented which illustrates the performance called for by Task 5. (See Task 5 example.) This example represents the task submitted by the same student whose tasks for Parts Two to Four were previously presented.

Additional examples for this and subsequent tasks are included in the *Student Guide* which accompanies this text.

Task 5 Example

Effect of Interactive Multimedia on the Achievement
of 10th-Grade Biology Students

Test One (from 11th <u>MMY</u>, test #160)

a) High-School Subject Tests, Biology - 1980-1990
American Testronics
$33.85 per 35 tests with administration directions;
$13.25 per 35 machine-scorable answer sheets; $19.45
per Teacher's Manual ('90, 110 pages).

b) The Biology test of the High-School Subject Tests is a
group administered achievement test which yields 10
scores (Cell Structure and Function, Cellular
Chemistry, Viruses/Monerans/Protists/Fungi, Plants,
Animals, Human Body Systems and Physiology, Genetics,
Ecology, Biological Analysis and Experimentation).

c) Reviewers state that reliability values (KR-20s) for
the various subject tests ranged from .85 to .93, with
a median of .88. Content validity should be examined
using the classification tables and objective lists
provided in the teacher's manual so that stated test
objectives and research objectives can be matched.

d) Grades 9-12

e) Administration time is approximately 40 minutes.

f) Scoring services are available from the publisher.

g) Reviewers recommend the test as a useful tool in the
evaluation of instructional programs, recognizing that
the test fairly represents the content for biology in
the high school curriculum. However, they do caution
that a match should be established between stated test
objectives and local objectives.

2

Test Two (from 11th <u>MMY</u>, test #256)

a) National Proficiency Survey Series: Biology (NPSS:B) -
1989
The Riverside Publishing Company
$34.98 per 35 test booklets including directions for
administration; $19.98 per 35 answer sheets; $9 per
technical manual (26 pages) (1990 prices)

b) The NPSS:B is a group administered achievement test
with 45 items designed to measure "knowledge about the
living world ranging from single-celled organisms to
the human body."

c) Content validity is good; items were selected from a
large item bank provided by classroom teachers and
curriculum experts. The manual alerts users that
validity depends in large measure upon the purpose of
the test. Although the standard error of measurement is
not given for the biology test, the range of KR-20s for
the entire battery is from .82 to .91 with a median
of .86.

d) Grades 9-12

e) Administration time is approximately 45 minutes.

f) Tests can be machine scored or self scored. A program
is available on diskette so that machine scoring may be
done on site. Both percentile rank and NCE scores are
used. NCEs allow users to make group comparisons.

g) The reviewer finds the reliability scores to be low if
the test is to be used to make decisions concerning
individual students. However, he praises the publishers
for their comments regarding content validity which
state that "information should always be interpreted in
relation to the user's own purpose for testing."

3

Test Three (from 11th <u>MMY</u>, test #135)

a) End of Course Tests (ECT) - 1986
   CTB/McGraw-Hill
   $21 per complete kit including 35 test booklets
   (Biology 13 pages) and examiner's manual.
b) The ECT covers a wide range of subjects in secondary
   school. Unfortunately, detailed information is not
   available for individual subjects. The number of
   questions range from 42 to 50 and are designed to
   measure subject matter content most commonly taught in
   a first one year course.
c) No statistical validity evidence is provided for the
   ECT and no demographic breakdown is provided to
   understand the representativeness of the
   standardization samples. However, reliability estimates
   were given and ranged from .80 to .89 using the KR-20
   formula.
d) Secondary school students
e) Administration time is from 45 to 50 minutes for any
   one subject test.
f) Both machine scoring and hand scoring are available. A
   Class Record Sheet is provided in the manual to help
   those who hand score to summarize the test results.
g) Users must be willing to establish local norms and
   validation evidence for effectual use of the ECT since
   no statistical validity evidence is provided.

4

Conclusion

All three batteries have a biology subtest; The High-School Subject Tests (HSST) and the NPSS:B are designed specifically for 10th-grade students, while the ECT is course, rather than grade, oriented. It is acknowledged that more data are needed for all three tests, but reported validity and reliability data suggest that they all would be at least adequate for the purpose of this study, i.e., to assess the effectiveness of the use of interactive multimedia in biology instruction.

Since of the three tests the least validity evidence is provided for the ECT, it was eliminated from contention first. Both the HSST and the NPSS:B provide tables and objective lists in their manuals which may be used to establish a match between stated test objectives and research objectives. The HSST and the NPSS:B both have good content validity but the HSST does not cross-index items to objectives, as does the NPSS:B. Also, norming information indicates that Catholic school students were included in the battery norm group. Therefore, of the three tests, the NPSS:B seems to be the most valid for the study.

With respect to reliability, all three tests provide a comparable range of KR-20 values for battery subtests. While specific figures are not given for the biology subtests, the reported ranges (low eighties to low nineties) suggest that they all have adequate internal consistency reliability.

The NPSS:B appears to be the most appropriate instrument for the study. The items (which were provided by both classroom teachers and curriculum experts) appear to match the objectives of the research study quite well. The

Task 5 Example (*continued*)

5

KR-20 reliability is good, both in absolute terms and as compared to that of the other available tests. Both machine- and self-scoring are options, but an added advantage is that machine scoring can be done on site using a program provided by the publisher.

Thus, the NPSS:B will be used in the current study. As a cross-check, internal consistency reliability will be computed based on the scores of the subjects in the study.

PART SIX

Types of Research

While research studies have a number of similar components, such as a defined problem and a set of conclusions, specific procedures in a study are to a great extent determined by the particular type of research involved. As each of the six types of research (historical, qualitative, descriptive, correlational, causal-comparative, experimental) has a unique purpose, application of each type entails a unique set of procedures and concerns. As suggested above, however, there are procedural steps common to all research studies; all studies, for example, involve some type of data collection and analysis.

The purpose of Parts One through Five was to give you an overview of the basic steps involved in conducting research and the major characteristics differentiating each of the types of research. The purpose of Part Six is to facilitate acquisition of specific competencies related to each of the types.

The goal of Part Six is for you to be able to describe the procedures involved in each of the types of research and apply them in designing specific studies. After you have read Part Six, you should be able to perform the following task.

■ TASK 6

Having stated a problem, formulated one or more hypotheses, described a sample, and selected one or more measuring instruments, develop the method section of a research report. This should include a description of subjects, instrument(s), research design, and specific procedures.

(See Performance Criteria, p. 411)

"Meder hypothesizes quite simply that Dracula was (is?!) a woman — 'a beautiful, seductive, evil noblewoman of highest society . . .' (p. 191)."

Historical Research

After reading Chapter 6, you should be able to:

1. Briefly state the purpose of historical research.

2. List and briefly describe the major steps involved in designing and conducting a historical research study.

3. Explain why primary sources of data are preferable to secondary sources.

4. Briefly describe external and internal criticism of data.

5. Briefly describe four factors which should be considered in determining the accuracy of documents.

DEFINITION AND PURPOSE

Historical research is the systematic collection and evaluation of data related to past occurrences in order to describe causes, effects, or trends of those events that may help to explain present events and anticipate future events. Many beginning researchers tend to think of historical research as a rather unscientific type of investigation. This is only true, however, of poorly designed and conducted historical research. Admittedly, the nature of historical research precludes exercise of many of the control procedures characteristic of other types; if well done, however, historical research also involves systematic, objective data collection and analysis.

Many current educational practices, theories, and issues can be better understood in light of past experiences. The grading issue, for example, is not a new one in education, nor is cooperative learning an innovation of the seventies. A knowledge of the history of education can yield insight into the circumstances involved in the evolution of the current educational system as well as practices and approaches that have been found to be ineffective or infeasible. In fact, studying the history of education might lead one to believe that not only is nothing new under the educational sun but also that educators never learn; some practices seem to appear and disappear with regularity. For over 150 years, for example, individualized instruction and group instruction have seemingly taken turns being the favored approach of the day. Miehl, however, does not view this constant shifting as the proverbial pendulum that swings from one approach to another and back, with no progress being made along the way. Instead, she sees educational change as a spiral phenomenon, with each ascending loop profiting from the former:

> In common with the pendulum swing, this view allows for renewed attention to a problem and line of solution which have been neglected for a time. The difference in the spiral view is that it accounts for the fact that proposals made at a later point in educational history usually are much more refined, with wisdom distilled from experience at both sides of the spiral built into them. At each new point on the upward and outward spiral the concepts are clearer and the language of education is more precise.[1]

Miehl has tested the spiral pattern on a number of educational issues, including the individualized versus group instruction question:

> During the depression years, when interest developed in helping children become more skillful, involved members of groups, new information on the dynamics of groups was available. The profession also could carry into the new movement better understanding of the individual within the group. At each new turn of the spiral the practices advocated could be more sophisticated, for educators could look back on the experiences had at previous positions on the lower levels of the spiral and could build into a new whole the useful residue from each previous stage.

As Miehl's position indicates, a knowledge of the history of education cannot only increase understanding of the present but also facilitate anticipation of future trends.

◼ THE HISTORICAL RESEARCH PROCESS

The steps involved in conducting a historical research study are essentially the same as for other types of research; definition of a problem, formulation of questions to be answered or hypotheses to be tested, systematic collection of data, evaluation of data, and production of a verbal synthesis of findings or confirmation/disconfirmation of hypotheses. In conducting a historical study, the researcher can neither manipulate nor control any of the variables. On the other hand, there is no way the researcher can affect events of the past; what has happened has happened. The researcher can, however, apply scientific objectivity in attempting to determine exactly what did happen in the past.

Definition of a Problem

The purpose of a historical research study should *not* be to find out what is already known about a topic and to retell it. Recall that the goal of all scientific research in

---

[1]Miehl, A. (1964). Reassessment of the curriculum—why? In D. Huebner (Ed.), *A reassessment of the curriculum*. New York: Teachers College Press.

general, and educational research in particular, is to explain, predict, and/or control phenomena. The nature of historical research, of course, eliminates control of phenomena; therefore, the purpose of a historical research study should be to explain or predict, not to rehash. The purpose of a historical research study should also *not* be to prove a point or to support a pet position of the researcher. One can easily verify almost any point of view by consciously or unconsciously "overlooking" evidence to the contrary. There are probably data available to support almost any position; the historical researcher's task is to objectively evaluate and weigh all evidence in arriving at the most tenable conclusion. For example, one could cite data which would seemingly support the position that having more highly educated and trained teachers has led to increased school vandalism. One could do a historical study describing how requirements for teacher certification and recertification have increased over the years and how school vandalism has correspondingly increased. Of course such a study would indicate very poor critical analysis since two separate, independent sets of factors are probably responsible for each of these trends rather than one being the cause or effect of the other. To avoid this sort of biased data collection and analysis, one should probably avoid topics about which one has strong feelings; it is a lot easier to be objective when you are not emotionally involved.

As with the other types of research, the purpose of a historical research study should be to discover new knowledge or to clarify, correct, or expand existing knowledge. Worthwhile historical research problems are identified much the same way as problems for other types of research. One especially valuable resource for acquainting beginning researchers with the kinds of historical research studies that have been conducted, and for suggesting possible future studies, is the *History of Education Quarterly*.[2] The *Quarterly,* for example, contains articles such as "Cathedral of Culture: The Schoolhouse in American Educational Thought and Practice since 1820" and "Do Young Children Need Intellectual Stimulation? Experts' Advice to Parents, 1900–1985."[3] It is just as important in historical research as in any other type to formulate a manageable, well-defined problem; otherwise it is likely that an overwhelming amount of data will be collected, considerably complicating analysis and synthesis of the data and the drawing of adequately documented conclusions. On the other hand, a concern unique to historical research is the possibility that a problem will be selected for which insufficient data are available. Unlike researchers utilizing the other types of research, the historical researcher cannot "create" data by administering instruments such as achievement tests, psychological inventories, or questionnaires to subjects.[4] The historical researcher is basically limited to whatever data are already available. Thus, if insufficient data are available, the problem will be inadequately investigated. It is better to study in depth a well defined problem with one or more specific, well stated questions or hypotheses, than to investigate either a too broadly stated problem, or a problem for which insufficient data are available.

[2]*History of Education Quarterly*. (1961 to date). New York: History of Education Society in cooperation with the School of Education, New York University.

[3]Cutler, W. W., III. (1989). Cathedral of culture: The schoolhouse in American educational thought and practice since 1820. *History of Education Quarterly, 29,* 1–40; *and* Wrigley, J. (1989). Do young children need intellectual stimulation? Experts' advice to parents, 1900–1985. *History of Education Quarterly, 29,* 41–76.

[4]A historical study may involve interviews with participants in, or observers of, an event. Even in these cases, however, the number of persons who can be interviewed, and the kinds of questions that can be asked, are usually limited.

Data Collection

In a historical research study, the review of related literature and the study procedures are part of the same process (remember, there are no measuring instruments).
The review of the literature does not take place before data collection; this does not
mean, of course, that the literature may not be consulted to initially identify a problem. The term "literature" takes on a much broader meaning in a historical study
and refers to all sorts of written communication; in addition, identification, acquisition, and review of such "literature" is considerably more complex. The written
communication may be in the form of legal documents, records, minutes of meetings, letters, and other documents which will not normally be indexed alphabetically by subject, author, and title in a library. Thus, identification of such data
requires considerably more "detective work" on the part of the researcher. Further,
unless the problem deals with a very local event or issue, it is not uncommon for
identified relevant documents to be available only at distant locations, in a special
library collection, for example. In such cases, proper examination of the data
requires either considerable travel or, when feasible, extensive reproduction. Both
of these alternatives present the researcher with problems. Travel requires that the
researcher have a healthy bank account (which very few do, as pointed out in
Chapter 4!) unless, of course, the effort is supported by a funding agency.
Reproduction (for example, acquiring photocopies of documents in a private collection) can also become costly and often wasteful; a 50-page document may turn
out to contain only one paragraph directly related to the problem under investigation. As an analogy, many legal cases involve extensive "historical research"; in the
pretrial investigation of the Iran-Contra affair, for example, Marine Lt. Col. Oliver
North's attorneys requested approximately 40,000 pages of classified documents.[5]
Obviously only a small portion of the information contained in those documents
was actually useful to the defense.

A historical research study in education may also involve interviews with persons who participated in the event or process under investigation, if it occurred in
the recent past (remember, it would be pretty tough to interview an observer of the
Boston tea party!), or an examination of relics and remains, such as textbooks.
Similar problems apply in these situations as when only written documents are
involved; they are more difficult to identify, they may be located some distance
from the researcher, and they may be unproductive sources after all. An interview
with a person believed to have been involved in an incident, for example, may
reveal that he or she was only peripherally involved or that he or she recollects only
partially, if at all, the details of the event. To use our legal analogy, we often read
accounts or view TV coverage of witnesses who state that they simply "don't
remember" or "have no recollection of" conversations or meetings.

Sources of data in a historical research study are classified as primary sources
or secondary sources. Primary sources constitute firsthand information, such as original documents and reports by actual participants or direct observers; secondary
sources constitute secondhand information, such as reference books (encyclopedias, for example) or reports by relatives of actual participants or observers. A student who participated in the takeover of the president's office at Rowdy U. would
be a primary source of data concerning the event; her or his mother would be a
secondary source. Primary sources are definitely to be preferred; the further
removed the evidence is, the less comprehensive and accurate the resulting data are
likely to be. You may have played a party game usually called "telephone" which

---

[5]Reagan for the defense? (1988, December 6). *The Miami Herald,* p. 26A.

illustrates how the facts get twisted as a story is passed from person to person. The first person hears the "true" story and whispers it to the second person, who whispers it to the third person, and so on until finally the last person tells out loud the story he or she was told. There is generally a considerable discrepancy between the first and the last version; "Greg and Muffy were seen holding hands at Bigger Burger" may well end up as "Greg and Muffy were kicked out of Club Yuppee because of their X-rated behavior on the dance floor!"

Because primary sources are admittedly more difficult to acquire, a common criticism of historical research is excessive reliance on secondary sources. It is better to select a "less grand" problem for which primary sources are available and accessible than to inadequately investigate the "problem of the year." Of course the further back in time the event under study occurred, the more likely it is that secondary sources may also have to be used. As a general rule, however, the more primary sources, the better.

The process of reviewing and abstracting pertinent data from primary and secondary sources is essentially the one described in Chapter 2: assessment of the source's relevancy to your problem; recording of complete bibliographic information; coding of the data from each source with respect to the hypothesis (or aspect of a hypothesis) to which it relates; summarization of the pertinent information; and notation of questions, comments, and quotations. One slight difference is that due to the nature of historical sources, several different note cards may be required for any one source. Minutes of a school board meeting, for example, might include information relating to two hypotheses; to facilitate later analysis and organization of data, they are best recorded separately. One major difference is that historical sources must also be subjected to a careful analysis to determine both their authenticity and their accuracy.

Data Analysis: External and Internal Criticism

When you read a report of a completed study in a professional journal, written by the person who conducted the research, you can generally assume that the report is accurate; the reported procedures and results can be assumed to be the procedure and results that actually occured. This is not the case with historical sources. Historical sources exist independently of your study; they were not written or developed for use in a research project. Thus, while they may very well serve the purpose for which they were created, they may not serve your purpose. Recall the previously discussed letter, allegedly written by Albert Einstein, containing an expression of concern regarding the amount of physical punishment in schools. Even if the letter were determined to be authentic, unless Albert Einstein could be shown to be a reliable source concerning educational practices of his day, his letter could not be used as evidence to support a position concerning widespread corporal punishment during his era.

All sources of historical data must be subjected to rigorous scientific analysis to determine both their authenticity (external criticism) and their accuracy (internal criticism). As with Aristotle and his fly with five legs, too often statements are uncritically accepted as factual statements if they are made by well-known persons. An authority in one area may have *opinions* concerning other areas, but they are not necessarily based on facts. Similarly, the fact that records are "official" does not necessarily mean that all information contained in those records is accurate. A school board member, for example, might state that teachers are losing control of their classrooms. This would be an opinion, however, and would not be objective evidence. Thus, for each source, first it must be determined whether it is authentic (was this letter really written by Albert Einstein?), and second, a judgment must be made concerning the accuracy of its contents.

External criticism, establishment of authenticity, is generally not the problem in educational research. The researcher does not usually have to worry about possible hoaxes or forgeries; there is not a big market for forged school board minutes! If the researcher is dealing with a problem for which sources are relatively old, and for which authenticity is not necessarily a given, there are a number of scientific techniques available to her or him. Age of document or relic, for example, can be fairly accurately estimated by applying various physical and chemical tests. Internal criticism, establishment of accuracy, is considerably more difficult. In determining the accuracy of documents, for example, there are at least four factors that must be considered:

1. Knowledge and competence of the author. It must be determined whether the person who wrote the document is, or was, a competent person and a person in a position to be knowledgeable concerning what actually occurred.
2. Time delay. An important consideration is how much time is likely to have elapsed between the event's occurrence and the recording of the facts. Reports written while an event is occurring (such as minutes of meetings), or shortly after (such as entries in a diary), are more likely to be accurate than reports written some time after, such as an anecdote in an autobiography.
3. Bias and motives of the author. People often report or record incorrect information. Such distortion of the truth may be intentional or unintentional. People, for example, tend to remember what they want to remember. People also tend to amplify, add little details, in order to make a story more interesting. A more serious problem occurs when the recorder has motives for consciously or unconsciously misinterpreting the facts; accounts of the same event given by the plaintiff and the defendant on *The People's Court* often differ considerably.
4. Consistency of data. Each piece of evidence must be compared with all other pieces to determine the degree of agreement. If one observer's account disagrees with those of other observers, his or her testimony may be suspect. Thus, in a sense, by the very fact that they agree, sources may validate their accuracy. Having reviewed, abstracted, and evaluated the data, the researcher then organizes and synthesizes the findings and prepares a research report.

Data Synthesis

As with a review of related literature, historical data should be organized and synthesized, and conclusions and generalizations formulated. Just as a review of literature should not be a series of annotations, the results of a historical study should not be a chronological listing of events. Critics of historical research question the validity of generalizations based on events that can never be exactly duplicated. This concern does have some merit and supports the need for extreme caution in forming generalizations. However, the generalization problem is not unique to historical research. It is virtually impossible to exactly duplicate any educational research study involving human beings, even highly controlled experimental studies. With historical research, as with other types of research, the more similar a new situation is to a former situation, the more applicable generalizations based on the past situation will be.

Since summarization of historical research data involves logical analysis rather than statistical analysis, the researcher must take care to be as objective as possible. It is very easy to "overlook" or to discard evidence that does not support, or contradicts, the research hypothesis. One may, for example, subconsciously apply stricter criteria when engaged in internal criticism of unwanted data. One way to avoid this is to adopt a caveat from the medical field; if in doubt, get a second opinion. From time to time even the most experienced experts in any field feel uncomfortable with a particular issue and find it helpful to find an unbiased and respected colleague just to say, "Take a look at this and tell me what you think."

You probably realize by now that there is a lot more to historical research than you originally thought. A historical research study is definitely not for rookies! The complex demands of data collection and analysis generally require skill, experience, and resources beyond those of the beginning researcher.[6]

■ AN EXAMPLE OF HISTORICAL RESEARCH

Many beginning researchers tend to have a preconceived notion that historical research (and history in general) is really quite dull. As the example to be discussed will illustrate, nothing could be further from the truth. Conducting a historical study can be a very challenging, exciting pursuit. Many of the characteristics that would make one a good detective— such as a desire to collect objective evidence and pursue clues—also make a good historical researcher. The following example is not presented as a model of historical research; by the researcher's own admission, it is based primarily on secondary sources, and it is of very little educational significance. It is presented because it does represent a fascinating area of research in which primary sources are hard to come by, or, as the researcher himself puts it, "It is fun to be in sort of scholarly disagreement in such a 'fun' area as this Dracula business . . ."[7]

Based on his experiences as a youth in Transylvania, his knowledge of the Romanian language, translations of court records, and other documentary evidence, Meder hypothesizes quite simply that Dracula was (is?!) a woman— "a beautiful, seductive, evil noblewoman of highest society. . . ."[8] As one piece of evidence, Meder cites the fact that "Dracula" translates into English literally as "the female devil." Further, there is a known historic figure, Countess Elizabeth Bathory of Transylvania, who in the 17th century was proven guilty in the highest court of the direct blood-ritual murders of more than 600 young girls. Convinced that the blood

---

[6]For more complete information on historical research, see Berlinger, R. E. (1978). *Historical analysis: Contemporary approaches to Clio's craft*. New York: John Wiley & Sons; *and* Brickman, W. W. (1982). *Educational historiography: Tradition, theory and technique*. Cherry Hill, NJ: Emeritus.

[7]Z. Meder. (personal communication, November 17, 1974)

[8]Meder, Z. *Dracula is a woman*. Manuscript in preparation. Note: When the first edition of this text was being written, Dr. Meder was contacted for additional information on his theory. During a lengthy visit, he was kind enough to share the picture of Elizabeth Bathory, which appears at the beginning of this chapter, and to discuss his work. He had spent his youth in Transylvania and, more recently, his summers. His goal was to spend an extended period of time there, collecting information related to his theory. Since then, attempts to contact him, in order to update this footnote and determine the status of his manuscript, have been futile. Letters sent to his last known address have been returned, and the university at which he taught claims no knowledge of his whereabouts. Honest.

of beautiful young virgins was the key to eternal beauty and youth, the Countess would bathe in the warm blood drained from their main blood vessel. According to Meder, "scores of legal documents still exist in the Hungarian archives to attest to the truth of these blood orgies." Because of her high rank, she was only locked up in her bed-chamber where she was later found dead, lying face down on the floor, the characteristic position of the undead in the Dracula legend. Since nobody actually saw her die, and since the guard who found her only saw her lying face down, it is easy to see how stories could be originated suggesting that she did not really die, but rather escaped to continue her ghastly pursuits.

As further evidence, Meder describes a painting titled *Elizabeth Bathory*, by István Csók, that seems to depict preparations for a blood bath. The female image of Dracula is also supported by another painting by Csók, titled *The Vampires*, showing a woman sucking blood from the neck artery of a young victim.

In his work, Meder also refutes the evidence presented by McNally and Florescu in *In Search of Dracula* identifying Dracula with a male Wallachian ruler who was known as Vlad the Impaler.[9] Meder questions not their evidence or its veracity, but rather its consistency with the Dracula legend. Regardless of who is correct, the question of Dracula's sex is, as Meder puts it, definitely a "fun" area of historical research.[10]

On the following pages an example of historical research is presented. Note that the study was based on primary sources of data.

---

[9]McNally, R. T., & Florescu, R. (1972). *In search of Dracula*. Greenwich, CT: New York Graphic Society.

[10]Fourth edition note (see footnote 8): Following publication of the third edition of this text, I discovered that in 1983 McGraw-Hill published a book titled *Dracula was a Woman*(!), written by R. T. McNally (!!), which includes the same information as the Meder manuscript. McNally (personal communication, June 21, 1990) claims no knowledge of Meder's existence or work. I swear, I'm not making this up.

JRME, VOLUME 38, NUMBER 2, PAGES 79–89

This article describes the development of Louisville public school music from its establishment in 1844 to its suspension in 1879. Rationales for music's introduction, debates over teaching methods, and choices of music curricula are examined within the context of Louisville society. Primary sources are used, including minutes and annual reports of the Louisville school board and accounts of mid–nineteenth-century historians. Although Louisville's early school music program had unique aspects, its development for the most part paralleled that of school music programs in other American cities. School board arguments in favor of music instruction focused on music's intellectual, physical, moral, and social benefits to students. Both "rote" and "note" teaching methods were used with success. Music curricula included books and series containing folk songs, songs by the authors of the books, and adaptations of songs by European composers. The music was simple in rhythm, melody, harmony, and form, and song texts were polite and sentimental.

Martha Chrisman Riley, *Purdue University*

Portrait of a Nineteenth-Century School Music Program

Each sketch of music education activities in a particular time or place contributes to the overall picture of American music education. This portrait of early school music education in Louisville, Kentucky, is particularly important since Louisville was one of the first cities to include music in the public school curriculum. One of the most influential American music educators of the nineteenth century, Luther Whiting Mason, began his career there. This article describes the beginning of public school music in Louisville, the subsequent struggles and strengths of the program, the debate over "note" versus "rote" teaching methods, and the music books and song repertoire chosen for instruction and performance. Was Louisville's early school music program unique, or was it typical of music education in other American cities during the same period? A study of this question provides insight into nineteenth-century music education in America.

This study is based on the author's doctoral dissertation, "Popular Songs of the Genteel Tradition: Their Influence on Music Education in Public Schools of Louisville, Kentucky, from 1850 to 1880," completed at the University of Minnesota, Minneapolis, in 1985. For copies of this article, contact Martha C. Riley, Division of Music, CA #3, Purdue University, West Lafayette, IN 47907.

193

Historical Setting

In the early 1800s, Louisville was a bustling and prosperous city. The town had grown rapidly since its establishment in the 1770s due to its accessible location on the southern bank of the Ohio River. River trade was brisk, and Louisville benefited greatly from the fact that all passengers and merchandise going between New England and New Orleans had to pass through the town. By 1820, the city had a population of 10,000 and had become a cultural center of the West.

Musical activities in Louisville reflected cultural trends of New England cities. In 1820, only five years after the founding of the Boston Handel and Haydn Society, a musical society was founded in Louisville (Casseday 1852). By the 1860s, there were at least seven musical societies, including the hundred-member Mozart Society, which presented monthly choral concerts, and the forty-member Musical Fund Society, which performed large instrumental works (Campbell 1864). Before railroads were in operation, concert artists made their way down the Ohio River to Louisville by steamboat. The arrival of railroads in the 1840s made the city even more accessible, and touring opera companies, minstrel troupes, and family singing groups performed there annually.

The public enthusiasm for parlor music that swept across the country around the middle of the century was evident in Louisville as well. In 1850, there were at least three music stores that sold sheet music and pianos, three music publishers, and one piano and organ manufacturer (Casseday 1852). Private music instruction was a booming business. Music lessons were fashionable, and many people considered them a necessary part of a nineteenth-century genteel education. Young ladies or gentlemen could receive music instruction from one of Louisville's thirty private teachers (Casseday 1852) or at any of the exclusive male or female seminaries. The decision to offer music in the public schools was, in part, an attempt by the school board to make the public school curriculum more like that of the private seminaries and thus more attractive to the general public.

Introduction of Music into the Louisville Schools

Music became an official part of the Louisville public school curriculum in 1844 (Louisville Board of Education 1844), just six years after Boston had established its public school music program. Boston's lead had been followed by Chicago, Baltimore, and a few small northern cities, but Louisville was the first southern city officially to include music.

The first music teacher was William C. Van Meter, who was paid a modest salary of $350 for the 1844–45 school year. Unfortunately, funding for the music position decreased the following year; in fact, Van Meter taught without pay for half the year (Louisville Board of Education 1845). He resigned his post in 1846 and was not immediately replaced.[1]

In 1852 the school board employed Luther Whiting Mason and William Fallin to teach in the city's six grammar schools. The original plan was to give each teacher three of the schools on a trial basis, hold an examination after three months to determine which teacher had made the most progress with his pupils, then hire the better of the two to instruct all six schools. The examination consisted of a public performance by each teacher's pupils, judged by five school board members and four "musical gentlemen" from the community (Louisville Board of Education 1853). The conclusion of the judges and the enthusiastic audience was that both teachers were equally competent, and so both were retained.

Mason and Fallin taught in the Louisville schools for several years. The primary schools were added to their schedules in 1853. This was a progressive action on the part of Louisville; even in Boston, music was not taught in primary schools until 1864. School board members heartily supported the music program, praising the physical, intellectual, social, and religious benefits gained from the study of music (Louisville Board of Education 1853). The superintendent felt music instruction was responsible for an increased interest of Louisville citizens in the schools as well (Board of Trustees 1853).[2] The importance of music instruction in the eyes of the school board is evident in the fact that Mason and Fallin were paid the highest salaries of any teachers in the school system (Board of Trustees 1853).

In June 1855, Fallin resigned for unexplained reasons. In the middle of the 1855–56 school year, Mason also resigned. Mason's resignation may have been due, in part, to his unpopularity in some of the schools. He had been reprimanded by the school board for losing his temper and speaking in a disrespectful manner, for pinching and pulling students' ears, and for hitting students on the head and hands with his violin bow (Louisville Board of Education 1854). On one occasion, the board had received a petition signed by forty-three people complaining of the "conduct of Mr. L. W. Mason, singing teacher for the Western district, and requesting his discontinuance" (Louisville Board of Education 1854, Vol. B, 264).[3] Mason and Fallin's positions were filled by several different music teachers over the next few years.[4]

In 1857, the Louisville music program was abruptly suspended. Although there is nothing in the school board minutes that states the reason for its suspension, it was no doubt related to the retirement of the president of the board, Reverend John H. Heywood, in 1856. Heywood had been the music program's most ardent supporter. It was he who had urged the board to hire Mason and Fallin in 1852, and who, the following year, had successfully introduced music into the primary schools as well. It was his influence that had obtained the high salaries for the music teachers. After Heywood's retirement, enthusiasm for the music program diminished, and it was nearly ten years before music regained a solid position in the curriculum.

Reestablishment of the Music Program

During the Civil War years, 1861–65, Louisville's primary and grammar schools were used as military hospitals. Classes continued to be held in church basements and rented buildings, but the financial situation made it impossible for any but the most basic subjects to be taught. Music was offered in the Female High School, however. For several years, Professor H. G. S. Whipple had taught music lessons independently at the high school, being paid directly by his students. In 1861, the school board officially hired him to teach three classes a week to all the young ladies.

Near the end of the war a demand arose for the reintroduction of music in the primary and grammar schools. Parents went so far as to collect enough money to rent pianos and employ teachers in several schools. Over $300 was collected in the Sixth Ward school alone, and there were five pianos in that building during the 1864–65 school year (Board of Trustees 1865).[5] The strong interest of parents in the matter forced the school board to reestablish the music program, and, in 1866, music was again made part of the curriculum. School board members justified music instruction on the basis of its moral, religious, and patriotic values. In addition, they felt music instruction would help children of lower social classes fit into the mainstream of Louisville's cultural society by enabling "the child of the humblest citizens [to] read the printed page of music by the side of the child of wealth." (Board of Trustees 1865, 59)

During the fall of 1866, Professor Whipple and his assistant attempted to teach music twice a week to every class in grades 1–8 and the Female High School, but the large number of schools made this schedule impossible to maintain. To ease the load, they dropped the primary grades from their schedules and offered methods courses to the primary teachers instead. In 1868, a third music teacher was employed. As the number of schools continued to increase, the music teachers cut the number of lessons from two to one per week. The board also hired a fourth teacher, Florence Hull, to teach music in the primary schools, the normal school's laboratory, and, for the first time, in the black schools (Louisville Board of Education 1872).

During the years immediately following the Civil War, the music program received strong support from the school board and the superintendent. The board defended music with references to improved discipline, physical health, class morale, and speech. The superintendent stressed the importance of music's aesthetic value. The strong Romantic influence of the nineteenth century is evident in his statement about the value of developing children's affective responses to music:

> Its study is the culture and embellishment of that portion of the human faculties usually included in the comprehensive term, the heart. Its tendencies are all refining, elevating, humanizing . . . . By the knowledge of music thus acquired, the child is made susceptible to the melting influences of songs sung round the fireside and the home, and the memory of which, in after years, when he has wandered far away from the parental roof, may bring back to him all the subtle influences linked therewith, tending to awaken in him the affections, soften the stubborn heart, and reclaim the wanderer. (Board of Trustees 1870, 110–111)

With the changing of school board members in 1872, interest in the program began to wane. The new president of the board felt that music instruction was a waste of time and that more attention should be paid to academic studies (Board of Trustees 1872). In 1876 there were four music teachers; in 1877, there were two; and in 1879, the music department was eliminated entirely.[6]

Thus, the first era of public school music education in Louisville came to an end. Although the program had known periods of considerable strength, its stability was always dependent on the attitudes of the current school board members. Its strongest years were the 1852–56 period when Reverend Heywood was president of the board and worked energetically to develop the program, and the ten-year period following the Civil War, when parents, board members, and the superintendent were outspoken advocates of the value of music instruction. Although music was taught by classroom teachers during the 1880s, it was not until 1892 that a unified course of music instruction began to be rebuilt.

Teaching Methods

Almost immediately after music was introduced into the Boston schools, the controversy over "note" teaching versus "rote" teaching commenced. Beginning with Joseph Bird's 1850 pamphlet, in which he voiced objections to Lowell Mason's rote song methods, advocates of both sides vigorously expressed their opinions through speeches and papers (John 1953). The debate was carried on in Louisville as well. In the 1850s, Luther Whiting Mason used a rote teaching approach while William Fallin stressed note reading. Fallin's approach, which followed the singing-school tradition, was the more generally accepted method. He drilled the children on the principles and symbols of music before allowing them to sing. When his students were finally given a piece of music, they were able to sing it at once at sight. In a letter to the *Louisville Journal* in 1854, one concerned citizen highly praised Fallin's teaching method while criticizing Mason's rote approach as unscientific and totally in error (McConathy 1922).

In spite of such skepticism, Mason's method was also quite successful. Mason had his students imitate intervals and tunes before presenting the notation. His students were able to sing scales by each of the intervals and to take difficult dictation exercises with complete accuracy. Members of the Boston Germania Band, while on a concert tour in 1854, observed Mason's classes and commended him for making his pupils "thoroughly acquainted with the rudiments of music without stuffing their heads with far-sought and, to children, incomprehensible expressions" (McConathy 1922, 161). The school board was unconcerned about the variance in teaching methods of the two music professors, allowing each to proceed in his own manner.

In the 1860s, the school board adopted a curriculum that all three music teachers were supposed to follow. The course of instruction was a combination of rote and note methods. The youngest children learned songs by imitation, but they also practiced drawing notes and reading simple scale exercises. Children in the middle grades learned songs by note as well as by rote, studied more advanced theory, and took dictation. Junior high and high school students were expected to be proficient sight-readers (Board of Trustees 1868). Although the instruction books adopted for the music classes changed every few years, the general course of instruction remained the same from that time until the 1880s. Students were required to purchase the music book assigned to their class.

Music Books and Song Repertoire

Eleven vocal instruction books were adopted by the Louisville school board during the first period of the music program. The first two were chosen by Mason and Fallin: William Bradbury's *The Singing Bird* (1852) and George F. Root's *The Academy Vocalist* (1852). *The Singing Bird* contained folk songs and composed songs for young children, with exercises interspersed among the songs. *The Academy Vocalist* began with a treatise on music theory followed by a large section of exercises. The repertoire was geared toward older students and included arrangements of songs by Donizetti, Rossini, Handel, Mendelssohn, and Bellini, as well as many songs by Root himself.

Following the Civil War, the board adopted Lowell Mason's three-volume *Song Garden* (1864). This was the first set of instruction books to be called a music "series," and the books were used by many school systems, including those of Washington, D.C. and St. Louis (John 1953). The repertoire of these volumes included a large number of German folk songs.

Three new instruction books were adopted in 1870. George Loomis' *First Steps in Music, Second Book*, whose first edition was published in 1868, was chosen for the youngest pupils. (Since no 1868 edition was available for study, the author examined the second edition [Loomis 1875] for analysis of contents.) Loomis' series enjoyed popularity as the first graded series that attempted to teach music reading in a child-developmental way, beginning with a one-line staff, then two lines, and so forth (John 1953). W. O. Perkins's *Golden Robin* (1868) was assigned to the intermediate grades, and Perkins's *The Laurel Wreath* (1870) was selected for the Female High School. Each of Perkins's books was divided into sections that included a theoretical introduction, exercises, a large number of part songs, and sacred songs. Perkins wrote many of the songs.

The last set of books to be adopted before the music program was suspended was the 1870–71 version of Luther Whiting Mason's *National Music Course* (Mason 1870, 1871a, 1871b). Complete sets of books and accompanying charts were donated to each school by a Louisville citizen "of high musical taste" (Board of Trustees 1871, 33). This series was widely used, not only in America but also in Germany and Japan (John 1953). The books contained no treatises on the elements of music; Mason advocated rote teaching in the beginning. The repertoire in these three relatively small books included folk songs and songs by European, particularly German, composers.

The music in all eleven books used in Louisville was simple with respect to rhythm, melody, harmony, and form. The songs were written for one to four voices, with rounds and three-part songs predominating. The standard form was the rounded binary (AABA), though bar form (AAB) was frequently found in the German folk songs. Rhythms were straightforward and repetitious. Melodies were nearly all major in tonality. Harmonies consisted of tonic and dominant chords, with some subdominants and secondary dominants. Texts were set syllabically. In general, the songs were quite tuneful and singable, though many had wide ranges and frequent large leaps.

Over one-fifth of the songs had religious or moral texts. These included hymns to open and close the school day and songs of praise to God. Though religious instruction was prohibited in the Louisville schools (*History of the Ohio Falls Cities* 1882), members of the school board approved of and encouraged the singing of religious songs. Their opinion was:

> If our children cannot all join in a common confession and prayer, they can all unite in a song of praise to the Creator. (Board of Trustees 1868, 31)

Songs of philosophy and advice were also common. Children were instructed to manage their time wisely, honor their elders, and stay out of trouble. Songs about nature were the most frequent type in the books for younger children. Each season was depicted romantically in song: spring songs featured birds and flowers, tinkling brooks, and gentle showers; summer songs described bright sun, blue skies, and warm breezes; autumn songs portrayed colorful forests and harvesttime. Other songs focused on specific aspects of nature, such as rainbows, mountains, or snow. Animal songs were also common in young children's books. The most popular creatures were lambs, foxes, ponies, dogs and cats, rabbits, fish, bees, butterflies, and many types of birds.

All the books contained songs about home and family. Images of the family sitting together around the fire, children playing, and babies sleeping were common. These happy songs portrayed in a romantic and rosy light such everyday activities as kissing mother good morning or waiting for papa to come home from work.

Songs of school were also found in all the books. Though some of these were intended for instructional purposes, such as to help memorize multiplication tables, most had texts of love and devotion to school, teachers, and classmates. Other categories included patriotic songs, songs about occupations or recreation, and songs in praise of music.

In general, a sentimental and genteel tone ran through all the song texts. Childhood was portrayed as a happy time, although children's songs were refined and polite, never silly, and rarely even humorous. Reverence for God, love of home and family, and loyalty to friends and country were set forth as important values. In addition, children were encouraged to study hard, avoid temptation, and follow the Golden Rule.

Public Performances

Music performances given by Louisville children were well received by parents, the school board, and the general public. Concerts of Professor Whipple's students were publicized in local newspapers. In 1863, the annual performance of a popular touring group, "The Continental Old Folks," generated a "Little Folks Old Folks Concert." Professor Whipple conducted this imitation of the adult concert, which included popular and patriotic songs, solos, and duets by such "artists" as Little Red Riding Hood, Goody Two Shoes, The First Bride of Huntsville, and Queen Elizabeth ([Louisville] *Daily Democrat* 1863). The program was such a success that the citizens demanded a repeat performance, which was cheerfully given. The following year, Whipple conducted his young ladies in a staged production of a children's operetta by George F. Root, *The Flower Queen, or The Coronation of the Rose* (1853).[7] This also was repeated a few years later.

Louisville citizens could also hear Whipple's students during the annual commencement exercises of the Female High School. These performances included opera arias, duets, and choruses, and were similar to the programs presented by touring concert artists of the mid-nineteenth century. Some of the composers represented in the programs were Mozart, Donizetti, Weber, Rossini, Meyerbeer, Bellini, Verdi, Mendelssohn, and Gounod.[8]

Conclusions

Louisville was pioneering in that it was the first southern city to include music in the school curriculum and the first city in the country to include music instruction in its primary schools. With respect to school board support, teaching methods, and choices of curricula, however, Louisville's music education program was typical of music programs in other major American cities during the same period.

The Louisville school board endorsed music instruction because of its perceived moral, intellectual, physical, patriotic, social, and religious benefits to the students. In addition, the superintendent stressed the importance of developing children's aesthetic responses to music. These arguments were similar to those used by the Boston School Committee and other school boards of the day. Additional reasons were the board's desire to make the public school curriculum more attractive to the general population, the need to satisfy parents who demanded music instruction, and the attempt to provide children of lower social classes with musical opportunities in order to help them fit into the genteel social and cultural life of the city.

Problems encountered by the Louisville music program were similar to difficulties faced by other nineteenth-century schools: (1) financial problems, resulting in the paring down of the curriculum and the maintenance of the "basics" at the expense of music; and (2) disinterest of school board members in the subject. In Louisville, the attitude of the school board determined the quality of the program. A respected, outspoken, and persuasive member was able to effect tremendous change. It is interesting to note that these same issues continue to challenge today's music educators.

The rote-versus-note question that emerged in Louisville was not unique, though it was perhaps unusual to have teachers with such distinctly opposing viewpoints teaching in the same school system at such an early date. Music teachers everywhere debated the same issue, however, and the argument continues in American schools today. Louisville's resolve to combine the two approaches in a unified curriculum proved to be a successful solution there.

The music books chosen for instruction in the Louisville schools are representative of music books of the time; in fact, many of the books were used in other cities. The songs in these books were European folk songs, songs by the authors of the books in the popular style of the day, and adaptations of songs by European masters. They were uniformly simple in rhythm, melody, harmony, and form. Nearly all were major in tonality. Texts ranged from serious subjects, such as God and morality, to lighter themes of music and recreation, but all were polite and sentimental in tone. Louisville children's performances also reflected national trends. Root's *Flower Queen* was one of the most popular children's operettas in the country, and the Female High School's renditions of European opera selections were an echo of concerts of the time.

Though Louisville's early school music program had unique aspects, its development for the most part paralleled that of other programs. Thus, this portrait of music education in Louisville provides not only a glimpse of the events in that colorful and lively city, but a clearer view of music education in nineteenth-century America.

REFERENCES

Annual Report for the Year Ending July 1, 1853. 1853. Louisville, KY: Board of Trustees of the Public Schools of Louisville.

Annual Report of the Board of Trustees of the Male High School, Female High School, and Public Schools of Louisville to the General Council of the City of Louisville for the Scholastic Year of 1864–65. 1865. Louisville, KY: Bradley and Gilbert.

Annual Report of the Board of Trustees of the Male High School, Female High School, and Public Schools of Louisville to the General Council of the City of Louisville for the Scholastic Year of 1866–67. 1867. Louisville, KY: Hull and Brother.

Annual Report of the Board of Trustees of the Male High School, Female High School, and Public Schools of Louisville to the General Council of the City of Louisville for the Year Ending June 30, 1868. 1868. Louisville, KY: Bradley and Gilbert.

Annual Report of the Board of Trustees of the Male High School, Female High School, and Public Schools of Louisville to the General Council of the City of Louisville for the Year Ending June 30, 1870. 1870. Louisville, KY: Bradley and Gilbert.

Annual Report of the Board of Trustees of the Male High School, Female High School, and Public Schools of Louisville to the General Council of the City of Louisville for the Year Ending June 30, 1871. 1871. Louisville, KY: Bradley and Gilbert.

Annual Report of the Board of Trustees of the Male High School, Female High School, and Public Schools of Louisville to the General Council of the City of Louisville for the Year Ending June 30, 1872. 1872. Louisville, KY: Bradley and Gilbert.

Bradbury, W. B. 1852. *The Singing Bird or Progressive Music Reader*. Chicago: S. C. Griggs and Co.

Campbell, J. D. 1864. *Louisville Business Directory for 1864*. Louisville, KY: L. A. Civill.

Casseday, B. 1852. *The History of Louisville from Its Earliest Settlement till the Year 1852*. Louisville, KY: Hull and Brother.

Chrisman, M. C. 1985. "Popular Songs of the Genteel Tradition: Their Influence on Music Education in Public Schools of Louisville, Kentucky, from 1850 to 1880." Ph.D. diss., University of Minnesota, Minneapolis.

History of the Ohio Falls Cities and Their Counties, Vol. I. 1882. Cleveland: L. A. Williams.

John, R. W. 1953. "History of Vocal Instruction Books in the United States." Ph.D. diss., Indiana University, Bloomington.

Kapfer, M. B. 1964. "Music Instruction and Supervision in the Public Schools of Columbus, Ohio, from 1845 to 1900." Ph.D. diss., Indiana University, Bloomington.

Keen, J. A. 1982. *A History of Music Education in the United States*. Hanover, NH: United Press of New England.

Loomis, G. B. 1875. *Loomis's Progressive Music Lessons, Book Two*. New York: Ivison, Blakeman.

Louisville Board of Education. 1844–1880. *Minutes of the Board of Education of Louisville*, Vols. A–D. Unpublished journals in the Louisville Board of Education Archives, Louisville, KY.

The [Louisville] *Daily Democrat*, June 9, 1863. University of Kentucky Library, Lexington, p. 2.

Mason, L. 1864–1866. *The Song Garden* (Vols. 1–3). New York: Mason Brothers.

Mason, L. W. 1870. *Second Music Reader*. Boston: Ginn, Heath.

———. 1871a. *First Music Reader*. Boston: New England Conservatory of Music.

———. 1871b. *Third Music Reader*. Boston: Ginn, Heath.

McConathy, O. 1922. "Evolution of Public School Music in the United States," in *Volume of Proceedings of the Music Teachers National Association*. Vol. 55, 163–74.

Perkins, W. O. 1868. *The Golden Robin*. Boston: Oliver Ditson.

———. 1870. *The Laurel Wreath*. Boston: G. D. Russell.

Podrovsky, R. 1978. "A History of Music Education in the Chicago Public Schools." Ph.D. diss., Northwestern University.

Root, D. L. 1981. *American Popular Stage Music, 1860–1880*. Ann Arbor, MI: UMI Research Press.

Root, G. F. 1852. *The Academy Vocalist*. Boston: Oliver Ditson.

———. 1853. *The Flower Queen, or the Coronation of the Rose*. New York: Mason Brothers.

———. 1891. *The Story of a Musical Life*. Cincinnati, OH: John Church.

Troiano, A. B. 1984. "A History of the Development and Determinants of Milwaukee Public School Arts Policy from 1870 to 1930." Ph.D. diss., University of Wisconsin–Milwaukee.

NOTES

1. William C. Van Meter subsequently moved to New York where he developed a reputation as a distinguished music teacher. In 1855, along with George F. Root, he led the first musical convention held in Virginia. Root described Van Meter as "a preacher, exhorter, singing-master . . . eloquent and magnetic as a speaker in his strange western

way . . . . Let Mr. Van Meter get an audience together and there was no resisting him. He could make people laugh or cry at will and paint in more glowing colors whatever he described than any man I ever knew. He always induced a large number of people to attend conventions" (G. F. Root 1891, 102).

2. In the 1840s, teachers and administrators in the public schools of Columbus, Ohio, also used music as a means of drawing public attention to the schools and increasing public interest and acceptance (Kapfer 1964).

3. After leaving Louisville, Mason took the position of superintendent of music in the Cincinnati schools, where he developed a strong and positive reputation as a successful music teacher. In 1864, he went to Boston where he introduced music into the primary schools and published his *National Music Course* (1870–75), one of the first graded music series. Mason later led music training institutes in Boston and served as governmental music supervisor for Japan, where his influence was so great that school music there was known as "Mason Song" (Keene 1982).

4. Louisville public school music teachers from 1855 to 1857 were Louis Tripp, who subsequently went into the music sales and publishing business, Nelson Hyatt, and John Harvey. Charles Godfrey taught music from 1858 to 1860.

5. Parental involvement in school music instruction was not unique to Louisville. In Chicago, money was collected to pay a public school music teacher as early as 1847 (Podrovsky 1978). Music lessons were also funded by parents in Milwaukee public schools in the 1860s, eventually forcing the school board there to hire a music teacher in order to control the instruction (Troiano 1984).

6. Music teachers between 1866 and 1879 were H. G. S. Whipple, M. F. Price, Herman Glagan, Joseph Clark, J. W. Lurton (who taught for only four months in 1869), Green H. Anderson, and Florence Hull.

7. *The Flower Queen* is the story of a gathering of flowers in the forest to choose a queen. A depressed recluse happens by and is drafted by the flowers to make the selection. As each flower sings a solo, the recluse is warmed by their teachings of love, goodwill, piety, kindness, and beauty. He chooses the rose to receive the crown while he, himself, is rescued from despair and solitude and returns to the world rejuvenated.

 The Flower Queen was Root's first children's cantata. It became popular immediately, and, within ten months of its publication, it had been performed in Maine, Rhode Island, New York, New Jersey, and Georgia (D. L. Root 1981)

8. The complete programs are listed in the annual reports of the Louisville Board of Trustees for 1867 through 1876 and in a doctoral dissertation by Martha C. Chrisman (1985).

September 6, 1988

■ SUMMARY/CHAPTER 6
DEFINITION AND PURPOSE

1. Historical research is the systematic collection and objective evaluation of data related to past occurrences in order to test hypotheses concerning causes, effects, or trends of these events that may help to explain present events and anticipate future events.

THE HISTORICAL RESEARCH PROCESS

2. The steps involved in conducting a historical research study are essentially the same as for other types of research; definition of a problem, formulation of questions to be answered or hypotheses to be tested, systematic collection of data, evaluation of data, and production of a verbal synthesis of findings or confirmation/disconfirmation of hypotheses.

Definition of a Problem

3. The purpose of a historical research study should be to explain or predict, not to rehash.
4. The historical researcher is basically limited to whatever data are already available.
5. It is much better to study in depth a well defined problem with one or more specific, well-stated questions or hypotheses, than to investigate either a too broadly stated problem or a problem for which insufficient data are available.

Data Collection

6. In a historical research study, the review of related literature and study procedures are part of the same process.
7. The term "literature" takes on a much broader meaning in a historical study and refers to all sorts of written communication; in addition, identification, acquisition, and review of such "literature" is considerably more complex.
8. The written communication may be in the form of legal documents, records, minutes of meetings, letters, and other documents which will not normally be indexed alphabetically by subject, author, and title in a library.
9. A historical research study in education may also involve interviews with persons who participated in the event or process under investigation, if it occurred in the recent past.
10. Primary sources constitute firsthand information, such as original documents and reports by actual participants or direct observers; secondary sources constitute secondhand information, such as reference books (encyclopedias, for example) or reports by relatives of actual participants or observers.
11. A common criticism of historical research is excessive reliance on secondary sources.

Data Analysis: External and Internal Criticism

12. All sources of historical data must be subjected to rigorous scientific analysis to determine both their authenticity (external criticism) and their accuracy (internal criticism).

13. In determining the accuracy of documents, there are at least four factors that must be considered: knowledge and competence of the author, the time delay between the occurrence and recording of events, biased motives of the author, and consistency of the data.

Data Synthesis

14. As with a review of related literature, historical data should be organized and synthesized, and conclusions and generalizations formulated.

15. Since summarization of historical research data involves logical analysis rather than statistical analysis, the researcher must take care to be as objective as possible.

"No qualitative researcher can be amazing enough, brilliant enough, or experienced enough to observe *everything* of interest in a given environment . . . (p. 213)."

Qualitative Research

After reading Chapter 7, you should be able to:

1. Briefly differentiate between the overall purpose of qualitative versus quantitative research.

2. Identify and briefly describe the major differences between sampling in a qualitative versus quantitative study.

3. Identify and briefly describe the major differences between measurement in a qualitative versus quantitative study.

4. Identify and briefly describe strategies used by qualitative researchers to insure the accuracy of data.

5. Identify and briefly describe the major differences between design and method in a qualitative versus quantitative study.

6. Identify and briefly describe the three major data collection strategies used in qualitative educational research.

7. Identify and briefly describe the two major types of fieldnotes.

8. Identify and briefly describe the major differences between data analysis in a qualitative versus quantitative study.

9. Briefly differentiate between conclusions and generalizations in a qualitative versus quantitative study.

10. Identify and briefly describe a major advantage and a major disadvantage of qualitative research.

■ DEFINITION AND PURPOSE

Simplistically put, qualitative research is the collection and analysis of extensive narrative data in order to gain insights into a situation of interest not possible using other types of research. But, you may be thinking, historical research fits that definition. And you are correct; historical research can definitely be considered to be a type of qualitative research. As the term is generally used, however, qualitative research is much broader in scope and its purpose is to promote greater understanding of not just the way things are, but also *why*. Thus, a qualitative study may well utilize historical methods in order to gain a better perspective on the person, place, object, or activity under study.

The term "qualitative research" is used not so much because it accurately describes a unique strategy of inquiry, but rather because it conveniently differentiates it from what we refer to as quantitative research. Descriptive, correlational, causal-comparative, and experimental research (to be discussed in Chapters 8–11) are all considered to be quantitative research because they all involve primarily the collection and analysis of *numerical* data, e.g., test scores. Qualitative research, on the other hand, involves for the most part nonnumerical data, such as extensive notes taken on site. Thus, in this and subsequent sections, an attempt will be made to facilitate your comprehension of both "qualitative" and "quantitative" research by comparing and contrasting the two. As you read this chapter, you will learn that qualitative research involves in- depth descriptions of who or what is being studied and you may wonder why this information is not included in Chapter 8, Descriptive Research. The reason is that the term "descriptive" research has traditionally been applied to studies which describe the way things are *using numbers,* questionnaire studies for example.

Definition

Qualitative research can best be "defined" by describing what it entails and its rationale. Qualitative research involves intensive data collection, that is, collection of extensive data on many variables over an extended period of time, in a naturalistic setting. The term "naturalistic setting" refers to the fact that the variables being investigated are studied *where* they naturally occur, *as* they naturally occur, not in researcher-controlled environments under researcher-controlled conditions, as is the case with quantitative studies. Because of the naturalistic settings characteristic of qualitative research, it is frequently referred to as naturalistic research, naturalistic inquiry, or field research. Further, because of its extensive use in the study of both human and animal cultures, it is also often referred to as ethnographic or anthropological research. In fact, some researchers use the terms "ethnographic" and "qualitative" interchangeably, while others consider ethnography to be *one kind* of qualitative research.[1] However, while some individuals may have strong feelings regarding the theoretically most appropriate label for such research, in practice it is generally referred to as qualitative research, at least in the field of education. And, while the frequency of qualitative studies has increased significantly in education, it is a strategy of inquiry which is by no means unique to education; it has been used for many years, as suggested above, in such diverse areas as anthropology, psychology, and sociology.

---

[1] Bogdan, R. C., & Biklen, S. K. (1992). *Qualitative research for education: An introduction to theory and methods* (2nd ed.). Boston: Allyn and Bacon.

The main reason for the growing enthusiasm for qualitative research in education is probably dissatisfaction with more traditional, quantitative approaches for investigating certain kinds of educational problems and questions, those which do not lend themselves well to numerical analysis. The rationale behind the use of qualitative inquiry is the research-based belief that behavior is significantly influenced by the environment in which it occurs. In other words, behavior occurs in a context and a more complete understanding of the behavior requires understanding of the context in which it occurs. Organizations such as schools, for example, definitely influence the behavior of persons within them.[2] Thus, qualitative researchers are not just concerned with describing the ways things are, but also with gaining insights into the "big picture." They seek answers to questions related to how things got to be the way they are, how people involved *feel* about the way things are, what they *believe*, what *meanings* they attach to various activities, and so forth. In other words, qualitative researchers attempt to obtain a holistic, in-depth understanding of the phenomenon under study. As qualitative researchers point out, if we wish our findings to have relevance to real-world settings, the findings should be derived from research conducted in real-world settings.

In order to achieve the objective of in-depth understanding, qualitative research utilizes a variety of methods and data collection strategies, and is often characterized as being "multimethod." The most common strategy used, however, is participant observation, usually supplemented by collection of relevant documents and extensive, informal interviewing. Participant observation (to be discussed later) basically involves the researcher immersing herself or himself in the setting of interest, observing as much as possible and taking extensive notes. *What* is observed is typically a single "unit" (or a small number of units). A unit may be (as examples) a school, a program, a classroom, an administrator, a teacher, or a student. A researcher, for instance, might be interested in gaining insight into what makes an outstanding teacher "outstanding." This is a complex question, to say the least. Having identified an outstanding teacher, perhaps the "teacher of the year" in a particular location, the researcher would observe factors such as the physical appearance of the teacher's classroom, the teacher's methods of instruction, and interactions between the teacher and his or her students. In addition to observing, the researcher would likely collect "documents" such as the teacher's lesson plans and instructional materials, and would interview the teacher, as well as a sample of the teacher's superiors (e.g., principal), colleagues, and students. This intensive data collection would go on for an extended period of time such as a semester or even a full school year.

In contrast, a quantitative study of outstanding teachers would involve the collection of limited, standardized, numerical data on a number of outstanding teachers. Questionnaires and/or rating scales, for example, might be administered to the students of 20 teachers identified as outstanding. Data for outstanding teachers might be compared to data for, shall we say, not-so-outstanding teachers. The objective would be to identify one or more generalizable variables which characterize outstanding teachers. This contrasting example is not meant to suggest that qualitative research and quantitative research are definitionally mutually exclusive. A qualitative study, for example, may include numerical data (such as attendance records) and a quantitative study may include narrative data (such as responses to an open-ended question on a questionnaire). There are, however, several major conceptual issues which differentiate the two approaches to inquiry.

---

[2]Wilson, S. (1977). The use of ethnographic techniques in educational research. *Review of Educational Research, 47,* 245–265.

At a very basic level is the question of values. Quantitative researchers are characterized by a desire to be totally objective, i.e., value-free, in their investigations. Qualitative researchers, on the other hand, argue that there is no such thing as "value-free science" and that the values and beliefs of both the researcher and the phenomena studied are important variables which, to the degree possible, should be taken into consideration when conducting, reporting, or reviewing research.[3] And, of course, they have a point. Even the most "objective" quantitative researcher, for example, has values and beliefs which affect her or his research.

At a more operational level, qualitative research is more holistic and process-oriented, whereas quantitative research is more focused and outcome-oriented. Qualitative researchers study many variables intensely over an extended period of time in order to find out the way things are, how and why they came to be that way, and what it all means, to both those directly involved and to consumers of the information. The fact that they study only one or a few "units" (e.g., classrooms) allows them to do this. Quantitative researchers, conversely, concentrate on rigorously measuring one or a small number of variables in order to describe current conditions or to investigate relationships, including cause-and-effect relationships (as in an experimental study). Because they are more concerned with the generalizability of their findings than with the meaning of those findings, quantitative researchers typically collect data from as many subjects as is feasible, using sampling techniques described in Chapter 4. Thus, for example, a qualitative researcher might observe many aspects of a cooperative learning environment in one class, for one entire school year, in order to get a handle on what made it effective or ineffective. A quantitative researcher, on the other hand, might compare the achievement scores of two comparable, relatively large, groups of students, one which had participated in cooperative learning for the entire school year and one which had not participated in cooperative learning, in order to determine if cooperative learning had a significant impact on achievement.

As the above discussion suggests, a very real difference between qualitative and quantitative research is the degree of control involved. Qualitative researchers do not wish to control anything; they want to study phenomena as they are, in natural settings. They therefore prefer research strategies such as observation and interviewing. Quantitative researchers attempt to control as many variables as possible. They therefore prefer research strategies such as random sampling, use of standardized instruments and, when appropriate, equalizing of conditions of groups to be compared. In other words, the issue really revolves around setting and degree of control sought, not methodology utilized, although various strategies of inquiry are typically associated with qualitative or quantitative research.[4]

The "power of qualitative data," as Patton (1990, p. 19) puts it, is illustrated by the outcome of an evaluation of a new accountability system which was implemented by the Kalamazoo, Michigan, school system in the seventies.[5] It was a "complex" system that included using both standardized achievement tests and criterion-referenced tests, performance objectives, ratings of teachers by peers, students, par-

---

[3]Denzin, N. K., & Lincoln, Y. S. (Eds.). (1994). *Handbook of qualitative research* (p. 3). Thousand Oaks, CA: Sage.

[4]Guba, E. G. (1981). Criteria for assessing the trustworthiness of naturalistic inquiries. *Educational Communication and Technology Journal, 29,* 75–91.

[5]Patton, M. Q. (1990). *Qualitative evaluation and research methods* (2nd ed.). Thousand Oaks, CA: Sage.

ents, and principals, as well as teacher self-ratings. While the new system attracted national attention and was given very positive reviews, the teachers involved definitely did not like it and the Kalamazoo Education Association claimed that the teachers were being demoralized. Some, however, felt that the teachers just did not want to be accountable. Subsequently, a survey of teachers was conducted to assess their views on the program. The results overwhelmingly confirmed that teachers believed the accountability system was a very bad one which did not contribute to enhancing teacher effectiveness. For example, 97% of those responding agreed that

> Accountability as practiced in Kalamazoo places too much
> emphasis on things that can be quantified so that it misses
> the results of teaching that are not easily measured.

But high-level school officials and school board members dismissed the results of the questionnaire and felt that they had been biased by teacher union leaders.

The questionnaire, however, had provided two places for teachers to make comments and 70% of those who responded to the questionnaire expressed their opinions. The decision makers were given all the open-ended responses and encouraged to select at random and to read as many as they wished. On virtually any page comments such as the following were found:

> In 10 years of teaching I have never ended a school year as
> depressed about "education" as I have this year. If things
> do not improve in the next 2 years, I will leave education.
> The Kalamazoo accountability system is oppressive and
> stifling.

> The superintendent with his accountability model and his
> abrasive condescending manner has managed in three short
> years to destroy teacher morale and effective creative class-
> room teaching.

Comments such as these had a definite effect on the attitude of the school board members. The discussion shifted from denouncement of the questionnaire results to "What do you think we should do?"

To make a long story short, the superintendent "resigned" and a new accountability system was developed, one which was mutually acceptable to both teachers and administrators. While the teacher comments represented but one of many factors which affected these developments, they definitely had a significant impact.

Purpose

Recall (from Chapter 1) that the scientific method involves *induction* of hypotheses based on observation, *deduction* of implications of the hypotheses, testing of the implications, and confirmation or disconfirmation of the hypotheses. Thus, qualitative and quantitative research represent complementary components of the scientific method.

Qualitative research is clearly inductive. Through intensive and extensive observation, the qualitative researcher seeks to derive and describe findings that promote greater understanding of how and why people behave the way they do. When they share their findings, they present tentative answers, suggestions as it were, as to what they think is/was going on. They believe that human behavior is too complex to explain or predict based solely on theoretical considerations. Some qualitative researchers do try to contribute directly to the development of theory, but it is *grounded theory,* i.e., theory based on data collected in real-world settings which reflect what naturally occurred over an extended period of time. Such researchers may well formulate a tentative hypothesis, but usually not prior to execution of the study. If a qualitative study is strictly descriptive, the guiding research question will differ somewhat than if grounded theory development is involved. For example, for a descriptive study the question might be something like "What can we learn by studying the outstanding teacher selected for this research effort?" For a more grounded theory-oriented study, the research question might be something like "What can we learn by studying the outstanding teacher (or teachers) selected for this study that might have implications regarding the behavior of outstanding teachers in general?" Such a study may well end with a tentative hypothesis.

Quantitative research is clearly deductive. The quantitative researcher isolates the variables to be studied, formulates *in advance* a specific statement of a problem and a specific hypothesis to be tested (or question to be answered), collects standardized (i.e., the same) data from all study participants, analyzes the data in a way which permits the original hypothesis to be supported or not, and states conclusions related to generalizability. Such researchers attempt to control all relevant variables *except* those being studied. In their attempt to do so they often create environments that are to varying degrees artificial. Even if the research is conducted in a natural setting, it is usually modified somewhat to facilitate the desired control.

Thus, questions formulated for a qualitative study are much more general than for a quantitative study. For example, if the topic of interest were teacher burnout, related questions might include: "To what factors do teachers attribute their burnout?" "What behaviors do 'burned out' teachers and their students exhibit?" This is not to say that a qualitative researcher never has a tentative hypothesis prior to a study, but the key word is *tentative.* Unlike a quantitative hypothesis, a qualitative hypothesis is subject to ongoing revision throughout the study. It follows that the review of related literature, the study of previous research and theory, plays a significantly different role in qualitative and quantitative studies. In a qualitative study, as stated, the review does not result in a testable hypothesis to be supported or not supported. At most, the study of previous work may result in a very tentative hypothesis. The qualitative researcher does not want to be overly influenced by findings produced by the application of other methods of research; such studies probably did not involve careful study of the environment in which the results were obtained or, more likely, the results were obtained in an environment different from the one to which the results were intended to be generalizable. Thus, an extensive review of the literature is not characteristic of qualitative research. The qualitative researcher wants to be open enough to get insights not necessarily predictable based on past research efforts.

As you have probably figured out by now, since qualitative and quantitative research have significantly different purposes, both in general and with respect to any given research topic to be studied, they also differ significantly with respect to various aspects of design, procedure, and analysis. Table 7.1 summarizes major differences discussed so far and those to be discussed in the remainder of the chapter. Prior to the beginning of subsequent sections, the relevant portion of Table 7.1 will be presented as a mini-overview. Keep in mind that to some degree the contents of Table 7.1 represent an oversimplification since differences between a given qualitative study and a given quantitative study are not always so clear-cut. Conceptually, however, Table 7.1 should help you to understand typical differences between the two approaches to inquiry.

■ SAMPLING AND MEASUREMENT

The contents of Chapter 4, Selection of a Sample, apply almost exclusively to quantitative studies. As you will soon see, sampling in a qualitative study is usually quite different. Similarly, Chapter 5, Selection of Measuring Instruments, includes concepts and guidelines related to measurement in quantitative research. Measurement in qualitative studies has very little in common with measurement in quantitative studies. In qualitative research, for example, the researcher herself or himself is usually the only instrument! Thus, while underlying concerns are similar, e.g., the appropriateness of the sample and the reliability of collected data, they are addressed in very different ways.

Sampling

Qualitative	Quantitative
Purposive: Intent to select "small," not necessarily representative, sample in order to acquire in-depth understanding	Random: Intent to select "large," representative sample in order to generalize results to a population

No qualitative researcher can be amazing enough, brilliant enough, or experienced enough to observe *everything* of interest in a given environment (or interview everyone who might have something to contribute). Therefore, by definition, whatever *is* observed represents a sample of what *could have been* observed. Thus, qualitative researchers try to make that sample the best one possible. Whereas the quantitative researcher approaches the problem by carefully (if possible, randomly) selecting a "large," representative sample, the qualitative researcher carefully selects a small, not necessarily representative, sample, one likely to yield the desired information. Further, while the quantitative researcher usually strives to maintain an objective, detached, "scientific" relationship with "subjects," the qualitative researcher is often involved in a very close relationship with study participants.

The reason for these differences is, of course, that qualitative and quantitative researchers select samples for different purposes. The quantitative researcher wants to generalize to a larger population, whereas the qualitative researcher wants to get the deepest understanding possible of the single situation studied. Thus, the quantitative researcher typically collects a limited amount of data for a larger group, while the qualitative researcher collects a great deal of data for a much smaller group, maybe even $N = 1$. At this point you may be getting confused as to what the word "sample" refers to. In a quantitative study, "sample" almost always refers to people, e.g., biology students. In a qualitative study, it refers not only to people, but also to environments. In a qualitative study the "sample" may be one school and selected individuals within that school, or one classroom, one teacher, and selected students. Generically, we can think of "sample" as being synonymous with "data source," i.e., the persons, places, or things on which data are collected.

In a qualitative study, the sampling is usually *purposive,* meaning that the sample is selected purposefully, i.e., precisely because it is believed to be a rich source

Table 7.1

Characteristics Which Differentiate Qualitative and Quantitative Research

Qualitative	Quantitative
Overall Purpose	
Explain, and gain insight and understanding of, phenomena through intensive collection of narrative data	Explain, predict, and/or control phenomena through focused collection of numerical data
Approach to Inquiry	
Inductive, value-laden (subjective), holistic, and process-oriented	Deductive, value-free (objective), focused, and outcome-oriented
Hypotheses	
Tentative, evolving, and based on particular study	Specific, testable, and stated prior to particular study
Review of Related Literature	
Limited, does not significantly affect particular study	Extensive, does significantly affect particular study
Research Setting	
Naturalistic (as is) to the degree possible	Controlled to the degree possible
Sampling	
Purposive: Intent to select "small," not necessarily representative, sample in order to acquire in-depth understanding	Random: Intent to select "large," representative sample in order to generalize results to a population
Measurement	
Nonstandardized, narrative, ongoing	Standardized, numerical, at the end

of the data of interest. A particular school, for example, is not selected randomly but *because* it exhibits some characteristic of interest, such as a high rate of violent incidents; a specific classroom is selected *because* it represents a successful integration of handicapped and nonhandicapped students. And so forth. Of course a particular case may well be selected because it is considered "typical," not necessarily because it is unusual in some identified way. However, even though the sampling is purposive, there is still a concern regarding representativeness. While qualitative researchers are not necessarily interested in generalizing results (although they may well be), they *are* concerned with the representativeness of the data they are collecting. In other words, they want their observations to at least accurately

Table 7.1 (continued)

Qualitative	Quantitative
Design and Method	
Flexible, specified only in general terms in advance of study	Structured, inflexible, specified in detail in advance of study
Involve nonintervention, minimal disturbance	Involve intervention, manipulation, and control
Historical	Descriptive
Ethnographic	Correlational
Case study	Causal-comparative
	Experimental
Data Collection Strategies	
Document collection	
Participant observation	Nonparticipant observation
Unstructured, informal interviews	Semistructured, formal interviews
Taking of extensive, detailed fieldnotes	Administration of tests and questionnaires
Data Analysis	
Raw data are words	Raw data are numbers
Essentially ongoing, involves synthesis	Performed at end of study, involves statistics
Data Interpretation	
Conclusions tentative, reviewed on an ongoing basis, generalizations speculative or nonexistent	Conclusions and generalizations formulated at end of study, stated with predetermined degree of certainty
Trends	
More-structured qualitative research	
Increased application of both inquiry strategies in same study	

reflect the situation under study, regardless of whether the dynamics of that situation are generalizable. Ideally, what is observed is not selected on the basis of convenience, but because of judgment on the part of the researcher.

Occasionally, a sample will be selected randomly, not for reasons of generalizability, but rather to increase credibility of findings.[6] Patton refers to this procedure as purposive random sampling. In an evaluation of a conflict resolution program, for example, the results of in-depth interviews with 10 randomly selected participants

---

[6]See footnote 5, pp. 179–180.

will carry more weight than similar results for 10 participants specifically selected by the evaluator. If, say, the program involved 200 participants in 8 schools, the opinions and feelings of the 10 participants would not necessarily generalize to all 200 participants, but at least they could not be suspected of being intentionally biased. In other words, no one could suggest that the 10 were selected because, for example, they were known to have favorable impressions of the program.

As you may have guessed, there are no guidelines for sample size in a qualitative study. In fact, the actual number of observations to be made (or the actual number of people to be interviewed) is rarely specified in advance. Such decisions are made as the study progresses. Given certain "up front" parameters, such as one researcher, one classroom, one semester, the attempt is made to make as many observations as possible and to conduct as many relevant in-depth interviews as possible.

Measurement

Qualitative	Quantitative
Nonstandardized, narrative, ongoing	Standardized, numerical, at the end

A major difference between measurement in a quantitative study and measurement in a qualitative study is that the former involves standardization and the latter does not. A second major difference is that for a quantitative study what is measured is expressed numerically, and for a qualitative study it is expressed narratively. In a quantitative study, the researcher carefully selects (or develops) the instrument(s) prior to execution of the study and then administers it to all subjects in the same way at the same time(s), usually at the end of the study, but possibly also at the beginning of the study, during the study, or some time after the study. Each subject is given a "score," and the scores are then analyzed collectively, either for the total group (e.g., 78% felt they were "well prepared" or "adequately prepared" for their career in teaching) or for two or more subgroups (e.g., teachers who had participated in conflict resolution training expressed significantly greater confidence in their ability to deal with classroom conflicts than those who had not). If observation is involved, predetermined observation codes and recording intervals are utilized (as will be discussed in Chapter 8). In a qualitative study, the researchers do not want to be restricted by predetermined questions or categories, except in the most general sense. They believe that what should specifically be observed or asked is best assessed as the study progresses, and that there should be few, if any, restrictions on the nature of the data collected. Whatever data will shed the most light on the general question of interest are the data that should be collected.

By the nature of the way in which qualitative data are collected, the researcher is the de facto instrument, in most cases the only instrument. And, while there is a trend in education toward team-oriented qualitative research, most is what is referred to as *Lone Ranger* research, i.e., one person collects all the data. Thus, the concepts of validity and reliability (as discussed in Chapter 5), while still very relevant, must be looked at differently in a qualitative study and cannot be expressed numerically.

For quantitative measurement, validity is the degree to which an instrument measures what it is intended to measure and, consequently, permits appropriate interpretation of scores. In qualitative "measurement," validity is the degree to which observations accurately reflect what was observed (and interviews accurately reflect the feelings, opinions, and so forth, of those interviewed) and, consequently, permit appropriate interpretation of narrative data. In a quantitative study, we can say that the "goodness" of the data depends on the "goodness" of the instrument used to collect it. In a qualitative study the "goodness" of the data depends on the "goodness" of the researcher. This is pretty heavy considering that qualitative data include not just what was observed (or reported), but also the researcher's personal reactions to same, i.e., the researcher's observations about what was observed. It is obvious then that to a much greater degree than in a quantitative study, the validity and reliability of measurement in a qualitative study are highly correlated with the competence, experience, and dedication of the person conducting the study.

The above discussion suggests one of the problems associated with qualitative research, namely, the inability to adequately assess the validity and reliability of the data because of lack of knowledge concerning the researcher who collected it. Usually we know very little about the researcher, who the researcher is, where the researcher is "coming from," the contents of the researcher's notes, how they were taken, and so forth. Qualitative researchers in general, however, are well aware of the potential sources of inaccurate data collection and utilize a number of strategies to deal with them. Use, and reporting, of these strategies diminishes the consumer's dependence on the competence of the researcher. One common strategy is referred to as *triangulation*. Triangulation is the term for the use of multiple methods, data collection strategies, and/or data sources. As mentioned earlier, this approach is characteristic of qualitative research. While participant observation, for example, may be the primary data collection strategy, collection of documents and use of interviews serves two purposes: 1) We get a more complete picture of what is being studied, and 2) we have a way to cross-check our information. If what we are surmising based on our observations "jibes" with what people are telling us, for example, we have more confidence in our data than if we depend solely on either our powers of observation or the motives, veracity, and openness of persons interviewed. Similarly, if several different people have similar stories, we have more confidence in the insights we are gaining than if only one person is interviewed. Even if their perceptions of reality are not accurate, we at least have evidence that the perception is a shared one. For example, if several teachers *believe* that the principal is "out to get them," this is important information, whether or not it is true. If, on the other hand, only one teacher is interviewed and expresses this belief, we don't know if this perception is shared by others or unique to the individual.

Of course qualitative researchers also utilize more traditional approaches to validity and reliability, comparing observations made at different times, for example, or interviewing the same person more than once. If more than one investigator is involved, the data and impressions of one can serve as a cross-check for the data and impressions of the other(s). In other words, qualitative researchers can look for consistency across observations over time, consistency of interview data among persons interviewed, consistency of interview data for the same person(s), consistency of researchers' data and impressions, and so forth.

Another major strategy of qualitative researchers for promoting accuracy of data is the use of recording devices such as audio and video equipment. Although such tools may be used by quantitative researchers, their utilization by qualitative researchers is much more common. And while there is no way that *everything* of interest can be recorded, use of these tools definitely enhances the effort. When their use is feasible, logistically and financially, they can be of invaluable assistance in both collecting accurate data and in verifying impressions based on that data. Of course, given that qualitative researchers take voluminous notes, their primary tools are still a good old-fashioned pen or pencil and a note pad. In addition to the staples and various recording devices (most often audio), however, they may use a range of tools from photographic equipment to lap-top computers. In other words, within given restrictions they use whatever it takes to complete the "mosaic."

The advantages of using recording devices (especially audio equipment) are fairly obvious. First, we are sure that we have an accurate and complete record of what was said (or what transpired). No matter how fast or furiously a person takes notes during an interview, for example, it is hard to equal a cassette recorder, not to mention the fact that manual recording can be very distracting to the person being interviewed. Of course, if a mechanical recording device is being used, it is very important that the person(s) being recorded is made aware of it and agrees to the procedure. Second, tapes can be replayed as many times as desired at a later time; we do not have to worry that we "missed" something. Also, we may replay them so that others may listen (or watch) and give us their impressions or opinions. Whenever mechanical tools of any kind are used, however, they should be of good quality and the researcher should be experienced with their use. As you may know from personal experience, there are very few things as annoying as taking the photo of the year only to find out later you forgot to take the lens cap off, or recording the wedding of the year and later not being able to hear the bride and groom's vows because of background noise.

■ DESIGN AND METHOD

Qualitative	Quantitative
Flexible, specified only in general terms in advance of study	Structured, inflexible, specified in detail in advance of study
Involve nonintervention, minimal disturbance	Involve intervention, manipulation, and control
Historical Ethnographic Case study	Descriptive Correlational Causal-comparative Experimental

In general, the design of a study is basically the overall approach used to investigate the problem of interest, i.e., to shed light on, or answer, the question(s) of interest or to test the intended hypothesis. It includes the method(s) of data collection and related specific strategies. For the sake of convenience and ease of reading, we will refer to design and method in our discussion as D & M (even though it does sound a little kinky). In a quantitative study, D & M are very structured and specified in detail prior to the execution of the study. They are then followed, to the degree possible, as planned; any unanticipated digressions are duly noted in the research report. In a qualitative study, however, D & M are much more flexible and are usually specified in only the most general terms prior to the actual study. It is expected, and considered desirable, that qualitative researchers will use any given technique at any given time, as they see fit. The fact that qualitative D & M are flexible and more spontaneous does not mean, however, that they are unsystematic or haphazard. Qualitative researchers are constantly making thoughtful, informed decisions concerning such issues as the most effective level of participation, the best way to proceed, what to observe, with whom they should interact, and the nature of the interactions (for example, what kinds of questions should be asked).

Another enormous difference between the D & M of quantitative and qualitative studies is the issue of intervention. A quantitative study almost demands intervention; variables and environments are manipulated and controlled, and participants may be subjected to various "treatments." Thus, descriptive, correlational, causal-comparative, and experimental research all represent quantitative D & M. Qualitative researchers engage in none of these activities but rather adhere to the Star Trek prime directive—nonintervention. They want to know the way things *are,* in their natural context, and they make every effort to minimize the effect of their presence in the environment of interest. Their overall D & M is referred to as *fieldwork* because their basic strategy is to spend considerable time "in the field," i.e., in the setting under study, to immerse themselves in this setting, and to collect as much relevant information as possible as unobtrusively as possible. As suggested earlier, they typically assume the role of participant observer (to be discussed shortly).

As discussed early in this chapter, some researchers use the terms "qualitative" and "ethnographic" interchangeably, while others consider ethnography to be *one kind,* or method, of qualitative research. Those who consider the ethnographic method to be distinct use it to refer to qualitative investigations that involve the study of a "culture." Any group of people who regularly associate with each other develop a culture, i.e., characteristic ways of behaving and thinking. Any given culture is associated with a set of shared, if not always articulated, beliefs, attitudes, values, mores, customs, and the like. Thus, particular neighborhoods, schools, classrooms, programs, and so forth, all represent cultures. Since these include typical objects of study in educational research, it is easy to see why the terms "ethnographic" and "qualitative" are often used interchangeably, at least in education.

Within the above context, it is safe to say that most qualitative research efforts represent case studies. A *case study* is the in-depth investigation of one "unit," e.g., individual, group, institution, organization, program, document, and so forth. In education, as also discussed early in this chapter, a unit is likely to be a school, a classroom, an administrator, a teacher, or a student. While not all case studies are qualitative, many are. In order to achieve a more complete understanding of a case under study, a qualitative researcher may well utilize historical research methods. Thus, while historical research may well be done for its own sake, it may also be used in conjunction with, say, participant observation in order to gain insights into how and why things came to be the way they are, i.e., to gain a historical perspective. While there are other methodologies used by qualitative researchers in general, their application in educational research studies is infrequent. A biographical or life history case study, which involves intensive interviews with one person, is an example.

As mentioned earlier, some qualitative researchers do try to contribute directly to theory, but it is *grounded theory,* i.e., theory based on data collected in real-world settings. Whether their studies involve a distinctly different methodology or simply the application of case study methodology *with a different intent,* is open to discussion. In any case (no pun intended), the D & M for grounded theory research is different in that it is more complex and involves data collection for *more than one unit*. Such research efforts are often referred to as *multicase studies* since several teachers, classrooms, schools, or whatever, are studied. The most sophisticated studies of this type are referred to as *multisite studies* because they involve more than the smaller number of cases characteristic of multicase studies. Of course, such studies are also usually undertaken by multiresearchers!

Data Collection Strategies—Fieldwork

Qualitative	Quantitative
Document collection	
Participant observation	Nonparticipant observation
Unstructured informal interviews	Semistructured, formal interviews
Taking of extensive, detailed fieldnotes	Administration of tests and questionnaires

As the evaluation of the Kalamazoo, Michigan, accountability system example illustrated, qualitative data may be no more complex than open-ended responses to items on a questionnaire. As the example also illustrated, however, such data are usually not the only data collected in a given study. The typical qualitative study involves a number of different data collection strategies and, although all options are open, some strategies are used more often than others.

Most qualitative studies, at least in education, are characterized by some type of overt participant observation and the taking of extensive fieldnotes (to be discussed shortly). Such observation is often supplemented by the collection of relevant documents (such as minutes of meetings and memoranda) and in-depth unstructured interviewing. Initial observation provides input that guides the researcher in applying other appropriate data collection strategies. Pelto and Pelto classify the possibilities as verbal and nonverbal.[7] Verbal techniques involve interactions between the researcher and persons in the research environment, mainly interviewing; nonverbal techniques are less obtrusive, that is, less likely to affect the behaviors being studied, and include such strategies as collection of written records.

It bears repeating that while the techniques to be described are the ones most commonly used, *all options are open*. A qualitative researcher may even collect statistical data, for example, if she or he feels that it will contribute to the overall understanding of the phenomenon under study. Just as the quantitative researcher may use a technique usually associated with qualitative research (e.g., participant observation), a qualitative researcher may use a technique usually associated with quantitative research (e.g., nonparticipant observation). To avoid confusion when you get to Chapter 8, Descriptive Research, it must be pointed out that qualitative and quanti-

---

[7]Pelto, P. J., & Pelto, G. H. (1978). *Anthropological research: The structure of inquiry* (2nd ed.). New York: Cambridge University Press.

tative researchers use data collection strategies which may *sound* similar but are really quite different. Both use observation and interviewing, for example, but in qualitative research the approaches are much less structured and yield narrative data, whereas in quantitative research they are highly structured and yield numerical data.

Participant Observation

While the unit(s) of observation in an educational research study may be smaller or larger, it is typically a classroom, an entire school, or some aspect of a school, such as principal-teacher interactions. In participant observation, the observer actually becomes a part of, a participant in, the situation to be observed. The rationale for participant observation is that in many cases the view from the inside is somewhat different than the view from the outside looking in. There are, of course, degrees of participation, and observation may be overt or covert. For example, if a researcher obtains permission to attend faculty meetings at a local high school in order to study principal-teacher interactions, the observation is more overt. If the researcher manages to get hired as a teacher, the intent being to study principal-teacher interactions without anyone being aware that such observation is occurring, the degree of participation is greater and the observation is covert. It is very likely that the conclusions drawn from the two approaches would differ. Although the covert observation might provide more valid findings, this type of observation has some obvious drawbacks. First and foremost is the highly questionable ethics involved in observing people without their knowledge. Thus, participant observation is usually overt.

The researcher allows for some time to get familiar with the environment and to get acquainted with the participants, and vice versa. The intent is for the people of interest to become comfortable with the researcher. The researcher gradually increases his or her degree of involvement and at all stages takes extensive notes (or otherwise records) as much as possible. These notes include not only what was seen, heard, experienced, and so forth, but also the researcher's reactions and reflections. If a researcher "sensed" tension during a meeting, for example, this would be recorded as well as any related observational data such as words and facial expressions.

Document Collection.   Qualitative researchers frequently supplement observation with document collection. A document may be any written or nonwritten record which exists and which may enhance the researcher's overall understanding of the situation under study. In education, such documents include (but are not limited to) minutes of meetings, attendance records, budget reports, policy statements, memoranda, and photographs. (Remember, a picture is worth 1,000 words!) Notice that these documents may contain numerical data; such data may be used in a number of ways in conjunction with other data. If at our faculty meeting, for example, several teachers expressed the sentiment that the new record keeping system was stressing them out, this might be supported by teacher sick leave data. Further, minutes of previous meetings might show that this is not the first time teachers have expressed their unhappiness.

Based on data collected to date, the researcher might well identify one or more teachers for possible interviews, perhaps including at least one teacher who had not made any overt or covert (e.g., absenteeism) statement concerning the new policy, or had made only a covert statement. Thus, the information contained in "documents" may support or not support data collected in other ways and/or may suggest future data collection strategies. Notice that documents often reveal information not available through other means. If teacher sick leave days were up, for example, this would suggest a problem, whether any teacher had voiced it or not. As will be discussed shortly, data from documents are especially valuable because they are "unobtrusive," i.e., not affected by the presence of the researcher. It must be kept in mind, however, that even if the documents are "public record," the anonymity of those involved in their contents should be protected, for ethical, if not legal, reasons.

Observer Bias.   As suggested above, the very presence of the researcher in the situation being observed creates potential problems. The situation may be "seen" differently than it would have been through the eyes of a different researcher (observer bias) and/or may be a somewhat different situation than it would have been if it were not observed (observer effect). While this problem is not unique to qualitative observation (as we shall see in subsequent sections), it is potentially more serious because of the more intimate involvement of the researcher and what is being researched.

Observer bias refers to invalid observations that result from the way in which the observer observes. Each researcher brings to a setting a highly individual background, set of experiences, perspectives, and the like, which in turn affect not only what and how he or she observes but also his or her personal reflections and interpretations. Relatedly, the qualitative researcher runs the risk of identifying with one or more participants or being judgmental towards others, with somewhat colored observations being the result. After attending a number of faculty meetings, for example, a researcher might tend to identify with the teachers, and observations and/or interpretations of principal-teacher interactions would be affected by this role identification. In other words, no two researchers in the same situation would have identical fieldnotes. (No, not even identical twins!) This apparently inevitable subjectivity is, however, both a weakness and a strength of participant observation. The more involved the researcher is, the greater the degree of subjectivity likely to creep into the observations; on the other hand, the greater the involvement, the greater the opportunity for acquiring in-depth understanding and insight.

Thus, qualitative researchers must walk a fine line in their attempt to be at the same time both involved and objective. But the point is that they *are aware* of the challenge and make every effort to meet it. They also try to minimize the effects of their personal biases on their findings by conscientiously recording their thoughts, feelings, and reactions, *about* what they observe, as well as *what* they observe. And, as discussed earlier, triangulation provides an additional, powerful safeguard; it is not likely that data derived from different sources and data collection strategies will all be biased in the same, unnoticed way. It is even less likely that data provided by several researchers will be so consistently biased that bias will be undetected. Of course detecting bias and eliminating it are not the same thing. Qualitative researchers, however, do not claim that they can eliminate all bias. They do maintain, however, and rightfully so, that they have a number of strategies for minimizing its effect on the results of their research.

Observer Effect.   The other side of the coin is called the observer effect and refers to the impact of the observer's participation on the situation being observed. In other words, the situation is somewhat different than it would have been if the observer did not participate; and, of course, the greater the participation the greater the likely impact. It is not news that persons being observed may behave atypically simply because they are being observed. Would you behave exactly the same as you normally would on a given day if you knew you were being *observed?* Probably not. Again, while this problem is by no means unique to qualitative research, it is potentially more serious since the researcher is trying to study how people *naturally* behave in their *natural* setting.

Thus, once again we see that qualitative researchers must walk a fine line in their attempt to be involved *enough* to gain the insights they are seeking and at the same time to be as unobtrusive, i.e., inconspicuous, as possible. One of their major strategies is to be as unassuming and nonthreatening as they can be as they gradually increase their participation. While initially persons in the observational setting may be highly conscious of the researcher's presence, the effect on their behavior typically decreases over time. Thus, for example, at the *first* faculty meeting attended by the observer, behavior may be somewhat artificial (more formal or more cordial, for example); but by say the *tenth* faculty meeting, people will tend to be their usual selves. It also helps if the exact nature of the researcher's inquiry is not described in any more detail than is necessary, ethically or legally. The fact that persons being observed may at least initially behave differently is bad enough; *focusing* their behavior change is worse! So, for example, it would probably be sufficient if the "official" reason given for the researcher's presence were "to observe high school faculty meetings," rather than "to observe principal-teacher interactions." Further, as with simulation observation, a quantitative strategy to be discussed in Chapter 8, if one is aware that people are behaving differently because of her or his presence, this recognition can lead to the collection of valuable data. The researcher can observe, for example, what people in the setting (e.g., teachers and administrators at a faculty meeting) *believe* is the appropriate way to behave and interact, even if this is not the way they *usually* behave or interact.

As with observer bias, triangulation represents an important safeguard which helps to detect a serious observer effect. Collection of documents is especially useful in this regard since, as mentioned, they are "unobtrusive" measures, i.e., they are not affected by the presence of the researcher. Teacher absenteeism records, for example, will not "behave" differently because they are being "observed." Such records might be one unobtrusive measure of teacher stress which would or would not yield data consistent with the researcher's observations. An amusing example of unobtrusive qualitative data is found in the statement of a police officer to the effect that one way to identify car thieves is by examining license plates. Police officers look for clean cars with dirty plates and dirty cars with clean plates, because thieves usually switch plates.[8]

Thus, qualitative researchers are well aware that they cannot totally eliminate observer effects. They do, however, make every effort to recognize, minimize, record, and report them.

Interviews

A typical qualitative interview is a one-on-one session in which the researcher asks a series of open-ended, probing questions. In addition to serving triangulation objectives, interviews have a unique purpose, namely, to acquire data not obtainable in any other way. There are certain things which simply cannot be observed, including (but not limited to) past events, events which occur outside of the researcher's sphere of observation, and mental processes. We cannot observe, for example, the way things "used to be" before Mr. Hardnozed became principal, the fact that Mr. Haddit, the math teacher, is seeing a psychiatrist to cope with job-related stress, or that Mr. Haddit is "thinking about" requesting a transfer to another school. Only a skilled interviewer would be likely to elicit such information. As mentioned previously, a qualitative researcher frequently attempts to gain a

---

[8]Reddy, J. (1965, February 28). Heady thieves find Wheeling their Waterloo. *Chicago Sun Times,* p. 66.

historical perspective on the situation of interest. The two major strategies for doing so are document collection and what are referred to as *retrospective interviews*.

Interviews vary in degree of structure and formality and include a range of questions which can be classified on a continuum of, for lack of a better word, sensitivity. At one end of the continuum we have questions of a factual nature, such as "How long have you been teaching?" and "Do you receive compensation for after-school responsibilites?" At the other end of the continuum are questions which deal with values, feelings, and opinions, questions such as "How did you feel when you found out that Mr. Hardnozed was going to be appointed principal?" and "How has teacher morale been affected?" Clearly, questions at this end require more skill, both methodological and interpersonal, on the part of the interviewer. Above all, of course, a good interviewer must be a good listener. In addition, he or she should be straightforward, nonthreatening, and nonjudgmental. It would be very ineffective, for example, for an interviewer to say "You did *what!?*" Obviously, being a good conversationalist in general comes in handy when conducting an interview. A good interviewer, however, is always looking for openings, ways to probe deeper. Although interviews typically begin with more mundane questions and gradually ease into more sensitive questions, the alert interviewer will be aware of opportunities as they arise. If in response to the apparently innocuous question "How long have you been teaching?" the teacher responds "Too-oo-oo long!", for example, the interviewer may chuckle and ask "Why do you say that?"

As the above illustrates, the typical qualitative interview is fairly unstructured and open-ended. The whole point is not to get answers to a predetermined set of standardized questions, but rather to find out where "they" are coming from, what they have experienced, feel, believe, and so forth. The typical interview is also quite informal in the sense that it is not, for example, scheduled. Rarely would you hear a qualitative researcher ask "What's a good time for an interview?" Rather, the researcher sees an opportunity to "chat" with a person of interest and seizes it. There are times, however, when varying degrees of structure are called for, given the purpose for which interviews are being conducted. The interviewer, for instance, may have a predetermined set of general questions or issues (an interview guide) which she or he wishes to explore with several interviewees. An example of this approach with which you may be familiar is the *focus group interview*. Focus group interviews, which are often used in evaluation efforts, involve a small number of people who have something of interest in common, e.g., participation in a particular program. They generally meet informally with an "interviewer" for several hours and respond to open-ended questions such as "What do you think you got out of the program?" and "What would have made the experience more positive for you?" The participants share their opinions and hear those of others. The objective is not debate or consensus, but rather expression of ideas and feelings. In a research study of principal-teacher interactions, those attending a faculty meeting might be considered a focus group, depending upon how it was conducted.

Occasionally, usually in multicase or multisite research, more standardized, open-ended interviews are utilized. In other words, each person interviewed is asked essentially the same questions in the same order. Such interviews are used when it is believed that the resulting comparability of responses is worth what insights may be lost as a result of inflexibility. In Chapter 8, we will discuss interviews as typically conducted in quantitative studies. Such interviews usually involve a semistructured approach, i.e., use of an interview guide which includes structured questions with fixed alternatives followed by clarifying unstructured, or open-ended questions. Structured, fixed-alternative questions are rarely used in qualitative research for obvious reasons.

Qualitative Data—Fieldnotes

Whereas quantitative data usually result from administration of some type of "test" or questionnaire, qualitative data are all the data collected, from whatever source, during fieldwork, including fieldnotes, documents, interview transcripts, photographs, and videotapes. Since participant observation is the major data collection strategy used in qualitative research, however, fieldnotes are obviously of prime importance. Whether taken in the actual setting or recorded as soon as possible after leaving the setting, they describe as accurately as possible and as comprehensively as possible all relevant aspects of the situation observed, and include both what was actually observed *and* the observer's reactions to same. What was actually observed represents the when, where, who, and what happened portion of the fieldnotes. To appreciate the enormity of the task, imagine yourself trying to describe, in writing, in excruciating detail, even one of your current research class meetings. What was the physical setting like? What did it look like? Who was present? What did they look like? How did they act? What about your instructor? How did he or she look and act? What was said? What interactions took place? And so on and so on.

The task appears even more awesome when you consider that descriptions must be very specific, and represent what was actually *seen* (or heard, or whatever), not your interpretation of what was seen. Instead of saying that someone was "happy" or "angry," for example, the fieldnotes should reflect how the person looked and acted. Patton (1990, pp. 240–241) gives several good examples which clearly illustrate the difference between "vague and overgeneralized notes" and "detailed and concrete notes." One of them is presented below:

> Vague: The next student who came in to take the test was very poorly dressed.

> Detailed: The next student who came into the room was wearing clothes quite different from the three students who'd been in previously. The three previous students looked like they'd been groomed before they came to the test. Their hair was combed, their clothes were clean and pressed, the colors of their clothes matched, and their clothes were in good condition. This new student had on pants that were soiled with a hole or tear in one knee and a threadbare seat. The flannel shirt was wrinkled with one tail tucked into the pants and the other tail hanging out. Hair was disheveled and the boy's hands looked like he'd been playing in the engine of a car.

Clearly, the "detailed" notes are superior to the "vague" notes. What constitutes being "very poorly dressed" may well vary from observer to observer (ever read the *STAR* tabloid?), but the detailed description speaks for itself, and anyone who reads it will have a similar mental picture of what the boy looked like.

In addition to literal descriptions, the observer also records personal reactions, generally referred to as *reflective fieldnotes*. These notes include interpretations, and other subjective thoughts and feelings, but they are clearly differentiated from the more objective, strictly descriptive, fieldnotes; typically a special code (e.g., PC = personal comment) is used. In these notes the observer is free to express any thoughts regarding how things are going, where things are going, and what might be concluded. Reflective fieldnotes might include statements such as the following:

PC I have the feeling that tension among faculty members has been growing for some time.

PC I think Mr. Haddit has been egging on other faculty members.

PC I'm finding it hard to be objective because Mr. Hardnozed is rather abrasive.

PC I think the transition would have been smoother if key faculty members had been informed and involved in the process.

Of course in a published report pseudonyms would be used, but you get the idea. Such insights add a significant dimension to the observations and thus contribute to producing a "rich" description, the objective of qualitative research.

Table 7.2, which represents an adaptation of Patton's "Top 10" guidelines, provides a useful summary of our discussion of fieldwork and fieldnotes.

Table 7.2

Summary Guidelines for Fieldwork and Fieldnotes

1. Be descriptive in taking fieldnotes.

2. Gather a variety of information from different perspectives.

3. Cross-validate and triangulate by gathering different kinds of data (e.g., observations, documents, interviews) and by using multiple methods.

4. Use quotations; represent people in their own terms. Capture their experiences in their own words.

5. Select "key informants" wisely and use them carefully. Draw on the wisdom of their informed perspectives, but keep in mind that their perspectives are limited.

6. Be aware of and sensitive to different stages of fieldwork.

   a) Build trust and rapport at the beginning. Remember that the observer is also being observed.

   b) Stay alert and disciplined during the more routine, middle phase of fieldwork.

   c) Focus on pulling together a useful synthesis as fieldwork draws to a close.

7. Be disciplined and conscientious in taking fieldnotes at all stages of fieldwork.

8. Be as involved as possible in experiencing the situation as fully as possible while maintaining an analytical perspective grounded in the purpose of the fieldwork.

9. Clearly separate description from interpretation and judgment.

10. Include in your fieldnotes and report your own experiences, thoughts, and feelings.

Note. From M. Q. Patton, 1990, *Qualitative evaluation and research methods* (2nd ed.), pp. 273–274. Copyright 1990 by Sage Publications. Adapted and reprinted with permission of the author and publisher.

■ DATA ANALYSIS AND INTERPRETATION

Data analysis for quantitative studies and qualitative studies is quite different. Whereas the "raw data" for quantitative studies are *numbers* (e.g., test scores), the raw data for qualitative studies are *words* (and possibly visual material such as photos). These data include primarily fieldnotes, often supplemented by documents and interview transcripts. Since the focus is on what people *actually said,* direct quotations are preferable to paraphrases or the observer's recollections. This is easier said than done, however. Having the bulk of the data represent quotations usually requires transcripts of many interview tapes, which is no mean task; it is both immensely time consuming and expensive. Nonetheless, they are highly preferred. Other major differences between quantitative and qualitative analysis are that while quantitative analysis is typically performed at the end of the study and usually involves application of descriptive and/or inferential statistics, qualitative analysis is essentially ongoing and infrequently involves application of statistics. In other words, the qualitative researcher does not wait until the study is over and then think "Hm-m-m, how shall I analyze these data?" While there will usually be at least some "at the end" analysis, the *process,* of necessity, must begin early on. Thinking about possible analyses will guide, for example, the formulation of coding strategies (to be discussed shortly).

Analysis

Qualitative	Quantitative
Raw data are words	Raw data are numbers
Essentially ongoing, involves synthesis	Performed at end of study, involves statistics

In a simplified nutshell, qualitative analysis involves making sense out of an enormous amount of narrative data. Given a "bunch" of fieldnotes, transcripts, documents, and so forth, the question is, what do they *say.* Thus, the qualitative researcher looks for categories, patterns, and themes which will facilitate a coherent synthesis of the data. This synthesis, including relevant illustrative examples and quotations, eventually represents the researcher's overall understanding of what the data mean. The process is similar in many ways to the one involved in generating a coherent review of related literature, as discussed in Chapter 2. Basically, if you recall (which I'm sure you do!), you went through the following process:

1. You entered the library, your "field," with a tentative problem statement and initial thoughts on sources and strategies for "data collection."
2. Over a period of time, you repeatedly returned to the "field" and collected a massive amount of notes and/or photocopies of portions of "documents" (e.g., journal articles).
3. As the search went on, you began to focus on the most useful sources and refined your strategies.

4. From day one you started getting ideas about ways to organize the material and coded each "piece of data" accordingly (e.g., O = opinion, S = study); as time went by, this process underwent constant refinement.
5. Eventually, you were home with a "pile of stuff" ready to be organized and synthesized into a report.
6. After reviewing and culling all your material, you finalized your organizational strategy and produced a written, coherent synthesis, which probably included one or more quotations.
7. Your final product presented, in a *relatively* small number of pages, a summary of all your "data."

As with a qualitative research report, "your" summary represented "your" choice of sources, "your" collection strategies, "your" interpretations, and so forth. Two students with identical research problems would not be expected to produce identical reports (They'd better not!). Similarly, two qualitative researchers independently investigating very similar problems or questions may well produce very different reports. Some will be "better" than others, depending upon such factors as diligence and experience.

Based on your experience, imagine the task of the qualitative researcher. Participant observation, for example, is characterized by the collection of large amounts of data that are, to say the least, not easy to analyze, as illustrated by the following statement made by a participant observer:

> . . . our files contain approximately five thousand single-spaced pages of such material. Faced with such a quantity of "rich" but varied data, the researcher faces the problem of how to analyze it systematically and then to present conclusions so as to convince other scientists of their validity.[9]

Thus, it is not surprising that one factor that has contributed significantly to the steady rise in the number of qualitative studies is the increasingly sophisticated technology available to researchers for data analysis. While index cards and the good old cut-and-paste approaches still live, most qualitative researchers use computers to assist them in a variety of data analysis procedures, sorting by code for example.

While specific instruction in coding techniques and strategies is beyond the scope of this text, it should be noted that coding of data is a critical aspect of most qualitative research. As with doing a review of related literature (analogy discussed above), coding involves critically analyzing the data and identifying themes and topics which represent categories into which numerous pieces of data can be classified. Specific categories can be labeled with words, letters, numbers, or symbols. Once coding categories have been identified and labeled, e.g., T = teacher, Q = quotation, any data entry can be coded and later sorted, e.g., TQ = teacher quotation. Aspects to be coded typically include variables such as persons, processes, and events observed, recollections, thoughts, and opinions reported, and the researcher's reactions to same (recall PC = personal comment). Analysis of collected documents involves essentially the same process; documents are reviewed and relevant portions are coded and later sorted as part of the synthesis effort.

Both quantitative and qualitative researchers report *how* the data were analyzed, not just the results, but the task is easier for the quantitative researchers; they

---

[9] Becker, H. S. (1958). Problems of inference and proof in participant observation. *American Sociological Review, 23,* 652–660.

simply state the statistics which were applied to the data, e.g., ". . . means, standard deviations, and a *t* test for independent samples were computed . . ." Qualitative researchers must report on a *process*, e.g., how they formulated their coding categories. To help you gain some conceptual understanding of what this involves, imagine not only producing a "Review of Related Literature," but also explaining in writing *how* you did it.

Interestingly, a current trend, particularly in the field of evaluation, is the collection and analysis of both quantitative and qualitative data. We will discuss this development further, later in this chapter.

Interpretation

Qualitative	Quantitative
Conclusions tentative, reviewed on an ongoing basis, generalizations speculative or nonexistent	Conclusions and generalizations formulated at end of study, stated with predetermined degree of certainty

As with data analysis, interpretation of results for qualitative research is very different than for quantitative research, reflecting the inductive versus deductive nature of the two approaches. While in a quantitative study conclusions and generalizations are formulated at the end of the study and are stated with a basically predetermined degree of certainty (to be discussed in Chapter 14, Inferential Statistics), in a qualitative study "conclusions" are drawn and reviewed on an ongoing basis and are more tentative, and generalizations are highly speculative or nonexistent. The conclusions in a qualitative study are the insights the researcher believes she or he has gleaned as the result of a lengthy, intensive effort. They are presented, as Rod Serling would say, "for your perusal" and consideration. (This is not to suggest in any way that qualitative research takes place in the Twilight Zone!) Further, since sampling is purposive and the "sample" size is small (representing, not atypically, a single case), no attempt is made to generalize findings to a larger population. The issue of generalizability is left up to consumers of the research and to other researchers. In other words, persons reading the report may believe that findings have a degree of applicability for *their* environment, and other researchers may conduct studies which support the credibility of the reported possibilities.

The application of qualitative research methodology to the investigation of educational problems is illustrated in a study by Schultz and Florio. A summary of their study is presented here to give you the flavor of qualitative research, including the kinds of "conclusions" it can yield.

The purpose of the research was to study the socialization process involved when children enter a school environment. Through socialization children learn which behaviors are appropriate and which are inappropriate in a variety of situations. One important aspect of socialization is recognizing when the context has changed sufficiently to necessitate a change in behavior. The prime agent for socialization in the school setting is, of course, the teacher. The Schultz and Florio study focused on the techniques used by one kindergarten teacher to alert students to a change in context. Specifically, the changes in context that occurred during an open activity period called "worktime" were studied. The research took place in a kindergarten/first grade classroom in a suburb of Boston. The study concentrated on identifying "what it is that children need to know in order to act in a manner that is considered appropriate in the classroom." Toward this end the researchers examined the various contexts as well as the related teacher-student interactions. Seventy hours of videotape were collected over a 2-year period, and supplementary field-notes were taken. During the second year of the study, a participant observer spent several days a week collecting information related to the vidoetaped behavior. Based on their analysis of the data, the authors concluded that consistent contextual changes in behavior required a systematic set of behaviors on the part of the teacher. Children associate certain behaviors with the requirement pay attention. If the teacher fails to exhibit these behaviors at any time, the children fail to pay attention and exhibit inappropriate behavior.[10]

■ QUALITATIVE VERSUS QUANTITATIVE RESEARCH

The word "versus" in the above heading is not used in the oppositional sense but rather in the compare/contrast sense. Each approach has its pluses and minuses and they may both be used in the same study.

Cautions and Contrasts

By now you should have a reasonably good basic understanding of qualitative research. Its drawbacks are obvious, although not necessarily unique (as we shall see in Chapters 8–11). Proper application of the approach requires the accurate recording of large amounts of data over long periods of time, by persons thoroughly trained in observational methods. Results are difficult to analyze, conclusions are highly tentative, and generalizations are minimal or nonexistent. At a practical level, qualitative research tends to be more costly. Thus, the good news is that qualitative research typically yields an abundance of potentially useful data and insights not obtainable using other methods, and the hypotheses generated by such research are in many cases more valid than those based on theory alone. The bad news is that collecting and analyzing such data and drawing defensible conclusions is not an easy task.

A current problem with qualitative research is not the fault of the approach, but rather the way in which it is being used. As more and more people have gotten into the qualitative act, some with little or no related training, there has been an increase in the number of poorly conducted, allegedly qualitative studies. As Rist puts it, qualitative research "is becoming a mantle to legitimate work that is shoddy, poorly conducted, and ill conceived." Such research is characterized by the taking of shortcuts such as minimal time being spent in the setting being studied.[11] In other words, the fact that you have studied this chapter (even a *lot!*) does not mean that you are capable of conducting a qualitative study. For a very narrowly focused

[10] Schultz, J., & Florio, S. (1979). Stop and freeze: The negotiation of social and physical space in a kindergarten/first grade classroom. *Anthropology & Education Quarterly, 10,* 166-181.

[11] Rist, R. C. (1980). Blitzkreig ethnography: On the transformation of a method into a movement. *Educational Researcher, 9*(2), 8–10.

question, such as what it's like to be the only handicapped student in a class, *and* with careful monitoring, you might get your feet wet, as they say, but doing a decent study would normally require at a minimum taking an entire course on qualitative methodology.

As you may have guessed, a major issue in educational research is the validity and preferability of qualitative versus quantitative approaches to inquiry, especially with respect to their potential for meaningfully investigating educational phenomena.[12] Both approaches have advocates who feel strongly that one or the other should be used exclusively. Other researchers feel that there may well be *a* best approach but have not been persuaded to favor one over the other; researchers in this camp call for further deliberation on the question. Other researchers take the position that neither is appropriate for all situations. These researchers believe that the choice of type of inquiry and corresponding methodologies depends upon the nature of the phenomena being studied. All things considered, the latter position appears to be the most reasonable one. It should be noted that at the present time more researchers prefer quantitative methodologies than prefer qualitative methodologies. The gap, however, is narrowing and, as a wise man once said, truth is not decided by a vote!

Trends

More-structured qualitative research
Increased application of both inquiry strategies in same study

---

In education, qualitative research design and methodology are undergoing constant refinement and adaptation in the direction of a more-structured (i.e., quantitative) approach. This trend is viewed as a positive one with the potential result being a research method incorporating the best features of the integrated approaches. When qualitative, or ethnographic, methodology was first applied to the investigation of educational problems, it was utilized by persons with training in anthropological methods. As its popularity has grown, it has increasingly been used by persons with more traditional, hypothesis-testing-oriented backgrounds. The result has been the emergence of a modified approach, an approach that could be characterized as more-structured. In 1980, Rist made the following statement which is even more valid today than it was when it was originally published:

> Finally, there is the matter of how to employ the method.
> The traditional assumption was that a single individual
> (sometimes a couple) would go to the field site, become
> enmeshed in the life of that site, and only after a long and
> involved period of time, begin to formulate a framework for
> the analysis. Theory was "grounded" in experience.
> Recently, there are several examples in which the number
> of ethnographers has not been one or two, but upwards to

---

[12] See, for example, Smith, J. K., & Heshius, L. (1986). Closing down the conversation: The end of the quantitative-qualitative debate among educational inquirers. *Educational Researcher, 15*(1), 4–12.

60 working on a single study. The conventional single site case study has been complemented by a multisite approach frequently used in policy analysis and program evaluation. Furthermore, the idea of going into the field and allowing the issues and problems to emerge from extensive time on site has also given way to the preformulation of research problems, to the specifying of precise activities that are to be observed, and to the analytic framework within which the study is to be conducted. And all of this prior to the *first* site visit. The end result is a structured and predetermined approach to data collection and analysis.[13]

Another major related trend is for studies to use a combination of methodologies, i.e., to use a multimethod approach, and to collect both qualitative and quantitative data in the same study. As currently utilized, this approach typically involves the use of qualitative data to gain insights into the *meaning* of quantitative results, or to support or corroborate such results (in other words, the concept of triangulation is applied to quantitative data by supplementing them with qualitative data). Degree of enthusiasm for this practice varies among researchers. Those who have reservations see the potential benefits but have concerns regarding its valid application, especially for single-researcher efforts. Specifically, they question whether one person can be sufficiently competent in both approaches. Their point is well taken in that there are few such individuals. However, if the qualitative data, for example, are merely supplemental data, or if more than one investigator is involved, most agree that the two kinds of data can be used together quite effectively, especially in evaluation research.

Based on personal experiences, Patton, for example, has found a combination of data types to be quite appropriate and useful, especially when testimonials and/or quotes are used in conjunction with descriptive statistics. An example which illustrates how qualitative data can add a very enhancing dimension to quantitative data is the case of the evaluation of the Technology for Literacy Center. The Center is a computer-based adult literacy program in Saint Paul, Minnesota, whose future funding following a three-year pilot effort hinged on an evaluation of its outcomes and cost-effectiveness. Quantitative data based on instruments such as reading tests and questionnaires clearly supported the effectiveness of the program. The qualitative data, however, gave depth and meaning to the "numbers" in a way which was very impactful. Based on a questionnaire, for example, it was found that 77% of the program participants were "very happy" with the program and 74% reported learning "a great deal." However, interview comments revealed just how much of a difference the program had made in the lives of many of the participants. Comments such as the following made the statistics come alive:[14]

> I love the newspaper now and actually read it.

> Helps me on the medicine. Now I can read the bottle and the directions! I was afraid to give the kids medicine before because I wasn't sure.

> My family is my motivation . . . Once you can read to your kids, it makes all the difference in the world . . . When I

---

[13] See footnote 11. Copyright 1980, American Educational Research Association, Washington, DC.

[14] See footnote 5, pp. 15–18.

can read myself, I can help them read so they can have a
better life. The kids love it when I read to them.

If only quantitative results were presented, one might easily ask "But what does it *mean* that 77% were 'very happy'?" If only the qualitative results were presented, they could easily be dismissed as being merely anecdotal. The combination was clearly more powerful.

While there are many excellent resources available on qualitative research, Bogdan and Biklen (1992) and Patton (1990) represent two very readable texts which you may wish to consult for in-depth discussion of topics discussed in this chapter.[15]

On the following pages an example of qualitative research is presented. Note that the study involved document analysis (specifically, analysis of reflective journals), multiple observations, and descriptive statistics.

This study is discussed further in the *Student Guide* which accompanies this text.

---

[15] See footnotes 1 and 5.

Reflective Thinking and Growth in Novices' Teaching Abilities

JOAN P. GIPE
University of New Orleans

JANET C. RICHARDS
The University of Southern Mississippi–Gulf Coast

ABSTRACT   Despite considerable differences in interpretations and agendas, reflective teaching programs are governed by the assumption that thoughtful and critically questioning novices will develop expertise in teaching abilities. However,
there is no reported research that specifically examines prospective teachers' reflective thoughts in relation to improvement in
teaching. This study examined the relationship between future
teachers' reflections and growth in their teaching abilities in an
early field placement. Data gathered over one semester from reflective journals and multiple observations were analyzed and
descriptive statistics included. Results suggest that teacher preparation programs should foster reflective thinking as an important facet of growth in teaching abilities.

The idea of reflection for prospective teachers is not
new. However, recent favorable reports have helped
place "reflective teaching" in vogue (Feiman-Nemser,
1990; Goodman, 1985; Zeichner, 1981–82). Teacher educators increasingly discuss the dimensions of reflection
and teaching. Teacher education institutions purchase
more reflective teaching materials than ever before
(Gore, 1987). Supervisors now urge prospective teachers
to think reflectively about their work. Novices in field
placements are asked to keep journals, participate in
seminars, or conduct mini-ethnographic studies. On a
broader scale, some colleges are so committed to producing reflective teachers that comprehensive "inquiry-oriented" programs have been designed for that purpose
(Korthagen, 1985; Korthagen & Verkuyl, 1987; Zeichner,
1981–82). Clearly, reflection "has become part of the [cur-
rent] language of teacher education" (Gore, 1987, p. 33).

The scope and depth of university reflective program
agendas differ considerably. Some education departments have tentatively begun to consider the merits of reflection; others have carefully monitored and continued
to refine their programs for over 10 years.

Teacher education departments and teacher educators
within those departments also differ in their interpretation of the widely used term *reflective teaching* (Beyer,
1984; Clift, Houston, & Pugach, 1990); that is, to think

in a reflective way about pedagogical actions and concerns. Those considered to have a more "technocratic
orientation" limit their interpretation of reflection to the
teaching act (i.e., "teachers thinking about what happened,
why it happened, and what else they could have done to
reach their goal") (Gore, 1987, p. 36). The major focus
of reflective thought is restricted to what occurs in classrooms.

Other inquiry-oriented pedagogists (Korthagen, 1985;
Schon, 1987; Zeichner, 1981–82; Zeichner & Teitelbaum,
1982) expanded the definition of reflective teaching to include a critical "consideration of ethical, moral, and political principles" (Gore, 1987, p. 33). Reflective thoughts
are extended beyond classroom walls to include "complexities inescapably linked with educational issues"
(Hartnett & Naish, 1980, p. 269). That more radical and
action-oriented perspective has the potential to stimulate
educational reform. It urges both novices and supervisors
to develop "habits of active, persistent, and careful examination of educational and social beliefs" (Zeichner,
Liston, Mahlios, & Gomez, 1987, p. 5).

Educators also debate the most appropriate and effective ways to promote novices' reflective attitudes. Some
educators believe that prospective teachers can objectively
and analytically learn how to reflect about their teaching
in a "complete and controlled clinical teaching experience" (Cruickshank, Holton, Fay, Williams, Kennedy,
Myers, & Hough, 1981, part 1, p. 4). For example, one
reflective teaching program requires novices to take turns
teaching identical subject-matter lessons by following
specifically stated manual guidelines. The lessons are
taught to small groups of peers who then immediately reflect upon the variables that affected the instruction
(Cruickshank & Applegate, 1981). Other experts emphat-
ically reject the idea that prospective teachers can learn
the skills of genuine reflective inquiry through a specific
instructional method. Rather, it is the development of

*Address correspondence to Joan P. Gipe, Department of
Curriculum & Instruction, University of New Orleans, New
Orleans, LA 70148.*

Gipe, J. P., & Richards, J. C. (1992). Reflective thinking and growth in novices' teaching abilities. *The Journal
of Educational Research, 86,* 52–57. Reprinted with the permission of the Helen Dwight Reid Educational
Foundation. Published by Heldref Publications, 1319 Eighteenth St., N.W., Washington, DC 20036-1802.
Copyright © 1992.

positive and sincere attitudes about the merits of reflection that "constitute the basis of truly reflective action" (Zeichner, 1981–82, p. 6). Therefore, a wholesome attitude about reflection is as imperative as demonstrating reflective abilities.

Despite such widespread differences in program interpretations and agendas, activities designed to promote novices' reflective thinking are governed by a common assumption. The assumption links prospective teachers' reflective thoughts to their teaching behaviors (Cruickshank, 1984; Dewey, 1904, 1933; Zeichner, 1981–82). That is, prospective teachers who in some way reflect about their work, or who extend their reflections to include broader educational concerns, will improve upon their teaching abilities. Yet, that assumption cannot be taken for granted. Enthusiastic "claims about reflective teaching are in advance of any solid empirical evidence" (Gore, 1987, p. 35). Two related studies do suggest that novices in reflective teaching programs, as opposed to counterparts in traditional programs, are less anxious about teaching and more able to think and talk about teaching and learning (Holton & Nott, 1980; Williams & Kennedy, 1980). However, those studies have been critiqued as narrowly focused (Gore, 1987). Moreover, they do not demonstrate a link between reflective thinking and growth in novices' teaching competencies. The idea that thoughtful and critically questioning prospective teachers will demonstrate growth in abilities to devise and present appropriate lessons has not been documented. There is no reported research that specifically examines prospective teachers' reflective thoughts in relation to improved teaching abilities over the course of a semester. We conducted our study to formally explore that assumptive theme.

Method

In this study, we used field research methodology, specifically analysis of reflective journals (Glaser & Strauss, 1967; Niemeyer & Moon, 1986; Yinger & Clark, 1981) and multiple observations (Medley & Mitzel, 1963; Meltzer, Petras, & Reynolds, 1975; Yonemura, 1987) coupled with some descriptive statistics. Research on journal writing supports the value of journals as a vehicle that promotes and documents reflective thinking (Erdman, 1983; Flower & Hayes, 1981; Gipe & Richards, 1990; Yinger & Clark, 1981). Observation produces insights about human behaviors that cannot be gained by any other method, and multiple observations substantially improve the reliability of behavioral data (Medley & Mitzel, 1963). Descriptive statistics quantify data so that comparisons can be more meaningfully interpreted (Gay, 1981).

The participants were 23 female elementary education majors enrolled in two reading/language arts methods courses designated as an early field experience. The novice teachers received 6 semester hours of credit for successful completion of the two courses. The semester's ac-

tivities (e.g., lectures, demonstration lessons, and student teaching) were conducted at an inner-city school two mornings a week from 8:00 a.m. to 10:45 a.m.

The program, in its third semester at the elementary school, was guided by an emerging "inquiry-oriented" perspective. Seminar discussions focused upon novices' teaching concerns (e.g., why lessons went well or poorly, classroom management concerns, worries about a particular child, suggestions for future lessons). However, because of the supervisor's expanding goals for an inquiry-oriented program, existing school policies and practices also were considered in relation to socio/political realities. The topics, which arose naturally from the context of the field placement, included (a) who ultimately is responsible when a child receives overly harsh punishment in the classroom—teacher, principal, superintendent, school board, citizens; (b) who controls what occurs in classrooms; (c) the meaning of "the hidden curriculum"; and (d) the difficulty of continuing to teach with a holistic, child-centered instructional philosophy without collegial or supervisory support.

Dialogue journal activities were extensively used, although journal writing was not a graded course assignment. Each week, for 15 weeks, the prospective teachers wrote their thoughts and feelings about teaching in their journals. Each week the program supervisor read the journals and then wrote feedback comments designed to encourage the novices to reflect in their journals (e.g., "What could you have done differently?" "Who really is responsible when children fail? Please answer!" "How have your views about education changed since the beginning of the semester?" "I noted your problem. What were you thinking?" "Try to find the answer to your teaching dilemma within yourself and write the possible solutions in your journal.").

Following course lectures and demonstration lessons (8:00–9:00 a.m. each Monday and Wednesday), each prospective teacher worked with her own small groups of children in four different grade-level classrooms (prekindergarten through sixth grades, including gifted and learning disabled; two grade levels on Monday and two grade levels on Wednesday). Four novice teachers were assigned to the same classroom[1] during each 50-min time period (9:00–9:50 a.m. and 9:55–10:45 a.m.) throughout the semester, relieving the classroom teacher of teaching responsibilities during that time. Thus, each novice teacher prepared and taught four separate 50-min reading/language arts lessons weekly. The lessons were informally but attentively observed over the semester by the participating classroom teachers ($N = 16$) and were formally observed by the program supervisor.

Data Collection and Analysis

Using a previously defined and agreed-upon criteria and rating scale (see Appendix B), the classroom teachers and the program supervisor independently evaluated the novices' teaching abilities at the end of the first month of the semester and during the last week of the semester. Each of 15 teachers rated their 4 novice teachers; the gifted classroom teacher rated 3 novices. Therefore, each novice was independently rated by four separate classroom teachers. Thus, the 23 prospective teachers each received five autonomous ratings of teaching ability at the end of the first month of the program and five autonomous ratings of teaching ability at the end of the program.

At the conclusion of the semester, the novices' initial five ratings for teaching ability were averaged and compared with their final teaching ability rating averages. For example, Novice 1 received end-of-first-month teaching ability ratings of 3, 2, 3, 2, 2, for an average of 2.4 (i.e., *occasionally* prepares and presents appropriate lessons). Final teaching ability ratings for Novice 1 were 4, 3, 4, 4, 4, for an average of 3.8 (i.e., *always* prepares and presents appropriate lessons). Table 1 contains results for all novices ($N = 23$).

Additionally, two university supervisors who use dialogue journals on a regular basis with their own students, scored the novices' reflective journal statements. Each rater independently documented and scored the number of reflective statements per journal entry. Reflective statements were defined prior to scoring as statements within a single entry that demonstrated that novices were (a) attempting to make sense of their teaching experiences, questioning the status quo, considering future teaching alternatives, and coming to conclusions about students' abilities and behaviors (e.g., "I want to provide my students with a technique for analyzing and remembering. I've been wracking my brain trying to think of what I can do. Maybe we should write a rap song and put on a little play.") and (b) attempting to consider and question the impact of broader, socio-political concerns on classroom teachers' practices (e.g., "Why do they use fourth grade material with all fourth grade students? Who decides this?").

Nonreflective journal statements were defined as statements that provided the reader with a "recap" of the teaching session and omitted any attempts to brainstorm

solutions to teaching dilemmas or questions about school policies. (See Appendix A for examples of journal entries reflecting teaching and broader educational concerns, as well as nonreflective journal entries.) Initial interrater reliability was .86. Differences in the two raters' opinions as to what they considered to be reflective statements were further resolved by discussion. Statements that were not agreed upon by both raters were excluded from the data analysis. The final analysis was a comparison of each novice's average teaching ability rating (end of first month and end of semester) with the number of reflective statements written in their reflective journals (see Table 1).

Six of the prospective teachers were rated at the end of the first month and at the end of the semester as "always prepares and presents appropriate lessons." The number of reflective journal statements written by those students for 15 journal entries ranged from 16 to 25 ($\bar{x} = 21.4$). Six of the prospective teachers were rated at the end of the first month of the semester as occasionally and at the end of the semester as always prepares and presents appropriate lessons. The number of reflective journal statements written by the students for 15 journal entries ranged from 34 to 42 ($\bar{x} = 40$). Eleven of the prospective teachers were rated at the end of the first month of the semester as occasionally and at the end of the semester as usually prepares and presents appropriate lessons. The number of reflective journal statements written by the students for 15 journal entries ranged from 4 to 20 ($\bar{x} = 12.2$). Many of the reflections written by the 11 students had a negative and blaming tone (e.g., "Spare the rod and spoil the child with these kids!" "One boy in second grade started telling me he had a twin brother and baby brother. I found out later that this was a pack of lies!!!").

The 6 prospective teachers who were rated as improving the most in ability to prepare and present appropriate lessons (i.e., occasionally to always) wrote the largest number of reflective journal statements. Conversely, the 11 prospective teachers who were rated as least improved in ability to prepare and present appropriate lessons (i.e., occasionally to usually) wrote the fewest number of reflective journal statements. The 6 prospective teachers who were rated at the beginning and at the end of the semester as always prepares and presents appropriate lessons wrote a midrange number of reflective journal statements.

Discussion

Research conducted within the classroom environment provides knowledge that cannot be gained by any other method. Yet, there are limitations to research conducted in a naturalistic setting. The dual role of the researcher as program supervisor and the idea that supervisors hold biases and beliefs that influence supervisory evaluations are acknowledged as possible limitations (Zeichner & Tabachnick, 1982). In this case, the researcher/supervisor

Table 1.—Novice Teachers' Initial and Final Teaching Ability Ratings—Range and Mean Number of Reflective Journal Statements

n	Initial	Final	Range	Mean
6	3.5–4.0	3.5–4.0	16–25	21.4
6	1.5–2.4	3.5–4.0	34–42	40.0
11	1.5–2.4	2.5–3.4	4–20	12.2

Note. No student received an initial teaching ability rating average in the 2.5–3.4 or 1.0–1.4 categories. 3.5–4.0 = *always* prepares and presents appropriate lessons; 2.5–3.4 = *usually* prepares and presents appropriate lessons; 1.5–2.4 = *occasionally* prepares and presents appropriate lessons; 1.0–1.4 = *never* prepares and presents appropriate lessons.

was not neutral, but wholeheartedly believed in and encouraged a reflective teaching program. The classroom teachers' subjective views also must be acknowledged as possible limitations.

The use of an arbitrarily defined teacher ability rating scale (see Appendix B), may also be viewed as a limitation of this study. Further, the rating scale may not accurately depict equal increments of change in novices' teaching abilities (e.g., the distance between a rating of 2 to 3 may not equal the distance between a rating of 3 to 4). The rating scale represents an admittedly gross measure of novices' teaching abilities; nevertheless, it is one that classroom teachers serving as raters of novices' teaching abilities can easily use without infringing upon their already busy days. A more sensitive measure may have been able to document pedagogical growth in the novices who were rated initially, and throughout the semester, as always prepares and presents appropriate lessons. However, although there are sophisticated measures available for teacher evaluation, there are none that measure pedagogical growth. Such a measure is needed. One suggestion is to provide opportunities for preservice and inservice teachers to dialogue with each other about their professional development. In this way, a sensitive measure of novices' pedagogical growth may emerge.

Additionally, journal writing that requires writers to reflect through recollection may not sufficiently reveal every prospective teacher's sincerity, willingness, or ability to reflect about teaching. Personal preferences for privacy and individual choices for reflective modalities must be considered. For example, one student was queried about the sparsity of her writing. She responded in her journal, "I do reflect. But, I do it naturally . . . like in the shower or driving or going to sleep. You've got to have time to write and I'm working 32 hours per week." Nonetheless, all 23 novices did have the same number of opportunities to reflect (i.e., 15 journal entries), and all 23 subjects did attempt to reflect in their journals, but not all were successful (e.g., "I gave out their papers. I went over their mistakes. They all seemed to enjoy the lesson using semantic maps. That's about it. Is this what you mean by reflection?").

The goal of the study was to investigate the assumptive theme linking prospective teachers' reflective thinking and improvement in teaching abilities. Although it is premature to conclude that the more that prospective teachers reflect about their work, the more their teaching abilities will improve, the results of the study suggest that the assumptive theme that links prospective teachers' reflective thinking to their teaching is an appropriate assumption. The first formal connection between future teachers' reflections and improvements in their teaching ability suggests that "teacher preparation should foster reflective capacities" (Doyle, 1990, p. 6). Teacher educators who are tentatively contemplating the merits of a reflective program may now wish to initiate such agendas.

The results also suggest that prospective teachers' reflections can help supervisors to analyze whether novices' classroom experiences provide the right conditions for growth (Maslow, 1968) and to prescribe appropriate contexts for novices' future field placements. For example, as indicated by their journals, the prospective teachers who were always unanimously rated high in teaching ability apparently did not feel compelled to reflect a great deal about their teaching (see Table 1). They did not have to worry about solving professional problems such as pondering alternatives to instruction. When they were urged to reflect more, one of the 6 highly rated students confidently wrote, "I don't need to reflect or worry about my work. I know that things will go OK and if they don't, I make them turn out OK." A second placement that provides some frustrations and dissonance may force the 6 pedagogically competent novices to reflect upon educational dilemmas to resolve uncertainties and, therefore, be "pulled into a new level of growth" (Bolin, 1987, p. 8).

Similarly, the accomplishments of the 6 novice teachers who increased their teaching ability the most by the end of the semester have more meaning when their journal reflections are considered. The 6 future teachers reflected considerably about their work, and they achieved substantial professional growth. Furthermore, the small amount and mainly negative tone of the reflections written by the 11 prospective teachers who were rated as improving the least in teaching abilities indicates that those students may need a second, more structured, nonthreatening field placement with nurturing, supportive supervision to advance professionally. There is a relationship between safety and growth; "Assured safety permits higher needs and impulses to emerge and to grow towards mastery" (Maslow, 1968, p. 49).

Finally, results of this study highlight the importance of the context of the field placement with respect to promoting prospective teachers' reflections about teaching. A nonchallenging field experience may provide few opportunities for reflective thought, because there are few problems to solve. An overly threatening field placement may promote negativism and stagnation. Reflection becomes subordinate to survival concerns. A field placement that offers moderate amounts of ambiguity and dissonance (Bolin, 1987; Hollingsworth, 1989) may provide opportunities for problem solving through reflection and thereby enhance professional growth.

APPENDIX A

Examples of Reflective Journal Statements Depicting Novices' Teaching Concerns

Journal No. 5

I think the children responded to these statements because it called attention to themselves. When I used declarative statements the children didn't respond. It seemed that by giving them a direct statement they believed that what I said was truth. When I used "wait time" one girl thought I was mad. They are too young and too inexperienced to understand that I wanted them to elaborate. Now I know that I have to guide them through a discussion.

Journal No. 12

I don't know if I can take this kind of pain. I feel a certain closeness with my group and now . . . also a sadness. We all know that we'll probably never see one another again. I'm really going to miss them. Teachers are special people, aren't they? They know things about kids that no one else could know.

Journal No. 21

I still don't see why everyone thinks that Sam [fictitious name] is such a good teacher. His class seems kind of dull to me. I think visuals in upper levels would help generate interest in the topics and stimulate a desire to learn. Why doesn't he let his students decorate the class with their work?

Journal No. 23

One student in particular was reluctant to get involved. So I just kept including her in the lesson—calling on her to take her turn, etc. She rolled her eyes, etc. but participated nonetheless. I'm concerned about why she was so lethargic and sleepy. It was almost as if she were drugged. I have to find out if this is her usual state or not. Maybe she's having personal troubles that lead to her behavior. It concerns me.

Examples of Reflective Journal Statements Depicting Novices' Broader Educational Concerns

Journal No. 2

I'm shocked! What a day! Why am *i* so shocked? I don't know. I guess I just didn't expect the kids to be so casual. Are all schools in the U.S. this way now? How did things change since I was in elementary school?

Journal No. 11

Guess what? I have had my eyes opened and I still want to teach. I love it! I guess sometimes we get so involved with just teaching that we don't stop to think clearly. When I think in this journal I think how much I've learned about teaching. I have a long way to go, but now I know that some teachers and some schools don't treat kids like real people. The worst part is I don't think anyone cares.

Journal No. 19

One problem is that these parents need to help their kids more by making sure they eat breakfast and get to bed on time. Another problem is that the kindergarten kids have to do too much paper work and ditto sheets. Another thing . . . Hannah [fictitious name] says she can't even teach the kids what she knows they need because she'll get into trouble if she doesn't follow the curriculum. Do you really have to follow a curriculum if it's not right for the kids?

Examples of Nonreflective Journal Statements

Journal No. 3

At first when I arrived there wasn't a soul in sight. The building looked old and broken down and it was very HOT! Soon after, people started coming so I went inside. You began our lecture and I learned different auding [listening] strategies to use with children. Thanks!

Journal No. 6

In my sixth grade group I had two new students. They hadn't been there before due to absences. There was a constant chatter among the people in my group. I asked one of them to leave the group. He couldn't be quiet and didn't want to participate in the group activity. I guess that's the way it is here. The kids have a lot of freedom.

Journal No. 14

The first thing they did was to read and write in their dialogue journals. After writing in their journals they made the final changes in their stories for the creative book. The stories are great! The rest of the time was spent on illustrating the books. They have to be completed by March 20th. I let them decide which parts they wanted to illustrate and then they were on their own. Everything's going fine!

Journal No. 16

I did teacher dictation and they seemed to like that. We did seven sentences and they all participated, even the ones I had put out of the group would listen and follow along. I hope that was okay? After we did this I read *The King Who Rained*, by Fred Gwynn, and I explained it as I went through it. As usual, it all is going well!

APPENDIX B

Criteria for Rating Prospective Teachers' Abilities to Prepare and Present Appropriate Reading/Language Arts Lessons

a. Creates and uses teacher-made games and learning aids.
b. Presents reading/language arts topics commensurate with children's cognitive development, instructional needs, and interests.
c. Uses current research-based reading/language arts instructional strategies.*

*Examples of Current Research-Based Reading/Language Arts Instructional Strategies

- Takes individual or group dictation.
- Assists children in creating puppet plays and drama activities.
- Encourages creative bookmaking.
- Teaches subprocesses of the writing process (e.g., planning, composing, revising, evaluating compositions).
- Teaches reading comprehension (e.g., uses cloze/maze procedures, directed reading-thinking activities, semantic mapping).
- Expands children's vocabularies and cognitive development through group discussions, experiential activities, and vicarious experiences.

Teaching Ability Rating Scale

4 = *Always* prepares and presents appropriate lessons.
3 = *Usually* prepares and presents appropriate lessons.
2 = *Occasionally* prepares and presents appropriate lessons.
1 = *Never* prepares and presents appropriate lessons.

NOTE

The gifted classroom received only 3 novice teachers because fewer numbers of children needed to be accommodated. Therefore, five classrooms received 4 novice teachers, and one classroom received 3 novices, totalling 23 novice teachers.

REFERENCES

Beyer, L. (1984). Field experience, ideology, and the development of critical reflectivity. *Journal of Teacher Education, 35*(3), 36–41.

Bolin, F. (1987, April). *Students' conceptions of teaching as revealed in preservice journals.* Paper presented at the annual meeting of the American Educational Research Association. Washington, DC.

Clift, R., Houston, W. R., & Pugach, M. (Eds.) (1990). Encouraging reflective practice in education: An analysis of issues and programs. New York: Teachers College Press.

Cruickshank, D. (1984). *Helping teachers achieve wisdom.* Unpublished manuscript. The Ohio State University, College of Education, Columbus, OH.

Cruickshank, D., & Applegate, J. (1981). Reflective teaching as a strategy for teacher growth. *Educational Leadership, 38*(7), 553–554.

Cruickshank, D., Holton, J., Fay, D., Williams, J., Kennedy, J., Myers, B., & Hough, J. (1981). *Reflective teaching.* Bloomington, IN: Phi Delta Kappa.

Dewey, J. (1904). The relation of theory to practice in education. In C. A. McMurray (Ed.), *The relation of theory to practice in the education of teachers* (Third Yearbook of the National Society for the Study of Education, Part 1, pp. 9–30). Bloomington, IL: Public School Publishing.

Dewey, J. (1933). *How we think: A restatement of the relation of reflective thinking to the educational process.* Boston: D. C. Heath.

Doyle, W. (1990). Themes in teacher education research. In W. R. Houston, M. Haberman, & J. Sikula (Eds.), *Handbook of research on teacher education* (pp. 3–24). New York: Macmillan.

Erdman, J. (1983). Assessing the purposes of early field placement programs. *Journal of Teacher Education, 34,* 27–31.

Feiman-Nemser, S. (1990). Teacher preparation: Structural and conceptual alternatives. In W. R. Houston, M. Haberman, & J. Sikula (Eds.), *Handbook of research on teacher education* (pp. 212–223). New York: Macmillan.

Flower, L., & Hayes, J. (1981). A cognitive process theory of writing. *College Composition and Communication, 32,* 365–387.

Gay, L. (1981). *Educational research* (2nd ed.). Columbus, OH: Charles E. Merrill.

Gipe, J. P., & Richards, J. C. (1990, Spring). Promoting reflection about reading instruction through journaling. *Journal of Reading Education, 15*(3), 6–13.

Glaser, B., & Strauss, A. (1967). The discovery of grounded theory: Strategies for qualitative research. Chicago: Aldine.

Goodman, J. (1985). What students learn from early field experiences: A case study and critical analysis. *Journal of Teacher Education, 36*(6), 42–48.

Gore, J. (1987). Reflecting on reflective teaching. *Journal of Teacher Education, 38*(2), 33–39.

Harnett, A., & Naish, M. (1980). Technicians or social bandits? Some moral and political issues in the education of teachers. In P. Woods (Ed.), *Teacher strategies* (pp. 225–274). London: Croom Helm.

Hollingsworth, S. (1989). Prior beliefs and cognitive change in learning to teach. *American Educational Research Journal, 26,* 160–189.

Holton, J., & Nott, D. (1980, April). *The experimental effects of reflective teaching on preservice teachers' ability to think and talk critically about teaching and learning.* Paper presented at the annual meeting of the American Educational Research Association, Boston, MA.

Korthagen, F. (1985). Reflective teaching and preservice teacher education in the Netherlands. *Journal of Teacher Education, 36*(5), 11–15.

Korthagen, F., & Verkuyl, H. (1987, April). *Supply and demand: Towards differentiation in teacher education, based on differences in learning orientations.* Paper presented at the annual meeting of the American Educational Research Association, Washington, DC.

Maslow, A. (1968). *Toward a psychology of being.* New York: Van Nostrand Reinhold.

Medley, D., & Mitzel, H. (1963). Measuring classroom behavior by systematic observation. In N. Gage (Ed.), *Handbook of research on teaching* (pp. 247–328). Chicago: Rand McNally.

Meltzer, B., Petras, J., & Reynolds, L. (1975). *Symbolic interactionism: Genesis, varieties and criticism.* London: Routledge and Kegan Paul.

Neimeyer, R, & Moon, A. (1986, April). *Researching decision-making in the supervision of student teachers.* Paper presented at the annual meeting of the American Educational Research Association, San Francisco.

Schon, D. (1987). *Educating the reflective practitioner.* San Francisco: Jossey-Bass.

Williams, F., & Kennedy, J. (1980, April). *The effects of reflective teaching relative to promoting attitudinal change.* Paper presented at the annual meeting of the American Educational Research Association, Boston, MA.

Yinger, R., & Clark, C. (1981). *Reflective journal writing: Theory and practice* (IRT Occasional Paper No. 50). East Lansing, MI: Institute for Research on Teaching, Michigan State University.

Yonemura, M. (1987). *A teacher at work: Professional development and the early childhood educator.* New York: Teachers College Press.

Zeichner, K. (1981–82). Reflective teaching and field-based experience in teacher education. *Interchange, 12,* 1–22.

Zeichner, K., Liston, D., Mahlios, M., & Gomez, M. (1987, April). *The structure and goals of a student teaching program and the character and quality of supervisory discourse.* Paper presented at the annual meeting of the American Educational Research Association, Washington, DC.

Zeichner, K., & Tabachnick, B. (1982). The belief systems of university supervisors in an elementary student-teaching program. *Journal of Education for Teaching, 8,* 34–54.

Zeichner, K., & Teitelbaum, K. (1982). Personalized and inquiry-oriented teacher education: An analysis of two approaches to the development of curriculum for field-based experience. *Journal of Education for Teaching, 8,* 95–117.

■ SUMMARY/CHAPTER 7
DEFINITION AND PURPOSE

1. Simplistically put, qualitative research is the collection and analysis of extensive narrative data in order to gain insights into a situation of interest not possible using other types of research.
2. A qualitative study may well utilize historical methods in order to gain a better perspective on the person, place, object, or activity under study.
3. Unlike quantitative research, qualitative research involves for the most part nonnumerical data such as extensive notes taken on site.

Definition

4. Qualitative research involves intensive data collection, that is, collection of extensive data on many variables over an extended period of time, in a naturalistic setting.
5. The term "naturalistic setting" refers to the fact that the variables being investigated are studied *where* they naturally occur, *as* they naturally occur, not in researcher-controlled conditions, as is the case with quantitative studies.
6. Some researchers use the terms "ethnographic" and "qualitative" interchangeably, while others consider ethnography to be *one kind* of qualitative research.
7. The rationale behind the use of qualitative inquiry is the research-based belief that behavior is significantly influenced by the environment in which it occurs.
8. Qualitative researchers are not just concerned with describing the way things are, but also with gaining insights into the "big picture"; they seek answers to questions related to how things got to be the way they are, how people involved *feel* about the way things are, what they *believe*, what *meanings* they attach to various activities, and so forth.
9. In order to achieve the objective of in-depth description and understanding, qualitative research utilizes a variety of methods and data collection strategies, and is often characterized as being "multimethod."
10. The most common strategy used, however, is participant observation, usually supplemented by collection of relevant documents and extensive, informal interviewing.
11. *What* is observed is typically a single "unit" (or a very small number of units); a unit may be (as examples) a school, a program, a classroom, an administrator, a teacher, or a student.
12. Unlike quantitative researchers, qualitative researchers argue that there is no such thing as "value-free science" and that the values of both the researcher and the phenomena studied are important variables which, to the degree possible, should be taken into consideration when conducting, reporting, or reviewing research.
13. At a more operational level, qualitative research is more holistic and process-oriented, whereas quantitative research is more focused and outcome-oriented.
14. Whereas quantitative researchers attempt to control as many variables as possible, qualitative researchers do not wish to control anything; they want to study phenomena as they are, in natural settings.

Purpose

15. Qualitative and quantitative research represent complementary components of the scientific method, i.e., inductive and deductive.
16. Some qualitative researchers do try to contribute directly to the development of theory, but it is *grounded theory,* i.e., theory based on data collected in real-world settings which reflect what naturally occurred over an extended period of time.
17. Questions formulated for a qualitative study are much more general than for a quantitative study.
18. Unlike a quantitative hypothesis, a qualitative hypothesis is tentative and subject to ongoing revision throughout the study.
19. At most, the study of previous work may result in a very tentative hypothesis; the qualitative researcher does not want to be overly influenced by findings produced by the application of other methods of research.
20. Thus, an extensive review of the literature is not characteristic of qualitative research.

SAMPLING AND MEASUREMENT

Sampling

21. By definition, whatever *is* observed represents a sample of what *could have been* observed.
22. The qualitative researcher carefully selects a small, not necessarily representative, sample, one likely to yield the desired information.
23. The qualitative researcher is often involved in a very close relationship with study participants.
24. The quantitative researcher wants to generalize findings to a larger population, whereas the qualitative researcher wants to get the deepest understanding possible of the situation studied.
25. In a qualitative study, the sampling is usually *purposive,* meaning that the sample is selected purposefully, i.e., precisely because it is believed to be a rich source of the data of interest.
26. While qualitative researchers are not necessarily interested in generalizing, they are concerned with the representativeness of the data they are collecting. In other words, they want their observations to at least accurately reflect the situation under study, regardless of whether the dynamics of that situation are generalizable.
27. There are no guidelines for sample size in a qualitative study.

Measurement

28. A major difference between measurement in a quantitative study and measurement in a qualitative study is that the former involves standardization and the latter does not.
29. A second major difference is that for a quantitative study what is measured is expressed numerically, and for a qualitative study it is expressed narratively.
30. In a qualitative study, the researcher does not want to be restricted by predetermined questions or categories, except in the most general sense.

31. By the nature of the way in which qualitative data are collected, the researcher is the de facto instrument, in most cases the only instrument.

32. Thus, the concepts of validity and reliability, while still very relevant, must be looked at differently in a qualitative study, and cannot be expressed numerically.

33. In qualitative "measurement," validity is the degree to which observations accurately reflect what was observed (and interviews accurately reflect the feelings, opinions, and so forth, of those interviewed) and, consequently, permit appropriate interpretation of narrative data.

34. It is obvious then that to a much greater degree than in a quantitative study, the validity and reliability of measurement in a qualitative study are highly correlated with the competence, experience, and dedication of the person conducting the study.

35. Qualitative researchers in general, however, are well aware of the potential sources of inaccurate data collection and utilize a number of strategies to deal with them. One common strategy is referred to as *triangulation;* triangulation is the term for the use of multiple methods, data collection strategies, and/or data sources.

36. Qualitative researchers can look for consistency across observations over time, consistency of interview data among persons interviewed, consistency of interview data for the same person(s), consistency of researchers' data and impressions, and so forth.

37. Another major strategy of qualitative researchers for promoting accuracy of data is the use of recording devices such as audio and video equipment.

DESIGN AND METHOD

38. In general, the design of a study is basically the overall approach used to investigate the problem of interest, i.e., to shed light on, or answer, the question(s) of interest or to test the intended hypothesis.

39. In a qualitative study, design and method (D & M) are more flexible (than in a quantitative study) and are usually specified in only the most general terms prior to the actual study.

40. Another enormous difference between the D & M of quantitative and qualitative studies is the issue of intervention; a quantitative study almost demands it, whereas a qualitative study tries to avoid it.

41. Most qualitative research efforts represent case studies; a *case study* is the in-depth investigation of one "unit," e.g., individual, group, institution, organization, program, document collection, and so forth.

42. In order to achieve a more complete understanding of a case under study, a qualitative researcher may well utilize historical research methods.

43. Some qualitative researchers do try to contribute to theory, but it is *grounded theory,* i.e., theory based on data collected in real-world settings.

44. Grounded theory research typically involves *multicase* and/or *multisite studies.*

Data Collection Strategies—Fieldwork

45. Most qualitative studies, at least in education, are characterized by some type of overt participant observation and the taking of extensive fieldnotes.

46. Such observation is often supplemented by the collection of relevant documents (such as minutes of meetings and memoranda) and in-depth, unstructured interviewing.
47. Qualitative and quantitative researchers use data collection strategies which may *sound* similar but are really quite different; both use observation and interviewing, for example, but in qualitative research the approaches are much less structured and yield narrative data.

Participant Observation

48. While the unit(s) of observation in an educational research study may be smaller or larger, it is typically a classroom, an entire school, or some aspect of a school, such as principal-teacher interactions.
49. In participant observation, the observer actually becomes a part of, a participant in, the situation to be observed.
50. The researcher gradually increases his or her degree of involvement and at all stages takes extensive notes (or otherwise records) as much as possible.

Document Collection

51. Qualitative researchers frequently supplement observation with document collection; a document may be any written or nonwritten record which exists and which may enhance the researcher's overall understanding of the situation under study.
52. These documents may contain numerical data; such data may be used in a number of ways in conjunction with other data.
53. The information contained in "documents" may support or not support data collected in other ways and/or may suggest future data strategies.
54. Documents often reveal information not available through other means.

Observer Bias

55. Observer bias refers to invalid observations that result from the way in which the observer observes.
56. The more involved the researcher is, the greater the degree of subjectivity likely to creep into the observations; on the other hand, the greater the involvement, the greater the opportunity for acquiring in-depth understanding and insight.
57. Qualitative researchers try to minimize the effects of their personal biases on their findings by conscientiously recording their thoughts, feelings, and reactions *about* what they observe, as well as *what* they observe.

Observer Effect

58. The other side of the coin is called the observer effect and refers to the impact of the observer's participation on the situation being observed.
59. Again, while this problem is by no means unique to qualitative research, it is potentially more serious since the researcher is trying to study how people normally behave in their *natural* setting.
60. A major strategy of qualitative researchers is to be as unassuming as they can be as they gradually increase their participation.
61. It also helps if the exact nature of the researcher's inquiry is not described in any more detail than is necessary, ethically or legally.
62. As with observer bias, triangulation represents an important safeguard which helps us to detect a serious observer effect.

63. Thus, qualitative researchers are well aware that they cannot totally eliminate observer effects; they do, however, make every effort to recognize, minimize, record, and report them.

Interviews

64. A typical qualitative interview is a one-on-one session in which the researcher asks a series of open-ended, probing questions.
65. In addition to serving triangulation objectives, interviews have a unique purpose, namely, to acquire data not obtainable in any other way.
66. The two major strategies for gaining a historical perspective on the situation of interest are document collection and what are referred to as *retrospective interviews*.
67. Interviews vary in degree of structure and formality and include a range of questions which can be classified on a continuum of, for lack of a better word, sensitivity.
68. Questions at the "more sensitive" end of the continuum require more skill, both methodological and interpersonal, on the part of the researcher.
69. The typical qualitative interview is fairly unstructured and open-ended.
70. The typical interview is also quite informal in the sense that it is not, for example, scheduled.
71. There are times, however, when varying degrees of structure are called for, given the purpose for which the interviews are being conducted.
72. A *focus group interview* involves a small number of people who have something of interest in common, e.g., participation in a particular program.
73. Occasionally, usually in multicase or multisite research, more standardized, open-ended interviews are utilized.

Qualitative Data—Fieldnotes

74. Qualitative data are all the data collected, from whatever source, during fieldwork, including fieldnotes, documents, interview transcripts, photographs, and videotapes.
75. Since participant observation is the major data collection strategy used in qualitative research, however, fieldnotes are obviously of prime importance.
76. Whether taken in the actual setting or recorded as soon as possible after leaving the setting, fieldnotes describe as accurately as possible and as comprehensively as possible all relevant aspects of the situation observed, and include both what was actually observed and the observer's reactions to same.
77. The task appears even more awesome when you consider that descriptions must be very specific and represent what was actually *seen* (or heard, or whatever), not your interpretation of what was seen.
78. In addition to literal descriptions, the observer also records personal reactions, generally referred to as *reflective fieldnotes*.

DATA ANALYSIS AND INTERPRETATION

79. Whereas the "raw data" for quantitative studies are *numbers* (e.g., test scores), the raw data for qualitative studies are *words* (and possibly visual material such as photos).

80. These data include primarily fieldnotes, often supplemented by documents and interview transcripts.
81. Since the emphasis is on what people *actually said*, direct quotations are preferable to paraphrases or the observer's recollections.
82. Other major differences between quantitative and qualitative analysis are that while quantitative analysis is typically performed at the end of the study and usually involves application of descriptive and/or inferential statistics, qualitative analysis is essentially ongoing and infrequently involves application of statistics.

Analysis

83. In a simplified nutshell, qualitative analysis involves making sense out of an enormous amount of narrative data.
84. The qualitative researcher looks for categories, patterns, and themes which will facilitate a coherent synthesis of the data.
85. The process is similar in many ways to the one involved in generating a coherent review of related literature, as discussed in Chapter 2.
86. Two qualitative researchers independently investigating very similar problems or questions may well produce very different reports.
87. Participant observation is characterized by the collection of large amounts of data that are, to say the least, not easy to analyze.
88. While index cards and the good old cut-and-paste approach still live, most qualitative researchers use computers to assist them in a variety of data analysis procedures, sorting by code for example.
89. Coding of data is a critical aspect of most qualitative research; coding involves critically analyzing the data and identifying themes and topics which represent categories into which numerous pieces of data can be classified.
90. Specific categories may be labeled with words, letters, numbers, or symbols.
91. Both quantitative and qualitative researchers report *how* the data were analyzed not just the results, but the task is more difficult for qualitative researchers since they must report on a *process,* e.g., how they formulated their coding categories.

Interpretation

92. While in a quantitative study conclusions and generalizations are formulated at the end of the study and are stated with a basically predetermined degree of certainty, in a qualitative study "conclusions" are drawn and reviewed on an ongoing basis and are more tentative, and generalizations are highly speculative or nonexistent.
93. The conclusions in a qualitative study are the insights the researcher believes she or he has gleaned as the result of a lengthy, intensive effort.
94. Since sampling is purposive and the "sample" size is small (representing, not atypically, a single case), no attempt is made to generalize findings to a larger population.
95. The issue of generalizability is left up to consumers of the research and to other researchers.

QUALITATIVE VERSUS QUANTITATIVE RESEARCH

Cautions and Contrasts

96. Proper application of the qualitative approach requires the accurate recording of large amounts of data over long periods of time, by persons thoroughly trained in observational methods.

97. Results are difficult to analyze, conclusions are highly tentative, and generalizations are minimal or nonexistent.

98. At a practical level, qualitative research tends to be more costly.

99. Thus, the good news is that qualitative research typically yields an abundance of potentially useful data and insights not obtainable using other methods, and the hypotheses generated by such research are in many cases more valid than those based on theory alone; the bad news is that collecting and analyzing such data and drawing defensible conclusions is not an easy task.

100. Although opinions vary, the most reasonable position appears to be that neither qualitative nor quantitative research is appropriate for all situations; the choice of type of inquiry and corresponding methodologies depends upon the nature of the phenomena being studied.

Trends

101. In education, qualitative research design and methodology are undergoing constant refinement and adaptation in the direction of a more-structured (i.e., quantitative) approach.

102. Another major related trend is for studies to use a combination of methodologies and to collect both qualitative and quantitative data in the same study.

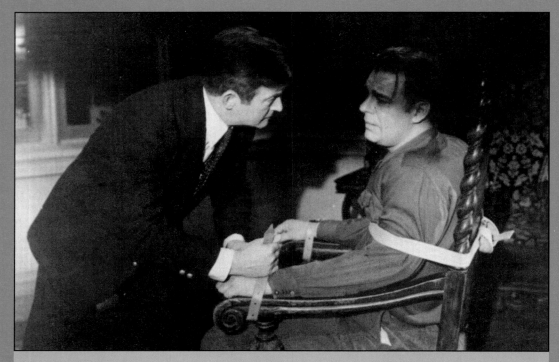

"The responses given by a subject may be biased and affected by her or his reaction to the interviewer . . . (p. 262)."

Descriptive Research

After reading Chapter 8, you should be able to:

1. Briefly state the purpose of descriptive research.

2. List the major steps involved in designing and conducting a descriptive research study.

3. State the major difference between self-report and observational research.

4. Briefly describe four types of self-report research.

5. List and briefly describe the steps involved in conducting a questionnaire study.

6. Identify and briefly describe four major differences between an interview study and a questionnaire study.

7. Briefly describe two types of observational research.

8. Briefly describe the steps involved in conducting an observational study.

DEFINITION, PURPOSE, AND PROCESS

Descriptive research involves collecting data in order to test hypotheses or to answer questions concerning the current status of the subject of the study. A descriptive study determines and reports the way things are. Descriptive research in general, and specific types of descriptive research in particular, will be discussed in some detail for two major reasons. First, a high percentage of reported research studies are descriptive in nature. Second, the descriptive method is useful for investigating a variety of educational problems. Typical descriptive studies are concerned with the assessment of attitudes, opinions, demographic information, conditions, and procedures. Descriptive data are usually collected through a questionnaire survey, interviews, or observation. Just as the historical researcher has no control over what *was,* the descriptive researcher has no control over what *is,* and can only measure what already exists.

Descriptive research sounds very simple; there is considerably more to it, however, than just asking questions and reporting answers. The same basic process is involved as for the other types of research, and each component must be just as conscientiously executed; for example, samples must be carefully selected, and appropriate relationships and conclusions must be derived from the data. In addition, descriptive studies involve a number of unique problems. For example, self-report studies, such as those utilizing questionnaires or interviews, often suffer from lack of response; many subjects do not return mailed questionnaires or attend scheduled interviews. In these situations it is very difficult to interpret findings since people who do not respond may feel very differently from those who do. Twenty percent of a sample, for example, might feel very negatively about the year-round school concept and might avail themselves of every opportunity to express their unhappiness, such as on your questionnaire. The other 80%, who feel neutrally or positively, might not be as motivated to respond. Thus, if conclusions were based only on those who responded, very wrong conclusions might be drawn concerning feelings toward the year-round school concept. Descriptive studies utilizing observational techniques to collect data also involve complexities that are not readily apparent. Observers must be trained and recording forms must be developed so that data will be collected objectively and reliably.

Once a descriptive problem has been defined, related literature has been reviewed, and hypotheses or questions stated, the researcher must give careful thought to sample selection and data collection. Which population has the desired information, for example, is not always readily apparent; this point is often not sufficiently thought through ahead of time. Also, there are frequently alternative methods available for collecting desired data, one of which is generally more appropriate. Suppose, for example, your problem was concerned with how elementary level teachers spend their time during the school day. You might hypothesize that they spend one-third of their time on noninstructional activities such as collecting milk money and maintaining order. Your first thought might be to mail a questionnaire to a sample of principals. This procedure, however, would be based on the assumption that principals *know* how teachers spend their time. While principals would of course be familiar with the duties and responsibilities of their teachers, it is not unlikely that teacher reports concerning time devoted to each activity would differ, perhaps significantly, from principal reports. Thus, directly asking the teachers themselves would probably result in more accurate information. On the other hand, it is possible that teachers might tend to subconsciously exaggerate the amount of time they spend on activities they consider to be distasteful, such as clerical operations (for example, grading papers). Thus, further thought might indicate that direct observation would probably yield the most objective, accurate data.

Having decided on a target population and a data collection strategy, the next steps are to identify your accessible population, determine needed sample size, select an appropriate sampling technique, and select or develop a data collection instrument. Frequently, since one is generally asking questions that have not been asked before, or seeking information that is not already available, a descriptive study requires the development of an instrument appropriate for obtaining the desired information. Of course if there is a valid, reliable instrument available, it can be used, but using an instrument just "because it is there" is not a good idea. If you want the correct answers, you have to ask the correct questions. If instrument development is necessary, the instrument should be tried out and revised where necessary before it is used in the actual study. Having identified an appropriate sample, and selected or developed a valid data collection instrument, the next step is to carefully plan and execute the specific procedures of the study (when the instrument will be administered, to whom, and how) and the data analysis procedures. Of course the basic steps in conducting a descriptive study will vary, depending upon the nature of the research. In a content analysis study, for example, human subjects are not involved.

There are many different types of descriptive studies, and classifying them is not easy. However, a logical way to initially categorize them is in terms of how data are collected, through self-report or observation. In a self-report study, information is solicited from individuals using, for example, questionnaires, interviews, or standardized attitude scales. In an observation study, individuals are not asked for information; rather, the researcher obtains the desired data through other means, such as direct observation. These two categories are not, of course, mutually exclusive; a self-report study may involve observation and vice versa.

■ SELF-REPORT RESEARCH

There are several major types of self-report research studies. The most well known and most often used is probably survey research, which generally utilizes questionnaires or interviews to collect data.

Types of Self-Report Research

While survey research is the most frequently encountered type of self-report research, developmental, follow-up, and sociometric studies also rely primarily on self-reported information.

Survey Research

A survey is an attempt to collect data from members of a population in order to determine the current status of that population with respect to one or more variables. Populations may be broadly defined, such as the American voting public, or narrowly defined, such as all parents of school-age children in Teenytown, U.S.A. Determining "current status . . . with respect to some variable" may involve assessment of a variety of types of information such as attitudes, opinions, characteristics, and demographic information. Surveys are generally viewed with some disdain because many people have encountered poorly planned, poorly executed survey studies utilizing poorly developed instruments. You should not condemn survey research, however, just because it has often been misused. After all, you do not dislike telephones just because a few people use them to make obscene phone calls. Descriptive research at its best can provide very valuable data. It represents considerably more than asking questions and reporting answers; it involves careful design and execution of each of the components of the research process, including the formulation of hypotheses, and may describe variables and relationships between variables. Surveys are used in many fields, including political science, sociology, economics, and education. In education their most common use is for the collection of data by schools or about schools. Surveys conducted by schools are usually prompted by a need for certain kinds of information related to instruction, facilities, or the student population. Surveys conducted to collect data about schools are initiated by a variety of groups, including governmental agencies and researchers.

Surveys are either sample surveys or census surveys, but usually the former. In a sample survey, as the name suggests, the researcher infers information about a population of interest based on the responses of a sample drawn from that population; preferably, the sample is either a simple-random or a stratified-random sample. In a census survey, an attempt is made to acquire data from each and every member of a population; a census survey is usually conducted when a population is relatively small and readily accessible, such as when a superintendent collects data from each principal in his or her system. Sample surveys are sometimes referred to as cross-sectional since information is collected at some point in time from a sample which hopefully represents all relevant subgroups in the population. Surveys concerned with the current status of construct variables (such as achievement or attitude), as opposed to concrete variables (such as number of professional journals to which English teachers subscribe, or number of pupils per class), not only involve careful selection from, and/or definition of, a population, but also require care in selection or development of the data-gathering instrument. It is considerably easier to develop a valid, reliable instrument for determining the percentage of teachers in each school who are teaching "out-of-field" than it is to develop one for assessing teachers' attitudes toward required, in-service teacher education programs.

There are a variety of types of surveys, many of which are familiar to most people. The results of various public opinion polls, for example, are frequently reported by the media. Such polls represent an attempt to determine how *all* the members of a population (be it the American public in general or citizens of Skunk Hollow) feel about a political, social, educational, or economic issue, not just vocal special-interest groups within the population. Public opinion polls are almost always sample surveys. Samples are selected to properly represent relevant subgroups (in terms of such variables as socioeconomic status, sex, and geographic location) and results are often reported separately for each of those subgroups as well as for the total group.

One type of survey unique to education is the school survey, which may involve the study of an individual school or of all the schools in a particular system. School surveys are generally conducted for the purpose of internal or external evaluation or for assessment and projection of needs and usually are conducted as a cooperative effort between local school personnel and a visiting team of experts, typically from local educational agencies and institutions. Resulting recommendations and/or projections are based upon the collection of data concerning the current status of variables such as community characteristics, institutional and administrative personnel, curriculum and instruction, finances, and physical facilities. School surveys can provide necessary and valuable information to both the schools studied and to other agencies and groups (such as boards of public instruction) whose operations are school related.

Developmental Studies

Developmental studies are concerned primarily with behavior variables that differentiate children at different levels of age, growth, or maturation. Developmental studies may investigate progression along a number of dimensions, such as intellectual, physical, emotional, or social development. The children under study may be a relatively heterogeneous group, such as fourth graders in general, or may comprise a more narrowly defined homogeneous group, such as the study of the gift-ed, children with high intellectual potential. Knowledge concerning developmental patterns of various student groups can be applied in order to make the curriculum and instruction for various student populations more appropriate and relevant. Knowing that 4-year-old and 5-year-old children typically enjoy skill-testing games (such as jumping rope and bouncing balls) but do not enjoy group work or activi-ties involving competition would certainly be helpful to a preschool teacher in developing lesson plans.[1]

Developmental studies may be cross-sectional or longitudinal; both methods have their own relative advantages and disadvantages. When the cross-sectional approach is used, different children at various stages of development are simulta-neously studied; when the longitudinal method is used, the same group of children is studied over a period of time as the children progress from level to level. Suppose, for example, you were interested in studying the development of abstract thinking in elementary school students. If you used a cross-sectional approach, you would study samples of children at each of the six grade levels, including first graders to sixth graders; the children studied at one level would be different chil-dren from those studied at another level. If you used a longitudinal approach, you could select a sample of first graders and study the development of their abstract thinking as they progressed from grade to grade; the group studied at the sixth-grade level would be the same group that was studied at the first-grade level. The advantage of the cross-sectional method is that larger groups can be studied. In lon-gitudinal studies, samples tend to shrink as time goes by; keeping track of subjects over periods of time can be difficult, as can maintaining their participation in the study. A major concern in a cross-sectional study is selecting samples of children that truly represent children at their level; a further related problem is selecting sam-ples at different levels that are comparable on relevant variables such as intelli-gence. An advantage of the longitudinal method is that this latter concern about comparability is not a problem in that the same group is involved at each level. A major disadvantage of the longitudinal method is that an extended commitment must be made by the researcher, the subjects, and all others involved. Although for particular problems one of the methods may be clearly more appropriate, the cross-sectional approach is generally preferable because of the typically larger samples.

Follow-Up Studies

A follow-up study is conducted to determine the status of a group of interest after some period of time. Like school surveys, follow-up studies are often conducted by educational institutions for the purpose of internal or external evaluation of their instructional program, or some aspect of it. Accreditation agencies, for example, typically require systematic follow-up of teacher education program graduates. Such follow-up efforts typically seek objective information regarding the current status of the former students (Are you presently employed?) as well as attitudinal and opin-ion data concerning the graduates' perceptions of the adequacy of their training. If a majority of graduates should indicate, for example, that they feel the career coun-seling they received was poor, this finding would suggest an area in need of improvement. Similarly, if a number of graduates should indicate that they have been unable to obtain employment due to a lack of certain competencies, this infor-mation would also be valuable input for the upgrading of the program of interest.

---

[1] Strang, R. M. (1959). *An introduction to child study.* New York: Macmillan.

Of course the results of such a follow-up study may also be very positive, indicating a high degree of satisfaction with the program.

Follow-up studies may also be conducted solely for research purposes. A researcher may be interested, for example, in assessing the degree to which initial treatment effects have been maintained over time. A study might demonstrate that students participating in preschool training are better adjusted socially and demonstrate higher academic achievement in the first grade. A follow-up study could be conducted to determine if this initial advantage is still in evidence at the end of the third grade. Many treatments which have an initial impact do not have a lasting effect; initial differences "wash out" or disappear after some period of time. A treatment may temporarily change attitudes, for example, but when the subjects are removed from the experimental setting they may gradually regress to their original point of view. Conversely, some treatments do not result in initial differences but may produce long-range effects. Delayed feedback concerning adequacy of test performance, for example, is a technique which does not necessarily improve initial achievement but does seem to facilitate long-term retention.[2] If follow-up data were not collected, it would be erroneously concluded that delayed feedback has no effect. Thus, in many areas of research, a follow-up study is essential to a more complete understanding of the effects of a given approach or technique.

Sociometric Studies

Sociometry is the assessment and analysis of the interpersonal relationships within a group of individuals. By analyzing the expressed choices or preferences of group members for other members of the group, degree of acceptance or rejection for members of the group can be determined. The basic sociometric process involves asking each member to indicate with which other members she or he would most like to engage in a particular activity. For example, you might ask subjects to list in order of preference the three individuals they would most like to work with on a cooperative project. As you well know, choices will vary depending upon the activity; the person you would most enjoy going with to a party is not necessarily the same person with whom you would like to write a joint term paper. The choices made by the group members are graphically depicted in a diagram called a sociogram. A sociogram may take many forms and use a variety of symbols, but basically it shows who chose whom. A sociogram will clearly identify "stars"—members chosen quite frequently, "isolates"—members not chosen, and "cliques"—small subgroups of individuals who mutually select each other.

Sociometric techniques are utilized by both researchers and practitioners. A number of educational research studies have been concerned with the relationship between group status and other variables such as personality characteristics. Another type of research study involves assessment of initial interpersonal relationship patterns, introduction of a treatment designed to change the existing pattern, and post-assessment to determine pattern changes. A similar procedure may be utilized by teachers in an attempt, for example, to bring isolates into the group. If Nell Nerdy were identified as being an isolate, her teacher could make a concerted effort to provide opportunities for Nell to interact with other members of the group. Thus, the sociometric process is one that is relatively simple to apply and can provide data

---

[2]See, for example, English, R. A., & Kinzer, J. R. (1966). The effect of immediate and delayed feedback on retention of subject matter. *Psychology in the Schools, 3,* 143–147.

useful for the solution of immediate social problems and for the development of theories concerning interpersonal relationships within a group.

Conducting Self-Report Research

Self-report research requires the collection of standardized, quantifiable information from all members of a population or sample. In other words, in order to obtain comparable data from all subjects, the same questions must be asked. Any of the types of tests described in Chapter 5 (i.e., achievement, personality, intelligence, aptitude) can be used in a self-report research study. Two additional commonly used procedures for collecting self-report data are the questionnaire study and the interview study.

Conducting a Questionnaire Study   *Mid-term !*

Criticisms of questionnaires are related not to their use but to their misuse. Too many carelessly and incompetently constructed questionnaires have unfortunately been administered and distributed. Development of a sound questionnaire requires both skill and time. However, the use of a questionnaire has some definite advantages over other methods of collecting data that are not available through other sources. In comparison to use of an interview procedure, for example, a questionnaire is much more efficient in that it requires less time, is less expensive, and permits collection of data from a much larger sample. Questionnaires may be administered to subjects but are usually mailed. Although a personally administered questionnaire has some of the same advantages inherent in the use of an interview, such as the opportunity to establish rapport with respondents, explain the purposes of the study, and clarify individual items, it is not usually the case that the members of a sample of interest are conveniently found together in one location. Attempting to travel to each respondent in order to administer the questionnaire is generally impracticable and eliminates the advantage of being able to contact a large sample.

The steps in conducting a questionnaire study are essentially the same as for other types of research, although data collection involves some unique considerations.

Statement of the Problem. The problem under investigation, and the topic of the questionnaire, must be of sufficient significance to motivate subjects to respond; questionnaires dealing with trivial issues usually end up in the circular file of potential respondents. The problem must be defined in terms of specific objectives concerning the kind of information needed; specific hypothesis of questions must be formulated and every item on the questionnaire should directly relate to them.

Selection of Subjects. Subjects should be selected using an appropriate sampling technique (or an entire population may be used), and identified subjects must be persons who (1) have the desired information and (2) are likely to be willing to give it. Individuals who possess the desired information but are not sufficiently interested, or for whom the topic under study has little meaning, are not likely to respond. It is sometimes worth the effort to do a preliminary check of potential responders to determine their receptivity. In some cases it is more productive to send the questionnaire to a person of authority rather than directly to the person with the desired information; if a person's boss passes along a questionnaire and asks the person to complete and return it, that person is more likely to do so than if *you* ask him or her!

Construction of the Questionnaire.   As a general guideline, the questionnaire should be as attractive and brief, and as easy to respond to, as possible. Sloppy looking questionnaires turn people off, lengthy questionnaires turn people off, questionnaires requiring lengthy responses to each question *really* turn people off! Turning people off is not the way to get them to respond. To meet this guideline you must carefully plan both the content and the format of the questionnaire. No item should be included that does not directly relate to the objectives of the study, and structured, or closed-form, items should be used if at all possible. A structured item consists of a question and a list of alternative responses from which the respondent selects. The list of alternatives should include all possible responses, and each possible response should be distinctly different from the rest. The difference between "often" and "frequently" as responses is not clear to many of us! In some cases, a very short written response may be required, but generally a structured item is multiple-choice in nature (yes or no, A, B, C, D, or E). In addition to facilitating response, structured items also facilitate data analysis; scoring is very objective and efficient. A potential disadvantage is the possibility that a subject's true response is not listed among the alternatives. Therefore, questionnaires should include an "other" category for each item (except for items such as Sex, M or F), and a space for a subject to write in a response not anticipated by the researcher. An unstructured item format, in which the responder has complete freedom of response (questions are asked with no possible responses indicated), is sometimes defended on the grounds that it permits greater depth of response and may permit insight into the reasons for responses. While this may be true, and unstructured items are simpler to construct, the disadvantages of this approach generally outweigh the advantages; subjects often provide information extraneous to the objectives of the study, responses are difficult to score and analyze, and subjects are not happy with an instrument that requires written responses. For certain topics or purposes unstructured items may be necessary and some questionnaires contain both structured and unstructured items. In general, however, structured items are to be preferred.

Individual items should also be constructed according to a set of guidelines. The number one rule is that each question should deal with a single concept and be worded as clearly as possible; any term or concept that might mean different things to different people should be defined. Do not ask, for example, "Do you spend a lot of time each week preparing for your classes?"; one teacher might consider one hour per day "a lot," while another might consider one hour per week "a lot." Instead, ask "How many hours per week do you spend preparing for your classes" or "How much time do you spend per week preparing for your classes—(A) less than 30 minutes, (B) between 30 minutes and an hour, (C) between 1 and 3 hours, (D) between 3 and 5 hours, (E) more than 5 hours." Also, when necessary, questions should indicate a point of reference. Do not ask, for example, "How much time do you spend preparing for your classes?" Instead, ask, "How much time do you spend *per day* (or per whatever time period you wish) preparing for your classes?" As another example, if you were interested not only in how many hours were actually spent in preparation but also in teachers' perceptions concerning that time, you would not ask, "Do you think you spend a lot of time preparing for classes?" Instead, you would ask, "Do you think you spend a lot of time *compared to other teachers* (or compared to whatever you wished) preparing for your classes?" As several of the above examples illustrate, underlining (in a typed questionnaire) or italicizing (in a printed one) key phrases may also help to clarify questions.

There are also a number of "don'ts" to keep in mind when constructing items. First, avoid leading questions which suggest that one response may be more appropriate than another. Second, avoid touchy questions to which the respondent might not reply honestly. Asking a teacher, for example, if he or she sets high standards for achievement is like asking a mother if she loves her children; the answer in both cases is going to be "of course!" Another major "don't" is not to ask a question that assumes a fact not necessarily in evidence; such questions present alternatives that are all unacceptable. The classic question of this nature is, "Have you stopped beating your wife?" The question calls for a simple "yes" or "no" response, but how does a husband respond who has never beaten his wife?! If he answers "yes," it suggests that he *used* to beat his wife but he has stopped; if he answers "no," it suggests that he is *still* beating his wife!

Typically, unwarranted assumptions are more subtle, and more difficult to spot. Several years ago, the author received a questionnaire on which appeared the question "Were you satisfied with the salary increase you received last year?" It so happened that the previous year had been a financially tough one; no faculty member had received a salary increase. Thus, there was no way to answer the question. A "yes" answer would have indicated satisfaction with no salary increase; a "no" response would have indicated dissatisfaction with whatever salary increase was received. The problem could have been avoided by the addition of a qualifying question such as "Did you receive a salary increase last year?"

Finally, you need to be careful about asking a series of questions that will allow a particular responder to be identified. You may well want to include demographic data items (e.g., sex, age, years in current position) so that you will be able to discuss subgroups within your overall population. In some cases, however, the questions will be such that only one member of the population could respond in a particular way. For example, if only one person received a doctoral degree from a specific university in 1989, an alumni questionnaire asking the responder to specify which degree was received and the year in which it was received would certainly identify the responder.

After the items have been developed, and their order determined, directions to respondents must be written. Standardized directions promote standardized, comparable responses. Directions should specify how the subject is to respond and where. When determining how subjects should respond, you should consider how the results will be tabulated. If results are to be machine-scored, for example, you might have subjects use a separate answer sheet and a number two pencil instead of having them circle responses on the questionnaire.

Validation of the Questionnaire.   A too-often-neglected procedure is validation of the questionnaire in order to determine if it measures what it was developed to measure. Validation is probably not done more often because it is not easy and requires much additional time and effort. However, anything worth doing is worth doing well. The appropriate validation procedure for a given questionnaire will depend upon the nature of the instrument. A questionnaire developed to determine the classroom behavior of teachers, for example, might be validated by observing a sample of respondents to determine the degree to which their actual behavior is consistent with their self-reported behavior.

Preparation of the Cover Letter.   Every mailed questionnaire must be accompanied by a cover letter that explains what is being asked of the respondent and why, and which hopefully motivates the responder to fulfill the request. The letter should be brief, neat, and addressed specifically to the potential responder (Dear Dr. Jekyll, not Dear Sir). Mercifully, there are database management computer programs which can assist you with the chore of personalizing your letters. The letter should also explain the purpose of the study, emphasizing its importance and significance, and give the responder a good reason for cooperating; the fact that you need the data for your thesis or dissertation is not a good reason. If at all possible, it should state a commitment to share the results of the study when completed. It usually helps if you can get the endorsement of an organization, institution, group, or administrator with which the responder is associated, or which the responder views with respect (such as a professional organization). If the group is too heterogeneous, or has no identifiable affiliation in common, a general appeal to professionalism can be made. Sometimes even humor and a little psychology are used. For example, a major car manufacturer sent out a questionnaire concerning one of their models to owners of that model. A quarter was enclosed along with a note indicating that the company was aware that the recipient of the questionnaire was quite busy and that the quarter was a gesture of appreciation for the anticipated cooperation. Besides being mildly amusing, the technique had the effect of making recipients feel like they "owed" the company a response. If possible, having the letter signed by a respected, well-known person also helps.

If the questions to be asked are at all threatening (such as items dealing with sex or attitudes toward the local administration), anonymity or confidentiality of responses must be assured. Complete anonymity probably increases the truthfulness of responses as well as the percentage of returns. On the other hand, anonymity makes follow-up efforts extremely difficult since you do not know who responded and who did not. It also makes subgroup comparisons impossible (for example, secondary teachers versus elementary teachers) unless specific classification items are included in the questionnaire itself (for example, "What grade do you teach?"). If identification is deemed necessary, complete confidentiality of responses must be guaranteed.

A specific deadline date by which the completed questionnaire is to be returned should be given. This date should give subjects enough time to respond but discourage procrastination; two to three weeks will usually be sufficient. Each letter to be sent should be signed individually. When many questionnaires are to be sent, individually signing each letter will admittedly take considerably more time than making copies of one signed letter, but it adds a personal touch which might make a difference in the potential responder's decision to comply or not comply. Again, some computer programs have the capacity to include signatures that appear to be individually done under all but the closest scrutiny. Finally, the act of responding should be made as painless as possible. A stamped, addressed, return envelope should be included; if not, your letter and questionnaire will very likely be placed into the circular file along with the mail addressed to "occupant"! (See Figure 8.1 for an example of a properly written cover letter.)

Pretesting the Questionnaire.   The questionnaire should be tried out in a field test just as a research plan should be executed first as a pilot study, and for essentially the same reasons. Few things are more disconcerting than sending out a questionnaire that was not pretested only to discover that the subjects didn't understand the directions or the questions. Pretesting the questionnaire yields data concerning instrument deficiencies as well as suggestions for improvement. Having two or three available people complete the questionnaire first will result in the identification of major problems. The subsequently revised instrument and the cover letter should then be sent to a small sample from your intended population or a highly similar population. Pretest subjects should be encouraged to make comments and suggestions concerning directions, recording procedures, and specific items. If the percentage of returns is very low, then both the letter and the instrument should be carefully reexamined. The feedback from those who do respond should be care-

K. Hanft
AT&T
Consumer Program Manager

Peter Diehl
7475 W. 18th Ave.
Hialeah FL 33014

Dear Peter Diehl:

On behalf of everyone at AT&T, I'd like to take this opportunity to wish you and those close to you the best this
holiday season and to extend my sincere thanks to you for
using AT&T as your long distance company.

All of us at AT&T appreciate your business. And we intend to
keep working hard to provide you with the highest quality of
long distance service.

As a valued AT&T customer, your opinion leads our efforts to
improve our service to meet your changing communications
needs. To help us meet those needs, please take a moment to
complete the enclosed questionnaire. In return, we'll send
you an AT&T Long Distance Gift Certificate which may be
redeemed for AT&T Long Distance Service.

Once again, our best wishes for a joyous holiday and a happy,
healthy year ahead.

Sincerely,

Kevin Hanft
AT&T
Consumer Program Manager

Figure 8.1. Sample cover letter for a questionnaire. *Note:* The accompanying questionnaire gave a return date, and a postage-paid return envelope was provided. Reprinted with
permission of AT&T.

fully studied and considered. Lastly, proposed data tabulation and analysis proce-dures should be applied to the pretest data. The end product of the pretest will be a revised instrument ready to be mailed to the already selected subjects.

Follow-Up Activities.   Not everyone to whom you send a questionnaire is going to return it (what an understatement!). Some recipients have no intention of com-pleting it, others mean to but put it off so long that they either forget it or lose it. It is for this latter group that follow-up activities are primarily conducted. The high-er your percentage of returns, the better. Although you should not expect 100%, you should not be satisfied with whatever you get after your first mailing. If your percentage of returns is not 70% or so, the validity of your conclusions will be weak. Given all the work you have already done, it makes no sense to end up with shaky findings and a study of limited value when some additional effort on your part can make a big difference.

An initial follow-up strategy is to simply send out a reminder postcard. This will prompt those who meant to fill it out but put it off and have not yet lost it! If responses are not anonymous you can mail a card only to those who have not responded. If they are anonymous, and you do not know who has and who has not responded, simply send a card to everyone; include a statement like the ones used by finance companies—"If you have already responded, please disregard this reminder and thank you for your cooperation." Full-scale follow-up activities are usually begun shortly after the deadline for responding has passed. A second set of questionnaires is sent to subjects, but with a new cover letter, and of course anoth-er stamped envelope. The new letter should suggest that you know they *meant* to respond but that they may have misplaced the questionnaire or maybe they never even received it. In other words, do not scold them; provide them with an accept-able reason for their nonresponse. The significance and purpose of the study should be repeated and the importance of *their* input should be reemphasized. The letter should suggest subtly that many others are responding; this implies that their peers have found the study to be important and so should they.

If the second mailing does not result in an overall acceptable percentage of return, be creative. Magazine subscription agencies have developed follow-up pro-cedures to a science and have become very creative. I once let a subscription to a popular weekly magazine lapse and received several gentle reminders and "sensa-tional one-time-only offers." One afternoon I received a long-distance call from sev-eral thousand miles away and the sweet voice at the other end suggested that my mail was apparently not getting through and wouldn't I like to renew my subscrip-tion. I bit! The point is that phone calls, if feasible, may be used, or any other method of written, verbal, or personal communication which might induce addi-tional subjects to respond. They may grow to admire your persistence!

If your questionnaire is well constructed, and your cover letter well written, you should get at least an adequate response rate. Research suggests that first mailings will typically result in close to a 50% return rate, and a second mailing will increase the percentage by about 20%; mailings beyond a second are generally not cost-effective, in that they each increase the percentage by about 10%.[3] After a second mailing, it is usually better to use other approaches until an acceptable percentage of returns is achieved.

Dealing with Nonresponse.   Despite all your initial and follow-up efforts, you may find yourself with an unacceptably low response percentage, say 60%. The

---

[3]Heberlein, T. A., & Baumgartner, R. (1978). Factors affecting response rates to mailed questionnaires: A quantitative analysis of the published literature. *American Sociological Review, 43*, 447–462.

problem is one of generalizability of results since you do not know if the 60% represents the population from which the sample was originally selected as well as the total original sample. If you knew that the responding subjects were essentially a random sample of the total sample, there would be no problem; but you do not know that. The subjects who responded may be different in some systematic way from nonresponders (the old volunteer syndrome); they may be better educated, feel more strongly about the issue (positively or negatively), or be more successful. In follow-up studies of program graduates discussed previously, successful graduates might tend to respond more than unemployed graduates or those in low-paying jobs. Generalizations based on information provided by responders only would suggest a rosier picture than if all graduates responded.

The usual approach to dealing with excessive nonresponse is to try to determine if nonresponders are different from responders in some systematic way by randomly selecting a small subsample of nonresponders and interviewing them, either in person or by phone. Through an interview, the researcher can not only obtain responses to questionnaire items but can also try to determine any distinguishing characteristics. If responses are essentially the same for the interviewed subjects as for the original responders, it may be assumed that the response group is representative and the results generalizable. If they are significantly different, such differences as well as resulting limitations to generalizability must be discussed in the research report. For example, instead of concluding that program graduates express general satisfaction with their training, you might conclude that at least *successful* program graduates express satisfaction (naturally!).

Analysis of Results.   When presenting the results of a questionnaire study, the response rate for each item should be given as well as the total sample size and the overall percentage of returns, since all respondents may not answer all questions. The simplest way to present the results is to indicate the percentage of responders who selected each alternative for each item. For example, "on item 4 dealing with possession of a master's degree, 50% said yes, 30% said no, and 20% said they were working on one." In addition to simply determining choices, relationships between variables can be investigated by comparing responses on one item with responses on other items. For example, it might be determined that 80% of those reporting possession of a master's degree expressed favorable attitudes toward personalized instruction, while only 40% of those reporting lack of a master's degree expressed a favorable attitude. Thus, possible explanations for certain attitudes and behaviors can be explored by identifying factors that seem to be related to certain responses. This type of relationship analysis can also be used to test hypotheses. For example, it might be hypothesized that teachers with advanced degrees are more receptive to nontraditional methods of instruction. The above finding concerning master's degrees and attitudes toward personalized instruction would be data in support of the hypothesis. Establishment of a direct cause-effect relationship between training and attitudes would not, however, be warranted. Due to lack of manipulation of variables it would not be possible to determine whether increased training *results* in increased receptivity to new ideas or whether receptive teachers seek out additional education. Resolution of such issues would require conducting a study using another method of research.

Conducting an Interview Study

An interview is essentially the oral, in-person, administration of a questionnaire to each member of a sample. The interview has a number of unique advantages and disadvantages. When well conducted it can produce in-depth data not possible with a questionnaire; on the other hand, it is expensive and time-consuming, and generally involves smaller samples. The interview is most appropriate for asking questions which cannot effectively be structured into a multiple-choice format, such as questions of a personal nature. In contrast to the questionnaire, the interview is flexible; the interviewer can adapt the situation to each subject. By establishing rapport and a trust relationship, the interviewer can often obtain data that subjects would not give on a questionnaire. The interview may also result in more accurate and honest responses since the interviewer can explain and clarify both the purpose of the research and individual questions. Another advantage of the interview is that the interviewer can follow up on incomplete or unclear responses by asking additional probing questions. Reasons for particular responses can also be determined.

Direct interviewer-interviewee contact also has its disadvantages. The responses given by a subject may be biased and affected by her or his reaction to the interviewer, either positive or negative. For example, a subject may become hostile or uncooperative if the interviewer reminds him of his first wife's mother! Another disadvantage is that it is very time-consuming and expensive, and the number of subjects that can be handled is generally considerably less than the number which can be sent a questionnaire; interviewing 500 people would be a monumental task as compared to mailing 500 questionnaires. Also, the interview requires a level of skill usually beyond that of the beginning researcher. It requires not only research skills, such as knowledge of sampling and instrument development, but also a variety of communication and interpersonal relations skills.

The steps in conducting an interview study are basically the same as for a questionnaire study, with some unique differences. The process of selecting and defining a problem and formulating hypotheses is essentially the same. Samples of subjects who possess the desired information are selected in the usual manner except that they are typically smaller. An effort must be made to get a commitment of cooperation from selected subjects. Subjects who do not attend interviews present the same problems as subjects who do not return questionnaires. The problem is more serious for interviews, however, since the sample size is smaller to begin with. The major differences between an interview study and a questionnaire study are the nature of the instrument involved (an interview guide versus a questionnaire), the need for human relations and communication skills, methods for recording responses, and the nature of pretest activities.

Construction of the Interview Guide.   The interviewer must have a written guide which indicates what questions are to be asked and in what order, and what additional prompting or probing is permitted. In order to obtain standardized, comparable data from each subject, all interviews must be conducted in essentially the same manner. As with a questionnaire, each question in the interview should relate to a specific study objective. Also as with a questionnaire, questions may be structured or unstructured. Since an interview is usually used when a questionnaire is not really appropriate, it usually involves unstructured or semistructured questions. Structured questions, which require the interviewee to select from alternatives, are of course easier to analyze but tend to defeat the purpose of an interview. Completely unstructured questions, on the other hand, which allow absolute freedom of response, can yield in-depth responses and provide otherwise unobtainable insights, but produce data that are very difficult to quantify and tabulate. Therefore, most interviews use a semistructured approach involving the asking of structured questions followed by clarifying unstructured, or open-ended, questions. The unstructured questions facilitate explanation and understanding of the responses to the structured questions. Thus, a combination of objectivity and depth can be obtained, and results can be tabulated as well as explained.

Many of the guidelines for constructing questionnaires apply to the construction of interview guides. The interview should be as brief as possible, and questions should be worded as clearly as possible. Terms should be defined when necessary and a point of reference given when appropriate. Also, leading questions should be avoided, as should questions based on the assumption of a fact not in evidence ("Tell me, have you stopped beating your wife?").

Communication During the Interview.   Effective communication during the interview is critical, and interviewers should be well trained before the study begins. Since first impressions can make a big difference, getting the interview "off on the right foot" is important. Before the first formal question is asked, some time should be spent in establishing rapport and putting the interviewee at ease. The purpose of the study should be explained and strict confidentiality of responses assured. As the interview proceeds, the interviewer should make full use of the advantages of the interview situation. The interviewer can, for example, explain the purpose of any question whose relevance to the purpose of the study is unclear to the subject. The interviewer should also be sensitive to the reactions of the subject and proceed accordingly. If a subject appears to be threatened by a particular line of questioning, for example, the interviewer should move on to other questions and return to the threatening questions later, when perhaps the interviewee is more relaxed. Or, if the subject gets carried away with a question and gets "off the track," the interviewer can gently get him or her back on target. Above all, the interviewer should avoid words or actions that may make the subject unhappy or feel threatened. Frowns and disapproving looks have no place in an interview!

Recording Responses.   Responses made during an interview can be recorded manually by the interviewer or mechanically by a recording device. If the interviewer records the responses, space is provided after each question in the interview guide, and responses are recorded either during the interview as it progresses or shortly after the interview is completed. If responses are recorded during the interview it may tend to slow things down, especially if responses are at all lengthy; it also may make some subjects nervous to have someone writing down every word they say. If responses are recorded after the interview, the interviewer is not likely to recall every response exactly as given, especially if many questions are asked. On the other hand, if a recording device such as an audiocassette recorder or video camcorder is used, the interview moves more quickly, and responses are recorded exactly as given. If responses need clarifying, several persons can listen to or view the recordings independently, and classifications can be compared. A recorder, of course, may initially make subjects nervous, but usually they tend to forget its presence as the interview progresses, whereas they are constantly aware when someone is writing down their responses. In general, mechanical recording is more objective. If mechanical recording devices are used, however, it is very important that subjects know they are being recorded and agree to the procedure.

Pretesting the Interview Procedure.   The interview guide, interview procedures, and analysis procedures should be tried out, before the main study begins, using a small sample from the same or a very similar population to the one being used in the study. Feedback from a small pilot study can be used to revise questions in the guide that are apparently unclear, do not solicit the desired information, or produce negative reactions in subjects. Insights into better ways to handle certain questions can also be acquired. Finally, the pilot study will determine whether the resulting data can be quantified and analyzed in the manner intended. As with the pretesting of a questionnaire, feedback should be sought from pilot subjects as well as from the interviewers. As always, a pretest of procedures is a good use of the researcher's time.

■ OBSERVATIONAL RESEARCH

In an observational study, the current status of a phenomenon is determined not by *asking* but by *observing*. For certain research questions, observation is clearly the most appropriate approach. For example, you could ask teachers how they handle discipline in their classrooms, but more objective information would probably be obtained by actually observing several of each teacher's classes. The value of observational research is illustrated by a study conducted in the Southwest on the classroom interaction between teachers and Mexican-American students.[4] Many teachers claimed that Mexican-American children are difficult to teach due to their lack of participation in classroom activities, their failure to ask or answer questions, and the like. Systematic observation, however, revealed that the main reason they did not answer questions, for example, was that they were not asked very many! Observation revealed that teachers tended to talk less often and less favorably to Mexican-American children and to ask them fewer questions. Thus, observation not only provided more accurate information than teacher reports but also made the teachers aware that they were unintentionally part of the problem. Observational techniques may also be used to collect data in nondescriptive studies. In an experimental study designed to determine the effect of behavior modification techniques on disruptive behavior, for example, students could be observed prior to and following the introduction of behavior modification in order to determine if instances of disruptive behavior were reduced in number. Observational data can be collected on inanimate objects such as books as well as human beings. In either case, an observational study must be planned and executed just as carefully as any other type of research study.

Types of Observational Research

The major types of quantitative observational research are nonparticipant observation and meta-analysis. Recall from Chapter 7 that participant observation is usually associated with qualitative research. Nonparticipant observation includes both naturalistic observation and simulation observation, and typically involves observation of human subjects. Meta-analysis involves observation and numerical analysis of a number of research reports. While some researchers feel uncomfortable classifying meta-analysis as a type of observational research, there does not seem to be a more appropriate classification. While it is true that it involves document (i.e., research report) analysis, the analysis is primarily statistical.

---

[4]Jackson, G., & Cosca, C. (1974). The inequality of educational opportunity in the Southwest: An observational study of ethnically mixed classrooms. *American Educational Research Journal, 11,* 219–229.

Nonparticipant Observation

In nonparticipant observation, the observer is not directly involved in the situation to be observed. In other words, the observer is on the outside looking in and does not intentionally interact with, or affect, the object of the observation.

Naturalistic Observation. Certain kinds of behavior can only be (or best be) observed as they occur naturally. In such situations the observer purposely controls or manipulates nothing, and in fact works very hard at not affecting the observed situation in any way.[5] The intent is to record and study behavior as it normally occurs. As an example, classroom behavior—behavior of the teacher, behavior of the student, and the interactions between teacher and student—can best be studied through naturalistic observation. Insights gained as a result of naturalistic observation often form the foundation for more controlled research in an area. The work of Piaget, for example, involved primarily naturalistic observation of children. His research and the research which it stimulated have provided education with many important findings regarding concept development in children.

Simulation Observation. In simulation observation the researcher creates the situation to be observed and tells subjects what activities they are to engage in. This technique allows the researcher to observe behavior that occurs infrequently in natural situations or not at all (for example, having a teacher trainee role-play a teacher-parent conference). The major disadvantage of this type of observation is of course that it is not natural, and the behavior exhibited by subjects may not be the behavior that would occur in a natural setting. Subjects may behave the way they think they should behave rather than the way they really would behave. In reality, this potential problem is not as serious as it may sound. Subjects tend to get carried away with their roles and often exhibit very true-to-life emotions. Besides, even if subjects "fake it," at least they show that they are aware of the correct way to behave. A student who demonstrates the correct way to interact with an irate parent at least *knows* what should be done.

Two major types of simulation are individual role playing and team role playing. In individual role playing the researcher is interested in the behavior of one person, although other "players" are involved. The individual is given a role, a situation, and a problem to solve. The observer then records and evaluates the subject's solution to the problem and the way in which she or he executes it. As an example, a teacher trainee might be told:

> Yesterday Billy Bungle was caught drawing pictures on his
> desk. You made him stay after school and wash and wax all
> the desks. The principal has just informed you that a very
> upset Mrs. Bungle is on her way to see you. What will you
> say to Mrs. Bungle?

In a team role-playing situation, a small group is presented with a situation and a problem and solutions are recorded and evaluated. Qualities such as leadership ability may also be studied. As an example, a group might be told:

> The faculty has appointed you a committee of six. Your
> charge is to come up with possible solutions to the problem

---

[5] Agnew, N. M., & Pyke, S. W. (1990). *The science game: An introduction to research in the behavioral sciences* (5th ed.). Englewood Cliffs, NJ: Prentice-Hall.

of student fights in the halls, an occurrence which has been increasing.

Meta-Analysis

Meta-analysis is a statistical approach to summarizing the results of many studies which have investigated basically the same problem. Given a number of studies, it provides a numerical way of expressing the "average" result. As you may have noticed when you reviewed the literature related to your problem, there are numerous variables which have been the subject of literally hundreds of studies, ability grouping, for example. Traditional attempts at summarizing the results of a number of related studies have basically involved classifying the studies in some defined way, noting the number of studies in which a variable was and was not significant, and drawing one or more conclusions. Thus, it might be stated that since in 45 of 57 studies the Warmfuzzy approach resulted in greater student self-esteem than the Nononsense approach, the Warmfuzzy approach appears to be an effective method for promoting self-esteem.

There are two major problems associated with the traditional, logical analysis, approach to summarizing studies. The first is the subjectivity involved. It has been documented that different authors use different criteria for selecting the studies to be included, use different review strategies, and often come to different (sometimes opposite) conclusions.[6] Thus, for example, some reviewers might conclude that the Warmfuzzy method is superior to the Nononsense method, while other reviewers might conclude that the results are inconclusive. The second major problem is that as the number of research studies available for reviewing increases over the years, so does the difficulty of the reviewing task. During the seventies, the need for a more efficient and more objective approach to research integration, or summarization, became increasingly apparent.

Meta-analysis is the alternative which was pioneered and developed by Glass and his colleagues. While much has been written on the subject, *Meta-analysis in Social Research* remains the classic work in the field (see footnote 6). In it, specific procedures are delineated for finding, describing, classifying, and coding the research studies to be included in a review, and for measuring and analyzing study findings. A central characteristic which distinguishes meta-analysis from more traditional approaches is the emphasis placed on having the review be as inclusive as possible. Thus, reviewers are encouraged to include results typically excluded, such as those presented in dissertation reports and unpublished works. Critics of meta-analysis claim that this strategy results in the inclusion in a review of a number of "poor" studies. Glass and his colleagues counter that there is no evidence that such is the case or that final conclusions are negatively affected and, further, there is evidence that dissertations, for example, on average exhibit higher design quality than published journal articles. They also note that experimental effects reported in journals are generally larger than those presented in dissertations; thus, if dissertations are excluded, effects will appear to be greater than they actually are.

The key feature of meta-analysis is that for each study results are translated into an effect size (ES), symbolized as Δ. Effect size is a numerical way of expressing the strength, or magnitude, of a reported relationship, be it causal or not. Thus, for an experimental study, for example, effect size expresses how much better (or

---

[6]Glass, G. V., McGaw, B., & Smith, M. L. (1981). *Meta-analysis in social research*. Beverly Hills, CA: Sage.

worse) the experimental group performed as compared to the control group. The basic formula is as follows:

$$\text{ES} = \frac{\overline{X}_e - \overline{X}_c}{SD_c}$$

where

$\overline{X}_e$ = the mean (average) score for the experimental group

$\overline{X}_c$ = the mean score for the control group

SD_c = the standard deviation (variability) of the scores for the control group

The formula may differ, depending upon the statistics actually presented in the study, but the objective is the same. After effect size has been calculated for each study, they are averaged, yielding one number which summarizes the overall, or typical, effect. Effect size is expressed as a decimal number and, while numbers greater than 1.00 are possible, they do not occur very often. Thus, an effect size near .00 means that, on average, experimental and control groups performed the same; a positive effect size means that, on average, the experimental group performed better; and a negative effect size means that, on average, the control group did better. For positive effect sizes, the larger the number the more effective the experimental treatment.

While there are no hard and fast rules, it is generally agreed that an effect size in the twenties (e.g., .28) indicates a treatment that makes a difference, but not much, whereas an effect size in the eighties (e.g., .81) indicates a powerful treatment. Just to give you a couple of examples, Walberg has reported that for cooperative learning studies effect size is .76.[7] This indicates that cooperative learning is a very effective instructional strategy. Walberg also reports that the effect size for assigned homework is .28, and for graded homework, .79. This suggests that homework makes a difference in achievement and that graded homework makes a big difference. (I'm sure there are many of you who can use this information to your advantage!)

As suggested earlier, meta-analysis is not without its critics. It must be recognized, however, that despite its perceived shortcomings, it still represents a significant improvement over traditional methods of summarizing literature. Further, it is not a fait accompli, but rather an approach in the process of refinement.[8]

Conducting Observational Research

The steps in conducting observational research are essentially the same as for other types of descriptive research. Selection and definition of the problem are essentially the same, as is "subject" selection. Like the interview technique, observation is time-consuming and typically involves smaller samples. It should be noted that the following discussion applies to conducting nonparticipant observational studies, but not to the execution of meta-analyses. Specific guidelines for conducting meta-analyses are beyond the scope of this text. (Hey, do you want a 1,000-page text?)

---

[7]Walberg, H. J. (1984). Improving the productivity of America's schools. *Educational Leadership, 41*(8), 19–27.

[8]For a discussion of problems in meta-analysis and proposed solutions, see Abrami, P. C., Cohen, P. A., & d'Apollonia, S. (1988). Implementation problems in meta-analysis. *Review of Educational Research, 58*, 151–179.

Definition of Observational Variables

There is no way that an observer can observe and record everything that goes on during a session, especially in a natural setting such as a classroom. What will be observed is determined by the research hypothesis or question. Thus, for a former example concerning the effectiveness of assertive discipline in reducing instances of disruptive behavior, attention would be focused only on "disruptive behavior." The term "disruptive behavior," however, does not have universal meaning; therefore, once the behavior to be observed is determined, the researcher must clearly define what specific behaviors do and do not match the intended behavior. In the above example, "disruptive behavior" might include talking out of turn, making extraneous noises, throwing things, and getting out of one's seat, whereas doodling would probably not be considered disruptive.

Once a behavioral unit is defined, observations must be quantified so that all observers will count the same way. If Gorgo screams *and* tips over his chair at the same time, that could be considered as one instance of disruptive behavior or as two instances. Researchers typically divide observation sessions into a number of specific observation periods, that is, they define a time unit. Thus, for a one-hour session, a time unit of 30 seconds might be agreed upon, resulting in a total of 120 observations per hour. The length of the time unit will usually be a function of both the behavior to be observed and the frequency with which it normally occurs. If it is simply a matter of observing and recording a high-frequency behavior, the time unit may be 10 seconds. If any judgments or inferences are required on the part of the observer, or if the behavior is a low-frequency behavior, the time unit is typically longer, perhaps 30 seconds or 1 minute. There should be correspondence between actual frequency and recorded frequency. Once the time unit has been established, the observer then records what occurred during the observation period. If during a 15-second interval a student exhibits disruptive behavior, this would be indicated, regardless of how often disruptive behavior occurred. After the variables have been defined and the time unit established, a decision must be made as to when observations will be made. For example, if behavior varies with factors such as day of the week and time of day, it would be unwise to observe every Tuesday morning only. One solution is to randomly select observation times so that different days and different times of day are reflected in the observations.

Recording of Observations

One point, which at first reading may seem obvious, is that observers should have to observe and record only one behavior at a time. Even if you are interested in two types of behavior, for example teacher behavior and student behavior, the observer should only have to make one decision at a time. Thus, if two types of behavior are to be observed they should probably be observed alternately. In other words, for the teacher-student observation example, teacher behavior might be observed during the first, third, fifth, seventh (and so forth) observation periods, and student behavior during the second, fourth, sixth, and eighth. Such a procedure would present a fairly accurate picture concerning what occurred in the observed classroom. It is also a good idea to alternate observation periods and recording periods, especially if any inference is required on the part of the observers. Thus we might have the observers observe for 15 seconds, record for 5 seconds, observe for 15 seconds, record for 5 seconds, and so forth. This approach controls for the fact that the observer is not paying complete attention while recording, and tends to increase the reliability of observations.

While the point is debatable, as a general rule it is probably better to record observations as the behavior occurs. Since each observation must be made within a set period of time, for example 15 seconds, the recording process should be as simplified as possible. Most observation studies facilitate recording by using an agreed-upon code, or set of symbols, and a recording instrument. Often the task is not just to determine whether a behavior occurred or not, but to record *what* occurred. The Flanders System, for example, which is widely used for classroom observation, classifies all teacher behavior and all student behavior into 1 of 10 categories, each of which is represented by a number.[9] Thus, if a teacher praises a student, the observer records that "2" occurred (see Figure 8.2)

Teacher Talk	Response	1. *Accepts feeling.* Accepts and clarifies an attitude or the feeling tone of a student in a nonthreatening manner. Feelings may be positive or negative. Predicting and recalling feelings are included. 2. *Praises or encourages.* Praises or encourages students; says "um hum" or "go on"; makes jokes that release tension, but not at the expense of a student. 3. *Accepts or uses ideas of students.* Acknowledges student talk. Clarifies, builds on, or asks questions based on student ideas.
		4. *Asks questions.* Asks questions about content or procedures, based on teacher ideas, with the intent that a student will answer.
	Initiation	5. *Lectures.* Offers facts or opinions about content or procedures; expresses *his* own ideas, gives *his* own explanation, or cites an authority other than a student. 6. *Gives directions.* Gives directions, commands, or orders to which a student is expected to comply. 7. *Criticizes students or justifies authority.* Makes statements intended to change student behavior from nonacceptable to acceptable patterns; corrects student behaviors; bawls someone out. Or, states why the teacher is doing what he is doing; uses extreme self-reference.
Student Talk	Response	8. *Student talk—response.* Student talk in response to teacher contact which structures or limits the situation. Freedom to express own ideas is limited.
	Initiation	9. *Student talk—initiation.* Students initiate or express own ideas either spontaneously or in response to teacher's soliciting initiation. Freedom to develop opinions and a line of thought; going beyond existing structure.
Silence	Silence	10. *Silence or confusion.* Pauses, short periods of silence, and periods of confusion in which communication cannot be understood by the observer.

Figure 8.2. Flanders' interaction analysis categories (FIAC).

---

[9] The Flanders System was developed at the Far West Laboratory for Educational Research and Development by the staff of the Teacher Education Division under the direction of N. A. Flanders. The interaction analysis materials are available from P. F. Amidon & Associates, 1966 Benson Avenue, St. Paul, MN 55116.

Some very good coding systems have been developed by researchers working in the area of behavior modification. Such codes are typically designed for recording the behavior of one individual. Bijou, Peterson, and Ault, for example, recorded occurrences of vocalizations (V), proximity (P) or physical contact (T) with another person, contact with physical objects (E) or with children, and whether the interaction was parallel play (A) or shared play (C). The basic symbols were adapted as needed. For example, aggressive vocalizations were recorded as Ⓥ. Other symbols were used as needed. A bracket on the top of the recording form at a particular number indicated a change in activity on the subject's part. An "x" indicated teacher approval for appropriate (i.e., verbal or proximity) behavior.[10] As Figure 8.3 (from the Bijou, Peterson, and Ault study) indicates, during 24 observation periods, the subject changed activities 12 times. During observation periods 16, 17, and 18, she talked (V), touched (T) and physically interacted with another child, and received approval (x) for these behaviors.

There are a number of different types of forms that are used to record observations. Probably the most often used, and the most efficient, is a checklist that lists all behaviors to be observed so that the observer can simply check each behavior as it occurs. This permits the observer to spend his or her time thinking about what is occurring rather than how to record it. The Flanders System, for example, uses a recording form which is basically a checklist (see Figure 8.4). In Figure 8.4, the various codes explained in Figure 8.2 are listed on the vertical axis, and the observation periods are indicated across the top (1–30). With the exception of categories 1 and 2, which must be specified, other categories are indicated with a checkmark. The time line shows the sequence of events that occurred over a period of time. During observation periods 1 and 2, the teacher was asking questions (4). During the next four periods students were expressing their ideas, and so forth. Thus, Figure 8.4 represents a classroom interaction in which the students are doing most of the talking and the teacher is encouraging and supporting their participation.

Rating scales are also sometimes used. These require the observer to evaluate the behavior and give it a rating from, for instance, 1 to 3. For example, an observer might rate a teacher's explanation as 1, not very clear, 2, clear, or 3, very clear. Although as many as five categories (infrequently more than five) are used, three is probably the ideal number. The more categories, the more difficult it becomes to

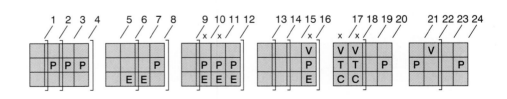

Figure 8.3. Sample line from a data sheet of a nursery school girl who changed activities with high frequency. (Table 1 from Bijou, Peterson, and Ault, 1968. Copyright 1968 by the Society for the Experimental Analysis of Behavior, Inc. Reproduced by permission.)

[10]Bijou, S. W., Peterson, R. F., & Ault, M. H. (1968). A method to integrate descriptive and experimental field studies at the level of data and empirical concepts. *Journal of Applied Behavior Analysis, 1,* 175–191.

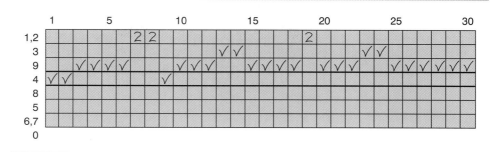

Figure 8.4. Recording form for Flanders' interaction analysis categories.

correctly classify. An observer could probably discriminate between "not very clear" and "clear" fairly easily; deciding between "very unclear" and "not very clear" would not be as simple.

Before developing your own observation form, you should check to see if there is a standardized observation form available that is appropriate for your study. Using a standardized observation form has the same advantages as using a standardized test in terms of time saved, validity, and reliability. Also, as with standardized tests, the results of your study can be compared with the results of other studies that have used the same form. The Flanders System, for example, has been used in a number of studies such as the one previously described dealing with the class participation of Mexican-American children. You should also check journals such as the *Journal of Applied Behavior Analysis* for observation systems that have been used in other studies. You may find one that appears to meet your needs.

Assessing Observer Reliability

Unreliable observations are as useless as data based on an unreliable test. Determining observer reliability generally requires that at least two observers independently make observations; their recorded judgments as to what occurred can then be compared to see how well they agree. If we wanted to estimate the reliability of scoring for a short-answer test, we could correlate the scores resulting from two independent scorings of the same answers. In other words, all of the tests would be scored twice, and the correlation between the two sets of scores would be our estimate of the reliability of scoring. When we observe behavior, however, we are not typically dealing with scores, but rather with frequencies, that is, how frequently certain behaviors occurred. In these cases reliability is generally calculated based on percent agreement. For example, we might have two independent observers recording number of disruptive behaviors exhibited by a selected student during a 1-hour period. If one observer recorded 20 incidents and the other observer recorded 25 incidents, we could compute interobserver reliability by dividing the smaller total (20) by the larger total (25) to obtain a percentage of agreement score of 80%.

As Barlow and Hersen point out, however, while 80% agreement may be considered satisfactory in most situations, if many frequencies are involved over a long

[11]Barlow, H., & Hersen, M. (1992). *Single-case experimental designs* (Rev. 2nd ed.). Des Moines, Iowa: Allyn & Bacon.

period of time, the possibility exists that the two observers are not recording the same behaviors at the same time.[11] One observer, for example, may have under-recorded during the first half of a session and over-recorded during the second half; the other observer may have done just the opposite. Thus, their totals might agree quite well even though their observations did not. One reasonable solution to this potential problem, as suggested by Bijou, Peterson, Harris, Allen, and Johnston, is to use shorter observation periods and to base reliability calculations on both agreements and disagreements on occurrences and nonoccurrences of behavior.[12] Bijou and associates argue that with shorter observation periods it is easier to determine whether observers are recording the same events at the same time. To calculate reliability using both observer agreement and disagreement, we divide the number of agreements by the total number of agreements and disagreements. To use our disruptive behavior example, suppose that during the first 30 minutes of the observation period the two observers agreed on the occurrence of 9 instances of disruptive behavior but disagreed on the occurrence of 3 instances. To calculate interobserver reliability we would divide the number of agreements (9) by the total of the agreements and the disagreements (9 + 3 = 12), and the resulting reliability estimate would be 9/12 or 75%. There are a number of different situations for which slightly different approaches for calculating reliability are recommended. Barlow and Hersen discuss a number of these situations and refer the reader to appropriate references.

Sometimes it is not possible to have several observers observe the same situation at the same time. One solution is to record the to-be-observed situation, with a video camcorder or audiocassette recorder, for example. This allows each observer to play back tapes at a time convenient for her or him. Another advantage to recording a situation is that you can replay it as often as you like. If behaviors to be observed are at all complex or occur at a fairly rapid rate, for example, it may be difficult to obtain reliable observations. If you record the behavior, you can play it back to your heart's content, as can other observers. This is especially useful if judgment and evaluation are required on the part of the observer. Regardless of whether observations are recorded as they occur or while viewing or listening to a tape, and assuming usage of a valid, reliable observation system, the best way to increase observer reliability is by thoroughly training and monitoring observers.

Training Observers

In order to determine agreement among observers, at least two observers are required. That means that there will be at least one other person besides yourself (or two, if you are not going to personally observe) who needs to be familiar with the observational procedures. Additional observers need to be trained in order to have some assurance that all observers are observing and recording the same behaviors in the same way. Thus, they must be instructed as to what behaviors to observe, how behaviors are to be coded, how behaviors are to be recorded, and how often (time unit). Observers should participate in numerous practice sessions at which they observe situations similar to those to be involved in the study and compare their recordings. Each point of disagreement should be discussed so that the observer who is incorrect understands why. Practice sessions using recordings of behavior are most effective since segments with which observers have difficulty can be replayed for discussion and feedback purposes. Estimates of observer relia-

---

[12]Bijou, S. W., Peterson, R. F., Harris, F. R., Allen, K. E., & Johnston, M. S. (1969). Methodology for experimental studies of young children in natural settings. *Psychological Record, 19,* 177–210.

bility should be calculated periodically to determine the effectiveness of the training and practice; observer reliability should increase with each session. Training may be terminated when a satisfactory level of agreement is achieved (say 80%).

Monitoring Observers

Training of observers only guarantees that the initial level of reliability is satisfactory. It does not guarantee that this level will be maintained throughout the study. Also, as we have noted, observers may be exhibiting acceptable levels of reliability and yet not be observing the same behaviors in the same way at the same time. As Barlow and Hersen point out, the major way to insure continued satisfactory levels of reliability is to monitor the recording activities of observers. The ideal would be to constantly monitor all observers. This technique is usually not feasible, however. At the very least, spot checks should be made.[13] As a general rule, the more monitoring that can reasonably be managed, the better.

Reducing Observation Bias

As discussed in Chapter 7, observers should be made aware of two factors that may seriously affect the validity of observations—observer bias and observer effect. Observer bias refers to invalid observations that result from the way in which the observer observes. Observer effect refers to invalid observations that result from the fact that those being observed (let's call them observees, with apologies to Webster!) behave differently simply because they are being observed. Each observer brings to the observation session a unique background that may affect the way he or she perceives the situation. Having observers record independently helps to detect the presence of bias but does not eliminate it. Training and practice sessions should help to reduce it by making observers aware of its existence and by providing feedback when it appears to be occurring. Other types of observer bias are similar to those described in Chapter 5 concerning rating scales and are referred to as response sets. A response set is the tendency of an observer to rate the majority of observees as above average, average, or below average regardless of the observees' actual behavior. A related problem is the "halo effect" whereby initial impressions concerning an observee (positive or negative) affect subsequent observations. A final major source of observer bias occurs when the observer's knowledge concerning observees or the purposes of the study affect observations. In the previously discussed study of the effectiveness of assertive discipline in reducing disruptive behavior, the observer might tend to see what was expected, namely a decrease in disruptive behavior. In this instance, having observers view recordings rather than live behavior would help since they would not have to be told which recordings were made *before* the introduction of behavior modification and which were made *after*.

The other side of the problem, observer effect, refers to the phenomenon whereby persons being observed behave atypically simply because they are being observed. Solutions to this problem such as those depicted on television crime shows (one-way mirrors, for example) may seem intriguing but are hardly ever practicable, never mind ethical, in observational settings. Classrooms, for example, rarely are equipped with such devices. The best way to handle the problem is to

---

[13]Reid, J. B., & DeMaster, B. (1972). The efficacy of the spot-check procedure in maintaining the reliability of data collected by observers in quasi-natural settings: Two pilot studies. *Oregon Research Bulletin, 12*(8).

make observers aware of it so that they can attempt to be as unobtrusive (inconspicuous) as possible. Observees apparently tend to ignore the presence of an observer after a few sessions. Thus, simply observing a few sessions prior to recording any data is an effective technique. Observers should also be instructed not to discuss the purpose of the observations with the observees. As discussed in Chapter 7, the fact that they may be behaving differently is bad enough; having them behave the way they think you want them to behave is worse! Another approach to the problem of observer effect is to eliminate observees. If the same information can be determined by observing inanimate objects (recall unobtrusive measures), use them. School suspension lists, for example, have never been known to act differently because they were being observed; such lists might be one unobtrusive measure of disruptive behavior on the part of students. The following newspaper article, although not necessarily sufficient to withstand the scrutiny of economics professors, does illustrate the concept of unobtrusive measures:

> Maury Graham—known in the world of freight train hoboes as "Steamtrain Maury"—reports that the current U.S. economy is in frightful shape.
> The former "King of the Hoboes" says that hoboes can gauge the seriousness of inflation by the length of the cigar and cigarette butts found along the streets.
> Says Steamtrain Maury, "The longer they are, the better times are. And right now the butts are awful short. People are smoking them right down to the end."[14]

On the following pages an example of descriptive research is presented. Note that the study involved a stratified random sample, a mailed questionnaire, a procedure for assuring anonymity of responses, a follow-up mailing, and telephone interviews to assess response bias (i.e., differences between mail responders and nonresponders).

---

[14]Krebs, A. Notes on people. *New York Times,* September 11, 1974, © 1974, by the New York Times Company. Reprinted by permission.

Reading Instruction: Perceptions of Elementary School Principals

JOHN JACOBSON
The University of Texas at Arlington

D. RAY REUTZEL
Brigham Young University

PAUL M. HOLLINGSWORTH
Brigham Young University

ABSTRACT   A stratified random sample of 1,244 U.S. elementary public school principals was surveyed to determine perceptions of their understanding of current issues in elementary reading instruction and the information sources that they use to learn about current issues in reading. The principals reported four major unresolved reading issues: (a) whole language versus basal approaches; (b) assessment of students' reading progress; (c) the use of tradebooks in place of basals; and (d) ability grouping students for reading instruction. Principals' priority ranking of the four most important unresolved reading issues were (a) whole language versus basal approaches; (b) effective alternative assessment of students' reading progress; (c) alternatives to ability grouping students for reading instruction; and (d) the necessity of phonics instruction as a prerequisite to formal reading instruction. The most frequently consulted reading information sources used by elementary school principals within the past 12 months included (a) professional education magazines, (b) personal contacts with specialists and colleagues, and (c) newspapers. Although college classes were the least used information resource of U.S. elementary school principals within the past 12 months, college courses in reading education rated high in utility along with personal contacts with reading specialists. The study concluded that U.S. elementary school principals report awareness of the important reading issues of the day, but that they may need readily accessible and practical information to significantly impact implementation of the current innovations in reading education.

No other area of the curriculum receives as much attention and generates as much debate as does reading instruction. For many years, research and practice have indicated that the success or failure of a school's reading program depends largely upon the quality of school principals' knowledge of and involvement in the school reading program (Ellis, 1986; McNinch & Richmond, 1983; McWilliams, 1981; Weber, 1971). One may conclude, then, that it is important for elementary principals to be informed, active participants in the national conversation about reading instructional issues. It is also an ipso facto conclusion that the quality of school principals' instructional leadership in school reading programs is directly linked to the quality of their knowledge about reading instruction (Barnard & Hetzel, 1982; Kean, Summers, Raivetz, & Tarber, 1979; McNinch & Richmond, 1983; Nufrio, 1987; Rausch & Sanacore, 1984). When principals lack necessary understanding of reading instruction, they tend to shun or delegate responsibility to others for the school reading program (Nufrio). Even worse, some researchers have determined that principals who lack sufficient knowledge of reading instruction tend to resort to misguided means for making decisions instead of grounding their decisions in reliable information and research (Roser, 1974; Zinski, 1975).

A synthesis of past and current research strongly suggests that elementary school principals should bear a major responsibility for the school reading program and have an ethical and professional obligation to be conversant in the same curriculum areas as those expected of elementary classroom teachers (Wilkerson, 1988). To do this, elementary school administrators must stay abreast of current critical reading issues to be effective instructional leaders in their own schools' reading programs.

Past research related to elementary school principals' understanding of reading instruction has been based primarily on surveys of teachers' impressions of principals' reading leadership capabilities. In other related studies, elementary school administrators have been queried about their familiarity with specific reading instructional concepts, their professional reading instruction preparation, and the amount of their own classroom reading teaching experience. Some past research has determined that principals understand reading instructional concepts fairly well (Aldridge, 1973; Gehring, 1977; Panchyshyn, 1971; Shelton, Rafferty, and Rose, 1990), while other research concluded that principals' reading instructional understanding is insufficient and their preparation inadequate to assume leadership roles for elementary school reading programs (Berger & Andolina, 1977; Kurth,

Address correspondence to Paul M. Hollingsworth, Brigham Young University, Department of Elementary Education, 215 McKay Building, Provo, UT 84602.

1985; Laffey & Kelly, 1983; Lilly, 1982; Moss, 1985; Nufrio, 1987; Rausch & Sanacore, 1984; Zinski, 1975).

Several problems have been associated with past attempts to research principals' knowledge of reading instruction. First, most past studies have been limited to a local area or single state. Few past studies go beyond state lines, and none of them have attempted to describe elementary school principals' perceived knowledge of reading instructional issues nationwide. Second, past survey studies have generally had marginally acceptable return rates, and no checks for response bias by comparing responders with nonresponders were made, thus severely limiting the generalizability of their conclusions.

An exhaustive search of the extant literature indicated that no national research study of principals' perceived knowledge of current critical issues in reading education has been conducted to date. Thus, little is known about the state of contemporary elementary school administrators' perceptions of current, critical issues in reading education. Furthermore, no research data are available on how these important leaders of school reading programs commonly access information regarding current issues in reading education. Thus, the purpose of this study focused on three research questions: (a) What do practicing elementary prinicipals perceive are the critical and unresolved issues in reading education? (b) What level of understanding do practicing elementary principals perceive that they have of each issue? (c) What sources do practicing elementary principals use and find helpful to inform themselves about current issues in reading education?

Method

Survey Instrument

A survey questionnaire consisting of several sections was constructed (see Appendix A). The first section requested the following standard demographic information from the elementary school principals surveyed: (a) school size and type (1–299, 300–599, or 600 or more students, and Grades K–3, K–6, etc.), (b) years of experience as a principal and educator, (c) state, and (d) type of reading approaches used in their schools. The second section of the survey instrument included three tasks. Task 1 presented principals with 11 reading issues and asked them to indicate whether each issue was resolved, unresolved, or never had been an issue in their own minds, experiences, or schools.[1] Task 2 requested that principals rank order from 1 to 3 the top three issues that they had classified as unresolved in Task 1. Task 3 requested that the principals perform a self-rating of their understanding level of each reading issue on a 4-point forced-choice scale: (a) understand well enough to describe underlying issues and give a reasoned argument, (b) understand most of the underlying issues and give a rationale in taking a position, (c) know problem exists, but not sure of basic issue, and (d) not aware of a problem.

In the third section of the questionnaire, Task 4 listed 16 different information sources that principals could use to learn about current reading instructional issues and related research. Principals were asked to respond whether they "had" or "had not" used each of the 16 information sources within the past 12 months. Finally, Task 5 asked principals to rate the usefulness of each reading information resource that they had used on a 3-point forced-choice scale: (1) quite helpful, (2) moderately helpful, and (3) not very helpful.

Procedures

Subjects for this study were randomly selected from a computerized list obtained from Quality Educational Data (QED) of elementary public school principals in the United States during the 1989–90 school year. A total of 1,261 principals from a possible population of 41,467 were selected. The sample represented approximately 3% of the total target population. A stratified random sampling design was used to increase the precision of variable estimates (Fowler, 1988). Elementary school principals were proportionately selected from school size and school types to yield 95% confidence intervals of within ± 1% for the total population from schools with a population of 1 through 299, 300 through 599, and 600 or more. Other subject schools included those having only Grades K through 3 and K through 6 (Fowler, 1988, p. 42).

To track the responses anonymously, we included a postcard (giving the principal's name and a code indicating the size of school) in the mailing. Respondents were asked to return the questionnaire and postcard to separate return addresses. The first mailing was sent in February 1990. Four weeks later, a second mailing (with an updated cover letter and survey form) was sent to those who had not responded to the initial mailing (Heberlein & Baumgartner, 1981).

Return rates on mailed educational survey instruments are frequently in the 40 to 60% range (Could-Silva & Sadoski, 1987). An unbiased final sample of 500 responses would still yield 95% confidence intervals of within ± 3% for the entire target population of U.S. elementary school administrators surveyed (Asher, 1976). To check for response bias among responders, a trained graduate student randomly selected and interviewed over the telephone a sample of 31 (5%) of the nonrespondents (Frey, 1989). The telephone interview consisted of 16 questions selected from the mailed questionnaire (11 questions relating to reading issues and 5 questions on reading information sources used). Telephone responses were then compared with mailed responses by using chi-square analyses of each item to learn if any systematic differences existed between the answers of the two groups. If significant differences were not found between the two groups, then responses for those who returned their survey by mail may be generalizable to the larger population of elementary school principals (Borg & Gall, 1989).

Results

Of the 1,261 surveys sent, 17 were returned because of inaccurate addresses. Thus, a total of 1,244 possible responses remained. Thirty percent (373) of the principals responded to the first mailing. The second mailing yielded an additional 17% or 208 principals, giving a total response rate of 47%, or 581 principals. In Table 1, we report the number of principals receiving and returning questionnaires from each state.

Because a 47% survey return rate is a figure that is minimally adequate to accurately reflect the perceptions of the target population (Dillman, 1978), a follow-up telephone interview of 5% of the nonrespondents was conducted. Responses to the telephone interview were compared with the mailed responses by constructing contingency tables from the responses of the two groups (responders and nonresponders). Chi-square statistics were calculated for each of the 16 questions. No significant differences ($p < .05$) were found for responses on 7 of 11 reading issues and 4 of 5 reading information sources. In other words, 64% of the responses between those who responded by telephone and those who responded by mail did not vary significantly on the 11 reading issues. And 80% of the responses between those who responded by telephone and those who responded by mail did not vary significantly on the sources of information that principals use to remain informed about reading issues. The differences between responders and nonresponders are described in Table 2.

In addition, chi-square analyses of responders from the first and second mailings yielded no significant differences, nor were measurable differences found between respondents resulting from school type or size ($p < .05$). Overall, the similarities between the two groups were determined sufficient to enable reasonably confident generalizations to the target population to be made by using the mail responses only (deVaus, 1986). Therefore, only the mail response data are reported.

Summary of Research Questions

Research Question 1: What do practicing elementary school principals perceive are the critical and unresolved issues in reading education? Of the 11 issues surveyed, 40% or more of the principals perceived 6 issues as *unresolved*: (a) use of whole language approaches instead of basal-reader approaches (73%); (b) assessment of students' reading progress (63%); (c) use of tradebooks instead of basal readers (56%); (d) use of ability grouping for reading instruction (48%); (e) whether kindergarten children should pass a screening test to enter kindergarten (46%); (f) whether at-risk readers should spend increased time reading or practicing skills (40%).

Table 1.—Number of Principals Receiving and Returning Questionnaires, by State

State	Sent	Returned	State	Sent	Returned
Alabama	21	5	Missouri	29	16
Alaska	5	3	Montana	7	3
Arizona	14	6	Nebraska	17	7
Arkansas	17	6	Nevada	6	2
California	125	38	New Hampshire	7	4
Colorado	23	12	New Jersey	36	13
Connecticut	18	7	New Mexico	11	8
Delaware	2	0	New York	68	27
District of Columbia	3	2	North Carolina	31	12
Florida	39	16	North Dakota	4	1
Georgia	27	16	Ohio	62	28
Hawaii	4	3	Oklahoma	21	10
Idaho	9	8	Oregon	21	8
Illinois	53	30	Pennsylvania	57	30
Indiana	33	19	Rhode Island	7	3
Iowa	25	12	South Carolina	17	5
Kansas	22	7	South Dakota	17	4
Kentucky	16	8	Tennessee	22	8
Louisiana	23	8	Texas	92	45
Maine	9	3	Utah	10	7
Maryland	24	12	Vermont	7	2
Massachusetts	32	11	Virginia	21	10
Michigan	56	24	Washington	24	12
Minnesota	24	12	West Virginia	19	10
Mississippi	12	6	Wisconsin	23	11
Total				1,244[a]	581

[a]1,261 surveys were sent, but 17 were not deliverable.

Table 2.—Percentage of Responders and Nonresponders Whose Answers Differed Significantly (Chi-Square) for the Resolvedness Question About Reading

Issue	Unresolved (%)	Resolved (%)	Never an issue (%)	No response	Total
Should schools be required to adopt a basal series?					
Responders	38.9	35.1	26.0	3	581
Nonresponders	48.4	51.6	.0	0	31
Should reading instruction be mastery based?					
Responders	37.3	46.0	16.7	5	581
Nonresponders	38.7	61.3	0.0	0	31
Should children's entry into kindergarten be delayed until they perform successfully on a screening test?					
Responders	45.7	29.1	25.3	3	581
Nonresponders	45.2	48.4	6.5	0	31
Should schools be required to use the same program in all grades (e.g., same basal series)?					
Responders	35.0	41.1	23.9	7	581
Nonresponders	51.6	45.2	3.2	0	31

Note. Critical value of chi-square = 5.99, $df = 2$, $p < .05$.

Of the 11 issues, 40% or more of the principals surveyed perceived the following 6 issues as *resolved*: (a) whether reading skills should be taught in isolation or integrated with the remaining language arts (63%); (b) whether phonics should be taught as a prerequisite to formal reading instruction (48%); (c) whether at-risk readers should spend increased time reading or practicing skills (47%); (d) whether reading instruction should be mastery based (46%); (e) use of ability grouping for reading instruction (43%); and (f) whether schools should be required to use the same reading instructional program in all grades (41%).

In 24% or more of the principals' responses, they indicated that certain reading issues had never been an issue in their perception. In order of *never been an issue*, the principals indicated (a) whether schools should be required to adopt basal reading series (26%); (b) whether tradebooks should be used in place of basal readers (25%); (c) whether kindergarten children should pass a screening test to enter kindergarten (25%); and (d) whether schools should be required to use the same reading instructional program in all grades (24%).

Of the issues that principals rated as unresolved, the top four items receiving the highest *priority ranking* in terms of their relative importance to improving reading instruction were (a) use of whole language approaches instead of basal reader approaches; (b) assessment of students' reading progress; (c) use of ability grouping for reading instruction; and (d) whether phonics should be

taught as a prerequisite to formal reading instruction. Of the 11 reading issues surveyed, the principals perceived the issue of requiring schools to use the same program in all grades (e.g., the same basal series) to be the issue of least importance. Table 3 gives the rankings of the surveyed elementary school principals for each reading issue.[2]

In summary, from among the 11 reading issues surveyed, elementary school principals rated the following as the single most important *unresolved* issue: use of whole language approaches instead of basal reader approaches (73%). The issue that the prinicipals perceived as most *resolved* was whether reading skills should be taught in isolation or integrated with the remaining language arts (63%). The *unresolved* issue that the principals ranked highest in relative importance was use of whole language approaches instead of basal reader approaches. Finally, the issue that most of the principals felt had *never been an issue* was whether schools should be required to adopt basal reading series (26%).

Research Question 2: What level of understanding do practicing elementary principals perceive they have of each issue? After the principals were asked to rank order the unresolved issues in terms of importance, we requested that they rate their understanding level for each of the 11 reading issues using a 4-point scale (1 being the highest). Therefore, the lower the mean score, the higher the principals rated their personal understanding of each reading issue. Percentages, along with means and standard deviations, are also presented in Table 3.

Table 3.—Classification, Rating, and Ranking of Reading Issues by U.S. Elementary School Principals

Reading issues	Unresolved (%)	Resolved (%)	Never an issue (%)	Issue ranking	Understanding of the issues[a]					
					1 (%)	2 (%)	3 (%)	4 (%)	M	SD
How should student reading progress be assessed?	65	26	9	2	60	33	5	2	1.48	.68
Should the whole language approach be used instead of the basal reader approach?	73	21	6	1	52	39	8	1	1.58	.67
Should tradebooks be used in place of basals?	56	19	25	7	43	15	31	11	1.93	1.0
Should reading skills be taught in isolation or integrated with other language arts curriculum?	23	63	14	8	76	18	3	3	1.34	.70
Should phonics be taught as a prerequisite to formal reading instruction?	39	48	13	4	67	27	4	2	1.42	.67
Should students be grouped by ability for reading instruction?	48	43	9	3	67	28	2	3	1.42	.69
Should schools be required to adopt a basal series?	39	35	26	10	57	26	6	11	1.72	1.0
Should at-risk readers spend more time reading connected text or on practicing isolated reading skills?	40	47	13	6	57	33	8	2	1.54	.71
Should reading instruction be mastery based?	37	46	17	9	45	39	11	5	1.76	.84
Should children's entrance into kindergarten be delayed until they perform successfully on a screening test?	46	29	25	5	58	28	9	5	1.62	.86
Should schools be required to use the same program in all grades (e.g., the same basal series)?	35	41	24	11	61	24	5	10	1.64	.96

[a]1 = understand well enough to describe underlying issues and give a reasoned argument; 2 = understand most of underlying issues and give a rationale in taking a position; 3 = know problem exists, but not sure of basic issue; 4 = not aware of problem.

Principals expressed *greatest* understanding of the following four issues: (a) teaching reading skills in isolation or integrated with other language arts curriculum ($M = 1.34$); (b) grouping students by reading ability for instruction in reading ($M = 1.42$); (c) teaching phonics as a prerequisite to reading instruction ($M = 1.42$); and (d) assessing students' reading progress. Principals expressed *least* confidence in their understanding of the following three issues: (a) using tradebooks in place of basals ($M = 1.93$); (b) using mastery-based reading instruction ($M = 1.76$); and (c) requiring schools to adopt a basal series ($M = 1.72$). Though principals reported a lack of confidence in their understanding of certain reading education issues, an overall mean score of 1.59 indicated that, generally, elementary school principals believed they understood most of the underlying issues, but, according to the survey criteria, they did not feel confident enough in their understanding of reading issues to give a good rationale for taking one side or the other.

Research Question 3: What sources do practicing elementary principals use and find helpful to inform themselves about current issues in reading education? Sixteen different information sources were listed on the questionnaire. Principals were to indicate if they had used each of the information sources in the past 12 months. They were asked also to rate the helpfulness of the sources that they had used. Percentages, along with means and standard deviations, were calculated and are reported in Table 4.

The principals reported that the top four reading information sources *used most* were (a) magazines for professional educators that carry articles about reading and literacy (96.6%); (b) personal contacts with specialists in the field (95.9%); (c) newspaper articles about reading issues (93.6%); and (d) magazines or newsletters focusing on reading issues (88.6%). The five reading information sources *used least* were, in order, (a) college or university reading courses (14.3%); (b) college textbooks focused on reading (24.9%); (c) reading articles in professional

Table 4.—Utility of Reading Education Information Sources as Rated by U.S. Elementary School Principals

Source	Percentage used	Rated utility in percentages			M	SD
		Quite	Moderately	Not very		
Personal contacts with specialists in the field	95.9	79.1	20.7	.2	1.2	.41
Professional association conventions	61.0	62.0	35.4	2.5	1.4	.54
Magazines or newsletters focusing on reading issues	88.6	52.5	46.3	1.2	1.5	.52
Literacy articles in magazines for professional educators	96.6	61.3	36.6	2.1	1.4	.53
Reading articles in magazines focused on techniques and instructional methods	81.3	46.2	51.5	2.3	1.6	.54
Reading articles in popular national magazines	74.4	17.6	55.4	27.0	2.1	.66
Journal articles reporting results of research	49.3	53.3	42.1	4.6	1.5	.59
Reading articles in professional handbooks	38.8	50.0	46.4	3.6	1.5	.57
College textbooks focused on reading	24.9	42.0	49.0	9.1	1.7	.64
Books about reading published by popular press	64.4	36.3	53.8	9.9	1.7	.63
TV or radio broadcasts about reading issues	77.7	19.3	55.6	25.1	2.1	.67
Newspaper articles about reading issues	93.6	18.3	55.8	25.9	2.1	.66
Reading reports from research agencies	42.3	49.6	46.7	3.7	1.5	.57
Reading reports and publications sponsored by governmental agencies	76.2	47.0	46.6	6.4	1.6	.61
College or university reading courses	14.3	61.3	35.0	3.8	1.4	.57
Workshops or organized study groups focused on reading issues	67.5	71.5	27.9	.5	1.3	.47

Note. Data represent only those principals who reported using the information resources in the past 12 months.

handbooks (38.8%); (d) reading reports from research agencies (42.3%); and (e) journal research articles (49.3%).

Also shown in Table 4 are the principals' rankings of the relative helpfulness of each used source. To calculate means and standard deviations for the relative helpfulness rating of each information resource, we converted category responses to numeric values, using a 3-point scale. The closer each mean approximated the value of 1, the higher the mean helpfulness utility rating for the information source. From an examination of the means, the following five reading information sources were reported as *most helpful: (a) personal contacts with specialists in the field* $(M = 1.2)$; (b) workshops or organized study groups focused on reading $(M = 1.3)$; (c) attendance at professional association conventions $(M = 1.4)$; (d) literacy articles in magazines for professional educators $(M = 1.4)$; and (e) college or university reading courses $(M = 1.4)$. Three information sources rated *least helpful* by elementary principals were (a) reading articles in popular national magazines $(M = 2.1)$; (b) watching

or listening to TV or radio broadcasts about reading issues $(M = 2.1)$; and (c) reading newspaper articles about reading issues $(M = 2.1)$.

Discussion

Among elementary school principals surveyed across the United States, the most unresolved reading issue is the controversy between the whole language versus basal approaches to reading instruction. The reading education issue rated least understood by principals was the use of tradebooks in place of basals. These findings are most interesting because of their immediate relationship to each other and to the whole language versus basal reader approaches to reading instruction issue. Explaining this finding is difficult because principals were not asked *why* they indicated that this issue is unresolved. One speculation might be that, in the minds of principals, part of the problem associated with deciding whether to implement tradebooks in reading instruction is the question of *how* to use tradebooks either to supplant or supplement the basal reader. However, further research is needed to determine the reasons *why* the issue surrounding the use of whole language versus basal readers is an issue of such great importance.

Also of note, the principals ranked as the second and third most important *unresolved* national reading issues, assessment of reading progress and use of ability grouping. Yet, when asked to rank their understanding of reading issues, the principals gave the second and most important unresolved issue, assessment of student reading progress, the fourth highest rating of understanding, indicating that although it is an unresolved issue, they understand it well. Additionally, the third most important unresolved issue, ability grouping students for reading instruction, received the second highest rating of understanding. Though principals rated their perceived understanding of the issue of ability grouping as being high, it remains an unresolved issue in the minds of principals nationally. Again, these issues share close philosophical proximity with the whole language versus basal reader issue. Because tradebook use calls into question accepted assessment practices and the use of ability groups, one can understand that these issues would loom as critical issues in the minds of U.S. principals.

Principals' perceived lack of understanding and priority rating of the whole language versus basal reader issue as unresolved reflects a widespread concern among principals nationally regarding this issue. One positive sign that principals may be attempting to deal with the whole language versus basal reader issue is the fact that only 77% of the principals surveyed reported that their schools used the basal reader as the major approach for reading instruction, as compared with other recent estimates indicating that basal reader use in American schools exceeds 90% (Goodman, Shannon, Freeman, & Murphy, 1988).

Although the principals rated their understanding of the whole language versus basal reader issue as one of the least understood issues, they reported less use of basal readers and greater use of tradebooks in schools than previous national estimates indicated. This finding suggests that the principals' perceived lack of understanding regarding the whole language versus basal reader issue may not be precluding their attempts to make greater use of tradebooks in their school reading programs. The means by which principals are learning to make these changes *may* be related to their use of reading information resources.

With respect to the information resources used and valued most by principals, this study revealed that the majority of principals surveyed relied on (a) professional education magazines, (b) personal contacts with specialists in reading, and (c) newspapers as their major sources for gaining information about reading education issues and practices. Nearly 90% of those principals surveyed indicated that they had used one of those top three information sources about reading education in the past 12 months. Of note, those sources tend to be interpretive sources and may give only surface-level information, as opposed to more in-depth original research sources. However, considering the constraints exigent upon principals' time, less formal research synthesis may be the most pragmatic means of acquiring current information regarding critical reading instructional issues and promising practices. This fact is substantiated in part by the information sources that the principals used least.

During the past 12 months, the information sources that principals used least were (a) college or university reading courses, (b) college textbooks on reading, (c) articles in professional handbooks, and (d) research reports from research agencies. Those sources tend to focus on theories, practices, techniques, and approaches verified by in-depth original research studies, and they require greater time commitments than do the less formal information resources used most by practicing principals. The finding that enrolling in college or university reading courses was least used was rather curious when juxtaposed against principals' rankings of the most helpful information sources. Although the principals tended not to enroll in college and university reading course work during the past 12 months, they ranked college and university reading courses in the top four reading information sources as most helpful ($M = 1.4$, on a 3-point, with 1 being the highest).

In summary, the principals chose print informational sources that were interpretive, informal, and less technical information sources, that is, newsletters, newspaper articles, and magazines. They tended not to use detailed research reports found in texts, journals, handbooks, and reading reports from research agencies. However, the principals' selection and use of less technical, more interpretive reading information sources, as well as accessible reading specialists, seems logical given the constraints upon their time. Although the principals tended to rate college courses as extremely helpful, enrolling in university course work might not always be accessible, convenient, or even feasible for many practicing principals.

Implications

From this study, one might conclude that the vast majority of U.S. elementary school principals do attempt to keep current on issues related to reading education. Although principals appear to be aware of current trends and issues in reading education, they may not feel sufficiently confident about their understanding of the issues to implement innovative changes in school reading programs. This conclusion is sustained by the principals' ranking of the issue regarding using whole language versus basal readers as the most unresolved issue while also ranking this issue as least understood.

The conclusion of this study, that U.S. elementary school principals prefer obtaining information about critical reading issues and practices from practical and accessible sources, suggests that authors of educational literature and reading specialists should be aware that principals not only need to understand the issues but also to receive specific guidance on *how* to select promising reading practices for use in their schools and *how* to implement reading program changes.

One paradoxical finding should give strong signals to colleges and universities. Although the principals valued university-level reading courses, many of them had not used that information resource within the past 12 months. This finding may indicate a need for institutions of higher learning to design more accessible means for disseminating current, practical information into schools and classrooms.

In conclusion, the majority of U.S. elementary principals perceived that they were aware of current, critical, and unresolved issues in reading education, that is, tradebooks, reading assessment, and ability grouping. However, according to the survey criteria, many principals did not have enough confidence in their understanding of reading issues to give a reasoned rationale for taking one side or the other. Finally, if principals are to remain informed, information related to innovative reading practices must be disseminated in easily accessible and understandable ways.

APPENDIX A

Reading Education in the United States: Elementary Principals' Involvement

ELEMENTARY SCHOOL PRINCIPALS' QUESTIONNAIRE

(This questionnaire takes approximately 10–15 minutes to complete)

Section 1. IMPORTANT Demographic Information

Please complete the following:
(Check)

School Size: _____ 1–299   _____ 300–599   _____ 600 +

School Type: _____ K–3   _____ K–6   _____ Other _____
(Specify)

Years of experience as an elementary school principal _____

Total years of experience as an educator _____

State in which your school is located _____

Give, in percentage, the kinds of reading approaches that are currently being used in your school. (e.g., 70% basal   20% literature based   10% whole language _____ other _____)
_____ basal   _____ literature based   _____ whole language   _____ other _____
(Specify)

SECTION 2. THIS SECTION ASKS YOU TO CONSIDER ELEVEN READING INSTRUCTION ISSUES. YOU WILL BE ASKED TO COMPLETE THREE TASKS RELATED TO THESE ELEVEN ISSUES.

Task 1. Classify
Eleven reading education issues are listed below. In your mind, which of these are:
UI: An *Unresolved Issue* (research is not conclusive)
RI: A *Resolved Issue* (research is conclusive—was once an issue but is no longer)
NI: *Never has been an issue* as far as I am concerned.
For each concern, circle the letter which designates the category you selected.

Task 2. Rank
After you have classified each statement, rank order the top three *unresolved issues* in terms of their relative importance to improving reading instruction from your point of view. Use the number "1" to indicate the issue which you believe is most important. Then use the numbers "2," "3," and so on to indicate the issues that are second, third. . . . Rank only the issues you classified as *unresolved*.

Task 3. Rate
Please rate your understanding of each issue (including any issues you added) as follows:
A. I understand this problem well enough to describe the underlying issues and can give a reasoned argument explaining my position.
B. I believe that I understand most of the underlying issues, but I can't give a good rationale for taking one side or the other.
C. I know that this problem exists, but I'm unsure of what the basic issues are.
D. I'm not aware of any problems in this area.

READING ISSUES:

	Task 1: Classify			Task 2: Rank	Task 3: Rate
1. How should students' reading progress be assessed?	UI	RI	NI	_____	_____
2. Should the whole language approach be used instead of the basal reader approach?	UI	RI	NI		
3. Should tradebooks be used in place of basals?	UI	RI	NI		
4. Should reading skills be taught in isolation or integrated with other language arts curriculum?	UI	RI	NI		
5. Should phonics be taught as a prerequisite to reading instruction?	UI	RI	NI		
6. Should students be grouped by reading ability for instruction in reading?	UI	RI	NI		
7. Should schools be required to adopt a basal reading series?	UI	RI	NI		
8. Should at-risk readers spend more time on reading connected text or on practicing isolated reading skills?	UI	RI	NI		
9. Should reading instruction be mastery based?	UI	RI	NI	_____	_____
10. Should children's entry into kindergarten be delayed until they perform successfully on a screening test?	UI	RI	NI	_____	_____
11. Should schools be required to use the same program in all grades (e.g., the same basal series)?	UI	RI	NI	_____	_____
12. (Other)_____	UI	RI	NI		

SECTION 3. THIS SECTION ASKS YOU TO CONSIDER SIXTEEN READING INFORMATION SOURCES AVAILABLE TO PRINCIPALS. YOU WILL BE ASKED TO DO TWO TASKS IN THIS SECTION.

Task 4
Which of the activities listed below have you personally participated in during the past 12 months as a means of keeping yourself informed about current issues in reading. Mark an "X" in the blank "Have Done" or "Have Not Done" for each source.

Task 5
After completing Task 4, rate the degree to which each source you have used was helpful by placing an "X" in the blank "Quite Helpful," "Moderately Helpful," or "Not Very Helpful." **DO NOT** rate sources that you have not used in the last 12 months.

SOURCES:	Task 4 Have Done	Have Not Done	Task 5 Quite Helpful	Moderately Helpful	Not Very Helpful
1. Personal contacts with specialists in the field (e.g., informal contacts with friends, colleagues, professors, and educators who have specialized in reading education)	_____	_____	_____	_____	_____
2. Attendance at conventions of professional associations (e.g., local, state, or national: International Reading Association, National Reading Conference)	_____	_____	_____	_____	_____
3. Reading magazines or newsletters which focus on reading issues (e.g., *Language Arts, Reading Teacher, Journal of Reading, Reading Horizons*)	_____	_____	_____	_____	_____
4. Reading articles about literacy issues in magazines for professional educators (e.g., *Phi Delta Kappan, The Principal, Elementary School Journal, Educational Leadership*)	_____	_____	_____	_____	_____
5. Reading articles in magazines focused on teaching techniques and instructional methods (e.g., *Instructor, Teacher, K-12 Learning*)	_____	_____	_____	_____	_____
6. Reading articles in popular national magazines (e.g., *Atlantic Monthly, Time, U.S. News, Reader's Digest, Parents, Family Circle*)	_____	_____	_____	_____	_____
7. Reading journal articles which focus on reporting the results of reading research (e.g., *Reading Research Quarterly, Journal of Reading Behavior, Journal of Educational Psychology, Journal of Educational Research*)	_____	_____	_____	_____	_____
8. Reading articles in professional handbooks (e.g., *Handbook of Reading Research, Handbook of Research on Teaching, Encyclopedia of Educational Research, Review of Research in Education*)	_____	_____	_____	_____	_____

Sources continued . . .

	Task 4	Task 5
9. Reading college textbooks focused on reading (e.g., Books on teaching language arts, reading)	___ ___	___ ___
10. Books about reading which have been published by popular press (e.g., *Cultural Literacy, Illiterate American, Why Johnny Still Can't Read, Closing of the American Mind, All I Ever Needed to Know I Learned in Kindergarten*)	___ ___	___ ___
11. Watching or listening to radio and television broadcasts about reading issues (e.g., news reports, documentaries, debates, interviews, commentaries)	___ ___	___ ___
12. Reading newspaper articles about reading issues.	___ ___	___ ___
13. Reading reports about reading from research agencies (e.g., Center for the Study of Reading, regional labs)	___ ___	___ ___
14. Reading reports and publications about reading sponsored by governmental agencies (e.g., *What Works, Becoming a Nation of Readers*)	___ ___	___ ___
15. Enrollment in college or university courses related to reading education.	___ ___	___ ___
16. Participation in workshops, seminars, or organized study groups focused on reading issues.	___ ___	___ ___
17. Other: _____	___ ___	___ ___

NOTES

1. The 11 issues included in the survey were selected by a panel of reading experts. Issues were selected based on attention that each has received in the recent reading education and research literature.

2. In the ranking of the reading issues, some respondents did not follow directions. They ranked all issues, instead of ranking only issues that they felt were unresolved. To adjust for the problem, we included only unresolved issues in the data analysis.

REFERENCES

Aldridge, T. (1973). *The elementary principal as an instructional leader for reading instruction.* Unpublished doctoral dissertation, University of Missouri.

Asher, J. W. (1976). *Educational research and evaluation methods.* Boston: Little, Brown.

Barnard, D., & Hetzel, R. (1982). *Principals handbook to improve reading instruction.* Lexington, MA: Ginn and Company.

Berger, A., & Andolina, C. (1977). How administrators keep abreast of trends and research in reading. *Journal of Reading, 21,* 121-125.

Borg, W. R., & Gall, M. D. (1989). *Educational research, 5th ed.* New York: Longman.

Could-Silva, C., & Sadoski, M. (1987). Reading teachers' attitudes toward basal reader use and state adoption policies. *Journal of Educational Research, 81,* (1), 5-16.

deVaus, D. A. (1986). *Surveys in social research.* Boston: George Allen and Unwin.

Dillman, D. A. (1978). *Mail and telephone surveys: The total design method.* New York: Wiley.

Ellis, T. (1986). The principal as instructional leader. *Research-Roundup, 3*(1), 6.

Fowler, F. J. (1988). *Survey research methods.* Newbury Park, CA: Sage.

Frey, J. H. (1989). *Survey research by telephone* (2nd ed.). Newbury Park, CA: Sage.

Gehring, R. (1977). *An investigation of knowledge of Clark County, Nevada, elementary school principals about the teaching of reading in primary grades.* Unpublished doctoral dissertation, University of Colorado, Boulder.

Goodman, K., Shannon, P., Freeman, Y., & Murphy, S. (1988). *Report card on basal readers.* Katohah, NY: Richard C. Owen Publishers.

Heberlein, T. A., & Baumgartner, R. (1981). Is a questionnaire necessary in a second mailing? *Public Opinion Quarterly, 45,* 102-108.

Kean, M., Summers, A., Raivetz, M., & Tarber, I. (1979). *What works in reading.* Office of Research and Evaluation, School Districts of Philadelphia, PA.

Kurth, R. J. (1985, December). *Problems court: The role of the reading educator in the training of elementary school principals.* Paper presented at the annual meeting of the American Reading Forum, Sarasota, FL.

Laffey, J., & Kelly, D. (1983). Survey of elementary principals. *The Journal of the Virginia State Reading Association* (a special edition), James Madison University, Harrisonburg, VA.

Lilly, E. R. (1982, September). *Administrative leadership in reading: A professional quagmire.* Paper presented at the meeting of the District of Columbia Reading Council of the International Reading Association, Washington, DC.

McNinch, G. H., & Richmond, M. G. (1983). Defining the principals' roles in reading instruction. *Reading Improvement, 18,* 235-242.

McWilliams, D. R. (1981). *The role of the elementary principal in the management of the primary reading program.* Unpublished doctoral dissertation, University of Pittsburgh, PA.

Moss, R. K. (1985). *More than facilitator: A principal's job in educating new and experienced reading teachers.* Paper presented at the annual meeting of the National Council of Teachers of English Spring Conference, Houston, TX. (ERIC Document Reproduction Service No. ED 253 856)

Nufrio, R. M. (1987). *An administrator's overview for teaching reading.* Opinion paper. (ERIC Document Reproduction Service No. ED 286 287)

Panchyshyn, R. (1971). *An investigation of the knowledge of elementary school principals about the teaching of reading in primary grades.* Unpublished doctoral dissertation, University of Iowa, Iowa City.

Rausch, S., & Sanacore, J. (1984). The administrator and the reading program: An annotated bibliography on reading leadership. *Reading World, 23,* 388-393.

Roser, N. L. (1974, February). Evaluation and the administrator: How decisions are made. *Journal of Education, 156*, 48–49.

Shelton, M., Rafferty, C., & Rose, L. (1990, Winter). The state of reading: What Michigan administrators know. *Michigan Reading Journal, 23*, 3–14.

Weber, G. (1971). *Inner-city children can be taught to read: Four successful schools.* New York: Council for Basic Education, Occasional Papers No. 18.

Wilkerson, B. (1988). A prinicipal's perspective. In J. L. Davidson (Ed.), *Counterpoint and beyond: A response to becoming a nation of readers.* Urbana, IL: National Council of Teachers of English.

Zinski, R. (1975). *The elementary school principals and the administration of a total reading program.* Unpublished doctoral dissertation, University of Wisconsin, Madison.

■ SUMMARY/CHAPTER 8

DEFINITION, PURPOSE, AND PROCESS

1. Descriptive research involves collecting data in order to test hypotheses or to answer questions concerning the current status of the subject of the study.
2. The researcher must give careful thought to sample selection and data collection; which population has the desired information is not always readily apparent.
3. Frequently, since one is generally asking questions that have not been asked before, or seeking information that is not already available, a descriptive study requires the development of an instrument appropriate for obtaining the desired information.
4. A logical way to initially categorize descriptive studies is in terms of how data are collected, through self-report or observation. In a self-report study, information is solicited from individuals using, for example, questionnaires, interviews, or standardized attitude scales. In an observation study, individuals are not asked for information; rather, the researcher obtains the desired data through other means, such as direct observation.

SELF-REPORT RESEARCH

Types of Self-Report Research

Survey Research

5. A survey is an attempt to collect data from members of a population in order to determine the current status of that population with respect to one or more variables.
6. In a sample survey, the researcher infers information about a population of interest based on the responses of a selected sample drawn from that population; preferably, the sample is either a simple-random or stratified-random sample.
7. In a census survey, an attempt is made to acquire data from each and every member of a population; a census survey is usually conducted when a population is relatively small and readily accessible.
8. Sample surveys are sometimes referred to as cross-sectional since information is collected at some point in time from a sample which hopefully represents all relevant subgroups in the population.
9. One type of survey unique to education is the school survey, which may involve the study of an individual school or of all the schools in a particular system.
10. School surveys are generally conducted for the purpose of internal or external evaluation or for assessment and projection of needs and usually are conducted as a cooperative effort between local school personnel and a visiting team of experts, typically from local educational agencies and institutions.

Developmental Studies

11. Developmental studies are concerned primarily with behavior variables that differentiate children at different levels of age, growth, or maturation.
12. When the cross-sectional approach is used, different children at various stages of development are simultaneously studied; when the longitudinal method is used, the same group of children is studied over a period of time as the children progress from level to level.

Follow-Up Studies

13. A follow-up study is conducted to determine the status of a group of interest after some period of time.
14. Like school surveys, follow-up studies are often conducted by educational institutions for the purpose of internal or external evaluation of their instructional programs.
15. Follow-up studies may also be conducted solely for research purposes.

Sociometric Studies

16. Sociometry is the assessment and analysis of the interpersonal relationships within a group of individuals.
17. The basic sociometric process involves asking each member to indicate with which other members she or he would most like to engage in a particular activity.
18. The choices made by the group members are graphically depicted in a diagram called a sociogram.

Conducting Self-Report Research

19. Self-report research requires the collection of standardized, quantifiable information from all members of a population or sample.

Conducting a Questionnaire Study

20. In comparison to use of an interview procedure, a questionnaire is much more efficient in that it requires less time, is less expensive, and permits collection of data from a much larger sample.
21. Questionnaires may be administered to subjects but are usually mailed.

Statement of the Problem

22. The problem under investigation, and the topic of the questionnaire, must be of sufficient significance to motivate subjects to respond.
23. The problem must be defined in terms of specific objectives concerning the kind of information needed; specific hypotheses or questions must be formulated and every item on the questionnaire should directly relate to them.

Selection of Subjects

24. Subjects should be selected using an appropriate sampling technique (or an entire population may be used), and identified subjects must be persons who (1) have the desired information and (2) are likely to be willing to give it.

Construction of the Questionnaire

25. As a general guideline, the questionnaire should be as attractive and brief, and as easy to respond to, as possible.
26. No item should be included that does not directly relate to the objectives of the study, and structured, or closed-form, items should be used if at all possible.
27. A structured item consists of a question and a list of alternative responses from which the respondent selects.
28. In addition to facilitating response, structured items also facilitate data analysis; scoring is very objective and efficient.
29. An unstructured item format, in which the responder has complete freedom of response (questions are asked with no possible responses indicated), is sometimes defended on the grounds that it permits greater depth of response and may permit insight into the reasons for responses.
30. With respect to item construction, the number one rule is that each question should deal with a single concept and be worded as clearly as possible; any term or concept that might mean different things to different people should be defined.
31. When necessary, questions should indicate a point of reference.
32. Avoid leading questions which suggest that one response may be more appropriate than another.
33. Do not ask a question that assumes a fact not necessarily in evidence.

Validation of the Questionnaire

34. A too-often-neglected procedure is validation of the questionnaire in order to determine if it measures what it was developed to measure.

Preparation of the Cover Letter

35. Every mailed questionnaire must be accompanied by a cover letter that explains what is being asked of the respondent, and why, and which hopefully motivates the responder to fulfill the request.
36. The cover letter should be brief, neat, and addressed specifically to the potential responder.
37. The letter should explain the purpose of the study, emphasizing its importance and significance, and give the responder a good reason for cooperating.
38. It usually helps if you can get the endorsement of an organization, institution, group, or administrator with which the responder is associated or which the responder views with respect (such as a professional organization).
39. If the questions to be asked are at all threatening (such as items dealing with sex or attitudes toward the local administration), anonymity or confidentiality of responses must be assured.
40. A specific deadline date by which the completed questionnaire is to be returned should be given.

41. The act of responding should be made as painless as possible. A stamped, addressed, return envelope should be included.

Pretesting the Questionnaire

42. The questionnaire should be tried out in a field test just as a research plan should be executed first as a pilot study, and for essentially the same reasons.

43. Pretesting the questionnaire yields data concerning instrument deficiencies as well as suggestions for improvement.

Follow-Up Activities

44. If your percentage of returns is not 70% or so, the validity of your conclusions will be weak.

45. An initial follow-up strategy is to simply send out a reminder postcard.

46. Full-scale follow-up activities are usually begun shortly after the deadline for responding has passed.

Dealing with Nonresponse

47. If your response rate is below 70%, you have a problem with generalizability of results since you do not know if the persons who did respond represent the population from which the sample was originally selected as well as the original sample.

48. The usual approach to dealing with excessive nonresponse is to try to determine if nonresponders are different from responders in some systematic manner by randomly selecting a small subsample of nonresponders and interviewing them, either in person or by phone.

Analysis of Results

49. The simplest way to present the results is to indicate the percentage of responders who selected each alternative for each item.

50. Relationships between variables can be investigated by comparing responses on one item with responses on other items.

Conducting an Interview Study

51. An interview is essentially the oral, in-person administration of a questionnaire to each member of a sample.

52. When well conducted an interview can produce in-depth data not possible with a questionnaire; on the other hand, it is expensive and time-consuming, and generally involves smaller samples.

53. The steps in conducting an interview study are basically the same as for a questionnaire study, with some unique differences.

Construction of the Interview Guide

54. The interviewer must have a written guide which indicates what questions are to be asked and in what order, and what additional prompting or probing is permitted.

55. In order to obtain standardized, comparable data from each subject, all interviews must be conducted in essentially the same manner.

56. As with a questionnaire, each question in the interview should relate to a specific study objective.

57. Most interviews use a semistructured approach involving the asking of structured questions followed by clarifying unstructured, or open-ended, questions.
58. Many of the guidelines for constructing a questionnaire apply to the construction of interview guides.

Communication During the Interview

59. Before the first formal question is asked, some time should be spent in establishing rapport and putting the interviewee at ease.
60. The interviewer should also be sensitive to the reactions of the subject and proceed accordingly.

Recording Responses

61. Responses made during an interview can be recorded manually by the interviewer or mechanically by a recording device.
62. In general, mechanical recording is more objective and efficient.

Pretesting the Interview Procedure

63. Feedback from a small pilot study can be used to revise questions in the guide that are apparently unclear, do not solicit the desired information, or produce negative reactions in subjects. Insights into better ways to handle certain questions can also be acquired.
64. The pilot study will determine whether the resulting data can be quantified and analyzed in the manner intended.

OBSERVATIONAL RESEARCH

Types of Observational Research

Nonparticipant Observation

65. In nonparticipant observation, the observer is not directly involved in the situation to be observed.

Naturalistic Observation

66. In naturalistic observation the observer purposely controls or manipulates nothing, and in fact works very hard at not affecting the observed situation in any way.

Simulation Observation

67. In simulation observation the researcher creates the situation to be observed and tells subjects what activities they are to engage in.
68. This technique allows the researcher to observe behavior that occurs infrequently in natural situations or not at all.
69. Two major types of simulation are individual role playing and team role playing.

Meta-Analysis

70. Meta-analysis is a statistical approach to summarizing the results of many studies which have investigated basically the same problem.
71. Given a number of studies, it provides a numerical way of expressing the "average" result.
72. A central characteristic which distinguishes meta-analysis from more traditional approaches is the emphasis placed on having the review be as inclusive as possible.
73. The key feature of meta-analysis is that for each study results are translated into an effect size (ES), symbolized as Δ.
74. Effect size is a numerical way of expressing the strength, or magnitude, of a reported relationship, be it causal or not.
75. After effect size has been calculated for each study, they are averaged, yielding one number which summarizes the overall, or typical, effect.
76. It is generally agreed that an effect size in the twenties (e.g., .28) indicates a treatment that makes a difference, but not much, whereas an effect size in the eighties (e.g., .81) indicates a powerful treatment.

Conducting Observational Research

77. The steps in conducting observational research are essentially the same as for other types of descriptive research.

Definition of Observational Variables

78. Once the behavior to be observed is determined, the researcher must clearly define what specific behaviors do and do not match the intended behavior.
79. Once a behavioral unit is defined, observations must be quantified so that all observers will count the same way.
80. Researchers typically divide observation sessions into a number of specific observation periods, that is, define a time unit. There should be correspondence between actual behavior frequency and recorded frequency.
81. Observation times may be randomly selected, so that different days and times of day are reflected in the observations.

Recording of Observations

82. Observers should have to observe and record only one behavior at a time.
83. It is also a good idea to alternate observation periods and recording periods, especially if any inference is required on the part of the observers.
84. As a general rule, it is probably better to record observations as the behavior occurs.
85. Most observation studies facilitate recording by using an agreed-upon code, or set of symbols, and a recording instrument.

86. Probably the most often used type of recording form, and the most efficient, is a checklist that lists all behaviors to be observed so that the
observer can simply check each behavior as it occurs. Rating scales are
also sometimes used.

Assessing Observer Reliability

87. Determining observer reliability generally requires that at least two
observers independently make observations; their recorded judgments as to
what occurred can then be compared to see how well they agree.
88. One approach to increasing reliability is to use shorter observation periods
and to base reliability calculations on both agreements and disagreements
on occurrences and nonoccurrences of behavior. With this approach it is
easier to determine whether observers are recording the same events at the
same time.
89. Recording situations to be observed allows each observer to play back
tapes at a time convenient for him or her, and to play them back as often
as needed.

Training Observers

90. Observers need to be trained in order to have some assurance that all
observers are observing and recording the same behaviors in the same
way.
91. Observers must be instructed as to what behaviors to observe, how behaviors are to be coded, how behaviors are to be recorded, and how often.
92. Practice sessions using recordings of behaviors are most effective since
segments with which observers have difficulty can be replayed for discussion and feedback purposes.
93. Training may be terminated when a satisfactory level of reliability is
achieved (say 80%).

Monitoring Observers

94. The major way to ensure continued satisfactory levels of reliability is to
monitor the recording activities of observers.
95. As a general rule, the more monitoring that can reasonably be managed,
the better.

Reducing Observation Bias

96. Observer bias refers to invalid observations that result from the way in
which the observer observes.
97. A response set is the tendency of an observer to rate the majority of
observees as above average, average, or below average, regardless of the
observees' actual behavior.
98. The "halo effect" refers to the phenomenon whereby initial impressions
concerning an observee (positive or negative) affect subsequent observations.

99. Observer effect refers to the phenomenon whereby persons being observed behave atypically simply because they are being observed.

100. The best way to handle the problem is to make observers aware of it so that they can attempt to be as unobtrusive as possible.

101. Another approach is to eliminate observees. If the same information can be determined by observing inanimate objects (referred to as unobtrusive measures), use them.

"Correlational research involves collecting data in order to determine whether, and to what degree, a relationship exists . . . (p. 296)."

Correlational Research

After reading Chapter 9, you should be able to:

1. Briefly state the purpose of correlational research.

2. List and briefly describe the major steps involved in the basic correlational research process.

3. Describe the range of numerical values associated with a correlation coefficient.

4. Describe how the size of a correlation coefficient affects its interpretation with respect to (a) statistical significance, (b) its use in prediction, and (c) its use as an index of validity and reliability.

5. State two major purposes of relationship studies.

6. Identify and briefly describe the steps involved in conducting a relationship study.

7. Briefly describe two methods for computing correlation coefficients.

8. Describe the difference between a linear and a curvilinear relationship.

9. Identify and briefly describe two factors that may contribute to an inaccurate estimate of relationship.

10. Briefly define or describe "predictor variables" and "criterion variables."

11. State three major purposes of prediction studies.

12. State the major difference between data collection procedures in a prediction study and a relationship study.

13. Explain why cross-validation is an important procedure associated with multiple regression equations.

■ DEFINITION AND PURPOSE

Correlational research is sometimes treated as a type of descriptive research, primarily because it does describe an existing condition. However, the condition it describes is distinctly different from the conditions typically described in self-report or observational studies; a correlational study describes in quantitative terms the degree to which variables are related. Correlational research involves collecting data in order to determine whether, and to what degree, a relationship exists between two or more quantifiable variables. Degree of relationship is expressed as a correlation coefficient. If a relationship exists between two variables, it means that scores within a certain range on one measure are associated with scores within a certain range on another measure. For example, there is a relationship between intelligence and academic achievement; persons who score highly on intelligence tests tend to have higher grade point averages, and persons who score low on intelligence tests tend to have lower grade point averages. The purpose of a correlational study may be to determine relationships between variables, or to use relationships in making predictions.

Relationship studies typically investigate a number of variables believed to be related to a major, complex variable such as achievement. Variables found not to be highly related are eliminated from further consideration; variables that are highly related may suggest causal-comparative or experimental studies to determine if the relationships are causal. As discussed in Chapter 1, the fact that there is a relationship between self-concept and achievement does not imply that self-concept "causes" achievement or that achievement "causes" self-concept. Regardless of whether a relationship is a cause-effect relationship, the existence of a high relationship permits prediction. For example, as discussed in Chapter 1, high school grade point average (GPA) and college GPA are highly related; students who have high GPAs in high school tend to have high GPAs in college, and students who have low GPAs in high school tend to have low GPAs in college. Therefore, high school GPA can be, and is, used to predict college GPA. Also, as discussed in Chapter 5, correlational procedures are used to establish certain types of instrument validity and reliability.

Correlational studies provide an estimate of just how related two variables are. If two variables are highly related, a correlation coefficient near +1.00 (or −1.00) will be obtained; if two variables are not related, a coefficient near .00 will be obtained. The more highly related two variables are, the more accurate are predictions based on their relationship. While relationships are rarely perfect, a number of variables are sufficiently related to permit useful predictions.

■ THE BASIC CORRELATIONAL RESEARCH PROCESS

While relationship studies and prediction studies have unique features which differentiate them, their basic processes are very similar.

Problem Selection

Correlational studies may be designed either to determine which variables of a list of likely candidates are related, or to test hypotheses regarding expected relationships. Variables to be included should be selected on the basis of either a deductive or an inductive rationale. In other words, the relationships to be investigated should be suggested by theory or derived from experience. Correlational treasure hunts in which the researcher correlates all sorts of variables to see "what turns up" are to be strongly discouraged. This research strategy (appropriately referred to as the "shotgun approach") does not involve hypothesis testing and is very inefficient. While it may lead to the discovery of an important relationship, it more often produces spurious correlation coefficients, that is, coefficients that do not accurately reflect the degree of relationship between two variables and which are not found if the variables are correlated again using another sample.

Sample and Instrument Selection

The sample for a correlational study is selected using an acceptable sampling method, and 30 subjects are generally considered to be a minimally acceptable sample size. As with any study, it is important to select or develop valid, reliable measures of the variables being studied. If inadequate data are collected, the resulting correlation coefficient will represent an inaccurate estimate of the degree of relationship. Further, if the measures used do not really measure the intended variables, the resulting coefficient will not indicate the intended relationships. Suppose, for example, you wanted to determine the relationship between achievement in mathematics and physics achievement. If you selected and administered a valid, reliable test of computational skill and a valid, reliable test of physics achievement, the resulting correlation coefficient would not be an accurate estimate of the intended relationship. Computational skill is only one kind of mathematical achievement; the resulting coefficient would indicate the relationship between physics achievement and *one kind* of mathematical achievement, computational skill. Thus, care must be taken to select measures that are valid *for your purposes*.

Design and Procedure

The basic correlational design is not complicated; two (or more) scores are obtained for each member of a selected sample, one score for each variable of interest, and the paired scores are then correlated. The resulting correlation coefficient indicates the degree of relationship between the two variables. Different studies investigate different numbers of variables, and some utilize complex statistical procedures, but the basic design is similar in all correlational studies.

Data Analysis and Interpretation

When two variables are correlated the result is a correlation coefficient. A correlation coefficient is a decimal number, between .00 and +1.00, or .00 and −1.00, which indicates the degree to which two variables are related. If the coefficient is near +1.00, the variables are positively correlated. This means that a person with a high score on one variable is likely to have a high score on the other variable, and a person with a low score on one is likely to have a low score on the other; an increase on one variable is associated with an increase on the other variable. If the coefficient is near .00, the variables are not related. This means that a person's score on one variable is no indication of what the person's score is on the other variable. If the coefficient is near −1.00, the variables are inversely related. This means that a person with a high score on one variable is likely to have a low score on the other variable, and a person with a low score on one is likely to have a high score on the other; an increase on one variable is associated with a decrease on the other variable, and vice versa (see Table 9.1). Table 9.1 presents four scores for each of eight 12th grade students: IQ, GPA, weight, and errors on a 20-item final exam. As Table 9.1 illustrates, IQ is positively related to achievement, not related to weight, and negatively, or inversely, related to errors. The students with progressively higher IQs have progressively higher GPAs. On the other hand, students with higher IQs tend to make fewer errors (makes sense!). The relationships are not perfect, and it would be very strange if they were. One's GPA, for example, is related to other variables besides intelligence, such as motivation. The data do indicate, however, that IQ is one major variable related to both GPA and examination errors. The data also illustrate an important concept often misunderstood by beginning researchers, namely that a high negative relationship is just as strong as a high positive relationship; −1.00 and +1.00 indicate equally perfect relationships. A coefficient near .00 indicates no relationship; the further away from .00 the coefficient is, in *either* direction (toward −1.00 or +1.00), the stronger the relationship. Both high positive and high negative relationships are equally useful for making predictions; knowing that Iggie has a low IQ score would enable you to predict both a low GPA and a high number of errors.

What a correlation coefficient *means* is difficult to explain. Some beginning researchers erroneously think that a correlation coefficient of .50 means that two variables are 50% related. Not true. In research talk, a correlation coefficient squared indicates the amount of common variance shared by the variables (WHAT??!!). Now, in English. Each of two variables will result in a range of scores; there will be score variance, that is, everyone will not get the same score. In Table 9.1, for example, IQ scores vary from 85 to 140 and GPAs from 1.0 to 3.8. Common variance refers to the variation in one variable that is attributable to its tendency to vary with the other. If two variables are not related, then the variability of one set of scores has nothing to do with the variability of the other set; if two variables are perfectly related, then variability of one set of scores has everything to do with variability in the other set. Thus with no relationship the variables have no common variance, but with a perfect relationship all variance, or 100% of the variance, is shared, common variance. The percent of common variance is generally less than the numerical

Table 9.1

Hypothetical Sets of Data Illustrating a High Positive Relationship Between Two Variables, No Relationship, and a High Negative Relationship

	High Positive Relationship		No Relationship		High Negative Relationship	
	IQ	GPA	IQ	Weight	IQ	Errors
1. Iggie	85	1.0	85	156	85	16
2. Hermie	90	1.2	90	140	90	10
3. Fifi	100	2.4	100	120	100	8
4. Teenie	110	2.2	110	116	110	5
5. Tiny	120	2.8	120	160	120	9
6. Tillie	130	3.4	130	110	130	3
7. Millie	135	3.2	135	140	135	2
8. Jane	140	3.8	140	166	140	1

value of the correlation coefficient. In fact, to determine common variance you simply square the correlation coefficient. A correlation coefficient of .80 indicates $(.80)^2$, or .64, or 64% common variance. A correlation coefficient of .00 indicates $(.00)^2$, or .00, or 00% common variance, and a coefficient of 1.00 indicates $(1.00)^2$, or 1.00, or 100% common variance. Thus, a coefficient of .50 may look pretty good at first but it actually means that the variables have 25% common variance.

Interpretation of a correlation coefficient depends upon how it is to be used. In other words, how large it needs to be in order to be useful depends upon the purpose for which it was computed. In a study designed to explore or test hypothesized relationships, a correlation coefficient is interpreted in terms of its statistical significance. In a prediction study, statistical significance is secondary to the value of the coefficient in facilitating accurate predictions. Statistical significance refers to whether the obtained coefficient is really different from zero and reflects a true relationship, not a chance relationship; the decision concerning statistical significance is made at a given level of probability.[1] In other words, based on one sample of a given size, you cannot determine positively whether there is or is not a true relationship between the variables, but you can say there probably is or probably is not such a relationship. Relatedly, a hypothesis concerning relationship or lack of it (the null hypothesis) can be supported or not supported, not proven or disproven. To determine statistical significance, you only have to consult a table that tells you how large your coefficient needs to be in order to be significant at a given probability level, and given the size of your sample (see Table A.2 in the Appendix). For the same probability level, or significance level, a larger coefficient is required when smaller samples are involved. We can generally have a lot more confidence in a coefficient based on 100 subjects than one based on 10 subjects. Thus, for example, at the 95% confidence level, with 10 cases, you would need a coefficient of at least .6319 in order to conclude the existence of a relationship; on the other hand, with 102 cases you would need a coefficient of only .1946.[2] This concept makes sense if you consider the case when you would collect data on *every* member of a population, not just a sample. In this case, no inference would be involved, and regardless of how small the actual correlation coefficient was, it would represent the true degree of relationship between the variables *for that population*. Even if the coefficient were only .11, for example, it would still indicate the existence of a relationship, a low one, but a relationship just the same. The larger the sample, the more closely it approximates the population and therefore the more probable it is that a given coefficient represents a true relationship.

You may also have noticed another related concept; for a given sample size, the value of the correlation coefficient needed for significance increases as the level of confidence increases. As the level of confidence increases, the p value in the table gets smaller; the 95% confidence level corresponds to $p = .05$ and the 99% level to $p = .01$. Thus for 10 subjects ($df = 8$), and $p = .05$, a coefficient of .6319 is required; for 10 subjects and $p = .01$, however, a coefficient of .7646 is required. In other words, the more confident you wish to be that your decision concerning significance is the correct one, the larger the coefficient must be. Beware, however, of

---

[1] The concepts of statistical significance, level of significance, and degrees of freedom will be discussed further in Chapter 14.

[2] In case you are trying to read Table A.2, a 95% level of confidence corresponds to $p = .05$, and 10 cases correspond to $df = 8$; degrees of freedom, df, are equal to N (number in the sample) $- 2$, thus $10 - 2$, or 8. For 100 cases, df equals $100 - 2$, which equals 98.

confusing significance with strength. No matter how significant a coefficient is, a low coefficient represents a low relationship. The level of significance only indicates the probability that a given relationship is a true one, regardless of whether it is a weak relationship or a strong relationship.

Prediction is another story. The utility of a correlation coefficient goes beyond its statistical significance in a prediction study. With a sample of 102 subjects, for example, a coefficient of .1946 is significant at $p = .05$. This relationship would be of little value for most prediction purposes. Since the relationship is so low (the common variance is only $[.1946]^2$, or .0379, or 3.8%), knowing a person's score on one variable would be of little help in predicting her or his score on the other. A correlation coefficient much below .50 is generally useless for either group prediction or individual prediction, although a combination of several variables in this range may yield a reasonably satisfactory prediction. Coefficients in the .60s and .70s are usually considered adequate for group prediction purposes, and coefficients in the .80s and above for individual prediction purposes.

When correlation coefficients are used to estimate the validity or reliability of measuring instruments, the criterion of acceptability is even higher. A correlation coefficient of .40, for example, would be considered useful in a relationship study, not useful in a prediction study, and terrible in a reliability study; a coefficient of .60 would be considered useful in a prediction study but would still probably be considered unsatisfactory as an estimate of reliability. As discussed in Chapter 5, what does constitute an acceptable level of reliability is partly a function of the type of instrument. While all reliabilities in the .90s are acceptable, for certain kinds of instruments, such as personality measures, a reliability in the low .70s might be acceptable. The standards for acceptable observer reliability are similar to those for test reliability. A researcher would be very happy with observer reliabilities in the .90s, satisfied with the .80s, minimally accepting of the .70s, and would be progressively more unhappy with the .60s, .50s, and so forth.

When interpreting a correlation coefficient you must always keep in mind that you are talking about a relationship only, not a cause-effect relationship. A significant correlation coefficient may *suggest* a cause-effect relationship but does not establish one. The only way to establish a cause-effect relationship is by conducting an experiment. When one finds a high relationship between two variables it is often very tempting to conclude that one "causes" the other. In fact, it may be that neither one is the cause of the other; there may be a third variable which "causes" both of them. To use a former example, the existence of a positive relationship between self-concept and achievement could mean one of three things: a higher self-concept leads to higher achievement, higher achievement tends to increase self-concept, or there is a variable which results in both higher self-concept and higher achievement. It might be, for example, that parental behavior is a major factor in both self-concept and achievement; parents who praise their children may also encourage them to do well in school. Which of the alternatives is in fact the true explanation cannot be determined through a correlational study.

◼ RELATIONSHIP STUDIES

Relationship studies are conducted in an attempt to gain insight into the factors or variables that are related to complex variables such as academic achievement, motivation, and self-concept. Variables found not to be related can be eliminated from further consideration. Identification of related variables serves several major purposes. First, such studies give direction to subsequent causal-comparative and experimental studies. Experimental studies are costly in more ways than one; correlational studies are an effective way of reducing unprofitable experimental studies and suggesting potentially productive ones. Also, in both causal-comparative and experimental research studies, the researcher is concerned with controlling for variables, other than the independent variable, which might be related to performance on the dependent variable. In other words, the researcher tries to identify variables that are correlated with the dependent variable and to remove their influence so that it will not be confused with that of the independent variable. Relationship studies help the researcher to identify such variables, to control for them, and therefore to investigate the effects of the intended variable. If you were interested in comparing the effectiveness of different methods of reading instruction for first graders, for example, you would probably want to control for initial differences in reading readiness.

The relationship study strategy of attempting to understand a complex variable by identifying and analyzing variables related to it has been more productive for some complex variables than for others. For example, while a number of variables correlated with achievement have been identified, factors significantly related to success in areas such as administration and teaching have not been as easy to pin down. Either some wholes are greater than the sum of their parts, or all the relevant parts have not yet been identified. If nothing else, however, relationship studies that have not uncovered useful relationships have at least identified variables which can be excluded from future studies, a necessary step in science.

Data Collection

In a relationship study the researcher first identifies, either inductively or deductively, variables potentially related to the complex variable under study. For example, if you were interested in factors related to self-concept, you might identify variables such as intelligence, past academic achievement, and socioeconomic status. As pointed out previously, you should have some reason for including variables in the study. The shotgun approach, which involves checking all conceivable variables for possible relationships, is very inefficient and often misleading. The more correlation coefficients that are computed at one time, the more likely it is that the wrong conclusion will be reached for some of them concerning the existence of a relationship. If only one correlation coefficient is computed, the odds are greatly in our favor that we are making the correct decision. On the other hand, if 100 coefficients are computed, and if we are working at $p = .05$, the odds are working against us since it is likely that we will erroneously conclude relationship. A smaller number of carefully selected variables is much to be preferred to a larger number of carelessly selected variables. We may find fewer significant correlation coefficients, but we can have more confidence that the ones we do find represent true relationships, not chance ones which are not likely to be found again.

The next step in data collection is to identify an appropriate population of subjects from which to select a sample. The population must be one for which data on each of the identified variables can be collected, and one whose members are available to the researcher. Although data on some variables can be collected without direct access to subjects, variables such as past achievement which can be found in cumulative records, many relationship studies require the administration of one or more instruments and in some cases observation. Any of the types of instruments so far discussed, such as standardized tests and questionnaires, may be used in a relationship study, and each must be selected with care. One advantage of a relationship study is that all the data may be collected within a relatively short period of time. Instruments may be administered at one session or several sessions in close succession. If school children are the subjects, as is often the case, time demands on students and teachers are relatively small compared to those required for experimental studies, and it is usually easier to obtain administrative approval.

Data Analysis and Interpretation

In a relationship study, the scores for each variable are in turn correlated with the scores for the complex variable of interest. Thus, there results one correlation coefficient for each variable; each coefficient represents the relationship between a particular variable and the complex variable under study. In a study investigating factors related to self-concept, a measure of self-concept might be correlated with a measure of intelligence, a measure of past achievement, a measure of socioeconomic status, and with each of any other identified variables. Since the end result in each case is a correlation coefficient, a number between −1.00 and +1.00, clearly each variable must be expressible in numerical form, that is, must be quantifiable. For the variable "past achievement," for example, simply classifying students as good students, average students, or poor students would not do. Past achievement would have to be expressed numerically, in terms of GPA, for example.

There are a number of different methods of computing a correlation coefficient; which one is appropriate depends upon the type of data represented by each variable.[3] The most commonly used technique is the product moment correlation coefficient, usually referred to as the Pearson *r*, which is appropriate when both variables to be correlated are expressed as ratio data or interval data. Since most instruments used in education, such as achievement measures and personality measures, are expressed in the form of interval data, the Pearson *r* is usually the appropriate coefficient for determining relationship. Further, since the Pearson *r* results in the most reliable estimate of correlation, its use is preferred even when other methods may be applied.

If the data for one of the variables are expressed as ranks, the appropriate correlation coefficient is the rank difference correlation coefficient, usually referred to as the Spearman rho.[4] Rank data are involved when, instead of using a score for each subject, subjects are arranged in order of score and each subject is assigned a rank from 1 to however many subjects there are. For a group of 30 subjects, for example, the subject with the highest score would be assigned a rank of 1, the subject with the second highest score 2, and the subject with the lowest score 30. If two subjects have the same score, their ranks are averaged; if two subjects, for example, have the same highest score they are each assigned the average of rank 1 and rank 2, namely 1.5. If only one of the variables to be correlated is in rank order, say class standing at the time of graduation, then the other variables to be correlated with it must also be expressed in terms of ranks in order to use the Spearman rho technique. Thus, if intelligence were to be correlated with class standing, students would have to be ranked in terms of intelligence, and IQ scores per se would not be involved in actual computation of the correlation coefficient.

---

[3]Actual computation of a correlation coefficient, as well as the various types of data, will be described and discussed in Chapters 12 and 13.

[4]Pearson and Spearman are the men credited with the development of their respective techniques for computing correlation coefficients.

Although the Pearson *r* is more precise, with a small number of subjects (less than 30) the Spearman rho is much easier to compute and results in a coefficient very close to the one which would have been obtained had a Pearson *r* been computed. When the number of subjects is large, however, the process of ranking becomes more time-consuming and the Spearman rho loses its only advantage over the Pearson *r*.

There are also a number of other correlational techniques which are encountered less often but which should be used when appropriate. Some variables, for example, can only be expressed in terms of a dichotomy. Since an individual is usually either male or female, the variable of sex cannot be expressed on a scale from 1 to 30. Thus sex is typically expressed as a 1 or 0 (female versus male) or as a 1 or 2 (female versus male). A 2, however, does not mean more of something than a 1, and 1 does not mean more than 0; these numbers indicate difference only, not difference in amount. Other variables which may be expressed as a dichotomy include political affiliation (Democrat versus Republican), smoking status (smoker versus nonsmoker), and educational status (high school graduate versus high school dropout). The above examples illustrate "true" dichotomies in that a person is or is not a female, a Democrat, a smoker, or a high school graduate. Artificial dichotomies may also be created by operationally defining a midpoint and categorizing subjects as falling above it or below it. Subjects with IQ scores of 100 or above might be classified as "high IQ subjects," for example, and subjects with IQ scores of 99 or below might be classified as "low IQ students." Such classifications are also typically translated into a "score" of 1 or 0.[5]

Most correlational techniques are based on the assumption that the relationship being investigated is a linear one. If a relationship is linear, then plotting the scores on the two variables will result in something resembling a straight line. If a relationship is perfect (+1.00 or −1.00), the line will be perfectly straight; if there is no relationship, the points will form no pattern but will instead be scattered in a random fashion. Figure 9.1, which plots the data presented in Table 9.1, illustrates the concept of a linear relationship. Not all relationships, however, are linear; some are curvilinear. If a relationship is curvilinear, an increase in one variable is associated with a corresponding increase in another variable to *a point,* at which point further increase in the first variable results in a corresponding decrease in the other variable (or vice versa). The relationship between age and agility, for example, is a curvilinear one (see Figure 9.2). As Figure 9.2 illustrates, agility increasingly improves with age, peaks or reaches its maximum somewhere in the twenties, and then progressively decreases as age increases. Two other examples of curvilinear relationships are age of car and dollar value, and anxiety and achievement. A car *decreases* in value as soon as it leaves the lot and continues to do so over time until it becomes an antique(!) and then it *increases* in value as time goes by. In contrast, increases in anxiety are associated with increases in achievement (no anxiety at all is not very conducive to learning) *to a point;* at some point anxiety becomes counterproductive and interferes with learning in that as anxiety increases, achievement *decreases*. If a relationship is suspected of being curvilinear, then a correlational technique which results in an eta ratio is required. If you try to use a correlational technique which assumes a linear relationship when the relationship is in fact curvilinear, your estimate of the degree of relationship will be way off base. Since it will in no way resemble a straight line, the coefficient will generally indicate little or no

---

[5]For additional discussion concerning alternative techniques for calculating correlation coefficients, see Glass, G. V., & Stanley, J. C. (1984). *Statistical methods in education and psychology* (2nd ed.). Englewood Cliffs, NJ: Prentice-Hall.

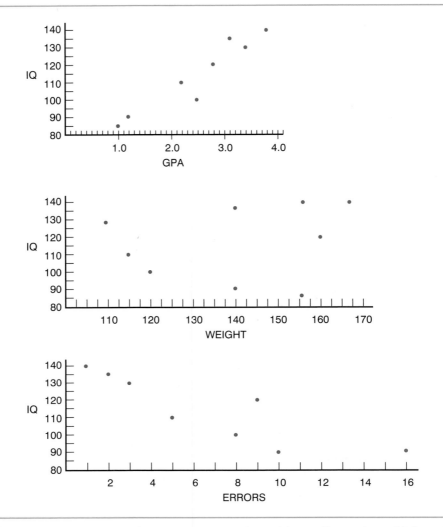

Figure 9.1. Data points for scores presented in Table 9.1 illustrating a high positive relationship (IQ and GPA), no relationship (IQ and weight), and a high negative relationship (IQ and errors).

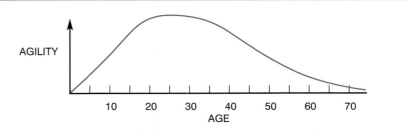

Figure 9.2. The curvilinear relationship between age and agility.

relationship; the positive relationship and negative relationship which combine to form a high curvilinear relationship will in a sense cancel each other out if a technique that assumes linearity (totally positive or totally negative) is applied.[6]

In addition to computing correlation coefficients for a total sample group, it is sometimes profitable to examine relationships separately for certain defined subgroups. The relationship between two variables may be different, for example, for females and males, college graduates and noncollege graduates, or high-ability students and low-ability students. When the subgroups are lumped together, such differential relationships may be obscured. There are also other factors that may contribute to an inaccurate estimate of relationship. Attenuation, for example, refers to the principle that correlation coefficients tend to be lowered due to the fact that less-than-perfectly-reliable measures are utilized. In relationship studies a correction for attenuation can be applied that provides an estimate of what the coefficient would be if both measures were perfectly reliable. If such a correction is used, it must be kept in mind that the resulting coefficient does not represent what was actually found. Such a correction is not used in prediction studies since predictions must be made based on existing measures, not hypothetical, perfectly reliable, instruments. Another factor that may lead to a coefficient representing an underestimate of the true relationship between two variables is a restricted range of scores. The more variability there is in each set of scores, the higher the coefficient is likely to be. The correlation coefficient for IQ and grades, for example, tends to decrease as these variables are measured at higher educational levels. Thus, the relationship will not be found to be as high for college seniors as for high school seniors. The reason is that not many low IQ individuals are college seniors; low IQ individuals either do not enter college or drop out long before their senior year. In other words, the range of IQ scores is much smaller, or more restricted, for college seniors, and a correlation coefficient based on such scores will tend to be reduced. There is also a correction for restriction in range that may be applied to obtain an estimate of what the coefficient would be if the range of scores were not restricted. It should be interpreted with the same caution as the correction for attenuation since it does not represent what was actually found.

■ PREDICTION STUDIES

If two variables are highly related, scores on one variable can be used to predict scores on the other variable. High school grades, for example, can be used to predict college grades. The variable upon which the prediction is made is referred to as the predictor, and the variable predicted is referred to as the criterion. Prediction studies are often conducted to facilitate decision making concerning individuals or to aid in the selection of individuals. Prediction studies are also conducted to test theoretical hypotheses concerning variables believed to be predictors of a criterion, and to determine the predictive validity of individual measuring instruments. The results of prediction studies are used, for example, to predict an individual's likely level of success in a specific course, such as first-year algebra, to predict which of a number of individuals are likely to succeed in college or in a vocational training program, and to predict in which area of study an individual is most likely to be

---

[6]For further discussion concerning eta, as well as other advanced correlational procedures such as factor analysis and partial correlation, see Nunnally, J. C. (1994). *Psychometric theory* (3rd ed.). New York: McGraw-Hill.

successful. Thus, the results of prediction studies are used by a number of groups besides researchers, such as counselors and admissions personnel. If several predictor variables each correlate well with a criterion, then a prediction based on a combination of those variables will be more accurate than a prediction based on any one of them. For example, a prediction of probable level of success (GPA) in college is usually based on a combination of factors such as high school GPA, rank in graduating class, and scores on college entrance exams. Although there are several major differences between prediction studies and relationship studies, both involve determining the relationship between a number of identified variables and a complex variable.

Data Collection

As with a relationship study, subjects must be selected from whom the desired data can be collected and who are available to the researcher. Instruments selected must also be valid measures of the variables of interest. It is especially important that the measure of the criterion variable be a valid one. If the criterion were "success on the job," success would have to be carefully defined in quantifiable terms. Size of desk would probably not be a valid measure of success (although you never know!), whereas number of promotions or salary increases probably would be. The major difference in data collection procedures for a relationship study and a prediction study is that in a relationship study data on all variables are collected within a relatively short period of time, whereas in a prediction study predictor variables are measured some period of time before the criterion variable is measured. In determining the predictive validity of a physics aptitude test, for example, success in physics would probably be measured at the end of a course of study, whereas the aptitude test would be administered some time prior to the beginning of the course.

Data Analysis and Interpretation

As with a relationship study, each predictor variable is correlated with the criterion variable. Since a combination of variables usually results in a more accurate prediction than any one variable, prediction studies often result in a prediction equation referred to as a multiple regression equation. A multiple regression equation uses all variables that individually predict the criterion to make a more accurate prediction. College admissions personnel, for example, use prediction equations that include a number of variables in order to predict college GPA. Since relationships are rarely perfect, predictions made by a multiple regression equation are not perfect. Thus, predicted scores are generally placed in a confidence interval. For example, a predicted college GPA of 1.20 might be placed in an interval of .80 to 1.60. In other words, students with a predicted GPA of 1.20 would be predicted to earn a GPA somewhere in the range between .80 and 1.60. A college that does not accept all applicants will probably as a general rule fail to accept any applicants with such a projected GPA range even though it is very likely that some of those students would be successful if admitted. Although the predictions for any given individual might be way off (either too high or too low), for the total group of applicants predictions are quite accurate on the whole; most applicants predicted to succeed, do so. As with relationship studies, and for similar reasons, prediction equations may be formulated for each of a number of subgroups as well as for a total group.

An interesting phenomenon characteristic of multiple regression equations is referred to as shrinkage; shrinkage is the tendency of a prediction equation to become less accurate when used with a different group, a group other than the one on which the equation was originally formulated. The reason for shrinkage is that an initial equation may be the result of chance relationships that will not be found again with another group of subjects. Thus, any prediction equation should be validated with at least one other group, and variables that are no longer found to be related to the criterion measure should be taken out of the equation; this procedure is referred to as cross-validation.

On the following pages an example of correlational research is presented. Note that the alpha reliability coefficients for the instruments used are given and they are satisfactory.

Explorations in Parent-School Relations

KATHLEEN V. HOOVER-DEMPSEY
OTTO C. BASSLER
JANE S. BRISSIE
Peabody College of Vanderbilt University

ABSTRACT   Grounded in Bandura's (1976, 1986) work, parent efficacy was defined as a parent's belief that he or she is capable of exerting a positive influence on children's school outcomes. Parents' sense of efficacy and its relationship to parent involvement were examined in this study. Parents (n = 390) of children in kindergarten through fourth grade in a metropolitan public school district responded to questionnaires assessing parent efficacy and parent involvement in five types of activities: help with homework, educational activities, classroom volunteering, conference participation, and telephone calls with teachers. Teachers (n = 50) from the same schools also participated, responding to questionnaires assessing teacher efficacy, perceptions of parent efficacy, and estimates of parent involvement. Findings revealed small but significant relationships between self-reported parent efficacy and three of the five indicators of parent involvement. Results for teachers revealed significant relationships among teacher efficacy, teacher perceptions of parent efficacy, and teacher reports of parent involvement in four areas. Results are discussed in relation to the patterns of involvement activities reported by parents and implications for research and intervention in parent-school relationships.

Bandura's (1977, 1984, 1986) work on personal efficacy considers the influence of beliefs that one is capable of achieving specific outcomes on behavior choices. In general, his work suggests that persons higher in efficacy will be more likely to engage in behaviors leading to a goal and will be more persistent in the face of obstacles than will persons with a lower sense of efficacy.

Hoover-Dempsey, Bassler, and Brissie (1987) earlier examined relationships between teacher efficacy and parent involvement. Building on Bandura's work and studies of the role of teacher efficacy in various educational outcomes (Ashton, Webb, & Doda, 1983; Dembo & Gibson, 1985), the authors defined teacher efficacy as "teachers' certainty that their instructional skills are effective" (p. 425). Hoover-Dempsey, Bassler, and Brissie found that teacher efficacy was significantly related to teacher reports of parents' involvement in conferences, volunteering, and home tutoring, as well as teacher perceptions of parent support.

Examination of specific parent variables often related to children's school performance suggests a complementary avenue of exploration in efforts to understand and improve parent-school relations. Some evidence that *parent* efficacy beliefs may be important in parent behaviors and child outcomes are reported in Baumrind's (1971, 1973) work on parenting styles, which established clear linkages between patterns of parenting behaviors and patterns of children's social and cognitive development. For example, the characteristics of Baumrind's authoritative style include consistent parental willingness to give reasons and explanations for requests and to consider and discuss alternative points of view. Because children of authoritative parents have consistent access to their parents' thinking—and because authoritative parents listen and take into account their children's reasoning— the children tend to develop higher levels of social and cognitive competence than do peers raised in other parenting styles.

Dornbusch, Ritter, Leiderman, Roberts, and Fraleigh (1987) recently demonstrated another specific outcome of an authoritative parenting style; they found that adolescents raised by authoritative parents, when compared with adolescents raised by authoritarian parents, have higher levels of academic performance in high school. In a related line of inquiry, Mondell and Tyler (1981) reported significant positive relationships between elements of parental competence and characteristics of parents' teaching interactions with their children, for example, more competent parents treat the child as an "origin," offer more approval and acceptance, and offer more helpful problem-solving questions and strategies.

In each set of findings, the qualities of parental behavior suggest the presence of strong parental beliefs in the abilities and "worthiness" of the child, for example, giving children reasons for requests and treating them as capable of solving problems. These behaviors suggest that parents believe in the abilities of the child and have

---

Address correspondence to Kathleen V. Hoover-Dempsey, Department of Psychology and Human Development, Box 512, Peabody College, Vanderbilt University, Nashville, TN 37203.

Hoover-Dempsey, K. V., Bassler, O. C., & Brissie, J. S. (1992). Explorations in parent-school relations. *The Journal of Educational Research, 85,* 287–294. Reprinted with the permission of the Helen Dwight Reid Educational Foundation. Published by Heldref Publications, 1319 Eighteenth St., N.W., Washington, DC 20036-1802. Copyright © 1992.

confidence in their own ability to guide the child's learning. Such attitudes and the behaviors that they enable are central to a parental sense of efficacy—parents' belief and knowledge that they can teach their children (content, processes, attitudes, and values) and that their children can learn what they teach.

Applied in this manner, Bandura's (1977, 1984, 1986) theory suggests that parents will hold personal efficacy beliefs about their ability to help their children learn. These efficacy beliefs will influence their decisions about the avenues and timing of efforts to become involved in their children's education. For example, parents with a strong sense of efficacy are more likely than low-efficacy parents are to help their children resolve a misunderstanding with the teacher, because they believe that they are capable of offering, and helping their child to act on, appropriate guidance. Overall, parents most likely become involved when they believe that their involvement will "make a difference" for their children.

Following Bandura's (1986) suggestion that assessments of perceived self-efficacy are appropriately "tailored to the domains of functioning being analyzed" (p. 360), the present study was designed to explore parent efficacy and the nature of its relationship to specific indicators of parents' involvement in their elementary school children's education. Although parent efficacy is likely only one of several contributors to parents' involvement decisions (Bandura 1986), we believe that it may operate as a fundamentally important mechanism, explaining variations in involvement decisions more fully than do some of the more frequently referenced status variables (e.g., parent income, education, employment). We believe that self-efficacy is more significant than such status variables because self-efficacy beliefs, far more than variables describing an individual's status, "function as an important set of proximal determinants of human motivation, affect, and action" (Bandura, 1989, p. 1175). Support for this position comes from related bodies of work, for example, Greenberger and Goldberg's (1989) findings that adults' commitment to parenting is "more consequential" for other parenting practices than is their involvement in work (30).

We also explored the replicability of previous results indicating a significant positive relationship between teachers' sense of efficacy and parent involvement. That relationship is grounded in the logical probability that teachers with a higher sense of personal teaching efficacy, being more confident of their teaching skills, are more likely to invite parent involvement and to accept parents' initiation of involvement activities (Hoover-Dempsey et al., 1987). Finally, we explored teachers' perceptions of parents' efficacy and involvement, based, in part, on earlier findings of a significant relationship between an "other's" perceptions of teacher efficacy and selected teacher outcomes (Brissie, Hoover-Dempsey, & Bassler, 1988). In general, we expected that higher levels of parent involvement would be associated with higher levels of parent efficacy, teacher efficacy, and teacher perceptions of parent efficacy. We expected to find those relationships because higher efficacy parents and teachers, being more confident of their skills and abilities related to children's learning, would more likely initiate and invite parent involvement in children's school-related learning activities.

Sample, Methods, and Procedures

Four elementary schools in a large public school district participated in the study. The schools varied in geographic location within the district, size (300 to 500 students), and mean annual family income reported by parents ($15,000 to $37,000). Because the purpose of the study was to examine a group of parents across varied school settings, data are not reported for individual schools.

We contacted principals from each school and obtained permission to solicit parent and teacher participation. Letters describing the study were put in teacher mailboxes at each school. Teachers choosing to participate were asked to complete a questionnaire that contained all teacher data needed for the study and to leave it in a sealed envelope in a collection box in the school office. All the teachers at each school, whether they choose to participate in the study or not, were asked to send parent letters and questionnaire packets home with students in their classes. The letter explained the study, solicited voluntary participation, and asked parents to complete an accompanying questionnaire and return it to school in a sealed envelope. We collected the sealed return envelopes from parents and teachers at the schools.

Parent Sample

Three hundred ninety parents participated in the study. The number represented approximately 30% of the children served by the four schools. Individual school response rates ranged from 24% to 36%. Given the relatively low response rate, the results must be interpreted with caution. It seemed probable that bias in the sample favored participation by parents who had stronger opinions about the issues involved. As a check on that possibility, we reviewed parents' comments at the end of the questionnaire (in a "comments" space used by approximately half of the participants). The comments revealed a wide range of positive and negative statements, indicating a varied set of parent experiences and attitudes (e.g., "I would appreciate more news on what the children are doing and why from teachers to parents, plus how to assist with that at home." "Conference times are inaccessible to people who work. Teachers do not like phone calls from parents in their off time and I understand this. You never hear from the schoolteacher unless they have a complaint or want something." "Our son's teacher this year and last has been a very positive influence on him. We're grateful for her caring the way she does.'' ''She never has homework. What is this teacher's problem? Is she too lazy to grade extra papers? My child is making Cs and Ds. Please help.''). Although the respondents may have had a higher-than-average level of interest in parent involvement issues, the variety of experiences reflected in their comments suggested that their reports would be useful in understanding many parents' patterns of school-related involvement.

In general, the respondents appeared to be an average group of elementary school parents (Table 1). Most of the respondents were mothers, most were married, and most were employed outside of the home. Education and income levels spanned a wide range. A comparison of that group with national data suggests that those parents were typical of many public school districts' parent population (e.g., compare Table 1 figures with national percentages for marital status in 1987—63% married, 36% not married—and for education—among the 25- to 34-year-old age group in 1984, 34% had a high school education and 16% had a college degree; U.S. Bureau of the Census, 1989).

Table 1.—Parent Characteristics

Elementary school parents	n	% of sample
Sex		
Female	326	84
Male	54	14
No response	8	2
Education		
Grade school	27	7
High school	131	34
Some college	125	32
BA/BS degree	50	13
Some graduate work	22	6
Graduate degree (MA/MS, PhD/MD)	24	7
No response	9	2
Marital status		
Married	259	67
Not married (includes single, separated, divorced, widowed)	124	32
No response	5	1
Employment status		
Employed out of the home	253	65
Not employed out of the home	118	30
No response	17	4
Family income		
≤ $5,000	25	6
$5,001–$10,000	42	11
$10,001–$20,000	78	20
$20,001–$30,000	76	20
$30,001–$40,000	75	20
$40,001–$50,000	36	9
$50,001 +	23	6
No response	10	8
Age of respondent	$M = 33.37$	$SD = 6.61$

Teacher Sample

Fifty teachers in the four schools (63% of the total possible) participated in the study and returned usable questionnaires. All the teachers were women, and their class enrollments averaged 21.06 ($SD = 5.20$). They had been teaching for an average of 15.76 years ($SD = 7.57$) and had been in their present schools for approximately 6.5 years ($SD = 5.73$). Their average age was 41.21 years ($SD = 8.73$). The majority of the teachers held a master's degree, and many had credits beyond the MA/MS degrees.

Measures

All data on the parents and teachers were derived from questionnaires returned by the respondents. The questionnaire for each set of respondents contained demographic items, a set of requests for estimates of participation in specific parent involvement activities, and a series of items designed to assess respondents' perceptions of parent or teacher efficacy.

Parent Questionnaire. The Parent Questionnaire asked participants to give specific information about themselves (employment status, education, family income, marital status, age, and sex) and estimates of their levels of involvement in various forms of parent-school activities—help with homework (hours in average week); other educational activities with children (hours in average week); volunteer work at school (hours in average week); telephone calls with teachers (number in average month); and parent-teacher conferences (average number in semester). Similar estimation procedures have been used successfully in other investigations (Grolnick & Ryan, 1989; Hoover-Dempsey, et al., 1987; Stevenson & Baker, 1987).

The Parent Questionnaire contained Likert-scale response items designed to assess parents' perceptions of their own efficacy. We developed the 12-item Parent Perceptions of Parent Efficacy Scale on the basis of the teaching efficacy and parenting literature cited earlier. Although efforts to develop an assessment of general parenting efficacy have been reported (Johnston & Mash, 1989), the teaching efficacy literature was used as the basis for this measure because interest in this study focused on parents' perceptions of personal efficacy specifically in relation to children's school learning. The scale included such items as "I know how to help my child do well in school" and "If I try hard, I can get through to my child even when he/she has trouble understanding something." Following the model set by previously reported scales of teacher efficacy, items in this scale focused on assessment of parents' general abilities to influence children's school outcomes and specific effectiveness in influencing children's school learning. Items were scored on a 5-point scale ranging from *strongly disagree* (1) to *strongly agree* (5). Negatively worded items were subsequently rescored so that higher scores uniformly reflected higher efficacy.

Possible total scores for the scale ranged from 12 to 60. Similarity to selected items of the Teacher Perceptions of Efficacy Scale (see below) and its grounding in related literature support the validity of this scale. Alpha reliability for this sample, .81, was judged satisfactory.

Teacher Questionnaire. The Teacher Questionnaire asked for specific information about teachers and their classes (grade, enrollment, percentage of students qualifying for free lunch, total years taught, years at present school, highest degree earned, sex, and age). Teachers were also asked to estimate the number of students in their classes whose parents participated in scheduled conferences, volunteer work at school, regular assistance with homework, regular involvement in other educational activities with children (e.g., reading and playing games), and telephone calls with the teacher. Again, such procedures have been used successfully in other investigations (Hoover-Dempsey et al., 1987; Stevenson & Baker, 1987).

We developed a seven-item Teacher Perceptions of Parent Efficacy Scale on the basis of the literature cited earlier. Items included such statements as "My students' parents help their children learn," and "My students' parents have little influence on their children's academic performance." All the items were scored on a scale ranging from *strongly disagree* (1) to *strongly agree* (5); negatively worded items were rescored so that higher scores consistently reflected more positive teacher perceptions of parent efficacy. Possible scores for the scale ranged from 7 to 35. Similarity to selected items of the Parent Perceptions of Parent Efficacy Scale and its grounding in the literature reviewed earlier support the validity of this scale. Alpha reliability of .79 for this sample was adequate.

Items on the 12-item Teacher Perceptions of Teacher Efficacy Scale (Hoover-Dempsey et al., 1987) included such statements as "I am successful with the students in my class" and "I feel that I am making a significant educational difference in the lives of my students." Items were scored on a scale ranging from *strongly disagree* (1) to *strongly agree* (5); negatively worded items were subsequently rescored so that higher scores uniformly reflected higher efficacy. Total scale scores ranged from 12 to 60. The scale's grounding in related literature, and its earlier successful use after substantial pretesting for clarity and content, support the validity of the scale. An alpha reliability of .83 for the scale with this sample was judged satisfactory.

Results

Correlations between parent efficacy and three indicators of parent involvement were statistically significant. Higher levels of parent efficacy were associated with more hours of classroom volunteering, more hours spent in educational activities with children, and fewer telephone calls with the teacher (see Table 2).

Parent efficacy scores did not reveal significant variations related to parents' sex, marital status, employment status, or family income. Parent education, however, was linked to some variations in efficacy scores, $F(5, 353) = 4.59$, $p < .01$. Parents with a grade school education had significantly lower efficacy scores than did parents with all levels of college education, and parents with a high school education were significantly lower than parents with some college work beyond the bachelor's degree.

Table 2.—Means, Standard Deviations, and Intercorrelations: Parent Involvement Variables and Parent Efficacy (N = 354)

	Homework	Educational activities	Volunteering	Telephone calls	Conferences	Parent efficacy
Homework (hours per week)	—					
Educational activities (hours per week)	.38**	—				
Volunteering (hours per week)	.07	.14**	—			
Telephone calls (number per month)	.09	.02	.02	—		
Conferences (number per semester)	.10*	.08	.08	.34**	—	
Parent efficacy	.06	.11*	.15**	−.14**	.02	—
M	4.54	4.84	.66	.49	1.45	45.71
SD	3.58	3.58	.21	1.06	1.99	5.82

*p < .05 (.11). **p < .01 (.14).

Parent reports of involvement were linked to some parent status characteristics. More hours of classroom volunteering were reported by females (0.74 hours per week v. 0.25 for males, $F[1, 352] = 8.53$, $p < .01$), married parents (0.81 hours per week v. 0.32 for not married, $F[1, 352] = 7.90$, $p < .01$), and unemployed parents (1.27 hours per week v. 0.34 for employed, $F[1, 352] = 8.82$, $p < .01$). More hours of homework help were reported by parents with lower education (high school at 4.80 hours per week v. college degree at 3.33, $F[5, 348] = 3.18$, $p < .01$), lower family income (3 lower income groups = 6.52 − 5.33 hours per week v. 3 higher income groups = 3.62 − 3.09, $F[6, 326] = 7.97$, $p < .01$), and single parent status (not married = 5.51 hours per week v. married = 4.05, $F[1, 352] = 13.83$, $p < .01$). More phone calls were reported by the lowest income parents (lowest income group = 1.38 calls per month v. 0.58 − 0.20 for all other income groups, $F[6, 326] = 3.90$, $p < .01$).

Teacher efficacy and teacher perceptions of parents' efficacy were both positively linked to teacher reports of parent involvement in homework, educational activities, volunteering, and conference participation (see Table 3). Teacher efficacy was also positively linked to teacher perceptions of parent efficacy. Although teacher efficacy did not show a significant relationship with the number of students qualifying for free lunch ($r = -.16$, ns), teacher perceptions of parent efficacy were significantly linked to the free lunch figure ($r = -.59$, $p < .01$).

Discussion

The finding that parent efficacy is related, at modest but significant levels, to volunteering, educational activities, and telephone calls suggests that the construct may contribute to an understanding of variables that influence parents' involvement in decisions and choices. Defined as a set of beliefs that one is capable of achieving desired outcomes through one's efforts and the effects of those efforts on others, parent efficacy appears to facilitate increased levels of parent activity in some areas of parent involvement. The correlational nature of our results suggests that just as efficacy may influence involvement choices, these varied forms of involvement may influence parents' sense of efficacy (e.g., parents may feel increased effectiveness when they observe, during their involvement activities, that their children are successful). Regardless of the direction of influence, however, the observed linkages seem logically based in dynamic aspects of the relationship between many parents and teachers.

Classroom volunteering, for example, may be linked to efficacy, because the decision to volunteer requires some sense that one has educationally relevant skills that can and will be used effectively. Similarly, the experiences implicit in classroom volunteering may offer parents new and positive information about their effectiveness with their own child. The decision to engage in educational activities with one's children at home may reflect a sense of personal efficacy ("I will do this because it will help my child learn."); in like manner, the activities undertaken may show up, from the parent's perspective, in improved school performance that, in turn, may enhance parent efficacy. The negative relationship between efficacy and telephone calls probably reflects the still-prevalent reality that calls to and from the school signal child difficulties. Lower efficacy parents, less certain of their ability to exert positive influence on their children's learning, may seek contact more often. Similarly, more school-initiated calls may signal to the parent that he or she is offering the child less-than-adequate help.

Overall, our findings suggest that the construct of parent efficacy warrants further investigation. Grounded in the teaching efficacy literature and theoretical work on personal efficacy, the Parent Perceptions of Parent Efficacy Scale achieved satisfactory reliability with this sample and emerged, as predicted, with modest but significant relationships with some indicators of parent involvement. Parents' average efficacy score, 45.71 ($SD = 5.82$) in a scale range of 12 to 60, indicated that those parents as a group had relatively positive perceptions of their own efficacy. The variations in efficacy by parental status characteristics suggested that, at least in this group, sex, marital status, employment status, and family income were *not* related to efficacy. The finding that parental education was significantly linked to efficacy is not surprising, given the probability that parents' own school experiences contribute to their sense of school-focused efficacy in relation to their children.

Parent efficacy may differ from parent education in the way it operates, however. Whereas higher levels of education may give parents a higher level of skill and knowledge, efficacy—a set of attitudes about one's ability to get necessary resources and offer effective help—increases the likelihood that a parent will *act* on his or her knowledge (or seek more information when available resources are insufficient). The explanatory function of efficacy is suggested by the finding that parent education was related to fewer and different outcomes than parent efficacy was. Parent efficacy was related to educational activities, volunteering and telephone calls, whereas education was significantly linked to homework alone. In that finding, parents with a high school education reported spending more time helping their children with homework than did parents with a college education. The fact that a group with lower education reported *more* homework help may reflect several different possibilities: the lower efficacy parents may be more determined to see their children succeed; they may use a set of less efficient helping strategies; or they may be responding to a pattern of greater school difficulty experienced by their children. Although our data do not permit an assessment of those possibilities, we suspect that the finding reflects less adequate knowledge of effective helping strategies. Be-

Table 3.—Means, Standard Deviations, and Intercorrelations Among Teacher Variables

	Homework	Educational activities	Volunteering	Telephone calls	Conferences	Free Lunch	Teacher efficacy	Perceptions of parent efficacy
Parents help with homework (number of students)	—							
Parents engage in educational activities with children (number of students)	.69**	—						
Parents do volunteer work at school (number of students)	.58**	.67**	—					
Telephone calls with parents (average number per month)	.25	.30	.12	—				
Parents attend scheduled conferences (number of students)	.62**	.52**	.49**	.10	—			
Number of students qualifying for free lunch	−.34*	−.48**	−.45**	−.25	−.38**	—		
Teacher efficacy	.42**	.39**	.54**	.17	.41**	−.16	—	
Perceptions of parent efficacy	.56**	.75**	.65**	.27	.59**	.44**	−.59**	—
M	8.72	8.06	2.96	4.74	9.98	9.94	43.28	24.09
SD	4.59	4.58	2.48	5.03	5.83	8.39	6.38	4.57

*$p < .05$ (.30). **$p < .01$ (.38).

cause many of our low-education parents were also unemployed, the finding may also reflect that they simply had more time for their children's homework activities than did the other parent groups. Whatever the explanations, the finding that education was related to fewer and different outcomes than efficacy suggests that the construct of parent efficacy warrants further investigation, perhaps particularly as it is distinguished from parent education.

Results for teachers support earlier findings (Hoover-Dempsey et al., 1987) of significant positive relationships between teacher efficacy and teacher reports of parent involvement. The general pattern—higher efficacy teachers reported high levels of parent participation in help with homework, educational activities, volunteering, and conferences—suggests that higher efficacy teachers may invite and receive more parent involvement or, conversely, that teachers who perceive and report higher levels of parent involvement develop higher judgments of personal teaching efficacy. It is also possible that both perceptions are operating. The absence of a significant positive relationship between teacher efficacy and the number of students in a school using the free lunch program also supports previous findings, suggesting again that teachers' personal efficacy judgments are to some extent independent of school socioeconomic status (SES). We suspect that the absence of a significant relationship reflects the probability that teacher judgments of personal ability to "make a difference" are related more powerfully to variables other than the status characteristics of their stu-

dents—for example, teaching skills, organizational support, and relations with colleagues (Brissie et al., 1988).

The strong positive linkages between teacher judgments of parents' efficacy and teacher reports of parent involvement likely point to the important role that parents' involvement efforts (and perhaps the visibility of those efforts) play in teachers' judgments of parents' effectiveness. In contrast to the absence of a significant relationship between teacher efficacy and school SES, teachers' judgments of *parent* efficacy were strongly and positively linked to school SES. Thus, although teachers appeared to distinguish between their own efficacy and the socioeconomic circumstances of the families that they serve, they did not appear to draw such boundaries between parents' SES and their judgments of parents' efficacy.

The further linkage between teacher efficacy and teacher judgments of parent efficacy suggests both that teachers with higher efficacy were likely to judge parents as more efficacious and that teachers who see their students' parents as more effective experience higher levels of efficacy themselves. We suspect that this relationship is an interactive one in reality, because, for example, high efficacy in each party would tend to allow each to act with more confidence and less defensiveness in the many forms of interaction that parents and teachers often routinely undertake.

The relationships between parent efficacy and some parent involvement outcomes, as well as those between teacher perceptions of parent efficacy and teacher effi-

May/June 1992 [Vol. 85(No. 5)]

cacy, suggest the potential importance of intervention strategies designed to increase parents' sense of efficacy and involvement. Bandura's (1977, 1984, 1986) work offers specific points of entry into the development of such interventions. For example, parents' *outcome expectancies*—their general beliefs that engaging in certain involvement behaviors will usually yield certain outcomes —should be examined in relation to parents' *personal efficacy* expectancies (beliefs that one's *own* involvement behaviors will yield desired outcomes). Future investigations might focus on parents' expectations about the outcomes of involvement, for example, do most parents really believe that their involvement is directly linked to child outcomes? If they believe so, what makes parents think that their *own* involvement choices are—or are not —important?

The findings reported here suggest the possibility that high-efficacy parents are more likely than those with low efficacy to believe that their efforts pay off. Therefore, the schools' best interests may be served by designing parent involvement approaches that focus specifically on increasing parents' sense of positive influence in their children's school success. This could be accomplished in a number of ways. For example, schools might regularly send home relatively specific instructions for parents about strategies for helping children with specific types of homework assignments. Schools might issue specific invitations related to volunteering for specific assignments (e.g., making posters, doing classroom aide work) and follow up with brief notes of thanks for a valued job well done. Teachers might routinely link some student accomplishments and positive characteristics to parent efforts as they conduct scheduled conference discussions. Many schools already engage in such practices, but the frequency and focus of such efforts might be increased in other schools as one means of communicating a basic efficacy-linked message to parents: "We think you're doing a good job of _____, and this is helping your child learn."

Similarly, the role and functions of teacher efficacy in the parent involvement process should be explored further. Is it the case, for instance, that higher efficacy teachers—more secure in and confident of their own roles in children's learning—invite (explicitly and implicitly) more frequent and significant parent involvement? Do more efficacious teachers, aware of children's specific learning needs, offer more specific suggestions or tasks for parent-child interaction? It may be true that teachers in schools with stronger parent involvement programs tend to receive more (and more positive) feedback on the value and impact of their teaching efforts. Also, teachers with varying levels of teaching efficacy perceive parent involvement and comments from parents differently (e.g., high-efficacy teachers may hear legitimate questions in a parent comment, whereas low-efficacy teachers hear criticism and threat).

The role and function of teachers' perceptions of parent efficacy also appear to warrant further examination. Teachers in this sample appeared able to give reliable estimates of their assessments of parents' efficacy. Of future interest would be an examination of the bases on which teachers make such evaluations and the role of those evaluations in teacher interactions with parents. Lightfoot (1978) suggested that parents and teachers participate in children's schooling with different interests and roles; the roles often engender conflict, but they may also be construed as complementary. Implicit in these relationships, whatever their form, is the assumption that parents and teachers watch and evaluate the actions of the other, equally essential, players in the child's school success. Closer examination of teachers' and parents' perceptions of their own roles and the "others' " roles in children's learning may yield information about an important source of influence on parent involvement and its outcomes.

The many calls over recent decades for increased parent involvement in children's education (Hess & Holloway, 1984; Hobbs, Dokecki, Hoover-Dempsey, Moroney, Shayne, & Weeks, 1984; Phi Delta Kappa, 1980) appear to have produced public and professional belief that parent involvement is one means of increasing positive educational outcomes for children. As yet, however, there has been little specific examination of the ways in which parent involvement—in general or in its varied forms—functions to produce those outcomes. With few exceptions (Epstein, 1986), little information on patterns of specific forms of parent involvement is available, underscoring the relatively unexamined nature of the causes, manifestations, and outcomes of parent involvement. The findings of this study suggest that further examination of parents' and teachers' sense of efficacy in relation to children's educational outcomes may yield useful information as both sets of participants work to increase the probabilities of children's school success.

NOTES

We appreciate the cooperation and support of the parents, teachers, principals, and other administrators who participated in this research.

We also gratefully acknowledge support from the H. G. Hill Fund of Peabody College, Vanderbilt University.

REFERENCES

Ashton, P. T., Webb, R. B., & Doda, N. (1983). *A study of teachers' sense of efficacy: Final report, executive summary.* Gainesville, FL: University of Florida.

Bandura, A. (1977). Self-efficacy: Toward a unifying theory of behavioral change. *Psychological Review, 84,* 191–215.

Bandura, A. (1984). Recycling misconceptions of perceived self-efficacy. *Cognitive Therapy and Research, 8,* 231–255.

Bandura, A. (1986). The explanatory and predictive scope of self-efficacy theory. *Journal of Social and Clinical Psychology, 4,* 359–373.

Bandura, A. (1989). Human agency in social cognitive theory. *American Psychologist, 44,* 1175–1184.

Baumrind, D. (1971). Current patterns of parental authority. *Developmental Psychology Monographs, 4,* 1–103.

Baumrind, D. (1973). The development of instrumental competence through socialization. In A. D. Pick (Ed.), *Minnesota Symposium on Child Psychology, Vol. 7,* 3–46. Minneapolis, MN: University of Minnesota Press.

Brissie, J. S., Hoover-Dempsey, K. V., & Bassler, O. C. (1988). Individual and situational contributors to teacher burnout. *Journal of Educational Research, 82,* 106–112.

Dembo, M. H., & Gibson, S. (1985). Teachers' sense of efficacy: An important factor in school achievement. *The Elementary School Journal, 86,* 173–184.

Dornbusch, S. M., Ritter, P. L., Leiderman, P. H., Roberts, D. F., & Fraleigh, M. J. (1987). The relation of parenting style to adolescent school performance. *Child Development, 58,* 1244–1257.

Epstein, J. L. (1986). Parents' reactions to teacher practices of parent involvement. *Elementary School Journal, 86,* 277–294.

Greenberger, E., & Goldberg, W. A. (1989). Work, parenting and the socialization of children. *Developmental Psychology, 25,* 22–35.

Grolnick, W. S., & Ryan, R. M. (1989). Parent styles associated with children's self-regulation and competence in school. *Journal of Educational Psychology, 81,* 143–154.

Hess, R. D., & Holloway, S. D. (1984). Family and school as educational institutions. In R. D. Parke, R. M. Emde, H. P. McAdoo, & G. P. Sackett (Eds.), *Review of child development research: Vol. 7.* The family (pp. 179–222). Chicago: University of Chicago Press.

Hobbs, N., Dokecki, P. R., Hoover-Dempsey, K. V., Moroney, R. M., Shayne, M. W., & Weeks, K. A. (1984). *Strengthening families.* San Francisco: Jossey-Bass.

Hoover-Dempsey, K. V., Bassler, O. C., & Brissie, J. S. (1987). Parent involvement: contributions of teacher efficacy, school socioeconomic status, and other school characteristics. *American Educational Research Journal, 24,* 417–435.

Lightfoot, S. L. (1978). *Worlds apart: Relationships between families and schools.* New York: Basic Books.

Johnston, C., & Mash, E. J. (1989). A measure of parenting satisfaction and efficacy. *Journal of Clinical Child Psychology, 18,* 167–175.

Mondell, S., & Tyler, F. B. (1981). Parental competence and styles of problem-solving/play behavior with children. *Developmental Psychology, 17,* 73–78.

Phi Delta Kappa (1980). *Why do some urban schools succeed?* Bloomington, IN: Author.

Stevenson, D. L., & Baker, D. P. (1987). The family-school relation and the child's school performance. *Child Development, 58,* 1348–1357.

U.S. Bureau of the Census (1989). *Statistical abstract of the United States.* Washington, DC: U.S. Government Printing Office.

■ SUMMARY/CHAPTER 9

DEFINITION AND PURPOSE

1. Correlational research involves collecting data in order to determine whether, and to what degree, a relationship exists between two or more quantifiable variables.
2. Degree of relationship is expressed as a correlation coefficient.
3. If a relationship exists between two variables, it means that scores within a certain range on one measure are associated with scores within a certain range on another measure.
4. The fact that there is a relationship between variables does not imply that one is the cause of the other.
5. Correlational studies provide an estimate of just how related two variables are. If two variables are highly related, a correlation coefficient near +1.00 (or −1.00) will be obtained; if two variables are not related, a coefficient near .00 will be obtained.
6. The more highly related two variables are, the more accurate are predictions based on their relationship.

THE BASIC CORRELATIONAL RESEARCH PROCESS

Problem Selection

7. Correlational studies may be designed either to determine which variables of a list of likely candidates are related or to test hypotheses regarding expected relationships.

Sample and Instrument Selection

8. The sample for a correlational study is selected using an acceptable sampling method, and 30 subjects are generally considered to be a minimally acceptable sample size.
9. It is important to select or develop valid, reliable measures of the variables being studied.

Design and Procedure

10. The basic correlational design is not complicated; two (or more) scores are obtained for all members of a selected sample, one score for each variable of interest, and the paired scores are then correlated.

Data Analysis and Interpretation

11. A correlation coefficient is a decimal number between .00 and +1.00, or .00 and −1.00, which indicates the degree to which the two variables are related.
12. If the coefficient is near +1.00, the variables are positively related. This means that a person with a high score on one variable is likely to have a high score on the other variable, and a person with a low score on one is

likely to have a low score on the other; an increase on one variable is associated with an increase on the other.

13. If the coefficient is near .00, the variables are not related.
14. If the coefficient is near −1.00, the variables are inversely related. This means that a person with a high score on one variable is likely to have a low score on the other variable, and a person with a low score on one is likely to have a high score on the other; an increase on one variable is associated with a decrease on the other variable, and vice versa.
15. A correlation coefficient squared indicates the amount of common variance shared by the variables.
16. How large a correlation coefficient needs to be in order to be useful depends upon the purpose for which it was computed.
17. In a study designed to explore or test hypothesized relationships, a correlation coefficient is interpreted in terms of its statistical significance.
18. In a prediction study, statistical significance is secondary to the value of the coefficient in facilitating accurate predictions.
19. Statistical significance refers to whether the obtained coefficient is really different from zero and reflects a true relationship, not a chance relationship.
20. To determine statistical significance you only have to consult a table that tells you how large your coefficient needs to be in order to be significant at a given level of confidence, and given the size of your sample.
21. For the same level of confidence, or significance level, a larger coefficient is required when smaller samples are involved.
22. For a given sample size, the value of the correlation coefficient needed for significance increases as the level of confidence increases.
23. No matter how significant a coefficient is, a low coefficient represents a low relationship.
24. A correlation coefficient much below .50 is generally useless for either group prediction or individual prediction, although a combination of several variables in this area may yield a reasonably satisfactory prediction.
25. Coefficients in the .60s and .70s are usually considered adequate for group prediction purposes, and coefficients in the .80s and above for individual prediction purposes.
26. While all reliabilities in the .90s are acceptable, for certain kinds of instruments, such as personality measures, a reliability in the low .70s might be acceptable.
27. When interpreting a correlation coefficient you must always keep in mind that you are talking about a relationship only, not a cause-effect relationship.

RELATIONSHIP STUDIES

28. Relationship studies are conducted in an attempt to gain insight into the factors, or variables, that are related to complex variables such as academic achievement, motivation, and self-concept.
29. Such studies give direction to subsequent causal-comparative and experimental studies. Also, in both causal-comparative and experimental research studies, the researcher is concerned with controlling for variables, other than the independent variable, which might be related to performance on the dependent variable. Relationship studies help the researcher to identify such variables.

Data Collection

30. In a relationship study the researcher first identifies, either inductively or deductively, variables potentially related to the complex variable under study.
31. The shotgun approach, which involves checking all conceivable variables for possible relationships, is very inefficient and often misleading.
32. A smaller number of carefully selected variables is much to be preferred to a large number of carelessly selected variables.
33. The population must be one for which data on each of the identified variables can be collected, and one whose members are available to the researcher.
34. One advantage of a relationship study is that all the data may be collected within a relatively short period of time.

Data Analysis and Interpretation

35. In a relationship study, the scores for each variable are in turn correlated with the scores for the complex variable of interest.
36. Each variable must be expressible in numerical form, that is, must be quantifiable.
37. The most commonly used technique is the product moment correlation coefficient, usually referred to as the Pearson *r*, which is appropriate when both variables to be correlated are expressed as ratio data or interval data.
38. If data for one of the variables are expressed as ranks, the appropriate correlation coefficient is the rank difference correlation coefficient, usually referred to as the Spearman rho.
39. There are also a number of other correlational techniques which are encountered less often but which should be used when appropriate.
40. Most correlational techniques are based on the assumption that the relationship being investigated is a linear one.
41. If a relationship is curvilinear, an increase in one variable is associated with a corresponding increase in another variable *to a point,* at which point further increase in the first variable results in a corresponding decrease in the other variable (or vice versa).
42. In addition to computing correlation coefficients for a total sample group, it is sometimes profitable to examine relationships separately for certain defined subgroups.
43. Attenuation refers to the principle that correlation coefficients tend to be lowered due to the fact that less-than-perfectly-reliable measures are utilized.
44. In relationship studies, a correction for attenuation can be applied that provides an estimate of what the coefficient would be if both measures were perfectly reliable.
45. Another factor that may lead to a coefficient representing an underestimate of the true relationship between two variables is a restricted range of scores.
46. There is a correction for restriction in range that may be applied to obtain an estimate of what the coefficient would be if the range of scores were not restricted.

PREDICTION STUDIES

47. If two variables are highly related, scores on one variable can be used to predict scores on the other variable.
48. The variable upon which the prediction is made is referred to as the predictor, and the variable predicted is referred to as the criterion.
49. Prediction studies are often conducted to facilitate decision making concerning individuals or to aid in the selection of individuals.
50. Prediction studies are also conducted to test theoretical hypotheses concerning variables believed to be predictors of the criterion, and to determine the predictive validity of individual measuring instruments.
51. If several predictor variables each correlate well with a criterion, then a prediction based on a combination of those variables will be more accurate than a prediction based on any one of them.

Data Collection

52. As with a relationship study, subjects must be selected from whom the desired data can be collected and who are available to the researcher.
53. The major difference in data collection procedures for a relationship study and a prediction study is that in a relationship study data on all variables are collected within a relatively short period of time, whereas in a prediction study predictor variables are measured some period of time before the criterion variable is measured.

Data Analysis and Interpretation

54. As with a relationship study, each predictor variable is correlated with the criterion variable.
55. Since a combination of variables usually results in a more accurate prediction than any one variable, prediction studies often result in a prediction equation referred to as a multiple regression equation.
56. A multiple regression equation uses all variables that individually predict the criterion to make a more accurate prediction.
57. Since relationships are not perfect, predictions made by a multiple regression equation are not perfect.
58. Predicted scores are generally placed in a confidence interval.
59. As with relationship studies, and for similar reasons, prediction equations may be formulated for each of a number of subgroups as well as for the total group.
60. Shrinkage is the tendency of a prediction equation to become less accurate when used with a different group, a group other than the one on which the equation was originally formulated.
61. Any prediction equation should be validated with at least one other group, and variables that are no longer found to be related to the criterion measure should be taken out of the equation; this procedure is referred to as cross-validation.

". . . the resulting matched groups are identical or very similar with respect to the identified extraneous variable (p. 327)."

Causal-Comparative Research

OBJECTIVES

After reading Chapter 10, you should be able to:

1. Briefly state the purpose of causal-comparative research.

2. State the major differences between causal-comparative and correlational research.

3. State one major way in which causal-comparative and experimental research are the same and one major way in which they are different.

4. Diagram and describe the basic causal-comparative design.

5. Identify and describe three types of control procedures that can be used in a causal-comparative study.

6. Explain why the results of causal-comparative studies must be interpreted very cautiously.

■ DEFINITION AND PURPOSE

Like correlational research, causal-comparative research is sometimes treated as a type of descriptive research since it too describes conditions that already exist. Causal-comparative research, however, also attempts to determine reasons, or causes, for the current status of the phenomena under study. Causal-comparative research entails procedures distinctly different from those involved in self-report or observational research, and qualifies as a separate type of research.

Causal-comparative, or ex post facto, research is that research in which the researcher attempts to determine the cause, or reason, for existing differences in the behavior or status of groups of individuals. In other words, it is observed that groups are different on some variable and the researcher attempts to identify the major factor that has led to this difference. Such research is referred to as "ex post facto" (Latin—"after the fact") since both the effect and the alleged cause have already occurred and are studied by the researcher in retrospect. For example, as a possible explanation of apparent differences in social adjustment among first graders, a researcher might hypothesize that participation in preschool education was the major contributing factor. The researcher would then select a group of first graders who had participated in preschool education and a group who had not and would then compare the social adjustment of the two groups. If the group that did participate in preschool education exhibited a higher level of social adjustment, the researcher's hypothesis would be supported.

The basic causal-comparative approach, therefore, involves starting with an effect and seeking possible causes. A variation of the basic approach involves starting with a cause and investigating its effect on some variable. Such research is concerned with "what is the effect of 'X'" questions. For example, a researcher might wish to investigate what long-range effect failure to be promoted to the seventh grade has on the self-concept of children not promoted. The researcher might hypothesize that children who are "socially promoted" have higher self-concepts at the end of the seventh grade than children who are "held back" and made to repeat the sixth grade. At the end of a school year, the researcher would identify a group of seventh graders who had been socially promoted to the seventh grade the year before, and a group of sixth graders who had been held back the year before and made to repeat the sixth grade. The self-concepts of the two groups would be compared. If the socially promoted group exhibited a higher level of self-concept, the researcher's hypothesis would be supported. The basic approach is sometimes referred to as *retrospective* causal-comparative research (since it starts with effects and investigates causes), and the variation as *prospective* causal-comparative research (since it starts with causes and investigates effects). Retrospective causal-comparative studies are by far more common in educational research.[1]

Beginning researchers often confuse causal-comparative research with both correlational research and experimental research. Correlational and causal-comparative research are probably confused because of the lack of manipulation common to both and the similar cautions regarding interpretation of results. There are definite differences, however. Causal-comparative studies *attempt* to identify cause-effect relationships, correlational studies do not. Causal-comparative studies typically involve two (or more) groups and one independent variable, whereas correlational studies typically involve two (or more) variables and one group. Also, causal-comparative studies involve comparison, whereas correlational studies involve correlation.

It is understandable that causal-comparative and experimental research are at first difficult to distinguish; both attempt to establish cause-effect relationships and both involve group comparisons. In an experimental study, however, the researcher creates the "cause," deliberately makes the groups different, and then observes what effect that difference has on some dependent variable. In contrast, in a causal-comparative study the researcher first observes an effect and then tries to determine the cause; in other words, the researcher attempts to determine what difference between the groups has led to the observed difference on some dependent variable. To put it as simply as possible, the major difference between them is that in experimental research the independent variable, the alleged cause, is manipulated; in causal-comparative research it is not, it has already occurred. In experimental

---

[1] Dunham, P. J. (1988). *Research methods in psychology* (pp. 195–211). New York: Harper & Row.

research, the researcher can randomly form groups and manipulate a variable—can determine "who" is *going to get* "what," "what" being the independent variable. In causal-comparative research, the groups are already formed and already different on the independent variable. Causal-comparative groups are *already different* in that one group may have had an experience which the other did not have, or one group may possess a characteristic which the other group does not. In any event, the difference between the groups (the independent variable) was not brought about by the researcher.

Independent variables in causal-comparative studies are variables that cannot be manipulated (such as socioeconomic status), should not be manipulated (such as number of cigarettes smoked per day), or simply are not manipulated but could be (such as method of reading instruction). There are a number of important educational problems for which it is impossible or not feasible to manipulate the independent variable. It is not possible to manipulate organismic variables such as sex, for example. Ethical considerations often prevent manipulation of a variable that *could be* manipulated but *should not be,* such as degree of drug use. If the nature of the independent variable is such that it may cause physical or mental harm to subjects, it should not be manipulated. For example, if a researcher were interested in determining the effect of prenatal care for the mother on the developmental status of a child at age one, it would not be ethical to deprive a group of mothers-to-be of prenatal care for the sake of science when such care is considered to be extremely important to both the mother's and the child's welfare. Thus, causal-comparative research permits investigation of a number of variables that cannot be studied experimentally. Table 10.1, which is by no means exhaustive, is presented to give you a feel for the types of independent variables studied in causal-comparative research.

Causal-comparative studies also identify relationships that may lead to experimental studies. As mentioned previously, experimental studies are costly in more ways than one and should be conducted only when there is good reason to believe the effort will be fruitful. Like correlational studies, causal-comparative studies help to identify variables worthy of experimental investigation. In fact, causal-comparative studies are sometimes conducted solely for the purpose of determining the probable outcome of an experimental study. Suppose, for example, a superintendent was considering the implementation of computer-assisted remedial math instruction in her or his school system. The superintendent might consider trying it out on an experimental basis for a year in a number of schools or classrooms before initiating total implementation. However, even such limited adoption would be costly in terms of equipment and teacher training. Thus, as a preliminary measure, to facilitate her or his decision, the superintendent might conduct a causal-comparative study and compare the math achievement of students in school districts currently using computer-assisted remedial math instruction with the math achievement of students in school districts not currently using computer-assisted remedial math instruction. Since most districts have yearly testing programs assessing the status of students in areas such as math, acquisition of the necessary data would not be difficult. If the results indicated that the students learning through computer-assisted remedial math instruction were achieving higher scores, the superintendent would probably decide to go ahead with an experimental tryout of computer-assisted remedial math instruction in her or his own district. If no differences were found, the superintendent would probably not go ahead with the experimental tryout and would thus not unnecessarily waste time, money, and effort.

Despite its many advantages, causal-comparative research does have some serious limitations which should also be kept in mind. Since the independent

Table 10.1

Examples of Independent Variables Investigated in Causal-Comparative Studies

Organismic Variables	**Family-Related Variables**
Age	Family Income
Sex	Socioeconomic Status
Ethnicity	Employment Status (of)
Ability Variables	Student
Intelligence	Mother
Scholastic Aptitude	Father
Specific Aptitudes	Marital Status of Parents
Perceptual Ability	Family Environment
Personality Variables	Birth Order
Anxiety Level	Number of Siblings
Introversion/Extroversion	**School-Related Variables**
Aggression Level	Preschool Attendance
Self-Concept	Size of School
Self-Esteem	Type of School (e.g.,
Aspiration Level	Public vs. Private)
Brain Dominance	Per Pupil Expenditure
Learning Style (e.g.,	Type of Curriculum
Field Independence/	Leadership Style
Field Dependence)	Teaching Style
	Peer Pressure

Note. A few of the variables *can be* manipulated, e.g., type of curriculum, but are frequently the object of causal-comparative research.

variable has already occurred, the same kinds of controls cannot be exercised as in an experimental study. Extreme caution must be applied in interpreting results. An apparent cause-effect relationship may not be as it appears. As with a correlational study, only a relationship is established, not necessarily a causal one. The alleged cause of an observed effect may in fact be the effect, or there may be a third variable that has "caused" both the identified cause and effect. For example, suppose a researcher hypothesized that self-concept is a determinant of achievement. The researcher would identify two groups, one group with high self-concepts and one group with low self-concepts, and would then compare their achievement. If the high self-concept group did indeed show higher achievement, the temptation would be to conclude that self-concept affects achievement. This conclusion would not be warranted since it would not be possible to establish that self-concept *comes before,* or precedes, achievement. The exact opposite might be true; it might be that achievement affects self-concept. Since both the independent and dependent variables would have already occurred, it would not be possible to determine which came first, which affected the other. If the study was reversed, and a group of high achievers was compared with a group of low achievers, it might well be that they would be different on self-concept, thus suggesting that achievement causes self-concept. Even worse, it would even be possible (in fact, very plausible) that some third variable, such as parental attitude, might be the "cause" of both self-concept and achievement; parents who praise their children might also encourage high academic achievement. Thus, cause-effect relationships established through causal-comparative research are at best tenuous and tentative. Only experimental research, which guarantees that the alleged cause, or independent variable, does *come before* the observed effect, or dependent variable, can truly establish cause-effect relationships. As discussed previously, however, causal-comparative studies do have their place; they permit investigation of variables that cannot or should not be investigated experimentally, facilitate decision making, provide guidance for experimental studies, and are less costly on all dimensions.

■ CONDUCTING A CAUSAL-COMPARATIVE STUDY

The basic causal-comparative design is quite simple, and although the independent variable is not manipulated, there are control procedures that can be exercised. Causal-comparative studies also involve a wider variety of statistical techniques than the other types of research thus far discussed.

Design and Procedure

The basic causal-comparative design involves selecting two groups differing on some independent variable and comparing them on some dependent variable (see Figure 10.1). As Figure 10.1 indicates, the researcher selects two groups of subjects, loosely referred to as experimental and control groups, although it is probably more accurate to refer to them as comparison groups. The groups may differ in that one

	Group	Independent Variable	Dependent Variable
Case A	(E)	(X)	O
	(C)		O

| | OR | |

	Group	Independent Variable	Dependent Variable
Case B	(E)	(X$_1$)	O
	(C)	(X$_2$)	O

Symbols:

(E) = Experimental group; ( ) indicates no manipulation
(C) = Control group
(X) = Independent variable
O = Dependent variable

Figure 10.1. The basic causal-comparative design.

group possesses a characteristic that the other does not or has had an experience which the other has not (Case A), or the groups may differ in degree; one group may possess more of a characteristic than the other or the two groups may have had different kinds of experiences (Case B). An example of Case A would be two groups, one of which was composed of brain-damaged children, or two groups, one of which received preschool training. An example of Case B would be two groups, one group composed of high self-concept individuals, and one group composed of low self-concept individuals or two groups, one which had learned algebra via traditional instruction and one which had learned algebra via computer-assisted instruction. In both cases, the groups are compared on some dependent variable. The researcher may administer a test of the dependent variable (any of the types of instruments thus far discussed) or collect already available data, such as the results of standardized testing conducted by a school.

Definition and selection of the comparison groups is a very important part of the causal-comparative procedure. The characteristic or experience differentiating the groups must be clearly and operationally defined, as each group will represent a different population. The way in which the groups are defined will affect the generalizability of the results. If a researcher was to compare a group of students with an "unstable" home life with a group of students with a "stable" home life, the terms unstable and stable would have to be operationally defined. An unstable home life could refer to any number of things, such as a home with a drinking mother, a brutal father, or a combination of factors. If samples are to be selected from the defined population, random selection is generally the preferred method of selection. The important consideration is to select samples that are representative of their respective populations and similar with respect to critical variables other than the independent variable. As with experimental studies, the goal is to have groups that are as similar as possible on all relevant variables except the independent variable. In order to determine the equality of groups, information on a number of background and current status variables may be collected. In order to promote equality, or to correct for identified inequalities, there are a number of control procedures available to the researcher.

Control Procedures

Lack of the randomization, manipulation, and control which characterize experimental studies are all sources of weakness in a causal-comparative design. Randomization of subjects to groups, for example, is probably the best single way to try to insure equality of groups. This is not possible in causal-comparative studies since the groups already exist, and furthermore, have already received the "treatment," or independent variable. A problem already discussed is the possibility that the groups are different on some other major variable besides the identified independent variable, and it is this other variable which is the real cause of the observed difference between the groups. For example, if a researcher simply compared a group of students who had received preschool education with a group who had not, the conclusion might be drawn that preschool education results in better reading achievement in first grade. What if, however, in the region in which the study was conducted, all preschool programs were private and required high tuitions. In this case, the researcher would really be investigating the effects not just of preschool education, but also of membership in a well-to-do family. It might very well be that mothers in such families provide early informal reading instruction for their children. It would be very difficult to evaluate only the effect of preschool education. If, however, the researcher was aware of the situation, he or she could *control* for this variable by only studying children of well-to-do parents. Thus, the two groups to be compared, one of which had attended a preschool program, would be equated with respect to income level of their parents, an extraneous variable. The above example is but one illustration of a number of statistical and nonstatistical methods that can be applied in an attempt to control for extraneous variables.[2]

Matching

Matching is a control technique that is also sometimes used in experimental studies (although not very often in either case). If a researcher has identified a variable believed to be related to performance on the dependent variable, she or he may control for that variable by pair-wise matching of subjects. In other words, for each subject in one group, the researcher finds a subject in the second group with the same or a similar score on the control variable. If a subject in either group does not have a suitable match, the subject is eliminated from the study. Thus, the resulting matched groups are identical or very similar with respect to the identified extraneous variable. For example, if a researcher matched on IQ, then a subject in one group with an IQ of 140 would have a match in the other group, a subject with an IQ at or near 140. As you may have deduced (if you have an IQ of 140!), a major problem with pair-wise matching is that there are invariably subjects who have no match and must therefore be eliminated from the study. The problem becomes even more serious when the researcher attempts to simultaneously match on two or more variables.

Comparing Homogeneous Groups or Subgroups

Another way of controlling an extraneous variable, which is also used in experimental research, is to compare groups which are homogeneous with respect to that variable. For example, if IQ were an identified extraneous variable, the researcher might limit groups to contain only subjects with IQs between 85 and 115 (average IQ). Of course this procedure also lowers the numbers of subjects in the study and additionally restricts the generalizability of the findings.

A similar but more satisfactory approach is to form subgroups within each group that represent all levels of the control variable. For example, each group might be divided into high (116 and above), average (85 to 115), and low (84 and below) IQ subgroups. The comparable subgroups in each group can be compared, for example, high IQ with high IQ. In addition to controlling for the variable, this technique has the added advantage of permitting the researcher to see if the independent variable affects the dependent variable differently at different levels of the control variable. If this question is of interest, the best approach is not to do several separate analyses but to build the control variable right into the design and analyze the results with a statistical technique called factorial analysis of variance. Factorial analysis of variance allows the researcher to determine the effect of the independent variable and the control variable, both separately and in combination. In other words, it permits the researcher to determine if there is an interaction between the independent variable and the control variable such that the independent variable operates differently at different levels of the control variable. For

---

[2] Several of these methods will be discussed further, and in more detail, in regard to their use in experimental research.

example, IQ might be a control variable in a causal-comparative study of the effects of two different methods of learning fractions. It might be found that a method involving manipulation of blocks is more effective for low IQ students who may have difficulty thinking abstractly.

Analysis of Covariance

The analysis of covariance, which is also used in experimental studies, is a statistical method that can be used to equate groups on one or more variables. In essence, analysis of covariance adjusts scores on a dependent variable for initial differences on some other variable (assuming that performance on the "other variable" is related to performance on the dependent variable, which is what control is all about anyway). For example, in the study comparing the effectiveness of two methods of learning fractions, one could covary on IQ, thus equating scores on a measure of achievement in fractions.[3] Analysis of covariance entails application of a nasty little formula, but fortunately there are computer programs readily available that can do the calculations for you if you know how to use them (or know somebody who knows!)

Data Analysis and Interpretation

Analysis of data in causal-comparative studies involves a variety of descriptive and inferential statistics. All of the statistics that may be used in a causal-comparative study may also be used in an experimental study, and a number of them will be described in Part Seven. Briefly, however, the most commonly used descriptive statistics are the mean, which indicates the average performance of a group on a measure of some variable, and the standard deviation, which indicates how spread out a set of scores is, that is, whether the scores are relatively close together and clustered around the mean or spread out covering a wide range of scores. The most commonly used inferential statistics are the *t* test, which is used to see if there is a significant difference between the means of two groups, analysis of variance, which is used to see if there is significant difference among the means of three or more groups, and the chi square test, which is used to compare group frequencies, that is, to see if an event occurs more frequently in one group than another.

As repeatedly pointed out, interpretation of the findings in a causal-comparative study requires considerable caution. Due to lack of randomization, manipulation, and other types of control characteristic of experimental studies, it is difficult to establish cause-effect relationships with any great degree of confidence. The cause-effect relationship may in fact be the reverse of the one hypothesized (the alleged cause may be the effect and vice versa), or there may be a third factor which is the "real" cause of both the alleged cause (independent variable) and effect (dependent variable). In some cases, reversed causality is not a reasonable alternative and need not be considered. For example, preschool training may "cause" increased reading achievement in first grade but reading achievement in first grade cannot "cause" preschool training. Similarly, one's sex may affect one's achievement in mathematics, but one's achievement in mathematics certainly does not affect one's sex! In other cases, however, reversed causality is more plausible and should be investigated. For example, it is equally plausible that achievement affects self-

---

[3] Analysis of variance, factorial analysis of variance, and analysis of covariance will be discussed further in Chapter 14.

concept and that self-concept affects achievement. It is also equally plausible that excessive absenteeism causes, or leads to, involvement in criminal activities as well as that involvement in criminal activity causes, or leads to, excessive absenteeism. The way to determine the correct order of causality, which variable caused which, is to determine which one occurred *first*. If, in the above example, it could be demonstrated that a period of excessive absenteeism was frequently followed by a student getting in trouble with the law, then it could more reasonably be concluded that excessive absenteeism leads to involvement in criminal activities. On the other hand, if it were determined that prior to a student's first involvement in criminal activities his or her attendance was good, but following it, poor, then the hypothesis that involvement in criminal activities leads to excessive absenteeism would be more reasonable.

The possibility of a third, common cause is plausible in many situations. Recall the example that parental attitude may affect both self-concept and achievement. One way to control for a potential common cause is to equate groups on the suspected variable. In the above example, students in both the high self-concept group and low self-concept group could be selected from among subjects whose parents had similar attitudes. It is clear that in order to investigate or control for alternative hypotheses, the researcher must be aware of them when they are plausible and must present evidence that they are not in fact the true explanation for the behavioral differences being investigated.

On the following pages an example of causal-comparative research is presented. Note that even though survey forms were used to collect data, the study was not descriptive because the purpose of the study was to investigate existing differences between groups.

Differing Opinions on Testing Between Preservice and Inservice Teachers

KATHY E. GREEN
University of Denver

ABSTRACT   Studies of teachers' use of tests suggest that classroom tests are widely used and that standardized test results are rarely used. What is the genesis of this lack of use? A previous comparison of pre- and inservice teachers' attitudes toward assessment suggested no differences. This study assessed the different opinions among sophomores ($n = 84$), seniors ($n = 152$), and inservice teachers ($n = 553$) about the use of classroom and standardized tests. Significant differences were found; preservice teachers had less favorable attitudes toward classroom testing than teachers did and more favorable attitudes toward standardized testing.

This study assessed differences among college students entering a teacher education program, students finishing a teacher education program, and inservice teachers concerning their opinions of some aspects of classroom and standardized testing. Although numerous studies of inservice teachers' attitudes toward testing have been conducted, little research is available regarding preservice teachers' views of testing and of the genesis of teachers' views of testing.

Interest in this topic stemmed from research findings suggesting that the results of standardized tests are not used by most teachers. If standardized testing is to continue, the failure to use results is wasteful. Other studies have identified some of the reasons for the lack of use. This study's purpose was to determine whether opinions about the usefulness of standardized and other tests were negative for students before they even entered the teaching profession. When were those attitudes developed? Are attitudes fixed by students' educational experiences *prior* to entry into a teacher education program? Are preservice teachers socialized by their educational programs into resistance to testing? Do negative attitudes appear upon entry into the profession because of socialization into the school culture? Or do they appear after several years of service as a teacher because of personal experiences in the classroom?

I found only one study that addressed differences in opinions of pre- and inservice teachers (Reeves & Kazelskis, 1985). That study examined a broad range of issues salient to first-year teachers; only one item addressed testing specifically. Reeves and Kazelskis found no significant differences between pre- and inservice teachers' opinions about testing, as measured by that item. In this study, I sought more information pertinent to the development of opinions about testing.

Test use in U.S. schools has been and continues to be extensive. It has been estimated that from 10 to 15% of class time is spent dealing with tests (Carlberg, 1981; Newman & Stallings, 1982). Gullickson (1982) found that 95% of the teachers he surveyed gave tests at least once every 2 weeks. The estimated percentage of students' course grades that are based on test scores is 40 to 50%, ranging from 0 to 100% (Gullickson, 1984; McKee & Manning-Curtis, 1982; Newman & Stallings). Classroom tests, thus, are used frequently and may, at times, be used almost exclusively in determining students' grades.

In contrast, a review of past practice suggests minimal teacher use of *standardized* test results in making instructional decisions (Fennessey, 1982; Green & Williams, 1989; Lazar-Morrison, Polin, Moy, & Burry, 1980; Ruddell, 1985). Stetz and Beck (1979) conducted a national study of over 3,000 teachers' opinions about standardized tests. They noted that 41% of the teachers surveyed reported making little use of test results, a finding consistent with that of Goslin (1967) from several decades ago and that of Boyd, McKenna, Stake, and Yachinsky (1975). Test results were viewed as providing information that was supplemental to the wider variety of information that the teachers already possessed. Reasons offered for why standardized tests are given but results not always used by teachers include resistance to a perceived narrowing of the curriculum, resistance to management control, accountability avoidance (Darling-Hammond,

Address correspondence to Kathy E. Green, University of Denver, School of Education, Denver, CO 80208.

1985), and a limited understanding of score interpretation resulting from inadequate preservice training (Cramer & Slakter, 1968; Gullickson & Hopkins, 1987). Marso and Pigge (1988) found that teachers perceive a lower need for standardized testing skills than for classroom testing skills. They also found that teachers reported lower proficiencies in standardized test score use and interpretation than in classroom test score use and interpretation.

The results of those studies suggest that inservice teachers use classroom tests extensively but make little use of standardized test results. This suggests that inservice teachers, in general, hold positive attitudes toward classroom tests and less positive attitudes toward standardized tests. The literature does not lead to any predictions about preservice teachers' attitudes toward tests.

This study assessed differences between preservice and inservice teachers' opinions about testing and test use. The following research hypotheses were formulated to direct the study.

H1. There are significant differences in opinions about the testing and test use between preservice and inservice teachers.
H2. There are significant differences in opinions about testing between students beginning their preparation (sophomores) and students finishing their preparation (seniors).
H3. There are significant differences among inservice teachers with differing years of experience.

Method

Samples

Three samples were drawn for this study. They were samples of (a) practicing teachers, (b) college sophomores beginning a teacher education program, and (c) college seniors completing a teacher education program (but prior to student teaching). For the first sample, survey forms were mailed in a rural western state to 700 teachers randomly selected from the State Department of Education list of all licensed educators. During the spring semester of 1986, teachers were sent a letter explaining the nature of the study, a survey form, and a stamped return envelope. With two follow-up mailings, a total of 555 questionnaires were received, or 81% of the deliverable envelopes. (Twelve questionnaires were undeliverable, 4 persons refused to respond, and 133 persons did not reply.) No compulsory statewide standardized testing program was in place in the state.

The second sample was a convenience sample of three sections of an educational foundations class typically taken by college sophomores who have just enrolled in a teacher preparation program ($n = 84$). The course examines educational thought and practice in the United States. The classes were taught in an 8-week block, meeting for 50 min per day, 4 days per week. Survey forms were distributed in class and completed during class time.

The third sample was also a convenience sample of four sections of a tests and measurement class taken by college seniors ($n = 152$). The course is typically taken after coursework is almost complete, but prior to student teaching. The course provides instruction in basic statistics, classroom test construction and analysis, and standardized test use and interpretation. The course was also taught in an 8-week block, with the same schedule as the foundations course. Survey forms were distributed during the first week of class and completed during class time. Survey forms took from 10 to 30 min to complete. Responses were anonymous. Both sophomores and seniors were attending a public university in a small western town.

Table 1 presents descriptive information for the three samples.

Instruments

Three different forms with overlapping questions were used in this study. The survey form sent to the teachers contained questions regarding training in tests and measurement, subject and grades taught, tests given, and attitudes toward both standardized and classroom tests. The questionnaire was two pages in length, double-sided and contained 49 questions. The form given to the sophomores had 43 questions and was one page in length, double-sided. The form given to the seniors was three pages in length, single-sided. The latter two forms differed by the inclusion of an evaluation anxiety scale and items eliciting importance of contemporary measurement practices for the seniors. Although different formats may have affected responses to some extent, all the forms began with several demographic questions followed by the items relevant to this study. Any form differences would, then, likely be minimized for those initial items.

There were 18 items common to the three forms. Sixteen of the items were Likert items with a 1 to 6 (*strongly disagree* to *strongly agree*) response format. Likert-scale items were drawn from a previously developed measure of attitudes toward both standardized and classroom testing (Green & Stager, 1986). Internal consistency reliabilities of the measures ranged from .63 to .75. The re-

Table 1.—Description of Samples

Item	Sophomores ($n = 84$)	Seniors ($n = 152$)	Teachers ($n = 553$)
Percentage female	84	152	553
Mean age	73.0	75.9	63.6
Age range	18–33	20–45	—
Mean years in teaching	—	—	12

maining two items asked how many hours per week teachers spend in testing activities and how much of a student's grade should be based on test results. The study examined differences found among groups on those items. Item content is presented in Table 2, in which items are grouped by content (opinions about standardized tests, classroom tests, and about personal liking for tests).

Data were analyzed using multivariate analyses of variance, followed by univariate analyses of variance. If univariate results were significant, I used Tukey's HSD test to assess the significance of pairwise post hoc differences. Samples of both items and persons were limited; therefore, results may not be widely generalizable.

Results

Significant multivariate differences were found across opinion items (Wilks's lambda = .70, $p < .001$) when the three samples were compared (Table 2). Hypothesis 1 was supported. Differences were found between teachers and students for all items, with significance levels varying from .02 to .001 for individual items. Opinions were not consistently more positive across all items for teachers or for students. For instance, whereas teachers were most likely to feel that standardized tests address important educational outcomes, teachers were least likely to find that standardized tests serve a useful purpose. In general, though, students favored use of standardized tests for student or teacher evaluation more than teachers did. Al-

Table 2.—Means and Standard Deviations for Opinions About Testing by Group

Variable	Sophomores ($n = 84$)	Seniors ($n = 152$)	Teachers ($n = 553$)	p	1	2	3
Hours spent in testing/week	10.43	9.18	4.37	.001	*	*	—
	(6.72)	(6.43)	(4.05)				
Percentage grade based on test	49.63	46.94	41.31	.001	*	*	—
	(15.48)	(18.71)	(22.68)				
Standardized test items							
Standardized tests are the best way to evaluate a teacher's effectiveness.	2.79	2.83	2.12	.001	*	*	—
	(1.03)	(1.10)	(1.18)				
Teachers whose students score higher on standardized tests should receive higher salaries.	2.53	2.33	1.74	.001	*	*	—
	(1.07)	(1.17)	(1.01)				
Requiring *students* to pass competency tests would raise educational standards.	4.14	3.89	3.69	.001	*	*	—
	(1.13)	(1.09)	(1.26)				
Requiring *teachers* to pass competency tests would raise educational standards.	4.35	4.09	3.30	.001	*	*	—
	(.90)	(1.27)	(1.34)				
Standardized tests assess important educational outcomes.	3.47	3.54	3.95	.001	*	*	—
	(1.04)	(.87)	(.88)				
Standardized tests serve a useful purpose.	4.02	3.97	2.93	.001	*	*	—
	(.83)	(.81)	(.97)				
Standardized tests force teachers to "teach to the test."	3.05	2.74	3.11	.02	—	*	—
	(1.19)	(.98)	(1.22)				
Classroom test items							
Test construction takes too much teacher time.	4.57	4.36	3.97	.001	*	*	—
	(1.02)	(.85)	(.88)				
Test scores are a fair way to grade students.	3.42	3.32	4.04	.001	*	*	—
	(1.02)	(1.13)	(.84)				
Testing has a favorable impact on student motivation.	4.00	3.88	4.16	.01	—	*	—
	(.71)	(1.00)	(.88)				
Tests are of little value in identifying learning problems.	1.76	1.43	1.44	.01	*	—	*
	(.96)	(.84)	(1.05)				
It is relatively easy to construct tests in my subject area.	4.11	3.51	4.35	.001	—	*	*
	(1.25)	(1.34)	(.89)				
Tests measure only minor aspects of what students can learn.	2.92	3.01	3.24	.01	*	—	—
	(1.13)	(1.13)	(1.00)				
Personal reflections							
I do(did) well on tests.	4.05	4.00	4.46	.001	*	*	—
	(1.04)	(1.10)	(.94)				
I personally dislike taking tests.	3.13	3.12	3.46	.01	—	*	—
	(1.35)	(1.14)	(1.16)				
The tests I have taken were generally good assessments of my knowledge of an area.	3.65	3.41	4.09	.001	*	*	—
	(1.08)	(1.10)	(.82)				

Note. For opinion items, the scale ranged from *strongly disagree* (1) to *strongly agree* (6). Standard deviations are presented in parentheses. Asterisks(*) indicate significant ($p < .05$) differences between groups: 1 = teachers versus sophomores, 2 = teachers versus seniors, 3 = sophomores versus seniors.

though the students were less likely to say that they do well on tests and that tests previously taken were good assessments of their ability, the students were also less likely to say that they disliked taking tests. Students' opinions about classroom testing were less favorable than were teachers' opinions for all but one item. Differences were also found between teachers and students in estimates of time spent in testing and in the percentage of students' grades based on test scores.

Hypothesis 2 was not supported. Only two significant differences in means were found between the sophomores and the seniors. One difference was found for the item "It is relatively easy to construct tests in my subject area." Sophomores tended to agree with that statement more than the seniors did. Because the seniors were required to complete a task involving test construction, the impending course requirement may have influenced their opinions. The second difference was found for the item "Tests are of little value in identifying learning problems," with more positive opinions expressed by seniors than by sophomores.

Hypothesis 3 was tested by dividing teachers into three groups: 0 to 1 years, 2 to 5 years, and 5+ years of experience as a teacher. No significant multivariate or univariate differences were found, so Hypothesis 3 was not supported. However, there were few teachers with 0 to 1 years of experience in the sample. Because of the small number of teachers with 0 to 1 years of teaching (46 teachers; 8.7% of the data file), groups were reformed as follows: 0 to 3 years, 4 to 6 years, and 6+ years of experience. Still, no significant multivariate or univariate differences were found. (In addition, no differences were found between teachers with 0 to 3 years of experience and those with 6 or more years of experience.)

Discussion

This study was undertaken to examine whether differences in opinions about testing would be discerned between preservice and inservice teachers and whether those differences would suggest a progression. The differences found suggest that teacher education students are less favorable to classroom testing and more favorable to standardized testing than teachers are. Differences were *not* found between sophomores and seniors, however. Nor were opinions about testing found to depend upon years of experience in teaching. Those results do not reflect a developmental progression. The shift in opinion seems to occur when beginning a teaching position, suggesting effects that result from job requirements or socialization as a teacher more than from a developmental trend. Differences between students and teachers, then, seem likely to be caused by direct teacher experience with creating, administering, and using tests or by acculturation into life as a teacher in a school. That conclusion suggests that if

one wishes to affect teachers' opinions about testing, provision of inservice experiences may be a more profitable avenue than additional preservice education.

Test use. The teachers sampled in this study reported spending an average of about 11% of their time in testing, which is consistent with estimates reported in the literature (10 to 15%). The finding in this study that an average of 41% of the students' grades was based on test results is also consistent with estimates reported in the literature (40 to 50%). Estimates of the time needed for testing activities obtained from students sampled in this study were much higher (23% and 26% for seniors and sophomores, respectively) than the estimates obtained from the teachers' reports. Although students' estimates of the percentage of grade based on test scores were significantly higher than those of teachers, they were within the range reported in the literature. Students, then, who lack an experiential base, seem either to have exaggerated views regarding the time that teachers spend on testing-related activities or think that it will take them longer to construct tests.

Beginning teachers also lack an experiential base. One might ask whether beginning teachers spend more time in test-related activities than do teachers with more experience, because beginning teachers may not have files of tests to draw upon. Mean reported time spent in testing was higher for first- and second-year teachers (means of 5.4 and 5.7 hours per week) than for teachers with more experience (mean for third year = 2.3, 4th year = 2.8, 5th year = 3.8). Thus, students may be accurate in their perception of the time needed by novices for testing-related activities.

Standardized testing. The students' opinions ranged from neutral to positive regarding the use of standardized tests and were, on average, significantly more positive than the teachers' opinions. One explanation for the positive opinions may be that students have extremely limited personal experience with standardized tests (their own or their friends) and so have a limited basis upon which to judge test effectiveness. By college level, most students have taken a number of standardized tests but may not be aware of the results, may not have been directly affected by the results, or may have been affected by the results at a time when they were too young to understand or argue. Students may believe that the tests must be useful because "authorities and experts" sanction their administration. Students' opinions may, then, be shaped by the positive *public* value placed on tests, as well as by their educational programs. The tests and measurement course taken by many preservice teachers emphasizes how tests can be valuable if used properly. One can argue that most students view themselves as intending to use tests properly. In contrast, many teachers are required to give standardized tests, and they may also be required to take them.

Preservice–inservice differences might be even more extreme in states where the stakes attached to standardized test use are higher—where the teacher's job or salary depends upon test results. Teachers develop a broader base of experience with standardized testing, and they may be more aware of the limitations of the tests and of the controversy surrounding standardized testing. The measurement profession is unclear about the value of standardized testing; it is not surprising that teachers also have reservations.

Classroom testing. Differences were also found between teachers and teacher education students for most classroom test items, though differences were not as pronounced for these items. The result is in contrast to Reeves and Kazelskis's (1985) finding of no differences between similar groups. The result of somewhat less favorable opinions of preservice than inservice teachers toward classroom testing may have stemmed from the frequent test taking by students versus the frequent use of tests by teachers. By the time students are seniors in college, they will have taken a larger number of classroom tests than standardized tests and thus will have considerably more experience in evaluating their effectiveness. Students undoubtedly encounter classroom tests and test questions that they consider to be unfair assessments of their knowledge. Such experiences may temper their opinions toward classroom tests. In contrast, because most teachers rely to some extent on test results in assigning grades and in evaluating instruction, opinions may change to conform with this behavior. Teachers' opinions may also be influenced by an experiential understanding of testing gained through learning how informative test results can be.

Because it is unlikely that the widespread use of classroom and standardized tests will diminish, teachers will continue to be called upon to use tests to make decisions that are important in the lives of students. Teachers need to be competent in test construction and interpretation. However, if tests are to be used effectively as part of the instructional process, teachers must perceive the positive aspects of test use. If a teacher finds that task impossible, that teacher should discontinue traditional test use and seek alternative assessment techniques, within the boundaries allowed by the district. Teachers should communicate positive feelings about the tests they give to their students. Teachers will probably be more likely to do so if they have positive opinions of tests. Tests are often viewed as evaluative; they may more effectively be viewed as informative and prescriptive.

If teacher educators wish to affect prospective teachers' views, they may need to both clarify their own views about the place of testing in instruction and clearly present arguments about testing, pro and con, to their classes. Well-constructed classroom assessments, whether paper-and-pencil, portfolio, or performance measures, provide diagnostic and prescriptive information about the students' progress and about the effectiveness of instruction. This information is valuable. Poorly constructed or standardized measures that do not address the curriculum provide little information of use in the classroom. The reasons for giving tests that do not provide information useful in instruction must be clearly explained. Such tests may be mandated to provide legitimate administrative, state, or national information.

But to what extent can teacher educators shape *prospective* teachers' views? The results of this study suggest that opinions held prior to and following preservice instruction may not survive the transition to the real world of the classroom. If this is the case, the preservice course —no matter how good it is—would be ineffective in influencing attitudes. (It may, however, be highly effective in influencing the quality of testing practices by providing basic skills in test construction and interpretation.) Inservice instruction may be a better vehicle to use to produce attitude change.

This study was cross-sectional in design. A longitudinal study that examined opinions over time (from preservice to inservice) is required to identify the extent to which opinions are shaped by school requirements. Additional information regarding school characteristics affecting preservice and inservice teachers' attitudes toward testing would be of interest, as would information about differences in testing skill levels between pre- and inservice teachers.

NOTES

An earlier version of this paper was presented at the 1990 annual meeting of the National Council on Measurement in Education, held April 1990 in Boston.

Appreciation is expressed to the *Journal of Educational Research* reviewers for their helpful suggestions.

REFERENCES

Boyd, J., McKenna, B. H., Stake, R. E., & Yachinsky, J. (1975). *A study of testing practices in the Royal Oak (MI) public schools.* Royal Oak, MI: Royal Oak City School District. (ERIC Reproduction Service No. 117 161)

Carlberg, C. (1981). South Dakota study report. Denver, CO: Midcontinent Regional Educational Laboratory.

Cramer, S., & Slakter, M. (1968). A scale to assess attitudes toward aptitude testing. *Measurement and Evaluation in Guidance, 1*(2).

Darling-Hammond, L., & Wise, A. E. (1985). Beyond standardization: State standards and school improvement. *Elementary School Journal, 85*, 315–336.

Fennessey, D. (1982). Primary teachers' assessment practices: Some implications for teacher training. Paper presented at the annual conference of the South Pacific Association for Teacher Education, Frankston, Victoria, Australia.

Goslin, D. A. (1967). *Teachers and testing.* New York: Russell Sage Foundation.

Green, K. E., & Stager, S. F. (1986–87). Testing: Coursework, attitudes, and practices. *Educational Research Quarterly, 11*(2), 48–55.

Green, K. E., & Stager, S. F. (1986). Measuring attitudes of teachers toward testing. *Measurement and Evaluation in Counseling and Development, 19*, 141–150.

Green, K. E., & Williams, E. J. (1989, March). Standardized test use by classroom teachers: Effects of training and grade level taught. Paper presented at the annual meeting of the National Council on Measurement in Education, San Francisco.

Gullickson, A. R. (1982). The practice of testing in elementary and secondary schools. (ERIC Reproduction Service No. ED 229 391)

Gullickson, A. R. (1984). Teacher perspectives of their instructional use of tests. *Journal of Educational Research, 77*, 244–248.

Gullickson, A. R, & Hopkins, K. D. (1987). The context of educational measurement instruction for preservice teachers: Professor perspectives. *Educational Measurement: Issues and Practice, 6*, 12–16.

Karmos, A. H., & Karmos, J. S. (1984). Attitudes toward standardized achievement tests and their relation to achievement test performance. *Measurement and Evaluation in Counseling and Development, 17*, 56–66.

Lazar-Morison, C., Polin, L., Moy, R., & Burry, J. (1980). A review of the literature on test use. Los Angeles: Center for the Study of Evaluation, California State University. (ERIC Reproduction Service No. 204 411)

Marso, R. N., & Pigge, F. L. (1988). Ohio secondary teachers' testing

needs and proficiencies: Assessments by teachers, supervisors, and principals. *American Secondary Education, 17*, 2–9.

McKee, B. G., & Manning-Curtis, C. (1982, March). Teacher-constructed classroom tests: The stepchild of measurement research. Paper presented at the National Council on Measurement in Education annual conference, New York.

Newman, D. C., & Stallings, W. M. (1982). Teacher competency in classroom testing, measurement preparation, and classroom testing practices. Paper presented at the American Educational Research Association annual meeting. New York. (ERIC Reproduction Service No. ED 220 491)

Reeves, C. K., & Kazelskis, R. (1985). Concerns of preservice and inservice teachers. *Journal of Educational Research, 78*, 267–271.

Ruddell, R. B. (1985). Knowledge and attitudes toward testing: Field educators and legislators. *Reading Teacher, 38*, 538–543.

Stetz, F. P., & Beck, M. D. (1979). Comments from the classroom: Teachers' and students' opinions of achievement tests. Paper presented at the annual meeting of the National Council on Measurement in Education, San Francisco.

■ SUMMARY/CHAPTER 10

DEFINITION AND PURPOSE

1. Causal-comparative, or ex post facto, research is that research in which the researcher attempts to determine the cause, or reason, for existing differences in the behavior or status of groups of individuals.
2. The basic causal-comparative approach (sometimes referred to as *retrospective*) involves starting with an effect and seeking possible causes.
3. A variation of the basic approach (sometimes referred to as *prospective*) involves starting with a cause and investigating its effect on some variable.
4. Causal-comparative studies *attempt* to identify cause-effect relationships; correlational studies do not.
5. The major difference between experimental research and causal-comparative research is that in experimental research the independent variable, the alleged cause, is manipulated, and in causal-comparative research it is not, it has already occurred.
6. In experimental research the researcher can randomly form groups and manipulate a variable—can determine "who" is *going to get* "what," "what" being the independent variable; in causal-comparative research the groups are already formed and *already different* on the independent variable.
7. Causal-comparative groups are already different in that one group may have had an experience which the other did not have, or one group may possess a characteristic which the other group does not; in any event, the difference between the groups (the independent variable) was not determined by the researcher.
8. Independent variables in causal-comparative studies are variables that cannot be manipulated (such as socioeconomic status), should not be manipulated (such as number of cigarettes smoked per day), or simply are not manipulated, but could be (such as method of reading instruction).
9. Causal-comparative studies identify relationships that may lead to experimental studies.
10. As with a correlational study, only a relationship is established, not necessarily a causal one.
11. The alleged cause of an observed effect may in fact be the effect, or there may be a third variable that has "caused" both the identified cause and effect.
12. Cause-effect relationships established through causal-comparative research are at best tenuous and tentative.
13. Only experimental research, which guarantees that the alleged cause, or independent variable, does come before the observed effect, or dependent variable, can truly establish cause-effect relationships.

CONDUCTING A CAUSAL-COMPARATIVE STUDY

Design and Procedure

14. The basic causal-comparative design involves selecting two groups differing on some independent variable and comparing them on some dependent variable.

15. The groups may differ in that one group possesses a characteristic that the other does not, *or* the groups may differ in degree; one group may possess more of a characteristic than the other or the two groups may have had different kinds of experiences.
16. The important consideration is to select samples that are representative of their respective populations and similar with respect to critical variables other than the independent variable.
17. In order to determine the equality of groups, information on a number of background and current status variables may be collected.

Control Procedures

18. Lack of the randomization, manipulation, and control which characterize experimental studies are all sources of weakness in a causal-comparative design.
19. A problem is the possibility that the groups are different on some other major variable besides the identified independent variable, and it is this other variable which is the real cause of the observed difference between the groups.

Matching

20. For each subject in one group the researcher finds a subject in the second group with the same or a similar score on the control variable.
21. A major problem with pair-wise matching is that there are invariably subjects who have no match and must therefore be eliminated from the study.

Comparing Homogeneous Groups or Subgroups

22. Another way of controlling an extraneous variable, which is also used in experimental research, is to compare groups which are as homogeneous as possible.
23. A similar but more satisfactory approach is to form subgroups within each group that represent all levels of the control variable. In addition to controlling for the variable, this technique has the added advantage of permitting the researcher to see if the independent variable affects the dependent variable differently at different levels of the control variable. If this question is of interest, the best approach is not to do several separate analyses but to build the control variable right into the design and analyze the results with a statistical technique called factorial analysis of variance.

Analysis of Covariance

24. The analysis of covariance, which is also used in experimental studies, is a statistical method that can be used to equate groups on one or more variables.
25. In essence, analysis of covariance adjusts scores on a dependent variable for initial differences on some other variable (assuming that performance on the "other variable" is related to performance on the dependent variable, which is what control is all about anyway).

Data Analysis and Interpretation

26. Analysis of data in causal-comparative studies involves a variety of descriptive and inferential statistics.
27. The most commonly used descriptive statistics are the mean, which indicates the average performance of a group on a measure of some variable, and the standard deviation, which indicates how spread out a set of scores is, that is, whether the scores are relatively close together and clustered around the mean or spread out covering a wide range of scores.
28. The most commonly used inferential statistics are the *t* test, which is used to see if there is a significant difference between the means of two groups, analysis of variance, which is used to see if there is a significant difference among the means of three or more groups, and the chi square test, which is used to compare group frequencies, that is, to see if an event occurs more frequently in one group than another.
29. As repeatedly pointed out, interpretation of the findings in a causal-comparative study requires considerable caution.
30. The alleged cause-effect relationship may in fact be the reverse of the one hypothesized (the alleged cause may be the effect and vice versa).
31. There may be a third factor which is the real "cause" of both the alleged cause (independent variable) and effect (dependent variable).
32. The way to determine the correct order of causality, which variable caused which, is to determine which one occurred *first*.
33. One way to control for a potential common cause is to equate groups on the suspected variable.

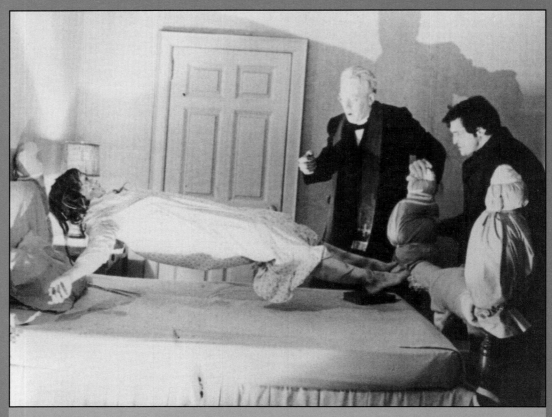

Single-subject experimental designs ". . . are typically used to study the behavior change an individual exhibits as a result of some intervention . . . (p. 374)."

Experimental Research

After reading Chapter 11, you should be able to:

1. Briefly state the purpose of experimental research.

2. List the basic steps involved in conducting an experiment.

3. Describe three ways in which a variable can be manipulated.

4. Explain the purpose of control.

5. Briefly define or describe "internal validity" and "external validity."

6. Identify and briefly describe eight major threats to the internal validity of an experiment.

7. Identify and briefly describe six major threats to the external validity of an experiment.

8. Briefly discuss the purpose of experimental design.

9. Identify and briefly describe five ways to control extraneous variables (and you better not leave out randomization!).

10. For each of the pre-experimental, true experimental, and quasi-experimental group designs discussed in this chapter, (a) draw a diagram, (b) list the steps involved in its application, and (c) identify major problems (e.g., sources of invalidity) with which it is associated.

11. Briefly describe the definition and purpose of a factorial design.

12. Briefly explain what is meant by the term interaction.

13. For each of the A-B-A single-subject designs discussed in this chapter, (a) draw a diagram, (b) list the steps involved in its application, and (c) identify major problems with which it is associated.

14. Briefly describe the procedures involved in using a multiple-baseline design.

15. Briefly describe an alternating treatments design.

16. Briefly describe how data resulting from the application of a single-subject design are analyzed.

17. Briefly describe three types of replication involved in single-subject research.

■ DEFINITION AND PURPOSE

Experimental research is the only type of research that can truly test hypotheses concerning cause-and-effect relationships. It represents the most valid approach to the solution of educational problems, both practical and theoretical, and to the advancement of education as a science. In an experimental study, the researcher manipulates at least one independent variable, controls over relevant variables, and observes the effect on one or more dependent variables. The researcher determines "who gets what," which group of subjects gets which treatment. This manipulation of the independent variable is the one characteristic that differentiates all experimental research from the other types of research. The independent variable, also referred to as the experimental variable, the cause, or the treatment, is that activity or characteristic believed to make a difference. In educational research independent variables typically manipulated include method of instruction, type of reinforcement, frequency of reinforcement, arrangement of learning environment, type of learning materials, and size of learning group. The above list is of course by no means exhaustive. The dependent variable, also referred to as the criterion variable, effect, or posttest, is the outcome of the study, the change or difference in groups that occurs as a result of manipulation of the independent variable. It is referred to as the dependent variable since it is "dependent" on the independent variable. The dependent variable may be measured by a test, but not necessarily. Since the independent variable is a variable which the researcher believes will make things "better," increase good things or decrease bad things, the dependent variable may also be such variables as attendance, number of suspensions, attention span, or even number of books checked out of the library. The only restriction on the dependent variable is that it represents an outcome that is measurable.

Experimental research is both the most demanding and the most productive type of research. When well conducted, experimental studies produce the soundest evidence concerning hypothesized cause-effect relationships. The results of experimental research permit prediction, but not the kind characteristic of correlational research. A correlational prediction is specific and predicts a particular score for a particular individual. Predictions based on experimental findings are more global and take the form, "if you use approach *X* you will probably get better results than if you use approach *Y*." Experimental research has repeatedly confirmed, for example, that systematically applied positive reinforcement leads to improved behavior. Although there are a number of alternative designs from which a researcher can select, the basic experimental process is the same in all studies.

The Experimental Process

The steps in an experimental study are basically the same as for other types of research: selection and definition of a problem, selection of subjects and measuring instruments, selection of a design, execution of procedures, analysis of data, and formulation of conclusions. An experimental study is guided by at least one hypothesis that states an expected causal relationship between two variables. The actual experiment is conducted in order to confirm (support) or disconfirm the experimental hypothesis. In an experimental study, the researcher is in on the action from the very beginning; the researcher forms or selects the groups, decides what is going to happen to each group, tries to control all relevant factors besides the change that she or he has introduced, and observes or measures the effect on the groups at the end of the study.

An experiment typically involves two groups, an experimental group and a control group (although as you will see later, there may be only one group, or there may be three or more groups). The experimental group typically receives a new, or novel treatment, a treatment under investigation, while the control group usually either receives a different treatment or is treated as usual. The control group is needed for comparison purposes to see if the new treatment is more effective than the usual or traditional approach, or to see if one approach is more effective than another. A common misconception among beginning researchers is that a control group always receives nothing. This would hardly be fair. If in a study, for example, the independent variable was the type of reading instruction, the experimental group might be instructed with a new method, while the control group was instructed with a traditional method. The control group would still receive reading instruction; it would not sit in a closet while the study was being conducted. Otherwise you would not be evaluating the effectiveness of a new method as compared to a traditional method, but rather the effectiveness of a new method as compared to no reading instruction at all! Any method of instruction is bound to be more effective than no instruction at all. Thus, the control group also receives a form of the independent variable. The two groups that are to receive different treatments are equated on all other variables that might be related to performance on the dependent variable, for example, reading readiness. In other words, the researcher makes every effort to ensure that the two groups are as equivalent as possible on all variables *except* the independent variable.

After the groups have been exposed to the treatment for some period of time, the researcher administers a test of the dependent variable (or otherwise measures it) and then determines whether there is a significant difference between the groups. In other words, the researcher determines whether the treatment *made a difference*. One problem associated with experimental studies in education is that subjects are often not exposed to the experimental treatment for a sufficient period of time. No matter how effective conflict resolution training is, for example, it is not likely to reduce suspensions if students are exposed to it for only one day. Thus, to adequately test a hypothesis concerning the effectiveness of conflict resolution training, the experimental group would need to be exposed to it over a period of time. The experimental treatment should be given a "chance to work."

Another problem associated with experimental research is that the treatments received by the groups are not sufficiently different to make a difference. For example, if your study were comparing team teaching with traditional teaching it would be vital that team teaching be operationalized according to its generally accepted meaning. If in your study team teaching meant nothing more than two teachers taking turns lecturing, it would not be very different from traditional teaching. Thus, you would be very unlikely to find a major difference between your experimental and control groups at the end of the study, even though you might have if team teaching had been correctly operationalized to include such things as large-group and small-group instruction.

Manipulation and Control

Direct manipulation by the researcher of at least one independent variable is the one single characteristic that differentiates all experimental research from other types of research. Manipulation of an independent variable seems to be a difficult concept for some beginning researchers to grasp. Quite simply it means that the researcher decides what forms or values the independent variable (or cause) will take and which group will get which form. For example, if the independent variable was number of reviews, the researcher might decide that there should be three groups, one group receiving no review, a second group receiving one review, and a third group receiving two reviews. There are many independent variables in education that can be manipulated (active variables), and many which cannot (assigned variables). You can manipulate such variables as method of instruction and size of group; you cannot manipulate such variables as sex or socioeconomic status. In other words, you can require students to receive one method of instruction or another, but you cannot require students to be male or female; they *already are* male or female. In order to manipulate a variable, *you* have to decide who is going to be what or who is going to get what. Although the design of an experimental study may include assigned variables, at least one variable must be manipulated.

The different values or forms that the independent variable may take are basically presence versus absence (A versus no A), presence in varying degrees (a lot of A versus a little A), or presence of one kind versus presence of another kind (A versus B). An example of A versus no A would be a study comparing the effectiveness of review versus no review in teaching history. An example of "a lot of A versus a little A" would be a study comparing the effectiveness of different numbers of examples in teaching algebra; one group might receive two examples per concept, and another group might receive five examples per concept. An example of A versus B would be a study to compare the effectiveness of the whole language approach to reading instruction versus the basal approach with respect to reading comprehension. Experimental designs may get quite complex and involve simultaneous manipulation of several independent variables. At this stage of the game, however, you had better stick to just one!

Control refers to efforts on the part of the researcher to remove the influence of any variable (other than the independent variable) that might affect performance on the dependent variable. In other words, the researcher wants the groups to be as similar as possible, so that the only major difference between them is the independent variable, the difference caused by the researcher. To illustrate the importance of control, suppose you conducted a study to compare the effectiveness of student tutors versus parent tutors in teaching first graders to read. Student tutors might be older children from higher grade levels, and parent tutors might be members of the PTA. Now suppose student tutors helped each member of one group for 1 hour per day for a month, while the parent tutors helped each member of a second group for 2 hours per week for a month. Would the comparison be fair? Certainly not. Subjects with the student tutors would have received two-and-one-half times as much help (5 hours per week versus 2 hours per week). Thus, one variable which would need to be *controlled* would be *time*. In order for the comparison to be fair, members of both groups would have to be helped in reading for the same amount of time. Then the researcher could truly compare the effectiveness of different *kinds* of help, not different *amounts*. The above is just one example of the kinds of factors which must be considered in planning an experiment. Some variables which need controlling may be relatively obvious; in the above example, variables such as reading readiness and intelligence would need to be considered. Other variables in need of control may not be as obvious; in the above study, for example, the researcher would need to ensure that both groups used the same reading texts and materials. Thus, we see that there are really two different kinds of variables that need to be controlled: subject variables (such as reading readiness), variables on which subjects in the different groups might differ; and environmental variables (such as learning materials), variables that might cause unwanted differences between groups. The researcher strives to ensure that the characteristics and experiences of the groups are as equal as possible on all important variables except, of course, the independent variable. If at the end of some period of time groups differ in performance on the dependent variable, the difference can be attributed to the independent variable, or treatment. Control is not easy in an experiment, especially in educational research where real live subjects are involved; it is a lot easier to control solids, liquids, and gases! The task is not an impossible one, however, since the researcher can concentrate on identifying and controlling only those variables that might really affect the dependent variable. If two groups differed significantly with respect to shoe size, for example, the results of the study would probably not be affected. Also, there are a number of techniques at the researcher's disposal that can be used to control for extraneous variables.[1]

You should keep in mind that, even though experimental research is the only type of research which can truly establish cause-effect relationships, it is only useful when it is appropriate. There are many problems in education for which the experimental method is inappropriate. For example, if a researcher wanted to determine at what ages children are capable of different levels of abstract thinking, a descriptive study would probably be the appropriate type of research.

■ THREATS TO EXPERIMENTAL VALIDITY

Any uncontrolled extraneous variables affecting performance on the dependent variable are threats to the validity of an experiment. An experiment is valid if results obtained are due only to the manipulated independent variable, and if they are generalizable to situations outside of the experimental setting. The two conditions which must be met are referred to as internal validity and external validity. *Internal validity* refers to the condition that observed differences on the dependent variable are a direct result of manipulation of the independent variable, not some other variable. In other words, the outcome of the study is the result of what the researcher did, not something else. If someone can come up with an alternative explanation (a rival hypothesis) for your results, your study was not internally valid. To use a former example, if the student tutors had worked with subjects for 5 hours per week, and the parent tutors only 2, and if the student-tutored group out-performed the parent-tutored group, then time, or amount of tutoring, would be a plausible

---

[1] These will be discussed later in the chapter.

alternative explanation for the results. The degree to which results are attributable to manipulation of the independent variable is the degree to which an experimental study is internally valid. *External validity* refers to the condition that results are generalizable, or applicable, to groups and environments outside of the experimental setting. In other words, the results of the study, the confirmed cause-effect relationship, can be expected to be reconfirmed with other groups, in other settings, at other times, as long as the conditions are similar to those of the study. If a study was conducted using groups of gifted ninth graders, for example, the results should be applicable to other groups of gifted ninth graders. As mentioned previously, if research results were not generalizable to any other situation outside of the experimental setting, then no one could profit from anyone else's research, and each and every effect would have to be reestablished over and over and over. An experimental study can only contribute to educational theory or practice if there is some assurance that confirmed relationships and observed effects are replicable and likely to occur at other times and places with other groups. The term *ecological validity* is sometimes used to refer to the degree to which results can be generalized to other environments. If results cannot be replicated in other environments by other researchers, the study has low ecological validity.

So all one has to do in order to conduct a valid experiment is to maximize internal validity and maximize external validity, right? Wrong. Unfortunately, there is a "catch-22" complicating the researcher's experimental life. Maximization of internal validity requires exercise of very rigid control over subjects and conditions in a laboratory-like environment. The more a situation is controlled, however, the less realistic it becomes, and the less generalizable to nonlaboratory settings the results become. In other words, lab findings are generalizable to other labs. A study can contribute little to educational practice, for example, if there is no assurance that a technique found to be effective in a controlled laboratory setting will also be effective in a natural classroom setting. On the other hand, the more natural the experimental setting becomes, the more difficult it becomes to control extraneous variables. It is very difficult, for example, to conduct a well controlled study in an actual classroom. Thus the researcher must strive for balance between control and realism. If a choice is involved, the researcher should err on the side of too much control rather than too little. A study that is not internally valid is worthless. In fact, one research strategy is first to demonstrate an effect in a highly controlled environment (for the sake of internal validity) and then to redo the study in a more natural setting (for the sake of external validity).

Although lab-like settings are generally preferred for the investigation of theoretical problems, experimentation in natural, or field, settings has its advantages, especially for certain practical problems. In the final analysis, however, the researcher usually strives for a compromise, or an environment somewhere between a lab setting and a natural educational setting. Many studies, for example, are conducted in simulated classroom settings that the researcher makes as much like a natural classroom as possible. This permits the researcher to exercise sufficient control to ensure adequate internal validity while at the same time maintaining a degree of realism necessary for generalizability.

In the pages to come many threats to internal and external validity will be discussed. Some extraneous variables are definite threats to internal validity, some are definite threats to external validity, and some may be threats to both. How potential threats are classified, or labeled, is not the important thing; what is important is that you, as a researcher, be aware of their existence and make efforts to control for them. As you read, you may begin to feel that there are just too many of them for one little researcher to control all at the same time. The task is not as formidable as it may at first appear, however. As you will see later, there are a number of experimental designs that control many threats for you; all you have to do is select a "good" design and go from there. Also, each of the threats to be discussed is only a potential threat that may not be a problem in a particular study.

Threats to Internal Validity

Probably the most authoritative source regarding experimental design and threats to experimental validity is the work of Donald Campbell and Julian Stanley.[2] Campbell and Stanley have identified eight major threats to internal validity, or to put it another way, sources of internal invalidity.

History

History refers to the occurrence of any event which is not part of the experimental treatment but which may affect performance on the dependent variable. The longer a study lasts, the more likely it is that history may be a problem. Happenings such as a bomb scare, an epidemic of measles, or even current events are examples of history. For example, suppose you conducted a series of in-service workshops designed to increase the morale of the teacher participants. Suppose that between the time you conducted the workshops and the time you administered some posttest measure of morale, the news media announced that, due to state-level budget problems, funding to the local school district was going to be significantly reduced and that it was likely that promised pay raises for teachers would have to be postponed. Such an event could easily wipe out any effect the workshops might have had; posttest morale scores might well be considerably lower than they otherwise might have been (to say the least!). Thus, while the researcher has no control over the occurrence of such events, he or she can select a design which controls *for* their occurrence.

Maturation

Maturation refers to physical or mental changes that may occur within the subjects over a period of time. These changes may affect the subjects' performance on the measure of the dependent variable. Especially in studies which last for any length of time, subjects may become, for example, older, more coordinated, unmotivated, anxious, or just plain bored. Maturation is more of a threat in some studies than in others. It would be much more likely to be a problem, for example, in a study designed to test the effectiveness of a psychomotor training program than in a study designed to compare two methods of teaching algebra, especially if preadolescent students were involved; such students are typically undergoing rapid biological changes. As with history, the researcher cannot control the occurrence of maturation but can control *for* its occurrence.

Testing

Testing, also referred to as pretest sensitization, refers to improved scores on a posttest resulting from subjects having taken a pretest. In other words, taking a

---

[2]Campbell, D. T., & Stanley, J. C. (1971). *Experimental and quasi-experimental designs for research.* Chicago: Rand McNally.

pretest may improve performance on a posttest, regardless of whether there is any treatment or instruction in between. Testing is more likely to be a threat when the time between testings is short; a pretest taken in September is not likely to affect performance on a posttest taken in June. This phenomenon is also more likely to occur in some studies than in others, for example, when the tests measure factual information that can be recalled; taking a pretest on algebraic equations, on the other hand, is much less likely to improve performance on a similar posttest. However, since analysis of a number of published research reports has indicated that testing can be a problem in any study, the decision to use a pretest should not be made lightly.[3] If a pretest is used, then whenever possible, a design should be selected which controls for testing.

Instrumentation

Instrumentation refers to unreliability, or lack of consistency, in measuring instruments which may result in an invalid assessment of performance. Instrumentation may occur in several different ways. If two different tests are used for pretesting and posttesting, and the tests are not of equal difficulty, instrumentation may occur; if the posttest is more difficult, it may fail to show improvement which is actually present, whereas if the posttest is less difficult, it may indicate an improvement that is not present. If data are collected through observation, observers may not be observing or evaluating behavior the same way at the end of the study as at the beginning. In fact, if they are aware of the nature of the study, they may unconsciously tend to see and record what they know the researcher is hypothesizing. If data are collected through the use of a mechanical device, such as a scale (in a study on the effectiveness of behavior modification for weight control, for example), it may be suffering from some malfunction resulting in inaccurate measurement. Thus, the researcher must take care in selecting tests, caution observers, and check mechanical devices. In addition, the researcher can select an experimental design that controls for this factor.

Statistical Regression

Statistical regression usually occurs when subjects are selected on the basis of their extreme scores and refers to the tendency of subjects who score highest on a pretest to score lower on a posttest, and of subjects who score lowest on a pretest to score higher on a posttest. The tendency is for scores to regress, or move toward, the mean (average) or expected score. For example, suppose a researcher wished to determine the effectiveness of a new method of spelling instruction in improving the spelling ability of poor spellers. The researcher might administer a 100-item, 4-alternative, multiple-choice spelling pretest. Each question might read, "Which of the following four words is spelled incorrectly?" The researcher might then select for the study the 30 students who scored lowest. Now suppose none of the pretested students knew *any* of the words and guessed on every single question. With 100 items, and 4 choices for each item, a student would be expected to receive a score of 25 just by guessing. Some students, however, just due to rotten guessing, would receive scores much lower than 25, and other students, just by chance, would receive much higher scores than 25. If they were administered the test a second

---

[3] Wilson, V. L., & Putnam, R. R. (1982). A meta-analysis of pretest sensitization effects in experimental design. *American Educational Research Journal, 19,* 249–258.

time, *without* any instruction intervening, their expected score would still be 25. Thus students who scored very low the first time would be expected to have a second score closer to 25, and students who scored very high the first time would also be expected to score closer to 25 the second time. In the above study, if students were selected because of their very low pretest scores, they would be expected to do better on the posttest, regardless of the treatment. The researcher might erroneously attribute their improved spelling ability to the new method of spelling instruction. The researcher must therefore be aware of statistical regression and if at all possible select a design that controls for this phenomenon.

Differential Selection of Subjects

Differential selection of subjects usually occurs when already formed groups are used and refers to the fact that the groups may be different before the study even begins, and this initial difference may at least partially account for posttest differences. Suppose, for example, you received permission to use two of Ms. Hynee's English classes in your study; there would be no guarantee that the two classes were at all equivalent. If your luck was really bad, one class might be the honors English class and one class might be the remedial English class. It would not be too surprising if the first class did much better on the posttest! Thus using already formed groups should be avoided if possible. If they must be used, groups should be selected which are as similar as possible, and a pretest should be administered to check for initial equivalence.

Mortality

First, let me make it perfectly clear that mortality *does not* mean that subjects die! Mortality, or attrition, is more likely to occur in longer studies and refers to the fact that subjects who drop out of a group may share a characteristic such that their absence has a significant effect on the results of the study. Subjects who drop out of a study may be less motivated, for example; this is especially a problem when volunteers are used. Volunteers rarely drop out of control groups because few or no demands are made on them. Volunteers may, however, drop out of an experimental group if too much effort is required for participation. The experimental group that remains at the end of the study may as a whole represent a more motivated group than the control group. As another example of the problem of mortality, suppose Suzy Shiningstar (high IQ and all that) got the measles and dropped out of one's control group. Now, suppose that before Suzy dropped out she managed to give the measles to her friends in the control group. Since birds of a feather flock together, Suzy's control group friends would probably also be "high IQ and all that." The experimental group might end up looking pretty good when compared to the control group simply because many of the good students dropped out of the control group. Thus, the researcher cannot assume that subjects drop out of a study in a random fashion and should if possible select a design that controls for mortality.

Selection-Maturation Interaction, Etc.

The "etc." means that selection may also interact with factors such as history and testing, although selection-maturation interaction is more common. What this means is that if already formed groups are used, one group may profit more (or less) from a treatment, or have an initial advantage, because of maturation, history, or testing factors. Suppose, for example, that you received permission to use two of Ms. Hynee's English classes, and both classes were average English classes and apparently equivalent on all relevant variables. Suppose, however, that for some reason one day Ms. Hynee had to miss one of her classes but not the other (maybe she had to have a root canal), and Ms. Alma Mater took over Ms. Hynee's class. Suppose further that as luck would have it Ms. Mater covered much of the material now included in your posttest (remember history?). Unbeknownst to you, your experimental group would have a definite advantage to begin with, and it might be this initial advantage which caused posttest differences, rather than your independent variable. Thus, the researcher must select a design that controls for this potential problem or make every effort to determine if it is operating in the study.

Threats to External Validity

There are also several major threats to external validity that limit, or make questionable, generalization to nonexperimental populations. Building on the work of Campbell and Stanley, Bracht and Glass refined and expanded discussion of threats to external validity, or sources of external invalidity.[4] Bracht and Glass classify threats to external validity into two categories. Threats affecting "to whom," to what persons, results can be generalized, are referred to as problems of *population validity;* threats affecting "to what," to what environments (settings, dependent variables, and so forth), results can be generalized, are referred to as problems of *ecological validity*. The discussion to follow incorporates the contributions of Bracht and Glass into Campbell and Stanley's original conceptualizations.

Pretest-Treatment Interaction

Pretest-treatment interaction occurs when subjects respond or react differently to a treatment because they have been pretested. A pretest may sensitize or alert subjects to the nature of the treatment. The treatment effect may be different than it would have been had subjects not been pretested. Thus results are only generalizable to other pretested groups. The results are not even generalizable to the unpretested population from which the sample was selected. This potential problem is more or less serious depending upon the subjects, the nature of the tests, the nature of the treatment, and the duration of the study. Studies involving self-report measures of personality, for example attitude scales, are especially susceptible to this problem. Campbell and Stanley illustrate the effect by pointing out the probable lack of comparability of one group viewing the antiprejudice film *Gentleman's Agreement* right after taking a lengthy pretest dealing with anti-Semitism, and another group viewing the movie without a pretest. Individuals in the unpretested group could quite conceivably enjoy the movie as a good love story and be unaware that it deals with a social issue; pretested individuals would have to be pretty dense not to see a connection between the pretest and the message of the film. On the other hand, taking a pretest on algebraic algorithms would probably affect very little a group's responsiveness to a new method of teaching algebra. The pretest-treatment interaction would also be expected to be minimized in studies involving very young children, who would probably not even see a connection between a pretest and a

---

[4]Bracht, G. H., & Glass, G. V. (1968). The external validity of experiments. *American Educational Research Journal, 5,* 437–474.

subsequent treatment, and in studies conducted over a relatively long period of time; any effects of a pretest taken in September would probably have worn off or greatly diminished by the time a posttest was given in June. Windle, for example, reviewed 41 studies involving pre- and posttesting with personality inventories and found a relationship between improved posttest scores and amount of time between pre- and posttesting; studies in which the interval between pretesting and posttesting was less than 2 months were more likely to find better adjustment scores on posttest measures.[5] Thus, for some studies the potential interactive effect of a pretest is a more serious consideration. In such cases the researcher should select a design which either controls for the effect or allows the researcher to determine the magnitude of the effect.

A possible parallel, as yet undocumented, threat to validity proposed by Bracht and Glass is posttest sensitization. Posttest sensitization refers to the possibility that treatment effects may only occur *if* subjects are posttested. In other words, the very act of posttesting "jells" treatment influences such that effects are manifested and measured which would not have occurred if a posttest had not been given. Suppose, for example, we have a study in which one randomly formed group views *Gentleman's Agreement* and another does not; both groups are then posttested with a self-report attitude scale dealing with anti-Semitism. Members of the experimental group, who saw the film, have time to process the film's message while completing the posttest. As with pretest-treatment interaction, it is possible that unposttested individuals could view the film and enjoy it as a good love story without being aware of the social issue being addressed. In studies in which there is a strong possibility that posttest sensitization may occur, unobtrusive measures are recommended, if feasible.

Multiple-Treatment Interference

Multiple-treatment interference can occur when the same subjects receive more than one treatment in succession; it refers to the carry-over effects from an earlier treatment which make it difficult to assess the effectiveness of a later treatment. Suppose you were interested in comparing two different approaches to improving classroom behavior—behavior modification and corporal punishment (admittedly an extreme example used to make a point!). Let us say that for 2 months behavior modification techniques were systematically applied to the subjects, and at the end of this period behavior was found to be significantly better than before the study began. Now suppose that for the next 2 months the same subjects were physically punished whenever they misbehaved (hand slappings, spankings, and the like), and at the end of the 2 months behavior was equally as good as after the 2 months of behavior modification. Could you then conclude that behavior modification and corporal punishment are equally effective methods of behavior control? Cer-tain-ly not. In fact, the goal of behavior modification is to produce behavior which is self-maintaining, that is, continues after direct intervention is stopped. Thus, the good behavior exhibited by the subjects at the end of the study could well be because of the effectiveness of the previous behavior modification and exist in spite of the corporal punishment. If it is not possible to select a design in which each group receives but one treatment, the researcher should try to minimize potential multiple-treatment interference by allowing sufficient time to elapse between treatments and by investigating distinctly different types of independent variables.

---

[5]Windle, C. (1954). Test-retest effects in personality questionnaires. *Educational and Psychological Measurement, 14,* 617–633.

Multiple-treatment interference may also occur when subjects who have already participated in a study are selected for inclusion in another, theoretically unrelated, study. Weitz, for example, found that college psychology students who had participated in a study of guilt were so suspicious during a subsequent study of cognitive dissonance that their responses could not be used.[6] Thus, if the accessible population for a study is one whose members are likely to have participated in other studies (psychology majors, for example), then information on previous participation should be collected and evaluated *before* subjects are selected for the current study. If any members of the accessible population are eliminated from consideration because of previous research activities, a note should be made of this limitation in the research report.

Selection-Treatment Interaction

Selection-treatment interaction is similar to the "differential selection of subjects" problem associated with internal invalidity and also occurs when subjects are not randomly selected for treatments. Interaction effects aside, the very fact that subjects are not randomly selected from a population severely limits the researcher's ability to generalize since representativeness of the sample is in question. Even if intact groups are randomly selected, the possibility exists that the experimental group is in some important way different from the control group, and/or from the larger population. This nonrepresentativeness of groups may also result in a selection-treatment interaction such that the results of a study hold only for the groups involved and are not representative of the treatment effect in the intended population. Bracht and Glass discuss what they refer to as *interaction of personological variables and treatment effects,* which they consider to be a *population validity* problem. Such an interaction occurs when actual subjects at one level of a variable react differently to a treatment than other potential subjects in the population, at another level, would have reacted. As an example, a researcher might conduct a study on the effectiveness of microcomputer-assisted instruction on the math achievement of junior high students. Classes available to the researcher (the accessible population) may represent an overall ability level at the lower end of the ability spectrum for all junior high students (the target population).[7] If a positive effect is found, it may be that it would not have been found if the subjects were truly representative of the target population. And similarly, if an effect is *not* found, it might have been. Thus, extra caution must be taken in stating conclusions and generalizations based on studies involving existing groups.

While selection-treatment interaction is a definite weakness associated with several of the less-than-wonderful designs, it is also an uncontrolled variable associated with the designs involving randomization. One's accessible population is often a far cry from one's target population, creating another population validity problem. The way in which a given population becomes available to a researcher may make generalizability of findings questionable, no matter how internally valid an experiment may be. As Campbell and Stanley point out, if a researcher is turned down by 9 school systems and accepted by a 10th, the accepting system is bound to be different from the other 9, and from the population of schools to which the researcher would like to generalize. Administrative and instructional personnel, in all proba-

[6]Weitz, J. (1967). Tiny theories. *American Psychologist, 22,* 157.

[7]Factorial designs, which intentionally compare performance at different levels of some variable, e.g., ability, will be discussed shortly.

bility, have "higher morale, less fear of being inspected, and more zeal for improvement" than personnel in an average school. It is therefore recommended that the researcher report problems involved in acquiring subjects, including the number of times he or she was turned down, so that the reader can judge the seriousness of a possible selection-treatment interaction.

Specificity of Variables

Like selection-treatment interaction, specificity of variables is a threat to generalizability regardless of the experimental design used. Specificity of variables refers to the fact that a given study is conducted (1) with a specific kind of subject; (2) based on a particular operational definition of the independent variable; (3) using specific measuring instruments; (4) at a specific time; and (5) under a specific set of circumstances. For example, use of manipulatives might be found to be effective *with* disadvantaged second graders, and *when* achievement is measured using the Baloney Achievement Test.

We have already discussed the importance of carefully describing the population from which subjects are selected and the method of sample selection. Care must also be taken in terms of generalization of results. A researcher would definitely be overgeneralizing, for example, if based on a study involving fourth graders, the researcher concluded that a treatment was effective for elementary students. We have also discussed the need to describe procedures in sufficient detail to permit another researcher to replicate your study. Of course, such detailed descriptions also permit interested readers to assess how applicable findings are to their situation. Experimental procedures represent an operational definition of the independent variable. When a number of studies which supposedly manipulated the same independent variable get different results, it is often difficult to determine reasons for discrepancies because of inadequate descriptions of treatment procedures. Wittrock, for example, noted that there have been many studies of the discovery method which have not clearly defined the independent variable, i.e., "discovery method."[8] Some of these studies have found no significant differences, others have found in favor of the discovery method; but because experimental procedures are not reported in sufficient detail, and because "discovery method" means different things to different people, it is impossible to know *what* discovery method was involved in the various studies and, consequently, what results should be generalized.

Relatedly, generalizability of results is tied to the definition of the dependent variable and to the actual instrument used to measure it. Defining achievement in geometry, for example, solely in terms of memorization of definitions would certainly not help the generalizability of a study since most geometry teachers measure achievement primarily in terms of problem solving. Further, the actual instrument administered represents an operational definition of the intended dependent variable, and there are often a number to select from. As Bracht and Glass point out, this raises the question of the comparability of instruments which supposedly measure the same thing, e.g., reading comprehension.

Generalizability of results may also be affected by short-term or long-term events which occur while the study is taking place. This potential threat is referred to as *interaction of history and treatment effects,* and describes the situation in which results are different than they might have been if events extraneous to the

[8] Wittrock, M. C. (1966). The learning by discovery process. In L. S. Shulman & E. R. Keisler (Eds.), *Learning by discovery: A critical appraisal* (pp. 33–76). Chicago: Rand McNally.

study had not occurred right before or during the study. Short-term, emotion-packed events, such as the firing of a superintendent or the NFL playoffs, for example, might affect the behavior of subjects. Usually, however, the researcher is aware of such happenings and can assess their possible impact on results. Of course, accounts of such events should also be included in the research report. The impact of more long-term events, such as wars and depressions, however, is more subtle and tougher to evaluate. The effects of such influences can only be detected through replication of the basic study over time.

Another threat to external validity related to time is what Bracht and Glass refer to as *interaction of time of measurement and treatment effect*. This threat results from the fact that posttesting may yield different results depending upon when it is done; a treatment effect which is found based on the administration of a posttest immediately following the treatment may not be found if a delayed posttest is given some time after treatment; conversely, a treatment may have a long-term, but not a short-term, effect. Recall the discussion of follow-up studies which suggested that attitude changes, for example, tend to dissipate over time, while delayed feedback promotes greater retention, but not greater immediate learning, than immediate feedback. Thus, really the only way to assess the generalizability of findings over time is to measure the dependent variable at various times following treatment.

To deal with the threats associated with specificity, the researcher must (1) operationally define variables in a way that has meaning outside of the experimental setting and (2) be careful in stating conclusions and generalizations. Also, as we shall see, it may be possible to deal with at least some of these threats through revisions or extensions of basic experimental designs.

Experimenter Effects

Interestingly enough, there is evidence to suggest that researchers may represent potential threats to the external validity of their own studies. Rosenthal has identified a number of ways in which the experimenter may unintentionally affect execution of study procedures, the behavior of subjects, or the assessment of their behavior, and hence results. Possible biasing influences may be passive or active. Passive elements include characteristics or personality traits of the experimenter such as sex, age, race, anxiety level, and hostility level; Rosenthal refers to these influences collectively as the *experimenter personal-attributes effect*.[9] Active bias results when the researcher's expectations affect his or her behavior and hence outcomes. Such behavior on the part of the researcher is referred to as the *experimenter bias effect*. In other words, the way an experimenter looks, feels, or acts may unintentionally affect study results, typically in the desired direction.

One form of experimenter bias occurs when the researcher affects subjects' behavior, or is inaccurate in evaluating their behavior, because of previous knowledge concerning the subjects. This problem is similar to the halo effect in that knowledge of a subject's behavior in one situation may color judgment concerning his or her behavior in another situation. Suppose a researcher hypothesizes that positive reinforcement improves behavior. If the researcher knows that Suzy Shiningstar is in the experimental group and that Suzy is a good student, he or she may give Suzy's behavior a higher rating than it actually warrants. This example also illustrates another way in which a researcher's expectations concerning study outcomes may actually contribute to producing those outcomes: Knowing which sub-

[9]Rosenthal, R. (1966). *Experimenter effects in behavioral research*. New York: Appleton-Century-Crofts.

jects are in which group may cause the researcher to be unintentionally biased in evaluating their performance.

Rosenthal has demonstrated the experimenter bias effect in a number of interesting studies. In one study, two groups of graduate students were given rats and instructions to train the rats to perform a discrimination-learning task.[10] One group of graduate students was told that due to selective breeding their rats were "maze-bright" and would learn quickly and well; the other graduate students were told that their rats were "maze-dull." In reality, both sets of rats were just average, run-of-the-mill rats which had been randomly assigned to the two groups of graduate students. Lo and behold, however, the "smart" rats significantly outperformed the "dumb" rats!

It should be noted that the studies of Rosenthal and his associates have been accused of being affected by experimenter bias! But seriously folks, some researchers have pointed out some methodological flaws, and others have suggested that the results would not have been obtained had properly trained observers been used. It is true that many of their findings have not been replicated and some researchers have concluded that the experimenter bias effect is apparently more difficult to demonstrate than one might believe based on Rosenthal's research.[11] Of course, Rosenthal might claim that *they* are victims of experimenter bias and failed to find an effect because they did not expect to! H-m-m-m.[12]

In any event, the message to the researcher is to be on the safe side and to not be directly involved in conducting her or his own study, if at all possible. Further, the researcher should avoid communicating outcome expectations to any personnel connected with the study.

Reactive Arrangements

Reactive arrangements refers to a number of factors associated with the way in which a study is conducted and the feelings and attitudes of the subjects involved. As discussed previously, in an effort to maintain a high degree of control for the sake of internal validity, a researcher may create an experimental environment that is highly artificial and hinders generalizability of findings to nonexperimental settings. Another type of reactive arrangement results from the subjects' knowledge that they are involved in an experiment or their feeling that they are in some way receiving "special" attention. The effect that such knowledge or feelings can have on the behavior of subjects was demonstrated at the Hawthorne Plant of the Western Electric Company in Chicago some years ago.[13] Studies were conducted to investigate the relationship between various working conditions and productivity. As part of their research, researchers investigated the relationship between light

---

[10] Rosenthal, R., & Fode, K. L. (1963). The effect of experimenter bias on the performance of the albino rat. *Behavioral Science, 8,* 183–189.

[11] See, for example, Barber, T. X., Forgione, A., Chaves, J. F., Calverley, D. S., McPeake, J. D., & Bowen, B. (1969). Five attempts to replicate the experimenter bias effect. *Journal of Consulting and Clinical Psychology, 33,* 1–6, *and* Barber, T. X. & Silver, M. J. (1968). Fact, fiction, and the experimenter bias effect. *Psychological Bulletin Monograph, 70* (6, Pt. 2), 1–29.

[12] For an interesting discussion of this controversial topic, see Wineburg, S. S. (1987). The self-fulfillment of the self-fulfilling prophecy. *Educational Researcher, 16*(9), 28–37, *and* Rosenthal, R. (1987). Pygmalion effects: Existence, magnitude, and social importance. (A reply to Wineburg.) *Educational Researcher, 16*(9), 37–41.

[13] Roethlisberger, F. S., & Dickson, W. J. (1939). *Management and the worker.* Cambridge, MA: Harvard University Press.

intensity and worker output. The researchers increased light intensity and production went up. They increased it some more and production went up some more.
The brighter the place became, the more production rose. As a check, the
researchers decreased illumination, and guess what—production went up! The
darker it got, the more workers produced. The researchers soon realized that it was
the attention the workers were receiving, and not the illumination, that was affecting production. To this day, the term *Hawthorne effect* is used to describe any situation in which subjects' behavior is affected not by the treatment per se, but by
their knowledge of participation in a study.

As with the experimenter bias effect, some researchers have criticized the
methodology used in these studies and have seriously questioned the validity of
results. Cook and Campbell, for example, point out that subjects were women, that
experimental group sizes were small, and that there was apparently considerable
variability in how the women reacted to treatments.[14] Further, attempts to replicate
the effect have not been too successful. Cook (no relation to the previous Cook),
for example, based on his own research and a comprehensive review of related literature, concluded that the Hawthorne effect probably does not affect the results of
studies in which achievement is measured nearly as much as is generally believed.[15]
As always, however, it is best for the researcher to be on the safe side and to take
appropriate precautions.

A related effect is known as the *John Henry effect*. Folk hero John Henry, you
may recall, was a "steel drivin' man" who worked for a railroad. When he heard
that a steam drill was going to replace him and his fellow steel drivers, he challenged, and set out to beat, the machine. Through tremendous effort he did manage to win the ensuing contest, dropping dead at the finish line. This phenomenon
has been shown to operate in research studies. If for any reason control groups or
their teachers feel threatened or challenged by being in competition with a new
program or approach, they may outdo themselves and perform way beyond what
would normally be expected—even if it "kills" them.[16] When this effect occurs, the
treatment under investigation does not appear to be very effective since posttest
performance of experimental subjects is not much (if at all) better than that of control subjects.

A similar phenomenon in medical research resulted in the *placebo effect,* which
is sort of the antidote for the Hawthorne and John Henry effects. In medical
research it was discovered that any "medication" could make subjects feel better,
even sugar and water. To counteract this effect, the placebo approach was developed in which half of the subjects receive the true medication and half receive a
placebo (sugar and water, for example); this fact is of course not known to the subjects. The application of the placebo effect in educational research is that all groups
in an experiment should *appear* to be treated the same. Subjects should not feel
special if they are in the experimental group, nor should they feel shortchanged if
they are in the control group. Suppose, for example, you have four groups of ninth
graders, two experimental and two control, and the treatment is a film designed to
promote a positive attitude toward a vocational career. If the experimental subjects

[14]Cook, T. D., & Campbell, D. T. (1979). *Quasi-experimentation: Design & analysis issues for field settings.* Boston: Houghton Mifflin.

[15]Cook, D. L. (1967). *The impact of the Hawthorne effect in experimental designs in educational
research* (Cooperative Research Project No. 1757). Washington, DC: U.S. Office of Education.

[16]See, for example, Saretsky, G. (1972). The OEO P. C. experiment and the John Henry effect. *Phi
Delta Kappan, 53,* 579–581.

are to be excused from several of their classes in order to view the film, then the control subjects too should be excused and shown another film whose content is unrelated to the purpose of the study (*Drugs and You: Just Say No!*, would do). As an added control you might have all the subjects told that there are two movies and that eventually all of them will see both movies. In other words, it should appear as if *all* the students are doing the same thing.

Another related effect is the *novelty effect*. The novelty effect refers to increased interest, motivation, or participation on the part of subjects simply because they are doing something different. In other words, a treatment may be effective because it is different, not better per se. To counteract the novelty effect, the study should be conducted over a period of time sufficient to allow the "newness" to wear off. This is especially true if the treatment involves activities very different from the subjects' usual routine.

▓ GROUP EXPERIMENTAL DESIGNS

The validity of an experiment is a direct function of the degree to which extraneous variables are controlled. If such variables are not controlled, it is difficult to evaluate the effects of an independent variable and the generalizability of effects. The term "confounding" is sometimes used to refer to the fact that the effects of the independent variable may be confounded by extraneous variables such that it is difficult to determine the effects of each. This is what experimental design is all about—control of extraneous variables; good designs control many sources of invalidity, poor designs control few. If you recall, two types of extraneous variables in need of control were previously identified, subject variables and environmental variables. Subject variables include organismic variables and intervening variables. Organismic variables, as the term implies, are characteristics of the subject, or organism (such as sex), which cannot be directly controlled, but which can be controlled *for*. Intervening variables, as the term implies, are variables that intervene between the independent variable and the dependent variable (such as anxiety or boredom), which cannot be directly observed or controlled, but which also can be controlled *for*.

Control of Extraneous Variables

Randomization is the best single way to attempt to control for many extraneous variables all at the same time. The logical implication of the above statement is that randomization should be used whenever possible; subjects should be randomly selected from a population whenever possible, subjects should be randomly assigned to groups whenever possible, treatments should be randomly assigned to groups whenever possible, and anything else you can think of should be randomly assigned, if possible! Recall that random selection means selection by pure chance and is usually accomplished using a table of random numbers. Random assignment means assignment by pure chance and is usually accomplished by again using the table of random numbers to select the members of the experimental group, or even by flipping a coin if two groups are involved, or by rolling a die if more than two groups are involved (heads, you are in the experimental group; tails, you are in the control group). Randomization is effective in creating equivalent, representative groups that are essentially the same on all relevant variables thought of by the researcher, and probably even a few not thought of. Randomly formed groups is a characteristic unique to experimental research; it is a control factor not possible with causal-comparative research. The rationale is that if subjects are assigned at random to groups, there is no reason to believe that the groups are greatly different in any systematic way. Thus, the groups would be expected to perform essentially the same on the dependent variable *if* the independent variable makes no difference; therefore, if the groups perform differently at the end of the study, the difference can be attributed to the treatment, or independent variable. The larger the groups, the more confidence the researcher can have in the effectiveness of randomization; recall that 15 subjects per group is an accepted minimum. In addition to equating groups on subject variables such as intelligence, randomization also equalizes groups on environmental variables. Teachers, for example, can be randomly assigned to groups so that the experimental groups will not have all the "Carmel Kandee" teachers or all the "Hester Hartless" teachers (and likewise the control groups). Clearly, the researcher should use as much randomization as possible. If subjects cannot be randomly selected, those available should at least be randomly assigned. If subjects cannot be randomly assigned to groups, then at least treatment condition should be randomly assigned to the existing groups.

In addition to randomization, there are other ways to control for extraneous variables. Certain environmental variables, for example, can be controlled by holding them constant for all groups. Recall the student tutor versus parent tutor study; help time was an important variable that had to be held constant, that is, be the same, for the two groups. Other such variables which might need to be held constant include: learning materials, meeting place and time (students might be more alert in the morning than in the afternoon), and years of experience of participating teachers. Controlling subject variables is critical. If the groups are not the same to start with, you have not even given yourself a fighting chance. Regardless of whether groups can be randomly formed, there are a number of techniques at your disposal that can be used to try to equate groups.

Matching

Matching is a technique for equating groups on one or more variables the researcher has identified as being highly related to performance on the dependent variable. The most commonly used approach to matching involves random assignment of pair members, one member to each group. In other words, for each of the available subjects, the researcher attempts to find another subject with the same or a similar score on the control variable (the variable on which subjects are being matched). If the researcher is matching on sex, obviously the "match" must be of the same sex, not a similar sex. If the researcher is matching on variables such as pretest scores, GRE scores, or IQ, however, the "similar score" concept makes sense. Unless the available number of subjects is very large, it is unreasonable to try to make exact matches. Thus, the researcher might decide that two GRE scores within 50 points of each other constitute an acceptable match. As the researcher identifies each matched pair, one member of the pair is randomly assigned to one group and the other member to the other group. If a subject does not have a suitable match, the subject is excluded from the study. The resulting matched groups are identical or very similar with respect to the identified extraneous variable.

A major problem with such matching is that there are invariably subjects who do not have a match and must be eliminated from the study. This factor may cost the researcher many subjects, especially if matching is attempted on two or more variables (imagine trying to find a match for a male with an IQ near 140 and a GPA between 1.00 and 1.50!). One way to combat loss of subjects is to match less close-ly. The researcher might decide that two IQ scores within 20 points constitute an acceptable match. This procedure may increase subjects but it tends to defeat the purpose of matching. A related procedure is to rank all of the subjects, from high-est to lowest, based on their scores on the control variable. The first two subjects (the subjects with the highest and next highest scores) are the first pair, no matter how far apart their scores are; one member is randomly assigned to one group and one member to the other. The next two subjects (the subjects with the third and fourth highest scores) are the next pair, and so on. The major advantage of this approach is that no subjects are lost; the major disadvantage is that it is a lot less precise than pair-wise matching. Advanced statistical procedures, such as analysis of covariance, and the availability of computer programs to compute such statistics have greatly reduced the research use of matching.

Comparing Homogeneous Groups or Subgroups

Another way of controlling an extraneous variable, which was discussed previous-ly with respect to causal-comparative research, is to compare groups that are homo-geneous with respect to that variable. For example, if IQ were an identified extra-neous variable, the researcher might select a group of subjects with IQs between 85 and 115 (average IQ). The researcher would then randomly assign half of the selected subjects to the experimental group and half to the control group. Of course this procedure also lowers the number of subjects in the study and additionally restricts the generalizability of the findings. Further, if random assignment is possi-ble, using only a homogeneous subgroup really only makes sense if one wants to have an additional guarantee concerning group equality on the control variable.

As with causal-comparative research, a similar, but more satisfactory approach is to form subgroups representing all levels of the control variable. For example, the available subjects might be divided into high (116 or above), average (85 to 115), and low (84 and below) IQ subgroups. Half of the selected subjects from each of the subgroups could then be randomly assigned to the experimental group and half to the control group. The procedure just described should sound familiar since it describes stratified sampling. (You knew that!) If the researcher is interested not just in controlling the variable but also in seeing if the independent variable affects the dependent variable differently at different levels of the control variable, the best approach is to build the control variable right into the design and to analyze the results with a statistical technique called factorial analysis of variance.[17]

Using Subjects as Their Own Controls

Using subjects as their own controls involves exposing the same group to the dif-ferent treatments, one treatment at a time. This helps to control for subject differ-ences since the same subjects get both treatments. Of course this approach is not always feasible; you cannot teach the same algebraic concepts twice to the same group using two different methods of instruction (well, you *could*, but it would not make much sense). A problem with this approach in some studies is carry-over effects of one treatment to the next. To use a previous example, it would be very difficult to evaluate the effectiveness of corporal punishment in improving behav-ior if the group receiving corporal punishment was the same group that had

---

[17] Analysis of variance and factorial analysis of variance will be discussed further in Chapter 14.

previously been exposed to behavior modification. If only one group is available, a better approach, if feasible, is to randomly divide the group into two smaller groups, each of which receives both treatments but in a different order. In the above example, the researcher could at least get some idea of the effectiveness of corporal punishment because there would be a group which received it *before* behavior modification.

Analysis of Covariance

The analysis of covariance is a statistical method for equating randomly formed groups on one or more variables. In essence, analysis of covariance adjusts scores on a dependent variable for initial differences on some other variable, such as pretest scores, IQ, reading readiness, or musical aptitude (assuming that performance on the "other variable" is related to performance on the dependent variable). In the example previously given, for a study comparing the effectiveness of two methods of learning fractions, the researcher could covary on IQ, thus equating scores on a measure of achievement in fractions. Although analysis of covariance can be used in studies when groups cannot be randomly formed, its use is most appropriate when randomization is used. Despite randomization, for example, it might be found that two groups differ significantly in terms of pretest scores. Analysis of covariance can be used in such cases to "correct" or adjust posttest scores for initial pretest differences.[18] Calculation of an analysis of covariance is quite a complex, lengthy procedure and you would not want to do many by hand. Fortunately, there are computer programs readily available that can do the work for you if you know how to use them.

Types of Group Designs

A selected experimental design dictates to a great extent the specific procedures of a study. Selection of a given design dictates such factors as whether there will be a control group, whether subjects will be randomly assigned to groups, whether each group will be pretested, and how resulting data will be analyzed. Depending upon the particular combination of such factors represented, different designs are appropriate for testing different types of hypotheses, and designs vary widely in the degree to which they control the various threats to internal and external validity. Of course there are certain threats to validity which no design can control for; experimenter bias, for example, is a potential threat with any design. However, some designs clearly do a better job than others. In selecting a design, you must first determine which designs are appropriate for your study, for testing your hypothesis. You then determine which of those that are appropriate are also feasible given any constraints under which you may be operating. If, for example, you must use existing groups, a number of designs will automatically be eliminated. From the designs that are appropriate and feasible, you select the one that controls the most sources of internal and external invalidity. In other words, you select the best design you possibly can that will yield the data you need to test your hypothesis or hypotheses.

---

[18]Another important function of analysis of covariance, its ability to increase the power of a statistical test, will be discussed in Chapter 14.

There are two major classes of experimental designs, single-variable designs, which involve one independent variable (which is manipulated), and factorial designs, which involve two or more independent variables (at least one of which is manipulated). Single-variable designs are classified as pre-experimental, true experimental, or quasi-experimental, depending upon the control they provide for sources of internal and external invalidity. Pre-experimental designs do not do a very good job of controlling threats to validity and should be avoided. In fact the results of a study based on such a design are so questionable, they are essentially worthless for all purposes except, *perhaps,* a preliminary investigation of a problem. The true experimental designs represent a very high degree of control and are always to be preferred. Quasi-experimental designs do not control as well as true experimental designs but do a much better job than the pre-experimental designs. To take a lighter look at the subject, if we were to assign letter grades to experimental designs, all true experimental designs would get an A, the quasi-experimental designs would get a B or a C (some are better than others), and pre-experimental designs would get a D or an F (there is at least one which is barely defensible for limited purposes). Thus, if you have a choice between a true experimental design and a quasi-experimental design, select the true design. If your choice is between a quasi-experimental design and a pre-experimental design, select the quasi-experimental design. If your choice is between a pre-experimental design or not doing the study at all, do not do the study at all, or do a follow-up study using an acceptable (C or better!) design. The poor designs will be discussed only so that (1) you will know what *not* to do, and (2) you will recognize their use in published research reports (heaven forbid) and be appropriately critical of findings.

Factorial designs are basically elaborations of true experimental designs and permit investigation of two or more variables, individually and in interaction with each other. In education, variables do not operate in isolation. After an independent variable has been investigated using a single-variable design, it is often useful to then study the variable in combination with one or more other variables; some variables work differently at different levels of another variable. Since a factorial design involves *two* or *more* variables, there is an almost infinite number of possibilities for such designs.

The designs to be discussed represent the basic designs in each category. Campbell and Stanley, and Cook and Campbell, present a number of variations (for those of you who are getting "hooked" on research).

Pre-Experimental Designs

Here is a research riddle for you: Can you do an experiment with only one group? The answer is . . . yes, but not a really good one. Two of the pre-experimental designs involve only one group. As Figure 11.1 illustrates, none of the pre-experimental designs does a very good job of controlling extraneous variables that jeopardize validity.

The One-Shot Case Study. The one-shot case study (It even *sounds* shoddy, doesn't it?) involves one group which is exposed to a treatment *(X)* and then posttested *(O)*. All of the sources of invalidity are not relevant; testing, for example, is not a concern since there is no pretest. As Figure 11.1 indicates, however, *none* of the threats to validity that are relevant is controlled. Even if the subjects score high on the posttest, you cannot attribute their performance to the treatment since

Designs	\multicolumn{8}{c}{Internal}	\multicolumn{2}{c}{External}
	History	Maturation	Testing	Instrumentation	Regression	Selection	Mortality	Selection Interactions	Pretest-X Interaction	Multiple-X Interference
One-Shot Case Study X O	−	−	(+)	(+)	(+)	(+)	−	(+)	(+)	(+)
One-Group Pretest–Posttest Design O X O	−	−	−	−	−	(+)	+	(+)	−	(+)
Static Group Comparison X_1 O X_2 O	+	−	(+)	(+)	(+)	−	−	−	(+)	(+)

(Table header: Sources of Invalidity)

Symbols:

X or X_1 = Unusual treatment
X_2 = Control treatment
O = Test, pretest or posttest

\+ = Factor controlled for
(+) = Factor controlled for because not relevant
− = Factor not controlled for

Each line of Xs and Os represents a group.

Note: Figures 11.1 and 11.2 basically follow the format used by Campbell and Stanley and are presented with a similar note of caution: The figures are intended to be supplements to, not substitutes for, textual discussions. You *should not* totally accept or reject designs because of their +s and −s; you *should* also be aware that which design is most appropriate for a given study is determined not only by the controls provided by the various designs but also by the nature of the study and the setting in which it is to be conducted.

While the symbols used in these figures, and their placement, vary somewhat from Campbell and Stanley's format, the intent, interpretations, and textual discussions of the two presentations are in agreement (Personal communication with Donald T. Campbell, April 22, 1975).

Figure 11.1. Sources of invalidity for pre-experimental designs.

you do not even know what they knew before you administered the treatment. So, if you have a choice between using this design and not doing a study—do not do the study.

The One-Group Pretest-Posttest Design. This design involves one group which is pretested *(O)*, exposed to a treatment *(X)*, and posttested *(O)*. The success of the treatment is determined by comparing pretest and posttest scores. However, although it controls invalidity not controlled by the one-shot case study, a number of additional factors are relevant to this design that are not controlled. If subjects do significantly better on the posttest, it cannot be assumed that the improvement is due to the treatment. History and maturation are not controlled; something may happen *to* the subjects or *inside* of the subjects to make them perform better the second time. The longer the study is, the more likely this becomes. Testing and instrumentation are not controlled; the subjects may learn something on the first test that helps them on the second test, or unreliability of the measures may be responsible for the apparent improvement. Statistical regression is also not controlled for. Even if subjects are not selected on the basis of extreme scores (high or low), it is possible that a group may do very poorly, just by poor luck, on the pretest; subjects may guess badly just by chance on a multiple-choice pretest, for example, and improve on a posttest simply because their score based on guessing is more in line with an expected score. The external validity factor pretest-treatment interaction is also not controlled. Pretest-treatment interaction may cause subjects to react differently to the treatment than they would have if they had not been pretested.

To illustrate the problems associated with this design, let us examine a hypothetical study. Suppose a professor teaches a very "heavy" statistics course and is concerned that the high anxiety level of students interferes with their learning. The kindly professor therefore prepares a 100-page booklet which explains the course and tries to convince students that they will have no problems and will receive all the help they need to successfully complete the course, even if they do have a poor math background and cannot "add 2 and 2." The professor wants to see if the booklet works; at the beginning of the term he or she administers an anxiety scale and then gives each student a copy of the booklet with instructions to read it as soon as possible. Two weeks later he or she administers the anxiety scale again and, sure enough, the students indicate much less anxiety than at the beginning of the term. The professor is well satisfied with the booklet and its effectiveness in reducing anxiety. However, this self-satisfaction is not warranted. If you think about it, you will see that there are a number of alternative factors that could explain the decreased anxiety. Students, for example, are typically more anxious at the beginning of a course because they do not know what is coming (fear of the unknown!). After being in a course for a couple of weeks students usually find that it is not as bad as they imagined (right?), or they have dropped it (remember mortality?). Besides, the professor would not even know if the students read the masterpiece! Unlike this example, the only situations for which the one-group pretest-posttest design is even remotely appropriate is when the behavior to be measured is not likely to change all by itself. Certain prejudices, for example, are not likely to change unless a concerted effort is made.

The Static-Group Comparison.   The static-group comparison involves at least two groups; one group receives a new, or unusual, treatment, the other receives a traditional, or usual, treatment, and both groups are posttested. The first group is usually referred to as the experimental group, and the second group as the control group. It is probably more accurate to call both groups comparison groups, since each really serves as the control for the other; each group receives some form of the independent variable. So, for example, if the independent variable is type of drill and practice, the "experimental" group (X_1) may receive computer-assisted drill and practice, and the "control" group may receive worksheet drill and practice. Occasionally, but not often, the experimental group may receive something while the control group receives nothing parallel. An experimental group of teachers, for example, may receive some type of in-service training while the control group of teachers does not. In this case, X_1 = in-service training and X_2 = no in-service training. The whole purpose of a control group is to indicate what the performance of the experimental group would have been *if* it had not received the experimental treatment. Of course, this purpose is fulfilled only to the degree that the control group is equivalent to the experimental group on other variables.

This design can be expanded to deal with any number of groups. For three groups, for example, the design would take the form:

$$X_1 \quad O$$
$$X_2 \quad O$$
$$X_3 \quad O$$

Which group is the control group? Basically, each group serves as a control, or comparison, group for the other two. For example, if the independent variable were number of reviews, then X_1 might represent two reviews, X_2 might represent one review, and X_3 no review. Thus X_3 (no review) would help us to assess the impact of X_2 (one review), and X_2 would help us to assess the impact of X_1 (two reviews). As stated above, the degree to which the groups are equivalent is the degree to which their comparison is reasonable. Since subjects are not randomly assigned to groups, and since there are no pretest data, however, it is difficult to determine just how equivalent they are. It is always possible that posttest differences are due to group differences, not just treatment effects (maturation, selection, and selection interactions). Mortality is also a problem since if you lose subjects from the study you have no information concerning what you have lost (no pretest data). On the positive side, the presence of a control group controls for history since it is assumed that events occurring outside of the experimental setting will equally affect both groups. Of course the existence of a control group (in this and other designs) permits the occurrence of events that are group-specific, events such as a power failure or a violent storm. These events, referred to as within-group, or intrasession, history, are more likely to occur when groups are "treated" at different times. If not controlled for in some way, their occurrence should be described fully in the research report.

Earlier it was suggested that at least one of the pre-experimental designs was "barely defensible." The static-group comparison design is occasionally employed in a preliminary, or exploratory, study. For example, one semester, early in the term, the author of this text wondered if the kind of test items given to educational research students affects their retention of course concepts. So, for the rest of the term, students in one section of the introductory educational research course were given multiple-choice tests, and students in another section were given short-answer tests. At the end of the term, group performance was informally compared. The short-answer test section had higher total scores for the course. Therefore, in a subsequent semester, a formal study was executed (with randomly formed groups and everything!). The results indicated that the short-answer test group performed as well as the multiple-choice group on the multiple-choice portion of the posttest, and significantly better on the short-answer portion. Thus, an exploratory study, based on a static-group comparison design (two sections, treated differently, and then posttested), led to a formal study which employed a true experimental design.[19]

True Experimental Designs

The true experimental designs control for nearly all sources of internal and external invalidity. As Figure 11.2 indicates, all of the true experimental designs have one characteristic in common that none of the other designs has—random assignment of subjects to groups. Ideally subjects should be randomly selected and randomly

[19] Gay, L. R. (1980). The comparative effects of multiple-choice versus short-answer tests on retention. *Journal of Educational Measurement, 17,* 45–50.

Designs	Sources of Invalidity									
	Internal								External	
	History	Maturation	Testing	Instrumentation	Regression	Selection	Mortality	Selection Interactions	Pretest-X Interaction	Multiple-X Interference
TRUE EXPERIMENTAL DESIGNS										
1. Pretest–Posttest Control Group Design $R\ O\ X_1\ O$ $R\ O\ X_2\ O$	+	+	+	+	+	+	+	+	−	(+)
2. Posttest-Only Control Group Design $R\quad X_1\ O$ $R\quad X_2\ O$	+	+	(+)	(+)	(+)	+	−	+	(+)	(+)
3. Solomon Four-Group Design $R\ O\ X_1\ O$ $R\ O\ X_2\ O$ $R\quad X_1\ O$ $R\quad X_2\ O$	+	+	+	+	+	+	+	+	+	(+)
QUASI-EXPERIMENTAL DESIGNS										
4. Nonequivalent Control Group Design $O\ X_1\ O$ $O\ X_2\ O$	+	+	+	+	−	+	+	−	−	(+)
5. Time Series Design $O\ O\ O\ O\ X\ O\ O\ O\ O$	−	+	+	−	+	(+)	+	(+)	−	(+)
6. Counterbalanced Design $X_1 O\ X_2 O\ X_3 O$ $X_3 O\ X_1 O\ X_2 O$ $X_2 O\ X_3 O\ X_1 O$	+	+	+	+	+	+	+	−	−	−

New Symbol:

R = Random assignment of subjects to groups

Figure 11.2. Sources of invalidity for true experimental designs and quasi-experimental designs.

assigned; however, *to qualify as a true design, at least random assignment must be involved*. Note too that all the true designs involve a control group. Also, while the posttest-only control group design may *look* like the static-group comparison design, random assignment makes them very different in terms of control.

The Pretest-Posttest Control Group Design.   This design involves at least two groups, both of which are formed by random assignment; both groups are administered a pretest of the dependent variable, one group receives a new, or unusual, treatment, and both groups are posttested.[20] Posttest scores are compared to determine the effectiveness of the treatment. The pretest-posttest control group design may also be expanded to include any number of treatment groups. For three groups, for example, this design would take the following form:

$$
\begin{array}{cccc}
R & O & X_1 & O \\
R & O & X_2 & O \\
R & O & X_3 & O
\end{array}
$$

The combination of random assignment and the presence of a pretest and a control group serve to control for all sources of internal invalidity. Random assignment controls for regression and selection factors; the pretest controls for mortality; randomization and the control group control for maturation; and the control group controls for history, testing, and instrumentation. Testing, for example, is controlled because if pretesting leads to higher posttest scores, the advantage should be equal for both the experimental and control groups. The only definite weakness with this design is a possible interaction between the pretest and the treatment which may make the results generalizable only to other pretested groups. As discussed before, the seriousness of this potential weakness depends upon such factors as the nature of the pretest, the nature of the treatment, and the length of the study. It is more likely to occur with reactive measures such as attitude scales and in short studies. When this design is used, the researcher should assess and report the probability of its occurrence. A researcher might indicate, for example, that possible pretest interaction was believed to be minimized by the nonreactive nature of the pretest (chemical equations), and by the length of the study (9 months).

There are three basic ways in which the data can be analyzed in order to determine the effectiveness of the treatment and to test the research hypothesis; one of them is clearly inappropriate, one is not very appropriate, and one is clearly the most appropriate. One approach is to compare the pretest and posttest scores of each group; if the experimental group improves significantly but not the control group, it is concluded that the treatment is effective. This approach is inappropriate because the real question is whether the experimental group is better than the control group; thus the appropriate comparison is of the posttest scores of each group. If the researcher finds that both groups have improved significantly (e.g., each group's average posttest reading score is significantly higher than its pretest reading score after 9 months of different instruction), this still does not indicate whether one group is significantly better than the other; we would expect both groups to improve their reading in 9 months, so the question involves which treatment has done a better job. A second approach is to compute gain, or difference, scores for each subject (posttest score minus pretest score) and then to compare the average gain of the experimental group with the average gain of the control group. Gain scores entail problems, however. For one thing, all students do not have the

---

[20]Although a number of measures may be administered before a study begins (for stratified sampling purposes, for example) the term *pretest* usually refers to a test of the dependent variable.

same "room" to gain. On a 100-item test, who is better, a student who goes from a pretest score of 80 to a posttest score of 99 (a gain of 19), or a student who goes from a pretest score of 20 to a posttest score of 70 (a gain of 50)? The third approach, and the one usually recommended, is to simply compare the posttest scores of the two groups. (Surprise! The simplest approach is recommended!) The pretest is used to see if the groups are essentially the same on the dependent variable. If they are, posttest scores can be directly compared using a *t* test; if they are not (random assignment does not *guarantee equality*), posttest scores can be analyzed using analysis of covariance.[21] Recall that covariance adjusts posttest scores for initial differences on any variable, including pretest scores.

A variation of the pretest-posttest control group design involves random assignment of members of matched pairs to the groups, one member to each group in order to more closely control for one or more extraneous variables. There is really no advantage to this technique, however, since any variable that can be controlled through matching can be better controlled using other procedures such as analysis of covariance.

Another variation of this design involves one or more additional posttests. For example:

$$R \quad O \quad X_1 \quad O \quad O$$
$$R \quad O \quad X_2 \quad O \quad O$$

This variation has the advantage of providing information on the effect of the independent variable both immediately following treatment *and* at a later date. Recall that *interaction of time of measurement and treatment effects* was discussed as a threat to external validity. It is a potential threat to generalizability because posttesting may yield different results depending upon when it is done; a treatment effect (or lack of same) which is found based on the administration of a posttest immediately following the treatment may not be found if a delayed posttest is given sometime after treatment. While the above variation does not completely solve the problem, it does greatly minimize it. Of course, how many additional posttests should be given, and when, depends upon the variables being investigated.

The Posttest-Only Control Group Design. This design is exactly the same as the pretest-posttest control group design *except* there is no pretest; subjects are randomly assigned to groups, exposed to the independent variable, and posttested. Posttest scores are then compared to determine the effectiveness of the treatment. As with the pretest-posttest control group design, the posttest-only control group design can be expanded to include more than two groups.

The combination of random assignment and the presence of a control group serves to control for all sources of internal invalidity except mortality. Mortality is not controlled for because of the absence of pretest data on subjects. However, mortality may or may not be a problem, depending upon the study. If the study is relatively short in duration, for example, no subjects may be lost. In this case the researcher may report that while mortality is a potential threat to validity with this design, it did not prove to be a threat in his or her particular study since the group sizes remained constant throughout the duration of the study. Thus, if the probability of differential mortality is low, the posttest-only design can be a very effective design. Of course if there is any chance that the groups may be different with respect to initial knowledge related to the dependent variable (despite random

---

[21] Even if groups are not significantly different initially, covariance may be used to increase the power of the statistical test. This concept will be discussed further in Chapter 14.

assignment), the pretest-posttest control group design should be used. Which design is "best" depends upon the study. If the study is to be short, and if it can be assumed that neither group has any knowledge related to the dependent variable, then the posttest-only design may be the "best." If the study is to be lengthy (good chance of mortality), or if there is a chance that the two groups differ on initial knowledge related to the dependent variable, then the pretest-posttest control group design may be the best. What if, however, you face the following dilemma:

1. The study is going to last 2 months.
2. Assessment of initial knowledge is essential.
3. The pretest is an attitude scale and the treatment is designed to change attitudes.

Here we have a classic case where pretest-treatment interaction is probable. Do we throw our hands up in despair? Of course not. One solution is to select the lesser of the two evils, perhaps take our chances with mortality. Another solution, if sufficient subjects are available, is to use the Solomon four-group design, to be discussed next. If you look at Figure 11.2 you will see that the Solomon four-group design is simply a combination of the pretest-posttest control group design (the top two lines) and the posttest-only control group design (the third and fourth lines).

A variation of the posttest-only control group design involves random assignment of members of matched pairs to the groups, one member to each group, in order to more closely control for one or more extraneous variables. As with the pretest-posttest control group design, however, there is really no advantage to this technique; any variable that can be controlled through matching can better be controlled using other procedures.

The Solomon Four-Group Design. The Solomon four-group design involves random assignment of subjects to one of four groups. Two of the groups are pretested and two are not; one of the pretested groups and one of the unpretested groups receive the experimental treatment. All four groups are posttested. As Figure 11.2 indicates, this design is a combination of the pretest-posttest control group design and the posttest-only control group design, each of which has its own major source of invalidity (pretest-treatment interaction and mortality, respectively). The combination of these two designs results in a design which controls for pretest-treatment interaction *and* for mortality. The correct way to analyze data resulting from application of this design is to use a 2×2 factorial analysis of variance. The two independent variables are the treatment variable and the pretest variable; in other words, whether a group is pretested or not is an independent variable, just as the experimental variable is. The factorial analysis tells the researcher whether the treatment is effective *and* whether there is an interaction between the treatment and the pretest. To put it as simply as possible, if the pretested experimental group performs differently on the posttest than the unpretested experimental group, there is probably a pretest-treatment interaction. If no interaction is found, then the researcher can have more confidence in the generalizability of treatment differences.

A common misconception among beginning researchers is that since the Solomon four-group design controls for so many sources of invalidity, it is the "best" design. This is not true. For one thing, this design requires twice as many subjects as either of the other true experimental designs, and subjects are often hard to come by. Further, if mortality is not likely to be a problem, and pretest data are not needed, then the posttest-only design may be the best; if pretest-treatment interaction is unlikely, and testing is a normal part of the subjects' environment (such as when classrooms are used), then the pretest-posttest control group design may be the "best." Which design is the "best" depends upon the nature of the study and the conditions under which it is to be conducted.

Quasi-Experimental Designs

Sometimes it is just not possible to randomly assign subjects to groups. In order to receive permission to use school children in a study, for example, a researcher often has to agree to use existing classrooms. When this occurs, however, there are still a number of designs available to the researcher that provide adequate control of sources of invalidity; these designs are referred to as quasi-experimental designs. Although Campbell and Stanley discuss a number of such designs, only three of the major ones will be discussed here. Keep in mind that designs such as these are *only* to be used when it is not feasible to use a true experimental design.

The Nonequivalent Control Group Design.   This design should be familiar to you since it looks very much like the pretest-posttest control group design; the only difference is that the nonequivalent control group design does not involve random assignment of subjects to groups (although treatment should be randomly assigned to groups, if possible). Two (or more) existing groups are pretested, administered a treatment, and posttested; three of six classrooms may be randomly designated to be the experimental group (X_1) for example, and the remaining three as the control group (X_2). The lack of random assignment adds sources of invalidity not associated with the pretest-posttest control group design—possible regression and interaction between selection and variables such as maturation, history, and testing. The more similar the groups are, the better; the researcher should make every effort to use groups that are as equivalent as possible. Comparing an advanced algebra class with a remedial algebra class, for example, would not do. If differences between the groups on any major extraneous variable are identified, analysis of covariance can be used to statistically equate the groups. An advantage of this design is that since classes are used "as is," possible effects from reactive arrangements are minimized. Subjects may not even be aware that they are involved in a study. As with the pretest-posttest control group design, the nonequivalent control group design may be extended to include more than two groups.

The Time-Series Design.   The time series design is actually an elaboration of the one-group pretest-posttest design. One group is repeatedly pretested (more than once, but not necessarily four times as shown in Figure 11.2), exposed to a treatment, and then repeatedly posttested. If a group scores essentially the same on a number of pretests and then significantly improves following a treatment, the researcher has more confidence in the effectiveness of the treatment than if just one pretest and one posttest are administered. To use a former example, if our statistics professor measured anxiety several times before giving the students the booklet, she or he would be able to see if anxiety was declining naturally. History is still a problem with this design, however, since something might happen between the last pretest and the first posttest, the effect of which might be confused with the treatment. Instrumentation may also be a problem but not an expected problem, unless for some reason the researcher changes measuring instruments during the study. Pretest-treatment interaction is also a validity problem. It should be clear that if one pretest can interact with a treatment, more than one pretest can only make matters worse. If instrumentation or pretest-treatment interaction occurs, however, you will probably at least be aware of the problem because scores will change *prior* to treatment.

While statistical analyses appropriate for this design are rather advanced, determining the effectiveness of the treatment basically involves analysis of the pattern of the test scores. Figure 11.3 illustrates several possible patterns which might be found; Campbell and Stanley discuss a number of other possibilities. In Figure 11.3 the vertical line between O_4 and O_5 indicates the point at which the treatment was introduced. Pattern A does not indicate a treatment effect; performance was increasing before the treatment was introduced, and continued to increase at the same rate following introduction of the treatment. In fact pattern A represents the reverse situation to that encountered by our statistics professor and the anxiety-reducing booklet. Patterns B and C do indicate a treatment effect; the effect appears to be more permanent in pattern C than in pattern B. Pattern D does not indicate a treatment effect even though student scores are higher on O_5 than O_4. The pattern is too erratic. Scores appear to be fluctuating up and down; the O_4 to O_5 fluctuation cannot be attributed to the treatment. The four patterns shown illustrate that just comparing O_4 and O_5 is not sufficient; in all four cases O_5 indicates a higher score than O_4, but only in two of the patterns does it appear that the difference is due to a treatment effect.

A variation of the time-series design, which is referred to as the multiple time-series design, involves the addition of a control group to the basic design as follows:

$$O \quad O \quad O \quad O \quad X_1 \quad O \quad O \quad O \quad O$$
$$O \quad O \quad O \quad O \quad X_2 \quad O \quad O \quad O \quad O$$

This variation eliminates history and instrumentation as threats to validity and thus represents a design with no probable sources of internal invalidity. This design can be more effectively used in situations where testing is a naturally occurring event not likely to be noticed, such as research involving school classrooms.

Counterbalanced Designs. In a counterbalanced design, all groups receive all treatments but in a different order. Although Figure 11.2 represents the design for three groups and three treatments, any number of groups may be involved (two or more); the only restriction is that the number of groups equals the number of treatments. The order in which the groups receive the treatments is randomly determined. While subjects may be pretested, this design is usually employed when

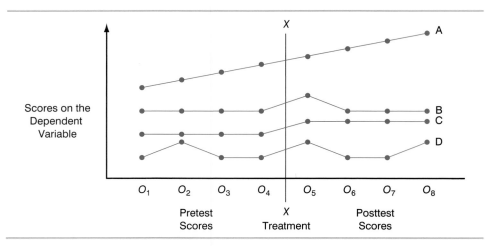

Figure 11.3. Possible patterns for the results of a study based on a time-series design.

intact groups must be used and when administration of a pretest is not possible or feasible. The static group comparison also can be used in such situations, but the counterbalanced design controls several additional sources of invalidity. In the situation shown in Figure 11.2, there are three groups and three treatments (or two treatments and a control group). The first horizontal line indicates that group 1 receives treatment 1 and is posttested, then receives treatment 2 and is posttested, and then treatment 3 and is posttested. The second line indicates that group 2 receives treatment 3, then treatment 1, and then treatment 2, and is posttested after each treatment. The third line indicates that group 3 receives treatment 2, then treatment 3, then treatment 1, and is posttested after each treatment. To put it another way, the first column indicates that at time 1, while group 1 is receiving treatment 1, group 2 is receiving treatment 3 and group 3 is receiving treatment 2. All three groups are posttested and the treatments are shifted to produce the second column. The second column indicates that at time 2, while group 1 is receiving treatment 2, group 2 is receiving treatment 1, and group 3 is receiving treatment 3. The groups are then posttested again and the treatments are again shifted to produce the third column. The third column indicates that now, at time 3, group 1 is receiving treatment 3, group 2 is receiving treatment 2, and group 3 is receiving treatment 1. All groups are posttested again. (This is *not* by the way a research variation of the old comedy routine "Who's on First?") Thus, each row represents a replication of the study. In order to determine the effectiveness of the treatments, the average performance of the groups for each treatment can be compared. In other words, the posttest scores for all the groups for the first treatment can be compared to the posttest scores of all the groups for the second treatment, and so forth, depending upon the number of groups and treatments.

A unique weakness of this design is potential multiple-treatment interference that can result when the same group receives more than one treatment. Thus, a counter-balanced design should really only be used when the treatments are such that exposure to one will not affect evaluation of the effectiveness of another. Of course, there are not too many situations in education where this condition can be met. You cannot, for example, teach the same geometric concepts to the same group using several different methods of instruction. There are, however, sophisticated analysis procedures which can be applied to determine both the effects of treatments and the effects of the order of those treatments.

Factorial Designs

Factorial designs involve two or more independent variables, at least one of which is manipulated by the researcher. They are basically elaborations of true experimental designs and permit investigation of two or more variables, individually and in interaction with each other. In education, variables do not operate in isolation. After an independent variable has been investigated using a single-variable design, it is often useful to then study the variable in combination with one or more other variables. Some variables work differently at different levels of another variable; one method of math instruction may be more effective for high-aptitude students while another method may be more effective for low-aptitude students. The term "factorial" refers to the fact that the design involves more than one independent variable, or factor; in the above example, method of instruction is a factor and aptitude is a factor. Each factor has two or more levels; in the above example, the factor "method of instruction" has two levels since there are two types of instruction, and the factor of aptitude has two levels, high aptitude and low aptitude. Thus, a 2 × 2 factorial design has two factors and each factor has two levels. The 2 × 2 is the simplest factorial design. As another example, a 2 × 3 factorial design has two factors; one factor has two levels and the second factor has three levels (such as high, average, and low aptitude). Suppose we have three independent variables, or factors: homework (required homework, voluntary homework, no homework); IQ (high, average, low); and sex (male, female). How would you symbolize this study? Right, it is a 3 × 3 × 2 factorial design.

The simplest factorial design, the 2 × 2, requires four groups, as Figure 11.4 illustrates. In Figure 11.4 there are two factors; one factor, type of instruction, has two levels, personalized and traditional, and the other factor, IQ, has two levels, high and low. Each of the groups represents a combination of one level of one factor and one level of the other factor. Thus, group 1 is composed of high IQ students receiving personalized instruction (PI), group 2 is composed of high IQ students receiving traditional instruction (TI), group 3 is composed of low IQ students receiving PI, and group 4 is composed of low IQ students receiving TI. If this design were used, a number of high IQ students would be randomly assigned to either group 1 or group 2, and an equal number of low IQ students would be randomly assigned to either group 3 or group 4. This should sound familiar since it represents stratified sampling. Also, in case the question crossed your mind, the study shown in Figure 11.4 *would not* require four classrooms; there would likely be two classes, the personalized class and the traditional class, and each class would contain equal numbers of high and low IQ students. In such a design both variables may be manipulated, but the 2 × 2 design usually involves one manipulated, or experimental, variable, and one nonmanipulated variable; the nonmanipulated variable is often referred to as a control variable. In the above example, IQ is a control variable. Control variables are usually physical or mental characteristics of the subjects such as sex, IQ, or math aptitude. When symbolizing such designs, the manipulated variable is traditionally placed first. Thus, a study with two independent variables, type of instruction (three types, manipulated), and sex (male, female), would be symbolized 3 × 2, not 2 × 3.

The purpose of a factorial design is to determine whether the effects of an experimental variable are generalizable across all levels of a control variable or whether the effects are specific to specific levels of the control variable. Also, a factorial design can demonstrate relationships that a single-variable experiment cannot. For example, a variable found not to be effective in a single-variable experiment may be found to interact significantly with another variable. The second example in Figure 10.5 illustrates this possibility.

Figure 11.5 represents two possible outcomes for an experiment involving a 2 × 2 factorial design. The number in each box, or cell, represents the average posttest score of that group. Thus, in the top example, the high IQ students under

Figure 11.4. An example of the basic 2 x 2 factorial design.

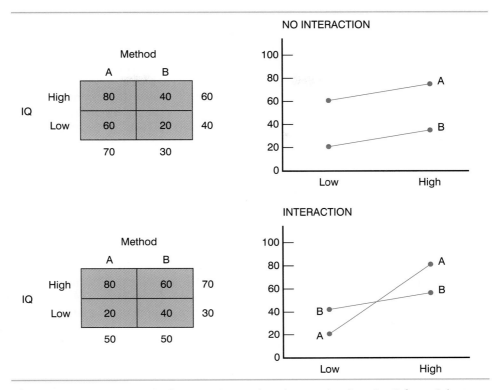

Figure 11.5. Illustration of interaction and no interaction in a 2 x 2 factorial experiment.

method A had an average posttest score of 80. The marginal row and column numbers outside of the boxes represent average scores across boxes, or cells. Thus, in the top example, the average score for high IQ subjects was 60 (found by averaging the scores for all high IQ subjects regardless of treatment), and for low IQ students the average score was 40. The average score for students under method A was 70 (found by averaging the scores of all the subjects under method A regardless of IQ level), and for students under method B, 30. By examining the cell averages, we see that method A was better than method B for high IQ students (80 versus 40), and method A was also better for low IQ students (60 versus 20). Thus, method A was better, regardless of IQ level; there was *no interaction* between method and IQ. The high IQ students in each method outperformed the low IQ students in each method (no big surprise), and the subjects in method A outperformed the subjects in method B at each IQ level. The graph to the right of the results illustrates the lack of interaction.

In the bottom example, which method was better, A or B? The answer is, it depends! Depends on what? Depends on which IQ level we are talking about. For high IQ students, method A was better (80 versus 60); for low IQ students, method B was better (20 versus 40). Even though high IQ students did better than low IQ students regardless of method, how well they did depended upon which method they were under. It cannot be said that either method was better in general; which method was better *depended* upon the IQ level. Now suppose the study had not used a factorial design but had simply compared two groups of subjects, one group receiving method A and one group receiving method B; each group would have been composed of both high and low IQ students. What would the researcher have concluded? The researcher would have concluded that method A and method B were equally effective, since the overall average score for method A was 50 and the overall average score for method B was 50! By using a factorial design it was determined that an *interaction* appears to exist between the variables such that each of the methods is differentially effective depending upon the IQ level of the subjects. The graph to the right of the results illustrates the interaction.

There are a lot of possible factorial designs depending upon the nature and the number of independent variables. Theoretically, a researcher could simultaneously investigate 10 factors in a $2 \times 2 \times 2 \times 2 \times 2 \times 3 \times 3 \times 3 \times 4 \times 4$ design, for example. In reality, however, more than 3 factors are rarely used. For one thing, each additional factor increases the number of subjects that are required. In Part Four, it was stated that the minimum number of subjects per group for an experimental study is 15. Thus, a pretest-posttest control group design with two groups requires at least 30 subjects (2×15). Since a 2×2 design involves 4 groups, 60 subjects (4×15) are required. Similarly, a $3 \times 3 \times 2$ design, which involves 18 groups, requires 270 subjects. It is easy to see that things quickly get out of hand. This is not to say that studies are not done with smaller group sizes—they are. But such situations are usually the result of the lack of an adequate number of subjects being available, or mortality during the study, not intentional planning. The results of such studies require cautious interpretation. For another thing, when too many factors are involved, resulting interactions become difficult, if not impossible, to interpret. Interpretation of a two-way interaction, such as the one illustrated in Figure 11.5, is relatively straightforward. But how, for example, would you interpret a five-way interaction between teaching method, IQ, sex, aptitude, and anxiety! Such interactions tend to have no meaning. Besides, it is not easy to graph a five-way interaction! When used correctly and reasonably, however, factorial designs are very effective for testing certain research hypotheses that cannot be tested with a single-variable design.

■ SINGLE-SUBJECT EXPERIMENTAL DESIGNS

As you would probably guess, single-subject experimental designs (also commonly referred to as single-case experimental designs) are designs that can be applied when the sample size is one. They can also be applied when a number of individuals are considered as one group. They are typically used to study the behavior change an individual exhibits as a result of some intervention, or treatment. In single-subject designs each subject serves as his or her own control in variations on a time-series design. Basically, the subject is alternately exposed to a nontreatment and a treatment condition, or phase, and performance is repeatedly measured during each phase. The nontreatment condition is symbolized as A and the treatment condition is symbolized as B. For example, we might (1) observe and record out-of-seat behavior on five occasions, (2) apply a behavior modification procedure and observe behavior on five more occasions, and (3) stop the behavior modification procedure and observe five more times. Our design would be symbolized as A-B-A. While single-subject designs have their roots in clinical psychology and psychiatry, they are useful in many educational settings. As an example, federally funded programs for handicapped students typically have a requirement that the effectiveness of the program be demonstrated for *each* participant.

The use of single-subject designs has increased steadily since about the mid sixties, paralleling the increased application of behavior modification techniques.

Publication of the first issue of the *Journal of Applied Behavior Analysis* in 1968 by The Society for the Experimental Analysis of Behavior, signaled a new acceptance for single-subject research, an acceptance based on an improved methodology. Whereas previously single-subject research was generally equated with a descriptive, case-study approach, it now became associated with a more controlled, experimental approach.

Single-Subject Versus Group Designs

As single-subject designs have become progressively more refined and capable of dealing with threats to experimental validity, they have come to be viewed as acceptable substitutes for traditional group designs in a number of situations. At the very least they are considered to be valuable complements to such designs.

Most experimental research problems require traditional group designs for their investigation. This is mainly because the results are intended to be applied to *groups,* for example, classrooms. As an example, if we were investigating the comparative effectiveness of two approaches to teaching reading, we would be interested in which approach *in general* produces better results. The schools cannot provide individual tutors or programs for each student and therefore seek strategies that are relatively more beneficial to groups of children. Our research study would, therefore, require the application of a group comparison design such as the pretest-posttest control group design. In addition to being inappropriate, a single-subject design would also be very impractical for such a research problem. Single-subject designs require multiple measurements during each phase (e.g., no treatment, treatment, no treatment) of the study. Recall that in a previous example 15 separate observation periods were involved (5 per phase). It would be highly impractical to administer a reading achievement test 15 times to the same students.

There are, however, a number of research questions for which traditional group designs are not appropriate for two major reasons. First, group comparison designs are frequently opposed on ethical or philosophical grounds. By definition such designs involve a control group that does not receive the experimental treatment. Withholding students with a demonstrated need from a potentially beneficial program, or intervention, may be opposed or actually prohibited, as in the case of certain federally funded programs. The fact that the effectiveness of the treatment has not yet been demonstrated, and in fact the purpose of the research is to assess its effectiveness, is irrelevant. That the treatment is *potentially* effective is sufficient to raise objections if an attempt is made to prevent any eligible subjects from receiving it. Second, application of a group comparison design is not possible in many cases because of the size of the population of interest. There may simply not be enough subjects of a given kind to permit the formulation of two equivalent groups. If the treatment, for example, is aimed at improving the social skills of profoundly retarded children, the number of such children available in any one locale may be quite small. If there are, say, 10 such children, application of a single-subject design is clearly preferable to the formulation of two more-or-less equivalent groups of 5 children each.

Further, single-subject designs are most frequently applied in clinical settings where the primary emphasis is on the therapeutic impact, not contribution to a research base. In such settings, the overriding objective is the identification of intervention strategies which will change the behavior of specific individuals. This is especially important when individuals are engaging in self-abusive or aggressive behavior. Of course it is hoped that a treatment found to be effective in changing a particular behavior of a particular subject in a particular setting will be found over time to be effective for other behaviors and subjects in various settings.

External Validity

A major criticism frequently leveled at single-subject research studies is that they suffer from low external validity, that is, results cannot be generalized to the population of interest as they can with group designs. While this allegation is basically true, it is also true that the results of a study using a group design cannot be directly generalized to any individual within the group. If we randomly select subjects and randomly assign them to groups, the result is two relatively heterogeneous groups. The average posttest performance of the treatment *group* may not adequately reflect the performance of any individual within the group. Thus, group designs and single-subject designs each have their own generalizability problems. If your concern is with improving the functioning of an individual, a group design is not going to be appropriate.

Usually, however, we are interested in generalizing the results of our research to persons other than those directly involved in the study. For single-subject designs, the key to generalizability is replication. If a researcher applies the same treatment using the same single-subject design to a number of subjects and gets essentially the same results in every case (or even in most cases), our confidence in the findings is increased; there is evidence for the generalizability of the results for other subjects. If other researchers in other settings apply the same treatment to other subjects and get essentially the same results, the case for the efficacy of the treatment becomes stronger. The more diverse the replications are (i.e., different kinds of subjects, different behaviors, different settings), the more generalizable the results are.

One generalizability problem associated with many single-subject designs is the possible effect of the baseline condition on the subsequent effects of the treatment condition. We can never be sure that the treatment effects are the same as they would have been if the treatment phase had been the *first* phase. This problem of course parallels the pretest-treatment interaction problem associated with a number of the group designs.

Internal Validity

If proper controls are exercised in connection with the application of a single-subject design, the internal validity of the resulting study may be quite good.[22]

Repeated and Reliable Measurement

As with a time-series design, pretest performance is measured a number of times prior to implementation of the treatment or intervention. In single-subject designs these sequential measures of pretest performance are referred to as baseline measures. As a result of these measures taken over some period of time, sources of invalidity such as maturation are controlled for in the same way as for the time-

[22]Much of the discussion to follow is based on discussion presented in Barlow, D. H., & Hersen, M. (1992). *Single-case experimental designs: Strategies for studying behavior change* (Rev. 2nd ed.). Des Moines, IA: Allyn & Bacon. You should consult this source for in-depth discussion of all topics in this section.

series design. Unlike the time-series design, however, performance is also measured at various points in time while the treatment is being applied. This added dimension greatly reduces the potential threat to validity from history, a threat to internal validity associated with the time-series design.

One very real threat to the internal validity of most single-subject designs is instrumentation. Recall that instrumentation refers to unreliability, or inconsistency, in measuring instruments that may result in an invalid assessment of performance. Since repeated measurement is a characteristic of all single-subject designs, it is especially important that measurement of the target behavior, or performance, be done in exactly the same way every time, or as nearly the same as is humanly possible. Thus, every effort should be made to promote observer reliability by clearly, and in sufficient detail, defining the target behavior, e.g., aggression. Typically, as suggested above, studies using single-subject designs are concerned with some type of behavior requiring observation as the major data collection strategy. In such studies it is critical that the observation conditions (e.g., location, time of day) be standardized. If one observer makes all the observations, then intraobserver reliability should be estimated. If more than one observer is involved, then interobserver reliability should be estimated. Consistency of measurement is especially crucial as we move from phase to phase. For example, if a change in measurement procedures occurs at the same time we move from a baseline to a treatment phase, the result will be an invalid assessment of the effect of the treatment.

Relatedly, the nature and conditions of the treatment should be specified in sufficient detail to permit replication. Some single-subject designs involve reinstatement of the treatment phase following measurement of posttest performance. For example, with an A-B-A-B design, we have a baseline phase, a treatment phase, a return to baseline conditions (withdrawal of the treatment), and a second treatment phase. If its effects are to be validly assessed, the treatment must involve precisely the same procedures every time it is introduced. Also, since the key to generalizability for single-subject designs is replication, it is clearly a necessity for the treatment to be sufficiently standardized to permit other researchers to apply it as it was originally applied and as it was intended to be applied.

Baseline Stability

Another factor related to the internal validity of single-subject designs is the length of the baseline and treatment phases. A major question is, "How many measurements of behavior should be taken before treatment is introduced?" There is no easy answer to this question. The purpose of the baseline measurements is to provide a description of the target behavior as it naturally occurs *without* the treatment. Thus, the baseline serves as the basis of comparison for assessing the effectiveness of the treatment.

If most behaviors were very stable, there would be no problem. But human behavior is variable (in some situations, very variable). For example, if the performance being measured were disruptive behavior, we would not expect a child to exhibit exactly the same number of disruptive acts during each observation period. There would be fluctuations and the child would be more disruptive at some times than at others. Such fluctuations, however, usually fall within some consistent range. Therefore, a sufficient number of baseline measurements are usually taken to establish a pattern. The establishment of a pattern is referred to as *baseline stability*. We might observe, for example, that the child normally exhibits between 5 and 10 disruptive behaviors during a 30-minute period. These figures then become our basis of comparison for assessing the effectiveness of the treatment. If during the treatment phase the number of disruptive behaviors ranges from, say, 0 to 3, or steadily decreases until it reaches 0, and if the number of disruptive behaviors increases when treatment is withdrawn, the effectiveness of the treatment is demonstrated. Also, the existence of an apparent trend affects the number of baseline data points. If the target behavior is found to be getting progressively worse—there are progressively more incidents of disruptive behavior, for example—fewer measurements are required to establish the baseline pattern. If, on the other hand, the behavior is naturally getting progressively better, at an acceptable rate, there is no point in introducing the treatment until, or unless, the behavior stabilizes and ceases to improve naturally. In general, however, three data points are usually considered the minimum number of measurements necessary to establish baseline stability.

Normally, the length of the treatment phase and the number of measurements taken during the treatment phase parallel the length and measurements of the baseline phase. If, for example, baseline stability is established after 10 observation periods, then the treatment phase will include 10 observation periods. There are reasons for varying phase length, however. In a study involving daily observations, for example, it might take 6 days to establish baseline, but 9 days to bring behavior to a criterion level.

The Single Variable Rule

An important principle of single-subject research is that only one variable at a time should be manipulated. In other words, as we move from phase to phase (any phase), only one variable should be changed, i.e., added or withdrawn. Sometimes an attempt is made to simultaneously manipulate two variables in order to assess their interactive effects. This practice is not sound and prevents us from assessing adequately the effects of either variable.

Types of Single-Subject Designs

Single-subject designs can be classified into three major categories: A-B-A withdrawal, multiple-baseline, and alternating treatments. A-B-A designs basically involve alternating phases of baseline (A) and treatment (B). Multiple-baseline designs entail the systematic addition of behaviors, subjects, or settings targeted for intervention. They are utilized mainly for situations in which baseline cannot be recovered once treatment is introduced, and for cases in which treatment cannot or should not be withdrawn once it is applied. An alternating treatments design involves the relatively rapid alternating of treatments for a single subject. Its purpose is to assess the relative effectiveness of two (or more) treatment conditions.

This section will describe the basic designs in each category and will present some common variations. The literature contains many additional variations.

A-B-A Withdrawal Designs

There are a number of variations of the basic A-B-A withdrawal design, the least complex of which is the A-B design. Since *withdrawal* refers to withdrawal of treatment and return to baseline, the A-B design is essentially a pre-withdrawal design, in the same sense that the one-shot case study (*XO*) group design is a pre-experimental design. Variations of the basic A-B-A withdrawal design not discussed in this section are used infrequently in educational research studies.

The A-B Design. Although this design is an improvement over the simple case-study approach, its internal validity is suspect. When this design is used baseline measurements are repeatedly made until stability is presumably established; treatment is then introduced and an appropriate number of measurements are made during treatment. If behavior improves during the treatment phase, the effectiveness of the treatment is allegedly demonstrated. We could symbolize this design as follows:

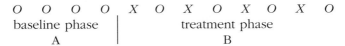

$$O \quad O \quad O \quad O \quad X \quad O \quad X \quad O \quad X \quad O \quad X \quad O$$

baseline phase	treatment phase
A	B

Of course the specific number of measurements (O) involved in each phase will vary from experiment to experiment. The problem is that we don't know if behavior improved *because of* the treatment or for some other reason. It is always possible that the observed behavior change occurred as a result of the influence of some other, unknown variable (such as the child's father returning to her or his home after a long marital separation), or that the behavior would have improved naturally without the treatment.

Additive designs, variations of the A-B design, involve the addition of another phase (or phases) in which the experimental treatment is supplemented with another treatment. An A-B-BC design, for example, might represent baseline (A), positive verbal reinforcement (B), and positive verbal reinforcement *plus* token reinforcement (BC). Such designs are usually used when an initial treatment is not satisfactory in terms of desired effects, and they suffer from the same validity problems as the basic A-B design.

The A-B-A Design. By simply adding a second baseline phase to the A-B design we get a much improved design, the A-B-A design. If the behavior is better during the treatment phase than during either baseline phase, the effectiveness of the treatment has presumably been demonstrated. Using familiar symbolism, we could represent this design in the following way:

$$O \quad O \quad O \quad O \quad X \quad O \quad X \quad O \quad X \quad O \quad X \quad O \quad O \quad O \quad O \quad O$$

baseline phase A	treatment phase B	baseline phase A

As an example, during an initial baseline phase we might observe on-task behaviors during 5 observation sessions. We might then introduce tangible reinforcement in the form of small toys for on-task behaviors and observe on-task behaviors during 5 observation periods in the treatment phase. Lastly, we might stop the tangible reinforcement and observe on-task behaviors during an additional 5 sessions. If on-task behavior was greater during the treatment phase, we would conclude that the tangible reinforcement was the probable cause.

The impact of positive reinforcement on the attending behavior of an easily distracted 9-year-old boy was clearly demonstrated in a study by Walker and Buckley which utilized the A-B-A design.[23] Initially, the subject exhibited a number of deviant behaviors, such as provoking other children, talking out of turn, and being easily distracted from tasks. Classroom observation indicated that he attended to assignments only 42% of the time. The subject was enrolled in an experimental class for behaviorally disordered children, and inappropriate behavior gradually

---

[23] Walker, H. M., & Buckley, N. K. (1968). The use of positive reinforcement in conditioning attending behavior. *Journal of Applied Behavior Analysis, 1,* 245–250.

decreased, with the exception of distractive behavior. Therefore, an individual reinforcement contingency program was developed. Prior to actual data collection, observer training was conducted until interrater reliability was .90 or above for 5 randomly selected time samples (10 minutes each) of attending behavior. Interrater reliabilities were calculated by a percent agreement method in which number of agreements was divided by the total number of time intervals. Interrater reliability was periodically checked throughout the experiment. During the initial baseline phase (A), percentage of attending behavior was recorded in 10-minute observation periods until a relatively stable pattern was observed (see Figure 11.6).

During the treatment phase B, the subject received points (160 points being exchangeable for a model of his choice) for time intervals of attending behavior. The time interval required for a point was gradually increased from 30 to 600 seconds (10 minutes). When the percentage of attending behavior was consistently at or near 100% for 10-minute observation periods, treatment was withdrawn. During the extinction phase (second A), percentage of attending behavior steadily decreased to near-baseline levels. Thus, the effectiveness of the reinforcement contingency program was convincingly demonstrated. Following the experiment, the boy was placed on a variable-interval reinforcement schedule and quickly achieved and maintained a high level of attending behavior.

In some cases, when it is feasible and ethical to do so, the treatment may actually be reversed during the second baseline phase. If such is the case, we refer to the design as a *reversal design*. In a reversal design the treatment phase is not followed by a control, baseline phase but rather by a treatment reversal phase. In other words, a condition that is essentially the opposite of the treatment condition

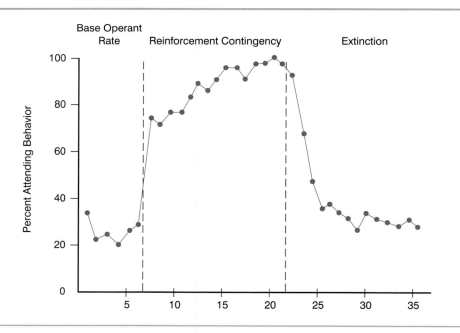

Figure 11.6. Percentage of attending behavior of a subject during successive observation periods in a study utilizing an A-B-A design. (Figure 2 from Walker and Buckley, 1968. Copyright 1968 by the Society for the Experimental Analysis of Behavior, Inc. Reproduced by permission.)

is implemented (think of it as an A-B-ᗺ design!). To use a former example, if the treatment phase (B) involved tangible reinforcement for on-task behavior, and a reversal design was used, then the treatment phase would be followed by a phase involving tangible reinforcement for *off-task* behavior. On-task behaviors would probably be dramatically reduced during this phase.

It should be noted that there is some terminology confusion in the literature concerning A-B-A designs. The A-B-A withdrawal designs are frequently referred to as reversal designs, which they are not, since treatment is generally withdrawn following baseline assessment, not reversed. A reversal design is but one kind of withdrawal design, representing a special kind of withdrawal.[24] When applicable, a reversal design typically produces more dramatic results than a nonreversal design. The major problem with this design is that its application is not very often feasible or desirable. If we were trying to reduce violent outbursts of behavior, for example, encouraging them for the sake of treatment reversal would not be advisable for obvious reasons.

The internal validity of the A-B-A design is superior to that of the A-B design. With the A-B design it is possible that behaviors would have improved without treatment intervention. It is very unlikely, however, that behavior would coincidentally improve during the treatment phase *and* coincidentally deteriorate during the subsequent baseline phase. The major problem with this design is an ethical one since the experiment ends with the subject *not* receiving the treatment. Of course if the treatment has not been shown to be effective, there is no problem. But if it has been found to be beneficial, the desirability of removing it is questionable.

A variation of the A-B-A design which eliminates this problem is the B-A-B design. As you have probably gathered, this design involves a treatment phase (B), a withdrawal phase (A), and a return to treatment phase (B). Although this design does yield an experiment that ends with the subject receiving treatment, the lack of an initial baseline phase makes it very difficult to assess the effectiveness of the treatment; in other words, we have no systematic data concerning the frequency of target behaviors prior to treatment. Some studies have involved a short baseline phase prior to application of the B-A-B design. Such a strategy, however, only approximates a better solution, which is application of an A-B-A-B design.

Before moving on to the A-B-A-B design, there is one other variation of the A-B-A design which should at least be mentioned, namely, the *changing criterion design*. In this design, a baseline phase is followed by successive treatment phases, each of which has a more stringent criterion for acceptable behavior level. Thus, each treatment phase becomes the baseline phase for the next treatment phase. The process continues until the final desired level of behavior is being achieved consistently. This design is useful for behaviors which involve step-by-step increases or decreases in frequency, completeness of assigned work, for example.

The A-B-A-B Design.   The A-B-A-B design is basically the A-B-A design with the addition of a second treatment phase. Not only does this design overcome the ethical objection to the A-B-A design, by ending the experiment during a treatment phase, it also greatly strengthens the conclusions of the study by demonstrating the effects of the treatment *twice;* the second treatment phase can of course be extended beyond the termination of the actual study, indefinitely if desired. If treatment effects are essentially the same during both B phases, the possibility that the effects are a result of extraneous variables, that just happened to be operating during the

---

[24] See, for example, Leitenberg, H. (1973). The use of single-case methodology in psychotherapy research. *Journal of Abnormal Psychology, 82,* 87–101.

treatment phase, is greatly reduced. The A-B-A-B design can be symbolized in the following manner:

$$O \ O \ O \ O \ X \ O \ X \ O \ X \ O \ X \ O \ O \ O \ O \ O \ X \ O \ X \ O \ X \ O \ X \ O$$

| baseline phase A | treatment phase B | baseline phase A | treatment phase B |

When application of this design is feasible, it provides very convincing evidence of treatment effectiveness.

The A-B-A-B design was utilized in a classic study conducted by Hall, Fox, Willard, Goldsmith, Emerson, Owen, Davis, and Porcia.[25] In a series of experiments, the disputing and "talking-out" behaviors of a number of students in special education classes and regular classes, from middle class and poverty areas, ranging from first grade to junior high school, were studied. As an example, in one experiment the talking-out behavior of a 10-year-old boy in a class for educable mentally retarded children was studied. His teacher indicated that his behavior greatly influenced the behavior of the other children. His talking-out behavior (instances when he spoke without the teacher's permission) was recorded during 15-minute periods. Behavior was observed by the teacher and also tape recorded. Another teacher made an independent tally of talking-out behavior, using the tape, as a reliability check. The correspondence between the two tallies was 100% for all phases of the experiment. The four phases of the experiment were as follows:

> Baseline (A): The teacher responded as usual to talking-out behavior. Talking-out behavior was recorded during a 15-minute period for 5 consecutive days (see Figure 11.7).

> Treatment (B): For the next 5 days the teacher ignored the subject when he exhibited talking-out behavior and paid him special attention when he was quiet and productive. As Figure 11.7 indicates, talking-out behavior had decreased to zero by the fourth day of the treatment phase (session 9).

> Baseline 2(A): The teacher again responded to talking-out behavior and ceased paying special attention to quiet, productive behavior. Talking-out behavior increased to its original level.

> Treatment 2(B): Treatment conditions were reinstated and talking-out behavior again decreased to zero by the fourth session of this phase (session 19).

Thus the effectiveness of paying attention only to appropriate behaviors was demonstrated twice. Note that if the experiment had ended after the second baseline phase (baseline$_2$), the design would have been an A-B-A design.

An interesting variation of the A-B-A-B design, which is used mainly when treatment involves reinforcement techniques, is the A-B-C-B design. The purpose of this design is to control for improvements in behavior which might result because the subject is receiving special attention (remember the Hawthorne effect?). For example, suppose the treatment, B, was reinforcement in the form of points, awarded contingent on the completion of assigned tasks. With the basic A-B-A-B design, the experiment would involve baseline, contingent reinforcement, baseline, and contingent reinforcement phases. With the A-B-C-B design, the C phase would involve an amount of noncontingent reinforcement equal to the amount of contingent rein-

[25]Hall, R. V., Fox, R., Willard, D., Goldsmith, L., Emerson, M., Owen, M., Davis, F., & Porcia, E. (1971). The teacher as observer and experimenter in the modification of disputing and talking-out behaviors. *Journal of Applied Behavior Analysis, 4,* 141–149.

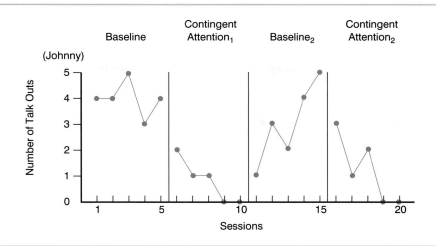

Figure 11.7. A record of talking-out behavior of an educable mentally retarded student. Baseline—before experimental conditions. Contingent Teacher Attention₁— systematic ignoring of talking-out and increased teacher attention to appropriate behavior. Baseline₂—reinstatement of teacher attention to talking-out behavior. Contingent Teacher Attention₂—return to systematic ignoring of talking-out and increased attention to appropriate behavior. (Figure 2 from Hall, Fox, Willard, Goldsmith, Emerson, Owen, Davis, and Porcia, 1971. Copyright 1971 by the Society for the Experimental Analysis of Behavior, Inc. Reproduced by permission.)

forcement received during B phases. In other words, the subject would receive an equal amount of attention, but not for exhibiting the desired behavior.

Multiple-Baseline Designs

Multiple-baseline designs are used when the only alternative would be an A-B design. This is the case when the treatment is such that it is not possible to withdraw it and return to baseline or when it would not be ethical to withdraw it or reverse it. In the most extreme case, the treatment might be some kind of surgical procedure. Multiple-baseline designs are also used when treatment can be withdrawn but the effects of the treatment "carry over" into the second baseline phase and a return to baseline conditions is difficult or impossible. The effects of many treatments do not disappear when treatment is removed (see Figure 11.3, pattern C): Actually, in many cases it is highly desirable if they do not. Reinforcement techniques, for example, are designed to produce improved behavior that will be maintained when external reinforcements are withdrawn.

There are three basic types of multiple-baseline designs: across behaviors, across subjects, and across settings designs. With a multiple-baseline design, instead of collecting baseline data for one target behavior for one subject in one setting, we collect data on several behaviors for one subject, one behavior for several subjects, or one behavior and one subject in several settings. We then systematically, over a period of time, apply the treatment to each behavior (or subject, or setting) one at a time until all behaviors (or subjects, or settings) are under treatment. If measured performance improves in each case only after treatment is introduced, then the treatment is judged to be effective. There are, of course, variations which can be applied. We might, for example, collect data on one target behavior for several subjects in several settings. In this case, performance for the group of subjects in each setting would be summed or averaged, and results would be presented for the group as well as for each individual.

When applying treatments across behaviors, it is important that the behaviors be able to be treated independently. If we apply treatment to behavior 1, for example, the other target behaviors should remain at baseline levels. If other behaviors change when behavior 1 is treated, the design is not valid for assessing treatment effectiveness. When applying treatment across subjects, the subjects should be as similar as possible (matched on key variables such as age and sex), and the experimental setting should be as identical as possible for each subject. When applying treatment across settings, it is preferable that the settings be natural, although that is not always possible. We might, for example, systematically apply treatment (e.g., tangible reinforcement) to successive class periods. Or we might apply treatment first in a clinical setting, then at school, and then at home. Sometimes it is necessary, due to the nature of the target behavior, to evaluate the treatment in a contrived, or simulation, setting. The target behavior, for example, may be an important one, but one which does not occur naturally very often (recall the discussion in Chapter 8 on simulation observation). If we are teaching a retarded child how to behave in various emergency situations (e.g., fires, injuries, intruders), for example, simulated settings may be the only feasible approach.

Application of the multiple-baseline designs might be symbolized as follows:

Case 1	**Case 2**	**Case 3**
behavior 1 A-B-B-B-B	subject 1 A-B-B-B-B	setting 1 A-B-B-B-B
behavior 2 A-A-B-B-B	subject 2 A-A-B-B-B	setting 2 A-A-B-B-B
behavior 3 A-A-A-B-B	subject 3 A-A-A-B-B	setting 3 A-A-A-B-B

The above would represent the situation in which the treatment, once applied, would not be withdrawn. We could also symbolize case 1 as follows:

behavior 1   *O O OXOXOXOXOXOXOXOXOXOXOXOXO*
behavior 2   *O O O O O OXOXOXOXOXOXOXOXOXO*
behavior 3   *O O O O O O O O OXOXOXOXOXOXOXO*

In this example, treatment was applied to behavior 1 first and then behavior 2 and then behavior 3 until all three behaviors were under treatment. If measured performance improved in each case only after treatment was introduced, then the treatment would be judged to be effective. We could symbolize cases 2 and 3 in the same manner. In all cases, the more behaviors, subjects, or settings involved, the more convincing the evidence is for the effectiveness of the treatment. What constitutes a sufficient *minimum* number of replications, however, is another issue (similar to the minimum number of subjects per group issue discussed in Chapter 4). While some investigators believe that four or more are necessary, three replications are generally accepted to be an adequate minimum.

In an interesting study by Bates, a multiple-baseline design was applied to an experimental group ($N = 8$) whose performance was also compared to that of a control group ($N = 8$).[26] The purpose of the study was to investigate the effectiveness of an interpersonal skill training package (i.e., verbal instruction, modeling, rehearsal, feedback, incentives, and homework) on the social skill performance of moderately and mildly retarded adults. Following initial assessments, the training

---

[26] Bates, P. (1980). Effectiveness of interpersonal skills training on the social skill acquisition of moderately and mildly retarded adults. *Journal of Applied Behavior Analysis, 13,* 237–248.

package was systematically applied to four social behaviors: introductions and small talk; asking for help; differing with others; and handling criticism. In two experiments, the targeted behaviors were approached in a different order. As Figure 11.8 shows, behavior improved in each case only after treatment. (The data in Figure 11.8 represent group means.) Some statistically significant differences were also found in favor of the experimental group. Although results do support the effectiveness of the treatment package, it should be noted that the study would have been strengthened if the baseline phase for introductions and small talk, and the treatment phase for handling criticism, had included at least three data points (especially given the downward trend of the latter). Also, as mentioned previously, results for individuals are expected to be presented in addition to group results. In the actual publication reporting the research, the author did indicate that individual multiple-baseline graphic displays for all experimental subjects are available upon request.[27]

While multiple-baseline designs are generally used when there is a problem with returning to baseline conditions, that is, baseline levels are not recoverable, they can be used very effectively for situations in which baseline is recoverable. We could, for example, target talking-out behavior, out-of-seat behavior, and aggressive

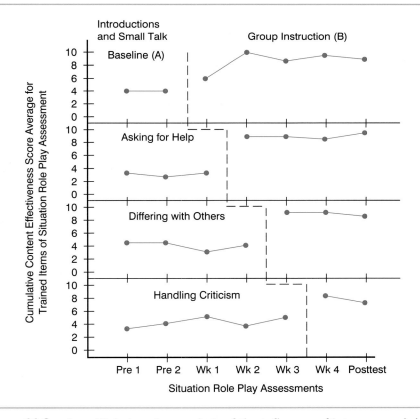

Figure 11.8. A multiple-baseline analysis of the influence of interpersonal skills training on Exp. 1's cumulative content effectiveness score across four social skill areas. (Figure 1 from Bates, 1980. Copyright 1980 by the Society for the Experimental Analysis of Behavior, Inc. Reproduced by permission.)

---

[27] Available from Paul Bates, Department of Special Education, Southern Illinois University, Carbondale, IL 62901.

behavior. It would be possible to return to baseline conditions with these behaviors. If we applied an A-B-A design within a multiple-baseline framework, the result could be symbolized as follows:

talking-out behavior	A-B-A-A-A
out-of-seat behavior	A-A-B-A-A
aggressive behavior	A-A-A-B-A

OR

talking-out behavior	O O OXOXOXO O O O O O O O O O
out-of-seat behavior	O O O O O OXOXOXO O O O O O O
aggressive behavior	O O O O O O O O OXOXOXO O O O

Such a design would combine the best features of an A-B-A design and a multiple-baseline design and would provide very convincing evidence regarding treatment effects. In essence it would represent three replications of an A-B-A experiment. Whenever baseline is recoverable and there are no carry-over effects, any of the A-B-A designs can be applied within a multiple-baseline framework.

Alternating Treatments Design

The number of experiments using an alternating treatments design has been steadily increasing since the late seventies. The main reason for this increase is the fact that the design currently represents the only valid approach to assessing the relative effectiveness of two (or more) treatments, within a single-subject context. Traditionally, comparative effectiveness has been studied using a group comparison design, such as the pretest-posttest control group design. The fact that a particular treatment is more effective for an identified group (or groups), however, tells us nothing concerning its effectiveness for any individual; the alternating treatments design serves this purpose.

In the literature, the alternating treatments design is referred to using a number of different terms: multiple schedule design, multi-element baseline design, multi-element manipulation design, randomization design, and simultaneous treatment design. There is some consensus, however, that "alternating treatments" most accurately describes the nature of the design. The *alternating treatments design* involves pretty much what it sounds like it involves—the relatively rapid alternation of treatments for a single subject. The qualifier "relatively" is attached to "rapid" because alternation does not *necessarily* occur within fixed intervals of time such as an hour, or even a day. If a child with behavior problems were to see a therapist every Tuesday, for example, then on some Tuesdays he or she would receive one treatment (e.g., verbal reinforcement), and on other Tuesdays another treatment (e.g., tangible reinforcement). As this example suggests, the treatments (let's refer to them as T_1 and T_2) are not typically alternated in a T_1-T_2-T_1-T_2 . . . fashion. Rather, to avoid potential validity threats such as ordering effects, treatments are alternated on a random basis, e.g., T_1-T_2-T_2-T_1-T_2-T_1-T_1-T_2 (see Figure 11.9). Figure 11.9 illustrates a situation for which treatment T_2 appears to be more effective *for the subject of the study;* determining whether it would be more effective for other subjects would require replication. Through visual analysis we can see that the data points are consistently higher for treatment T_2 than for T_1.

This design has several pluses which make it attractive to investigators. First, no withdrawal is necessary; thus, if one treatment is found to be more effective, it may be continued beyond the termination of the experiment. Incidentally, this design may also be used to alternate treatment and no-treatment conditions, also with the

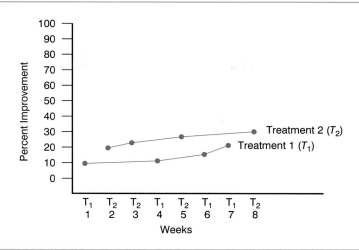

Figure 11.9. Hypothetical example of an alternating treatments design comparing treatments T_1 and T_2. (Figure 8-1, p. 254 from Barlow and Hersen, 1992. Copyright 1992 by Allyn & Bacon. Reproduced by permission.)

advantage of not having to withdraw an effective treatment. Second, no baseline phase is necessary since we are usually attempting to determine which treatment is more effective, not whether a treatment is better than no treatment. For the case where we are alternating treatment and no-treatment, baseline (no-treatment) phases are incorporated into the design on a random basis. The above advantages contribute to another major advantage, namely, that a number of treatments can be studied more quickly and efficiently than with other designs. One potential problem with this design, multiple-treatment interference (carryover effects from one treatment to the other), is believed by many investigators to be minimal; researchers have consistently observed such effects to be short-lived and to occur mainly when subjects have difficulty discriminating between treatments, which does not happen often.[28]

Data Analysis and Interpretation

Data analysis in single-subject research typically involves visual inspection and analysis of a graphic presentation of results. First, an evaluation is made concerning the adequacy of the design, e.g., were there a sufficient number of data points within each phase? Second, assuming a sufficiently valid design, an assessment of treatment effectiveness is made. The primary criterion is typically the *clinical significance* of the results, rather than the statistical significance. Effects which are small, but statistically significant, may not be large enough to make a sufficient difference in the behavior of a subject.[29] As an example, suppose the subject is an 8-year-old male who exhibits dangerous, aggressive behavior toward other children. A 5% reduction in such behavior, as a result of treatment, may be statistically significant, but it is clearly not good enough.

---

[28] See, for example, Blough, P. M. (1983). Local contrast in multiple schedules: The effect of stimulus discriminability. *Journal of the Experimental Analysis of Behavior, 39,* 427–437.

[29] See, for example, Kazdin, A. E. (1977). Assessing the clinical or applied importance of behavior change through social validation. *Behavior Modification, 1,* 427–452.

Kazdin, who has published extensively in the behavioral change journals, believes that statistical analyses may provide a valuable supplement to visual analysis.[30] They may be useful, for example, in identifying promising approaches in need of further refinement and study. There are a number of statistical analyses available to the single-subject researcher, including t and F tests (to be discussed in Chapter 14). Each design involves two or more phases which can be compared statistically. For example, if we apply an A-B-A-B design, behavior in the two A phases combined can be compared to performance in the two B phases combined using a t test.

Whether statistical tests should be used in single-subject research is currently a controversial issue. To date they have not been used much and their future application in single-subject research is uncertain. As Kazdin emphasizes, however, the key to sound data evaluation is judgment, and the use of statistical analyses does not remove this responsibility from the researcher. This principle is as important for group-oriented research, which regularly applies statistical techniques, as it is for single-subject research, which rarely does.

Replication

Replication is a vital part of all research and especially single-subject research since initial findings are generally based on one, or a small number, of subjects. The more results are replicated, the more confidence we have in the procedures that produced those results. Also, replication serves to delimit the generalizability of findings, i.e., provides data concerning the subjects, behaviors, and settings to which results are applicable. There are three basic types of replication of single-subject experiments: direct, systematic, and clinical. *Direct replication* refers to replication by the same investigator, with the same subject or with different subjects, in a specific setting (e.g., a classroom). Generalizability is promoted when replication is done with other subjects, matched as closely as possible on relevant variables, who share the same problem. When replication is done on a number of subjects with the same problem at the same location, at the same time, the process is referred to as *simultaneous replication;* while intervention involves a small group, results are presented separately for each subject.[31] When an effective approach is subsequently directly replicated at least three times, the next step is systematic replication. *Systematic replication* refers to replication which follows direct replication, and which involves different investigators, behaviors, or settings. Over an extended period of time, techniques are identified which are consistently effective in a variety of situations. We know, for example, that teacher attention can be a powerful factor in behavior change. At some point, enough data is amassed to permit the third stage of replication, clinical replication.

Clinical replication involves the development of treatment packages, composed of two or more interventions which have been found to be effective individually, designed for persons with complex behavior disorders. Autistics, for example, exhibit a number of characteristics, including apparent sensory deficit, mutism, and self-injurious behavior. Clinical replication would utilize research on each of

---

[30] Kazdin, A. E. (1992). Statistical analyses for single-case experimental designs. In D. H. Barlow & M. Hersen, *Single-case experimental designs: Strategies for studying behavior change* (Rev. 2nd ed., pp. 285–324). Des Moines, IA: Allyn & Bacon.

[31] See, for example, Fisher, E. B., Jr. (1979). Overjustification effects in token economies. *Journal of Applied Behavior Analysis, 12,* 407–415.

these to develop a total program, which would then be applied to a number of autistic individuals. Such research has, in fact, been carried out by Lovaas, Koegel, Simmons, and Long, an effort involving 13 autistic children.[32] Although the variation was large, all of the children showed at least some improvement. Results ranged from return to a normal classroom setting to continued institutionalization. Thus, clinical replication represents a very promising approach which is likely to become more effective as time goes by and the research base for such replications grows.

On the following pages an example of experimental research is presented. See if you can figure out which experimental design was used. Hint: Students were randomly assigned to one of three treatment groups. Also, don't be concerned because you don't understand the statistics; focus on the problem, the procedures, and the conclusions.

---

[32]Lovaas, O. I., Koegel, R., Simmons, J. Q., & Long, J. D. (1973). Some generalization and follow-up measures on autistic children in behavior therapy. *Journal of Applied Behavior Analysis, 5,* 131–166.

Effects of Word Processing on Sixth Graders' Holistic Writing and Revisions

GAIL F. GREJDA
Clarion University of Pennsylvania

MICHAEL J. HANNAFIN
Florida State University

ABSTRACT   The purpose of this study was to examine the effects of word processing on overall writing quality and revision patterns of sixth graders. Participants included 66 students who were randomly assigned to one of three revision treatments: paper and pencil, word processing, and a combination of the two techniques. Training in word processing was provided, and instruction was subsequently given during the 3-week study. The students were given a standard composition to revise and were also required to write and revise an original composition. Significant differences were found for both mechanical and organizational revisions in favor of the word-processing group. In addition, word-processing students tended to correct more first-draft errors and to make fewer new errors than their counterparts did. Although a similar pattern was found, no significant differences were discovered for holistic writing quality.

Interest in the potential of word processors to improve writing has grown substantially during the past decade. Various authorities have lauded the capability to increase writer productivity (Zaharias, 1983), to reduce the tediousness of recopying written work (Bean, 1983; Daiute, 1983; Moran, 1983, to increase the frequency of revising (Bridwell, Sirc, & Brooke, 1985; Daiute, 1986), and to improve both attitudes toward writing (Rodriguez, 1985) and the writing process (McKenzie, 1984; Olds, 1982). Some researchers have argued that word processors alter both individuals' writing styles and the methods used to teach writing (Bertram, Michaels, & Watson-Geges, 1985).

Yet, research findings on the effects of word processing have proved inconsistent (Fitzgerald, 1987). Some researchers have reported positive effects on writing (Daiute, 1985), whereas others have reported mixed effects (Wheeler, 1985). Although word processing seems to increase the frequency of revision, the revisions are often surface level and do little to improve the overall quality of composition (Collier, 1983; Hawisher, 1987). In some cases, word processing has actually hampered different aspects of writing (Grejda & Hannafin, in press; Perl, 1978).

However, comparatively little has been demonstrated conclusively. Attempts to study word processing have been confounded by both typing requirements and limited word-processing proficiency. Inadequate definition has also plagued word-processing research. Many studies have isolated only mechanical attributes of revision, such as punctuation, requiring only proofreading rather than sophisticated revision skills (Collier, 1983; Dalton & Hannafin, 1987). Other research has focused only on global writing measures, with little attribution possible for observed changes in writing quality (Boone, 1985; Woodruff, Bereiter, & Scardamalia, 1981–82). Both mechanical and holistic aspects of writing are important, but they are rarely considered concurrently (cf. Humes, 1983).

Although comparatively few studies have focused on young writers, the results have been encouraging. Daiute (1986) reported that junior high school students using word processors were more likely to expand their compositions, as well as to identify and correct existing errors, than were paper-and-pencil students. Likewise, word-processing students were more likely than paper-and-pencil students were to revise their language-experience stories (Barber, 1984; Bradley, 1982). Boone (1985) reported that the compositions of fourth, fifth, and sixth graders became increasingly sophisticated through revisions focusing on both mechanics and higher level organizations. In contrast, despite improving students' attitudes, word processing has failed to improve overall compositions based upon holistic ratings of writing quality (Woodruff, Bereiter, & Scardamalia, 1981–82).

The purpose of this study was to examine the effects of word processing on the holistic writing quality and revision patterns of sixth graders. We predicted that word processing would improve both the accuracy of revisions as well as the overall holistic quality of student writing.

Address correspondence to Gail F. Grejda, Education Department, 110 Stevens Hall, Clarion University of Pennsylvania, Clarion, PA 16214.

Methods

Subjects

The subjects included 66 sixth graders (23 girls and 43 boys), and 3 classroom teachers. The students were enrolled in a school in a rural university community. Overall language achievement of the participating students, based upon the Language Scale of the Stanford Achievement Test, was at the 79th percentile.

Preliminary Training

Prior to the study, the sixth-grade teachers and the students in word-processing groups received 1 hour of word-processing training during each of 5 days. The *Bank Street Writer* was used because of its widespread availability and popularity among elementary school teachers. The training included entering text, deleting and inserting characters, capitalizing letters, moving the cursor, centering, indenting, making corrections, moving and returning blocks of text, erasing and unerasing, saving, retrieving, and printing. In addition, the purpose and design of the study, as well as procedural information and materials required, were presented.

Revision Instruction

An hour of daily instruction on mechanical and organizational revisions was provided for 10 days of the 3-week study. The instruction reviewed previously taught revision rules commonly found in sixth-grade language books and focused on errors typical of those in the compositions of young writers.

The first 5 days included instruction on five mechanical error categories: capitalization, commas, punctuation, possessive nouns, and sentence structure. Daily lessons included rules for the error category under consideration, pertinent examples of each rule, and a paragraph containing numerous violations of the rules that were subsequently identified and revised by the students. During the next 5 days, the subjects focused on revising the following organizational errors, phrasing the main idea, adding relevant detail sentences, deleting irrelevant sentences, sequencing or ordering sentences, and, finally, applying the rhetorical devices vital to paragraph unity and coherence.

Original Writing Sample

All the students were allotted 60 min to write an original composition on a given topic. The task was to describe a planned trip itinerary to Canada, a topic based on a recently completed unit of study. The writing sample was obtained to provide a unique composition for each student, and it was subsequently used to identify and to make needed revisions in individual writing. All the students used paper and pencil to create the initial compositions.

Standard Composition

A standard composition was developed to determine each student's ability to identify and revise typical mechanical and organizational errors. The writing yielded a common metric from which revision comparisons could be made across students. The composition contained 57 mechanical errors and eight organizational writing errors. The errors, violations of rules found in typical sixth-grade language books, required the application of rules stressed during the daily lessons.

Instructional Groups

The students were assigned to one of three groups, depending on how revisions were made: exclusively with computer word processing (C-C); exclusively with paper and pencil (P-P); or a combination of the two techniques (C-P). All the treatment groups received identical revision instruction.

In the C-C group, the students used word-processing software during all phases of the study. That gorup examined the influence of continuous access to word processing on student editing, revising, and writing quality. The students in the P-P treatment group used paper and pencil to make all revisions on both compositions throughout the 10 days of instruction. That group approximated writing without the aid of the word processor. In the C-P treatment, the students used a word processor to revise the 10 daily lessons and paper and pencil to revise the compositions. That method examined the potential transfer of word-processing skills to non-computer writing and approximated the circumstances encountered when word processors were provided for some, but not all, of a student's writing needs.

Design and Data Analysis

In this study we used a one-way design, featuring three word-processing groups: pencil-pencil (P-P), computer-computer (C-C), and computer-pencil (C-P). Individual scores on the Stanford Achievement Test–Language Scale were used as a covariate in the analysis to adjust for potential prestudy writing differences. In addition, because of the relatively high prior achievement in the sample (only 4 students scored below the 50th percentile on the language scale) and the high correlation between writing and general language, the use of the standardized test scores as a covariate in the analysis permitted greater precision in isolating true treatment effects. The highly significant effect for the covariate, paired with the nonsignificant preliminary test for homogeneity of slopes, further supported the analysis.

A one-way multivariate analysis of covariance (MANCOVA), with the four composition subscale scores and the holistic writing rating, was run to test for treatment group effects. Analysis of covariance (ANCOVA) procedures were subsequently executed for each measure: a priori contrasts were constructed to test for differences between the C-C group and each of the other word-processing groups. The remaining scores were used to provide descriptive data related to revision strategies.

Procedures

Regularly assigned sixth-grade classroom teachers were presented an overview of the purpose and design of the study, procedural information, and required materials. The students were randomly assigned to one of the three treatment groups. The students and teachers in both word-processing groups (C-C and C-P) were then given word-processing training.

The students in each group were allotted 60 min to write their original composition. All students wrote the preliminary composition with pencil and paper. The compositions of students in the C-C group were subsequently entered electronically by a typist, because those students were required to revise the writing via word processing.

Next, instruction on revising mechanical and organizational writing error categories was provided. Each lesson included rules for the error category under consideration, pertinent examples of each rule, and a paragraph containing violations of the rules to be identified and revised by the students. After discussing the rules and examples of applications, the students revised the given paragraph, using their designated writing instrument. Upon completion, the students were given an errorless copy of the paragraph and were instructed to correct any existing errors. On subsequent days the subjects followed the same format, each day focusing on another of the mechanical and organizational error categories. During the study, the first author scheduled regular conferences with the classroom teachers to ensure compliance with current instruction topics as well as to preview upcoming lessons. In addition, the first author randomly rotated among the classes to ensure that planned activities were implemented as scheduled.

After the 10 daily lessons were completed, the students revised both the standard composition and the original composition. On the standard composition, students were allotted 60 min to revise mechanical errors in capitalization, punctuation, commas, possessive nouns, sentence structure, and organizational errors, including rephrasing the main idea, adding relevant detail sentences, deleting irrelevant sentences, sequencing sentences, and applying rhetorical devices vital to paragraph unity and coherence. None of the mechanical or organizational errors were cued in any way. The score for each measure was a percentage of the number of correct revisions to the total possible errors (57 mechanical, 8 organizational) on the standard composition.

The students were also provided 60 min to revise the mechanical and organizational errors on their original composition. The number of possible errors varied in each student's composition, so percentage correction scores were derived to account for differences in the number of mechanical and organizational errors. The score was a percentage of the correct revisions versus the total number of initial mechanical and organizational errors on the students' original composition.

Each original composition was then evaluated holistically for overall writing quality based on the procedures developed by Myers (1980) and Potkewitz (1984). Three trained composition instructors, experienced in both process writing and holistic scoring, served as raters; none of them were participants in the study. Each composition was evaluated "blind" by at least two of the raters by comparing the works to a rubric consisting of six competency levels ranging from lowest (1) to highest (6). If the two ratings were within one point of one another, the ratings were summed to yield a total rating score. If discrepancies of greater than one point were found, the third evaluator rated the composition independently, and the most discrepant rating of the three was discarded. Interrater agreement, based upon the percentage of rating pairs identical or within one point of one another, was .91. Discrepancies of more than one point in the initial ratings occurred on only 6 of the 66 compositions.

The students inadvertently introduced additional errors in their revisions, so new errors in the final compositions were also tallied. New errors, mechanical as well as organizational, were computed beyond those provided in the standard composition or generated by the students in the original composition. The errors were tallied according to the same criteria established for mistakes in the standard and original compositions.

Finally, revisions on both the standard and original compositions were classified to examine the nature of editorial revisions made by different writing groups. The instructors tallied word insertions and deletions, sentence insertions and deletions, sentences moved, sentence fragments and run-on sentences inserted, and sentence fragments or run-on sentences corrected.

All compositions were typed, printed, coded, and randomized to prevent rater bias. In addition, that step allowed the students to work with comparably "clean" copies, and equalized the time spent revising versus recopying: To isolate specific revision skills without the confounding of either excessive typing or manual recopying, we provided the students with typed versions of their work.

Results

The means for each of the subscales, adjusted for the influence of the covariate, are contained in Table 1. The one-way MANCOVA revealed a significant difference among word-processing groups, $F(2, 62) = 9.28$, $p < .001$. ANCOVA results, shown in Table 2, revealed a sig-

Table 1.—Adjusted Percentage Means for Composition Subscales

Source	C-C	C-P	P-P
Standard composition			
Mechanical revisions	74.86	68.59	68.23
Organizational revisions	81.14	58.82	66.18
Original composition			
Mechanical revisions	57.32	42.91	45.00
Organizational revisions	63.64	48.55	42.73

Table 2.—ANCOVA Source Data for Composition Subscales

Source	df	M	F	p<
Standard composition				
Mechanical revisions				
Covariate (prior achievement)	1	7,915.55	76.11	.0001
Writing group	2	459.58	4.42	.016
Error	62	104.00		
Organizational revisions				
Covariate (prior achievement)	1	8,463.83	13.62	.0001
Writing group	2	3,353.83	5.40	.007
Error	62	621.48		
Original composition				
Mechanical revisions				
Covariate (prior achievement)	1	5,156.74	6.27	.015
Writing group	2	1,590.89	1.93	nsd
Error	62	822.93		
Organizational revisions				
Covariate (prior achievement)	1	5,027.33	7.69	.007
Writing group	2	2,818.37	4.31	.018
Error	62	653.86		

nificant difference among treatment groups for all scales except for the mechanical revisions on the original composition. A priori contrasts for each significant difference indicated that the C-C students corrected a higher percentage of mechanical and organizational errors than the C-P or P-P groups did, on both the standard and original compositions (min. $p < .05$ in each case). No differences were found between the C-P and P-P groups for any of the subscales. In addition, although not statistically significant, the performance pattern for the mechanical revisions on original compositions was similar to the other subscales, with the C-C group performing best.

A profile of revision errors is shown in Table 3. The C-C word-processing group made fewer new mechanical and organizational errors than the other groups on both the standard and the original compositions. The C-C students also made fewer new errors on their own compositions. Paper-and-pencil and mixed-writing groups corrected a comparable percentage of organizational errors on both compositions.

Revision patterns, summarized in Table 4, suggest different strategies among the three groups. On the original composition, word-processing students inserted more words and sentences, moved more sentences, and corrected more sentence fragments or run-on sentences than did students in the remaining groups. On the standard composition, word-processing students were more likely to insert words and move sentences, but less likely to delete words, than their counterparts.

Students in all groups revised the standard composition more effectively than their original compositions; that was true for both mechanical and organizational revisions. Comparatively few new mechanical and organization errors were made by the word-processing students, whereas new errors were substantially more common for the other writing groups.

Although adjusted means for holistic ratings fell in the predicted direction, there were only marginal differences in

Table 3.—Frequency of New Errors Introduced During Final Revision

Revision type	C-C	C-P	P-P
Original			
Mechanical	12	20	39
Organizational	2	45	56
Standard			
Mechanical	0	7	12
Organizational	5	38	43

Table 4.—Revision Types for Original and Standard Compositions

Revision activity	C-C	C-P	P-P
Original composition			
Words inserted	167	52	31
Words deleted	13	9	17
Sentences inserted	121	47	64
Sentences deleted	9	14	3
Sentences moved	27	3	0
Sentence fragments/run-on sentences inserted	2	19	13
Sentence fragments/run-on sentences corrected	26	12	18
Standard composition			
Words inserted	9	0	0
Words deleted	0	15	23
Sentences inserted	0	1	0
Sentences deleted	59	43	38
Sentences moved	31	3	0
Sentence fragments/run-on sentences inserted	0	4	5
Sentence fragments/run-on sentences corrected	37	29	23

overall writing quality, $F(2, 62) = 2.31$, $p > .107$. Computer word-processing students (6.36) and the mixed-treatment group (6.27) were marginally higher than the paper-and-pencil group (5.00).

Discussion

Several findings warrant further discussion. Consistent with much research on revising (Bridwell, Sirc, & Brooke, 1985; Daiute, 1986), word-processing students performed consistently better than other students did. Those students were more successful in revising existing as well as original writing, and they made more revisions to their work. In the present study, face evidence for improving editing via word processing is strong.

Yet, consistent with other researchers (Collier, 1983; Hawisher, 1987), overall quality did not improve significantly. Though word-processing groups performed marginally better than the paper-and-pencil group did, reliable differences were not detected. Despite strong evidence that mechanical and organizational revisions improved significantly, holistic writing quality was only marginally affected. Overall quality improvements may require substantially more time to develop (Riel, 1984). Word processing may, in the absence of concerted efforts to offset the tendency, inadvertently direct proportionately more attention to structural than holistic aspects of writing. Structural skills are important and yield the most visible features of composition, but they do not, by themselves, ensure improvement in the holistic quality of compositions (Flower & Hayes, 1981).

Editing is a necessary, but not sufficient, skill for effective writing (cf. Hodges, 1982; Sommers, 1980). The conceptual aspects of holistic writing, although not diminished in our study by word processing, require more than simple mechanical and even organizational changes in written products (Hairston, 1986; Humes, 1983; Kintsch & van Dijk, 1978). Yet, word processors seem to bias students toward mechanical editing. A spelling or capitalization error is substantially more apparent than an error of logic, argumentation, or internal inconsistency. Process-writing advocates promote recursive methods in the teaching of writing—methods designed to promote writer-level problem solving in their expression. Though such goals are likely attainable and supportable through well-constructed writing-via-word-processing efforts, they are less likely to be supported directly in typical word-processing software. Mechanical improvements may be necessary to overall quality, but they are clearly insufficient when emphasized exclusively.

Contrary to the findings of some researchers (Bartlett, 1982), more revisions were made and a higher proportion of initial errors were detected on the standard composition than on the original composition. That finding is not surprising because the standard composition was essentially an editing task. On the other hand, the students were more likely to embellish their own compositions by inserting words and sentences. In this study, in which we used both types of composition, different revision patterns clearly emerged for student- versus instructor-generated compositions.

In contrast to the findings of others, the students in this study focused principally on in-text revisions, and they made few new additions during revisions. Daiute (1986) noted that word-processing students appended words to their text rather than making corrections within the text. In this study, however, word-processing students made both mechanical and organizational revisions throughout the text. They also corrected more first-draft errors and made fewer new errors than did students in the other treatment groups. The emphasis on identifying and revising in-text errors rather than on adding new text during the instructional phase of the study might account for that difference.

Various authorities have expressed concern that providing writing instruction exclusively via word processors may ultimately interfere with conventional writing (Keifer & Smith, 1983). The rationale has been that students develop writing strategies that are dependent upon technological capabilities of limited accessibility. The combined word-processing and paper-and-pencil group was designed to test the transfer of revision skills developed via word processing to traditional writing tools. Consistent with previous research (Grejda & Hannafin, in press), intermittent word processing neither improved nor impeded transfer to paper-and-pencil formats.

Several other aspects of the present study are noteworthy. The initial training provided to both students and teachers, paired with control of supporting instruction, permitted increased precision in localizing those effects reasonably attributable to word processing. The short-term effects of word processing appear most pronounced for structural revisions; the long-term effects on both structural and holistic aspects remain unproved. Likewise, examining revision skills on both standard and student-generated compositions allowed us to focus on both specific editing and the constructive aspects of process writing.

Considerable work is needed to refine both research methods and instructional practices. Keyboarding, although not a major issue in our study, remains a concern. Young students can be trained nominally, but few of them actually develop proficiency. Daiute (1983) suggested that sustained word-processing training, for as much as 1 year, may be needed before sufficient technical proficiency is acquired to improve writing. In addition, the potential antagonism between the structural versus holistic approaches to word processing is troublesome. Methods designed to optimize both are needed, but the present findings suggest that one often benefits at the expense of the other.

From a research perspective, we have not generated clear-cut answers but, rather, clarifications regarding the relevant questions and needed methods of study. Neither writing nor the tools available to improve writing are likely to be advanced appreciably through studies that simplify complex processes artificially or control everyday factors unrealistically. From an academic perspective, educators must temper the enthusiasm for technologies and tools of such high-face validity with the sobering reality that a word processor "does not a writer make."

REFERENCES

Barber, B. (1984). Creating Bytes of language. *Language Arts, 59,* 472–475.

Bartlett, E. J. (1982). Learning to revise. In M. Nystrand (Ed.), *What writers know* (pp. 345–363). New York: Academic Press.

Bean, H. C. (1983). Computerized word processing as an aid to revision. *College Composition and Communication, 34,* 146–148.

Bertram, B., Michaels, S., & Watson-Geges, K. (1985). How computers can change the writing process. *Language Arts, 2,* 143–149.

Boone, R. A. (1985). *The revision processes of elementary school students who write using a word processing computer program.* Unpublished doctoral dissertation. University of Oregon, Eugene, OR.

Bradley, V. (1982). Improving students' writing with microcomputers. *Language Arts, 59,* 732–743.

Bridwell, L., Sirc, G., & Brooke, R. (1985). Revising and computing: Case studies of student writers. In S. W. Fredman (Ed.), *The acquisition of written language: Response and revision* (pp. 172–194). Norwood, NJ: Ablex.

Collier, R. M. (1983). The word processor and revison strategies. *College Composition and Communication, 34,* 149–155.

Daiute, C. (1983). The computer as stylus and audience. *College Composition and Communication, 34,* 134–145.

Daiute, C. (1985). *Writing and computers.* Reading, MA: Addison-Wesley.

Daiute, C. (1986). Physical and cognitive factors in revising: Insights from studies with computers. *Research in the Teaching of English, 20,* 141–159.

Dalton, D., & Hannafin, M. J. (1987). The effects of word processing on written composition. *Journal of Educational Research, 80,* 338–342.

Fitzgerald, J. (1987). Research on revision in writing. *Review of Educational Research, 57(4),* 481–506.

Flower, L., & Hayes, J. (1981). A cognitive process theory of writing. *College Composition and Communication, 32,* 365–387.

Grejda, G. F., & Hannafin, M. J. (in press). The influence of word processing on the revisions of fifth graders. *Computers in the Schools.*

Hairston, M. (1986). *Different products, different processes: A theory about writing.* College Composition and Communication, *37,* 12.

Hawisher, G. (1987). The effects of word processing on the revision strategies of college freshmen. *Research in the Teaching of English, 21,* 145–159.

Hodges, K. (1982). A history of revision: Theory versus practice. In R. Sudol (Ed.), *Revising: New essays for teachers of writing* (pp. 24–42). Urbana, IL: National Council of Teachers of English.

Humes, A. (1983). Research on the composing process. *Review of Educational Research, 53,* 201–216.

Keifer, K., & Smith, C. (1983). Textual analysis with computers: Tests of Bell Laboratories' computer software. *Research in the Teaching of English, 17,* 201–214.

Kintsch, W., & van Dijk, T. (1978). Toward a model of text comprehension and production. *Psychological Review, 85,* 363–394.

McKenzie, J. (1984). Accordion writing: Expository composition with the word processor. *English Journal, 73,* 56–58.

Moran, C. (1983). Word processing and the teaching of writing. *English Journal, 72,* 113–115.

Myers, M. (1980). *A procedure for writing assessment and holistic scoring.* Urbana, IL: National Council of Teachers of English.

Olds, H. (1982). Word processing: How will it shape the student as writer? *Classroom Computer News, 3,* 24–26.

Perl, S. (1979). The composing process of unskilled college writers. *Research in the Teaching of English, 13,* 317–336.

Potkewitz, R. (1984). *The effect of writing instruction on the written language proficiency of fifth and sixth grade pupils in remedial reading programs.* Unpublished doctoral dissertation.

Riel, M. M. (1984). *The computer chronicles newswire: A functional learning environment for acquiring skills.* Paper developed for Laboratory of Comparative Human Cognition, San Diego, CA.

Rodrigues, D. (1985). Computers and basic writers. *College Composition and Communication, 36,* 336–339.

Sommers, N. (1980). Revision strategies of student writers and experienced adult writers. *College Composition and Communication, 31,* 378–388.

Wheeler, F. (1985). "Can word processing help the writing process?" *Learning, 3,* 54–62.

Woodruff, E., Bereiter, C., & Scardamalia, M. (1981–82). On the road to computer-assisted composition. *Journal of Educational Technology Systems, 10,* 133–148.

Zaharias, J. (1983). Microcomputers in the language arts classroom: Promises and pitfalls. *Language Arts, 60,* 990–995.

■ SUMMARY/CHAPTER 11
DEFINITION AND PURPOSE

1. In an experimental study, the researcher manipulates at least one independent variable, controls other relevant variables, and observes the effect on one or more dependent variables.
2. The independent variable, also referred to as the experimental variable, the cause, or the treatment, is that activity or characteristic believed to make a difference.
3. The dependent variable, also referred to as the criterion variable, effect, or posttest, is the outcome of the study, the change or difference in groups that occurs as a result of manipulation of the independent variable.
4. When well conducted, experimental studies produce the soundest evidence concerning hypothesized cause-effect relationships.
5. Predictions based on experimental findings (in contrast to those based on correlational studies) are more global and take the form "if you use approach *X* you will probably get better results than if you use approach *Y*."

The Experimental Process

6. The steps in an experimental study are basically the same as for other types of research: selection and definition of a problem, selection of subjects and measuring instruments, selection of a design, execution of procedures, analysis of data, and formulation of conclusions.
7. An experimental study is guided by at least one hypothesis that states an expected causal relationship between two variables.
8. In an experimental study, the researcher is in on the action from the very beginning; the researcher forms or selects the groups, decides what is going to happen to each group, tries to control all other relevant factors besides the changes that she or he has introduced, and observes or measures the effect on the groups at the end of the study.
9. An experiment typically involves two groups, an experimental group and a control group (although there may be only one group, or there may be three or more groups).
10. The experimental group typically receives a new, or novel, treatment, a treatment under investigation, while the control group either receives a different treatment, or is treated as usual.
11. The two groups that are to receive different treatments are equated on all other variables that might be related to performance on the dependent variable.
12. After the groups have been exposed to the treatment for some period of time, the researcher administers a test of the dependent variable (or otherwise measures it) and then determines whether there is a significant difference between the groups.

Manipulation and Control

13. Direct manipulation by the researcher of at least one independent variable is the one single characteristic that differentiates all experimental research from other types of research.

14. The different values or forms that the independent variable may take are basically presence versus absence (A versus no A), presence in varying degrees (a lot of A versus a little A), or presence of one kind versus presence of another kind (A versus B).

15. Control refers to efforts on the part of the researcher to remove the influence of any variable (other than the independent variable) that might affect performance on the dependent variable.

16. There are really two different kinds of variables that need to be controlled, subject variables, such as reading readiness, variables on which subjects in the different groups might differ, and environmental variables, variables such as learning materials, variables which might cause unwanted differences between groups.

THREATS TO EXPERIMENTAL VALIDITY

17. Any uncontrolled extraneous variables affecting performance on the dependent variable are threats to the validity of an experiment.

18. An experiment is valid if results obtained are due only to the manipulated independent variable, and if they are generalizable to situations outside of the experimental setting.

19. *Internal validity* refers to the condition that observed differences on the dependent variable are a direct result of manipulation of the independent variable, not some other variable.

20. *External validity* refers to the condition that results are generalizable, or applicable, to groups and environments outside of the experimental setting.

21. The term *ecological validity* is sometimes used to refer to the degree to which results can be generalized to other environments.

22. The researcher must strive for a balance between control and realism. If a choice is involved, the researcher should err on the side of too much control rather than too little.

23. Although lab-type settings are generally preferred for the investigation of theoretical problems, experimentation in natural, or field, settings has its advantages, especially for certain practical problems.

Threats to Internal Validity

History

24. History refers to the occurrence of any event that is not part of the experimental treatment but which may affect performance on the dependent variable.

Maturation

25. Maturation refers to physical or mental changes that may occur within the subjects over a period of time. These changes may affect the subjects' performance on the measure of the dependent variable.

Testing

26. Testing refers to improved scores on a posttest resulting from subjects having taken a pretest.

Instrumentation

27. Instrumentation refers to unreliability, or lack of consistency, in measuring instruments which may result in invalid assessment of performance.

Statistical Regression

28. Statistical regression usually occurs when subjects are selected on the basis of their extreme scores and refers to the tendency of subjects who score highest on a pretest to score lower on a posttest, and of subjects who score lowest on a pretest to score higher on a posttest.

Differential Selection of Subjects

29. Differential selection of subjects usually occurs when already formed groups are used and refers to the fact that the groups may be different before the study even begins, and this initial difference may at least partially account for posttest differences.

Mortality

30. Mortality, or attrition, is more likely to occur in longer studies and refers to the fact that subjects who drop out of a study may share a characteristic such that their absence has a significant effect on the results of the study.

Selection-Maturation Interaction, Etc.

31. The "etc." means that selection may also interact with factors such as history and testing, although selection-maturation interaction is more common. What this means is that if already formed groups are used, one group may profit more (or less) from a treatment or have an initial advantage (or disadvantage) because of maturation, history, or testing factors.

Threats to External Validity

32. Threats affecting "to whom," to what persons, results can be generalized, are referred to as problems of *population validity*.
33. Threats affecting "to what," to what environments (settings, dependent variables, and so forth) results can be generalized, are referred to as problems of *ecological validity*.

Pretest-Treatment Interaction

34. Pretest-treatment interaction occurs when subjects respond or react differently to a treatment because they have been pretested. The treatment effect is different than it would have been had subjects not been pretested.
35. Posttest sensitization refers to the possibility that treatment effects may occur only *if* subjects are posttested. In other words, the very act of

posttesting "jells" treatment influences such that effects are manifested and measured which would not have occurred if a posttest had not been given.

Multiple-Treatment Interference

36. Multiple-treatment interference can occur when the same subjects receive more than one treatment in succession; it refers to the carryover effects from an earlier treatment which make it difficult to assess the effectiveness of a later treatment.
37. Multiple-treatment interference may also occur when subjects who have already participated in a study are selected for inclusion in another, theoretically unrelated study.

Selection-Treatment Interaction

38. Selection-treatment interaction is similar to the "differential selection of subjects" problem associated with internal validity and also occurs when subjects are not randomly selected for treatments.
39. Interaction effects aside, the very fact that subjects are not randomly selected from a population severely limits the researcher's ability to generalize since representativeness of the sample is in question.
40. This nonrepresentativeness of groups may also result in a selection-treatment interaction such that the results of a study hold only for the groups involved and are not representative of the treatment effect in the intended population.
41. *Interaction of personological variables and treatment effects* occurs when actual subjects at one level of a variable react differently to a treatment than other, potential subjects in the population, at another level, would have reacted.
42. While selection-treatment interaction is a definite weakness associated with several of the poorer experimental designs, it is also an uncontrolled variable associated with the designs involving randomization. One's accessible population is often a far cry from one's target population, creating another population validity problem.

Specificity of Variables

43. Specificity is a threat to generalizability regardless of the experimental design used.
44. Specificity of variables refers to the fact that a given study is conducted: (1) with a specific kind of subject; (2) based on a particular operational definition of the independent variable; (3) using specific measuring instruments; (4) at a specific time; and (5) under a specific set of circumstances.
45. Generalizability of results may be affected by short-term or long-term events which occur while the study is taking place. This potential threat is referred to as *interaction of history and treatment effects*.
46. *Interaction of time of measurement and treatment effects* results from the fact that posttesting may yield different results depending upon when it is done.

47. To deal with the threats associated with specificity, the researcher must (1) operationally define variables in a way that has meaning outside of the experimental setting, and (2) be careful in stating conclusions and generalizations.

Experimenter Effects

48. Passive elements include characteristics or personality traits of the experimenter such as age, race, anxiety level, and hostility level (*experimenter personal-attributes effect*).
49. Active bias results when the researcher's expectations affect his or her behavior and hence outcomes (*experimenter bias effect*).
50. One form of experimenter bias occurs when the researcher affects subjects' behavior, or is inaccurate in evaluating their behavior, because of previous knowledge concerning the subjects.
51. Knowing which subjects are in which group may cause the researcher to be unintentionally biased in evaluating their performance.

Reactive Arrangements

52. Reactive arrangements refers to a number of factors associated with the way in which a study is conducted and the feelings and attitudes of the subjects involved.
53. In an effort to maintain a high degree of control for the sake of internal validity, a researcher may create an experimental environment that is highly artificial and hinders generalizability of findings to nonexperimental settings.
54. Another type of reactive arrangement results from the subjects' knowledge that they are involved in an experiment or their feeling that they are in some way receiving "special" attention (*Hawthorne effect*).
55. If for any reason control groups or their teachers feel threatened or challenged by being in competition with a new program or approach, they may outdo themselves and perform way beyond what would normally be expected (*John Henry effect*).
56. The *placebo effect* is sort of the antidote for the Hawthorne and John Henry effects. Its application in educational research is that all groups in an experiment should appear to be treated the same.
57. The *novelty effect* refers to increased interest, motivation, or participation on the part of subjects simply because they are doing something different.

GROUP EXPERIMENTAL DESIGNS

58. The validity of an experiment is a direct function of the degree to which extraneous variables are controlled.
59. This is what experimental design is all about—control of extraneous variables; good designs control many sources of invalidity, poor designs control few.
60. Subject variables include organismic variables and intervening variables.

61. Organismic variables are characteristics of the subject, or organism (such as sex), which cannot be directly controlled, but which can be controlled *for.*
62. Intervening variables are variables that intervene between the independent variable and the dependent variable (such as anxiety or boredom), which cannot be directly observed or controlled, but which can be controlled *for.*

Control of Extraneous Variables

63. Randomization is the best single way to attempt to control for many extraneous variables at the same time.
64. Randomization should be used whenever possible; subjects should be randomly selected from a population whenever possible, subjects should be randomly assigned to groups whenever possible, treatments should be randomly assigned to groups whenever possible, and anything else you can think of should be randomly assigned if possible!
65. Randomization is effective in creating equivalent, representative groups that are essentially the same on all relevant variables thought of by the researcher, and probably even a few not thought of.
66. Randomly formed groups are a characteristic unique to experimental research; they are a control factor not possible with causal-comparative research.
67. Certain environmental variables can be controlled by holding them constant for all groups.
68. Controlling subject variables is critical.

Matching

69. Matching is a technique for equating groups on one or more variables the researcher has identified as being highly related to performance on the dependent variable.
70. The most commonly used approach to matching involves random assignment of pair members, one member to each group.
71. A major problem with such matching is that there are invariably subjects who do not have a match and must be eliminated from the study.
72. One way to combat loss of subjects is to match less closely.
73. A related procedure is to rank all of the subjects, from highest to lowest, based on their scores on the control variable; each two adjacent scores constitute a pair.

Comparing Homogeneous Groups or Subgroups

74. Another way of controlling an extraneous variable is to compare groups that are homogeneous with respect to that variable.
75. As with causal-comparative research, a similar, but more satisfactory approach is to form subgroups representing all levels of the control variable.
76. If the researcher is interested not just in controlling the variable but also in seeing if the independent variable affects the dependent variable differently at different levels of the control variable, the best approach is to build the control variable right into the design and to analyze the results with a statistical technique called factorial analysis of variance.

Using Subjects as Their Own Controls

77. Using subjects as their own controls involves exposing the same group to the different treatments, one treatment at a time.

Analysis of Covariance

78. The analysis of covariance is a statistical method for equating randomly formed groups on one or more variables.
79. In essence, analysis of covariance adjusts scores on a dependent variable for initial differences on some other variable, such as pretest scores, IQ, reading readiness, or musical aptitude (assuming that performance on the "other variable" is related to performance on the dependent variable).

Types of Group Designs

80. A selected experimental design dictates to a great extent the specific procedures of a study.
81. Selection of a given design dictates such factors as whether there will be a control group, whether subjects will be randomly assigned to groups, whether each group will be pretested, and how resulting data will be analyzed.
82. Depending upon the particular combination of such factors represented, different designs are appropriate for testing different types of hypotheses and designs vary widely in the degree to which they control the various threats to internal and external validity.
83. From the designs that are appropriate and feasible, you select the one that controls the most sources of internal and external invalidity.
84. There are two major classes of experimental designs, single-variable designs, which involve one independent variable (which is manipulated), and factorial designs, which involve two or more independent variables (at least one of which is manipulated).
85. Single-variable designs are classified as pre-experimental, true experimental, or quasi-experimental, depending upon the control they provide for sources of internal and external invalidity.
86. Pre-experimental designs do not do a very good job of controlling threats to validity and should be avoided.
87. The true experimental designs represent a very high degree of control and are always to be preferred.
88. Quasi-experimental designs do not control as well as true experimental designs but do a much better job than the pre-experimental designs.
89. Factorial designs are basically elaborations of true experimental designs and permit investigation of two or more variables, individually and in interaction with each other.

Pre-Experimental Designs

The One-Shot Case Study

90. The one-shot case study involves one group which is exposed to a treatment (X) and then posttested (O).
91. None of the threats to validity that are relevant is controlled.

The One-Group Pretest-Posttest Design

92. This design involves one group which is pretested (*O*), exposed to a treatment (*X*), and posttested (*O*).
93. Although it controls several sources of invalidity not controlled by the one-shot case study, a number of additional factors are relevant to this design that are not controlled.

The Static-Group Comparison

94. The static-group comparison involves at least two groups; one receives a new, or unusual, treatment and both groups are posttested.
95. Since subjects are not randomly assigned to groups, and since there is no pretest data, it is difficult to determine just how equivalent they are.

True Experimental Designs

96. The true experimental designs control for nearly all sources of internal and external invalidity.
97. All of the true experimental designs have one characteristic in common that none of the other designs has—random assignment of subjects to groups.
98. Ideally, subjects should be randomly selected and randomly assigned; however, *to qualify as a true design, at least random assignment must be involved*.
99. Note too that all the true designs involve a control group.

The Pretest-Posttest Control Group Design

100. This design involves at least two groups, both of which are formed by random assignment; both groups are administered a pretest of the dependent variable, one group receives a new, or unusual, treatment, and both groups are posttested.
101. The combination of random assignment and the presence of a pretest and a control group serve to control for all sources of internal invalidity.
102. The only definite weakness with this design is a possible interaction between the pretest and the treatment which may make the results generalizable only to other pretested groups.
103. The best approach to data analysis is to simply compare the posttest scores of the two groups. The pretest is used to see if the groups are essentially the same on the dependent variable. If they are, posttest scores can be directly compared using a *t* test; if they are not (random assignment does not *guarantee* equality), posttest scores can be analyzed using analysis of covariance.
104. A variation of the pretest-posttest control group design involves random assignment of members of matched pairs to the groups, one member to each group, in order to more closely control for one or more extraneous variables.

The Posttest-Only Control Group Design

105. This design is exactly the same as the pretest-posttest control group design *except* there is no pretest; subjects are randomly assigned to groups, exposed to the independent variable, and posttested. Posttest scores are then compared to determine the effectiveness of the treatment.
106. The combination of random assignment and the presence of a control group serves to control for all sources of invalidity except mortality. Mortality is not controlled for because of the absence of pretest data on the subjects.

107. A variation of the posttest-only control group design involves random assignment of members of matched pairs to the groups, one member to each group, in order to more closely control for one or more extraneous variables.

The Solomon Four-Group Design

108. The Solomon four-group design involves random assignment of subjects to one of four groups. Two of the groups are pretested and two are not; one of the pretested groups and one of the unpretested groups receive the experimental treatment. All four groups are posttested.

109. This design is a combination of the pretest-posttest control group design and the posttest-only control group design, each of which has its own source of invalidity (pretest-treatment interaction and mortality, respectively). The combination of these two designs results in a design which controls for pretest-treatment interaction *and* for mortality.

110. The correct way to analyze data resulting from application of this design is to use a 2×2 factorial analysis of variance. The factorial analysis tells the researcher whether there is an interaction between the treatment and the pretest.

111. Which design is the "best" depends upon the nature of the study.

Quasi-Experimental Designs

112. Sometimes it is just not possible to randomly assign subjects to groups. When this occurs, however, quasi-experimental designs are available to the researcher. They provide adequate control of sources of invalidity.

The Nonequivalent Control Group Design

113. This design looks very much like the pretest-posttest control group design; the only difference is that the nonequivalent control group design does not involve random assignment.

114. The lack of random assignment adds a source of invalidity not associated with the pretest-posttest control group design—possible interactions between selection and variables such as maturation, history, and testing.

115. The researcher should make every effort to use groups that are as equivalent as possible.

116. If differences between the groups on any major extraneous variable are identified, analysis of covariance can be used to statistically equate the groups.

117. An advantage of this design is that since classes are used "as is," possible effects from reactive arrangements are minimized.

The Time-Series Design

118. The time-series design is actually an elaboration of the one-group pretest-posttest design. One group is repeatedly pretested, exposed to a treatment, and then repeatedly posttested.

119. If a group scores essentially the same on a number of pretests and then significantly improves following a treatment, the researcher has more confidence in the effectiveness of the treatment than if just one pretest and one posttest are administered.

120. History is still a problem, however, since something might happen between the last pretest and the first posttest, the effect of which might be confused with the treatment. Pretest-treatment interaction is also a validity problem.

121. While statistical analyses appropriate for this design are rather advanced, determining the effectiveness of the treatment basically involves analysis of the pattern of the test scores.
122. A variation of the time-series design, which is referred to as the multiple time-series design, involves the addition of a control group to the basic design. This variation eliminates history and instrumentation as threats to validity, and thus represents a design with no probable sources of internal invalidity.

Counterbalanced Designs

123. In a counterbalanced design, all groups receive all treatments but in a different order.
124. The only restriction is that the number of groups equals the number of treatments.
125. While subjects may be pretested, this design is usually employed when intact groups must be used and when administration of a pretest is not possible or feasible.
126. In order to determine the effectiveness of the treatments, the average performance of the groups for each treatment can be compared.
127. A unique weakness of this design is potential multiple-treatment interference that can result when the same group receives more than one treatment.
128. A counterbalanced design should really only be used when the treatments are such that exposure to one will not affect evaluation of the effectiveness of another.

Factorial Designs

129. Factorial designs involve two or more independent variables, at least one of which is manipulated by the researcher.
130. They are basically elaborations of true experimental designs and permit investigation of two or more variables, individually and in interaction with each other.
131. In education, variables do not operate in isolation.
132. The term "factorial" refers to the fact that the design involves several factors. Each factor has two or more levels.
133. The 2×2 is the simplest factorial design.
134. Both variables may be manipulated, but the 2×2 design usually involves one manipulated, or experimental, variable and one nonmanipulated variable; the nonmanipulated variable is often referred to as a control variable.
135. Control variables are usually physical or mental characteristics of the subjects such as sex, IQ, or math aptitude.
136. The purpose of a factorial design is to determine whether the effects of an experimental variable are generalizable across all levels of a control variable or whether the effects are specific to specific levels of the control variable. Also, a factorial design can demonstrate relationships that a single-variable experiment cannot.
137. If one value of the independent variable is more effective regardless of level of the control variable, there is no interaction.
138. If an interaction exists between the variables, different values of the independent variable are differentially effective depending upon the level of the control variable.

139. Theoretically, a researcher can simultaneously investigate any number of factors.
140. In reality, however, more than three factors are rarely used.

SINGLE-SUBJECT EXPERIMENTAL DESIGNS

141. Single-subject experimental designs are commonly referred to as single-case experimental designs.
142. Single-subject experimental designs are designs that can be applied when the sample size is one.
143. Single-subject designs are typically used to study the behavior change an individual exhibits as a result of some intervention, or treatment.
144. Basically, the subject is alternately exposed to a nontreatment and a treatment condition, or phase, and performance is repeatedly measured during each phase.
145. The nontreatment condition is symbolized as A and the treatment condition is symbolized as B.

Single-Subject Versus Group Designs

146. At the very least, single-subject designs are considered to be valuable complements to group designs.
147. Most experimental research problems require traditional group designs for their investigation. This is mainly because the results are intended to be applied to *groups,* e.g., classrooms.
148. There are a number of research questions for which traditional group designs are not appropriate for two major reasons. First, group comparison designs are frequently opposed on ethical or philosophical grounds since by definition such designs involve a control group that does not receive the experimental treatment. Second, application of a group comparison design is not possible in many cases because of the small size of the population of interest. Further, single-subject designs are most frequently applied in clinical settings where the primary emphasis is on therapeutic impact, not contribution to a research base.

External Validity

149. Results of single-subject research cannot be generalized to the population of interest as they can with group design research.
150. It is also true that the results of a study using a group design cannot be directly generalized to any individual within the group.
151. For single-subject designs, the key to generalizability is replication.
152. One generalizability problem associated with many single-subject designs is the possible effect of the baseline condition on the subsequent effects of the treatment condition.

Internal Validity

Repeated and Reliable Measurement

153. As with a time-series design, pretest performance is measured a number of times prior to implementation of the treatment or intervention. In single-

subject designs these sequential measures of pretest performance are referred to as baseline measures.

154. As a result of these measures taken over some period of time, sources of invalidity such as maturation are controlled for in the same way as for the time-series design.

155. Unlike the time-series design, however, performance is also measured at various points in time while the treatment is being applied. This added dimension greatly reduces the potential threat to validity from history.

156. One very real threat to the internal validity of most single-subject designs is instrumentation. Since repeated measurement is a characteristic of all single-subject designs, it is especially important that measurement of the target behavior, or performance, be done in exactly the same way every time, or as nearly the same as is humanly possible.

157. In single-subject studies it is critical that the observation conditions (e.g., location, time of day) be standardized.

158. If one observer makes all the observations, then intraobserver reliability should be estimated. If more than one observer is involved, then interobserver reliability should be estimated.

159. The nature and conditions of the treatment should be specified in sufficient detail to permit replication. If its effects are to be validly assessed, the treatment must involve precisely the same procedures every time it is introduced, either in the same study or in another study by another researcher.

Baseline Stability

160. The purpose of the baseline measurements is to provide a description of the target behavior as it naturally occurs *without* the treatment. The baseline serves as the basis of comparison for assessing the effectiveness of the treatment.

161. A sufficient number of baseline measurements are usually taken to establish a pattern. The establishment of a pattern is referred to as *baseline stability*.

162. Normally, the length of the treatment phase and the number of measurements taken during the treatment phase parallel the length and measurements of the baseline phase.

The Single Variable Rule

163. An important principle of single-subject research is that only one variable at a time should be manipulated.

Types of Single-Subject Designs

A-B-A Withdrawal Designs

The A-B Design

164. When this design is used baseline measurements are repeatedly made until stability is presumably established, treatment is then introduced and an appropriate number of measurements are made during treatment. If behavior improves during the treatment phase, the effectiveness of the treatment is allegedly demonstrated.

165. The problem is that we don't know if behavior improved *because* of the treatment or for some other reason.

166. *Additive designs,* variations of the A-B design, involve the addition of another phase (or phases) in which the experimental treatment is supplemented with another treatment.

The A-B-A Design

167. By simply adding a second baseline phase to the A-B design we get a much improved design, the A-B-A design.

168. In some cases when it is feasible and ethical to do so, the treatment may actually be reversed during the second baseline phase. If such is the case, we refer to the design as a *reversal design,* and a condition that is essentially the opposite of the treatment condition is implemented.

169. The internal validity of the A-B-A design is superior to that of the A-B design. With the A-B design it is possible that behaviors would have improved without treatment intervention. It is very unlikely, however, that behavior would coincidentally improve during the treatment phase *and* coincidentally deteriorate during the subsequent baseline phase.

170. The major problem with this design is an ethical one since the experiment ends with the subject *not* receiving the treatment.

171. The B-A-B design involves a treatment phase (B), a withdrawal phase (A), and a return to treatment phase (B).

172. Although the B-A-B design does yield an experiment that ends with the subject receiving treatment, the lack of an initial baseline phase makes it very difficult to assess the effectiveness of treatment.

173. In the *changing criterion design,* a baseline phase is followed by successive treatment phases, each of which has a more stringent criterion for acceptable behavior level.

The A-B-A-B Design

174. The A-B-A-B design is basically the A-B-A design with the addition of a second treatment phase.

175. Not only does this design overcome the ethical objection to the A-B-A design, by ending the experiment during a treatment phase, it also greatly strengthens the conclusions of the study by demonstrating the effects of the treatment *twice.*

176. The second treatment phase can be extended beyond the termination of the actual study, indefinitely if desired.

177. When application of the A-B-A-B design is feasible, it provides very convincing evidence of treatment effectiveness.

178. An interesting variation of the A-B-A-B design, which is used mainly when treatment involves reinforcement techniques, is the A-B-C-B design.

179. With the A-B-C-B design, the C phase would involve, for example, an amount of noncontingent reinforcement equal to the amount of contingent reinforcement received during B phases.

Multiple-Baseline Designs

180. *Multiple-baseline designs* are used when the only alternative would be an A-B design. This is the case when the treatment is such that it is not possible to withdraw it and return to baseline or when it would not be ethical to withdraw it or reverse it.

181. Multiple baseline designs are also used when treatment can be withdrawn but the effects of the treatment "carry over" into the second baseline phase and a return to baseline conditions is difficult or impossible.

182. There are three basic types of multiple-baseline designs: across behaviors, across subjects, and across settings designs.

183. With a multiple-baseline design, instead of collecting baseline data for one target behavior for one subject in one setting, we collect data on several behaviors for one subject, one behavior for several subjects, or one behavior and one subject in several settings. We then systematically, over a period of time, apply the treatment to each behavior (or subject, or setting) one at a time until all behaviors (or subjects, or settings) are under treatment. If measured performance improves in each case only after treatment is introduced, then the treatment is judged to be effective.

184. When applying treatment across behaviors, it is important that the behaviors be able to be treated independently.

185. When applying treatment across subjects, the subjects should be as similar as possible (matched on key variables such as age and sex), and the experimental setting should be as identical as possible for each subject.

186. When applying treatment across settings, it is preferable that the settings be natural, although this is not always possible.

187. In all cases, the more behaviors, subjects, or settings involved, the more convincing the evidence is for the effectiveness of the treatment. Three replications are generally accepted to be an adequate minimum.

188. Whenever baseline is recoverable and there are no carryover effects, any of the A-B-A designs can be applied within a multiple-baseline framework.

Alternating Treatments Design

189. The alternating treatments design currently represents the only valid approach to assessing the relative effectiveness of two (or more) treatments, within a single-subject context.

190. The *alternating treatments design* involves pretty much what it sounds like it involves—the relatively rapid alternation of treatments for a single subject.

191. To avoid potential validity threats such as ordering effects, treatments are alternated on a random basis, e.g., T_1-T_2-T_2-T_1-T_2-T_1-T_1-T_2.

192. This design has several pluses which make it attractive to investigators. First, no withdrawal is necessary. Second, no baseline phase is necessary. Third, a number of treatments can be studied more quickly and efficiently than with other designs.

193. One potential problem with this design, multiple-treatment interference (carryover effects from one treatment to the other), is believed by many investigators to be minimal.

Data Analysis and Interpretation

194. Data analysis in single-subject research typically involves visual inspection and analysis of a graphic presentation of results. First, an evaluation is made concerning the adequacy of the design. Second, assuming a sufficiently valid design, an assessment of treatment effectiveness is made.

195. The primary criterion is typically the *clinical significance* of the results, rather than the statistical significance. Effects which are small, but statistically significant, may not be large enough to make a sufficient difference in the behavior of a subject.

196. Statistical analyses may provide a valuable supplement to visual analysis.

197. There are a number of statistical analyses available to the single-subject researcher, including *t* and *F* tests.
198. The key to sound data evaluation is judgment, and the use of statistical analyses does not remove this responsibility from the researcher.

Replication

199. The more results are replicated, the more confidence we have in the procedures that produced those results.
200. Also, replication serves to delimit the generalizability of findings.
201. *Direct replication* refers to replication by the same investigator, with the same subject or with different subjects, in a specific setting (e.g., a classroom).
202. When replication is done on a number of subjects with the same problem, at the same location, at the same time, the process is referred to as *simultaneous replication;* while intervention involves a small group, results are presented separately for each subject.
203. *Systematic replication* refers to replication which follows direct replication, and which involves different investigators, behaviors, or settings.
204. *Clinical replication* involves the development of a treatment package, composed of two or more interventions which have been found to be effective individually, designed for persons with complex behavior disorders.

TASK 6 PERFORMANCE CRITERIA

The description of subjects should describe the population from which the sample was selected (allegedly of course!), including its size and major characteristics.

The description of the instrument(s) should describe the purpose of the instrument (what it is intended to measure), and available validity and reliability coefficients.

The description of the design should indicate why it was selected, potential threats to validity associated with the design, and aspects of the study that are believed to have minimized their potential effects. A figure should be included illustrating how the selected design was applied in the study. For example, you might say:

> Since random assignment of subjects to groups was possible, and since administration of a pretest was not advisable due to the reactive nature of the dependent variable (attitudes toward school), the posttest-only control group design was selected for this study (see Figure 1).

Group	Assignment	n	Treatment	Posttest
I	Random	25	Daily Homework	So-so Attitude Scale
II	Random	25	No Homework	So-so Attitude Scale

Figure 1. Experimental design.

The description of procedures should describe in detail all steps which were executed in conducting the study. The description should include: (1) the manner in which the sample was selected and the groups formed; (2) how and when pretest data were collected; (if applicable) (3) the ways in which the groups were different (the independent variable, or treatment); (4) aspects of the study that were the same or similar for all groups; and (5) how and when posttest data were collected. (*Note:* If the dependent variable was measured with a test, the specific test or tests administered should be named. If a test was administered strictly for selection-of-subjects purposes, that is, not as a pretest of the dependent variable, it too should be described.)

On the following pages, an example is presented which illustrates the performance called for by Task 6. (See Task 6 example.) Again, the task was prepared by the same student who developed previous task examples, and you should therefore be able to see how Task 6 builds on previous tasks. Note especially how Task 3, the research plan, has been refined and expanded. Keep in mind that Tasks 3, 4, and 5 will not appear in your final research report; Task 6 will. Therefore, all of the important points in those previous tasks should be included in Task 6.

Additional examples for this and subsequent tasks are included in the *Student Guide* which accompanies this text.

1

Effect of Interactive Multimedia on the Achievement
of 10th-Grade Biology Students

Method

Subjects

The sample for this study was selected from the total
population of 213 10th-grade students at an upper middle class
all-girls Catholic high school in Miami, Florida. The
population was 90% Hispanic, mainly of Cuban-American descent,
9% Caucasian non-Hispanic and 1% African-American. Sixty
students were randomly selected (using a table of random
numbers) and randomly assigned to two groups of 30 each.

Instrument

The biology test of the National Proficiency Survey
Series (NPSS) was used as the measuring instrument. The test
was designed to measure individual student performance in
biology at the high school level but the publishers also
recommended it as an evaluation of instructional programs.
Content validity is good; items were selected from a large
item bank provided by classroom teachers and curriculum
experts. High school instructional materials and a national
curriculum survey were extensively reviewed before objectives
were written. The test objectives and those of the biology
classes in the study were highly correlated. Although the
standard error of measurement is not given for the biology
test, the range of KR-20s for the entire battery is from .82
to .91 with a median of .86. This is satisfactory since the
purpose of the test was to evaluate instructional programs not
to make decisions concerning individuals. Catholic school
students were included in the battery norming which procedures
were carried out in April and May of 1988 using 22,616

students in grades 9-12 from 45 high schools in 20 states.

<u>Experimental Design</u>

        The design used in this study was the posttest-only control group design (see Figure 1). This design was selected because it provides control for most sources of invalidity and random assignment to groups was possible. A pretest was not necessary since the final science grades from June 1993 were available to check initial group equivalence and to help control mortality, a potential threat to internal validity with this design. Mortality, however, was not a problem as no students dropped from either group.

Group	Assignment	<u>n</u>	Treatment	Posttest
1	Random	30	IMM instruction	NPSS:B[a]
2	Random	30	Traditional instruction	NPSS:B

[a]National Proficiency Survey Series: Biology

<u>Figure 1.</u> Experimental design.

<u>Procedure</u>

        Prior to the beginning of the 1993-94 school year, before classes were scheduled, 60 of the 213 10th-grade students were randomly selected and randomly assigned to two groups of 30 each, the average biology class size; each group became a biology class. One of the classes was randomly chosen to receive IMM instruction. The same teacher taught both classes.

        The study was designed to last eight months beginning on the first day of class. The control group was taught using traditional methods of lecturing and open class discussions. The students worked in pairs for laboratory investigations

3

which included the use of microscopes. The teacher's role was one of information disseminator.

The experimental classroom had 15 workstations for student use, each one consisting of a laserdisc player, a video recorder, a 27 inch monitor, and a Macintosh computer with a 40 MB hard drive, 10 MB RAM and a CD-ROM drive. The teacher's workstation incorporated a Macintosh computer with CD-ROM drive, a videodisc player and a 27 inch monitor. The workstations were networked to the school library so students had access to online services such as Prodigy and Infotrac as well as to the card catalogue. Two laser printers were available through the network for the students' use.

In the experimental class the teacher used a videodisc correlated to the textbook. When barcodes provided in the text were scanned a section of the videodisc was activated and appeared on the monitor. The section might be a motion picture demonstrating a process or a still picture offering more detail than the text. The role of the teacher in the experimental group was that of facilitator and guide. After the teacher had introduced a new topic, the students worked in pairs at the workstations investigating topics connected to the main idea presented in the lesson. Videodiscs, CD-ROM's and online services were all available as sources of information. The students used HyperStudio to prepare multimedia reports which they presented to the class.

Throughout the study the same subject matter was covered and the two classes used the same text. Although the students of the experimental group paired up at the workstations, the other group worked in pairs during lab time thus equalizing any effect from cooperative learning. The classes could not meet at the same time as they were taught by

4

the same teacher, so they met during second and third periods. First period was not chosen as the school sometimes has a special schedule which interferes with first period. Both classes had the same homework reading assignments which were reviewed in class the following school day. Academic objectives were the same for each class and all tests measuring achievement were identical.

During the first week of May, the biology test of the NPSS was administered to both classes to compare their achievement in biology.

PART SEVEN

Data Analysis and Interpretation
Or . . .
The Word Is "Statistics," not "Sadistics"

Statistics is a set of procedures for describing, synthesizing, analyzing, and interpreting quantitative data. One thousand scores, for example, can be represented with a single number. As another example, you would not expect two groups to perform *exactly* the same on a posttest, even if they were essentially equal. Application of the appropriate statistic helps you to decide if the difference between groups is big enough to represent a true difference, not a chance difference.

Choice of appropriate statistical techniques is determined to a great extent by the design of the study and by the kind of data to be collected. The posttest-only control group design and the Solomon four-group design, for example, suggest different statistical analyses for investigating group differences. As with the design, statistical procedures and techniques are identified and described in detail in the research plan. Analysis of the data is as important as any other component of the research process. Regardless of how well the study is conducted, inappropriate analyses can lead to inappropriate conclusions. The complexity of the analysis is not an indication of its "goodness"; a simple statistic is often more appropriate than a more complicated one. The choice of statistical techniques is largely determined by the research hypothesis to be tested.

There are a wide variety of statistics available to the researcher. This part will describe and explain only those commonly used in educational research. The intent is that you be able to apply and interpret these statistics, *not* that you necessarily understand their theoretical rationale and mathematical derivation. Despite what you have heard, statistics is easy. In order to calculate the statistics to be described you only need to know how to add, subtract, multiply, and divide. That is all there is. All formulas, no matter how gross they may look, turn into arithmetic problems when applied to your data. The arithmetic problems involve only the operations of addition, subtraction, multiplication, and division; the formulas tell you how often, and in what order, to perform those operations. Now, you might be thinking, "H-m-m-m, what about square roots?" While it is true that many of the formulas involve square roots, you do not have to know how to find the square root of anything. Virtually all calculators have a square root button; you may not have noticed it before because it doesn't come in real handy for everyday calculator uses such as balancing your checkbook.

Even if you have a hangup about math and have not had a math course since junior high school, you will be able to calculate statistics; no calculus is required. The very hardest formula still requires arithmetic, maybe sixth-grade arithmetic if you have to divide by a big number, but arithmetic just the same. In fact, you do not even have to divide big numbers if you do not want to. You are *encouraged* to use a calculator! All you have to do is follow the steps as presented, and you cannot go wrong. You are going to be pleasantly surprised to see just how easy statistics is. Trust me.

The goal of Part Seven is for you to be able to select, apply, and correctly interpret analyses appropriate for a given study. After you have read Part Seven, you should be able to perform the following task.

■ TASK 7

Based on Tasks 2–6, which you have already completed, write the results section of a research report. Specifically:

1. Generate data for each of the subjects in your study.
2. Summarize and describe the data using descriptive statistics.
3. Statistically analyze the data using inferential statistics.
4. Interpret the results in terms of your original research hypothesis.
5. Present the results of your data analyses in a summary table.

If STATPAK, the microcomputer program which accompanies this text, is available to you, use it to check your work.

(See Performance Criteria, p. 525.)

CHAPTER 12

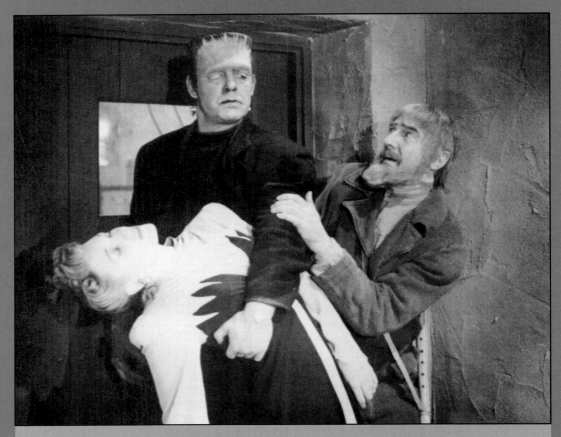

"Thus, with a ratio scale we can say that . . . Frankenstein is seven-fifths as tall as Igor (p. 422)."

Preanalysis Considerations

OBJECTIVES

After reading Chapter 12, you should be able to:

1. Identify and describe the four scales of measurement.

2. List three examples of each of the four scales of measurement.

3. List the steps involved in scoring
   (a) standardized tests and
   (b) self-developed tests.

4. Describe the process of coding data, and give three examples of variables which would require coding.

5. Define the following terms:
   (a) "hardware,"
   (b) "software,"
   (c) "hardcopy," and
   (d) "modem."

■ TYPES OF MEASUREMENT SCALES

Data for analysis result from the measurement of one or more variables. Depending upon the variables, and the way in which they are measured, different kinds of data result, representing different scales of measurement. There are four types of measurement scales: nominal, ordinal, interval, and ratio. It is important to know which type of scale is represented by your data since different statistics are appropriate for different scales of measurement.

There is a difference of opinion concerning where in the text this information should be presented. Some would prefer that it be included in Chapter 5, Selection of Measuring Instruments. This position makes perfect sense since various instruments represent various scales of measurement. Others, however, myself included (obviously!), believe that it should be included here, prior to discussion of statistics. The rationale for this position is that the topic relates more to choice of statistical techniques for data analysis than to concepts such as validity and reliability. Just keep in mind that all test items, whether from an achievement test or an attitude scale, represent one of the scales of measurement.

Nominal Scales

A nominal scale represents the lowest level of measurement. Such a scale classifies persons or objects into two or more categories. Whatever the basis for classification, a person can only be in one category, and members of a given category have a common set of characteristics. Categories may be referred to as *true* or *artificial*. True categories are categories into which persons or objects naturally fall, independently of the research study. Variables which involve true categories include:

sex (female versus male)

number of siblings (0 versus 1 versus 2 versus 3, etc.)

employment status of mother (full-time versus part-time versus unemployed)

preschool attendance (attended preschool versus did not attend preschool)

type of school (e.g., public versus private)

Artificial categories are categories which are operationally defined by the researcher. Variables which require artificial categories include:

height (e.g., tall versus short)

trait anxiety (e.g., high anxious versus low anxious)

IQ (e.g., high IQ versus average IQ versus low IQ)

family income (e.g., above average versus below average)

learning style (e.g., field independent versus field dependent)

For IQ, for example, a researcher might operationally define high IQ as an IQ greater than 115, average IQ as an IQ between 85 and 115, and low IQ as an IQ below 85. Unlike true category variables, with artificial category variables a researcher may create as many categories as she or he wishes. Thus, for IQ for example, a researcher might define 6 categories: A = below 71; B = 71–85; C = 86–100; D = 101–115; E = 116–130; F = over 130. When a nominal scale is used, the data simply indicate how many subjects are in each category. For 100 first graders, for example, it might be determined that 40 attended preschool and 60 did not.

For identification purposes, categories are sometimes numbered from 1 to however many categories there are, say 4. It is important to realize, however, that the category labeled 4 is only different from the category labeled 3; 4 is not more, or higher, than 3, only different from 3. To avoid confusion, it is sometimes a good idea to label categories with letters instead of numbers, in other words, A, B, C, D instead of 1, 2, 3, 4 (as illustrated above). While nominal scales are not very precise, occasionally their use is necessary.

Ordinal Scales

An ordinal scale not only classifies subjects but also ranks them in terms of the degree to which they possess a characteristic of interest. In other words, an ordinal scale puts the subjects in order from highest to lowest, from most to least. With respect to height, for example, 50 subjects might be ranked from 1 to 50; the subject with rank 1 would be the tallest and the subject with rank 50 would be the shortest. It would be possible to say that one subject was taller or shorter than another subject. Indicating one's rank in a graduating class, or expressing one's score as a percentile rank, are measures of relative standing that represent ordinal scales.

Although ordinal scales do indicate that some subjects are higher, or better, than others, they do not indicate how much higher or how much better. In other words, intervals between ranks are not equal; the difference between rank 1 and rank 2 is not necessarily the same as the difference between rank 2 and rank 3, as the example below illustrates:

Rank	Height
1	6'2"
2	6'1"
3	5'11"
4	5'7"
5	5'6"
6	5'5"
7	5'4"
8	5'3"
9	5'2"
10	5'0"

The difference in height between the subject with rank 1 and the subject with rank 2 is 1 inch; the difference between rank 2 and rank 3 is 2 inches. In the example given, differences in height represented by differences in rank range from 1 inch to 4 inches. Thus, while an ordinal scale results in more precise measurement than a nominal scale, it still does not allow the level of precision usually desired in a research study.

Interval Scales

An interval scale has all the characteristics of a nominal scale and an ordinal scale, but in addition it is based upon predetermined equal intervals. Most of the tests used in educational research, such as achievement tests, aptitude tests, and intelligence tests, represent interval scales. Therefore, you wll most often be working with statistics appropriate for interval data. When we talk about "scores," we are usually referring to interval data. When scores have equal intervals it is assumed, for example, that the difference between a score of 30 and a score of 40 is essentially the same as the difference between a score of 50 and a score of 60, and the difference between 81 and 82 is approximately the same as the difference between 82 and 83. And, similarly, for IQ, the difference between an IQ of 130 and an IQ of 140 (10 points) is considered to be the same as the difference between an IQ of 60 and an IQ of 70. Thus, with an interval scale we can say not just that Hornrim has a higher measured IQ than Norm, but also that Hornrim's IQ is 140 and Norm's is 100. Interval scales, however, do not have a true zero point. Such scales typically have an arbitrary maximum score and an arbitrary minimum score, or zero point. If an IQ test produces scores ranging from 0 to 200, a score of 0 does not indicate the absence of intelligence, nor does a score of 200 indicate possession of the ultimate intelligence. A score of 0 only indicates the lowest level of performance possible on that particular test and a score of 200 represents the highest level. Thus, scores resulting from administration of an interval scale can be added and subtracted, but not multiplied or divided. We can say that an achievement test score of 90 is 45 points higher than a score of 45, but we cannot say that a person scoring 90 knows twice as much as a person scoring 45. Similarly, a person with a measured IQ of 140 is not necessarily twice as smart, or twice as intelligent, as a person with a measured IQ of 70. For most educational measurement, however, such generalizations are not needed.

Ratio Scales

A ratio scale represents the highest, most precise, level of measurement. A ratio scale has all the advantages of the other types of scales and in addition it has a meaningful, true zero point. Height, weight, time, distance, and speed are examples of ratio scales. The concept of "no time," for example, is a meaningful one. Because of the true zero point, not only can we say that the difference between a height of 3'2" and a height of 4'2" is the same as the difference between 5'4" and 6'4", but also that a man 6'4" is twice as tall as a child 3'2". Similarly, 60 minutes is 3 times as long as 20 minutes, and 40 pounds is 4 times as heavy as 10 pounds. Thus, with a ratio scale we can say that Frankenstein is tall and Igor is short (nominal scale), Frankenstein is taller than Igor (ordinal scale), Frankenstein is 7 feet tall and Igor is 5 feet tall (interval scale), *and* Frankenstein is seven-fifths as tall as Igor. Since most physical measures represent ratio scales, but not psychological measures, ratio scales are not used very often in educational research.

A statistic appropriate for a lower level of measurement may be applied to data representing a higher level of measurement. A statistic appropriate for ordinal data, for example, may be used with interval data, since interval data possess all the characteristics of ordinal data and more. The reverse, however, is not true. A statistic appropriate for interval data cannot be applied to ordinal data since such a statistic requires equal intervals.

■ PREPARING DATA FOR ANALYSIS

Execution of a research study usually produces a mass of raw data resulting from the administration of one or more standardized or self-developed instruments or from the collection of naturally available data (such as grade point averages). Collected data must be accurately scored, if appropriate, and systematically organized in a manner that facilitates analysis.

Scoring Procedures

All instruments administered should be scored accurately and consistently; each subject's test should be scored using the same procedures and criteria. When a standardized instrument is used, the scoring process is greatly facilitated. The test manual usually spells out the steps to be followed in scoring each test (or answer sheet), and a scoring key is often provided. If the manual is followed conscientiously and each test is scored carefully, scoring errors are minimized. As an extra check it is usually a good idea to recheck all tests, or at least some percentage of them, say 25% (every fourth test).

Scoring self-developed instruments is more complex, especially if open-ended items are involved.[1] There is no manual to follow, and the researcher has to develop and refine a scoring procedure. Steps for scoring each item and for arriving at a total score must be delineated and carefully followed. If other than objective-type items (such as multiple-choice questions) are to be scored, it is advisable also to have at least one other person score the tests as a reliability check. Tentative scoring procedures should always be tried out beforehand by administering the instrument to a group of subjects from the same or a similar population as the one from which subjects will be selected for the actual study. Problems with the instrument or with scoring procedures can be identified and corrected before it is too late to do anything about them. The procedure ultimately used to score study data should be described in detail in the final research report.

If a test scoring service is available on your campus, and if your test questions can be responded to on a standard, machine-scorable answer sheet, you can save yourself a lot of time and increase the accuracy of the scoring process if you take advantage of the service. If tests are to be machine scored, answer sheets should be checked carefully for stray pencil marks and a percentage of them should be scored by hand just to make sure that the key is correct and that the machine is scoring properly. The fact that your tests are being scored by a machine does not relieve you of the responsibility of carefully checking your data before and after processing.

Tabulation and Coding Procedures

After instruments have been scored, the results are transferred to summary data sheets and/or data cards. Recording of the scores in a systematic manner facilitates examination of the data as well as data analysis. If analysis is to consist of a simple comparison of the posttest scores of two or more groups, data are generally placed in columns, one for each group, in ascending or descending order. If pretest scores are involved, similar, additional columns are formed. If planned analyses involve subgroup comparisons, scores should be tabulated separately for each subgroup. For example, in a study investigating the interaction between two types of mathematics instruction and two levels of aptitude (a 2×2 factorial design), four subgroups are involved, as shown in Table 12.1. The same is true for questionnaires. If the research hypotheses or questions are concerned with subgroup comparisons, responses to each should be tallied by subgroup. To use a former example, a superintendent might be interested in comparing the attitude toward unions of elementary-level teachers with those of secondary teachers. Thus, for a question such as, "Would you join a union if given the opportunity?" the superintendent would tally the number of "yes," "no," and "undecided" responses separately for elementary- and secondary-level teachers.

When a number of different kinds of data are collected for each subject, such as demographic information and several test scores, both the variable names and

---

[1] Projective tests also involve complex scoring procedures. The skills and experience required for valid scoring and interpretation of such tests are generally beyond the capabilities of beginning researchers.

Table 12.1

Hypothetical Results of a Study Based on a 2 × 2 Factorial Design

	Method A	Method B
High Aptitude	68	55
	72	60
	76	65
	78	70
	80	72
	84	74
	84	74
	85	75
	86	75
	86	76
	88	76
	90	76
	91	78
	92	82
	96	87
	50	60
Low Aptitude	58	66
	60	67
	62	68
	64	69
	64	69
	65	70
	65	70
	66	71
	67	71
	70	72
	72	75
	72	76
	75	77
	78	79

the actual data are frequently coded. The variable "pretest reading comprehension scores," for example, may be coded as PRC, and gender of subject may be recorded as "1" or "2" (male versus female). When a number of different analyses are to be performed, data cards (one card for each subject) may be used to facilitate analysis since they can be easily sorted and re-sorted to form the piles, or subgroups, required for each analysis. An alternative, and often more attractive, strategy is to use a computerized database management program. Use of the computer is particularly to be recommended if complex or multiple analyses are to be performed, or if a large number of subjects are involved. In these cases, coding of the data is especially important. Data for all variables and subjects are usually converted to numerical values when the data are entered into the database management program since long entries take up considerable space and contribute to typographical and spelling errors that mess up subsequent manipulations. The major advantage of database management programs is the capacity to rearrange data by subgroups and extract information without reentering all the data.

The first step in coding data is to give each subject an ID number. If there are 50 subjects, for example, they are numbered from 01 to 50. As this example illustrates, if the highest value for a variable is 2 digits (e.g., 50), then all represented values must be 2 digits. Thus, the first subject is 01, not 1. Similarly, IQ scores, for example, which range from, say 75 to 132, are coded 075 to 132. The next step is to make decisions as to how nonnumerical, or categorical, data will be coded and, if more than one person is involved in coding, to communicate coding rules. Categorical data include such variables as sex, group membership, and college level (e.g., sophomore). Thus, if the study involves 50 subjects, 2 groups of 25, then group membership may be coded "1" or "2" for "experimental" and "control" respectively. Categorical data also refer to the case where subjects choose from a small number of alternatives representing a wider range of values, and are most often associated with survey instruments. For example, teachers might be asked the following question:

12. How many hours of classroom time do you spend per
    week in nonteaching activities?
    (a) 0–5
    (b) 6–10
    (c) 11–15
    (d) 16–20

Responses might be coded (a) = 1, (b) = 2, (c) = 3, and (d) = 4.

Once the data have been prepared for analysis, the choice of statistical procedures to be applied is determined not only by the research hypothesis and design, but also by the type of measurement scale represented by the data.

■ USING A COMPUTER

If sample sizes are not large, if a limited number of variables are involved, and if relatively simple statistical analyses are to be performed, use of a calculator may be the most efficient approach to data analysis. Of course, if the opposite is true, the computer is a logical choice of an analysis tool. A good guideline for beginning researchers, however, is that you should not use the computer to perform an analysis that you have never done yourself by hand, or at least studied extensively. After you have performed several analyses of variance on various sets of data, for example, you will have the knowledge and comprehension necessary to effectively use the computer for subsequent analyses. Instructions for preparing data for computer processing will make sense to you and you will know what the resulting output should look like.

There is really no need for anyone to do an analysis without at least a calculator when they are so readily available. In fact, purchase of an inexpensive one (they sell for under $10) is an excellent investment for a beginning researcher. Besides making life easier for you, it also reduces the likelihood of computational errors. If you punch the correct numbers in, it almost always gives you the correct answer. At some point, after you have acquired experience performing various analyses, you might want to invest in a more sophisticated handheld calculator. For around $50 there are models which allow you to enter sets of data and select from a number of statistical keys, e.g., *SD*. In other words, by pushing the appropriate button, a desired analysis is performed on entered data and the result displayed.

If complex analyses are to be performed, however, or if a large number of subjects is involved, researchers usually use computers to do the calculations. Some people feel the same way about using computers that they feel about doing statistics—not good! As with statistics, however, it is a lot easier than it might seem. Rapid technological advances, and the development of "user friendly" equipment and programs, have made it possible for researchers to easily perform a wide variety of analyses. Using the computer may be as simple as selecting from a list of available statistics (a menu) and typing in your data as directed. It is definitely worth your time to learn how to use computers for data analysis (as well as a variety of other applications, such as word processing).

A computer system entails the use of hardware and software. *Hardware* refers to the actual equipment, the computer itself and related accessories such as printers. *Software* refers to the programs which give instructions to the computer concerning desired operations, i.e., which tell the computer what we would like it to do for us. Of course the computer has limited capabilities in terms of what it can do, but what it does do, it does very quickly and accurately. The computer, for example, cannot write your review of the literature (at least not yet!), but it can facilitate the task by quickly generating references and abstracts related to your topic. A computer system, like all systems, involves input, process, and output. In other words, you give information to the computer, it does as instructed, and gives you back what you asked for. In the case of statistical analysis, the input is your data and analysis instructions (your program); the process is the requested data analyses; and the output is the results of the analyses. Output that is printed out on paper is referred to as *hardcopy.* Many microcomputer programs present the question "Do you want a hardcopy?" on the screen, with instructions to type "Y" or "Yes" if you do, and "N" or "No" if you just want the results displayed on the screen.

There are two basic kinds of computers which are used for statistical analysis— mainframe computers, which are generally referred to as mainframes, and microcomputers, which are commonly called micros. Mainframes are very large and very fast, and are capable of processing and storing tremendous quantities of data simultaneously for many users. Most colleges and universities have a mainframe, more than likely an IBM or VAX system. The first step in using a mainframe is to select an appropriate program, one which performs desired analyses, from the statistical package available to you. One of the most useful and popular statistical packages, the one that is probably available at more university and college centers than any other, is some version of the *Statistical Package for the Social Sciences* (SPSS). SPSS includes programs for many statistics, from the most basic to the most sophisticated, frequently used in research studies. The good news concerning SPSS usage is that no mathematical or programming background is required, only the ability to follow instructions (although some instruction or assistance is usually initially necessary). If multiple analyses are to be performed over time on the same data, SPSS programs may be created, modified, and stored and may be reaccessed any number of times. For most analyses, the information you need for using SPSS will be included in manuals available in your campus bookstore.

More and more researchers (and lots of other people!), however, are obtaining micro, or personal, computers because they are relatively small and inexpensive, and yet they can perform many of the same tasks that mainframes do. The rapid growth of microcomputer technology has revolutionized the computer industry in general and computer data processing in particular. Given how far micro technology has come in a relatively short period of time, it is difficult to predict what the state of the art will be in even 5 years. However, at the time of the writing of this text, information is usually inputted into a micro by typing it in directly, by insertion of a disk, or by some combination of the two. A statistical program, for example, may be on a disk; once inserted into the micro, the program will appear on a screen with instructions for entering data using the keyboard. Output is typically displayed on the screen, and the user is usually given the option to get a hardcopy (i.e., to have the results printed out on paper). This operation, of course, requires that a printer be connected to the micro. Micros can also exchange information with mainframes through the addition of a modem. A *modem* permits telephone communication between two computers by converting computer language into audiotones. Thus, if you have a micro at home, and the required telephone hookup, you can access your university's mainframe as needed (cool, huh?).

Most researchers who invest in a computer come to wonder how they ever lived without it. A nice fringe benefit is that if you use your computer in your work, the purchase may actually be tax deductible! Additional good news, as mentioned, is that a lot of software, including word processing and statistical programs, is available and much of it is "user friendly," meaning that little or no experience or background is required or assumed for its use. STATPAK, the program which accompanies this text, was designed specifically for use with the text. It is menu driven and performs all of the statistics which are computed in Chapters 13 and 14. It is very easy to use, and it is free for the asking.[2]

SUMMARY/CHAPTER 12
TYPES OF MEASUREMENT SCALES

1. Data for analysis result from the measurement of one or more variables. Depending upon the variables, and the way in which they are measured, different kinds of data result, representing different scales of measurement.
2. It is important to know which type of scale is represented by your data since different statistics are appropriate for different scales of measurement.

Nominal Scales

3. A nominal scale represents the lowest level of measurement.
4. Such a scale classifies persons or objects into two or more categories.
5. Whatever the basis for classification, a person can only be in one category, and members of a given category have a common set of characteristics.
6. Categories may be referred to as *true* or *artificial*. True categories are categories into which persons or objects naturally fall; artificial categories are categories which are operationally defined by the researcher.

---

[2]Frisbie, L. H. (1992). STATPAK: Some common educational statistics [Computer software]. Columbus, OH: Merrill. Detailed instructions for using STATPAK are presented in the *Student Guide* and *Instructor's Manual* which accompany this text.

Ordinal Scales

7. An ordinal scale not only classifies subjects but also ranks them in terms of the degree to which they possess a characteristic of interest.
8. Intervals between ranks are not equal.

Interval Scales

9. An interval scale has all the characteristics of a nominal scale and an ordinal scale, but in addition it is based upon predetermined equal intervals.
10. Most of the tests used in educational research, such as achievement tests, aptitude tests, and intelligence tests, represent interval scales.
11. Interval scales do not have a true zero point.

Ratio Scales

12. A ratio scale represents the highest, most precise, level of measurement.
13. A ratio scale has all the advantages of the other types of scales and in addition it has a meaningful, true zero point.
14. Because of the true zero point, not only can we say that the difference between a height of 3'2" and a height of 4'2" is the same as the difference between 5'4" and 6'4", but also that a man 6'4" is twice as tall as a child 3'2".
15. Since most physical measures represent ratio scales, but not psychological measures, ratio scales are not used very often in educational research.
16. A statistic appropriate for a lower level of measurement may be applied to data representing a higher level of measurement; the reverse is not true.

PREPARING DATA FOR ANALYSIS

Scoring Procedures

17. All instruments administered should be scored accurately and consistently; each subject's test should be scored using the same procedures and criteria.
18. When a standardized instrument is used, the scoring process is greatly facilitated; the test manual usually spells out the steps to be followed in scoring each test (or answer sheet), and a scoring key is often provided.
19. Scoring self-developed instruments is more complex, especially if open-ended items are involved. Steps for scoring each item and for arriving at a total score must be delineated and carefully followed. If other than objective-type items are to be scored, it is advisable to also have at least one other person score the tests as a reliability check. Tentative scoring procedures should always be tried out beforehand by administering the instrument to a group of subjects from the same or a similar population as the one from which subjects will be selected for the actual study.
20. If a test scoring service is available on your campus, and if your questions can be responded to on a standard, machine-scorable answer sheet, you can save yourself a lot of time and increase the accuracy of the scoring process if you take advantage of the service.

Tabulation and Coding Procedures

21. After instruments have been scored, the results are transferred to summary data sheets and/or data cards.
22. If planned analyses involve subgroup comparisons, scores should be tabulated for each subgroup.
23. When a number of different kinds of data are collected for each subject, such as several test scores and biographical information, data are sometimes recorded on data cards, one card for each subject.
24. The card for each subject follows the same format, and both the variable names and the actual data are frequently coded.
25. An alternative, and often more attractive, strategy is to use a computerized database management program; data for all variables and subjects are usually converted to numerical values when the data are entered into the data management program.

USING A COMPUTER

26. If sample sizes are not large, if a limited number of analyses are involved, and if relatively simple statistical analyses are to be performed, use of a calculator may be the most efficient approach to data analysis; of course, if the opposite is true, the computer is a logical choice.
27. A good guideline for beginning researchers is that you should not use the computer to perform an analysis that you have never done yourself by hand, or at least studied extensively.
28. *Hardware* refers to the actual equipment, the computer itself and related accessories such as printers; *software* refers to the programs which give instructions to the computer concerning desired operations, i.e., which tell the computer what we would like it to do for us.
29. A computer system, like all systems, involves input, process, and output.
30. Output that is printed out on paper is referred to as *hardcopy*.
31. There are two basic kinds of computers which are used for statistical analysis—mainframe computers, which are generally referred to as mainframes, and microcomputers, which are commonly called micros.
32. One of the most useful and popular statistical packages, the one that is probably available at more university and college centers than any other, is some version of the *Statistical Package for the Social Sciences* (SPSS).
33. More and more researchers, however, are obtaining micro, or personal, computers because they are relatively small and inexpensive, and yet they can perform many of the same tasks that mainframes do.
34. Information is usually inputted into a micro by typing it in directly, by insertion of a disk, or by some combination of the two.
35. Output is typically displayed on the screen, and the user is usually given the option to get a hardcopy.
36. Micros can exchange information with mainframes through the addition of a modem; a *modem* permits telephone communication between two computers by converting computer language into audiotones.

"Looks bad, right? (p. 449)."

Descriptive Statistics

After reading Chapter 13, you should be able to:

1. List the steps involved in constructing a frequency polygon.

2. Define or describe three measures of central tendency.

3. Define or describe three measures of variability.

4. List four characteristics of normal distributions.

5. List two characteristics of
   (a) positively skewed distributions and
   (b) negatively skewed distributions.

6. Define or describe two measures of relationship.

7. Define or describe four measures of relative position.

8. Generate a column of 10 numbers each between 1 and 10 (in other words, make them up). You may use any number more than once. Assume those numbers represent scores on a posttest. Using these "scores," give the formula and compute the following (show your work):
   (a) mean,
   (b) standard deviation,
   (c) z scores, and
   (d) Pearson r (divide the column in half and make two columns of five scores each).

If STATPAK, the microcomputer program which accompanies this text, is available to you, use it to check your work. Isn't this fun?

■ TYPES OF DESCRIPTIVE STATISTICS

The first step in data analysis is to describe, or summarize, the data using descriptive statistics. In some studies, such as certain questionnaire surveys, the entire analysis procedure may consist solely of calculating and interpreting descriptive statistics. Descriptive statistics permit the researcher to meaningfully describe many, many scores with a small number of indices. If such indices are calculated for a sample drawn from a population, the resulting values are referred to as *statistics;* if they are calculated for an entire population, they are referred to as *parameters*.

The major types of descriptive statistics are measures of central tendency, measures of variability, measures of relative position, and measures of relationship. Measures of central tendency are used to determine the typical or average score of a group of scores; measures of variability indicate how spread out a group of scores are; measures of relative position describe a subject's performance compared to the performance of all other subjects; and measures of relationship indicate to what degree two sets of scores are related. Before actually calculating any of these measures, it is often useful to present the data in graphic form.

Graphing Data

As discussed previously, data are sometimes recorded on summary sheets, in columns, and placed in ascending order. Data in this form are easily graphed. Graphing data permits the researcher to see what the distribution of scores looks like. The shape of the distribution may not be self-evident, especially if a large number of scores are involved, and, as we shall see later, the shape of the distribution may influence our choice of certain descriptive statistics.

The most common method of graphing research data is to construct a frequency polygon. The first step in constructing a frequency polygon is to list all scores and to tabulate how many subjects received each score. If 85 10th-grade students were administered an achievement test, the results might be as shown in Table 13.1.

Once the scores are tallied, the steps are as follows:

1. Place all the scores on a horizontal axis, at equal intervals, from lowest score to highest.
2. Place the frequencies of scores at equal intervals on the vertical axis, starting with zero.
3. For each score, find the point where the score intersects with its frequency of occurrence and make a dot.
4. Connect all the dots with straight lines (see Figure 13.1).[1]

From Figure 13.1 we can see that most of the 10th graders scored at or near 85, with progressively fewer students achieving higher or lower scores. In other words, the scores appear to form a relatively normal distribution, a concept to be discussed a little later. This knowledge would be helpful in selecting an appropriate measure of central tendency.

Measures of Central Tendency

Measures of central tendency give the researcher a convenient way of describing a set of data with a single number. The number resulting from computation of a

---

[1]Computer software is readily available which will graph your data and compute all of the statistics to be discussed.

Table 13.1

Frequency Distribution Based on 85 Hypothetical Achievement Test Scores

Score	Frequency of Score
78	1
79	4
80	5
81	7
82	7
83	9
84	9
85	12
86	10
87	7
88	6
89	3
90	4
91	1
	Total: 85 students

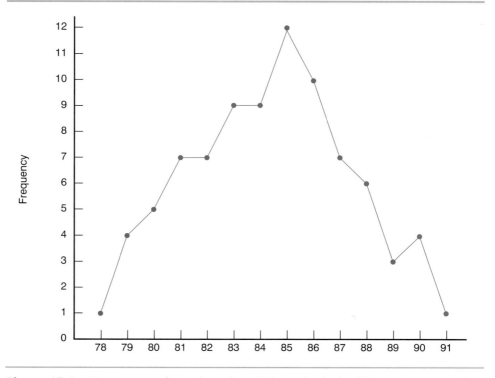

Figure 13.1.　Frequency polygon based on 85 hypothetical achievement test scores.

measure of central tendency represents the average or typical score attained by a group of subjects. The three most frequently encountered indices of central tendency are the mode, the median, and the mean. Each of these indices is appropriate for a different scale of measurement; the mode is appropriate for nominal data, the median for ordinal data, and the mean for interval or ratio data. Since most measurement in educational research represents an interval scale, the mean is the most frequently used measure of central tendency.

The Mode

The mode is the score that is attained by more subjects than any other score. For the data presented in Figure 13.1, for example, the mode is 85 since 12 subjects achieved that score. The mode is not established through calculation; it is determined by looking at a set of scores or at a graph of scores and seeing which score occurs most frequently. There are several problems associated with the mode, and it is therefore of limited value and seldom used. For one thing, a set of scores may have two (or more) modes, in which case it is referred to as bimodal. Another problem with the mode is that it is an unstable measure of central tendency; equal-sized samples randomly selected from the same accessible population are likely to have different modes. When nominal data are involved, however, the mode is the only appropriate measure of central tendency.

The Median

The median is that point in a distribution above and below which are 50% of the scores; in other words, the median is the midpoint (like the median strip on a highway). If there are an odd number of scores, the median is the middle score (assuming the scores are arranged in order). For example, for the scores 75, 80, 82, 83, 87, the median is 82, the middle score. If there is an even number of scores, the median is the point halfway between the two middle scores. For example, for the scores 21, 23, 24, 25, 26, 30, the median is 24.5; for the scores 50, 52, 55, 57, 59, 61, the median is 56. Thus, the median is not necessarily the same as one of the scores.

The median is only the midpoint of the scores and does not take into account each and every score; it ignores, for example, extremely high scores and extremely low scores. Two quite different sets of scores may have the same median. For example, for the scores 60, 62, 65, 67, 72, the median is 65; for the scores 60, 62, 65, 67, 89, the median is also 65. As we shall see shortly, this apparent lack of precision may be advantageous at times.

The median is the appropriate measure of central tendency when the data represent an ordinal scale. For certain distributions, the median may be selected as the most appropriate measure of central tendency even though the data represent an interval or ratio scale. While the median appears to be a rather simple index to determine, it cannot always be arrived at by simply looking at the scores; it does not always neatly fall between two different scores. For example, determining the median for the scores 80, 82, 84, 84, 84, 88 would require application of a relatively complex formula.[2]

---

[2]For an explanation of the procedure used to determine the median, see Downie, N. M., & Heath, R. W. (1983). *Basic statistical methods* (5th ed.). New York: HarperCollins.

The Mean

The mean is the arithmetic average of the scores and is the most frequently used measure of central tendency. It is calculated by adding up all of the scores and dividing that total by the number of scores. By the very nature of the way in which it is computed, the mean takes into account, or is based on, each and every score. Unlike the median, the mean is definitely affected by extreme scores. Thus, in certain cases, the median may actually give a more accurate estimate of the typical score.

In general, however, the mean is the preferred measure of central tendency. It is appropriate when the data represent either an interval or a ratio scale and is a more precise, stable index than both the median and the mode. If equal-sized samples are randomly selected from the same population, the means of those samples will be more similar to each other than either the medians or the modes. While the mode is almost never the most appropriate measure of central tendency when the data represent an interval or ratio scale, the median may be. In the situation described previously, in which there are one or more extreme scores, the median will not be the most accurate representation of the performance of the total group but it will be the best index of typical performance. As an example of this concept, suppose you had the following IQ scores: 96, 96, 97, 99, 100, 101, 102, 104, 155. For these scores, the measures of central tendency are:

mode = 96 (most frequent score)

median = 100 (middle score)

mean = 105.6 (arithmetic average)

In this case, the median clearly best represents the typical score. The mode is too low, and the mean is higher than all of the scores except one. The mean is "pulled up" in the direction of the 155 score whereas the median essentially ignores it. The different pictures presented by the different measures are part of the reason for the phrase "lying with statistics." And in fact, by selecting one index of central tendency over another one may present a particular point of view in a stronger light. In a labor-versus-management union dispute over salary, for example, very different estimates of typical employee salaries will be obtained depending upon which index of central tendency is used. Let us say that the following are typical of employee salaries in a union company: $12,000, $13,000, $13,000, $15,000, $16,000, $18,000, $45,000. For these salaries, the measures of central tendency are:

mode = $13,000 (most frequent score)

median = $15,000 (middle salary)

mean = $18,857 (arithmetic average)

Both labor and management could overstate their case, labor by using the mode and management by using the mean. The mean is higher than every salary except one, $45,000, which in all likelihood would be the salary of a company manager. Thus, in this case, the most appropriate, and most accurate, index of typical salary would be the median.

In research, we are not interested in "making cases" but rather in describing the data in the most accurate way. For the majority of sets of data the mean is the appropriate measure of central tendency.

Measures of Variability

Although measures of central tendency are very useful statistics for describing a set of data, they are not sufficient. Two sets of data that are very different can have identical means or medians. As an example, consider the following sets of data:

set A:	79	79	79	80	81	81	81
set B:	50	60	70	80	90	100	110

The mean of both sets of scores is 80 and the median of both is 80, but set A is very different from set B. In set A the scores are all very close together and clustered around the mean. In set B the scores are much more spread out; in other words, there is much more variation, or variability, in set B. Thus, there is a need for a measure that indicates how spread out the scores are, how much variability there is. There are a number of descriptive statistics that serve this purpose, and they are referred to as measures of variability. The three most frequently encountered are the range, the quartile deviation, and the standard deviation. While the standard deviation is by far the most often used, the range is the only appropriate measure of variability for nominal data, and the quartile deviation is the appropriate index of variability for ordinal data. As with measures of central tendency, measures of variability appropriate for nominal and ordinal data may be used with interval or ratio data even though the standard deviation is generally the preferred index for such data.

The Range

The range is simply the difference between the highest score and the lowest score in a distribution and is determined by subtraction. As an example, the range for the scores 79, 79, 79, 80, 81, 81, 81, is 2, while the range for the scores 50, 60, 70, 80, 90, 100, 110 is 60. Thus, if the range is small the scores are close together, whereas if the range is large the scores are more spread out. Like the mode, the range is not a very stable measure of variability, and its chief advantage is that it gives a quick, rough estimate of variability.

The Quartile Deviation

In "research talk" the quartile deviation is one-half of the difference between the upper quartile and the lower quartile in a distribution. In English, the upper quartile is the 75th percentile, that point below which are 75% of the scores; the lower quartile, correspondingly, is the 25th percentile, that point below which are 25% of the scores. By subtracting the lower quartile from the upper quartile and then dividing the result by two, we get a measure of variability. If the quartile deviation is small the scores are close together, whereas if the quartile deviation is large the scores are more spread out. The quartile deviation is a more stable measure of variability than the range and is appropriate whenever the median is appropriate. Calculation of the quartile deviation involves a process very similar to that used to calculate the median, which just happens to be the second quartile.[3]

The Standard Deviation

The standard deviation is appropriate when the data represent an interval or ratio scale and is by far the most frequently used index of variability. Like the mean, its

---

[3] For an explanation of the procedure used to determine the quartile deviation, see Downie & Heath.

counterpart measure of central tendency, the standard deviation is the most stable measure of variability and takes into account each and every score. In fact, the first step in calculating the standard deviation involves finding out how far each score is from the mean, that is, subtracting the mean from each score. Now (concentrate!), if we square each difference, add up all the squares, and divide by the number of scores, we have a measure of variability called variance. If the variance is small, the scores are close together; if the variance is large, the scores are more spread out. The square root of the variance is called the standard deviation and, like variance, a small standard deviation indicates that scores are close together and a large standard deviation indicates that the scores are more spread out.

If you know the mean and the standard deviation of a set of scores you have a pretty good picture of what the distribution looks like. An interesting phenomenon associated with the standard deviation is the fact that if the distribution is relatively normal (about which we will have more to say shortly), then the mean plus 3 standard deviations and the mean minus 3 standard deviations encompasses just about all the scores, over 99% of them. In other words, each distribution has its own mean and its own standard deviation that are calculated based on the scores. Once they are computed, 3 times the standard deviation added to the mean, and 3 times the standard deviation subtracted from the mean, includes just about all the scores. The number 3 is a constant. In other words, for any normal distribution of scores, the standard deviation multiplied by 3 and then added to the mean and subtracted from the mean will include almost all the scores in the distribution. The symbol for the mean is $\overline{X}$ and the standard deviation is usually abbreviated as *SD*. Thus, the above described concept can be expressed as follows:

$$\overline{X} \pm 3\,SD = 99+\% \text{ of the scores}$$

As an example, suppose that for a set of scores the mean $(\overline{X})$ is calculated to be 80 and the standard deviation (*SD*) to be 1. In this case the mean plus 3 standard deviations, $\overline{X} + 3\,SD$, is equal to $80 + 3(1) = 80 + 3 = 83$. The mean minus 3 standard deviations, $\overline{X} - 3\,SD$, is equal to $80 - 3(1) = 80 - 3 = 77$. Thus, almost all the scores fall between 77 and 83. This makes sense since, as we mentioned before, a small standard deviation (in this case *SD* = 1) indicates that the scores are close together, not very spread out.

As another example, suppose that for another set of scores the mean $(\overline{X})$ is again calculated to be 80, but this time the standard deviation (*SD*) is calculated to be 4. In this case the mean plus three standard deviations, $\overline{X} + 3\,SD$, is equal to $80 + 3(4) = 80 + 12 = 92$. In case you still do not see,

80 plus 1 *SD* = 80 + 4 = 84
80 plus 2 *SD* = 80 + 4 + 4 = 88
80 plus 3 *SD* = 80 + 4 + 4 + 4 = 92

Or, to explain it another way, 80 plus 1 *SD* = 80 + 4 = 84, plus another *SD* = 84 + 4 = 88, plus one more (the third) *SD* = 88 + 4 = 92. Now, the mean minus three standard deviations, $\overline{X} - 3\,SD$, is equal to $80 - 3(4) = 80 - 12 = 68$. In other words,

80 minus 1 *SD* = 80 − 4 = 76
80 minus 2 *SD* = 80 − 4 − 4 = 72
80 minus 3 *SD* = 80 − 4 − 4 − 4 = 68

Or, to explain it another way, 80 minus 1 *SD* = 80 − 4 = 76, minus another *SD* = 76 − 4 = 72, minus one more (the third) *SD* = 72 − 4 = 68. Thus, almost all the scores fall between 68 and 92. This makes sense since a larger standard deviation (in this case *SD* = 4) indicates that the scores are more spread out. Clearly, if you know the mean and standard deviation of a set of scores you have a pretty good idea of what the scores look like. You know the average score and you know how spread out, or how variable, the scores are. Thus, together they describe a set of data quite well.

The Normal Curve

The ±3 concept is valid only when the scores are normally distributed, that is, form a normal, or bell-shaped, curve. Most of you are probably familiar with the concept of grading "on the normal curve." When this is done, a certain percentage of students receive a grade of C, a smaller percentage receive Bs and Ds, and an even smaller percentage receive As and Es, or Fs. Such grading is based on the assumption (which may or may not be true in a given case) that the students' scores do indeed form a normal curve. Many, many variables, such as height, weight, IQ scores, and achievement scores, do yield a normal curve if a sufficient number of subjects are measured.

Normal Distributions

If a variable is normally distributed, that is, does form a normal curve, then several things are true:

1. Fifty percent of the scores are above the mean and 50% are below the mean.
2. The mean, the median, and the mode are the same.
3. Most scores are near the mean and the farther from the mean a score is, the fewer the number of subjects who attained that score.
4. The same number, or percentage, of scores is between the mean and plus one standard deviation ($\overline{X}$ + 1 *SD*) as is between the mean and minus one standard deviation ($\overline{X}$ − 1 *SD*), and similarly for $\overline{X}$ ± 2 *SD* and $\overline{X}$ ± 3 *SD* (See Figure 13.2).

In Figure 13.2, the symbol σ (the Greek letter sigma) is used to represent the standard deviation, that is, 1σ = 1 *SD,* and the mean ($\overline{X}$) is designated as 0 (zero). The vertical lines at each of the *SD* (σ) points delineate a certain percentage of the total area under the curve. As Figure 13.2 indicates, if a set of scores forms a normal distribution, the $\overline{X}$ + 1 *SD* includes 34.13% of the scores and the $\overline{X}$ − 1 *SD* includes 34.13% of the scores. Each succeeding standard deviation encompasses a constant percentage of the cases. Since the $\overline{X}$ ± 2.58 *SD* (approximately 2½ *SD*s) includes 99% of the cases, we see that $\overline{X}$ ± 3 *SD* includes almost all the scores, as pointed out previously.

Below the row of *SD*s is a row of percentages. As you move from left to right, from point to point, the cumulative percentage of scores which fall below each point is indicated. Thus, at the point which corresponds to − 3 *SD*, we see that only .1% of the scores fall below this point. The numerical value corresponding to + 1 *SD,* on the other hand, is a figure higher than 84.1% (rounded to 84% on the next row) of the scores. Relatedly, the next row, percentile equivalents, also involves cumulative percentages. The figure 20 in this row, for example, indicates that 20% of the scores fall below this point. While we will discuss percentiles and the remaining rows further as we proceed through this chapter, we will look at one more row at this time. Near the bottom of Figure 13.2, under Wechsler Scales, is a row labeled Deviation IQs. This row indicates that the mean IQ for the Wechsler

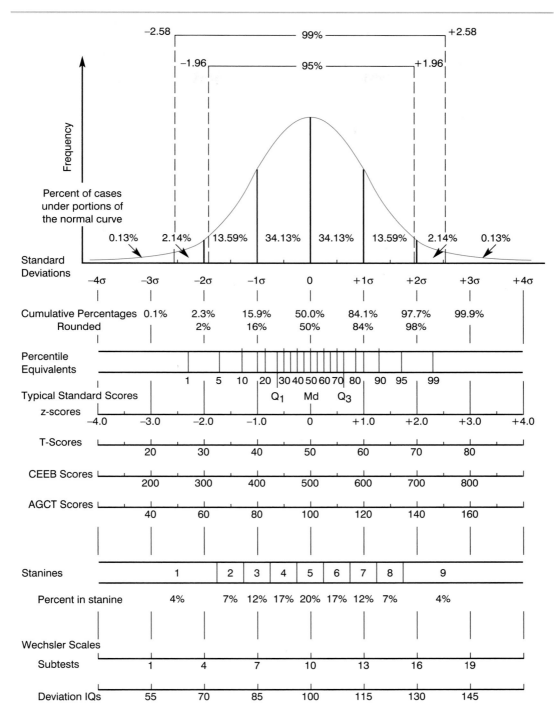

Note. This chart cannot be used to equate scores on one text to scores on another test. For example, both 600 on the CEEB and 120 on the AGCT are one standard deviation above their respective means, but they do not represent "equal" standings because the scores were obtained from different groups.

Figure 13.2. Characteristics of the normal curve. *Note.* Based on a figure appearing in *Test Service Bulletin* No. 48, January, 1955, of The Psychological Corporation.

Scale is 100 and the standard deviation is 15 (115 is in the column corresponding to + 1 *SD* [+1σ]) and since the mean is 100, 115 represents $\overline{X}$ + 1 *SD* = 100 + 15 = 115. An IQ of 145 represents a score 3 *SD*s above the mean (average) IQ. If your IQ is in this neighborhood, you are certainly a candidate for Mensa! An IQ of 145 corresponds to a percentile of 99.9. On the other side of the curve we see that an IQ of 85 corresponds to a score one standard deviation below the mean ($\overline{X}$ – 1 *SD* = 100 – 15 = 85) and to the 16th percentile. Note that the mean always corresponds to the 50th percentile. In other words, the average score is always that point above which are 50% of the cases and below which are 50% of the cases. Thus, if scores are normally distributed the following statements are true:

$$\overline{X} \pm 1.0\ SD = \text{approximately 68\% of the scores}$$

$$\overline{X} \pm 2.0\ SD = \text{approximately 95\% of the scores}$$
$$(1.96\ SD \text{ is exactly 95\%})$$

$$\overline{X} \pm 2.5\ SD = \text{approximately 99\% of the scores}$$
$$(2.58\ SD \text{ is exactly 99\%})$$

$$\overline{X} \pm 3.0\ SD = \text{approximately 99+ \% of the scores}$$

And similarly, the following are always true:

$$\overline{X} - 3.0\ SD = \text{approximately the .1 percentile}$$

$$\overline{X} - 2.0\ SD = \text{approximately the 2nd percentile}$$

$$\overline{X} - 1.0\ SD = \text{approximately the 16th percentile}$$

$$\overline{X} \qquad\quad = \text{the 50th percentile}$$

$$\overline{X} + 1.0\ SD = \text{approximately the 84th percentile}$$

$$\overline{X} + 2.0\ SD = \text{approximately the 98th percentile}$$

$$\overline{X} + 3.0\ SD = \text{approximately the 99+ percentile}$$

You may have noticed that the ends of the curve never touch the baseline and that there is no definite number of standard deviations which corresponds to 100%. This is because the curve allows for the existence of unexpected extremes at either end and because each additional standard deviation includes only a tiny fraction of a percent of the scores. As an example, for the IQ test the mean plus 5 standard deviations would be 100 + 5(15) = 100 + 75 = 175. Surely 5 *SD*s would include everyone. Wrong! There has been a very small number of persons who have scored near 200, which corresponds to + 6.67 *SD*s. Thus, while ± 3 *SD*s includes just about everyone, the exact number of standard deviations required to include every score varies from variable to variable.

As mentioned earlier, many variables form a normal distribution, including physical measures, such as height and weight, and psychological measures, such as intelligence and aptitude. In fact, most variables measured in education form normal distributions *if* enough subjects are tested. In other words, a variable that is normally distributed in a population may not be in a small sample. In Figure 13.2, the standard deviation is symbolized as σ, instead of *SD*, to indicate that the curve represents the scores of a population, not a sample; thus, σ represents a parameter, whereas *SD* represents a statistic. Depending upon the size and nature of a particular sample, the assumption of a normal curve may or may not be a valid one. Since research studies deal with a finite number of subjects, and often a not very large number, research data only more or less approximate a normal curve; correspondingly all of the equivalencies (standard deviation, percentage of cases, and percentile) are also only approximations.[4] This is an important point since most statistics used in educational research are based on the assumption that the variable is normally distributed. If this assumption is badly violated in a given sample, then certain statistics should not be used.

In general, however, the fact that most variables are normally distributed allows us to quickly determine many useful pieces of information concerning a set of data.

Skewed Distributions

When a distribution is not normal, it is said to be skewed. A normal distribution is symmetrical and the values of the mean, the median, and the mode are the same. A distribution which is skewed is not symmetrical, and the values of the mean, the median, and the mode are different. In a symmetrical distribution, there are approximately the same number of extreme scores (very high and very low) at each end of the distribution. In a skewed distribution there are more extreme scores at one end than the other. If the extreme scores are at the lower end of the distribution, the distribution is said to be negatively skewed; if the extreme scores are at the upper, or higher, end of the distribution, the distribution is said to be positively skewed (see Figure 13.3).

As we can see by looking at the negatively skewed distribution, most of the subjects did well but a few did very poorly. Conversely, for the positively skewed distribution, most of the subjects did poorly but a few did very well. In both cases, the mean is "pulled" in the direction of the extreme scores. Since the mean is affected by extreme scores and the median is not, the mean is always closer to the extreme scores than the median. Thus, for a negatively skewed distribution the mean ($\overline{X}$) is always lower, or smaller, than the median (md); for a positively skewed distribution the mean is always higher, or greater, than the median. Since the mode is not affected by extreme scores, no "always" statements can be made concerning its relationship to the mean and the median in a skewed distribution. Usually, however, as Figure 13.3 indicates, in a negatively skewed distribution the mean and the median are lower, or smaller, than the mode, whereas in a positively skewed

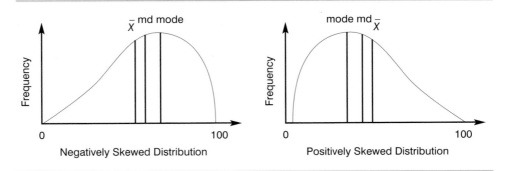

Figure 13.3. A positively skewed distribution and a negatively skewed distribution, each resulting from the administration of a 100-item test.
Note. $\overline{X}$ = mean. md = median.

[4] Thus, we see the fallacy of some normal-curve grading which assumes that each class forms a normal distribution of ability and effort, a highly improbable event.

distribution the mean and the median are higher, or greater, than the mode. To summarize:

negatively skewed: mean < median < mode
positively skewed: mean > median > mode

Since the relationship between the mean and the median is a constant, the skewness of a distribution can be determined without constructing a frequency polygon. If the mean is less than the median, the distribution is negatively skewed; if the mean and the median are the same, or very close, the distribution is symmetrical; if the mean is greater than the median, the distribution is positively skewed. The farther apart the mean and the median are, the more skewed is the distribution. If the distribution is very skewed, then the assumption of normality required for many statistics is violated.

Measures of Relative Position

Measures of relative position indicate where a score is in relation to all other scores in the distribution. In other words, measures of relative position permit you to express how well an individual has performed as compared to all other individuals in the sample who have been measured on the same variable. A major advantage of such measures is that they make it possible to compare the performance of an individual on two or more different tests. For example, if Ziggy's score in reading is 40 and his score in math is 35, it does not follow that he did better in reading; 40 may have been the lowest score on the reading test and 35 the highest score on the math test! Measures of relative position express different scores on a common scale, a common frame of reference. The two most frequently used measures of relative position are percentile ranks and standard scores.

Percentile Ranks

A percentile rank indicates the percentage of scores that fall at or below a given score. If a score of 65 corresponds to a percentile rank of 80, the 80th percentile, this means that 80% of the scores in the distribution are lower than 65. Or, to put it another way, if Suzy Smart scored at the 95th percentile, this would mean that she did better than 95% of the other students who took the same test. Conversely, if Dudley Veridull scored at the 2nd percentile this would mean that Dudley only did better than, or received a higher score than, 2% of the students.

Percentiles are appropriate for data representing an ordinal scale, although they are frequently computed for interval data. The median of a set of scores corresponds to the 50th percentile, which makes sense since the median is the middle point and therefore the point below which are 50% of the scores. While percentile ranks are not used very often in research studies, they are frequently used in the public schools to report test results of students in a form which is understandable by most audiences.

Standard Scores

Figure 13.2 depicts a number of standard scores. Basically, a standard score is a derived score that expresses how far a given raw score is from some reference point, typically the mean, in terms of standard deviation units. A standard score is a measure of relative position which is appropriate when the test data represent an interval or ratio scale of measurement. The most commonly reported and used standard scores are z scores, T scores (or Z scores), and stanines. Standard scores allow scores from different tests to be compared on a common scale and, unlike percentiles, we can validly perform mathematical operations on them in order to average them, for example. Averaging scores on a series of tests in order to obtain an overall average score is like averaging apples and oranges and getting an "orapple." Such tests are likely to vary in level of difficulty and variability of scores. By converting test scores to standard scores, however, we can average them and arrive at a valid final index of average performance.

The normal curve equivalencies indicated in Figure 13.2 for the various standard scores are accurate only to the degree to which the distribution is normal. Further, standard score equivalencies hold only if all the derived scores are based on the raw scores of the same group. A CEEB (College Entrance Examination Board) score of 700, for example, is not equivalent to a Wechsler IQ of 130 because the tests were normed on different groups. If a set of raw scores is normally distributed, then so are the standard score equivalents. But all distributions are not normal, even if the variable being measured is. Height, for example, is normally distributed, but the measured heights of the girls in a seventh-grade gym class may not be for a variety of reasons. There is a procedure for transforming a set of raw scores which ensures that the distribution of standard scores will be normal. Raw scores thus transformed are referred to as normalized scores. All resulting standard scores are normally distributed and the normal curve equivalencies are accurate.

z Scores. A z score is the most basic standard score. It expresses how far a score is from the mean in terms of standard deviation units. A score which is exactly "on" the mean corresponds to a z of 0; a score which is exactly 1 standard deviation above the mean (such as an IQ of 115) corresponds to a z of +1.00; a z score which is exactly 2 standard deviations below the mean (such as an IQ of 70) corresponds to a z of −2.00. Get it? As Figure 13.2 indicates, if a set of scores is transformed into a set of z scores (each score is expressed as a z score), the new distribution has a mean of 0 and a standard deviation of 1.

The major advantage of z scores is that they allow scores from different tests or subtests to be compared. As an example, suppose Bobby Bonker's mother, a woman who is really on top of things, comes in and asks his teacher, "How is Bobby doing in the basic skills area?" If the teacher tells her that Bobby's reading score was 50 and his math score was 40, she still does not know how well Bobby is doing. In fact, she might get the false impression that he is better in reading when in fact 50 might be a very low score on the reading test and 40 may be a very good score on the math test. Now suppose Bobby's teacher also tells his mother that the average score (the mean, $\overline{X}$) on the reading test was 60, and the average score on the math test was 30. Aha! Now it looks as if Bobby is better in math than in reading. Further, if the standard deviation (*SD*) on both tests was 10, Bobby's true status becomes even more evident. Since his score in reading is exactly 1 *SD* below the mean ($60 - 10 = 50$), his z score is −1.00. On the other hand, his score in math is 1 *SD* above the mean ($30 + 10 = 40$) and his z score is +1.00. Converting z scores to percentiles shows that Bobby is clearly better in math than in reading:

	Raw Score	$\overline{X}$	SD	z	Percentile
Reading	50	60	10	−1.00	16th
Math	40	30	10	+1.00	84th

We can use Figure 13.2 to estimate percentile equivalents for given z scores, but this becomes more difficult for z scores that fall between values given in Figure 13.2 (e.g., z = .65). A better approach is to use Table A.3 in the Appendix. For each z between −3.00 and +3.00, in the column labeled Area, Table A.3 gives the proportion of cases which are included up to this point. In other words, for any z on the horizontal axis, we can erect a straight line up to the curve; the area created to the left of this line represents the proportion of cases that falls below that z score. Thus, for z = .00 (the mean score), we go down the z columns until we come to .00 and we see that the corresponding area to the left is .5000, representing 50% of the cases and the 50th percentile. For Bobby, we simply go down the z columns until we come to −1.00 (his z score for reading), and we see that the corresponding area under the curve is .1587. By multiplying by 100 and rounding, we see that Bobby's reading score corresponds to approximately the 16th percentile (16% of the cases fall below z = −1.00). Similarly, for his math score of +1.00, the area is .8413, or approximately the 84th percentile.

Of course there are lots of other fun things we can do with Table A.3. If we want to know the proportion of cases in the area to the *right* of a given z score, for example, we simply subtract the *left* area value from 1.00, since the total area under the curve equals unity, or 1.00 (100% of the cases).[5] So, if we want to know the percentage of students who did *better* than Bobby on the reading test, we subtract .1587 from 1.00 and we get .8413, or approximately 84%. Similarly, if we want to know the percentage of scores *for any test* that falls between z = −1.00 and z = +1.00, we subtract .1587 from .8413 and we get .6826, or approximately 68%. In other words, approximately 68% (68.26% to be exact) of the scores fall between z = −1.00 and z = +1.00 (as indicated by Figure 13.2, 34.13% + 34.13% = 68.26%). Thus, we can find the percentage of cases that falls between any two z scores by subtracting their Table A.3 area values.

We can also find the percentage of cases that falls between the mean (z = .00, area = .5000) and any other z score by subtraction. A-a-and, we can also reverse the process to find, for example, the z score that corresponds to a given percentile. To become a member of Mensa, for example, you have to have an IQ at the 98th percentile (or better). The closest area value in Table A.3 which reflects at least the 98th percentile is .9803, which corresponds to z = 2.06. In other words, your IQ has to be approximately two standard deviations (+2 SD) above average, which corresponds to an IQ of 130 (see Figure 13.2).

Of course, as mentioned previously and as Table A.3 indicates, scores do not always happen to be exactly 1 SD (or 2 SD or 3 SD) above or below the mean. Usually we have to apply the following formula to convert a raw score to a z score.

$$z = \frac{X - \overline{X}}{SD}, \quad \text{where } X = \text{the raw score}$$

The only problem with z scores is that they involve negative numbers and decimals. It would be pretty hard to explain to Mrs. Bonker that her son was a −1.00. How do you tell a mother her son is a negative?! A simple solution is to transform z scores into T (or Z) scores. As Figure 13.2 indicates, z scores are actually the building blocks for a number of standard scores. Other standard scores represent transformations of z scores that communicate the same information in a more generally understandable form by eliminating negatives and/or decimals.

---

[5] Don't be confused. This 1.00 just means "all of them," 100% of the cases, and has nothing to do with one standard deviation (1 SD) or with a z score of 1.00.

T Scores. A *T* score is nothing more than a *z* score expressed in a different form. To transform a *z* score to a *T* score, you simply multiply the *z* score by 10 and add 50. In other words, $T = 10z + 50$. Thus a *z* score of 0 (the mean score) becomes a *T* score of 50 [$T = 10(0) + 50 = 0 + 50 = 50$]. A *z* score of +1.00 becomes a *T* score of 60 [$T = 10(1.00) + 50 = 10 + 50 = 60$], and a *z* score of –1.00 becomes a *T* score of 40 [$T = 10(-1.00) + 50 = -10 + 50 = 40$]. Thus, when scores are transformed to *T* scores, the new distribution has a mean of 50 and a standard deviation of 10 (see Figure 13.2). It would clearly be much easier to communicate to Mrs. Bonker that Bobby is a 40 in reading and a 60 in math and that the average score is 50 than to tell her that he is a +1.00 and a –1.00 and the average score is .00.

If the raw score distribution is normal, then so is the *z* score distribution. If this is the case, then the transformation $10z + 50$ produces a *T* distribution. If, on the other hand, the original distribution is not normal (such as when a small sample group is involved), then neither is the *z* score distribution. In such cases the distribution resulting from the $10z + 50$ transformation is more accurately referred to as a *Z* distribution. Of course, even with a set of raw scores that are not normally distributed, we can produce a set of normalized *Z* scores. In either case, we can use the normal curve equivalencies to convert such scores into corresponding percentiles, or vice versa. As Figure 13.2 indicates, for example, a *T* of 50 = P_{50}. Similarly, the second percentile corresponds to a *T* of 30 and a *T* of 60 corresponds to the 84th percentile. The same is true for the other standard score transformations illustrated in Figure 13.2. The CEEB distribution is formed by multiplying *T* scores by 10 to eliminate decimals; it is calculated directly using $CEEB = 100z + 500$. The AGCT (Army General Classification Test) distribution is formed by multiplying *T* scores by 2, and is formed directly using $AGCT = 20z + 100$. In both cases, given values can be converted to percentiles (and vice versa) using normal curve equivalencies. Thus, a CEEB score of 400 corresponds to the 16th percentile and the 98th percentile corresponds to an AGCT score of 140.

Stanines. Stanines are standard scores that divide a distribution into nine parts. Stanine (short for "standard nine") equivalencies are derived using the formula $2z + 5$ and rounding resulting values to the nearest whole number. Stanines 2 through 8 each represent $\frac{1}{2}$ *SD* of the distribution; stanines 1 and 9 include the remainder. In other words, stanine 5 includes $\frac{1}{2}$ *SD* around the mean ($\overline{X}$); that is, it equals $\overline{X}$ ± $\frac{1}{4}$ *SD*. Stanine 6 goes from + $\frac{1}{4}$ *SD* to + $\frac{3}{4}$ *SD* ($\frac{1}{4}$ *SD* + $\frac{1}{2}$ *SD* = $\frac{3}{4}$ *SD*), and so forth. Stanine 1 includes any score that is less than $-1\frac{3}{4}$ *SD* (–1.75 *SD*) below the mean, and stanine 9 includes any score that is greater than + $1\frac{3}{4}$ *SD* (+1.75 *SD*) above the mean. As Figure 13.2 indicates (see the row of figures directly beneath the stanines), stanine 5 includes 20% of the scores, stanines 4 and 6 each contain 17%, stanines 3 and 7 each contain 12%, 2 and 8 each contain 7%, and 1 and 9 each contain 4% of the scores (percentages approximate).

Like percentiles, stanines are very frequently reported in norms tables for standardized tests. They are very popular with school systems because they are so easy to understand and to explain to others. While they are not as exact as other standard scores, they are useful for a variety of purposes. They are frequently used as a basis for grouping and are also used as a criterion for selecting students for special programs. A remediation program, for example, may select students who scored in the first and second (and perhaps the third) stanines on a standardized reading test.

Measures of Relationship

Correlational research was discussed in detail in Chapter 9. You will recall that correlational research involves collecting data in order to determine whether and to what degree, a relationship exists between two or more quantifiable variables—not a causal relationship, just a relationship. Degree of relationship is expressed as a correlation coefficient which is computed based on the two sets of scores. The correlation coefficient provides an estimate of just how related two variables are. If two variables are highly related, a correlation coefficient near +1.00 (or −1.00) will be obtained; if two variables are not related, a coefficient near .00 will be obtained. There are a number of different methods of computing a correlation coefficient; which one is appropriate depends upon the scale of measurement represented by the data. The two most frequently used correlational analyses are the rank difference correlation coefficient, usually referred to as the Spearman rho, and the product moment correlation coefficient, usually referred to as the Pearson *r*.

The Spearman Rho

If the data for one of the variables are expressed as ranks instead of scores, the Spearman rho is the appropriate measure of correlation.[6] The Spearman rho is thus appropriate when the data represent an ordinal scale (although it may be used with interval data) and is used when the median and quartile deviation are used.[7] If only one of the variables to be correlated is in rank order, for example, class standing at time of graduation, then the other variable to be correlated with it must also be expressed in terms of ranks in order to use the Spearman rho technique. Thus, if intelligence were to be correlated with class standing, students would have to be ranked in terms of intelligence, and IQ scores per se would not be involved in actual computation of the correlation coefficient.

The Spearman rho is interpreted in the same way as the Pearson *r* and also produces a coefficient somewhere between −1.00 and +1.00. If a group of subjects achieves identical ranks on two variables, for example, the coefficient will be +1.00. If more than one subject receives the same score, then the corresponding ranks are averaged. So, for example, if two subjects have the same, highest score, they are each assigned the average of rank 1 and rank 2, namely rank 1.5, and the next highest score is assigned rank 3. Similarly, the 24th and 25th highest scores, if identical, would each be assigned the rank 24.5.[8]

The Pearson r

The Pearson *r* is the most appropriate measure of correlation when the sets of data to be correlated represent either interval or ratio scales. Like the mean and the standard deviation, the Pearson *r* takes into account each and every score in both distributions; it is also the most stable measure of correlation. Since most educational measures represent interval scales, the Pearson *r* is usually the appropriate coefficient for determining relationship. An assumption associated with the application of the Pearson *r* is that the relationship between the variables being correlated is a linear one. If this is not the case, the Pearson *r* will not yield a valid indication of relationship. If there is any question concerning the linearity of the relationship, the two sets of data should be plotted as previously shown in Figure 9.1.

---

[6] Rho is a Greek letter and is pronounced like row, row, row your boat.

[7] Statistics appropriate for ordinal data are referred to as nonparametric. This concept will be discussed in Chapter 14.

[8] For a description of the procedures involved in calculating the Spearman rho, see Downie & Heath. Also, STATPAK will calculate it for you.

■ CALCULATION FOR INTERVAL DATA

Since most data in educational research studies represent interval scales, we will calculate the measure of central tendency, variability, relationship, and relative position appropriate for interval data. There are several alternate formulas available for computing each of these measures; in each case, however, we will use the easiest formula, the raw score formula. At first glance some of the formulas may look scary but they are really easy. The only reason they look hard is because they involve symbols with which you are unfamiliar. As promised, however, each formula transforms "magically" into an arithmetic problem in one easy step; all you have to do is substitute the correct numbers for the correct symbols.

For those of you who have not done any arithmetic problems lately and would like a little review of the basics, worksheets and step-by-step answer keys are provided in Appendix D. Appendix D is taken from *Statistics with a Sense of Humor: A Humorous Workbook and Guide to Study Skills,* which also includes worksheets and step-by-step answer keys for all of the statistics to be discussed in this text. If you enjoy the review and would like to obtain a copy of the complete workbook, write to Fred Pyrczak, Publisher, P.O. Box 39731, Los Angeles, CA 90039.

Following the various calculations, the corresponding STATPAK printout is presented. Because of differences in "rounding off" strategies, the text values may not *exactly* match the STATPAK values. Similarly, for any analysis you might check using STATPAK, your result may not match exactly.

Symbols

Before we start calculating you should get acquainted with a few basic symbols. First, "X" is usually used to symbolize a raw score, any score. If you see a column of numbers, and at the top of that column is an X, you know that the column represents a set of scores. If there are two sets of scores they may be labeled X_1 and X_2 or X and Y, it does not matter which.

Another symbol used frequently is the Greek letter Σ, which is used to indicate addition; Σ means "the sum of," or "add them up." Thus ΣX means "add up all the Xs," and ΣY means "add up all the Ys." Isn't this easy?

Now, if any symbol has a bar over it, such as $\overline{X}$, that indicates the mean, or arithmetic average, of the scores. Thus $\overline{X}$ refers to the mean of the X scores and $\overline{Y}$ refers to the mean of the Y scores.

A capital N refers to the number of subjects; $N = 20$ means that there are 20 subjects (N for number makes sense, doesn't it?). If one analysis involves several groups, the number of subjects in each group is indicated with a lowercase letter n and a subscript indicating the group. If there are three groups, and the first group has 15 subjects, the second group has 18 subjects, and the third group has 20 subjects, this is symbolized as $n_1 = 15$, $n_2 = 18$, and $n_3 = 20$. The total number of subjects is represented as $N = 53$ ($15 + 18 + 20 = 53$).

Finally, you must get straight the difference between ΣX^2 and $(\Sigma X)^2$; they do not mean the same thing. Different formulas may include one or the other or both and it is very important to interpret each correctly; a formula tells you what to do and you must do exactly what it tells you. Now let us look at ΣX^2. What does it tell you? The Σ tells you that you are supposed to add something up. What you are supposed to add up are X^2s. What do you suppose X^2 means? Right. It means the square of the score; if $X = 4$, then $X^2 = 4^2 = 4 \times 4 = 16$. Thus, ΣX^2 says to square each score and then add up all the squares. Now let us look at $(\Sigma X)^2$. Since whatever is in the parentheses is always done first, the first thing we do is ΣX. You already know what that means, it means "add up all the scores." And then what? Right. You add up all the scores and *then* you square the total. As an example:

X	X^2	
1	1	
2	4	$\Sigma X^2 = 55$
3	9	
4	16	$(\Sigma X)^2 = 225$
5	25	
$\Sigma X = 15$	$\Sigma X^2 = 55$	

As you can see, there is a big difference between ΣX^2 and $(\Sigma X)^2$, so watch out! To summarize, symbols commonly used in statistical formulas are as follows:

X = any score

Σ = the sum of; add them up

ΣX = the sum of all the scores

$\overline{X}$ = the mean, or arithmetic average, of the scores

N = total number of subjects

n = number of subjects in a particular group

ΣX^2 = the sum of the squares; square each score and add up all the squares

$(\Sigma X)^2$ = the square of the sum; add up the scores and square the sum, or total

If you approach each statistic in an orderly fashion, it makes your statistical life easier. A suggested procedure is to:

1. Make the columns required by the formula, e.g., X, X^2, as shown above, and find the sum of each column.
2. Label the sum of each column; in the above example, the label for the sum of the X column = ΣX, and the label for the sum of the X^2 column = ΣX^2.
3. Write the formula.
4. Write the arithmetic equivalent of the formula, e.g., $(\Sigma X)^2 = (15)^2$.
5. Solve the arithmetic problem, e.g., $(15)^2 = 225$.

The Mean

Although a sample size of 5 is hardly ever considered to be acceptable, we will work with this number for the sake of illustration. In other words, all of our calculations will be based on the test scores for 5 subjects so that you can concentrate on how the calculation is being done and will not get lost in the numbers. For the same reason we will also use very small numbers. Now let us assume we have the following scores for some old friends of ours and we want to compute the mean, or arithmetic average.

	X
Iggie	1
Hermie	2
Fifi	3
Teenie	4
Tiny	5

Remember that a column labeled *X* means "here come the scores!"

The formula for the mean is $\overline{X} = \dfrac{\Sigma X}{N}$

You are now looking at a statistic. Looks bad, right? Now let us first see what it really says. It reads "the mean ($\overline{X}$) is equal to the sum of the scores (ΣX) divided by the number of subjects (N)." So, in order to find $\overline{X}$ we need ΣX and N.

$$
\begin{array}{c}
X \\
1 \\
2 \\
3 \\
4 \\
\underline{5} \\
\Sigma X = 15
\end{array}
$$

Clearly, $\Sigma X = 1 + 2 + 3 + 4 + 5 = 15$

$N = 5$ (there are 5 subjects, right?)

Now we have everything we need to find the mean and all we have to do is substitute the correct number for each symbol.

$$\overline{X} = \frac{\Sigma X}{N} = \frac{15}{5}$$

Now what do we have? Right! An arithmetic problem. A hard arithmetic problem? No! An elementary school arithmetic problem? Yes! And all we did was to substitute each symbol with the appropriate number. Thus,

$$\overline{X} = \frac{\Sigma X}{N} = \frac{15}{5} = 3 \ (3.00)$$

and the mean is equal to 3.00. If you look at the scores you can see that 3 is clearly the average score. Since traditionally statistical results are given with 2 decimal places, our "official" answer is 3.00.

Was that hard? Cer-tain-ly not! And guess what—you just learned how to do a statistic! Are they all going to be that easy? Of course!

The Standard Deviation

Earlier we discussed the fact that the standard deviation is the square root of the variance, which is based on the distance of each score from the mean. To calculate the standard deviation (*SD*), however, we do not have to calculate deviation scores; we can use a raw score formula which gives us the same answer with less grief. Now, before you look at the formula remember that no matter how bad it looks it is going to turn into an easy arithmetic problem. Ready?

$$SD = \sqrt{\frac{SS}{N-1}} \text{ where } SS = \Sigma X^2 - \frac{(\Sigma X)^2}{N}$$

OR

$$SD = \sqrt{\dfrac{\sum X^2 - \dfrac{(\sum X)^2}{N}}{N - 1}}$$

In other words, the *SD* is equal to the square root of the sum of squares (*SS*) divided by $N - 1$.

If the standard deviation of a population is being calculated, the formula is exactly the same, except we divide *SS* by *N*, instead of $N - 1$. The reason is that a sample standard deviation is considered to be a biased estimate of the population standard deviation. When we select a sample, especially a small sample, the probability is that subjects will come from the middle of the distribution and that extreme scores will not be represented. Thus, the range of sample scores will be smaller than the population range, as will be the sample standard deviation. As the sample size increases, so do the chances of getting extreme scores; thus, the smaller the sample, the more important it is to correct for the downward bias. By dividing by $N - 1$ instead of *N*, we make the denominator (bottom part!) smaller, and thus $\dfrac{SS}{N - 1}$ is larger, closer to the population SD than $\dfrac{SS}{N}$. For example, if *SS* = 18 and $N = 10$, then

$$\frac{SS}{N - 1} = \frac{18}{9} = 2.00; \qquad \frac{SS}{N} = \frac{18}{10} = 1.80$$

Now just relax and look at each piece of the formula; you already know what each piece means. Starting with the easy one, *N* refers to what? Right—the number of subjects. How about $(\sum X)$? Right—the sum of the scores. And $(\sum X)^2$? Right—the square of the sum of the scores. That leaves $\sum X^2$, which means the sum of what? . . . Fantastic. The sum of the squares. Okay, let us use the same scores we used to calculate the mean. The first thing we need to do is to square each score and then add those squares up—while we are at it we can also go ahead and add up all the scores.

	X	X^2	
Iggie	1	1	
Hermie	2	4	$\sum X = 15$
Fifi	3	9	$\sum X^2 = 55$
Teenie	4	16	$N = 5$
Tiny	5	25	$N - 1 = 4$
	$\sum X = 15$	$\sum X^2 = 55$	

Do we have everything we need? Does the formula ask for anything else? We are in business. Substituting each symbol with its numerical equivalent we get:

$$SS = \sum X^2 - \frac{(\sum X)^2}{N} = 55 - \frac{(15)^2}{5}$$

Now what do we have? A statistic? No! An arithmetic problem? Yes! A hard arithmetic problem? No! It is harder than 15/5 but it is not *hard*. If we just do what the formula tells us to do we will have no problem at all. The first thing it tells us to do is to square 15:

$$SS = \sum X^2 - \frac{(\sum X)^2}{N} = 55 - \frac{(15)^2}{5} = 55 - \frac{225}{5}$$

So far so good? The next thing the formula tells us to do is divide 225 by 5:

$$= 55 - 45$$

It is looking a lot better; now it is *really* an easy arithmetic problem. Okay, the next step is to subtract 45 from 55:

$$SS = 10$$

Mere child's play. Think you can figure out the next step? Terrific! Now that we have *SS,* we simply substitute it into the *SD* formula as follows:

$$SD = \sqrt{\frac{SS}{N-1}} = \sqrt{\frac{10}{4}} = \sqrt{2.5}$$

To find the square root of 2.5, simply enter 2.5 into your calculator and hit the square root button ($\sqrt{\ }$); the square root of 2.5 is 1.58. Substituting in our square root we have:

$$SD = \sqrt{2.5} = 1.58$$

and the standard deviation is 1.58. If we had calculated the standard deviation for the IQ distribution shown in Figure 13.2, what would we have gotten? Right—15. Now you know how to do *two* statistics. Were they hard? No! (STATPAK printout below.)

```
=================================================================
        STANDARD DEVIATION FOR SAMPLES AND POPULATIONS
=================================================================
  STATISTIC                                            VALUE
-----------------------------------------------------------------

  NO. OF SCORES (N)                                       5

  SUM OF SCORES (ΣX)                                   15.00

  MEAN (X̄)                                              3.00

  SUM OF SQUARED SCORES (ΣX²)                          55.00

  SUM OF SQUARES (SS)                                  10.00

  STANDARD DEVIATION FOR A POPULATION                   1.41

  STANDARD DEVIATION FOR A SAMPLE                       1.58

=================================================================
```

Standard Scores

Your brain has earned a rest, and the formula for a *z* score is a piece of cake:

$$z = \frac{X - \overline{X}}{SD}$$

To convert scores to z scores we simply apply that formula to each score. We have already computed the mean and the standard deviation for the following scores:

	X	
Iggie	1	
Hermie	2	$\overline{X} = 3$
Fifi	3	
Teenie	4	$SD = 1.58$
Tiny	5	

Let's see how Iggie works out:

$$\text{Iggie} \quad z = \frac{X - \overline{X}}{SD} = \frac{1 - 3}{1.58} = \frac{-2}{1.58} = -1.26$$

This tells us that Iggie's score was 1.26 standard deviations *below* average. In case you have forgotten, if the signs are the same (two positives or two negatives), the answer in a multiplication or division problem is a positive number; if the signs are different, the answer is a negative number, as in Iggie's case. For the rest of our friends, the results are:

$$\text{Hermie} \quad z = \frac{X - \overline{X}}{SD} = \frac{-1}{1.58} = -.63$$

$$\text{Fifi} \quad z = \frac{X - \overline{X}}{SD} = \frac{0}{1.58} = .00$$

$$\text{Teenie} \quad z = \frac{X - \overline{X}}{SD} = \frac{1}{1.58} = +.63$$

$$\text{Tiny} \quad z = \frac{X - \overline{X}}{SD} = \frac{2}{1.58} = +1.26$$

Notice that since Fifi's score was the same as the mean score, her z score is .00; her score is *no* distance from the mean. On the other hand, Iggie's and Hermie's scores were below the mean so their z scores are negative, whereas Teenie and Tiny scored above the mean and their z scores are positive.

If we want to eliminate the negatives, we can convert each z score to a Z score. Remember those? To do that we multiply each z score by 10 and add 50:

$$Z = 10z + 50$$

If we apply this formula to our z scores we get the following results:

$$\text{Iggie} \quad Z = 10z + 50 = 10(-1.26) + 50$$
$$= -12.6 + 50$$
$$= 50 - 12.6$$
$$= 37.40$$

$$\text{Hermie} \quad Z = 10z + 50 = 10(-.63) + 50$$
$$= -6.3 + 50$$
$$= 50 - 6.3$$
$$= 43.70$$

$$\text{Fifi} \quad Z = 10z + 50 = 10(.00) + 50$$
$$= .00 + 50$$
$$= 50 + .00$$
$$= 50.00$$

$$\text{Teenie} \quad Z = 10z + 50 = 10(+.63) + 50$$
$$= 6.3 + 50$$
$$= 50 + 6.3$$
$$= 56.30$$

$$\text{Tiny} \quad Z = 10z + 50 = 10(+1.26) + 50$$
$$= 12.6 + 50$$
$$= 50 + 12.6$$
$$= 62.60$$

I told you it would be easy! (STATPAK printout below.)

```
==============================================================================
                STANDARD SCORES FOR SAMPLES AND POPULATIONS
==============================================================================
    STATISTIC                                                    VALUE
------------------------------------------------------------------------------

    NO. OF SCORES (N)                                              5
         _
    MEAN (X)                                                     3.00

    STANDARD DEVIATION FOR A POPULATION                          1.41

    STANDARD DEVIATION FOR A SAMPLE                              1.58

------------------------------------------------------------------------------

                       z   A N D   T - S C O R E S

                  RAW           POPULATION            SAMPLE
                 SCORE      z-SCORE  T-SCORE    z-SCORE  T-SCORE

------------------------------------------------------------------------------

     ITEM NO:  1   1.00      -1.41    35.86      -1.26    37.35
     ITEM NO:  2   2.00      -0.71    42.93      -0.63    43.68
     ITEM NO:  3   3.00       0.00    50.00       0.00    50.00
     ITEM NO:  4   4.00       0.71    57.07       0.63    56.32
     ITEM NO:  5   5.00       1.41    64.14       1.26    62.65

==============================================================================
```

The Pearson *r*

Now that your brain is rested (!), you are ready for the Pearson *r*. The formula for the Pearson *r looks* very, very complicated, but it is not (have I lied to you so far?). It looks bad because it has a lot of pieces, but each piece is quite simple to calculate. Now, to calculate a Pearson *r* we need two sets of scores. Let us assume we have the following sets of scores for two variables for our old friends:

	X	Y
Iggie	1	2
Hermie	2	3
Fifi	3	4
Teenie	4	3
Tiny	5	5

The question is, "Are these two variables related?" Positively? Negatively? Not at all?

In order to answer those questions we apply the formula for the Pearson *r* to the data. Here goes!

$$r = \frac{\sum XY - \dfrac{(\sum X)(\sum Y)}{N}}{\sqrt{\left[\sum X^2 - \dfrac{(\sum X)^2}{N}\right]\left[\sum Y^2 - \dfrac{(\sum Y)^2}{N}\right]}}$$

Now, if you look at each piece you will see that you already know how to calculate all of them except one. You should have no problem with $\sum X$, $\sum Y$, $\sum X^2$, or $\sum Y^2$. And even though there are 10 scores there are only 5 subjects, so $N = 5$. What is left? The only new symbol in the formula is $\sum XY$. What could that mean? Well, you know that it is the sum of something, namely the *XY*s, whatever they are. An *XY* is just what you would guess it is—the product of an *X* score and its corresponding *Y* score. Thus, Iggie's *XY* score is 1 x 2 = 2, and Teenie's *XY* score is 4 x 3 = 12. Okay, let us get all the pieces we need:

	X	Y	X²	Y²	XY
Iggie	1	2	1	4	2
Hermie	2	3	4	9	6
Fifi	3	4	9	16	12
Teenie	4	3	16	9	12
Tiny	5	5	25	25	25
	15	17	55	63	57
	$\sum X$	$\sum Y$	$\sum X^2$	$\sum Y^2$	$\sum XY$

Now guess what we are going to do. Right! We are going to turn that horrible-looking statistic into a horrible-looking arithmetic problem! Just kidding. Of course it will really be an easy arithmetic problem if we do it one step at a time.

$$r = \frac{\sum XY - \dfrac{(\sum X)(\sum Y)}{N}}{\sqrt{\left[\sum X^2 - \dfrac{(\sum X)^2}{N}\right]\left[\sum Y^2 - \dfrac{(\sum Y)^2}{N}\right]}} = \frac{57 - \dfrac{(15)(17)}{5}}{\sqrt{\left[55 - \dfrac{(15)^2}{5}\right]\left[63 - \dfrac{(17)^2}{5}\right]}}$$

It still does not look good, but you have to admit it looks better! Let us start with the numerator (for you nonmathematical types, the top part). The first thing the formula tells you to do is multiply 15 by 17:

$$= \cfrac{57 - \dfrac{255}{5}}{\sqrt{\left[55 - \dfrac{(15)^2}{5}\right]\left[63 - \dfrac{(17)^2}{5}\right]}}$$

The next step is to divide 255 by 5:

$$= \cfrac{57 - 51}{\sqrt{\left[55 - \dfrac{(15)^2}{5}\right]\left[63 - \dfrac{(17)^2}{5}\right]}}$$

The next step is a real snap. All you have to do is subtract 51 from 57:

$$= \cfrac{6}{\sqrt{\left[55 - \dfrac{(15)^2}{5}\right]\left[63 - \dfrac{(17)^2}{5}\right]}}$$

So much for the numerator. Was that hard? NO! *Au contraire,* it was very easy. Right? Right. Now for the denominator (the bottom part). If you think hard, you will realize that you have seen part of the denominator before. Hint: It was not in connection with the mean. Let us go through it step by step anyway just in case you did not really understand what we were doing the last time we did it. The first thing the formula says to do is to square 15:

$$= \cfrac{6}{\sqrt{\left[55 - \dfrac{225}{5}\right]\left[63 - \dfrac{(17)^2}{5}\right]}}$$

Now we divide 225 by 5:

$$= \cfrac{6}{\sqrt{\left[55 - 45\right]\left[63 - \dfrac{(17)^2}{5}\right]}}$$

Did you get that? All we did was divide 225 by 5 and we got 45. Can you figure out the next step? Good. We subtract 45 from 55:

$$= \cfrac{6}{\sqrt{\left[10\right]\left[63 - \dfrac{(17)^2}{5}\right]}}$$

It is looking a lot better, isn't it? Okay, now we need to square 17; 17 x 17 = 289.

$$= \cfrac{6}{\sqrt{\left[10\right]\left[63 - \dfrac{289}{5}\right]}}$$

Next, we divide 289 by 5 (Sorry, life doesn't always come out even):

$$= \frac{6}{\sqrt{[10][63-57.8]}}$$

We are getting there. Now we subtract 57.8 from 63. Do not let the decimals scare you:

$$\frac{6}{\sqrt{[10][63-57.8]}} = \frac{6}{\sqrt{[10][5.2]}}$$

Can you figure out what to do next? If you can, you are smarter than you thought. Next, we multiply 10 by 5.2:

$$\frac{6}{\sqrt{[10][5.2]}} = \frac{6}{\sqrt{52}}$$

Next, we find the square root of 52:

$$\frac{6}{\sqrt{52}} = \frac{6}{7.2}$$

Almost done. All we have to do is divide 6 by 7.2:

$$\frac{6}{7.2} = .83$$

Fanfare! Ta-ta-ta-ta! We are through. In case you got lost in the action, .83 is the correlation coefficient, the Pearson *r*. In other words, *r* = +.83. (STATPAK printout below).

==

PEARSON'S PRODUCT MOMENT CORRELATION

==

STATISTIC	VALUE
N	5
ΣX	15.00
ΣY	17.00
ΣX^2	55.00
ΣY^2	63.00
MEAN OF 'X' SCORES	3.00
MEAN OF 'Y' SCORES	3.40
ΣXY	57.00
PEARSON'S r	0.83
df	3

==

Is .83 good? Does it represent a true relationship? Is .83 significantly different from .00? If you recall the related discussion in Chapter 9, you know that to determine whether .83 represents a true relationship we need a table. We need a table which indicates how large our *r* needs to be in order to be significant, given the number of subjects we have and the level of significance at which we are working (see Table A.2 in the Appendix). The number of subjects affects the degrees of freedom, which for the Pearson r are always computed by the formula $N - 2$. Thus, for our example, degrees of freedom $(df) = N - 2 = 5 - 2 = 3$. If we select $\alpha = .05$ as our level of significance, we are now ready to use Table A.2.[9] Look at Table A.2 and find the column labeled df and run your left index finger down the column until you hit 3, the df associated with our r; keep your left finger right there for the time being. Now run your right index finger across the top of the table until you come to .05, the significance level we have selected. Now, run your left finger straight across the table and your right finger straight down the table until they meet. If you follow directions well, you should have ended up at .8783, which rounds off to .88. Now we compare our coefficient to the table value. Is $.83 \geq .88$? No, .83 is not greater than or equal to .88. Therefore, our coefficient does not indicate a true relationship between X and Y. Even though it *looks* big, it is not big enough given that we only have five subjects. We are not positive that there is no relationship, but the odds are against it. Note that if we had had just one more subject ($N = 6$) our df would have been 4 ($N - 2 = 6 - 2 = 4$) and our coefficient would have indicated a significant relationship ($.83$ is $\geq .81$). Note, too, that the same table would have been used if r had been a negative number, $- .83$. The table does not know or care whether the r is positive or negative. It only tells you how large r must be in order to indicate a relationship significantly different from .00, a true relationship.

Do not forget, however, that even if a correlation coefficient is statistically significant it does not necessarily mean that the coefficient has any practical significance. Whether the coefficient is useful depends upon the use to which it will be put; a coefficient to be used in a prediction study needs to be much higher than a coefficient to be used in a relationship study.

Postscript

Almost always in a research study, descriptive statistics such as the mean and standard deviation are computed separately for each group in the study. A correlation coefficient is usually only computed in a correlational study (unless it is used to compute the reliability of an instrument used in a causal-comparative or experimental study). Standard scores are rarely used in research studies. In order to test our hypothesis, however, we almost always need more than descriptive statistics; application of one or more inferential statistics is usually required.

▪ SUMMARY/CHAPTER 13
TYPES OF DESCRIPTIVE STATISTICS

1. The first step in data analysis is to describe, or summarize, the data using descriptive statistics.
2. Descriptive statistics permit the researcher to meaningfully describe many, many scores with a small number of indices.
3. If such indices are calculated for a sample drawn from a population, the resulting values are referred to as statistics; if they are calculated for an entire population, they are referred to as parameters.

---

[9] Degrees of freedom and levels of significance will be explained further in Chapter 14.

Graphing Data

4. The shape of the distribution may not be self-evident, especially if a large number of scores are involved.
5. The most common method of graphing research data is to construct a frequency polygon.
6. The first step in constructing a frequency polygon is to list all the scores and to tabulate how many subjects received each score. Once the scores are tallied, the steps are as follows: place all the scores on a horizontal axis, at equal intervals, from lowest score to highest; place the frequencies of scores at equal intervals on the vertical axis, starting with zero; for each score, find the point where the score intersects with its frequency of occurrence and make a dot; connect all the dots with straight lines.

Measures of Central Tendency

7. Measures of central tendency give the researcher a convenient way of describing a set of data with a single number.
8. The number resulting from computation of a measure of central tendency represents the average or typical score attained by a group of subjects.
9. Each index of central tendency is appropriate for a different scale of measurement; the mode is appropriate for nominal data, the median for ordinal data, and the mean for interval or ratio data.

The Mode

10. The mode is the score that is attained by more subjects than any other score.
11. The mode is not established through calculation; it is determined by looking at a set of scores or at a graph of scores and seeing which score occurs most frequently.
12. There are several problems associated with the mode, and it is therefore of limited value and seldom used. For one thing, a set of scores may have two (or more) modes, in which case it is referred to as bimodal. Another problem with the mode is that it is an unstable measure of central tendency; equal-sized samples randomly selected from the same accessible population are likely to have different modes.
13. When nominal data are involved, however, the mode is the only appropriate measure of central tendency.

The Median

14. The median is that point in a distribution above and below which are 50% of the scores; in other words, the median is the midpoint.
15. The median does not take into account each and every score; it ignores, for example, extremely high scores and extremely low scores.

The Mean

16. The mean is the arithmetic average of the scores and is the most frequently used measure of central tendency.

17. By the very nature of the way in which it is computed, the mean takes into account, or is based on, each and every score.
18. It is appropriate when the data represent either an interval or a ratio scale and is a more precise, stable index than both the median and the mode.
19. In situations in which there are one or more extreme scores, the median will be the best index of typical performance.

Measures of Variability

20. Two sets of data that are very different can have identical means or medians.
21. Thus, there is a need for a measure that indicates how spread out the scores are, how much variability there is.
22. While the standard deviation is by far the most often used, the range is the only appropriate measure of variability for nominal data, and the quartile deviation is the appropriate index of variability for ordinal data.
23. As with measures of central tendency, measures of variability appropriate for nominal and ordinal data may be used with interval or ratio data even though the standard deviation is generally the preferred index of variability.

The Range

24. The range is simply the difference between the highest and lowest score in a distribution and is determined by subtraction.
25. Like the mode, the range is not a very stable measure of variability, and its chief advantage is that it gives a quick, rough estimate of variability.

The Quartile Deviation

26. The quartile deviation is one-half of the difference between the upper quartile (the 75th percentile) and lower quartile (the 25th percentile) in a distribution.
27. The quartile deviation is a more stable measure of variability than the range and is appropriate whenever the median is appropriate.

The Standard Deviation

28. Like the mean, its counterpart measure of central tendency, the standard deviation is the most stable measure of variability and takes into account each and every score.
29. If you know the mean and the standard deviation of a set of scores, you have a pretty good picture of what the distribution looks like.
30. If the distribution is relatively normal, then the mean plus 3 standard deviations and the mean minus 3 standard deviations encompasses just about all the scores, over 99% of them.

The Normal Curve

31. Many, many variables do yield a normal curve if a sufficient number of subjects are measured.

Normal Distributions

32. If a variable is normally distributed, that is, does form a normal curve, then several things are true. First, 50% of the scores are above the mean and 50% of the scores are below the mean. Second, the mean, the median, and the mode are the same. Third, most scores are near the mean and the further from the mean a score is, the fewer the number of subjects who attained that score. Fourth, the same number, or percentage, of scores is between the mean and plus one standard deviation ($\overline{X} + 1\,SD$) as is between the mean and minus one standard deviation ($\overline{X} - 1\,SD$), and similarly for $\overline{X} \pm 2\,SD$ and $\overline{X} \pm 3\,SD$.

33. If scores are normally distributed, the following are true statements:

$$\overline{X} \pm 1.0\,SD = \text{approximately 68\% of the scores}$$

$$\overline{X} \pm 2.0\,SD = \text{approximately 95\% of the scores}$$
$$\text{(1.96 } SD \text{ is exactly 95\%)}$$

$$\overline{X} \pm 2.5\,SD = \text{approximately 99\% of the scores}$$
$$\text{(2.58 } SD \text{ is exactly 99\%)}$$

$$\overline{X} \pm 3.0\,SD = \text{approximately 99+ \% of the scores}$$

And similarly, the following are always true:

$$\overline{X} - 3.0\,SD = \text{approximately the .1 percentile}$$

$$\overline{X} - 2.0\,SD = \text{approximately the 2nd percentile}$$

$$\overline{X} - 1.0\,SD = \text{approximately the 16th percentile}$$

$$\overline{X} \quad\quad = \text{the 50th percentile}$$

$$\overline{X} + 1.0\,SD = \text{approximately the 84th percentile}$$

$$\overline{X} + 2.0\,SD = \text{approximately the 98th percentile}$$

$$\overline{X} + 3.0\,SD = \text{approximately the 99+ percentile}$$

34. Many variables form a normal distribution, including physical measures, such as height and weight, and psychological measures, such as intelligence and aptitude.

35. Since research studies deal with a finite number of subjects, and often a not very large number, research data only more or less approximate a normal curve.

Skewed Distributions

36. When a distribution is not normal, it is said to be skewed.

37. A distribution which is skewed is not symmetrical, and the values of the mean, the median, and the mode are different.

38. In a skewed distribution, there are more extreme scores at one end than the other. If the extreme scores are at the lower end of the distribution, the distribution is said to be negatively skewed; if the extreme scores are at the upper, or higher, end of the distribution, the distribution is said to be positively skewed.

39. In both cases, the mean is "pulled" in the direction of the extreme scores.

40. For a negatively skewed distribution the mean ($\overline{X}$) is always lower, or smaller, than the median (md); for a positively skewed distribution the mean is always higher, or greater, than the median. Usually, in a negatively skewed distribution the mean and the median are lower, or smaller, than the mode, whereas in a positively skewed distribution the mean and the median are higher, or greater, than the mode.

Measures of Relative Position

41. Measures of relative position indicate where a score is in relation to all other scores in the distribution.
42. A major advantage of such measures is that they make it possible to compare the performance of an individual on two or more different tests.

Percentile Ranks

43. A percentile rank indicates the percentage of scores that fall at or below a given score.
44. Percentiles are appropriate for data representing an ordinal scale, although they are frequently computed for interval data.
45. The median of a set of scores corresponds to the 50th percentile.

Standard Scores

46. A standard score is a measure of relative position which is appropriate when the data represent an interval or ratio scale.
47. A z score expresses how far a score is from the mean in terms of standard deviation units.
48. If a set of scores is transformed into a set of z scores, the new distribution has a mean of 0 and a standard deviation of 1.
49. The major advantage of the z score is that it allows scores from different tests to be compared.
50. A table of normal curve areas corresponding to various z scores can be used to determine the proportion (and percentage) of cases that falls below a given z score, above a given z score, and between any two z scores.
51. The only problem with z scores is that they involve negative numbers and decimals. A simple solution is to transform z scores into Z scores. To do this you simply multiply the z score by 10 and add 50.
52. Stanines are standard scores that divide a distribution into nine parts.

Measures of Relationship

53. Degree of relationship is expressed as a correlation coefficient which is computed based on the two sets of scores.
54. If two variables are highly related, a correlation coefficient near +1.00 (or −1.00) will be obtained; if two variables are not related, a coefficient near .00 will be obtained.

The Spearman Rho

55. If the data for one of the variables are expressed as ranks instead of scores, the Spearman rho is the appropriate measure of correlation.
56. The Spearman rho is thus appropriate when the data represent an ordinal scale (although it may be used with interval data) and is used when the median and quartile deviation are used.
57. If only one of the variables to be correlated is in rank order, for example, class standing at time of graduation, then the other variable to be correlated with it must also be expressed in terms of ranks.
58. The Spearman rho is interpreted in the same way as the Pearson *r* and produces a coefficient somewhere between −1.00 and +1.00.
59. If more than one subject receives the same score, then their corresponding ranks are averaged.

The Pearson r

60. The Pearson *r* is the most appropriate measure of correlation when the sets of data to be correlated represent either interval or ratio scales.
61. Like the mean and the standard deviation, the Pearson *r* takes into account each and every score in both distributions; it is also the most stable measure of correlation.
62. Since most educational measures represent interval scales, the Pearson *r* is usually the appropriate coefficient for determining relationship.
63. An assumption associated with the application of the Pearson *r* is that the relationship between the variables being correlated is a linear one.

CALCULATION FOR INTERVAL DATA

Symbols

64. Symbols commonly used in statistical formulas are as follows:

$$X = \text{any score}$$
$$\Sigma = \text{the sum of; add them up}$$
$$\Sigma X = \text{the sum of all the scores}$$
$$\overline{X} = \text{the mean, or arithmetic average, of the scores}$$
$$N = \text{total number of subjects}$$
$$n = \text{number of subjects in a particular group}$$
$$\Sigma X^2 = \text{the sum of the squares; square each score and add up all the squares}$$
$$(\Sigma X)^2 = \text{the square of the sum; add up the scores and square the sum, or total}$$

The Mean

65. The formula for the mean is $\overline{X} = \dfrac{\Sigma X}{N}$

The Standard Deviation

66. The formula for the standard deviation is

$$SD = \sqrt{\frac{SS}{N-1}} \text{ where } SS = \sum X^2 - \frac{(\sum X)^2}{N}$$

Standard Scores

67. The formula for a z score is $z = \dfrac{X - \overline{X}}{SD}$

68. The formula for a Z score is $Z = 10z + 50$.

The Pearson r

69. The formula for the Pearson r is

$$r = \frac{\sum XY - \dfrac{(\sum X)(\sum Y)}{N}}{\sqrt{\left[\sum X^2 - \dfrac{(\sum X)^2}{N}\right]\left[\sum Y^2 - \dfrac{(\sum Y)^2}{N}\right]}}$$

70. The formula for degrees of freedom for the Pearson r is $N - 2$.

C H A P T E R 14

"Does it look bad? Is it? What will it turn into? (p. 486)."

Inferential Statistics

After reading Chapter 14, you should be able to:

1. Explain the concept of standard error.

2. Describe how sample size affects standard error.

3. Define or describe the null hypothesis.

4. State the purpose of a test of significance.

5. Define or describe Type I and Type II errors.

6. Define or describe the concept of significance level (probability level).

7. Describe one-tailed and two-tailed tests.

8. Explain the difference between parametric tests and nonparametric tests.

9. State the purpose, and explain the strategy, of the t test.

10. Define or describe independent and nonindependent samples.

11. State the purpose of the t test for independent samples (when is it used).

12. State the purpose of the t test for nonindependent samples.

13. Describe one major problem associated with analyzing gain scores (difference scores).

14. State the purpose of the simple analysis of variance.

15. State the purpose of multiple comparison procedures.

16. State the purpose of a factorial analysis of variance.

17. State a major purpose of analysis of covariance.

18. State two (2) uses of multiple regression.

19. State the purpose of chi square.

20. Generate three columns of five one-digit numbers ("scores"), compute each of the following statistics (give the formula and show your work), state whether each result is statistically significant at α = .05, and interpret each result:

   (a) t test for independent samples (use columns 1 and 2),

   (b) t test for nonindependent samples (use columns 2 and 3),

   (c) simple analysis of variance for 3 groups (use all 3 columns),

   (d) the Scheffé test (based on [c] above), and

   (e) chi square (sum the numbers in each column and treat them as if they were the total number of people responding "yes," "no," and "undecided," respectively, in a survey).

If STATPAK, the microcomputer program which accompanies this text, is available to you, use it to check your work.

CONCEPTS UNDERLYING APPLICATION

Inferential statistics deal with, of all things, inferences. Inferences about what? Inferences about populations based on the behavior of samples. Most educational research studies deal with samples. Recall that "goodness" of the various sampling techniques is a function of their effectiveness in producing representative samples; the more representative a sample is, the more generalizable the results will be to the population from which the sample was selected. Results which only hold for the sample upon which they are based are of very limited value. Consequently, random samples are preferred since they seem to do the job best. Inferential statistics are concerned with determining how likely it is that results based on a sample or samples are the same results that would have been obtained for the entire population.

As mentioned in Chapter 13, sample values, such as the mean, are referred to as *statistics*. The corresponding values in the population are referred to as *parameters*. Thus, if a mean is based on a sample, it is a statistic; if it is based on an entire population, it is a parameter. Inferential statistics are used to make inferences concerning parameters, based on sample statistics. If a difference between means is found for two groups at the end of a study, the question of interest is whether a similar difference exists in the population from which the samples were selected. It could be that no real difference exists in the population and that the difference found for the samples was a chance one; if two different samples had been used it is likely that no difference would have been found. And now we get to the heart of inferential statistics, the concept of "how likely is it"; if I find a difference between two sample means and conclude that the difference is large enough to infer that a true difference exists in the population, how likely is it that I am wrong? In other words, inferences concerning populations are only probability statements; the researcher is only probably correct when he or she makes an inference and concludes that there is a true difference, or true relationship, in the population.

There are a number of concepts underlying the application of inferential statistics with which you should be familiar. Before the various types of inferential statistics are described, and several major ones calculated, these concepts will be discussed.

Standard Error

Inferences concerning populations are based on the behavior of samples. The chances of the composition of a sample being identical to that of its parent population, however, are virtually nil. If we randomly select a number of samples from the same population and compute the mean for each, it is very likely that each mean will be somewhat different from each other mean, and that none of the means will be identical to the population mean. This expected, chance variation among the means is referred to as sampling error. Recall that in Chapter 4 we discussed the fact that unlike sampling bias, sampling error is not the researcher's fault. Sampling error just happens and is as inevitable as taxes! Thus, if a difference is found between sample means, the question of interest is whether the difference is a result of sampling error or a reflection of a true difference.

An interesting characteristic of sampling errors is that they are normally distributed. Errors vary in size (small errors versus large errors) and these errors form a normal curve. Although sampling errors are random fluctuations, they actually behave in a very orderly manner. Thus, if a sufficiently large number of equal-sized large samples are randomly selected from a population, all samples will not have the same mean on the variable measured, *but* the means of those samples will be normally distributed around the population mean. The mean of all the sample means will yield a good estimate of the population mean.[1] Most of the sample means will be very close to the population mean; the number of means which are considerably different from the population mean (as estimated by the mean of the sample means) will decrease as the size of the difference increases. In other words, very few means will be much higher or much lower than the population mean. An example may help to clarify this concept.

Let us suppose that we do not know what the population mean IQ is on the Stanford-Binet, Form L.M. Further, suppose we randomly select a sample of $N = 100$. We might get the following results:

64	82	87	94	98	100	104	108	114	121
67	83	88	95	98	101	104	109	115	122
68	83	88	96	98	101	105	109	116	123
70	84	89	96	98	101	105	110	116	124
71	84	90	96	98	102	105	110	117	125
72	84	90	97	99	102	106	111	117	127
74	84	91	97	99	102	106	111	118	130
75	85	92	97	99	103	107	112	119	131
75	86	93	97	100	103	107	112	119	136
78	86	94	97	100	103	108	113	120	142

If we compute the mean, we get 10,038/100 = 100.38, which is a darn good estimate of the population mean, which we know is 100. Further, if you check the scores, you will discover that 71% of the scores fall between 84 and 116, and 96% fall between 68 and 132. Since we know that the standard deviation is 16, our distribution approximates a normal curve quite well; the percentage of cases falling

---

[1]To find the mean of the sample means you simply add up all the sample means and divide by the number of means, assuming that the size of each sample is the same as the size of every other sample.

within each successive standard deviation is very close to the percentage characteristic of a normal curve (71% as compared to 68%, and 96% as compared to 95%). The concept illustrated by the above example is a comforting one. It tells us, in essence, that most of the sample means we obtain will be close to the population mean and only a few will be very far away. In other words, once in a while, just by chance, we will get a sample which is quite different from the population, but not very often.

As with any normally distributed set of scores, a distribution of sample means has not only its own mean but also its own standard deviation. The standard deviation of the sample means (the standard deviation of sampling errors) is usually referred to as the standard error of the mean. The standard error of the mean ($SE_{\bar{x}}$) tells us by how much we would expect our sample means to differ if we used other samples from the same population. According to normal curve percentages, we can say that approximately 68% of the sample means will fall between plus and minus one standard error of the mean (remember, the standard error of the mean is a standard deviation), 95% will fall between plus and minus two standard errors, and 99+ % will fall between plus and minus three standard errors. In other words, if the mean is 60, and the standard error of the mean is 10, we can expect 95% of the sample means to fall between 40 and 80 [60 ± 2(10)]. Thus a sample mean might very well be 65, but a sample mean of 95 is highly unlikely. Thus, given a number of large, randomly selected samples we can estimate quite well population parameters by computing the mean and standard deviation of the sample means.

It is not necessary, however, to select a large number of samples in order to estimate standard error. If we know the standard deviation of the population, we can estimate the standard error of the mean by dividing the standard deviation by the square root of our sample size ($\sqrt{N}$). In most cases, however, we do not know the mean or standard deviation of the population. In these cases, we estimate the standard error by dividing the standard deviation of the sample by the square root of the sample minus one:

$$SE_{\bar{x}} = \frac{SD}{\sqrt{N-1}}$$

Using this estimate of the $SE_{\bar{x}}$, the sample mean, $\bar{X}$, and characteristics of the normal curve, we can estimate probable limits within which the population mean falls. These limits are referred to as confidence limits. Thus, if a sample $\bar{X}$ is 80 and the SE_{x} is 1.00, if we say that the population mean falls between 79 and 81 ($\bar{X} \pm 1\ SE_{\bar{x}}$), we have approximately a 68% chance of being correct; if we say that the population mean falls between 78 and 82 ($\bar{X} \pm 2\ SE_{\bar{x}}$), we have approximately a 95% chance of being correct; if we say that the population mean falls between 77 and 83 ($\bar{X} \pm 3\ SE_{\bar{x}}$), we have approximately a 99+ % chance of being correct. In other words, the probability of the population mean being less than 78 or greater than 82 is only 5/100, or 5%. Note that as our degree of confidence increases, the limits get farther apart. This makes sense since we are 100% confident that the population mean is somewhere between our sample mean plus infinity and minus infinity!

You have probably come to the realization by now that the smaller the standard error of the mean is, the better; a smaller standard error indicates less sampling error. The major factor affecting the standard error of the mean is sample size. As the size of the sample increases, the standard error of the mean decreases. This makes sense since if we used the whole population there would be no sampling error at all. A large sample is more likely to represent a population than a small sample. This discussion should help you to understand why samples should be as large as possible; smaller samples entail more error than larger samples. Another factor affecting the standard error of the mean is the size of the population standard deviation. If it is large, members of the population are very spread out on the variable of interest, and sample means will also be very spread out. Of course the researcher has no control over the size of the population standard deviation, but the researcher can control sample size to some extent. Thus, the researcher should make every effort to acquire as many subjects as possible so that inferences about the population of interest will be as correct as possible.

All of the above discussion has been in reference to the standard error of a mean. An estimate of standard error, however, can also be computed for other measures of central tendency as well as measures of variability, relationship, and relative position. Further, an estimate of standard error can also be determined for the difference between means. In other words, at the conclusion of an experimental study we may have two sample means, one mean for the experimental group and one for the control group. In order to determine whether or not the difference between those means probably represents a true population difference, we need an estimate of the standard error of the difference between two means. Differences between two sample means are normally distributed around the mean difference in the population. Most differences will be close to the true difference and a few will be way off. In order to determine whether a difference found between sample means probably represents a true difference or a chance difference, tests of significance are applied to the data; tests of significance allow us to determine whether or not there is a significant difference between the means. Many tests of significance are based upon an estimate of standard error and they typically test a null hypothesis.

The Null Hypothesis

When we talk about the difference between two sample means being a true difference we mean that the difference was caused by the treatment (the independent variable), and not by chance. In other words, the difference is either caused by the treatment, as stated in the research hypothesis, or is the result of chance, random sampling error. The chance explanation for the difference is called the null hypothesis. The null hypothesis says in essence that there is no true difference or relationship between parameters in the populations and that any difference or relationship found for the samples is the result of sampling error. A null hypothesis might state:

> There is no significant difference between the mean reading
> comprehension of first-grade students who receive whole
> language reading instruction and first-grade students who
> receive basal reading instruction.

This hypothesis says that there really is not any difference between the two methods and if you find one in your study, it is not a true difference, but a chance difference resulting from sampling error.

The null hypothesis for a study is usually (although not necessarily) different from the research hypothesis.[2] The research hypothesis usually states that one method is expected to be more effective than another. Why have both? It is difficult to explain simply, but essentially the reason is that rejection of a null

---

[2]Sometimes our research hypothesis states the expectation that two approaches are equally effective. Recall a previous example concerning the comparative effectiveness of parent volunteers versus paid paraprofessionals.

hypothesis is more conclusive support for a positive research hypothesis. In other words, if the results of your study support your research hypothesis, you only have one piece of evidence based upon one situation. If you reject a null hypothesis, your case is stronger. As an analogy, suppose you hypothesize that all research textbooks contain a chapter on sampling. If you examine a research textbook and it does contain such a chapter, you have not *proven* your hypothesis, you have just found one little piece of evidence to support your hypothesis. If, on the other hand, the textbook you examine does not contain a chapter on sampling, your hypothesis is *disproven*. In other words, 1 book is enough to disprove your hypothesis, but 1,000 books are not enough to prove it; there may always be a book somewhere that does not contain a chapter on sampling. In a research study, the test of significance selected to determine whether a difference between means is a true difference provides a test of the null hypothesis. As a result, the null hypothesis is either rejected, as being probably false, or not rejected, being probably true. Notice the word "probably." We never know for sure whether we are making the correct decision; what we can do is estimate the probability of our being wrong. After we make the decision to reject or not reject the null hypothesis, we make an inference back to our research hypothesis. If, for example, our research hypothesis states that *A* is better than *B*, and if we reject the null hypothesis that *A* = *B*, and if the mean for *A* is greater than the mean for *B* (and not vice versa), then we conclude that our research hypothesis was supported. If we do not reject the null hypothesis *A* = *B*, then we conclude that our research hypothesis was not supported.

In order to test a null hypothesis we need a test of significance and we need to select a probability level which indicates how much risk we are willing to take that the decision we make is wrong.

Tests of Significance

At the end of an experimental research study the researcher typically has two or more group means. These means are very likely to be at least a little different. The researcher must then decide whether the means are significantly different, different enough to conclude that they represent a true difference. In other words, the researcher must make the decision whether or not to reject the null hypothesis. The researcher does not make this decision based on her or his own best guess. Instead, the researcher selects and applies an appropriate test of significance. The test of significance helps us to decide whether we can reject the null hypothesis and infer that the difference is significantly greater than a chance difference. If the difference is too large to attribute to chance, we reject the null hypothesis; if not, we do not reject it.

The test of significance is made at a preselected probability level and allows us to state that we have rejected the null hypothesis because we would expect to find a difference as large as we have found by chance only 5 times out of every 100 studies, or only 1 time in every 100 studies, or whatever; therefore, we conclude that the null hypothesis is *probably* false and reject it. Obviously, if we can say we would expect such a difference by chance only 1 time in 100 studies, we are more confident in our decision than if we say we would expect such a chance difference 5 times in 100. How confident we are depends upon the level of significance, or probability level, at which we perform our test of significance.

There are a number of different tests of significance which can be applied in research studies, one of which is more appropriate in a given situation. Factors such as the scale of measurement represented by the data, method of subject selection, the number of groups, and the number of independent variables determine which test of significance should be selected for a given experiment. Shortly, we will discuss and calculate several frequently used tests of significance—the *t* test, analysis of variance, and chi square.

Decision Making: Levels of Significance and Type I and Type II Errors

Based on a test of significance the researcher will either reject or not reject the null hypothesis as a probable explanation for results. In other words, the researcher will make the decision that the difference between the means is, or is not, too large to attribute to chance. The researcher never knows for sure whether he or she is right or wrong, only whether he or she is probably correct. Actually, there are four possibilities. If the null hypothesis is really true, and the researcher agrees that it is true (does not reject it), the researcher makes the correct decision. Similarly, if the null hypothesis is false, and the researcher rejects it (says there *is* a difference), the researcher also makes the correct decision. But what if the null hypothesis is true, there really is no difference, and the researcher rejects it and says there is a difference? The researcher makes an incorrect decision. Similarly, if the null hypothesis is false, there really is a significant difference between the means, but the researcher concludes that the null hypothesis is true and does not reject it, the researcher also makes an incorrect decision. In other words, the four possibilities are:

1. The null hypothesis is true ($A = B$), and the researcher concludes that it is true.
   Correct!
2. The null hypothesis is false ($A \neq B$), and the researcher concludes that it is false.
   Correct!
3. The null hypothesis is true ($A = B$), and the researcher concludes that it is false.
   Oops!
4. The null hypothesis is false ($A \neq B$) and the researcher concludes that it is true.
   Ooops!

The wrong decisions (Oops and Ooops) that can be made by researchers have "official" names. If the researcher rejects a null hypothesis that is really true (3 above), the researcher makes a Type I error; if the researcher fails to reject a null hypothesis that is really false (4 above), the researcher makes a Type II error. Figure 14.1 illustrates the four possible outcomes of decision making.

When the researcher makes the decision to reject or not reject the null hypothesis, she or he does so with a given probability of being correct. This probability of being correct is referred to as the significance level, or probability level, of the test of significance. If the decision is made to reject the null hypothesis, the means are concluded to be significantly different—too different to be the result of chance error. If the null hypothesis is not rejected, the means are determined to be not significantly different. The level of significance, or probability level, selected determines how large the difference between the means must be in order to be declared significantly different. The most commonly used probability level (symbolized as α) is the .05 level. Some studies use $\alpha = .01$ and occasionally an exploratory study will use $\alpha = .10$.

The true status of the null
hypothesis. It is really

		True (should not be rejected)	False (should be rejected)
The researcher's decision. The researcher concludes that the null hypothesis is	True (does not reject)	Correct Decision	Type II Error
	False (rejects)	Type I Error	Correct Decision

Figure 14.1. The four possible outcomes of decision making concerning rejection
of the null hypothesis.

The probability level selected determines the probability of committing a Type I error, that is, of rejecting a null hypothesis that is really true. Thus, if you select $\alpha = .05$, you have a 5% probability of making a Type I error, whereas if you select $\alpha = .01$, you have only a 1% probability of committing a Type I error. The less chance of being wrong you are willing to take, the greater the difference between the means must be. As an example, examine the six possible outcomes presented below and decide whether you think the means are significantly different. Assume that the means indicate the mean final performance on a 100-item test for two groups of 20 subjects each:

	Group A	*Group B*
1.	70.0	70.4
2.	70.0	71.0
3.	70.0	72.0
4.	70.0	75.0
5.	70.0	80.0
6.	70.0	90.0

How about outcome 1? Is 70.0 significantly different from 70.4 (a difference of .4)? Probably not; such a difference could easily occur by chance. How about outcome 2, 70.0 versus 71.0 (a difference of 1.0)? Probably not significantly different. How about outcome 6, 70.0 versus 90.0 (a difference of 20.0)? That difference probably is significant. How about 5, 70.0 versus 80.0? Probably a significant difference. How about 4, 70.0 versus 75.0? H-m-m-m. Is a 5-point difference a big enough difference? Up to a point the difference is probably too small to represent a true difference. Beyond a certain point the difference becomes large enough to be probably a true difference. Where is that magic point? At what point does a difference stop being too small and become "big enough"? The answer to these questions depends upon the probability level at which we perform our selected test of significance. The smaller our probability level is, the larger the difference must be. In the above example, if we were working at $\alpha = .05$, then a difference of 5 (say 70.0 versus 75.0) might be big enough. If, on the other hand, we were working at $\alpha = .01$ (a smaller chance of being wrong), a difference of at least 10 might be required (say 70.0 versus 80.0). Got the idea?

Thus, if you are working at $\alpha = .05$, and as a result of your test of significance you reject the null hypothesis, you are saying in essence that you do not believe the null hypothesis is true because the chances are only 5 out of 100 (.05) that a difference as large (or larger) as the one you have found would occur just by chance as a result of sampling error. In other words, there is a 95% chance that the difference resulted from manipulation of the independent variable, not chance. Similarly, if you are working at $\alpha = .01$ and reject the null hypothesis, you are saying that a difference as large as the one you have found would be expected to occur by chance only once for every 100 studies (1 out of 100, or .01). So why not set α at .000000001 and hardly ever be wrong? Good question; I am glad you asked it. If you select α to be very, very small, you definitely decrease your chances of committing a Type I error; you will hardly ever reject a true null hypothesis. *But*, guess what happens to your chances of committing a Type II error? Right. As you decrease the probability of committing a Type I error, you increase the probability of committing a Type II error, that is, of not rejecting a null hypothesis when you should (catch-22 again!). For example, you might conduct a study for which a mean difference of 9.5 represents a true difference. If you set α at .0001, however, you might require a mean difference of 20.0. If the difference actually found was 11.0, you would not reject the null hypothesis (11.0 is less than 20.0) although there really is a difference (11.0 is greater than 9.5). How do you decide which α level to work at, and when do you decide?

The choice of a probability level, α, is made prior to execution of the study. The researcher considers the relative seriousness of committing a Type I versus a Type II error and selects α accordingly. In other words, the researcher compares the consequences of making the two possible wrong decisions. As an example, suppose you are a teacher and one day your principal comes up to you and says: "I understand you have research training and I want you to do a study for me. I'm considering implementing the Whoopee Reading System in the school next year. This System is very costly, however; if implemented, we will have to spend a great deal of money on materials and inservice training. I don't want to do that unless it *really* works. I want you to conduct a pilot study this year with several groups and then tell me if the Whoopee System really results in better reading achievement. You know what you're doing, so you'll have my complete support in setting up the groups the way you want to and in implementing the study." In this case, which would be more serious, a Type I error or a Type II error? Suppose you conclude that the groups are significantly different, that the Whoopee System really works. Suppose it really does not. Suppose you make a Type I error. In this case, the principal is going to be *very* upset if a big investment is made based on your decision and at the end of a year's period there is no difference in achievement. On the other hand, suppose you conclude that the groups are not significantly different, that the Whoopee System does not really make a difference. Suppose it really does. Suppose you make a Type II error. In this case, what will happen? Nothing. You will tell the principal the System does not work, you will be thanked for the input, the System will not be implemented, and life will go on as usual. No one will ever know you made the wrong decision. Therefore, for this situation, which would *you* rather commit, a Type I error or a Type II error? Obviously, a Type II error. You want to be very sure you do not commit a Type I error. Therefore you would select a very small α, perhaps $\alpha = .01$ or even $\alpha = .001$. You want to be pretty darn sure there is a difference before you say there is.

As another example, suppose you are going to conduct an exploratory study to investigate the effectiveness of a new counseling technique. If you conclude that it is more effective, does make a difference, further research will be conducted. If you conclude that it does not make a difference, the new technique will be labeled as being not very promising. Now, which would be more serious, a Type I error or a

Type II error? If you conclude there is a difference, and there really is not (Type I error), no real harm will be done and the only real consequence will be that further research will probably disconfirm your finding. If, on the other hand, you conclude that the technique makes no difference, and it really does (Type II error), a technique may be prematurely abandoned; with a little refinement, this new technique might make a real difference. In this case, you would probably rather commit a Type I error than a Type II error. Therefore, you might select an α level as low as .10.

For most studies, α = .05 is a reasonable probability level. The consequences of committing a Type I error are usually not too serious. A no-no in selecting a probability level is to compute a test of significance, such as a *t* test, and then see "how significant it is." If the results just happen to be significant at α = .01 you do not say "oh goodie" and report that the *t* was significant at the .01 level. You put your cards on the table before you play the game.

A common misconception among beginning researchers is the notion that if you reject a null hypothesis you have "proven" your research hypothesis. Rejection of a null hypothesis, or lack of rejection, only supports or does not support a research hypothesis. If you reject a null hypothesis and conclude that the groups are really different, it does not mean that they are different for the reason you hypothesized. They may be different for some other reason. On the other hand, if you fail to reject the null hypothesis, it does not necessarily mean that your research hypothesis is wrong. The study, for example, may not have represented a fair test of your hypothesis. To use a former example, if you were investigating cooperative learning, and the cooperative learning group and the control group each received its respective treatment for one day, you probably would not find any differences between the groups. This would not mean that cooperative learning is not effective; if your study were conducted over a 6-month period, it might very well make a difference.

Two-Tailed and One-Tailed Tests

Tests of significance are almost always two-tailed. The null hypothesis states that there is no difference between the groups ($A = B$), and a two-tailed test allows for the possibility that a difference may occur in either direction; either group mean may be higher than the other ($A > B$ or $B > A$). A one-tailed test assumes that a difference can only occur in one direction; the null hypothesis states that one group is not better than another ($A \not> B$), and the one-tailed test assumes that if a difference occurs it will be in favor of that particular group ($A > B$). As an example, suppose a research hypothesis were:

> Kindergarten children who receive a mid-morning snack exhibit better behavior during the hour before lunch than kindergarten students who do not receive a mid-morning snack.

For this research hypothesis the null hypothesis would state:

> There is no difference between the behavior during the hour before lunch of kindergarten students who receive a mid-morning snack and kindergarten students who do not receive a mid-morning snack.

A two-tailed test of significance would allow for the possibility that either the group that received a snack or the group that did not might exhibit better behavior. For a one-tailed test, the hypothesis might state:

> Kindergarten children who receive a mid-morning snack do
> not exhibit better behavior during the hour before lunch
> than kindergarten children who do not receive a mid-morn-
> ing snack.

In this case, the assumption would be that if a difference were found between the groups it would be in favor of the group that received the snack. In other words, the researcher would consider it highly unlikely that not receiving a snack could result in better behavior than receiving one (although it *could* if they were fed sugar-coated chocolate twinkos!).

As mentioned before, tests of significance are almost always two-tailed. To select a one-tailed test of significance the researcher has to be pret-ty darn sure that a difference can only occur in one direction; this is not very often the case. When appropriate, a one-tailed test has one major advantage. The value resulting from application of the test of significance required for significance is smaller. In other words, it is "easier" to find a significant difference. It is difficult to explain simply why this is so, but it has to do with α. Suppose you are computing a *t* test of significance at $\alpha = .05$. If your test is two-tailed, you are allowing for the possibility of a positive *t* or a negative *t;* in other words, you are allowing that the mean of the first group may be higher than the mean of the second group ($\overline{X}_1 - \overline{X}_2$ = a positive number), or that the mean of the second group may be higher than the mean of the first group ($\overline{X}_1 - \overline{X}_2$ = a negative number). Thus, our α value, say .05, has to be divided in half, half for each possibility, .025 and .025 (.025 + .025 = .05). For a one-tailed test, the entire α value, say .05, is concentrated on one possible outcome, a positive *t*. Since .025 is a smaller probability of committing a Type I error than .05, for example, a larger *t* value is required. The above explanation applies to any α value and to other tests of significance besides the *t* test. While the above is definitely not the most scientific explanation of two-tailed and one-tailed tests, it should give you some conceptual understanding.

Degrees of Freedom

After you have determined whether the test will be two-tailed or one-tailed, selected a probability level, and computed a test of significance, you are ready to consult the appropriate table in order to determine the significance of your results. As you may recall from our discussion of the significance of *r* in Chapter 9, the appropriate table is usually entered at the intersection of your probability level and your degrees of freedom, *df.* Degrees of freedom are a function of such factors as the number of subjects and the number of groups. Recall that for the correlation coefficient, *r,* the appropriate degrees of freedom were determined by the formula $N - 2$, number of subjects minus 2. It is difficult to explain in plain English what the concept of degrees of freedom *means* but an illustration may help. Suppose I ask you to name any five numbers. You agree and say "25, 44, 62, 84, 2." In this case *N* is equal to 5 and you had 5 choices, or 5 degrees of freedom. Now suppose I tell you to name 5 more and you say "1, 2, 3, 4, . . . ," and I say "Wait! The mean of the five numbers must be 4." Now you have no choice—the last number *must be* 10 because 1 + 2 + 3 + 4 + 10 = 20 and 20 divided by 5 = 4. You lost one degree of freedom because of that one restriction, the restriction that the mean must be 4. In other words, instead of having $N = 5$ degrees of freedom, you only had $N = 4$ (5 – 1) degrees of freedom. Got the idea?

Each test of significance has its own formula for determining degrees of freedom. For the correlation coefficient, *r,* for example, the formula is $N - 2$. The number 2 is a constant. In other words, degrees of freedom are always determined for *r* by subtracting 2 from *N,* the number of subjects. Each of the inferential statistics we are about to discuss also has its own formula for degrees of freedom.

■ TESTS OF SIGNIFICANCE: TYPES

Different tests of significance are appropriate for different sets of data. It is important that the researcher select an appropriate test; an incorrect test can lead to incorrect conclusions. The first decision in selecting an appropriate test of significance is whether a parametric test may be used or whether a nonparametric test must be selected. Parametric tests are usually more powerful and generally to be preferred. By "more powerful" is meant more likely to reject a null hypothesis that is false; in other words, the researcher is less likely to commit a Type II error, less likely to not reject a null hypothesis that should be rejected.

Parametric tests, however, require that certain assumptions be met in order for them to be valid. One of the major assumptions underlying use of parametric tests is that the variable measured is normally distributed in the population (or at least that the form of the distribution is known). Since most variables studied in education are normally distributed, this assumption is usually met. A second major assumption is that the data represent an interval or a ratio scale of measurement. Again, since most measures used in education represent interval data, this assumption is usually met. In fact, this is one major advantage of using an interval scale—it permits application of a parametric test to the data. A third assumption is that subjects are selected independently for the study; in other words, that selection of one subject in no way affects selection of any other subject. Recall that the definition of random sampling is sampling in which every member of the population has an equal and *independent* chance of being selected for the sample. Thus, if randomization is involved in subject selection, the assumption of independence is met. Another assumption is that the variances of the population comparison groups are equal (or at least that the ratio of the variances is known). Recall that the variance of a group of scores is nothing more than the standard deviation squared.

With the exception of independence, some violation of one or more of these assumptions usually does not make too much difference, in other words, the same decision is made concerning the statistical significance of the results. However, if one or more assumptions are greatly violated, such as if the distribution is extremely skewed, parametric statistics should not be used. In such cases, a nonparametric test should be used. Nonparametric tests make no assumptions about the shape of the distribution. They are usually used when the data represent an ordinal or nominal scale, when a parametric assumption has been greatly violated, or when the nature of the distribution is not known.

If the data represent an interval or ratio scale, a parametric test should be used unless another of the assumptions is greatly violated. As mentioned before, parametric tests are more powerful. It is more difficult with a nonparametric test to reject a null hypothesis at a given level of significance; it usually takes a larger sample size to reach the same level of significance. Another advantage of parametric statistics is that they permit tests of a number of hypotheses that cannot be tested with a nonparametric test; there are a number of parametric statistics that have no counterpart among nonparametric statistics. Since parametric statistics seem to be relatively hardy, that is, do their job even with moderate assumption violation, they will usually be selected for analysis of research data.

With one exception, all of the statistics to be discussed are parametric statistics. Of course, we are not going to discuss each and every statistical test available to the researcher. A number of useful, commonly used statistics will be described, and a smaller number of frequently used statistics will be calculated. Although the statistics to be calculated are considered to be basic-level statistics, an analysis of research articles published over the 5-year period 1979–83 in the *American Educational Research Journal* and the *Journal of Educational Psychology* revealed that about one-third of them used one of these statistics as the major analysis.[3]

The *t* Test

The *t* test is used to determine whether two means are significantly different at a selected probability level. In other words, for a given sample size the *t* indicates how often a difference ($\overline{X}_1 - \overline{X}_2$) as large or larger would be found when there is no true population difference. The *t* test makes adjustments for the fact that the distribution of scores for small samples becomes increasingly different from a normal distribution as sample sizes become increasingly smaller. Distributions for smaller samples, for example, tend to be higher at both the mean and the ends. For a given α level, the values of *t* required to reject a null hypothesis are progressively higher for progressively smaller samples; as the size of the samples becomes larger (approaches infinity) the score distribution approaches normality.

The strategy of the *t* test is to compare the *actual* mean difference observed ($\overline{X}_1 - \overline{X}_2$) with the difference *expected* by chance. The *t* test involves forming the ratio of these two values. In other words, the numerator for a *t* test is the difference between the sample means $\overline{X}_1$ and $\overline{X}_2$, and the denominator is the chance difference which would be expected if the null hypothesis were true—the standard error of the difference between the means. The denominator, or error term, is a function of both sample size and group variance. Smaller sample sizes and greater variation within groups are associated with an expectation of greater random differences between groups. To explain it one more way, even if the null hypothesis is true you do not expect two sample means to be identical; there is going to be some chance variation. The *t* ratio determines whether the observed difference is sufficiently larger than a difference which would be expected by chance. After the numerator is divided by the denominator, the resulting *t* value is compared to the appropriate *t* table value (depending upon the probability level and the degrees of freedom); if the calculated *t* value is equal to or greater than the table value, then the null hypothesis is rejected.

There are two different types of *t* tests, the *t* test for independent samples and the *t* test for nonindependent samples.

The t *Test for Independent Samples*

Independent samples are samples that are randomly formed, that is, formed without any type of matching. The members of one group are not related to members of the other group in any systematic way other than that they are selected from the same population. If two groups are randomly formed, the expectation is that they are essentially the same at the beginning of a study with respect to performance on

---

[3]Goodwin, L. D., & Goodwin, W. L. (1985). Statistical techniques in AERJ articles, 1979–1983. The preparation of graduate students to read the educational research literature. *Educational Researcher, 14*(2), 5–11.

the dependent variable. Therefore, if they are essentially the same at the end of the study, the null hypothesis is probably true; if they are different at the end of the study, the null hypothesis is probably false, that is, the treatment does make a difference. The key word is *essentially*. We do not expect them to be identical at the end, they are bound to be somewhat different; the question is whether they are significantly different. Thus, the *t* test for independent samples is used to determine whether there is probably a significant difference between the means of two independent samples.

The t Test for Nonindependent Samples

Nonindependent samples are samples formed by some type of matching. The ultimate matching, of course, is when the two samples are really the same sample group at two different times, such as one group which receives two different treatments at two different times or which is pretested before a treatment and then posttested. When samples are not independent, the members of one group are systematically related to the members of a second group (especially if it is the same group at two different times). If samples are nonindependent, scores on the dependent variable are expected to be correlated and a special *t* test for correlated, or nonindependent, means must be used. When samples are nonindependent, the error term of the *t* test tends to be smaller and therefore there is a higher probability that the null hypothesis will be rejected. Thus, the *t* test for nonindependent samples is used to determine whether there is probably a significant difference between the means of two matched, or nonindependent, samples or between the means for one sample at two different times.

Analysis of Gain Scores (Difference Scores)

When two groups are pretested, administered a treatment, and then posttested, the *t* test may or may not be the appropriate analysis technique. Many beginning researchers (and some not-so-beginning researchers) assume that the logical procedure is to (1) subtract each subject's pretest score from his or her posttest score (resulting in a gain, or difference, score), (2) compute the mean gain, or difference, score for each group, and (3) calculate a *t* value for the difference between the two average mean differences. There are a number of problems associated with this approach, however, the major one being lack of equal opportunity to grow. Every subject does not have the same room to gain. A subject who scores very low on a pretest has a lot of room, and a subject who scores very high only has a little room (referred to as the ceiling effect). Who has improved, or gained, more—a subject who goes from 20 to 70 (a gain of 50) or a subject who goes from 85 to 100 (a gain of only 15 but perhaps a perfect score)?

The correct analysis of posttest scores for two groups depends upon the performance of the two groups on the pretest. If both groups are essentially the same on the pretest, for example, neither group knows anything, then posttest scores can be directly compared using a *t* test. If, on the other hand, there is a difference between the groups on the pretest, the preferred posttest analysis is analysis of covariance. Recall that analysis of covariance adjusts posttest scores for initial differences on some variable (in this case the pretest) related to performance on the dependent variable. Thus, in order to determine whether analysis of covariance is necessary, a Pearson *r* can be calculated to determine if there is a significant relationship between pretest scores and posttest scores. If not, a simple *t* test can be computed on posttest scores (or as we shall see shortly, analysis of covariance may be computed anyway, but for a different reason).

Simple Analysis of Variance

Simple, or one-way, analysis of variance (ANOVA) is used to determine whether there is a significant difference between two or more means at a selected probability level. In a study involving three groups, for example, the ANOVA is the appropriate analysis technique. Three (or more) posttest means are bound to be different; the question is whether the differences represent true differences or chance differences resulting from sampling error. To answer this question at a given probability level the ANOVA is applied to the data and an F ratio is computed. You may be wondering why you cannot just compute a lot of t tests, one for each pair of means. Aside from some statistical problems concerning resulting distortion of your probability level, it is more convenient to perform one ANOVA than several ts. For four means, for example, six separate t tests would be required ($\overline{X}_1 - \overline{X}_2$, $\overline{X}_1 - \overline{X}_3$, $\overline{X}_1 - \overline{X}_4$, $\overline{X}_2 - \overline{X}_3$, $\overline{X}_2 - \overline{X}_4$, $\overline{X}_3 - \overline{X}_4$).

The concept underlying ANOVA is that the total variation, or variance, of scores can be attributed to two sources—variance between groups (variance caused by the treatment) and variance within groups (error variance). As with the t test, a ratio is formed (the F ratio) with group differences as the numerator (variance between groups) and an error term as the denominator (variance within groups). Randomly formed groups are assumed to be essentially the same at the beginning of a study on a measure of the dependent variable. At the end of the study, after administration of the independent variable (treatment), we determine whether the between groups (treatment) variance differs from the within groups (error) variance by more than what would be expected by chance. In other words, if the treatment variance is enough larger than the error variance, a significant F ratio results, the null hypothesis is rejected, and it is concluded that the treatment had a significant effect on the dependent variable. If, on the other hand, the treatment variance and error variance are essentially the same (do not differ by more than what would be expected by chance), the resulting F ratio is not significant and the null hypothesis is not rejected. The greater the difference, the larger the F ratio. To determine whether or not the F ratio is significant an F table is entered at the place corresponding to the selected probability level and the appropriate degrees of freedom. The degrees of freedom for the F ratio are a function of the number of groups and the number of subjects.

Multiple Comparisons

If the F ratio is determined to be nonsignificant, the party is over. But what if it is significant? What do you know? All you know is that there is at least one significant difference somewhere, you do not know where that difference is; you do not know which means are significantly different from which other means. It might be, for example, that three means are equal but all greater than a fourth mean, that is, $\overline{X}_1 = \overline{X}_2 = \overline{X}_3$ and each mean is $> \overline{X}_4$ ($\overline{X}_1$, $\overline{X}_2$, and $\overline{X}_3$ might represent three treatments and $\overline{X}_4$ might represent a control group). Or it might be that $\overline{X}_1 = \overline{X}_2$, and $\overline{X}_3 = \overline{X}_4$, but $\overline{X}_1$ and $\overline{X}_2$ are each greater than $\overline{X}_3$ and $\overline{X}_4$. When the F ratio is significant, and more than two means are involved, multiple comparison procedures are used to determine which means are significantly different from which other means. There are a number of different multiple comparison techniques available to the researcher. In essence, they involve calculation of a special form of the *t* test, a form for which the error term is based on the combined variance of all the groups, not just the groups being compared. This special *t* adjusts for the fact that many tests are being executed. What happens is that when many tests are performed, the probability level, α, tends to increase; if α is supposed to be .05, it will actually end up being greater, maybe .90, if many tests are performed. Thus, the chance of finding a significant difference is increased but so is the chance of committing a Type I error. Which mean comparisons are to be made should generally be decided upon *before* the study is conducted, not after, and should be based upon research hypotheses. In other words, application of a multiple comparison technique should not be essentially a "fishing expedition" in which the researcher looks for any difference she or he can find.[4]

Of the many multiple comparison techniques available probably the most often used is the Scheffé test. The Scheffé test is appropriate for making any and all possible comparisons involving a set of means. The calculations for this approach are quite simple and sample sizes do not have to be equal, as is the case with some multiple comparison techniques. The Scheffé test is very conservative, which is good news and bad news. The good news is that the probability of committing a Type I error for any comparison of means is never greater than the α level selected for the original analysis of variance. The bad news is that it is entirely possible, given the comparisons selected for investigation, to find no significant differences even though the *F* for the analysis of variance was significant. In general, however, the flexibility of the Scheffé test and its ease of application make it useful for a wide variety of situations.

Factorial Analysis of Variance

If a research study is based upon a factorial design and investigates two or more independent variables and the interactions between them, the appropriate statistical analysis is a factorial, or multifactor, analysis of variance. Such an analysis yields a separate *F* ratio for each independent variable and one for each interaction. Analysis of the data presented in Figure 11.5, for example, would yield three *F*s— one for the manipulated, independent variable, Method, one for the control independent variable, IQ, and one for the interaction between Method and IQ. For the No Interaction example, the *F* for Method would probably be significant since method *A* appears to be significantly more effective than method *B* (70 versus 30); the *F* for IQ would also probably be significant since high IQ subjects appear to have performed significantly better than low IQ subjects (60 versus 40); the *F* for the interaction between Method and IQ would not be significant since method *A* is more effective than method *B* for both IQ groups, not differentially effective for one level of IQ or another (80 > 40, 60 > 20). On the other hand, for the Interaction example, the *F* for Method would not be significant since method *A* is equally as effective as method *B* overall (50 = 50); the *F* for IQ would probably be significant since high IQ subjects still appear to have performed significantly better than low IQ subjects (70 versus 30); the *F* for the interaction between Method and IQ, however, would probably be significant since the methods appear to be differentially

---

[4]It is possible to obtain a nonsignificant *F* ratio and yet to find a significant difference between two or more means. Some statisticians believe that it is legitimate to investigate this possibility if the *F* ratio is nonsignificant (most do not). All statisticians and researchers, however, agree that multiple comparison techniques should not be applied with abandon in the hopes that "something will turn up."

effective depending upon the IQ level; method *A* is better for high IQ subjects (80 versus 60) and method *B* is better for low IQ subjects (20 versus 40). Another way of looking at it is to see that for the No Interaction example (80 + 20) = (60 + 40); for the Interaction example (80 + 40) ≠ (20 + 60).

A factorial analysis of variance is not as difficult to calculate as you may think. If no more than two variables are involved, and if you have access to a calculator, one can be performed without too much difficulty. Most statistics texts outline the procedure to be followed. If more than two variables are involved, it is usually better to use a computer if possible.

Analysis of Covariance

Analysis of covariance (ANCOVA) is used in two major ways, as a technique for controlling extraneous variables and as a means of increasing power. Covariance is a form of ANOVA and is a statistical, rather than an experimental, method that can be used to equate groups on one or more variables. Use of covariance is essentially equivalent to matching groups on the variable or variables to be controlled. In a number of situations, covariance is the preferred approach to control. As pointed out previously, for example, analysis of pretest-posttest gain scores has several disadvantages. Thus, for a study based on a pretest-posttest control group design, covariance is a superior method for controlling for pretest differences.

Essentially, ANCOVA adjusts posttest scores for initial differences on some variable and compares adjusted scores. In other words, the groups are equalized with respect to the control variable and then compared. It's sort of like handicapping in bowling; in an attempt to equalize teams, high scorers are given little or no handicap, low scorers are given big handicaps, and so forth. Any variable that is correlated with the dependent variable can be controlled for using covariance. Pretest performance, IQ, readiness, and specific aptitude are frequently controlled for in educational research studies through the use of analysis of covariance. If the variable to be controlled is a variable such as IQ which is very unlikely to be affected by manipulation of the independent variable under study, then it does not really matter when such data are collected—prior to, during, or following the experiment. Otherwise, as in the case of a pretest of the dependent variable, the covariate data must be collected prior to the initiation of treatments. By using covariance we are attempting to reduce variation in posttest scores which is attributable to another variable. Ideally, we would like all posttest variance to be attributable to the treatment conditions.

Analysis of covariance is a control technique used in both causal-comparative studies in which already formed, not necessarily equal groups are involved and in experimental studies in which either existing groups or randomly formed groups are involved; randomization does not guarantee that groups will be equated on all variables. Unfortunately, the situation for which ANCOVA is least appropriate is the situation for which it is most often used. Covariance is based on the assumption that subjects have been randomly assigned to treatment groups. It is therefore best used in conjunction with true experimental designs. If existing, or intact, groups are involved but treatments are assigned to groups randomly, covariance may still be used but results must be interpreted with due caution. If covariance is used with existing groups and nonmanipulated independent variables, as in causal-comparative studies, the results are likely to be misleading at best. There is evidence, for example, that improper use of covariance tends to give an artificial advantage to whichever group scores higher initially on the variable to be controlled. Thus, for example, if an experimental group has a higher pretest score than a control group, it is difficult to interpret results if the experimental group scores significantly higher than the control group on the posttest.[5] There are other assumptions associated with the use of analysis of covariance. Violation of these assumptions is not as serious, however, if subjects have been randomly assigned to treatment groups.[6]

A second, not previously discussed, function of ANCOVA is that it increases the power of a statistical test by reducing within-group (error) variance. Although increasing sample size also increases power, the researcher is often limited to samples of a given size because of financial and practical reasons. The power-increasing function of ANCOVA is directly related to the degree of randomization involved in formation of the groups; the results of ANCOVA are least likely to be valid when already formed groups to which treatments have not been randomly assigned are used. Further, since randomization increases the validity of ANCOVA, and since randomization can generally be counted on to equate groups on relevant variables, Huck and others urge that researchers consider the primary value of analysis of covariance to be its ability to increase power rather than its ability to equate groups on extraneous variables.[7]

As pointed out before, application of the analysis of covariance technique is quite a complex, lengthy procedure which is hardly ever hand calculated. Almost all researchers use computer programs for reasons of accuracy and sanity!

Multiple Regression

As discussed in Part Six, since a combination of variables usually results in a more accurate prediction than any one variable, prediction studies often result in a prediction equation referred to as a multiple regression equation. A multiple regression equation uses variables that are known to individually predict (correlate with) the criterion to make a more accurate prediction. Thus, for example, we might use high school GPA, Scholastic Aptitude Test (SAT) scores, and rank in graduating class to predict college GPA at the end of the first semester of college. Use of multiple regression is increasing, primarily because of its versatility and precision. It can be used with data representing any scale of measurement and can be used to analyze the results of experimental and causal-comparative, as well as correlational, studies. It determines not only whether variables are related, but also the degree to which they are related.

To see how multiple regression works, we will use the above example concerning college GPA. The first step in multiple regression is to identify the variable which *best* predicts the criterion, that is, is most highly correlated with it. Since past performance is generally the best predictor of future performance, high school GPA would probably be the best predictor. The next step is to identify the variable that

---

[5] Campbell, D. T., & Boruch, R. F. (1975). Making the case for randomized assignment to treatments by considering the alternatives: Six ways in which quasi-experimental evaluations in compensatory education tend to underestimate effects. In C. A. Bennett and A. A. Lumsdaine (Eds.), *Evaluation and experiment: Some critical issues in assessing social programs.* Seattle: Academic Press.

[6] For further discussion of these concepts, see: Elasoff, J. D. (1969). Analysis of covariance: A delicate instrument. *American Educational Research Journal, 6,* 383–401; Evans, S. H., & Anastasio, E. J. (1968). Misuse of analysis of covariance when treatment effect and covariate are confounded. *Psychological Bulletin, 69,* 225–234; *and* Winer, B. J. (1991). *Statistical principles in experimental design* (3rd ed.) New York: McGraw-Hill.

[7] Huck, S. W. (1972). The analysis of covariance: Increased power through reduced variability. *Journal of Experimental Education, 41*(1), 42–46.

most improves the prediction which is based on the first variable only. In other words, in our case, the question would be "Do we get a more accurate prediction using high school GPA and SAT scores *or* using high school GPA and rank in graduating class?" The results of multiple regression would give us the answer to that question and would also tell us *by how much* the prediction was improved. In our case, the answer might be high school GPA and SAT scores. That would leave rank in graduating class. For this last variable, the results of multiple regression would tell us by how much our prediction would be improved if we included it. Since our three predictors would most probably all be correlated with each other, as well as with the criterion, it might be that rank in graduating class adds very little to the accuracy of a prediction based on high school GPA and SAT scores. A study involving more than three variables works exactly the same way; at each step it is determined which variable adds the most to the prediction and how much it adds.

It should be noted that the sign, positive or negative, of the relationship between a predictor and the criterion has nothing to do with how good a predictor it is. Recall that $r = -1.00$ represents a relationship just as strong as $r = +1.00$; the only difference indicated is the nature of the relationship. It should also be noted that the number of predictor variables is related to the needed sample size; the greater the number of variables, the larger the sample size needs to be. The larger the sample size is in relation to the number of variables, the greater the probability is that the prediction equation will work with groups other than those involved in creating the equation.

With increasing frequency, multiple regression is being used as an alternative to the various analysis of variance techniques. When this is the case, the dependent variable, or posttest scores, becomes the criterion variable, and the predictors include group membership (e.g., experimental versus control) and any other appropriate variables, such as pretest scores. The results indicate not only whether group membership is significantly related to posttest performance, but also the magnitude of the relationship. For analyses such as these, the researcher typically specifies the order in which variables are to be checked. For analysis of covariance, with pretest scores as the covariate, for example, the researcher specifies that pretest scores be entered into the equation first; it can then be determined whether group membership significantly improves the equation.

Chi Square

Chi square, symbolized as χ^2, is a nonparametric test of significance appropriate when the data are in the form of frequency counts (or percentages or proportions which can be converted to frequencies) occurring in two or more mutually exclusive categories.[8] Thus, chi square is appropriate when the data represent a nominal scale, and the categories may be true categories (e.g., male vs. female) or artificial categories (e.g., tall vs. short). (See Chapter 12.) A chi square test compares proportions actually observed in a study with proportions expected, to see if they are significantly different. Expected proportions are usually the frequencies which would be expected if the groups were equal, although they may be based on past data. The chi square value increases as the difference between observed and expected frequencies increases. Whether the chi square is significant is determined by consulting a chi square table.

---

[8]Chi is pronounced KEYE, like those things you see with; not CHI as in child.

One-Dimensional Chi Square

The chi square can be used to compare frequencies occurring in different categories or the categories may be groups, so that the chi square is comparing groups with respect to the frequency of occurrence of different events. As an example, suppose you stopped 90 shoppers in a supermarket and asked them to taste three different brands of peanut butter (unidentified to the shoppers, of course) and to tell you which one tasted best. Suppose that 40 shoppers chose brand X, 30 chose brand Y, and 20 chose brand Z. If the null hypothesis were true, if the three brands tasted essentially the same, we would expect an equal number of shoppers to select each brand—30, 30, and 30 (there were 90 shoppers who "voted"). We can present our data in what is called a *contingency table* as shown below:

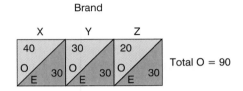

where
$\qquad$ O = observed frequencies
$\qquad$ E = expected frequencies

To determine whether the observed frequencies (40, 30, 20) were significantly different from the expected frequencies (30, 30, 30), a chi square test could be applied. If the chi square were significant, the null hypothesis would be rejected, and it would be concluded that the brands do taste different.

As another example, you might wish to investigate whether college sophomores prefer to study alone or with others. Tabulation, based on a random sample of 100 sophomores, might reveal that 45 prefer to study alone, and 55 prefer to study with others. The null hypothesis of no preference would suggest a 50-50 split. The corresponding contingency table would look as follows:

Study Preference

Alone	Others	
45	55	
O / E 50	O / E 50	Total O = 100

In order to determine whether the groups were significantly different, you would compare the observed frequencies (45, 55) with the expected frequencies (50, 50) using a chi square test of significance.

Two-Dimensional Chi Square

The chi square may also be used when frequencies are categorized along more than one dimension, sort of a factorial chi square. In the above study, for example, you might select a stratified sample, comprising 50 males and 50 females. Responses could then be classified by study preference and by sex, a two-way classification, in order to see if study preference is related to the sex of the subject. The corresponding contingency table would be set up as follows:

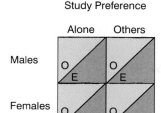

Although 2 x 2 applications are quite common, contingency tables may be based on any number of categories; thus, such tables may be, as examples, 2 x 3, 3 x 3, 2 x 4, and so forth. When a two-way classification is used, calculation of expected frequencies is a little more complex, but not difficult (as you will see later in the chapter).

Figure 14.2 summarizes the conditions for which each of the statistics discussed in this section are appropriate.

■ CALCULATION AND INTERPRETATION OF SELECTED TESTS OF SIGNIFICANCE

There are many tests of significance available to the researcher, some of which are used much more frequently than others. We will calculate and interpret those which are both frequently appropriate and not beyond your current level of research competence: the *t* test for independent samples, the *t* test for nonindependent samples, simple (or one-way) analysis of variance, the Scheffé test, and chi square. In each case the easiest formula will be used. At first glance some of the formulas may look horrible, but they are really easy. Just like the descriptive statistics, they only *look* hard. You are already familiar with most of the symbols involved, so they may not look so scary after all. Regardless of how it looks, however, each formula will transform "magically" into an arithmetic problem in one easy step. Although a sample size of 5 is hardly ever considered to be acceptable, we will again work with this number for the sake of illustration. In other words, all of our calculations (except for the chi square) will be based on the scores for groups each containing 5 subjects so that you can concentrate on how the calculation is being done and will not get lost in the numbers. For the same reason, we will also use very small numbers.

The *t* Test for Independent Samples

Suppose we have the following sets of posttest scores for two randomly formed groups:

Group 1	Group 2
3	2
4	3
5	3
6	3
7	4

Statistic	Number of Groups	Number of Independent Variables	Type of Data	Related Designs[a]
t test for independent samples	2	1	interval or ratio	1,2,4[b]
t test for nonindependent samples	2	1	interval or ratio	4 (if groups are matched)
simple ANOVA	≥2	1	interval or ratio	1,2,4
Scheffé test	≥2	1	interval or ratio	1,2,4
factorial ANOVA	≥2	≥2	interval or ratio	3
analysis of covariance	≥2	≥2	interval or ratio	1,2,3,4
multiple regression	≥1	≥1	all	1,2,3,4
chi square	≥2	≥1	nominal	1,2,3,4

[a] See Figure 11.2

[b] The *t* test for independent samples is appropriate for designs 1 and 4 *if* there is no relationship between pretest scores and posttest scores. If there is, analysis of covariance is required.

Figure 14.2.   **Summary of conditions for which selected statistics are appropriate.**

Are these two sets of scores significantly different? They are different, but are they *significantly* different? The appropriate test of significance to use in order to answer this question is the *t* test for independent samples. The formula is:

$$t = \frac{\overline{X}_1 - \overline{X}_2}{\sqrt{\left(\dfrac{SS_1 + SS_2}{n_1 + n_2 - 2}\right)\left(\dfrac{1}{n_1} + \dfrac{1}{n_2}\right)}}$$

Does it look bad? Is it? What will it turn into? (The answers are: Yes! No! An arithmetic problem. See Chapter 14 photo.) If you look at the formula you will see that you are already familiar with each of the pieces. The numerator is simply the difference between the two means $\overline{X}_1$ and $\overline{X}_2$. Each of the *n*s refers to the number of subjects in each group; thus, $n_1 = 5$ and $n_2 = 5$. What about the *SS*s? How do we find them? Right! We calculate each *SS* in the same way as we did for the standard deviation. Thus:

$$SS_1 = \sum X_1^2 - \frac{(\sum X_1)^2}{n_1} \text{ and } SS_2 = \sum X_2^2 - \frac{(\sum X_2)^2}{n_2}$$

Remember? Okay, now let's find each piece.

First, let's calculate means, sums, and sums of squares, and let's label the scores for group 1 as X_1 and the scores for group 2 as X_2:

X_1	X_1^2	X_2	X_2^2
3	9	2	4
4	16	3	9
5	25	3	9
6	36	3	9
7	49	4	16
$\Sigma X_1 = 25$	$\Sigma X_1^2 = 135$	$\Sigma X_2 = 15$	$\Sigma X_2^2 = 47$

$$\overline{X}_1 = \frac{25}{5} = 5 \qquad\qquad \overline{X}_2 = \frac{15}{5} = 3$$

Next, we need the *SS*s:

$$SS_1 = \Sigma X_1^2 - \frac{(\Sigma X_1)^2}{n_1} \qquad SS_2 = \Sigma X_2^2 - \frac{(\Sigma X_2)^2}{n_2}$$

$$= 135 - \frac{(25)^2}{5} \qquad\qquad = 47 - \frac{(15)^2}{5}$$

$$= 135 - 125 \qquad\qquad = 47 - 45$$

$$= 10 \qquad\qquad\qquad = 2$$

Now we have everything we need and all we have to do is substitute the correct number for each symbol in the formula:

$$t = \frac{\overline{X}_1 - \overline{X}_2}{\sqrt{\left(\dfrac{SS_1 + SS_2}{n_1 + n_2 - 2}\right)\left(\dfrac{1}{n_1} + \dfrac{1}{n_2}\right)}} = \frac{5 - 3}{\sqrt{\left(\dfrac{10 + 2}{5 + 5 - 2}\right)\left(\dfrac{1}{5} + \dfrac{1}{5}\right)}}$$

Now what do we have? A statistic? No! An arithmetic problem? Yes! A hard arithmetic problem? No! Now, if we just do what the formula tells us to do we will have no problem at all. The first thing it says to do is to subtract 3 from 5:

$$= \frac{2}{\sqrt{\left(\dfrac{10 + 2}{5 + 5 - 2}\right)\left(\dfrac{1}{5} + \dfrac{1}{5}\right)}}$$

So far so good? Terrific. Now, the next thing it says is to add 10 and 2. That does not sound too tough:

$$= \frac{2}{\sqrt{\left(\dfrac{12}{5 + 5 - 2}\right)\left(\dfrac{1}{5} + \dfrac{1}{5}\right)}}$$

Okay, the next step is to add 5 and 5 and subtract 2:

$$= \frac{2}{\sqrt{\left(\dfrac{12}{8}\right)\left(\dfrac{1}{5}+\dfrac{1}{5}\right)}}$$

Did you follow that? $5 + 5 - 2 = 10 - 2 = 8$. Next, we add $1/5$ to $1/5$ and get guess what:

$$= \frac{2}{\sqrt{\left(\dfrac{12}{8}\right)\left(\dfrac{2}{5}\right)}}$$

Right! $1/5 + 1/5 = 2/5$. Before we go any further, this would be a good time to convert those fractions to decimals. To convert a fraction to a decimal you simply divide the numerator by the denominator. If you are using a calculator, you enter the top number (e.g., 12) first, hit the ÷ key, and then enter the bottom number (e.g., 8). Thus, $12/8 = 1.5$ and $2/5 = .4$.

Substituting the decimals for the fractions we have:

$$t = \frac{2}{\sqrt{\left(\dfrac{12}{8}\right)\left(\dfrac{2}{5}\right)}} = \frac{2}{\sqrt{(1.5)\,(.4)}}$$

Since the parentheses indicate multiplication, we next multiply 1.5 by $.4$. Now we have:

$$t = \frac{2}{\sqrt{(1.5)\,(.4)}} = \frac{2}{\sqrt{.60}}$$

We are almost through, but now we have to find the square root of $.60$; the square root of $.60$ is $.74$. Substituting in our square root we have:

$$t = \frac{2}{\sqrt{.60}} = \frac{2}{.774}$$

One more step! Once we divide 2 by $.774$ we will be through.

$$\text{Therefore, } t = \frac{2}{.774} = 2.58$$

Assuming we selected $\alpha = .05$, the only thing we need before we go to the t table is the appropriate degrees of freedom. For the t test for independent samples, the formula for degrees of freedom is $n_1 + n_2 - 2$. For our example, $df = n_1 + n_2 - 2 = 5 + 5 - 2 = 8$. Therefore, $t = 2.58$, $\alpha = .05$, $df = 8$. (STATPAK printout on next page).

```
================================================================
                   t-TEST FOR INDEPENDENT SAMPLES
================================================================
     STATISTIC                                          VALUE
----------------------------------------------------------------
     NO. OF SCORES IN GROUP ONE                            5

     SUM OF SCORES IN GROUP ONE                         25.00

     MEAN OF GROUP ONE                                   5.00

     SUM OF SQUARED SCORES IN GROUP ONE                135.00

     SS OF GROUP ONE                                    10.00

     NO. OF SCORES IN GROUP TWO                            5

     SUM OF SCORES IN GROUP TWO                         15.00

     MEAN OF GROUP TWO                                   3.00

     SUM OF SQUARED SCORES IN GROUP TWO                 47.00

     SS OF GROUP TWO                                     2.00

     t-VALUE                                             2.58

     DEGREES OF FREEDOM (df)                               8
================================================================
```

Now go to Table A.4 in the Appendix. The p values in the table are the probabilities associated with various α levels. In our case, we are really asking the following question: Given α = .05, and df = 8, what is the probability of getting $t \geq 2.58$ if there really is no difference? Okay, now run the index finger of your right hand across the probability row at the top of the table until you get to .05. Now run the index finger of your left hand down the degrees of freedom column until you get to 8. Now move your right index finger down the column and your left index finger across; they intersect at 2.306. The value 2.306, or 2.31, is the t value required for rejection of the null hypothesis with α = .05 and df = 8. Is our t value 2.58 > 2.31? Yes, and therefore we reject the null hypothesis. Are the means different? Yes. Are they significantly different? Yes. Was that hard? Of course not. Are all the tests of significance going to be that easy? Of course!

Note that the table value, 2.306 or 2.31, was the value required to reject the null hypothesis given α *equal to* .05. If, instead of t = 2.58, we got t = 2.31, then our probability of committing a Type I error would be *exactly* .05, i.e., p = .05. But, since our value, t = 2.58, was *greater* than the table value, 2.31, our probability of committing a Type I error is *less,* i.e., $p < .05$. In other words, we got *more* than we needed so our chances of being wrong are less.

Suppose our t value were 2.29. What would we conclude? We would conclude that there is no significant difference between the groups, because 2.29 < 2.31. We could express this conclusion by stating $p > .05$; in other words, because our value is *less* than required for α = .05, our probability of committing a Type I error is *greater.* Usually, however, if results are not significant, the abbreviation N.S. is used to represent *not* significant. How about if we concluded that our t was *almost* significant? Boooo! A *t* is not *almost* significant or *really* significant; it is or it is not significant. You will never see a research report that says "rats, almost made it" or "pret-ty close"!

What if we selected $\alpha = .01$? Table A.4 indicates that 3.355, or 3.36, is the *t* value required for rejection of the null hypothesis with $\alpha = .01$ and *df* = 8. Is our value 2.58 > 3.36? No, and therefore we would *not* reject the null hypothesis. Are the means different? Yes. Are they significantly different? For $\alpha = .05$, the answer is yes, but for $\alpha = .01$ the answer is no. Thus, we see that the smaller the risk we are willing to take of committing a Type I error, the larger our *t* value has to be.

What if our *t* value had been −2.58? (Table A.4 has no negative values.) We would have done exactly what we did; we would have looked up 2.58. The only thing that determines whether the *t* is positive or negative is the order of the means; the denominator is always positive. In our example we had a mean difference of 5 − 3, or 2. If we had reversed the means, we would have had 3 − 5, or −2. As long as we know which mean goes with which group, the order is unimportant. The only thing that matters is the size of the difference. So, if you do not like negative numbers, put the larger mean first. Remember, the table is two-tailed; it is prepared to deal with a difference in favor of either group.

Are we having fun yet?

The *t* Test for Nonindependent Samples

Let us assume that we have the following sets of scores for two matched groups:

X_1	X_2
2	4
3	5
4	4
5	7
6	10

Are these two sets of scores significantly different? They are different, but are they significantly different? The appropriate test of significance to use in order to answer this question is the *t* test for nonindependent samples. The formula is:

$$t = \frac{\overline{D}}{\sqrt{\dfrac{\sum D^2 - \dfrac{(\sum D)^2}{N}}{N(N-1)}}}$$

Except for the *D*s the formula should look very familiar. If the *D*s were *X*s, you would know exactly what to do. Whatever *D*s are, we are going to find their mean, $\overline{D}$, add up their squares, $\sum D^2$, and square their sum $(\sum D)^2$. What do you suppose *D* could possibly stand for? Right! *D* stands for difference. The difference between what? Right, *D* is the difference between the matched pairs. Thus, each *D* equals $X_2 - X_1$. For our data, the first pair of scores is 2 and 4 and *D* = +2. Got it? Okay, let us find the *D*s for each pair of scores. While we are at it we might as well get the squares, the sums, and the mean. The mean of the *D*s is found the same way as any other mean, by adding up the *D*s and dividing by the number of *D*s:

X_1	X_2	D	D^2
2	4	+2	4
3	5	+2	4
4	4	0	0
5	7	+2	4
6	10	+4	16
		$\sum D = 10$	$\sum D^2 = 28$

$$\bar{D} = \frac{\sum D}{N} = \frac{10}{5} = 2$$

Now we have everything we need, and all we have to do is substitute the correct number for the correct symbol in the formula:

$$t = \frac{\bar{D}}{\sqrt{\dfrac{\sum D^2 - \dfrac{(\sum D)^2}{N}}{N(N-1)}}} = \frac{2}{\sqrt{\dfrac{28 - \dfrac{(10)^2}{5}}{5(5-1)}}}$$

Now what do we have? Right! An easy arithmetic problem. Now that you are an old pro, we can solve this arithmetic problem rather quickly. Below, the steps are executed one at a time with an explanation for each step to the right of the step:

$$t = \frac{2}{\sqrt{\dfrac{28 - \dfrac{(10)^2}{5}}{5(5-1)}}}$$

$$= \frac{2}{\sqrt{\dfrac{28 - \dfrac{100}{5}}{5(5-1)}}} \qquad 10^2 = 100$$

$$= \frac{2}{\sqrt{\dfrac{28 - 20}{5(5-1)}}} \qquad \frac{100}{5} = 20$$

$$= \frac{2}{\sqrt{\dfrac{8}{5(5-1)}}} \qquad 28 - 20 = 8$$

$$= \frac{2}{\sqrt{\dfrac{8}{5\,(4)}}} \qquad\qquad (5-1) = 4$$

$$= \frac{2}{\sqrt{\dfrac{8}{20}}} \qquad\qquad 5(4) = 20$$

$$= \frac{2}{\sqrt{.4}} \qquad\qquad \frac{8}{20} = \frac{4}{10}$$

$$= \frac{2}{.63} \qquad\qquad \sqrt{.4} = .63$$

$$t = 3.17$$

Thus, $t = 3.17$. Assuming $\alpha = .05$, the only thing we need before we go to the t table is the appropriate degrees of freedom. For the t test for nonindependent samples, the formula for degrees of freedom is $N - 1$, the number of pairs minus 1. For our example, $N - 1 = 5 - 1 = 4$. Therefore, $t = 3.17$, $\alpha = .05$, $df = 4$ (STATPAK printout below).

```
===============================================================================
                     t-TEST FOR NONINDEPENDENT SAMPLES
===============================================================================
    STATISTIC                                                      VALUE
-------------------------------------------------------------------------------

   NO. OF PAIRS OF SCORES                                            5

   SUM OF "D"                                                      10.00

   MEAN OF D'S                                                      2.00

          2
   SUM OF "D "                                                     28.00

   t-VALUE                                                          3.17

   DEGREES OF FREEDOM (df)                                           4

===============================================================================
```

Now go to Table A.4 again (the t table does not know whether our t is for independent or nonindependent samples). For $p = .05$ and $df = 4$, the table value for t required for rejection of the null hypothesis is 2.776, or 2.78. Is our value 3.17 > 2.78? Yes, and therefore we reject the null hypothesis. Are the groups different? Yes. Are they significantly different? Yes. We are really rolling now, aren't we?

Simple Analysis of Variance (ANOVA)

Suppose we have the following sets of posttest scores for three randomly formed groups:

X_1	X_2	X_3
1	2	4
2	3	4
2	4	4
2	5	5
3	6	7

These sets of data are different, but are they significantly different? The appropriate test of significance to use in order to answer this question is the simple, or one-way, analysis of variance. Recall that the total variation, or variance, is a combination of between (treatment) variance and within (error) variance. In other words:

$$\text{total sum of squares} = \text{between sum of squares} + \text{within sum of squares or,}$$

$$SS_{total} = SS_{between} + SS_{within}$$

In order to compute an ANOVA we need each term, *but,* since $C = A + B$, or $C\ (SS_{total}) = A(SS_{between}) + B(SS_{within})$, we only have to compute any two terms and we can easily get the third. Since we only have to calculate two we might as well do the two easiest, SS_{total} and $SS_{between}$. Once we have these we can get SS_{within} by subtraction; SS_{within} will equal $SS_{total} - SS_{between}$ $(B = C - A)$. The formula for SS_{total} is as follows:

$$SS_{total} = \Sigma X^2 - \frac{(\Sigma X)^2}{N}$$

How easy can you get? First, we need ΣX^2. You know how to get that; all we have to do is square *every* score in all three groups and add up the squares. For the second term all we have to do is add up *all* the scores $(X_1 + X_2 + X_3)$, square the total, and divide by $N(n_1 + n_2 + n_3)$. Now let's look at the formula for $SS_{between}$:

$$SS_{between} = \frac{(\Sigma X_1)^2}{n_1} + \frac{(\Sigma X_2)^2}{n_2} + \frac{(\Sigma X_3)^2}{n_3} - \frac{(\Sigma X)^2}{N}$$

This formula has more pieces, but each piece is *easy*. For the first three terms all we have to do is add up all the scores in each group, square the total for each group, and divide by the number of scores in each group. We already know what the fourth term, $(\Sigma X)^2/N$ is equal to after we calculate SS_{total}. Note that if an X or N refers to a particular group it is subscripted $(X_1, X_2, X_3$ and $n_1, n_2, n_3)$. If an X or N is not subscripted it refers to the total for all the groups. So, what do we need? We need the sum of scores for each group and the total of all the scores, and the sum of all the squares. That should be easy; let's do it:

X_1	X_1^2	X_2	X_2^2	X_3	X_3^2
1	1	2	4	4	16
2	4	3	9	4	16
2	4	4	16	4	16
2	4	5	25	5	25
3	9	6	36	7	49
10	22	20	90	24	122
ΣX_1	ΣX_1^2	ΣX_2	ΣX_2^2	ΣX_3	ΣX_3^2

$$\Sigma X = \Sigma X_1 + \Sigma X_2 + \Sigma X_3 = 10 + 20 + 24 = 54$$

$$\Sigma X^2 = \Sigma X_1^2 + \Sigma X_2^2 + \Sigma X_3^2 = 22 + 90 + 122 = 234$$

$$N = n_1 + n_2 + n_3 = 5 + 5 + 5 = 15$$

Now we are ready. First let us do SS_{total}:

$$SS_{total} = \Sigma X^2 - \frac{(\Sigma X)^2}{N}$$

$$= 234 - \frac{(54)^2}{15}$$

$$= 234 - \frac{2916}{15} \qquad (54^2 = 2916)$$

$$= 234 - 194.4 \qquad (2916 \div 15 = 194.4)$$

$$= 39.6$$

That was easy, easy, easy. Now let us do $SS_{between}$:[9]

$$SS_{between} = \frac{(\Sigma X_1)^2}{n_1} + \frac{(\Sigma X_2)^2}{n_2} + \frac{(\Sigma X_3)^2}{n_3} - \frac{(\Sigma X)^2}{N}$$

(We already computed the last term, remember?)

$10^2 = 100$
$20^2 = 400$
$24^2 = 576$

$$= \frac{(10)^2}{5} + \frac{(20)^2}{5} + \frac{(24)^2}{5} - 194.4$$

$$= \frac{100}{5} + \frac{400}{5} + \frac{576}{5} - 194.4$$

$\dfrac{100}{5} = 20$

$\dfrac{400}{5} = 80$

$$= 20 + 80 + 115.2 - 194.4$$

$\dfrac{576}{5} = 115.2$

$$= 215.2 - 194.4$$

$$= 20.8$$

$20 + 80 + 115.2 = 215.2$

---

[9] For more than three groups, the ANOVA procedure is exactly the same except that $SS_{between}$ has one extra term for each additional group. For four groups, for example,

$$SS_{between} = \frac{(\Sigma X_1)^2}{n_1} + \frac{(\Sigma X_2)^2}{n_2} + \frac{(\Sigma X_3)^2}{n_3} + \frac{(\Sigma X_4)^2}{n_4} - \frac{(\Sigma X)^2}{N}$$

Now how are we going to get SS_{within}? Right. We subtract $SS_{between}$ from SS_{total}:

$$SS_{within} = SS_{total} - SS_{between}$$
$$= 39.6 - 20.8$$
$$= 18.8$$

Now we have everything we need to begin! Seriously, we have all the pieces but we are not quite there yet. Let us fill in a summary table with what we have and you will see what is missing:

Source of Variation	Sum of Squares	df	Mean Square	F
Between	20.8	$(K - 1)$		
Within	18.8	$(N - K)$		
Total	39.6	$(N - 1)$		

The first thing you probably noticed is that each term has its own formula for degrees of freedom. The formula for the between term is $K - 1$, where K is the number of treatment groups; thus, the degrees of freedom are $K - 1 = 3 - 1 = 2$. The formula for the within term is $N - K$, where N is the total sample size and K is still the number of treatment groups; thus, degrees of freedom for the within term $N - K = 15 - 3 = 12$. We do not need them, but for the total term $df = N - 1 = 15 - 1 = 14$. Now what about mean squares? Mean squares are found by dividing each sum of squares by its appropriate degrees of freedom. In other words,

$$\text{mean square} = \frac{\text{sum of squares}}{\text{degrees of freedom}}$$

or,

$$MS = \frac{SS}{df}$$

For between, MS_B, we get:

$$MS_B = \frac{SS_B}{df}$$
$$= \frac{20.8}{2}$$
$$= 10.40$$

For within, MS_W, we get:

$$MS_W = \frac{SS_W}{df}$$
$$= \frac{18.8}{12}$$
$$= 1.57$$

Now all we need is our F ratio. The F ratio is a ratio of MS_B and MS_W:

$$F = \frac{MS_B}{MS_W}$$

Therefore, for our example:

$$F = \frac{MS_B}{MS_W}$$

$$= \frac{10.40}{1.57}$$

$$= 6.62$$

Filling in the rest of our summary table we have:

Source of Variation	Sum of Squares	df		Mean Square	F
Between	20.8	$(K-1)$	2	10.40	6.62
Within	18.8	$(N-K)$	12	1.57	
Total	39.6	$(N-1)$	14		

Note that we simply divided across (20.8 ÷ 2 = 10.40 and 18.8 ÷ 12 = 1.57) and then down (10.40 ÷ 1.57 = 6.62). Thus, *F* = 6.62 with 2 and 12 degrees of freedom (STATPAK printout on next page).

Assuming α = .05, we are now ready to go to our *F* table, Table A.5 in the Appendix. Across the top of Table A.5 the row labeled n_1 refers to the degrees of freedom for the between term, in our case 2. Find it? Down the extreme left-hand side of the table, in the column labeled n_2, are the degrees of freedom for the within term, in our case 12. Find it? Good. Now, where these two values intersect (go down the 2 column and across the 12 row) we find 3.88, the value of *F* required for significance (required in order to reject the null hypothesis) if α = .05. The question is whether our *F* value 6.62 is greater than 3.88. It is. Therefore we reject the null hypothesis and conclude that there is a significant difference among the group means. Note that because two separate degrees of freedom, 2 and 12, are involved, a separate table is required for each α level. Thus, for example, the .05 table is on one page and the .01 table another.

WHEW!! That was long, *but* it was not hard, was it?

The Scheffé Test

In the above example the only thing the *F* ratio told us was that there was at least one significant difference *somewhere*. In order to find out *where* we will apply the Scheffé test. The Scheffé test involves calculation of an *F* ratio for each mean comparison of interest. As you study the following formula, you will notice that we already have almost all of the information we need to apply the Scheffé test:

$$F = \frac{(\overline{X}_1 - \overline{X}_2)^2}{MS_W \left(\frac{1}{n_1} + \frac{1}{n_2} \right)(K-1)} \quad \text{with } df = (K-1), (N-K)$$

Where in the world do we get MS_W? Correct! MS_W is the MS_W from the analysis of variance, which is 1.57. The degrees of freedom are also from the ANOVA, 2 and 12. Of course the above formula is for the comparison of $\overline{X}_1$ and $\overline{X}_2$. To compare any other two means we simply change the $\overline{X}$s and the *n*s. So before we can apply the Scheffé test, the only thing we have to calculate is the mean for each group.

```
===============================================================
              SIMPLE ANALYSIS OF VARIANCE (A N O V A)
===============================================================

      STATISTIC              VALUE
-----------------------------------------------------------------

      N      =                  5
      1

      ΣX     =               10.00
       1
      _
      X      =                2.00
      1

      ΣX²    =               22.00
        1

      N      =                  5
      2

      ΣX     =               20.00
        2
      _
      X      =                4.00
      2

      ΣX²    =               90.00
        2

      N      =                  5
      3

      ΣX     =               24.00
        3
      _
      X      =                4.80
      3

      ΣX²    =              122.00
        3
```

SOURCE OF VARIATION	SUM OF SQUARES	df		MEAN SQUARE	F RATIO
BETWEEN	20.80	(K - 1)	2	10.40	6.64
WITHIN	18.80	(N - K)	12	1.57	
TOTAL	39.60	(N - 1)	14		

Looking back at our ANOVA example, the sums for each group were 10, 20, and 24, respectively. Thus, the three means are:

$$\overline{X}_1 = \frac{\Sigma X_1}{n_1} = \frac{10}{5} = 2.00$$

$$\overline{X}_2 = \frac{\Sigma X_2}{n_2} = \frac{20}{5} = 4.00$$

$$\overline{X}_3 = \frac{\Sigma X_3}{n_3} = \frac{24}{5} = 4.80$$

Applying the Scheffé test to $\overline{X}_1$ and $\overline{X}_2$ we get:

$$F = \frac{(\overline{X}_1 - \overline{X}_2)^2}{MS_W \left(\dfrac{1}{n_1} + \dfrac{1}{n_2} \right)(K - 1)} = \frac{(2.00 - 4.00)^2}{1.57 \left(\dfrac{1}{5} + \dfrac{1}{5} \right) 2}$$

$$= \frac{(-2.00)^2}{1.57 \left(\dfrac{2}{5} \right) 2}$$

$$= \frac{4}{1.57(.4)2}$$

$$= \frac{4}{1.57(.8)}$$

$$= \frac{4}{1.256}$$

$$= 3.18$$

Since the value of F required for significance is 3.88 if $\alpha = .05$ and $df = 2$ and 12, and since $3.18 < 3.88$, we conclude that there is no significant difference between $\overline{X}_1$ and $\overline{X}_2$.

Applying the Scheffé test to $\overline{X}_1$ and $\overline{X}_3$ we get:

$$F = \frac{(\overline{X}_1 - \overline{X}_3)^2}{MS_W \left(\dfrac{1}{n_1} + \dfrac{1}{n_3} \right)(K - 1)} = \frac{(2.00 - 4.80)^2}{1.57 \left(\dfrac{1}{5} + \dfrac{1}{5} \right) 2}$$

$$= \frac{(-2.80)^2}{1.256}$$

$$= \frac{7.84}{1.256}$$

$$= 6.24$$

Since $6.24 > 3.88$, we conclude that there is a significant difference between $\overline{X}_1$ and $\overline{X}_3$. Note that since the ns are equal in our example, that is, $n_1 = n_2 = n_3$, the denominator is the same as for the $\overline{X}_1$ and $\overline{X}_2$ comparison. And similarly for $\overline{X}_2$ and $\overline{X}_3$ we get:

$$F = \frac{(\overline{X}_2 - \overline{X}_3)^2}{MS_W \left(\dfrac{1}{n_2} + \dfrac{1}{n_3} \right)(K-1)} = \frac{(4.00 - 4.80)^2}{1.57 \left(\dfrac{1}{5} + \dfrac{1}{5} \right) 2}$$

$$= \frac{(-.80)^2}{1.256}$$

$$= \frac{.64}{1.256}$$

$$= .51$$

Since .51 < 3.88, we conclude that there is no significant difference between $\overline{X}_2$ and $\overline{X}_3$. In other words, group 3 performed significantly better than group 1 and that is the only significant difference. Even though group 2 performed better than group 1 ($\overline{X}_1 = 2.00$, $\overline{X}_2 = 4.00$) the difference, 2.00, is not a significant difference (STATPAK printout below).

```
==================================================================
SCHEFFÉ  TESTS
------------------------------------------------------------------

GROUP  ONE  VS  GROUP  TWO              3.19

GROUP  ONE  VS  GROUP  THREE            6.26

GROUP  TWO  VS  GROUP  THREE            0.51

==================================================================
```

The Scheffé test can also be used to compare combinations of means. Suppose, for example, that group 1 was a control group and we wanted to compare the mean of group 1 to the mean of groups 2 and 3 combined. First we would have to combine the means for groups 2 and 3 as follows:

$$\overline{X}_{2+3} = \frac{n_2 \overline{X}_2 + n_3 \overline{X}_3}{n_2 + n_3} = \frac{5(4.00) + 5(4.80)}{5 + 5}$$

$$= \frac{20.00 + 24.00}{10}$$

$$= \frac{44.00}{10}$$

$$= 4.40$$

Of course, since $n_2 = n_3$, we could have simply averaged the means as follows:

$$\overline{X}_{2+3} = \frac{\overline{X}_2 + \overline{X}_3}{2} = \frac{4.00 + 4.80}{2} = \frac{8.80}{2} = 4.40$$

Next, we calculate the F ratio using $\overline{X} = 2.00$ and the combined mean $\overline{X}_{2+3} = 4.40$:

$$F = \frac{(\overline{X}_1 - \overline{X}_{2+3})^2}{MS_W \left(\dfrac{1}{n_1} + \dfrac{1}{n_2 + n_3} \right)(K - 1)} = \frac{(2.00 - 4.40)^2}{1.57 \left(\dfrac{1}{5} + \dfrac{1}{10} \right) 2}$$

$$= \frac{(-2.4)^2}{1.57(.2 + .1)2}$$

$$= \frac{5.76}{1.57(.3)2}$$

$$= \frac{5.76}{.94}$$

$$= 6.13$$

Since $6.13 > 3.88$, we would conclude that there is a significant difference between $\overline{X}_1$ and $\overline{X}_{2+3}$. In other words, the experimental groups performed significantly better than the control group.

Chi Square

A one-dimensional chi square (χ^2) is the easiest statistic of all. To use our peanut butter example, we asked 90 people to indicate which brand they thought tasted best; 40 picked brand X, 30 picked brand Y, and 20 picked brand Z. If there were no difference between the brands we would expect the same number of people to choose each brand, 30 ($90 \div 3 = 30$). Therefore, we have the following table:

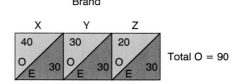

where

> O = observed frequencies
> E = expected frequencies

In order to determine whether the observed frequencies are significantly different from the expected frequencies we apply the following formula:

$$\chi^2 = \sum \left[\frac{(fo - fe)^2}{fe} \right]$$

Now that is some sum sign! All this formula says, however, is that for each cell, or category (X, Y, and Z) we subtract the expected frequency (*fe*) from the observed frequency (*fo*), square the difference $(fo - fe)^2$, and then divide by the expected frequency, *fe*. The big $\sum$ says that after we do the above for each term we add up the resulting values. Thus, substituting our table values into the formula we get:

	X		Y		Z

$$\chi^2 = \frac{\overset{fo \ fe}{(40 - 30)^2}}{30} + \frac{\overset{fo \ fe}{(30 - 30)^2}}{30} + \frac{\overset{fo \ fe}{(20 - 30)^2}}{30}$$

$$= \frac{\overset{fe}{(10)^2}}{30} + \frac{\overset{fe}{(0)^2}}{30} + \frac{\overset{fe}{(-10)^2}}{30}$$

$$= \frac{100}{30} + 0 + \frac{100}{30}$$

$$= 3.333 + 0 + 3.333$$

$$= 6.67$$

Thus, $\chi^2 = 6.67$. The degrees of freedom for a one-dimensional chi square are determined by the formula (C − 1), where C equals the number of columns, in our case 3. Thus, $df = C - 1 = 3 - 1 = 2$. Therefore, we have $\chi^2 = 6.67$, $\alpha = .05$, $df = 2$. (STATPAK printout below).

```
============================================================================
             C E L L    C H I - S Q U A R E    V A L U E S

ROW 1 COL 1 "O"=     40.000 "E"=     30.000 CHI-SQUARE        3.333
ROW 1 COL 2 "O"=     30.000 "E"=     30.000 CHI-SQUARE        0.000
ROW 1 COL 3 "O"=     20.000 "E"=     30.000 CHI-SQUARE        3.333

C H I - S Q U A R E   =        6.667

THERE WAS   1 ROW AND THERE WERE   3 COLUMNS IN THE CONTINGENCY TABLE.

DEGREES OF FREEDOM = (C - 1) = ( 3   - 1) =   2

============================================================================
```

To determine whether the differences between observed and expected frequencies are significant, we compare our chi square value to the appropriate value in Table A.6 in the Appendix. Run the index finger of your right hand across the top until you find $p = .05$. Now run the index finger of your left hand down the extreme left-hand column and find $df = 2$. Run your left hand across and your right hand down and they will intersect at 5.991, or 5.99. Is our value of 6.67 > 5.99? Yes. Therefore, we reject the null hypothesis. There is a significant difference between observed and expected proportions; the brands of peanut butter compared do taste different! Suppose we selected α = .01. The chi square value required for significance would be 9.210, or 9.21. Is our value of 6.67 > 9.21? No. Therefore, we would not reject the null hypothesis and we would conclude that there is no significant difference between observed and expected proportions; the three brands of peanut butter taste the same. Thus, once again you can see that selection of an α level is important; different conclusions may very well be drawn with different α levels.

Now let's look at our study preference example. We asked 100 college sophomores whether they preferred to study alone or with others; 45 said alone and 55 said with others. Under a null hypothesis of no preference we would expect a 50-50 split. Therefore, we have the following table:

Study Preference

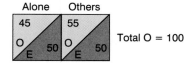

Applying the chi square formula we get:

$$\chi^2 = \frac{(45 - 50)^2}{50} + \frac{(55 - 50)^2}{50}$$

$$= \frac{(-5)^2}{50} + \frac{(5)^2}{50}$$

$$= \frac{25}{50} + \frac{25}{50}$$

$$= .50 + .50$$

$$\chi^2 = 1.00$$

Since degrees of freedom are C − 1, we have 2 − 1, or 1. Thus, χ^2 = 1.00, α = .05, *df* = 1 (STATPAK printout below).

```
:================================================================================:
            C E L L   C H I - S Q U A R E     V A L U E S

   ROW 1 COL 1 "O"=    45.000 "E"=    50.000 CHI-SQUARE        0.500
   ROW 1 COL 2 "O"=    55.000 "E"=    50.000 CHI-SQUARE        0.500

   C H I - S Q U A R E  =        1.000

   THERE WAS  1 ROW AND THERE WERE  2 COLUMNS IN THE CONTINGENCY TABLE.

   DEGREES OF FREEDOM = (C - 1) = ( 2  - 1) =  1

:================================================================================:
```

Table A.6 indicates that for α = .05 and *df* = 1, the required value is 3.841, or 3.84. Is our value of 1.00 > 3.84? No. Therefore, we do not reject the null hypothesis. There is not a significant difference between observed and expected proportions; sophomores do not prefer to study alone or with others.

Now, suppose as discussed previously, we wanted to know if study preference is related to the sex of the student. Our 2 x 2 contingency table might look as follows:

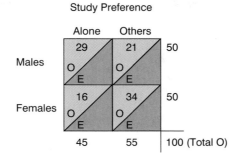

To find the expected frequency for a particular cell, or category, we multiply the corresponding row total by the corresponding column total and divide by the overall total. I know it sounds bad, but it isn't. So, for males who prefer to study alone, the observed frequency is 29. To find the expected frequency, we multiply the total for the male row (50) by the total for the alone column (45) and divide by the overall total (100):

$$\text{males} - \text{alone} = \frac{50 \times 45}{100} = \frac{2250}{100} = 22.5$$

Similarly, for the other cells, we get:

$$\text{males} - \text{others} = \frac{50 \times 55}{100} = \frac{2750}{100} = 27.5$$

$$\text{females} - \text{alone} = \frac{50 \times 45}{100} = \frac{2250}{100} = 22.5$$

$$\text{females} - \text{others} = \frac{50 \times 55}{100} = \frac{2750}{100} = 27.5$$

Now we can fill in the expected frequencies in our table and it looks as follows:

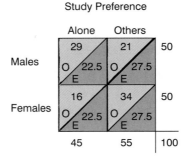

Chi square is calculated in the same way as for the other examples except now we have four terms:

$$\chi^2 = \frac{(29-22.5)^2}{22.5} + \frac{(21-27.5)^2}{27.5} + \frac{(16-22.5)^2}{22.5} + \frac{(34-27.5)^2}{27.5}$$

$$= \frac{(6.5)^2}{22.5} + \frac{(-6.5)^2}{27.5} + \frac{(-6.5)^2}{22.5} + \frac{(6.5)^2}{27.5}$$

$$= \frac{42.25}{22.5} + \frac{42.25}{27.5} + \frac{42.25}{22.5} + \frac{42.25}{27.5}$$

$$= 1.88 + 1.54 + 1.88 + 1.54$$

$$\chi^2 = 6.84$$

The degrees of freedom for a two-dimensional chi square are determined by the following formula:

$$df = (R-1)(C-1)$$

where

R = the number of rows in the contingency table
C = the number of columns in the contingency table

Since we have two rows and two columns,

$$df = (R-1)(C-1) = (2-1)(2-1) = 1 \times 1 = 1$$

Therefore, we have $\chi^2 = 6.84$, $\alpha = .05$, $df = 1$ (STATPAK printout below and on next page). The table value for $\alpha = .05$ and df = 1 is 3.841, or 3.84. Is our value of 6.84 > 3.84? Yes. Therefore, we conclude that sex is related to study preference.

For larger contingency tables (e.g., a 3 x 2), expected frequencies and chi square are calculated in the same way as above. The only difference is that the number of terms increases; for a 3 x 2, for example, the number of terms is 6 (3 x 2 = 6).

---

2 X 2 CONTINGENCY TABLE

O = 29.000	O = 21.000	
E = 22.500	E = 27.500	50.000
X^2 = 1.878	X^2 = 1.536	
O = 16.000	O = 34.000	
E = 22.500	E = 27.500	50.000
X^2 = 1.878	X^2 = 1.536	
45.000	55.000	100.000

PRESS ANY KEY TO CONTINUE:

```
================================================================================
              C E L L   C H I - S Q U A R E    V A L U E S
     ROW 1 COL 1 "O"=     29.000 "E"=     22.500 CHI-SQUARE      1.878
     ROW 1 COL 2 "O"=     21.000 "E"=     27.500 CHI-SQUARE      1.536
     ROW 2 COL 1 "O"=     16.000 "E"=     22.500 CHI-SQUARE      1.878
     ROW 2 COL 2 "O"=     34.000 "E"=     27.500 CHI-SQUARE      1.536

     C H I - S Q U A R E   =       6.828

     THERE WERE 2 ROWS AND 2 COLUMNS IN THE CONTINGENCY TABLE.

     DEGREES OF FREEDOM = (R - 1)(C - 1) = (2 - 1)(2 - 1) =   1
================================================================================
```

■ Summary/Chapter 14
Concepts Underlying Application

1. Inferential statistics deal with inferences about populations based on the behavior of samples.
2. Inferential statistics are concerned with determining how likely it is that results based on a sample or samples are the same results that would have been obtained for the entire population.
3. Sample values, such as the mean, are referred to as statistics. The corresponding values in the population are referred to as parameters.
4. Inferential statistics are used to make inferences concerning parameters, based on sample statistics.
5. If a difference between means is found for two groups at the end of a study, the question of interest is whether a similar difference exists in the population from which the samples were selected.
6. Inferences concerning populations are only probability statements; the researcher is only probably correct when he or she makes an inference and concludes that there is true difference, or true relationship, in the population.

Standard Error

7. Expected, chance variation among the means is referred to as sampling error.
8. If a difference is found between sample means, the question of interest is whether the difference is a result of sampling error or a reflection of a true difference.
9. An interesting characteristic of sampling errors is that they are normally distributed.
10. If a sufficiently large number of equal-sized large samples are randomly selected from a population, all samples will not have the same mean on the variable measured, *but* the means of those samples will be normally distributed around the population mean. The mean of all the sample means will yield a good estimate of the population mean.
11. As with any normally distributed set of scores, a distribution of sample means has not only its own mean but also its own standard deviation. The standard deviation of the sample means (the standard deviation of sampling errors) is usually referred to as the standard error of the mean.

12. The standard error of the mean ($SE_{\bar{x}}$) tells us by how much we would expect our sample means to differ if we used other samples from the same population.

13. According to normal curve percentages, we can say that approximately 68% of the sample means will fall between plus and minus one standard error of the mean (remember the standard error of the mean is a standard deviation), 95% will fall between plus and minus two standard errors, and 99+ % will fall between plus and minus three standard errors.

14. If we know the standard deviation of the population, we can estimate the standard error of the mean by dividing the standard deviation by the square root of our sample size ($\sqrt{N}$).

15. In most cases, however, we do not know the mean or standard deviation of the population. In these cases, we estimate the standard error by dividing the standard deviation of the sample by the square root of the sample minus one:

$$SE_{\bar{x}} = \frac{SD}{\sqrt{N-1}}$$

16. The smaller the standard error of the mean is, the better; a smaller standard error indicates less sampling error.

17. The major factor affecting the standard error of the mean is sample size. As the size of the sample increases, the standard error of the mean decreases.

18. The researcher should make every effort to acquire as many subjects as possible so that inferences about the population of interest will be as correct as possible.

19. An estimate of standard error can also be computed for other measures of central tendency as well as measures of variability, relationship, and relative position. Further, an estimate of standard error can also be determined for the difference between means.

20. Differences between two sample means are normally distributed around the mean difference in the population.

The Null Hypothesis

21. When we talk about the difference between two sample means being a true difference we mean that the difference was caused by the treatment (the independent variable), and not by chance.

22. The null hypothesis says in essence that there is no true difference or relationship between parameters in the populations and that any differences or relationship found for the samples is the result of sampling error.

23. The null hypothesis for a study is usually (although not necessarily) different from the research hypothesis.

24. Rejection of a null hypothesis is more conclusive support for a positive research hypothesis.

25. In a research study, the test of significance selected to determine whether a difference between means is a true difference provides a test of the null hypothesis. As a result, the null hypothesis is either rejected, as being probably false, or not rejected, being probably true.

26. After we make the decision to reject or not reject the null hypothesis, we make an inference back to our research hypothesis.

27. In order to test a null hypothesis we need a test of significance, and we need to select a probability level which indicates how much risk we are willing to take that the decision we make is wrong.

Tests of Significance

28. The test of significance helps us to decide whether we can reject the null hypothesis and infer that the difference is a true one, a population difference, not a chance one resulting from sampling error.
29. The test of significance is made at a preselected probability level and allows us to state that we have rejected the null hypothesis because we would expect to find a difference as large as we have found by chance only 5 times out of every 100 studies, or only 1 time in every 100 studies, or whatever; therefore we conclude that the null hypothesis is *probably* false and reject it.
30. There are a number of different tests of significance which can be applied in research studies, one of which is more appropriate in a given situation.
31. Factors such as the scale of measurement represented by the data, method of subject selection, the number of groups, and the number of independent variables determine which test of significance should be selected for a given experiment.

Decision Making: Levels of Significance and Type I and Type II Errors

32. The researcher makes a decision that the difference between the means is, or is not, too large to attribute to chance. The researcher never knows for sure whether he or she is right or wrong, only whether he or she is probably correct.
33. There are four possibilities. If the null hypothesis is really true, and the researcher agrees that it is true (does not reject it), the researcher makes the correct decision. Similarly, if the null hypothesis is false, and the researcher rejects it (says there *is* a difference), the researcher also makes the correct decision. But if the null hypothesis is true, there really is no difference, and the researcher rejects it and says there is a difference, the researcher makes an incorrect decision referred to as a Type I error. Similarly, if the null hypothesis is false, there really is a significant difference between the means, but the researcher concludes that the null hypothesis is true and does not reject it, the researcher also makes an incorrect decision referred to as a Type II error.
34. When the researcher makes the decision to reject or not reject the null hypothesis, she or he does so with a given probability of being correct. This probability of being correct is referred to as the significance level, or probability level, of the test of significance.
35. If the decision is made to reject the null hypothesis, the means are concluded to be significantly different—too different to be the result of chance error. If the null hypothesis is not rejected, the means are determined to be not significantly different.
36. The level of significance, or probability level, selected determines how large the difference between the means must be in order to be declared significantly different.

37. The most commonly used probability level (symbolized as α) is the .05 level. Some studies use α = .01 and occasionally an exploratory study will use α = .10.
38. The probability level selected determines the probability of committing a Type I error, that is, of rejecting a null hypothesis that is really true.
39. The smaller our probability level is, the larger the mean difference must be in order to be a significant difference.
40. As you decrease the probability of committing a Type I error, you increase the probability of committing a Type II error, that is, of not rejecting a null hypothesis when you should.
41. The choice of a probability level, α, is made prior to execution of the study. The researcher considers the relative seriousness of committing a Type I versus a Type II error and selects α accordingly.
42. Rejection of a null hypothesis, or lack of rejection, only supports or does not support a research hypothesis; it does not "prove" anything.

Two-Tailed and One-Tailed Tests

43. Tests of significance are almost always two-tailed.
44. The null hypothesis states that there is no difference between the groups (A = B) and a two-tailed test allows for the possibility that a difference may occur in either direction; either group mean may be higher than the other (A > B or B > A).
45. A one-tailed test assumes that a difference can only occur in one direction; the null hypothesis states that one group is not better than another (A ≯ B), and the one-tailed test assumes that if a difference occurs it will be in favor of that particular group (A > B).
46. To select a one-tailed test of significance the researcher has to be pret-ty sure that a difference can only occur in one direction; this is not very often the case.
47. When appropriate, a one-tailed test has one major advantage. The value resulting from application of the test of significance required for significance is smaller. In other words, it is "easier" to find a significant difference.

Degrees of Freedom

48. After you have determined whether the test will be two-tailed or one-tailed, selected a probability level, and computed a test of significance, you are ready to consult the appropriate table in order to determine the significance of your results.
49. The appropriate table is usually entered at the intersection of your probability level and your degrees of freedom, *df*.
50. Degrees of freedom are a function of such factors as the number of subjects and the number of groups.
51. Each test of significance has its own formula for determining degrees of freedom.

TESTS OF SIGNIFICANCE: TYPES

52. Different tests of significance are appropriate for different sets of data.

53. It is important that the researcher select an appropriate test; an incorrect test can lead to incorrect conclusions.

54. The first decision in selecting an appropriate test of significance is whether a parametric test may be used or whether a nonparametric test must be selected.

55. Parametric tests are more powerful and are generally to be preferred. By "more powerful" is meant more likely to reject a null hypothesis that is false; in other words, the researcher is less likely to commit a Type II error, less likely to not reject a null hypothesis that should be rejected.

56. Parametric tests require that certain assumptions be met in order for them to be valid.

57. One of the major assumptions underlying use of parametric tests is that the variable measured is normally distributed in the population (or at least that the form of the distribution is known).

58. A second major assumption is that the data represent an interval or ratio scale of measurement.

59. A third assumption is that subjects are selected independently for the study; in other words, that selection of one subject in no way affects selection of any other subject. Recall that the definition of random sampling is sampling in which every member of the population has an equal and independent chance of being selected for the sample.

60. Another assumption is that the variances of the population comparison groups are equal (or at least that the ratio of the variances is known).

61. With the exception of independence, some violation of one or more of these assumptions usually does not make too much difference, in other words, the same decision is made concerning the statistical significance of the results.

62. If one or more of the parametric assumptions are greatly violated, a nonparametric test should be used. Nonparametric tests make no assumptions about the shape of the distribution.

63. Nonparametric tests are used when the data represent an ordinal or nominal scale, when a parametric assumption has been greatly violated, or when the nature of the distribution is not known.

64. If the data represent an interval or ratio scale, a parametric test should be used unless another of the assumptions is greatly violated.

65. Besides being more powerful, parametric tests also have the advantage that they permit tests of a number of hypotheses that cannot be tested with a nonparametric test; there are a number of parametric statistics that have no counterpart among nonparametric statistics.

66. Typically, the results of single-subject research are presented graphically and summarized using simple descriptive statistics. The need for inferential statistics depends somewhat on the nature of the results.

The *t* Test

67. The *t* test is used to determine whether two means are significantly different at a selected probability level.

68. For a given sample size, the *t* indicates how often a difference as large or larger ($\overline{X}_1 - \overline{X}_2$) would be found when there is no true population difference.

69. The *t* test makes adjustments for the fact that the distribution of scores for small samples becomes increasingly different from a normal distribution as sample sizes become increasingly smaller.
70. Distributions for smaller samples, for example, tend to be higher at both the mean and the ends.
71. For a given α level, the values of *t* required to reject a null hypothesis are progressively higher for progressively smaller samples; as the size of the samples becomes larger (approaches infinity) the score distribution approaches normality.
72. The strategy of the *t* test is to compare the *actual* mean difference observed $(\overline{X}_1 - \overline{X}_2)$ with the difference *expected* by chance. The *t* test involves forming the ratio of these two values. In other words, the numerator for a *t* test is the difference between the sample means $\overline{X}_1$ and $\overline{X}_2$ and the denominator is the chance difference which would be expected if the null hypothesis were true—the standard error of the difference between the means.
73. The denominator is a function of both sample size and group variance.
74. Smaller sample sizes and greater variation within groups are associated with an expectation of greater random differences between groups.
75. The *t* ratio determines whether the observed difference is sufficiently larger than a difference which would be expected by chance.
76. After the numerator is divided by the denominator, the resulting *t* value is compared to the appropriate *t* table value (depending upon the probability level and the degrees of freedom); if the calculated *t* value is equal to or greater than the table value, then the null hypothesis is rejected.
77. There are two different types of *t* tests, the *t* test for independent samples and the *t* test for nonindependent samples.

The t Test for Independent Samples

78. Independent samples are samples that are randomly formed, that is, formed without any type of matching.
79. If two groups are randomly formed, the expectation is that they are essentially the same at the beginning of a study with respect to performance on the dependent variable. Therefore, if they are essentially the same at the end of the study, the null hypothesis is probably true; if they are different at the end of the study, the null hypothesis is probably false, that is, the treatment probably makes a difference.
80. The *t* test for independent samples is used to determine whether there is a significant difference between the means of two independent samples.

The t Test for Nonindependent Samples

81. Nonindependent samples are samples formed by some type of matching. The ultimate matching, of course, is when the two samples are really the same sample group at two different times, such as one group which receives two different treatments at two different times or which is pretested before a treatment and then posttested.
82. When samples are not independent, the members of one group are systematically related to the members of a second group (especially if it is the same group at two different times).

83. If samples are nonindependent, scores on the dependent variable are expected to be correlated and a special *t* for correlated, or nonindependent, means must be used.

84. The *t* test for nonindependent samples is used to determine whether there is probably a significant difference between the means of two matched, or nonindependent, samples or between the means for one sample at two different times.

Analysis of Gain Scores (Difference Scores)

85. There are a number of problems associated with this approach, the major one being lack of equal opportunity to grow. Every subject does not have the same room to gain.

86. If two groups are essentially the same on a pretest, their posttest scores can be directly compared using a *t* test.

87. If there is a difference between the groups on the pretest the preferred posttest analysis is analysis of covariance.

Simple Analysis of Variance

88. Simple, or one-way, analysis of variance (ANOVA) is used to determine whether there is a significant difference between two *or more* means at a selected probability level.

89. The concept underlying ANOVA is that the total variation, or variance, of scores can be attributed to two sources—variance between groups (variance caused by the treatment) and variance within groups (error variance).

90. As with the *t* test, a ratio is formed (the *F* ratio) with group differences as the numerator (variance between groups) and an error term as the denominator (variance within groups).

91. At the end of the study, after administration of the independent variable (treatment), we determine whether the between groups (treatment) variance differs from the within groups (error) variance by more than what would be expected by chance.

92. The degrees of freedom for the *F* ratio are a function of the number of groups and the number of subjects.

Multiple Comparisons

93. Multiple comparison procedures are used following ANOVA to determine which means are significantly different from which other means.

94. In essence, they involve calculation of a special form of the *t* test, a form for which the error term is based on the combined variance of all the groups, not just the groups being compared. This special *t* adjusts for the fact that many tests are being executed. When many tests are performed, the probability level, *p,* tends to increase; if α is supposed to be .05, it will actually end up being greater, maybe .90, if many tests are performed.

95. Which mean comparisons are to be made should generally be decided upon *before* the study is conducted, not after, and should be based upon the research hypotheses.

96. Of the many multiple comparison techniques available probably the most often used is the Scheffé test, which is a very conservative test.

97. The Scheffé test is appropriate for making any and all possible comparisons involving a set of means.
98. The calculations for the Scheffé test are quite simple and sample sizes do not have to be equal.

Factorial Analysis of Variance

99. If a research study is based upon a factorial design and investigates two or more independent variables and the interactions between them, the appropriate statistical analysis is a factorial, or multifactor, analysis of variance.
100. Such an analysis yields a separate F ratio for each independent variable and one for each interaction.

Analysis of Covariance

101. Analysis of covariance (ANCOVA) is used in two major ways, as a technique for controlling extraneous variables and as a means of increasing power.
102. Covariance is a form of ANOVA and is a statistical, rather than experimental, method that can be used to equate groups on one or more variables.
103. Essentially, ANCOVA adjusts posttest scores for initial differences on some variable (such as pretest performance or IQ) and compares adjusted scores.
104. Covariance is based on the assumption that subjects have been randomly assigned to treatment groups. It is therefore best used in conjunction with true experimental designs. If existing, or intact, groups are involved but treatments are assigned to groups randomly, covariance may still be used but results must be interpreted with due caution.
105. Covariance increases the power of a statistical test by reducing within-group (error) variance.

Multiple Regression

106. A multiple regression equation uses variables that are known to individually predict (correlate with) the criterion to make a more accurate prediction.
107. Use of multiple regression is increasing, primarily because of its versatility and precision. It can be used with data representing any scale of measurement, and can be used to analyze the results of experimental and causal-comparative, as well as correlational, studies.
108. It determines not only whether variables are related, but also the degree to which they are related.
109. The first step in multiple regression is to identify the variable which *best* predicts the criterion, that is, is most highly correlated with it.
110. The next step is to identify the variable that most improves the prediction which is based on the first variable only, and so on for other variables.
111. With increasing frequency, multiple regression is being used as an alternative to the various analysis of variance techniques. When this is the case, the dependent variable, or posttest scores, becomes the criterion variable, and the predictors include group membership (e.g., experimental versus control) and any other appropriate variables, such as pretest scores.

Chi Square

112. Chi square, symbolized as χ^2, is a nonparametric test of significance appropriate when the data are in the form of frequency counts occurring in two or more mutually exclusive categories.
113. Chi square is appropriate when the data represent a nominal scale, and the categories may be true categories (e.g., male versus female) or artificial categories (e.g., tall versus short).
114. Expected frequencies are usually the frequencies which would be expected if the groups were equal, although they may be based on past data.

One-Dimensional Chi Square

115. The chi square can be used to compare frequencies occurring in different categories or the categories may be groups, so that the chi square is comparing groups with respect to the frequency of occurrence of different events.
116. We can present our data in what is called a *contingency table*.

Two-Dimensional Chi Square

117. The chi square may also be used when frequencies are categorized along more than one dimension, sort of a factorial chi square.
118. Although 2 x 2 applications are quite common, contingency tables may be based on any number of categories; such tables may be, as examples, 2 x 3, 3 x 3, 2 x 4, and so forth.

CALCULATION AND INTERPRETATION OF SELECTED TESTS OF SIGNIFICANCE

The *t* Test for Independent Samples

119. The formula is:

$$ t = \frac{\overline{X}_1 - \overline{X}_2}{\sqrt{\left(\dfrac{SS_1 + SS_2}{n_1 + n_2 - 2} \right) \left(\dfrac{1}{n_1} + \dfrac{1}{n_2} \right)}} $$

120. The formula for the degrees of freedom is

$$ n_1 + n_2 - 2 $$

121. If your *t* value is equal to or greater than the *t* table value, you reject the null hypothesis; the means are significantly different at a selected α level.
122. If our *t* value is *greater* than the table value for a given α, our probability of committing a Type I error is *less,* e.g., $p < .05$.
123. If our *t* value is *less* than the table value for a given α, we can express the nonsignificance as $p > .05$ or N.S.

The *t* Test for Nonindependent Samples

124. The formula is:

$$t = \frac{\overline{D}}{\sqrt{\dfrac{\sum D^2 - \dfrac{(\sum D)^2}{N}}{N(N-1)}}}$$

125. The formula for degrees of freedom is $N - 1$, the number of pairs minus 1.
126. If your t value is equal to or greater than the t table value, you reject the null hypothesis; the means are significantly different at a selected α level.

Simple Analysis of Variance (ANOVA)

127. $SS_{\text{total}} = SS_{\text{between}} + SS_{\text{within}}$

128. $SS_{\text{total}} = \sum X^2 - \dfrac{(\sum X)^2}{N}$

129. $SS_{\text{between}} = \dfrac{(\sum X_1)^2}{n_1} + \dfrac{(\sum X_2)^2}{n_2} + \dfrac{(\sum X_3)^2}{n_3} + \ldots + \ldots - \dfrac{(\sum X)^2}{N}$

130. The formula for degrees of freedom for the between term is $K - 1$, where K is the number of groups.
131. The formula for the degrees of freedom for the within term is $N - K$, where N is the total sample size and K is still the number of treatment groups.

132. Mean square $= \dfrac{\text{sum of squares}}{\text{degrees of freedom}}$

133. $F = \dfrac{MS_B}{MS_W}$

If your F value is greater than the F table value, you reject the null hypothesis; there is a significant difference among the means.

The Scheffé Test

134. The Scheffé test involves calculation of an F ratio for each mean comparison.
135. For example, to compare $\overline{X}_1$ with $\overline{X}_2$ the formula is:

$$F = \frac{(\overline{X}_1 - \overline{X}_2)^2}{MS_W \left(\dfrac{1}{n_1} + \dfrac{1}{n_2} \right)(K-1)} \quad \text{with } df = (K-1), (N-K)$$

136. The MS_W in the formula is the MS_W from the analysis of variance.
137. The significance of each F is determined using the degrees of freedom from the analysis of variance.

Chi Square

138. $$\chi^2 = \sum \left[\frac{(fo - fe)^2}{fe} \right]$$

139. The formula for degrees of freedom for a one-dimensional chi square is C − 1, where C equals the number of columns.

140. The formula for degrees of freedom for a two-dimensional chi square is (R − 1)(C − 1), where R equals the number of rows in the contingency table and C equals the number of columns in the contingency table.

141. If your chi square value is equal to or greater than the chi square table value, you reject the null hypothesis; there is a significant difference between observed and expected proportions.

". . . all subsequent records have been given a royal escort whenever similar journeys have been called for (p. 519)."

Postanalysis Considerations

After reading Chapter 15, you should be able to:

1. List at least six guidelines to be followed in verifying and storing data.

2. Explain how a rejected null hypothesis relates to a research hypothesis.

3. Explain how a null hypothesis which is not rejected relates to a research hypothesis.

4. Identify the major use of significant unhypothesized relationships.

5. Explain the difference between statistical and practical significance.

6. Define or describe replication.

■ VERIFICATION AND STORAGE OF DATA

After you have completed all the statistical analyses necessary to describe your data and test your hypothesis, you do not say, "thank goodness, I'm done!" and happily throw away all your data and your work sheets. Whether you do your analyses by hand, with the aid of a calculator, or with the aid of a computer, all data must be thoroughly checked and stored in an organized manner.

Verification

Verification involves double-checking the input and evaluating the output. Double-checking input may seem a bit excessive, but output is only valid to the degree that input is accurate. There is an old but apt expression, GIGO—garbage in . . . garbage out. Thus, original scores should be rechecked (or some percentage of them), as well as data sheets. Coded data should be compared with uncoded data to make sure all data were coded properly. If a computer has been used and data files created, they should be printed out, or "listed," and compared with data sheets. Considering that the entire study is worthless if inaccurate data are analyzed, and considering all the effort that has been expended at this point on the entire study, time involved in rechecking input is time well spent.

When analyses are done by hand, or with a calculator, both the accuracy of computations and the reasonableness of the results need to be checked. You may have noticed that we applied each statistic step by step, leaving no steps to the imagination. This was probably helpful to some and annoying to others. Math superstar types seem to derive great satisfaction from doing several steps in a row "in their heads" and writing down the results instead of separately recording the result of each step. This may save time in the short run but not necessarily in the long run. If you end up with a result that just does not look right, it is a lot easier to spot an error if every step is in front of you.

Also, do not just check the steps you followed after you had an arithmetic problem; check every value that you substituted into the formula in order to make it an arithmetic problem. A very frustrated student once came to me with the very sad tale that he had been up all night, had rechecked his work over and over and over, and still kept getting a negative sum of squares in his ANOVA. He was at the point where he could easily have been convinced that squares can be negative! An inspection of his work revealed very quickly that the problem was not in his execution of ANOVA but in the numbers he was trying to do ANOVA with. Early in the game he had added ΣX_1, ΣX_2, and ΣX_3 and obtained a number much, much larger than their actual sum. From that point on, he was doomed. The moral of the story is that if you have checked a set of figures several times and they are still correct, do not check them 50 more times, look elsewhere. Make sure you are using the correct formula and make sure you have substituted the correct numbers. The anecdote also illustrates that the results should make sense. If your scores range from 20 to 94 and you get a standard deviation of 1.20 you have probably made a mistake somewhere because 1.20 does not look reasonable. Similarly, if your means are 24.20 and 26.10 and you get a t ratio of 44.82 you had better recheck everything ve-ry carefully.

When analyses are done by computer, output must be checked very carefully. Some people are under the mistaken impression that if a result was produced by a computer, it is automatically correct. Wrong! Computers may not make mistakes but people do, and people write the programs and input the data. A student once came to me excitedly waving a printout. It had run! No error messages! Finis! As I looked at the printout I noticed that the mean IQ scores for the groups were numbers like 10.42. The student had obviously given the computer an incorrect instruction concerning placement of decimal places. Hating to kill the mood, but being obligated to say something, I casually asked the student if those results looked OK to him, hoping he would spot the error. Response: "They *must* be right, the *computer* did them!" 'Nuff said.

The "blind faith" problem illustrated above is compounded by the number of persons who use the computer to perform analyses they do not understand. Computer usage has almost been made *too* easy. A person with little or no knowledge of analysis of covariance, for example, can, by following directions, have a computer perform the analysis. Such a person could not possibly know whether the results make sense. You may now be beginning to see the wisdom of the advice to never use the computer to apply a statistic that you have not previously done by hand. Also, although you can usually be pretty safe in assuming that the computer will accurately execute each analysis, it is a good idea to spot check. The computer only does what it has been programmed to do and programming errors do occur. Thus, if the computer gives you six F ratios, calculate at least one yourself; if it agrees with the one the computer gave you, the rest are most probably correct. This may sound a little extreme. A former student, however, did indeed use a statistics program that did just fine until it got to the actual F ratios, all of which were computed incorrectly.

Storage

When you are convinced that your work is accurate, all data sheets or cards, work sheets, records of calculations, printouts, and computer disks should be labeled, organized, and filed in a safe place. You never know when you might need your data again. Sometimes an additional analysis is desired either by the original researcher or by another researcher who wishes to analyze the data using a different statistical technique. Also, it is not highly unusual to use data from one study in a later study. Therefore, all of the data should be carefully labeled with as many identification labels as possible, labels such as the dates of the study, the nature of each treatment group, and whether data are pretest data, posttest data, or data for a control variable (such as IQ). All work sheets should also be clearly labeled to indicate the identity of the group(s), the analysis, and the scores, for example, "social reinforcement group/standard deviation/posttest." If the same analysis covers more than one page, fully label each page and indicate "page 1 of 4, page 2 of 4 . . ." A convenient, practical way to store printed data is in loose-leaf ring binders or notebooks. Notebooks can be labeled on the binding, for example, "Reinforcement Study, Spring, 1995," and pages are not likely to slip out and become lost as when manila folders are used. Lastly, find a safe place for all and guard it very carefully. Years ago the author learned a lesson the hard way. In the process of moving from one location to another, the box containing all the data for a major study got lost in the action, never to be seen again (you know, like socks in the dryer). Naturally, since that time several requests for the data have been received. Also, since that tragic event, all subsequent records have been given a royal escort whenever similar journeys have been called for.

■ INTERPRETATION OF RESULTS

The result of the application of a test of significance is a number and only a number, a value which is statistically significant or not statistically significant. What it actually *means* requires interpretation by the researcher. The results of statistical analyses need to be interpreted in terms of the purpose of the study, the original research hypothesis, and with respect to other studies that have been conducted in the same area of research.

Hypothesized Results

The researcher must discuss whether the results support the research hypothesis and why or why not, and whether the results are in agreement with other findings and why or why not. Minimally, this means that you will state, for example, that hypotheses one and two were supported, and that hypothesis three was not. The supported hypotheses are relatively simple to deal with; unsupported hypotheses require some explanation regarding possible reasons. There may have been validity problems in your study, for example. Similarly, if your results are not in agreement with other research findings, reasons for the discrepancy must be discussed. There may have been validity problems in your study or you may have discovered a relationship previously not uncovered. The work of Yvonne Brackbill is a good example of the latter. The results of her studies suggested that contrary to previous evidence derived from animal studies, immediate feedback is not necessarily superior to delayed feedback when human beings are involved, especially with respect to delayed retention.[1] Subsequent studies have confirmed her findings. On the other hand, if you reject a null hypothesis, your research hypothesis may be supported but it is not proven. One study does not prove anything; it only shows that in one instance the hypothesis was supported. Also, a supported research hypothesis does not necessarily mean that your treatment would "work" with different populations, different materials, and different dependent variables. As an example, if token reinforcement is found to be effective in improving the behavior of first graders, this does not mean that token reinforcement will necessarily be effective in reducing referrals to the principal at the high school level. In other words, do not overgeneralize.

If you do not reject the null hypothesis, and your research hypothesis is not supported, you do not apologize. The natural reaction in this situation for beginning researchers is to be very disappointed. In the first place, failure to reject a null hypothesis does not necessarily mean that your research hypothesis is false, but even if it is, it is just as important to know what does not work as what does, which variables are not related as which are. Of course if there were some serious validity problems with your study, you should describe them in detail. Also, if for some reason you lost a lot of subjects you should discuss why, and how the study may have been affected.[2] But do not rationalize. If your study was well planned and well conducted, and no unforeseen mishaps occurred, do not try to come up with *some* reason why your study did not "come out right." It may very well have "come out right"; the null hypothesis might be true. But you do not know that. All you know is that it was not rejected in your study. In other words, there is no evidence either way concerning the truth or falsity of the hypothesized relationship.

Unhypothesized Results

Unhypothesized results should be interpreted with great care. Often during a study an apparent relationship will be noticed which was not hypothesized. You might notice, for example, that experimental subjects appear to require fewer examples to learn new math concepts, an unhypothesized relationship. You do not go and change your original hypothesis, nor do you slip in a new one; hypothesis must be formulated a priori based on deductions from theory and/or experience. A true test of a hypothesis comes from its ability to explain and predict what *will* happen, not

---

[1] See, for example, Brackbill, Y., & Kappy, M. S. (1962). Delay of reinforcement and retention. *Journal of Comparative and Physiological Psychology, 55*(1), 14–18.

[2] Recall that an insufficient number of subjects affects the power of a study and that power refers to statistical ability to reject a false null hypothesis. In other words, if your sample size is too small you may lack the power to reject the null hypothesis even if it is false. Power is also affected by the type of statistic used (parametric tests are more powerful than nonparametric tests) and by group variance on the dependent variable.

what *is* happening. You can, however, collect and analyze data on these unforeseen relationships and present your results as such. These findings may then form the basis for a later study, conducted by yourself or another investigator, specifically designed to test a hypothesis related to your findings. Do not fall into the trap, however, of searching frantically for *something* that might be significant if your study does not appear to be going as hypothesized. Fishing expeditions in experimental studies are just as bad as fishing expeditions in correlational studies.

Statistical Versus Practical Significance

The fact that results are statistically significant does not automatically mean that they are of any educational value. Statistical significance only means that your results would be likely to occur by chance a certain percentage of the time, say 5%. This only means that the observed relationship or difference is probably a real one, not necessarily an important one. With very large samples, for example, a very small correlation coefficient may be statistically significant but of no real practical use to anybody. Similarly, the error term of the *t* test is affected by the sample size; as the sample size increases, the error term (denominator) tends to decrease, and thus the *t* ratio increases. Thus, with very large samples a very small mean difference may yield a significant *t*. A mean difference of two points might be statistically significant but probably not worth the effort of revising a curriculum.

Thus, in a way, the smaller sample sizes typically used in educational research studies actually have a redeeming feature. Given that smaller sample sizes mean less power, and given that a greater mean difference is probably required for rejection of the null hypothesis, more observed relationships are probably practically significant than if larger samples were involved. Of course, by the same token, our lack of power may keep us from finding some important relationships. In any event, you should always take care in interpreting results. The fact that method *A* is significantly more effective than method *B statistically* does not mean that the whole world should immediately adopt method *A*!

Replication of Results

Perhaps the strongest support for a research hypothesis comes from replication of results. Replication means that the study is done again. The second (third, etc.) study may be a repetition of the original study, using the same or different subjects, or it may represent an alternative approach to testing the same hypothesis. Although repeating the study with the same subjects (which is feasible only in certain types of research, such as those involving single-subject designs) supports the reliability of results, repeating the study with different subjects in the same or different settings increases the generalizability of the findings.[3] Brackbill's hypothesis concerning the effectiveness of delayed feedback, for example, was increasingly supported as other researchers repeatedly demonstrated the effect with other types of subjects and other learning tasks. The need for replication is especially great when an unusual or new relationship is found in a study, or when the results have practical significance and the treatment investigated might really make a difference. Interpretation and discussion of a replicated finding will invariably be less "hedgy" than a first-time-ever finding, and rightly so.

---

[3]Sidman, M. (1960). *Tactics of scientific research: Evaluating experimental data in psychology.* New York: Basic Books.

The significance of a relationship may also be enhanced if it is replicated in a more natural setting. A highly controlled study, for example, might find that method *A* is more effective than method *B in a laboratory-like environment.* Interpretation and discussion of the results in terms of practical significance and implications for classroom practice would have to be stated with due caution. If the same results could then be obtained in a classroom situation, however, the researcher could be less tentative concerning their generalizability.

◼ Summary/Chapter 15
Verification and Storage of Data

1. Whether you do your analyses by hand, with the aid of a calculator, or with the aid of a computer, all data must be thoroughly checked and stored in an organized manner.

Verification

2. Verification involves double-checking the input and evaluating the output. Double-checking input may seem a bit excessive, but output is only valid to the degree that input is accurate.
3. Original scores should be rechecked (or some percentage of them), as well as data sheets.
4. Coded data should be compared with uncoded data to make sure all data were coded properly.
5. If a computer has been used and data files created, they should be printed out, or "listed," and compared with data sheets.
6. When analyses are done by hand, or with a calculator, both the accuracy of the computations and the reasonableness of the results need to be checked.
7. Do not just check the steps you followed after you had an arithmetic problem; check every value that you substituted into the formula in order to make it an arithmetic problem.
8. When analyses are done by computer, output must be checked very carefully.
9. Although you can usually be pretty safe in assuming that the computer will accurately execute each analysis, it is a good idea to spot check.

Storage

10. When you are convinced that your work is accurate, all data sheets or cards, work sheets, and records of calculations should be labeled, organized, and filed in a safe place.
11. All of the data should be carefully labeled with as many identification labels as possible, labels such as the dates of the study, the nature of each treatment group, and whether data are pretest data, posttest data, or data for a control variable (such as IQ).
12. A convenient, practical way to store data is in loose-leaf ring binders or notebooks.
13. Find a nice, safe place for it all and guard it very carefully.

INTERPRETATION OF RESULTS

14. The results of statistical analyses need to be interpreted in terms of the purpose of the study, the original research hypothesis, and with respect to other studies that have been conducted in the same area of research.

Hypothesized Results

15. The researcher must discuss whether the results support the research hypothesis and why or why not, and whether the results are in agreement with other findings and why or why not.
16. If you reject a null hypothesis, your research hypothesis may be supported but it is not proven.
17. A supported research hypothesis does not necessarily mean that your treatment would "work" with different populations, different materials, and different dependent variables.
18. Failure to reject a null hypothesis does not necessarily mean that your research hypothesis is false, but even if it is, it is just as important to know what does not work as what does, which variables are not related as which are.
19. If you do not reject the null hypothesis, there is no evidence either way concerning the truth or falsity of the hypothesized relationship.

Unhypothesized Results

20. Unhypothesized results should be interpreted with great care.
21. Often during a study an apparent relationship will be noticed which was not hypothesized.
22. A true test of a hypothesis comes from its ability to explain and predict what *will* happen, not what *is* happening.
23. You can, however, collect and analyze data on these unforeseen relationships and present your results as such.
24. These findings may then form the basis for a later study, conducted by yourself or another investigator, specifically designed to test a hypothesis related to your findings.

Statistical Versus Practical Significance

25. The fact that results are statistically significant does not automatically mean that they are of any educational value.
26. With very large samples a very small mean difference may yield a significant t. A mean difference of two points might be statistically significant but probably not worth the effort of revising a curriculum.

Replication of Results

27. Perhaps the strongest support for a research hypothesis comes from replication of results.
28. Replication means that the study is done again. The second study may be a repetition of the original study, using different subjects, or it may represent an alternative approach to testing the same hypothesis.

29. The need for replication is especially great when an unusual or new relationship is found in a study, or when the results have practical significance and the treatment investigated might really make a difference.
30. The significance of a relationship may also be enhanced if it is replicated in a more natural setting.

TASK 7 PERFORMANCE CRITERIA

The data which you generate (scores you make up for each subject) should make sense. If your dependent variable is IQ, for example, do not generate scores for your subjects like 2, 11, and 15; generate scores like 84, 110, and 120. Got it? Unlike a real study, you can make your study turn out any way you want!

Depending upon the scale of measurement represented by your data, select and compute the appropriate descriptive statistics.

Depending upon the scale of measurement represented by your data, your research hypothesis, and your research design, select and compute the appropriate test of significance. Determine the statistical significance of your results for a selected probability level. Present your results in a summary statement and in a summary table, and relate how the significance or nonsignificance of your results supports or does not support your original research hypothesis. For example, you might say:

> Computation of a *t* test for independent samples (α = .05) indicated that the group which received weekly reviews retained significantly more than the group which received daily reviews (see Table 1). Therefore, the original hypothesis that "ninth-grade algebra students who receive a weekly review will retain significantly more algebraic concepts than ninth-grade algebra students who receive a daily review" was supported. *Note:* Task 7 should look like the results section of a research report. Although your actual calculations should not be part of Task 7, they should be attached to it.

Table 1

Means, Standard Deviations, and t *for the Daily-Review and Weekly-Review Groups on the Delayed Retention Test*

	Review Group		*t*
	Daily	**Weekly**	
M	44.82	52.68	2.56*
SD	5.12	6.00	

Note: Maximum score = 65.

*df = 38, *p* < .05.

On the following pages, an example is presented which illustrates the performance called for by Task 7. (See Task 7 example.) Note that the scores are based on the administration of the test described in Task 5. Note also that the student calculated effect size (ES) as described in Chapter 8.

Additional examples for this and subsequent tasks are included in the *Student Guide* which accompanies this text.

1

Effect of Interactive Multimedia on the Achievement of
10th-Grade Biology Students

Results

Prior to the beginning of the study, after the 60
students were randomly selected and assigned to experimental
and control groups, final science grades from the previous
school year were obtained from school records in order to
check initial group equivalence. Examination of the means and
a t test for independent samples (α = .05) indicated
essentially no difference between the groups (see Table 1). A
t test for independent samples was used because the groups
were randomly formed and the data were interval.

Table 1

Means, Standard Deviation and t Tests for the Experimental and
Control Groups

Score	Group		
	IMM instruction[a]	Traditional instruction[a]	t
Prior Grades			
M	87.47	87.63	−0.08*
SD	8.19	8.05	
Posttest NPSS:B			
M	32.27	26.70	4.22**
SD	4.45	5.69	

Note. Maximum score for prior grades = 100. Maximum score for
posttest = 40.

[a]n = 30.

*p > .05. **p < .05.

526

2

       At the completion of the eight-month study, during the first week in May, scores on the NPSS:B were compared, also using a $\underline{t}$ test for independent samples. As Table 1 indicates, scores of the experimental and control groups were significantly different. In fact, the experimental group scored approximately one standard deviation higher than the control group (ES=.98). Therefore, the original hypothesis that "10th-grade biology strudents whose teachers use IMM as part of their instructional technique will exhibit significantly higher achievement than 10th-grade biology students whose teachers do not use IMM" was supported.

PRIOR GRADES

S	EXPERIMENTAL X_1	X_1^2	CONTROL X_2	X_2^2
1	72	5184	71	5041
2	74	5476	75	5625
3	76	5776	75	5625
4	76	5776	77	5929
5	77	5929	78	6084
6	78	6084	78	6084
7	78	6084	79	6241
8	79	6241	80	6400
9	80	6400	81	6561
10	84	7056	83	6889
11	85	7225	85	7225
12	87	7569	88	7744
13	87	7569	88	7744
14	88	7744	89	7921
15	89	7921	89	7921
16	89	7921	89	7921
17	90	8100	90	8100
18	91	8281	91	8281
19	92	8464	92	8464
20	93	8649	92	8464
21	93	8649	93	8649
22	93	8649	94	8836
23	94	8836	94	8836
24	95	9025	95	9025
25	95	9025	96	9216
26	97	9409	96	9216
27	97	9409	97	9409
28	98	9604	97	9409
29	98	9604	98	9604
30	99	9801	99	9801
	2624 ΣX_1	231,460 ΣX_1^2	2629 ΣX_2	232,265 ΣX_2^2

$$\overline{X_1} = \frac{\Sigma X_1}{n_1} = \frac{2624}{30} = 87.47$$

$$\overline{X_2} = \frac{\Sigma X_2}{n_2} = \frac{2629}{30} = 87.63$$

$$SD_1 = \sqrt{\frac{SS_1}{n_1 - 1}} \qquad\qquad SD_2 = \sqrt{\frac{SS_2}{n_2 - 1}}$$

$$SS_1 = \sum x_1^2 - \frac{\left(\sum x_1\right)^2}{n_1} \qquad SS_2 = \sum x_2^2 - \frac{\left(\sum x_2\right)^2}{n_2}$$

$$= 231{,}460 - \frac{(2624)^2}{30} \qquad\qquad = 232{,}265 - \frac{(2629)^2}{30}$$

$$= 231{,}460 - \frac{6885376}{30} \qquad\qquad = 232{,}265 - \frac{6911641}{30}$$

$$= 231{,}460 - 229{,}512.53 \qquad\qquad = 232{,}265 - 230388.03$$

$$SS_1 = 1947.47 \qquad\qquad SS_2 = 1876.97$$

$$SD_1 = \sqrt{\frac{1947.47}{29}} \qquad\qquad SD_2 = \sqrt{\frac{1876.97}{29}}$$

$$= \sqrt{67.154} \qquad\qquad\qquad = \sqrt{64.72}$$

$$SD_1 = 8.19 \qquad\qquad\qquad SD_2 = 8.05$$

$$t = \frac{\bar{x}_1 - \bar{x}_2}{\sqrt{\left(\frac{SS_1 + SS_2}{n_1 + n_2 - 2}\right)\left(\frac{1}{n_1} + \frac{1}{n_2}\right)}} = \frac{87.47 - 87.63}{\sqrt{\left(\frac{1947.47 + 1876.97}{30 + 30 - 2}\right)\left(\frac{1}{30} + \frac{1}{30}\right)}}$$

$$= \frac{-0.16}{\sqrt{\left(\frac{3824.44}{58}\right)\left(\frac{1}{15}\right)}}$$

Note: the t table does not have $df = 58$. To be conservative I used $df = 40$. For $df = 40$ the table value is 2.021

$$= \frac{-0.16}{\sqrt{(65.9386)(.0667)}}$$

$$= \frac{-0.16}{\sqrt{4.398}}$$

$$= \frac{-0.16}{2.097}$$

$$t = -.08 \qquad df = 58 \qquad p < .05$$

POSTTEST   NATIONAL PROFICIENCY SURVEY SERIES: BIOLOGY

	EXPERIMENTAL			CONTROL	
S	X_1	X_1^2		X_2	X_2^2
1	20	400		15	225
2	24	576		16	256
3	26	676		18	324
4	27	729		20	400
5	28	784		21	441
6	29	841		22	484
7	29	841		22	484
8	29	841		23	529
9	30	900		24	576
10	31	961		24	576
11	31	961		25	625
12	31	961		25	625
13	32	1024		25	625
14	32	1024		26	676
15	33	1089		26	676
16	33	1089		27	729
17	33	1089		27	729
18	34	1156		28	784
19	34	1156		29	841
20	35	1225		29	841
21	35	1225		30	900
22	35	1225		30	900
23	36	1296		31	961
24	36	1296		31	961
25	36	1296		32	1024
26	37	1369		33	1089
27	37	1369		34	1156
28	38	1444		35	1225
29	38	1444		36	1296
30	39	1521		37	1369
	968	31808		801	22327
	ΣX_1	ΣX_1^2		ΣX_2	ΣX_2^2

$$\overline{X}_1 = \frac{\Sigma x_1}{n_1} = \frac{968}{30} = 32.27 \qquad \overline{X}_2 = \frac{\Sigma x_2}{n_2} = \frac{801}{30} = 26.70$$

$$SD_1 = \sqrt{\frac{SS_1}{n_1 - 1}} \qquad\qquad SD_2 = \sqrt{\frac{SS_2}{n_2 - 1}}$$

$$SS_1 = \sum x_1^2 - \frac{\left(\sum x_1\right)^2}{n_1} \qquad SS_2 = \sum x_2^2 - \frac{\left(\sum x_2\right)^2}{n_2}$$

$$= 31808 - \frac{(968)^2}{30} \qquad\qquad = 22327 - \frac{(801)^2}{30}$$

$$= 31808 - \frac{937024}{30} \qquad\qquad = 22327 - \frac{641601}{30}$$

$$= 31808 - 31234.13 \qquad\qquad = 22327 - 21386.70$$

$$SS_1 = 573.87 \qquad\qquad SS_2 = 940.30$$

$$SD_1 = \sqrt{\frac{573.87}{29}} \qquad\qquad SD_2 = \sqrt{\frac{940.30}{29}}$$

$$= \sqrt{19.789} \qquad\qquad = \sqrt{32.424}$$

$$SD_1 = 4.45 \qquad\qquad SD_2 = 5.69$$

$$t = \frac{\bar{x}_1 - \bar{x}_2}{\sqrt{\left(\frac{SS_1 + SS_2}{n_1 + n_2 - 2}\right)\left(\frac{1}{n_1} + \frac{1}{n_2}\right)}} \qquad = \frac{32.27 - 26.70}{\sqrt{\left(\frac{573.87 + 940.30}{30 + 30 - 2}\right)\left(\frac{1}{30} + \frac{1}{30}\right)}}$$

$$= \frac{5.57}{\sqrt{\left(\frac{1514.17}{58}\right)\left(\frac{1}{15}\right)}}$$

$$= \frac{5.57}{\sqrt{(26.1064)(.0667)}}$$

$$= \frac{5.57}{\sqrt{1.7404}}$$

$$= \frac{5.57}{1.3192}$$

$$t = 4.22 \qquad df = 58 \qquad p < .05$$

Prior Grades

Descriptive Statistics

EXPERIMENTAL GROUP

==

STANDARD DEVIATION FOR SAMPLES AND POPULATIONS

==

STATISTIC	VALUE
NO. OF SCORES (N)	30
SUM OF SCORES (ΣX)	2624.00
MEAN ($\overline{X}$)	87.47
SUM OF SQUARED SCORES (ΣX^2)	231460.00
SUM OF SQUARES (SS)	1947.47
STANDARD DEVIATION FOR A POPULATION	8.06
STANDARD DEVIATION FOR A SAMPLE	8.19

==

CONTROL GROUP

==

STANDARD DEVIATION FOR SAMPLES AND POPULATIONS

==

STATISTIC	VALUE
NO. OF SCORES (N)	30
SUM OF SCORES (ΣX)	2629.00
MEAN ($\overline{X}$)	87.63
SUM OF SQUARED SCORES (ΣX^2)	232265.00
SUM OF SQUARES (SS)	1876.97
STANDARD DEVIATION FOR A POPULATION	7.91
STANDARD DEVIATION FOR A SAMPLE	8.05

==

===

t-TEST FOR INDEPENDENT SAMPLES

===

STATISTIC	VALUE
NO. OF SCORES IN GROUP ONE	30
SUM OF SCORES IN GROUP ONE	2624.00
MEAN OF GROUP ONE	87.47
SUM OF SQUARED SCORES IN GROUP ONE	231460.00
SS OF GROUP ONE	1947.47
NO. OF SCORES IN GROUP TWO	30
SUM OF SCORES IN GROUP TWO	2629.00
MEAN OF GROUP TWO	87.63
SUM OF SQUARED SCORES IN GROUP TWO	232265.00
SS OF GROUP TWO	1876.97
t-VALUE	-0.08
DEGREES OF FREEDOM (df)	58

===

STATPAK PRINTOUTS
NPSS:B Scores
Descriptive Statistics

EXPERIMENTAL GROUP

==

STANDARD DEVIATION FOR SAMPLES AND POPULATIONS

==

STATISTIC	VALUE
NO. OF SCORES (N)	30
SUM OF SCORES (ΣX)	968.00
MEAN ($\bar{X}$)	32.27
SUM OF SQUARED SCORES (ΣX^2)	31808.00
SUM OF SQUARES (SS)	573.87
STANDARD DEVIATION FOR A POPULATION	4.37
STANDARD DEVIATION FOR A SAMPLE	4.45

==

CONTROL GROUP

==

STANDARD DEVIATION FOR SAMPLES AND POPULATIONS

==

STATISTIC	VALUE
NO. OF SCORES (N)	30
SUM OF SCORES (ΣX)	801.00
MEAN ($\bar{X}$)	26.70
SUM OF SQUARED SCORES (ΣX^2)	22327.00
SUM OF SQUARES (SS)	940.30
STANDARD DEVIATION FOR A POPULATION	5.60
STANDARD DEVIATION FOR A SAMPLE	5.69

==

STATPAK PRINTOUTS

NPSS:B Scores

Inferential Statistic

===

t-TEST FOR INDEPENDENT SAMPLES

===

STATISTIC	VALUE
NO. OF SCORES IN GROUP ONE	30
SUM OF SCORES IN GROUP ONE	968.00
MEAN OF GROUP ONE	32.27
SUM OF SQUARED SCORES IN GROUP ONE	31808.00
SS OF GROUP ONE	573.87
NO. OF SCORES IN GROUP TWO	30
SUM OF SCORES IN GROUP TWO	801.00
MEAN OF GROUP TWO	26.70
SUM OF SQUARED SCORES IN GROUP TWO	22327.00
SS OF GROUP TWO	940.30
t-VALUE	4.22
DEGREES OF FREEDOM (df)	58

===

PART EIGHT

Research Reports

There are a variety of reasons for which people conduct research. The motivation for doing a research project may be no more than that such a project is a degree requirement, or it may come from a strong desire to contribute to educational theory or practice. Whatever the reason for their execution, most research studies culminate with the production of a research report.

A number of manuals are available which describe various formats and styles for writing research reports, although there are a number of elements which are common to most reports regardless of the format followed. Virtually all research reports, for example, contain a statement of the problem, a description of procedures, and a presentation of results. Further, all research reports have a common purpose, namely, to communicate as clearly as possible the purpose, procedures, and findings of the study. A well written report describes a study in sufficient detail to permit replication by another researcher.

You have already written many of the components of a research report through your work in Parts Two through Seven. In Part Eight you will integrate all your previous efforts to produce a complete report.

The goal of Part Eight is for you, having conducted a study, to be able to produce a complete report. After you have read Part Eight, you should be able to perform the following task.

■ TASK 8

Based on Tasks 2.6, and 7, prepare a research report which follows the general format for a thesis or dissertation.

(See Performance Criteria, p. 560)

"The research report should . . . reflect scholarship (p. 540)."

Preparation of a Research Report

OBJECTIVES

After reading Chapter 16, you should be able to:

1. List 10 general rules for writing and preparing a research report.
2. Identify and briefly describe the major sections and subsections of a research report.
3. List four major differences between a research report prepared as a thesis or dissertation and a research report prepared as a manuscript for publication.
4. List two guidelines for presenting a paper at a professional meeting.

GENERAL GUIDELINES

If you carefully prepare a research plan before you conduct your study, you have a good head start on writing your research report, especially the introduction section. While you are conducting your study, you can profitably utilize any free time you have by revising and refining the introduction and method sections of the report. The study may not be executed exactly as planned, but the procedures should not diverge drastically from the original plan. When the study is completed, the final draft of the method section can incorporate any final changes in procedures. After all the data are analyzed you are ready to write the final sections of the report. The major guideline previously described for analyzing, organizing, and reporting related literature is applicable to this task—make an outline. The chances of your results and conclusions being presented in an organized, logical manner are greatly increased if the sequence is thought through before anything is actually written. Formulation of an outline greatly facilitates the "thinking through" process. To review briefly, development of an outline involves identification and ordering of major topics followed by differentiation of each major heading into logical sub-headings. The time spent in working on an outline is well worth it since it is much easier to reorganize an outline that is not quite right than to reorganize a document written in paragraph form. Of course this does not mean that your first report draft will be your last. Two or three revisions of each section are to be expected. Each time you read a section you will see ways to improve its organization or clarity. Also, other persons who review your report for you will see areas in need of rethinking or rewording that you have not noticed.

While the research plan may have been written in the future tense ("subjects *will* be randomly selected . . .") by the time you get to the research report the party is over and each section is written in the past tense ("subjects *were* randomly select-ed"). Further, in addition to conscientiously following a selected style and format, there are several general rules of good report writing which the researcher should be aware of and follow.

General Rules for Writing and Typing

Probably the foremost rule of research report writing is that the writer must be as objective as possible in reporting the study. A research report is a scientific docu-ment, not a novel or treatise. In other words, the report should not contain subjec-tive statements ("*clearly* group instruction is no good"), overstatements ("wow, what fantastic results!"), or emotional statements ("every year thousands of school chil-dren are the poor, innocent victims of an ineffective reading program"). Further, the report should not be written as if it were a legal brief intended to present arguments in favor of a position ("the purpose of this study was to prove . . ."). The research report should contain an objective, factual description of past research and the study upon which the report is based.[1] Consistent with the goal of objective reporting, personal pronouns such as *I* and *we* should be kept to a minimum. Instead, imper-sonal pronouns and the passive voice should be used. Phrases such as "*it* was deter-mined" and "subjects *were* randomly *selected*" should be used instead of "*I* deter-mined" and "*I* randomly selected subjects." On the other hand, personal pronouns may be used when it would be awkward not to. For example, it would sound a lit-tle strange to say "Subjects were told that the experimenter would send them per-sonalized profiles . . ." if the experimenter were in fact yourself.

The research report should be written in a clear, simple, straightforward style; you do not have to be boring, just concise. In other words, say what you have to say in the fewest number of words and using the simplest language. For example, instead of saying "the population comprised all students who matriculated for the fall semester at Egghead University," it would be better to say "the population was all students enrolled for the fall semester at Egghead University." The research report should also reflect scholarship; correct spelling, grammatical construction, and punctuation are not too much to expect of a scientific report. And do not say that you are the world's worst speller; even if you don't have a spelling program on your computer, you do have access to a dictionary. If there is any doubt in your mind concerning the correct spelling of a word, correct construction of a sentence, or correct punctuation, consult the appropriate reference book. It is also a good idea to have someone you know, someone who is perhaps stronger in these areas, review your manuscript for you and indicate errors.

---

[1]A little more latitude is permitted the researcher in discussing implications of the study and in making recommendations for future research or action.

While different style manuals suggest different rules of writing, there are several which are common to most manuals. Use of abbreviations and contractions, for instance, is generally discouraged. Do not say, for example, "the American Psychological Assn.," say "the American Psychological Association." Also, words like *shouldn't, isn't,* and *won't* should be avoided. Exceptions to the abbreviation rule include commonly used and understood abbreviations (such as IQ and GPA) and abbreviations defined by the researcher to promote clarity, simplify presentation, or reduce repetition. If the same sequence of words is going to be used repeatedly, the researcher will often define an abbreviation in parentheses the first time the sequence is used and thereafter use only the abbreviation. In a study by Skaalvik and Rankin (1995), for example, the Self-Description Questionnaire was referred to throughout the research report as the SDQ.[2] Also, as the above sentence illustrates, authors of cited references are usually referred to by last name only in the main body of the report; first names, initials, and titles are not given. Instead of saying "Professor Dudley Q. McStrudle (1995) concluded . . ." you normally would say "McStrudle (1995) concluded . . ." The above described guidelines, of course, hold only for the main body of the report. Tables, figures, footnotes, and references may include abbreviations; footnotes and references usually give at least the author's initials. Another convention followed by most style manuals is with respect to numbers. If the first word of a sentence is a number ("Six schools were contacted . . ."), or if the number is nine or less ("a total of five lists . . ."), numbers are usually expressed as words. Otherwise, numbers are generally expressed as arabic numerals ("a total of 500 questionnaires was sent to the various groups of interest").

The same standards of scholarship should be applied to the typing of the report as to the writing of the report. When you read a report full of typos you cannot help but wonder if the study was conducted in the same careless manner as the report was proofread. If you are not highly proficient in typing, find yourself a typist who is. Present the typist with a manuscript which is in final, correct form; the typist's job is to type, not to polish, your report. I once gave a paper to my secretary that I was going to read at a meeting. In the middle of page 7 I wrote a note which said "see attached document"; the attached document had a paragraph marked that I wanted included in the paper. While proofreading the typed paper, much to my chagrin, I discovered that she had typed "see attached document" right in the middle of a page. When I asked her about it she told me sweetly "I type what I see, not what you mean!" The point is that you should not expect your typist to "know" what you want. If you have any special instructions (such as not to split words at the end of a line), share them with your typist and be sure they are understood. It is also a good idea to give your typist a copy of the style manual you are following to ensure that required guidelines (such as size of margins) are followed. Finally, no matter how good your typist is, nobody is perfect. The final typed report should be proofread carefully at least twice. Reading the report silently to yourself will usually be sufficient to identify major typing errors. If you have a willing listener, however, reading the manuscript out loud often helps you to identify grammatical or constructional errors. Sometimes sentences do not make nearly as much sense when you hear them as when you write them; also, your listener will frequently be helpful in bringing to your attention sections that are unclear. Reading the report backwards, last sentence first, will also help you to identify poorly constructed or unclear sentences.

---

[2]Skaalvik, E. M., & Rankin, R. J. (1990). Math, verbal, and general academic self-concept: The internal/external frame of reference model and gender differences in self-concept structure. *Journal of Educational Psychology, 82,* 546–554.

The process of preparing a research report has been greatly facilitated by the development of word processing software for micros. A word processor provides so many features not available with a typewriter that it is probably safe to say that the old electric typewriter can be added to the endangered species list. When using a word processing program, you type in your text and it is displayed on the screen; it is then stored and available for additions, deletions, and changes. A high-quality printer allows you to print out results which are virtually identical to typed copy. While different programs have different capabilities, commonly available features include: automatic page numbering and heading centering; the ability to rearrange words, sentences, and paragraphs; and spelling checkers. Yes, alas, we may soon be adding Webster to our endangered species list!

Format and Style

Most research reports consistently follow a selected system for format and style. While many such systems are available, a given report usually strictly follows one of them. Format refers to the general pattern of organization and arrangement of the report. The number and types of headings and subheadings to be included in the report are determined by the format used. Style refers to the rules of spelling, capitalization, punctuation, and typing followed in preparing the report. While specific formats may vary in terms of specific headings included, all research reports follow a very similar format that parallels the steps involved in conducting a study. One format may call for a discussion section, for example, while another may require a summary, conclusions, and recommendations section (or both), but all formats for a research report entail a section in which the results of the study are discussed and interpreted. All research reports also include a condensed description of the study, whether it be a summary of a dissertation or an abstract of a journal article.

Most colleges, universities, and professional journals either have developed their own, required style manual or have selected one that must be followed. One such manual, which is increasingly being adopted as the required guide for theses and dissertations, is the *Publication Manual of the American Psychological Association*.[3] This format is becoming increasingly popular, primarily because it eliminates the need for formal footnotes. If you are not bound by any particular format and style system, the APA manual is recommended. In addition to acquiring and studying a copy of the selected manual, it is also very helpful to study several reports that have been written following the same manual. Such reports serve as useful models and help the writer translate abstract guidelines into practice. To the degree possible, e.g., with respect to tables, figures, references, and student examples of tasks, this text reflects APA guidelines, as does the discussion below. Figure 16.1 illustrates some of the basic APA guidelines using a page from the Task 8 example which appears at the end of this chapter.

■ TYPES OF RESEARCH REPORTS

Research reports usually take the form of a thesis, dissertation, journal article, or paper to be read at a professional meeting. In fact, the same report may take sev-

---

[3]American Psychological Association. (1994). *Publication manual of the American Psychological Association* (4th ed.). Washington, DC: Author.

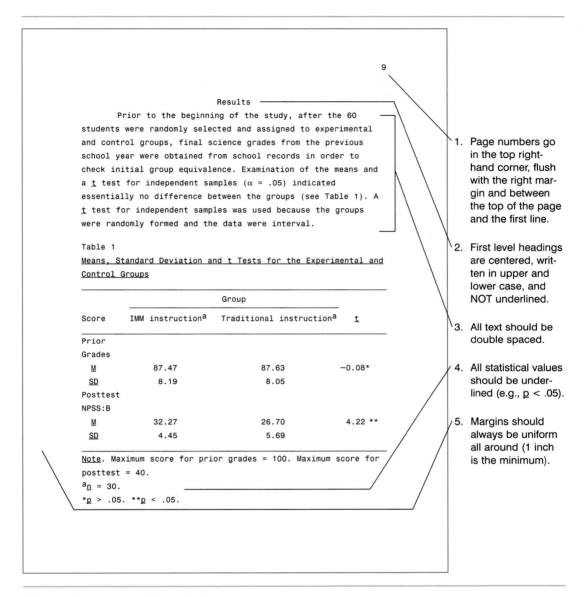

Figure 16.1. Some APA guidelines for preparing your paper.

eral forms; dissertation studies are frequently described at professional meetings and prepared for publication. As mentioned previously, and as you probably noticed when you reviewed the literature related to your problem, the components of all research reports are very similar. Depending upon its form, the report may be divided into sections or chapters but these divisions are similar in content.

Theses and Dissertations

While specifics will vary considerably, most research reports prepared for a degree requirement follow the same general format. Table 16.1 presents an outline of the typical contents of such a report. As Table 16.1 indicates, theses and dissertations

Table 16.1

Common Components of a Research Report Submitted for a Degree Requirement

PRELIMINARY PAGES

Title page

Acknowledgment page

Table of Contents

List of Tables and Figures

Abstract

MAIN BODY OF THE REPORT

Introduction

Statement of the Problem

Review of Related Literature

Statement of the Hypothesis

Method

Subjects

Instruments

Design

Procedure

Results

Discussion (Conclusions and Recommendations)

References (Bibliography)

APPENDIXES

include a set of fairly standard preliminary pages, components which directly parallel the research process, and supplementary information, which is included in appendices.

Preliminary Pages

The preliminary pages set the stage for the report to follow and indicate where in the report each component, table, and figure can be found.

The Title Page.   The title page usually includes the title of the report, the author's name, the degree requirement being fulfilled, the name and location of the college or university awarding the degree, the date of submission of the report, and signatures of approving committee members (although approvals are often listed on a separate page). The title should be brief (10 to 12 words, as a rule of thumb), and at the same time it should describe the purpose of the study as clearly as possible. One way to reduce the size of the title is to omit unnecessary words such as "a study of . . . ," "an investigation of . . . ," and "an experimental study to determine. . . ." The title should, however, at least indicate the major independent and dependent variables, and sometimes it identifies the population studied. Volume 85, issue 3, of *The Journal of Educational Research,* for example, includes the following titles:

Effects of Word Processing on Sixth Graders' Holistic
Writing and Revisions[4]

Effects of Frequent Testing of Secondary Algebra Students[5]

Effects of Peer Interaction During Computer-Based
Mathematics Instruction[6]

Each one of these titles specifies the cause-effect relationship that was investigated. A good title should clearly communicate what the study was about. Recall that when you reviewed the literature and looked under key words in the various indexes, you made decisions based on titles listed concerning whether the articles were probably related or not related to your problem. When the titles were well constructed it was fairly easy to determine probable relationship or lack of relationship to your problem; when they were vaguely worded it was often difficult to determine without examining the report of the study. Thus, after you write your title apply the communication test: Would *you* know what the study was about if you read the title in an index?

The Acknowledgment Page.   Most theses and dissertations include an acknowledgment page. This page permits the writer to express appreciation to persons who have contributed significantly to the completion of the report. Notice the word significant. Everyone who had anything to do with the study or the report cannot (and should not!) be mentioned. It is acceptable to thank your major professor for his or her guidance and assistance; it is not acceptable to thank your third-grade teacher for giving you confidence in your ability. (Remember the Academy Awards!)

The Table of Contents and List of Tables and Figures.   The table of contents is basically an outline of your report which indicates on which page each major section (or chapter) and subsection begins. The list of tables and figures, which is presented on a separate page, gives the number and title of each table and figure and the page on which it can be found. As an example:

List of Tables and Figures

Table	Page
1. Means and standard deviations for all tests by group and experiment	22
2. Analysis of variance of delayed retention scores for review and nonreview subjects for experiment II	25

Figure	
1. Experimental designs for experiment I and experiment II	14
2. Plot of test scores for all groups before and after each learning and review session	23

Entries listed in the table of contents should be identical to headings and subheadings in the report, and table titles and figure titles should be the same titles that are given for the actual tables and figures in the main body of the report.

---

[4] Grejda, G. F., & Hannafin, M. J. (1992). Effects of word processing on sixth graders' holistic writing and revisions. *The Journal of Educational Research, 85,* 144–149.

[5] Kika, F. M., McLaughlin, T. F., & Dixon, J. (1992). Effects of frequent testing of secondary algebra students. *The Journal of Educational Research, 85,* 159–162.

[6] Hooper, S. (1992). Effects of peer interaction during computer-based mathematics instruction. *The Journal of Educational Research, 85,* 180–189.

Abstract.   Some colleges and universities require an abstract, while others require a summary, and the current trend is in favor of abstracts. The content of abstracts and summaries is identical, only the positioning differs; whereas an abstract precedes the main body of the report, a summary follows the Discussion section. The size of the abstract will determine the amount of detail permitted and its emphasis. Abstracts are often required to be no more than a given maximum number of words, usually between 100 and 500. As the APA manual points out, many institutions require abstracts to be no more than 350 words, the maximum allowed by *Dissertation Abstracts International,* whereas most APA journals require abstracts which are between 100 and 150 words. Shorter abstracts usually concentrate more on the problem and on the results than on the method. Since the abstract of a report is often the only part read (remember when you did your review of the literature?) it should describe the most important aspects of the study, including the problem investigated, the type of subjects and instruments involved, the design, the procedures, and the major results and the major conclusions. A reader should be able to tell from an abstract exactly what a study was about and what it found. For example, a 100-word abstract for a study investigating the effect of a writing-oriented curriculum on the reading comprehension of fourth-grade students might read as follows:

> The purpose of this study was to determine the effectiveness of a curriculum that emphasized writing with respect to the reading comprehension of fourth-grade students reading at least one level below grade level. Using a posttest-only control group design and the *t* test for independent samples, it was found that after 8 months the students ($n = 20$) who participated in a curriculum which emphasized writing achieved significantly higher scores on the reading comprehension subtest of the Stanford Achievement Test, Primary Level 3 (grades 3.5—4.9) than the students ($n = 20$) who did not [$t (38) = 4.83, p < .05$]. It was concluded that the curriculum emphasizing writing was more effective in promoting reading comprehension.[7]

The Main Body of the Report

With the exception of the section for Discussion, you are already quite familiar with the components of a research report. Therefore, we will review each of these components briefly and will discuss the Discussion section in more depth.

Introduction.   As mentioned previously, the introduction to a research report is already written and in pretty good shape if the researcher carefully developed a research plan prior to conducting the study. The introduction section includes a description of the problem, a review of related literature, a statement of hypotheses, and definition of terms. A well written statement of a problem generally indicates the variables, and the specific relationship between those variables, investigated in the study. The statement of the problem should be accompanied by a presentation of the background of the problem, including a justification for the study in terms of the significance of the problem.

The review of related literature describes and analyzes what has already been done related to your problem. The review of related literature is not a series of abstracts or annotations but rather an analysis of the relationships and differences among related studies and reports. The review should flow in such a way that the least related references are discussed first and the most related references are dis-

---

[7]Based on a paper by E. Batten. (1990). Florida International University, Miami, FL. Used by permission.

cussed last, just prior to the statement of the hypothesis. The review should conclude with a brief summary of the literature and its implications.

A good hypothesis states as clearly and concisely as possible the expected relationship (or difference) between two variables and defines those variables in operational, measurable terms. The hypothesis (or hypotheses) logically follows the review of related literature and it is based upon the implications of previous research. A well-developed hypothesis is testable, that is, can be confirmed or disconfirmed.

The introduction also includes operational definition of terms used in the study which do not have a commonly known meaning. Some institutions require that one section of the introduction be devoted to defining all the terms in one place. Usually, however, it is better to define each term the first time it appears in the report.

Method.   As with the introduction, the method section of the report is already written and included in the research plan. The procedure section may require some revision, but it should be in reasonably good shape. The method section includes a description of subjects, instruments, design, procedure, assumptions, and limitations. The description of subjects includes a definition and description of the population from which the sample was selected and may describe the method used in selecting the sample or samples (or the method of selection may be described in the procedure section). The description of the population should indicate its size and major characteristics such as age, grade level, ability level, and socioeconomic status. Information should be provided on any variables which might be related to performance on the dependent variable. A good description of the population enables the reader of the report to determine how similar study subjects were to the population with which she or he is involved, and thus, how applicable results might be. If method of sample selection is presented here it should be very specific.

The description of instruments should identify and describe all instruments used to collect data pertinent to the study, be they tests, questionnaires, interview forms, or observation forms. The description of each instrument should relate the function of the instrument in the study (for example, selection of subjects or a measure of the dependent variable), what the instrument is intended to measure, and data related to validity and reliability. If an instrument has been developed by the researcher, the description needs to be more detailed and should also relate the manner in which it was developed, a description of pretesting efforts and subsequent instrument revisions, steps involved in scoring, and guidelines for interpretation. A copy of the instrument itself, accompanying scoring keys, and other pertinent data related to a newly developed test are generally placed in the appendix of the thesis or dissertation.

The description of the design is especially important in an experimental study. In other types of research the description of the design may be combined with procedure. In an experimental study, the description of the basic design (or variation of a basic design) applied in the study should include a rationale for selection and a discussion of sources of invalidity associated with the design, and why they may have been minimized in the study being reported.

The procedure section should describe each step followed in conducting the study, in chronological order, in sufficient detail to permit the study to be replicated by another researcher. If not done so earlier, the method of subject selection should be described in detail. It should be clear exactly how subjects were assigned to groups and how treatments were assigned to groups. Time and conditions of pretest administration (if appropriate) should be described, followed by a detailed explanation of the study itself. The ways in which groups were different (treatment) should be clearly delineated as well as ways in which they were similar (control procedures). Any unforeseen events which occurred which might have affected the results should be discussed in terms of their seriousness and probable consequences. Also, any insights regarding ways to improve procedures should be shared so that other researchers may profit from the investigator's experiences.

Results.   The results section describes the statistical techniques that were applied to the data, preselected α levels, and the results of each analysis. For each hypothesis, the statistical test of significance selected and applied to the data is described, followed by a statement indicating whether the hypothesis was supported or not supported. Tables and figures are used to present findings in summary or graph form and add clarity to the presentation. Tables present numerical data in rows and columns and usually include descriptive statistics, such as means and standard deviations, and the results of tests of significance, such as t and F ratios. While a figure may be any nontabular presentation of information (such as a diagram or chart), figures in the results sections are usually graphical presentations of data. Figures can often be used to show relationships not evident in tabular presentations of data. Interactions, for example, are clearer when illustrated in a figure. If figures are based on numerical data, that data should be presented in a table or in the figure itself. Good tables and figures are uncluttered and self-explanatory; it is better to use two tables (or figures) than one that is crowded. They should stand alone, that is, be interpretable without the aid of related textual material. Tables and figures follow their related textual discussion and are referred to by number, not name or location. In other words, the text should say "see Table 1," not "see the table with the means" or "see the table on the next page."

Figure 16.2 illustrates appropriate use and format of tables and figures. It presents Table 1 and Figure 1 adapted from a study by Fantuzzo, Riggio, Connelly, and Dimeff which appeared in an issue of the *Journal of Educational Psychology*.[8] Table 1 includes descriptive statistics (means, *M,* and standard deviations, *SD*). Figure 1 graphically presents the means from Table 1 and clearly depicts interactions which are not evident from an examination of Table 1.

Discussion.   Every research report has a section that discusses and interprets the results, draws conclusions and implications, and makes recommendations. Interpretation of results may be presented in a separate section titled "Discussion" or it may be included in the same section as the other analysis of results items. If only one hypothesis was tested, and (or) if the discussion is brief, it may be included in the results section. What this section (or sections) is called is unimportant; what is important is how well it is done. Each result is discussed in terms of the original hypothesis to which it relates, and in terms of its agreement or disagreement with previous results obtained by other researchers in other studies. For example, in a study investigating the effectiveness of reviews in increasing retention of mathematical rules (Gay, 1973), it was hypothesized that ". . . for the mathematical task involved in this study . . . one review will significantly enhance retention . . ." and "temporal position of one review will not be a significant effect . . ."[9] The

---

[8]Fantuzzo, J. W., Riggio, R. E., Connelly, S., & Dimeff, L. A. (1989). Effects of reciprocal peer tutoring on academic achievement and psychological adjustment: A component analysis. *Journal of Educational Psychology, 81,* 173–177.

[9]Gay, L. R. (1973). Temporal position of reviews and its effect on the retention of mathematical rules. *Journal of Educational Psychology, 64,* 171–182. Temporal position refers to when the review was received. In this study subjects received a review 1 day, 1 week, or 2 weeks following the day of original learning.

Table 1
Means, Standard Deviations, for the BDI scale

Measure and Group	Preassessment		Postassessment[a]	
	M	SD	M	SD
BDI scale				
DS	6.6	3.9	3.1	4.3
DU	3.9	3.6	8.5	6.6
IS	5.7	5.5	7.1	9.8
IU	7.1	8.4	5.5	8.8

Note. DS = dyadic structured format group; DU = dyadic unstructured format group; IS = independent structured format group; IU = independent unstructured format group; and BDI = Beck Depression Inventory.
[a]Posttest means are adjusted for pretest scores.

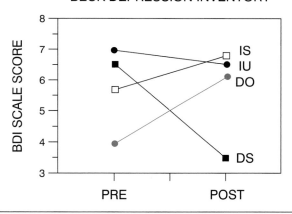

BECK DEPRESSION INVENTORY

Figure 1. Pre- and posttest group means are displayed for the Beck Depression Inventory (DS = dyadic structured format group; DU = dyadic unstructured format group; IS = independent structured format group; IU = independent unstructured format group).

Figure 16.2. Example of a table and figure illustrating appropriate use and format. (From Fantuzzo, Riggio, Connelly and Dimeff, 1989; only a portion of the original table and figure is presented. Copyright 1989 by the American Psychological Association. Reprinted by permission.)

results section of the research report stated that: "It was found that while review groups retained significantly more than the no-review group (F = 6.96, df = 1/48, p < .05) the effect of temporal position of the reviews was not significant." And the Discussion section stated that "The results of experiment I indicate that the temporal position of one review is not an important factor in retention of mathematical rules. These findings are consistent with those of Peterson et al. (1935), Sones and Stroud (1940), and Ausubel (1966) involving meaningful verbal learning."[10]

Two common errors committed by beginning researchers are to confuse results and conclusions and to overgeneralize results. A result is the outcome of a test of significance, for example, the mean of group 1 is found to be significantly larger than the mean of group 2. The corresponding conclusion is that the original hypothesis was supported and that method *A* was more effective than method *B*. Overgeneralization refers to the statement of conclusions that are not warranted by the results. For example, if a group of first graders receiving personalized instruction were found to achieve significantly higher on a test of reading comprehension than a group receiving traditional instruction, it would be an overgeneralization to conclude that personalized instruction is a superior method of instruction for elementary students.

The researcher should also discuss the theoretical and practical implications of the findings and make recommendations for future research or future action. In this portion of the report the researcher is permitted more freedom in expressing opinions that are not necessarily direct outcomes of data analysis. The researcher is free to discuss any possible revisions or additions to existing theory and to encourage studies designed to test hypotheses suggested by the results. The researcher may also discuss implications of the findings for educational practice and suggest studies designed to replicate the study in other settings, with other subjects, and in other curricular areas, in order to increase the generalizability of the findings. The researcher may also suggest next-step studies designed to investigate another dimension of the problem investigated. For example, a study finding type of feedback to be a factor in retention might suggest that amount of feedback may also be a factor and recommend further research in that area.

References.   The references, or bibliography, section of the report lists all the sources, alphabetically by authors' last names, that were directly used in writing the report. Most of the references will, of course, appear in the introduction section of the report. Every source cited in the paper must be included in the references, and every entry listed in the references must appear in the paper; in other words, the sources in the paper and the sources in the references must correspond exactly. If the APA style manual is being followed, secondary sources are not included in the references. Citations in the text for such sources should indicate the primary source from which they were taken; the primary source should be included in the references. For example, you might say:

Nerdfais (cited in Snurd, 1995) found that yellow chalk . . .

The Snurd source would be listed in the references. Note that no year would be given for the Nerdfais study. For thesis and dissertation studies, if sources were consulted that were not directly cited in the main body of the report, these may be included in an appendix. Also, in thesis and dissertation studies, since the list of references is likely to be lengthy, references are often subdivided into sections such as Books, Articles, and Unpublished.

The style manual being followed will determine the form which each reference must take. This form is usually different for journal articles and books. It is impor-

---

[10]Peterson, H. A., Ellis, M., Toohill, N., & Kloess, P. (1935). Some measurements of the effects of reviews. *Journal of Educational Psychology, 26,* 65–72; Sones, A. M., & Stroud, J. B. (1940). Review, with special reference to temporal position. *Journal of Educational Psychology, 31,* 665–676; *and* Ausubel, D. P. (1966). Early versus delayed review in meaningful learning. *Psychology in the Schools, 3,* 195–198.

tant that whatever form is used be followed consistently. If the style manual to be used is known while the review of related literature is being conducted, the researcher can save time by writing each reference in the proper form initially.

Appendixes

Appendixes are usually necessary in thesis and dissertation reports. Appendixes include information and data pertinent to the study which either are not important enough to be included in the main body of the report or are too lengthy. Appendixes contain such entries as materials especially developed for the study (for example, tests, questionnaires, and cover letters), raw data, and data analysis sheets. Infrequently, an index may be required. An index alphabetically lists all items of importance or interest in the report and the page on which each can be found. The longer the document, the more useful an index will be. Also, a number of universities ask that a vita be included. A vita is a short autobiography describing professionally related activities and experiences of the author. Information typically included in a vita describes educational training and degrees earned, professional work experience, memberships in professional organizations, and publications, if any.

Journal Articles

Preparation of a research report for publication in a professional journal serves the interests of the professional community as well as those of the researcher. Progress in educational research requires that researchers share their efforts so that others may profit from and build upon them. Dissertations and theses are not read nearly as often as professional journals; thus, publication in a frequently read journal permits the largest possible audience to read about and use the findings of a research study. From a personal point of view, it is definitely to the researcher's advantage, especially the new graduate, to have a publication. When applying for a position, for example, most of what a prospective employer knows about you is what he or she reads about you in your vita. Since a newly graduated individual is likely to be short on professional experience, having a publication definitely gives her or him an edge. Having a publication in a respected journal indicates not only that you conducted a worthwhile study but also that you had the ability *and* the energy to prepare, submit, and publish a scholarly report.

Selection and Analysis of a Journal

Based on your review of related literature and your references, you should be able to identify two or three journals which publish studies in the area of research represented by your study. If you do not know, you should check with someone who does in order to determine which journal of those identified is the most respected in your field. Examination of a recent issue should give you some guidance concerning the format, style, and length acceptable to the selected journal. There is usually a section in the front or back of the journal that gives instructions for submitting manuscripts. The *Journal of Educational Psychology,* for example, strongly advises authors to use the *Publication Manual of the American Psychological Association* in preparing the manuscript and requires an abstract of 100 to 120 words. Authors are instructed to submit manuscripts in triplicate to the editor. Although the journal may not specify a definite maximum manuscript length, shorter manuscripts, all things being equal, have a higher probability of being published. Space in a journal is at a premium and most editors try to publish as many articles per issue as possible. If too long, an otherwise acceptable manuscript may be returned for revision and shortening.

Preparation of the Manuscript

The contents and format of a journal article are very similar to those of a thesis or dissertation except that, as just pointed out, the journal article is much shorter. In fact, some complex or lengthy theses or dissertations may best be submitted as two shorter articles; this is especially true in studies with two or more substudies. None of the preliminary pages of a thesis or dissertation becomes part of a journal article; only the title remains. The introduction section is usually considerably shorter, describing primarily those studies directly related to the hypothesis of the study. The method section is also much shorter, describing the subjects, instruments, design, and procedure in much less detail. The author must exercise judgment in determining which are the critical aspects of the study and which components require more in-depth description. The results section is usually of greater interest to the reader and thus typically gets reduced less than preceding sections of the paper. Correspondingly, the discussion section will probably not require too much revision. Instead of a summary, many journals require an abstract of a given length, usually between 100 and 150 words. The abstract, as discussed earlier, serves the same purpose as a summary but is not included as part of the manuscript; it is submitted on a separate sheet. When published, the abstract generally precedes the complete description of the study. Limits are not usually put on the number of references permitted, and all pertinent sources are included. As with the preliminary pages, the supplementary pages of the thesis or dissertation are not part of the manuscript. Usually a footnote in the manuscript is used to indicate how and where interested readers may obtain copies of tests and other materials usually included in appendixes.

Submission and Evaluation of Manuscripts

Before submitting a manuscript to a journal editor, you should have at least one other person read it. If you are in a university setting, you will probably know several persons who have publications who can read your manuscript with the critical eye of a journal review editor. The required number of copies of the manuscript and a brief cover letter indicating the title of the article and your mailing address should be mailed first class to the journal. The editorial board members who review your manuscript will independently determine whether your research, in their opinion, represents a significant contribution, was well conducted, and is well reported. The fact that you are a novice researcher should not affect their evaluation of your manuscript. Most research journals use what is referred to as *blind review;* this means that information which identifies you or your institutional affiliation is removed from the manuscript before it is reviewed. If your manuscript is not accepted for publication, you will usually be given copies of the reviewers' comments or be informed in a summary statement as to the reasons for its rejection. Often you can use this input to revise your manuscript before submitting it to another journal. While it is not ethical to send your article to several journals simultaneously, it is perfectly all right to send it to a second journal after you have been rejected by another.

Papers Presented at Professional Meetings

There are a number of professional organizations that hold annual national meetings and in some cases more frequent regional meetings. Some of these organizations include members from a wide variety of professional areas; this is the case with the American Educational Research Association and the American Psychological Association. Others, such as the National Association of Social Studies Teachers, are more specialized and members represent either one specific professional area or a small number of related areas. Whatever their scope, the major focus of their meetings is typically to have members share new knowledge and research findings. While a great deal of informal exchange occurs, the structured, scheduled portion of meetings usually takes the form of paper presentations. A new PhD, for example, may describe his or her dissertation study. Papers with a common theme (such as retention of verbal learning, programs for the culturally disadvantaged, or computer-assisted instruction) are presented together at one (or several) sessions. Thus, while at any given time a number of different paper sessions may be going on simultaneously in different locations, a person is free to select and attend those sessions that appear to be most closely related to her or his personal interests or needs.

Usually at least 6 months prior to the date of the meeting, the sponsoring association publishes a "call for papers" in one of its journals or newsletters. The call for papers indicates guidelines and deadlines for submitting papers. An understood restriction is that the information to be presented has not already been published and truly represents "new" knowledge. Typically a full report is not required but rather an abstract of a specified length (1,000 words, for example). Submitted abstracts are sent out for review and a certain number selected for presentation. If you receive notification that your paper has been accepted, you are committed to being present at the meeting to give your paper and to having copies of a complete report available.

Research reports presented at meetings follow the same general format as all research reports and, in fact, the paper you prepare for presentation may resemble very closely a manuscript you are submitting to a journal.[11] It is not unethical to present the results of a study which is to be published as long as the publication date follows the paper presentation date. In fact, a major purpose of professional meetings is to share knowledge more quickly than can be done through the reading of journals. The length of time that typically elapses between the date on which a manuscript is submitted and the date on which it first appears in print in a journal is considerably longer than the 6 to 9 months that typically elapse between a call for papers and a professional meeting.

Since the time allotted for presenting a given paper is generally in the neighborhood of 10 minutes (the range is normally from 5 to 20 minutes), it is usually not possible to read the entire research report. In fact, reading a report verbatim is not a good idea anyway, especially since copies of a complete report should be available to interested persons.[12] It is a much more efficient use of limited time to give a brief informal summary of the study, emphasizing results, conclusions, and

---

[11] If a journal article represents a version of a paper previously presented at a professional meeting, this fact should be discussed in a footnote at the beginning of the manuscript. This footnote should indicate the name, location, and date of the meeting at which it was presented.

[12] Most presenters bring a limited number of copies of the complete report to the meeting itself and honor additional requests by mailing copies. Sometimes a request for a paper will be received months after a presentation is made; these requests must also be honored, just as promptly as initial requests.

any other important aspects of the study. An audience appreciates a presenter who *talks* to them rather than *reads* to them. It is usually helpful to prepare either an outline of what you want to say or a set of note cards. It is also a good idea to practice your presentation by making it to anyone who will listen. You should practice until your presentation is within your alloted time (fellow presenters are not thrilled with persons who go over their limit) and you feel comfortable making it.

■ SUMMARY/CHAPTER 16
GENERAL GUIDELINES

1. If you carefully prepare a research plan before you conduct your study, you have a good head start on writing your research report.
2. The major guideline previously described for analyzing, organizing, and reporting related literature is applicable to this task—make an outline.
3. Development of an outline involves identification and ordering of major topics followed by differentiation of each major heading into logical sub-headings.
4. A research report is written in the past tense.

General Rules for Writing and Typing

5. Probably the foremost rule of research report writing is that the writer must be as objective as possible in reporting the study.
6. Consistent with the goal of objective reporting, personal pronouns such as *I* and *we* should be kept to a minimum; instead impersonal pronouns and the passive voice should be used.
7. The research report should be written in a clear, simple, straightforward style; you do not have to be boring, just concise.
8. Correct spelling, grammatical construction, and punctuation are not too much to expect of a scientific report.
9. Use of abbreviations and contractions is generally discouraged.
10. Authors of cited references are usually referred to by last name only in the main body of the report; first names, initials, and title are not given. Tables, footnotes, and references may include abbreviations; footnotes and references usually give at least the author's initials.
11. If the first word of a sentence is a number, or if the number is nine or less, numbers are usually expressed as words. Otherwise, numbers are generally expressed as arabic numerals.
12. The same standards of scholarship should be applied to the typing of the report as to the writing of the report.
13. Present the typist with a manuscript which is in final, correct form; the typist's job is to type, not to polish, your report.
14. If you have any special instructions, share them with the typist and be sure they are understood.
15. It is also a good idea to give your typist a copy of the style manual you are following to insure that required guidelines (such as size of margins) are followed.
16. The final typed report should be proofread carefully.

17. The process of preparing a research report has been greatly facilitated by the development of word processing software for micros.
18. While different programs have different capabilities, commonly available features include: automatic page numbering and heading centering; the ability to rearrange words, sentences, and paragraphs; and spelling checkers.

Format and Style

19. Most research reports consistently follow a selected system for format and style.
20. Format refers to the general pattern of organization and arrangement of the report.
21. Style refers to the rules of spelling, capitalization, punctuation, and typing followed in preparing the report.
22. While specific formats may vary in terms of specific headings included, all research reports follow a very similar format that parallels the steps involved in conducting a study.
23. Most colleges, universities, and professional journals either have developed their own, required style manual or have selected one that must be followed.
24. In addition to acquiring and studying a copy of the selected manual, it is also very helpful to study several reports that have been written following the same manual.

TYPES OF RESEARCH REPORTS

25. Research reports usually take the form of a thesis, dissertation, journal article, or paper to be read at a professional meeting.
26. Depending upon its form, the report may be divided into sections or chapters, but these divisions are similar in content.

Theses and Dissertations

Preliminary Pages

The Title Page

27. The title page usually includes the title of the report, the author's name, the degree requirement being fulfilled, the name and location of the college or university awarding the degree, the date of submission of the report, and signatures of approving committee members (although approvals are often listed on a separate page).
28. The title should be brief (10 to 12 words, as a rule of thumb), and at the same time it should describe the purpose of the study as clearly as possible.
29. The title should, however, at least indicate the major independent and dependent variables, and sometimes it names the population studied.

The Acknowledgment Page

30. This page permits the writer to express appreciation to persons who have contributed significantly to the completion of the report.

The Table of Contents and List of Tables and Figures

31. The table of contents is basically an outline of your report which indicates on which page each major section (or chapter) and subsection begins.
32. The list of tables and figures, which is presented on a separate page, gives the number and title of each table and figure and the page on which it can be found.

Abstract

33. Some colleges and universities require an abstract, while others require a summary, and the current trend is in favor of abstracts.
34. The content of abstracts and summaries is identical; only the positioning differs.
35. Summaries are often required to be no more than a given maximum number of words, usually between 100 and 500.
36. Since the abstract of a report is often the only part read, it should describe the most important aspects of the study, including the problem investigated, the type of subjects and instruments, the design, the procedures, and the major results and the major conclusions.

The Main Body of the Report

Introduction

37. The introduction section includes a description of the problem, a review of related literature, a statement of the hypothesis, and definition of terms.
38. A well-written statement of a problem generally indicates the variables, and the specific relationship between those variables, investigated in the study.
39. The review of related literature describes and analyzes what has already been done related to your problem.
40. A good hypothesis states as clearly and concisely as possible the expected relationship (or difference) between two variables, and defines those variables in operational, measurable terms.
41. The introduction also includes operational definition of terms used in the study which do not have a commonly known meaning.

Method

42. The method section includes a description of subjects, instruments, design, procedure, assumptions, and limitations.
43. The description of subjects includes a definition and description of the population from which the sample was selected and may describe the method used in selecting the sample or samples (or the method of selection may be described in the procedure section).
44. The description of each instrument should relate the function of the instrument in the study (for example, selection of subjects or a measure of the dependent variable), what the instrument is intended to measure, and data related to validity and reliability.
45. In an experimental study, the description of the basic design (or variation of a basic design) applied in the study should include a rationale for selection and a discussion of sources of invalidity associated with the design, and why they may have been minimized in the study being reported.
46. The procedure section should describe each step followed in conducting the study, in chronological order, in sufficient detail to permit the study to be replicated by another researcher.

Results

47. The results section describes the statistical techniques that were applied to the data, preselected α levels, and the results of each analysis.
48. For each hypothesis, the statistical test of significance selected and applied to the data is described, followed by a statement indicating whether the hypothesis was supported or not.
49. Tables and figures are used to present findings in summary or graph form and add clarity to the presentation.
50. Tables present numerical data in rows and columns and usually include descriptive statistics, such as means and standard deviations, and the results of tests of significance such as t and F ratios.
51. Good tables and figures are uncluttered and self-explanatory; it is better to use two tables (or figures) than one that is crowded.
52. Tables and figures follow their related textual discussion and are referred to by number, not name or location.

Discussion

53. Every research report has a section that discusses and interprets the results, draws conclusions and implications, and makes recommendations.
54. Each result is discussed in terms of the original hypothesis to which it relates, and in terms of its agreement or disagreement with previous results obtained by other researchers in other studies.
55. A result is the outcome of a test of significance; the corresponding conclusion is whether or not an original hypothesis was supported.
56. Overgeneralization refers to the statement of conclusions that are not warranted by the results.
57. The researcher should discuss the theoretical and practical implications of the findings and make recommendations for future research or future action.

References

58. The references, or bibliography, section of the report lists all the sources, alphabetically by authors' last names, that were directly used in writing the report.
59. Every source cited in the paper must be included in the references, and every entry listed in the references must appear in the paper; in other words, the sources in the paper and the sources in the references must correspond exactly.
60. If the APA style manual is being followed, secondary sources are not included in the references.
61. Citations in the text for secondary sources should indicate the primary source from which they were taken; the primary source should be included in the references.
62. If sources were consulted that were not directly cited in the main body of the report, these may be included in an appendix.
63. In thesis and dissertation studies, since the list of references is likely to be lengthy, references are often subdivided into sections such as Books, Articles, and Unpublished.

Appendixes

64. Appendixes include information and data pertinent to the study which either are not important enough to be included in the main body of the report or are too lengthy.

65. Appendixes contain such entries as materials especially developed for the study (for example, tests, questionnaires, and cover letters), raw data, and data analysis sheets.
66. An index alphabetically lists all items of importance or interest in the report and the page on which each can be found.
67. A vita is a short autobiography describing professionally related activities and experiences of the author.

Journal Articles

Selection and Analysis of a Journal

68. Based on your review of related literature and your references, you should be able to identify two or three journals which publish studies in the area of research represented by your study.
69. Examination of a recent issue should give you some guidance concerning the format, style, and length acceptable to the selected journal.
70. All things being equal, shorter manuscripts have a higher probability of being published.

Preparation of the Manuscript

71. The contents and format of a journal article are very similar to those of a thesis or dissertation except that the journal article is much shorter.
72. None of the preliminary pages of a thesis or dissertation becomes part of a journal article; only the title remains.
73. The results section is usually of greater interest to the reader and thus typically gets reduced less than preceding sections of the paper. Correspondingly, the discussion section will probably not require too much revision.
74. Instead of a summary, many journals require an abstract of a given length, usually between 100 and 150 words.
75. Limits are not usually put on the number of references permitted, and all pertinent sources are included.
76. Supplementary pages of the thesis or dissertation are not part of the manuscript.

Submission and Evaluation of Manuscripts

77. Before submitting a manuscript to a journal editor, you should have at least one other person read it.
78. The required number of copies of the manuscript and a brief cover letter indicating the title of the article and your mailing address should be mailed first class to the journal.

Papers Presented at Professional Meetings

79. The major focus of professional meetings is typically to have members share new knowledge and research findings.
80. While a great deal of informal exchange occurs, the structured, scheduled portion of meetings usually takes the form of paper presentations.

81. If you receive notification that your paper has been accepted, you are committed to being present at the meeting to give your paper and to having copies of a complete report available.

82. Research reports presented at meetings follow the same general format as all other reports and, in fact, the paper you prepare for presentation may resemble very closely a manuscript you are submitting to a journal.

83. A major purpose of professional meetings is to share knowledge more quickly than can be done through the reading of journals.

84. Reading a report verbatim is not a good idea, especially since copies of a complete report should be available to interested persons.

85. It is usually helpful to prepare either an outline of what you want to say or a set of note cards.

86. It is also a good idea to practice your presentation by making it to anyone who will listen.

TASK 8 PERFORMANCE CRITERIA

Your research report should include all the components presented in Figure 16.1 with the possible exceptions of an acknowledgment page and appendixes.

Development of Task 8 basically involves combining Tasks 2, 6, and 7, writing a Discussion section, and preparing the appropriate preliminary pages (including an Abstract) and References. In other words, you have already written most of Task 8.

On the following pages, an example is presented which illustrates the performance called for by Task 8 (see Task 8 example). This example represents the synthesis of the previously presented tasks related to the effects of interactive multimedia on biology achievement. To the degree possible with a student paper, this example follows the guidelines of the *Publication Manual of the American Psychological Association*.

Additional examples for this and other tasks are included in the *Student Guide* which accompanies this text.

Effect of Interactive Multimedia on the Achievement
of 10th-Grade Biology Students
Sara Jane Calderin
Florida International University

Submitted in partial fulfillment of
the requirements for EDF 5481
April, 1994

Task 8 Example (*continued*)

Table of Contents

i

Task 8 Example (*continued*)

List of Tables and Figures

ii

563

Task 8 Example (*continued*)

Abstract

The purpose of this study was to investigate the effect of interactive multimedia on the achievement of 10th-grade biology students. Using a posttest-only control group design and a t test for independent samples, it was found that after approximately 8 months the students ($\underline{n}$ = 30) who were instructed using interactive multimedia achieved significantly higher scores on the biology test of the National Proficiency Survey Series than did the students ($\underline{n}$ = 30) whose instruction did not include interactive multimedia, $\underline{t}$ (58) = 4.22, $\underline{p}$ < .05. It was concluded that the interactive multimedia instruction was effective in raising the achievement level of the participating students.

iii

564

1

Introduction

One of the major concerns of educators and parents
alike, is the decline in student achievement. An area of
particular concern is science education where the higher-level
thinking skills and problem solving techniques so necessary
for success in our technological society need to be developed
(Smith & Westhoff, 1992).

Research is constantly providing new proven methods for
educators to use, and technology has developed many kinds of
tools ideally suited to the classroom. One such tool is
interactive multimedia (IMM). IMM provides teachers with an
extensive amount of data in a number of different formats
including text, sound, and video. This makes it possible to
appeal to all the different learning styles of the students
and to offer a variety of material for students to analyze
(Howson & Davis, 1992).

When teachers use IMM, students become highly motivated
which results in improved class attendance and more completed
assignments (O'Connor, 1993). In addition, students also
become actively involved in their own learning, encouraging
comprehension rather than mere memorization of facts
(Kneedler, 1993; Reeves, 1992).

Statement of the Problem

The purpose of this study was to investigate the effect
of IMM on the achievement of 10th-grade biology students. IMM
was defined as "a computerized database that allows users to
access information in multiple forms, including text,
graphics, video and audio" (Reeves, 1992, p. 47).

2

<u>Review of Related Literature</u>

Due to modern technology, such as video tapes and video discs, students receive more information from visual sources than they do from the written word (Helms & Helms, 1992), and yet in school the majority of information is still transmitted through textbooks. While textbooks cover a wide range of topics superficially, IMM can provide in-depth information on essential topics in a format that students find interesting (Kneedler, 1993). Smith and Westhoff (1992) note that when student interest is sparked, curiosity levels are increased and students are motivated to ask questions. The interactive nature of multimedia allows students to seek out their own answers, and by so doing they become owners of the concept involved. Ownership translates into comprehension (Howson & Davis, 1992).

Many science concepts are learned through observation of experiments. By using IMM, students can participate in a variety of experiments which are either too expensive, too lengthy or too dangerous to carry out in the school laboratory (Howson & Davis, 1992; Leonard, 1989; Louie, Sweat, Gresham & Smith, 1991). While observing experiments students can discuss what is happening and ask questions. At the touch of a button teachers are able to replay any part of the proceedings, and they also have random access to related information which can be used to illustrate completely the answer to the question (Howson & Davis, 1992). By answering students' questions in this detailed way, the content becomes more relevant to the needs of the students (Smith & Westhoff, 1992). When knowledge is relevant students are able to use it to solve problems and in so doing develop higher-level thinking skills (Helms & Helms, 1992; Sherwood, Kinzer, Bransford, & Franks, 1987).

3

A major challenge of science education is to provide students with large amounts of information that will encourage them to be analytical (Howson & Davis, 1992; Sherwood et al. 1987). IMM offers electronic access to extensive information allowing students to organize, evaluate and use it in the solution of problems (Smith & Wilson, 1993). When information is introduced as an aid to problem solving it becomes a tool with which to solve other problems, rather than a series of solitary, disconnected facts (Sherwood et al. 1987).

Although critics complain that IMM is entertainment and students do not learn from it (Corcoran, 1989), research has shown that student learning does improve when IMM is used in the classroom (Sherwood et el. 1987; Sherwood & Others, 1990). A 1987 study by Sherwood et al., for example, showed that seventh- and eighth-grade science students receiving instruction enhanced with IMM had better retention of that information, and O'Connor (1993) found that the use of IMM in high school mathematics and science increased the focus on students' problem solving and critical thinking skills.

Statement of the Hypothesis

The quality and quantity of software available for science classes has dramatically improved during the past decade. Although some research has been carried out on the effects of IMM on student achievement in science, due to promising updates in the technology involved, further study is warranted. Therefore, it was hypothesized that 10th-grade biology students whose teachers use IMM as part of their instructional technique will exhibit significantly higher achievement than 10th-grade biology students whose teachers do not use IMM.

4

Method

Subjects

The sample for this study was selected from the total population of 213 tenth-grade students at an upper middle class all girls Catholic high school in Miami, Florida. The population was 90% Hispanic, mainly of Cuban-American descent. Sixty students were randomly selected (using a table of random numbers) and randomly assigned to two groups of 30 each.

Instrument

The biology test of the National Proficiency Survey Series (NPSS) was used as the measuring instrument. The test was designed to measure individual student performance in biology at the high school level but the publishers also recommended it as an evaluation of instructional programs. Content validity is good; items were selected from a large item bank provided by classroom teachers and curriculum experts. High school instructional materials and a national curriculum survey were extensively reviewed before objectives were written. The test objectives and those of the biology classes in the study were highly correlated. Although the standard error of measurement is not given for the biology test, the range of KR-20s for the entire battery is from .82 to .91 with a median of .86. This is satisfactory since the purpose of the test was to evaluate instructional programs not to make decisions concerning individuals. Catholic school students were included in the battery norming procedures which were carried out in April and May of 1988 using 22,616 students in grades 9-12 from 45 high schools in 20 states.

Experimental Design

The design used in this study was the posttest-only control group design (see Figure 1). This design was selected

Task 8 Example (*continued*)

5

because it provides control for most sources of invalidity and
random assignment to groups was possible. A pretest was not
necessary since the final science grades from June 1993 were
available to check initial group equivalence and to help
control mortality, a potential threat to internal validity
with this design. Mortality, however, was not a problem as no
students dropped from either group.

Group	Assignment	n	Treatment	Posttest
1	Random	30	IMM instruction	NPSS:B[a]
2	Random	30	Traditional instruction	NPSS:B

[a]National Proficiency Survey Series: Biology

<u>Figure 1</u>. Experimental design.

Procedure

   Prior to the beginning of the 1993-94 school year,
before classes were scheduled, 60 of the 213 tenth-grade
students were randomly selected and randomly assigned to two
groups of 30 each, the average biology class size; each group
became a biology class. One of the classes was randomly chosen
to receive IMM instruction. The same teacher taught both
classes.

   The study was designed to last eight months beginning
on the first day of class. The control group was taught using
traditional methods of lecturing and open class discussions.
The students worked in pairs for laboratory investigations

6

which included the use of microscopes. The teacher's role was one of information disseminator.

The experimental classroom had 15 workstations for student use, each one consisting of a laserdisc player, a video recorder, a 27 inch monitor, and a Macintosh computer with a 40 MB hard drive, 10 MB RAM and a CD-ROM drive. The teacher's workstation incorporated a Macintosh computer with CD-ROM drive, a videodisc player and a 27 inch monitor. The workstations were networked to the school library so students had access to online services such as Prodigy and Infotrac as well as to the card catalogue. Two laser printers were available through the network for the students' use.

In the experimental class the teacher used a videodisc correlated to the textbook. When barcodes provided in the text were scanned, a section of the videodisc was activated and appeared on the monitor. The section might be a motion picture demonstrating a process or a still picture offering more detail than the text. The role of the teacher in the experimental group was that of facilitator and guide. After the teacher had introduced a new topic, the students worked in pairs at the workstations investigating topics connected to the main idea presented in the lesson. Videodiscs, CD-ROMs and online services were all available as sources of information. The students used HyperStudio to prepare multimedia reports which they presented to the class.

Throughout the study the same subject matter was covered and the two classes used the same text. Although the students of the experimental group paired up at the workstations, the other group worked in pairs during lab time thus equalizing any effect from cooperative learning. The classes could not meet at the same time as they were taught by

7

the same teacher, so they met during second and third periods. First period was not chosen as the school sometimes has a special schedule which interferes with first period. Both classes had the same homework reading assignments which were reviewed in class the following school day. Academic objectives were the same for each class and all tests measuring achievement were identical.

During the first week of May, the biology test of the NPSS was administered to both classes to compare their achievement in biology.

Task 8 Example (*continued*)

Results

Prior to the beginning of the study, after the 60 students were randomly selected and assigned to experimental and control groups, final science grades from the previous school year were obtained from school records in order to check initial group equivalence. Examination of the means and a t test for independent samples (α = .05) indicated essentially no difference between the groups (see Table 1). A t test for independent samples was used because the groups were randomly formed and the data were interval.

Table 1

Means, Standard Deviation and t Tests for the Experimental and Control Groups

Score	IMM instruction[a]	Traditional instruction[a]	t
	Group		
Prior Grades			
M	87.47	87.63	−0.08*
SD	8.19	8.05	
Posttest NPSS:B			
M	32.27	26.70	4.22 **
SD	4.45	5.69	

Note. Maximum score for prior grades = 100. Maximum score for posttest = 40.

[a]n = 30.

*p > .05. **p < .05.

9

At the completion of the eight-month study, during the first week in May, scores on the NPSS:B were compared, also using a t test for independent samples. As Table 1 indicates, scores of the experimental and control groups were significantly different. In fact, the experimental group scored approximately one standard deviation higher than the control group (ES=.98). Therefore, the original hypothesis that "10th-grade biology students whose teachers use IMM as part of their instructional technique will exhibit significantly higher achievement than 10th-grade biology students whose teachers do not use IMM" was supported.

Task 8 Example (*continued*)

Discussion

The results of this study support the original hypothesis: 10th-grade biology students whose teachers used IMM as part of their instructional technique did exhibit significantly higher achievement than 10th-grade biology students whose teachers did not use IMM. The IMM students' scores were 5.57 (13.93%) points higher than those of the other group. Also, it was informally observed that the IMM instructed students were eager to discover information on their own and to carry on the learning process outside scheduled class hours.

Results cannot be generalized to all classrooms since the study took place in an all-girls Catholic high school with the majority of the students having an Hispanic background. However, the results were consistent with research on IMM in general, and in particular with the findings of Sherwood et. al. (1987) and O'Connor (1993) concerning the improvement of student achievement.

IMM appears to be a viable educational tool with applications in a variety of subject areas and with both cognitive and psychological benefits for students. While further research is needed, especially using other software and in other subject areas, the suggested benefits to students' learning offered by IMM warrant that teachers should be cognizant of this instructional method. In this technological age it is important that education takes advantage of available tools which increase student motivation and improve academic achievement.

Task 8 Example (*continued*)

11

References

Corcoran, E. (1989, July). Show and tell: Hypermedia turns
    information into a multisensory event. <u>Scientific American,</u>
    <u>261,</u> 72, 74.

Helms, C. W., & Helms, D. R. (1992, June). <u>Multimedia in</u>
    <u>education</u> (Report No. IR-016-090). Proceedings of the 25th
    Summer Conference of the Association of Small Computer
    Users in Education. North Myrtle Beach, SC. (ERIC Document
    Reproduction Service No. ED 357 732)

Howson, B.A., & Davis, H. (1992). Enhancing comprehension with
    videodiscs. <u>Media and Methods, 28</u>(3), 12-14.

Kneedler, P. E. (1993). California adopts multimedia science
    program. <u>Technological Horizons in Education Journal,</u>
    <u>20</u>(7), 73-76.

Lehmann, I.J. (1990). Review of National Proficiency Survey
    Series. In J. J. Kramer & J. C. Conoley (Eds.), <u>The</u>
    <u>eleventh mental measurements yearbook</u> (pp. 595-599).
    Lincoln: University of Nebraska, Buros Institute of Mental
    Measurement.

Leonard, W. H. (1989). A comparison of student reaction to
    biology instruction by interactive videodisc or
    conventional laboratory. <u>Journal of Research in Science</u>
    <u>Teaching, 26,</u> 95-104

Louie, R., Sweat, S., Gresham, R., & Smith, L. (1991).
    Interactive video: Disseminating vital science and math
    information. <u>Media and Methods, 27</u>(5), 22-23.

O'Connor, J. E. (1993, April). <u>Evaluating the effects of</u>
    <u>collaborative efforts to improve mathematics and science</u>
    <u>curricula</u> (Report No. TM-019-862). Paper presented at the
    Annual Meeting of the American Educational Research
    Association, Atlanta, GA. (ERIC Document Reproduction
    Service No. ED 357 083)

12

Reeves, T. C. (1992). Evaluating interactive multimedia. <u>Educational Technology, 32</u> (5), 47-52.

Sherwood, R. D., Kinzer, C. K., Bransford, J. D., & Franks, J. J. (1987). Some benefits of creating macro-contexts for science instruction: Initial findings. <u>Journal of Research in Science Teaching, 24,</u> 417-435.

Sherwood, R. D., & Others. (1990, April). <u>An evaluative study of level one videodisc based chemistry program</u> (Report No. SE-051-513). Paper presented at a Poster Session at the 63rd Annual Meeting of the National Association for Research in Science Teaching, Atlanta, GA. (ERIC Document Reproduction Service No. ED 320 772)

Smith, E. E., & Westhoff, G. M. (1992). The Taliesin project: Multidisciplinary education and multimedia. <u>Educational Technology, 32.</u> 15-23.

Smith, M. K., & Wilson, C. (1993, March). <u>Integration of student learning strategies via technology</u> (Report No. IR-016-035). Proceedings of the Fourth Annual Conference of Technology and Teacher Education. San Diego, CA. (ERIC Document Reproduction Service No: ED 355 937)

PART NINE

Research Critiques

Anyone who reads a newspaper, listens to the radio, or watches television is a consumer of research. We are constantly bombarded with the latest research findings concerning the relationship between diet and heart disease, the wrinkle-reducing powers of face creams, and the positive effects of aspirin, to name a few. Many people tend to uncritically accept and act on such findings if they are labeled the results of "scientific research" or if they are transmitted by anyone in a white lab coat. Very few people question the control procedures utilized or the generalizability of findings based on rats to human beings. You, as a professional, are required to possess critical evaluation skills. In addition to being critical of data transmitted by the media, you have a responsibility to be informed concerning the latest findings in your professional area and to be able to differentiate "good" research from "poor" research. Decisions made based on invalid research are likely to be bad ones and may result in the adoption of ineffective procedures.

Just because a study is reported in a journal does not necessarily mean that it was a good study; results are frequently published which are based on research involving one or more serious flaws. When you reviewed the literature related to your problem, you did not critically evaluate references; you simply determined whether or not each was related to your problem and, if so, in what way. Normally a researcher critically evaluates each reference and does not consider the results of poorly executed research. When you reviewed the literature you did not yet possess the competencies required to make quality discriminations. Competent evaluation of a research study requires knowledge of each of the components of the research process. Your work in previous chapters has given you that knowledge.

The goal of Part Nine is for you to be able to critically analyze and evaluate research reports. After you have read Part Nine, you should be able to perform the following task.

◼ TASK 9

Given a reprint of a research report and an evaluation form, evaluate the components of the report.

(See Performance Criteria, p. 590.)

"Normally a researcher critically evaluates each reference and does not consider the results of poorly executed research (p. 578)."

Evaluation of a Research Report

After reading Chapter 17, you should be able to:

1. For *each* of the major sections and subsections of a research report, list at least three questions which should be asked in determining its adequacy.
2. For each of the following types of research, list at least three questions which should be asked in determining the adequacy of a study representing that type:

    Historical Research
    Qualitative Research
    Descriptive Research
      Questionnaire Studies
      Interview Studies
      Observation Studies
    Correlational Research
      Relationship Studies
      Prediction Studies
    Causal-Comparative Research
    Experimental Research

GENERAL EVALUATION CRITERIA

As mentioned in the introduction to Part Nine, the fact that a study is published in a journal does not necessarily mean that it was a good study or that it was reported adequately. Hall, Ward, and Comer (1988) asked highly qualified judges to evaluate research articles which had already been published.[1] An unsettling 42% of the articles were "judged to be either unacceptable for publication or in need of major revisions to make them acceptable" (p. 186). The most often identified flaw was lack of validity and reliability information for data-gathering procedures, e.g., instruments. Table 17.1 presents the top 10 shortcomings cited by the judges (and David Letterman had nothing to do with them!). The results of the above study reinforce the importance of being a competent consumer of research reports; they also highlight common pitfalls to be avoided in your own research.

At your current level of expertise you will not be able to evaluate every component of every study. You would not be able to determine, for example, whether the appropriate degrees of freedom were used in the calculation of an analysis of covariance. There are, however, a number of basic errors or weaknesses which you should be able to detect in a research study. You should, for example, be able to identify the sources of invalidity associated with a study based on a one-group pretest-posttest design. You should also be able to detect obvious indications of experimenter bias which may have affected the results. A statement in a research report that "the purpose of this study was to prove . . ." should alert you to a probable bias effect.

As you read a research report, either as a consumer of research keeping up with the latest findings in your professional area or as a producer of research reviewing literature related to a defined problem, there are a number of questions you should ask yourself concerning the adequacy of execution of the various components. The

Table 17.1

Specific Shortcomings Cited by Judges to Substantiate Decisions to Reject or Require Major Revisions in Articles

Specific shortcoming	% of the 54 articles cited
1. Validity and reliability of data-gathering procedures not established[a]	43
2. Research design not free of specific weaknesses[a]	39
3. Limitations of study not stated[a]	31
4. Research design not appropriate to solution of the problem[a]	28
5. Method of sampling is inappropriate[a]	28
6. Results of the analysis not presented clearly[a]	28
7. Inappropriate methods selected to analyze data[a]	26
8. Report is not clearly written	26
9. Assumptions are not clearly stated	22
10. Data-gathering methods or procedures not described	22

[a]Among 10 most frequently cited shortcomings in 1971 study.

Journal of Educational Research, 81, 1988. Reprinted with permission of the Helen Dwight Reid Educational Foundation. Published by Heldref Publications, 1319 Eighteenth St., N.W., Washington, D.C. 20036-1802. Copyright © 1988.

---

[1]Hall, B. W., Ward, A. W., & Comer, C. B. (1988). Published educational research: An empirical study of its quality. *Journal of Educational Research, 81,* 182–189.

answers to some of these questions are more critical than the answers to others. An inadequate title is not a critical flaw; an inadequate design is. Some questions are difficult to answer if the study is not directly in your area of expertise. If your area of specialization is reading, for example, you are probably not in a position to judge the adequacy of a review of literature related to anxiety effects on learning. And, admittedly, the answers to some questions are more subjective than objective. Whether or not a good design was used is pretty objective; most everyone would agree that the randomized posttest-only control group design is a good design. Whether or not the most appropriate design was used, given the problem under study, involves a degree of subjective judgment; the need for inclusion of a pretest, for example, might be a debatable point. Despite the lack of complete precision, however, evaluation of a research report is a worthwhile process. Major problems and shortcomings are usually readily identifiable, and by mentally responding to a number of questions one formulates an overall impression concerning the validity of the study. For each component of a research report a number of evaluative questions are listed for your consideration. This forthcoming list is by no means exhaustive and, as you read it, you may very well think of additional questions which might be asked.

Introduction

Problem

Is there a statement of the problem?
Is the problem "researchable," that is, can it be investigated through the collection and analysis of data?
Is background information on the problem presented?
Is the educational significance of the problem discussed?
Does the problem statement indicate the variables of interest and the specific relationship between those variables which were investigated?
When necessary, are variables directly or operationally defined?

Review of Related Literature

Is the review comprehensive?
Are all references cited relevant to the problem under investigation?
Are most of the sources primary, i.e., are there only a few or no secondary sources?
Have the references been critically analyzed and the results of various studies compared and contrasted, i.e., is the review more than a series of abstracts or annotations?
Is the review well organized, i.e., does it logically flow in such a way that the references least related to the problem are discussed first and the most related references are discussed last?
Does the review conclude with a brief summary of the literature and its implications for the problem investigated?
Do the implications discussed form an empirical or theoretical rationale for the hypotheses which follow?

Hypotheses

Are specific questions to be answered listed or specific hypotheses to be tested stated?
Does each hypothesis state an expected relationship or difference?

If necessary, are variables directly or operationally defined?
Is each hypothesis testable?

Method

Subjects

Are the size and major characteristics of the population studied described?
If a sample was selected, is the method of selecting the sample clearly described?
Is the method of sample selection described one that is likely to result in a representative, unbiased sample?
Did the researcher avoid the use of volunteers?
Are the size and major characteristics of the sample described?
Does the sample size meet the suggested guideline for minimum sample size appropriate for the method of research represented?

Instruments

Is the rationale given for the selection of the instruments (or measurements) used?
Is each instrument described in terms of purpose and content?
Are the instruments appropriate for measuring the intended variables?
Is evidence presented that indicates that each instrument is appropriate for the sample under study?
Is instrument validity discussed and coefficients given if appropriate?
Is reliability discussed in terms of type and size of reliability coefficients?
If appropriate, are subtest reliabilities given?
If an instrument was developed specifically for the study, are the procedures involved in its development and validation described?
If an instrument was developed specifically for the study, are administration, scoring or tabulating, and interpretation procedures fully described?

Design and Procedure

Is the design appropriate for answering the questions or testing the hypotheses of the study?
Are the procedures described in sufficient detail to permit them to be replicated by another researcher?
If a pilot study was conducted, are its execution and results described as well as its impact on the subsequent study?
Are control procedures described?
Did the researcher discuss or account for any potentially confounding variables that he or she was unable to control for?

Results

Are appropriate descriptive statistics presented?
Was the probability level, α, at which the results of the tests of significance were evaluated, specified in advance of the data analyses?
If parametric tests were used, is there evidence that the researcher avoided violating the required assumptions for parametric tests?
Are the tests of significance described appropriate, given the hypotheses and design of the study?

Was every hypothesis tested?
Are the tests of significance interpreted using the appropriate degrees of freedom?
Are the results clearly presented?
Are the tables and figures (if any) well organized and easy to understand?
Are the data in each table and figure described in the text?

Discussion (Conclusions and Recommendations)

Is each result discussed in terms of the original hypothesis to which it relates?
Is each result discussed in terms of its agreement or disagreement with previous
    results obtained by other researchers in other studies?
Are generalizations consistent with the results?
Are the possible effects of uncontrolled variables on the results discussed?
Are theoretical and practical implications of the findings discussed?
Are recommendations for future action made?
Are the suggestions for future action based on practical significance or on statistical
    significance only, i.e., has the author avoided confusing practical and statistical
    significance?
Are recommendations for future research made?

Abstract (or Summary)[2]

Is the problem restated?
Are the number and type of subjects and instruments described?
Is the design used identified?
Are procedures described?
Are the major results and conclusions restated?

■ TYPE-SPECIFIC EVALUATION CRITERIA

In addition to general criteria that can be applied to almost any study, there are
additional questions that should be asked depending upon the type of research represented by the study. In other words, there are concerns that are specific to historical studies, and likewise to qualitative, descriptive, correlational, causal-comparative, and experimental studies.

Historical Research

Were the sources of data related to the problem mostly primary?
Was each piece of data subjected to external criticism?
Was each piece of data subjected to internal criticism?

Qualitative Research

Is each data collection strategy described?

---

[2]The abstract is evaluated last because you are in a better position to critique it *after* you have evaluated the complete report.

Was more than one data collection strategy used?

Were the data collection strategies used appropriate, given the purpose of the study?

Were strategies used to strengthen the validity and reliability of the data, e.g., triangulation?

If participant observation was used, are strategies for minimizing observer bias and observer effect described?

Are the researcher's reactions reported?

If the researcher's reactions are given, are they differentiated from descriptive field-notes?

Are data coding strategies described and examples of coded data given?

Are conclusions supported by data, e.g., are direct quotes used to illustrate points made?

Descriptive Research

Questionnaire Studies

Are questionnaire validation procedures described?

Was the questionnaire pretested?

Are pilot study procedures and results described?

Are directions to questionnaire respondents clear?

Does each item in the questionnaire relate to one of the objectives of the study?

Does each questionnaire item deal with a single concept?

When necessary, is a point of reference given for questionnaire items?

Are leading questions avoided in the questionnaire?

Are there sufficient alternatives for each questionnaire item?

Does the cover letter explain the purpose and importance of the study and give the potential responder a good reason for cooperating?

If appropriate, is confidentiality of responses assured in the cover letter?

Was the percentage of returns approximately 70% or greater?

Are follow-up activities described?

If the response rate was low, was any attempt made to determine any major differences between responders and nonresponders?

Interview Studies

Were the interview procedures pretested?

Are pilot study procedures and results described?

Does each item in the interview guide relate to a specific objective of the study?

When necessary, is a point of reference given in the guide for interview items?

Are leading questions avoided in the interview guide?

Does the interview guide indicate the type and amount of prompting and probing that was permitted?

Are the qualifications and special training of the interviewers described?

Is the method that was used to record responses described?

Did the researcher use the most reliable, unbiased method of recording responses that could have been used?

Did the researcher specify how the responses to semistructured and unstructured items were quantified and analyzed?

Observation Studies

Are observational variables defined?
Were observers required to observe only one behavior at a time?
Was a coded recording instrument used?
Are the qualifications and special training of the observers described?
Is the level of observer reliability reported?
Is the level of observer reliability sufficiently high?
Were possible observer bias and observer effect discussed?
Was observation of subjects the best approach for data collection (as opposed to use of some unobtrusive measure)?

Correlational Research

Relationship Studies

Were variables carefully selected, i.e., was a shotgun approach avoided?
Is the rationale for variable selection described?
Are conclusions and recommendations based on values of correlation coefficients corrected for attenuation or restriction in range?
Do the conclusions avoid suggesting causal relationships between the variables investigated?

Prediction Studies

Is a rationale given for selection of predictor variables?
Is the criterion variable well defined?
Was the resulting prediction equation validated with at least one other group?

Causal-Comparative Research

Are the characteristics or experiences that differentiate the groups (the independent variable) clearly defined or described?
Are critical extraneous variables identified?
Were any control procedures applied to equate the groups on extraneous variables?
Are causal relationships found discussed with due caution?
Are plausible alternative hypotheses discussed?

Experimental Research

Was an appropriate experimental design selected?
Is a rationale for design selection given?
Are sources of invalidity associated with the design identified and discussed?
Is the method of group formation described?
Was the experimental group formed in the same way as the control group?
Were groups randomly formed and the use of existing groups avoided?
Were treatments randomly assigned to groups?
Were critical extraneous variables identified?
Were any control procedures applied to equate groups on extraneous variables?
Were possible reactive arrangements (e.g., the Hawthorne effect) controlled for?

■ SUMMARY/CHAPTER 17

GENERAL EVALUATION CRITERIA

1. There are a number of basic errors or weaknesses which even a beginning researcher should be able to detect in a research study.
2. You should be able to detect obvious indications of experimenter bias which may have affected the results.
3. As you read a research report, either as a consumer of research keeping up with the latest findings in your professional area or as a producer of research reviewing literature related to a defined problem, there are a number of questions you should ask yourself concerning the adequacy of execution of the various components.
4. The answers to some of these questions are more critical than the answers to others.
5. Major problems and shortcomings are usually readily identifiable, and by mentally responding to a number of questions one formulates an overall impression concerning the validity of the study.

Introduction

6. Problem	See page 583.
7. Review of Related Literature	See page 583.
8. Hypotheses	See page 583.

Method

9. Subjects	See page 584.
10. Instruments	See page 584.
11. Design and Procedure	See page 584.

Results

12.	See page 584.

Discussion (Conclusions and Recommendations)

13.	See page 585.

Abstract (or Summary)

14.	See page 585.

TYPE-SPECIFIC EVALUATION CRITERIA

15. In addition to general criteria which can be applied to almost any study, there are additional questions which should be asked depending upon the type of research represented by the study.

Historical Research

Qualitative Research

Descriptive Research

Correlational Research

Causal-Comparative Research

Experimental Research

TASK 9 PERFORMANCE CRITERIA

The evaluation form will list a series of questions about an article to which you must indicate a yes or no response. For example, you might be asked if there is a statement of hypotheses. If the answer is yes, you must indicate where the asked-for component is located in the study. For example, you might indicate a statement of a hypothesis on page 32, paragraph 3, lines 2–6.

In addition, if the study is experimental you will be asked to identify and diagram the experimental design which was applied.

On the following pages a research report is reprinted. (See Task 9 example.) Following the report, a form is provided for you to use in evaluating the report. In answering the questions, use the following code:

Y = Yes

N = No

NA = Question not applicable (e.g., a pilot study was not done)

?/X = Cannot tell from information given or, given your current level of expertise, you are not in a position to make a judgment

Effects of Using an Instructional Game on Motivation and Performance

JAMES. D. KLEIN
ERIC FREITAG
Arizona State University

ABSTRACT Although many educators theorize that instructional games are effective for providing students with motivating practice, research on instructional gaming is inconclusive. The purpose of this study was to determine the effect on motivation and performance of using an instructional game. The effect of using a supplemental reading on motivation and performance was also examined. We randomly assigned 75 undergraduates to one of two treatments after they had attended a lecture on the information-processing model of learning. The subjects in one treatment group used an instructional board game to practice the material presented in the lecture, while those in the other group practiced using a traditional worksheet. Results indicated that using the instructional game significantly affected the four motivational components of attention, relevance, confidence, and satisfaction. The instructional game did not influence performance. The results also suggested that the subjects who reported completion of a supplemental reading had significantly better performance and confidence than did the subjects who reported that they had not completed the reading. Implications for the design of practice are discussed.

Providing students with an opportunity to practice newly acquired skills and knowledge is an important component in designing an instructional strategy. Although many instructional design theories include recommendations for designing practice activities, Salisbury, Richards, and Klein (1986) have emphasized that most of the theories fail to address how to design practice that is motivational.

Some educators have theorized that instructional games are effective for providing motivating practice of newly acquired skills and information. They have argued that instructional games are motivational because they generate enthusiasm, excitement, and enjoyment, and because they require students to be actively involved in learning (Coleman, 1968; Ernest, 1986; Rakes & Kutzman, 1982; Wesson, Wilson, & Mandlebaum, 1988). Other scholars have theorized that instructional games decrease student motivation. Those authors have suggested that the motivational aspects of instructional games are limited to those who win, and that losing an instructional game produces a failure syndrome and reduces self-esteem (Allington & Strange, 1977; Andrews & Thorpe, 1977).

Whereas theorists have argued about the motivational aspects of instructional games, researchers have investigated the effect of using games on student motivation. Some researchers have reported that the use of instructional gaming increases student interests, satisfaction, and continuing motivation (DeVries & Edwards, 1973; Sleet, 1985; Straus, 1986). In addition, investigators have reported that instructional games influence school attendance. Allen and Main (1976) found that including instructional gaming in a mathematics curriculum helped to reduce the rate of absenteeism of students in inner-city schools. Studies by Raia (1966) and Boseman and Schellenberger (1974) indicated that including games in a college business course has a positive affect on course attendance but not on expressed interest and satisfaction. Others have reported that playing a game does not influence student satisfaction or attitude toward school (DeVries & Slavin, 1978).

In addition to the possible motivational benefits of games, many educators have theorized that games are effective for increasing student performance. They have argued that instructional games make practice more effective because students become active participants in the learning process (Ernest, 1986; Rakes & Kutzman, 1982; Wesson et al., 1988). Others have suggested that games foster incorrect responding and inefficiently use instructional time; also, the rate of practice in a game cannot compare with that of a flashcard drill or reading a connected text (Allington & Strange, 1977; Andrews & Thorpe, 1977).

Researchers have attempted to answer whether instructional games are an effective method for learning. Some

Address correspondence to James D. Klein, Learning and Instruction, College of Education, Arizona State University, Tempe, AZ 85287-0611.

Journal of Educational Research

investigators have reported that instructional games are effective for assisting students to acquire, practice, and transfer mathematical concepts and problem-solving abilities (Bright, 1980; Bright, Harvey, & Wheeler, 1979; DeVries & Slavin, 1978; Dienes, 1962; Rogers & Miller, 1984). Others have reported that using an instructional game to practice mathematics skills assists slow learners but not more able students (Friedlander, 1977). Research on the use of instructional games in college business courses has produced inconclusive or nonsignificant findings in many studies (Boseman & Schellenberger, 1974; Greenlaw & Wyman, 1973; Raia, 1966), whereas instructional games have positively influenced learning in actual business training settings (Jacobs & Baum, 1987; Pierfy, 1977). Even advocates of instructional gaming are unsure whether games teach intellectual content and skills (Boocock, 1968).

There are several explanations for the inconsistent findings from research concerning the effect of instructional games on motivation and learning. A few authors (Reiser & Gerlach, 1977; Remus, 1981; Stone, 1982) have suggested that much of the research on instructional gaming has been conducted using flawed experimental designs and methods. Another explanation is that many studies on instructional gaming have not investigated the integration of games in an instructional system. Gaming advocates have suggested that games should be used with other instructional methods such as lecture and textbooks (Clayton & Rosenbloom, 1968). A third explanation is that researchers examining the effect of instructional gaming on motivation have not adequately defined and operationalized the variable of motivation. After an extensive review of instructional gaming, Wolfe (1985) indicated, "No rigorous research has examined a game's motivational power, [or] what types of students are motivated by games" (p. 279).

Our purpose in this article is to describe the results of a study conducted to determine the effects on student motivation and performance of using an instructional game as practice. Because the study was designed to integrate the game into an instructional system, we also attempted to determine how using a supplemental reading affects student motivation and performance. Motivation was defined using the ARCS model of motivation (Keller, 1987a). The model suggests that motivation in an instructional setting consists of four conditions: attention, relevance, confidence, and satisfaction. According to Keller (1987a), all four conditions must be met for students to become and remain motivated. We hypothesized that students using an instructional game to practice newly acquired information would indicate that the method enhanced their attention, relevance, confidence, and satisfaction. We also believed that students who reported that they had completed a supplemental reading would perform better on a posttest than would those who reported that they did not complete the reading.

Method

Subjects

Our subjects were 75 undergraduate education majors enrolled in a required course in educational psychology at a large southwestern university. Although students in this class were required to participate in one research study during the semester, participation in this particular study was not mandatory.

Materials

Materials used in this study were an instructional game and a worksheet (both designed to provide practice of information and concepts presented in a lecture), the textbook *Essentials of Learning for Instruction* by Gagne & Driscoll (1988), the Instructional Materials Motivation Scale (Keller, 1987b), and a measure of performance.

The term *game* has various meanings, and several characteristics are important to understand the construct of game. In general, most games include a model or representation of reality, a set of rules that describe how to proceed, a specified outcome, and a group of players who act individually or collectively as a team (Atkinson, 1977; Coleman, 1968; Fletcher, 1971; Shubik, 1975, 1989). Games usually require active participation by players and can include elements of competition and cooperation (Orbach, 1979; Shubik, 1989). Games used for instructional purposes should be based on specific educational objectives and provide immediate feedback to participants (Atkinson, 1977; Jacobs & Baum, 1987; Orbach, 1979).

The instructional game used in this study included the elements listed above. We developed the game to provide students with practice on objectives from a unit on the information-processing model of learning. The instructional game consisted of a board that graphically represented the information-processing model, a direction card that explained the rules of the game, and a set of 25 game cards. Each game card had a practice question about the information-processing model of learning on the front and feedback with knowledge of correct results on the back. The rules were developed to encourage cooperation, competition, and active participation. The rules specified that team members should discuss each question among themselves before providing an answer. Teams were also told that they would be playing against another team.

We also developed the worksheet to provide subjects with practice on the information-processing model of learning. The worksheet was four pages in length and included the same 25 questions that appeared on the game cards. After subjects completed a set of five questions, the worksheet instructed subjects to turn to the last page for feedback.

Task 9 Example (*continued*)

May/June 1991 [Vol. 84(No. 5)]

We used the Instructional Materials Motivation Scale (IMMS) developed by Keller (1987b), to measure student perception of the motivational characteristics of the instructional materials. The IMMS includes four subscales to measure the degree to which subjects believe that a set of instructional materials address the motivational components of attention, relevance, confidence, and satisfaction. Keller reported that Cronbach's alpha reliability of the instrument is .89 for attention, .81 for relevance, .90 for confidence, .92 for satisfaction, and .96 for overall motivation.

A 15-item constructed response posttest was used to measure student performance. We developed the items on this posttest to determine subject mastery of the information-processing model. The Kuder-Richardson internal consistency reliability of this measure was .77.

Procedures

All of the subjects attended a 50-min lecture on the information-processing model of learning and were told afterward to read chapter 2 in the textbook, *Essentials of Learning for Instruction*, by Gagne & Driscoll (1988). Two days later, the subjects were randomly assigned to one of two treatment groups. The subjects in both groups were given 30 min to practice the information presented in the lecture and assigned reading by using either the instructional game or the worksheet.

One group of subjects used the instructional game to practice the information-processing model. Those subjects were randomly placed in groups of 8 to 10 and formed into two teams of players. Each group received the game materials described above, and the experimenter read the game rules aloud. Subjects in this group played the game for 30 min. The other group of subjects used the worksheet to practice the same items. The latter group worked individually for 30 min to complete the worksheet. The subjects were told to review incorrect items if time permitted.

Upon completion of the practice activity, all the subjects completed the Instructional Materials Motivation Scale and then took the posttest. The subjects also were asked if they had attended the lecture on the information-processing model and if they had completed the assigned reading from the textbook. Completion of the activities took approximately 15 min.

Results

Motivation

We used a multivariate analysis of variance (MANOVA) to test for an overall difference between groups on the motivation scales. Stevens (1986) indicated that MANOVA should be used when several dependent variables are correlated and share a common conceptual meaning. An alpha level of .05 was set for the MANOVA tests. The analyses were followed by univariate analyses on each of the four IMMS subscales. To account for the possibility of inflated statistical error, we set the alpha at .0125 for the univariate analyses, using the Bonferroni method (Stevens, 1986). To determine the size of the treatment effect for each variable, we calculated effect-size estimates expressed as a function of the overall standard deviation (Cohen, 1969).

Results indicated that using the instructional game to practice information had a significant effect on motivation. A significant MANOVA effect, $F(4, 64) = 6.57$, $p < .001$, was found for the treatment on the motivation measures. Univariate analyses revealed that subjects who played the game rated this method of practice as motivational in the four areas of attention, $F(1, 67) = 21.91$, $p < .001$; relevance, $F(1, 67) = 15.05$, $p < .001$; confidence, $F(1, 67) = 16.80$, $p < .001$; and satisfaction, $F(1, 67) = 24.71$, $p < .001$. Effect-size estimates for each motivation variable were .61 for attention, .91 for relevance, 1.01 for confidence, and 1.23 for satisfaction. Cohen (1969) indicated that an effect size of .80 should be considered large for most statistical tests in psychological research. Table 1 includes a summary of means and standard deviations on each motivation subscale for the game and the nongame groups.

Results also suggested that subject self-report about completion of the reading assignment was significantly related to motivation. A significant MANOVA effect $F(4, 64) = 2.94$, $p < .05$, was found for this variable on the motivation measures. Follow-up univariate analyses revealed that the motivational area of consdience was sig-

Table 1.—Means and Standard Deviations on Attention (A), Relevance (R), Confidence (C), Satisfaction (S), and Performance (P) Measures, by Treatment Group

Group	A	R	C	S	P
Game	4.22	3.71	4.06	3.88	10.49
(*n* = 37)	(0.58)	(0.58)	(0.57)	(0.86)	(3.20)
Nongame	3.77	3.13	3.31	2.72	9.39
(*n* = 38)	(0.89)	(0.69)	(0.90)	(1.02)	(3.60)

Note. Maximum scores = 5.00 for A, R, C, S and 15.00 for P.

nificantly related to completion of reading assignment, $F(1, 67) = 6.52$, $p < .0125$. Attention, relevance, and satisfaction were not significantly related to self-reported completion of reading assignment. In addition, a test of the interaction between self-reported completion of reading assignment and the treatment was not statistically significant, $F(4, 64) = 0.97$, $p > .05$.

Performance

We measured performance using a 15-item constructed response posttest. Analysis of variance (ANOVA) was used to test for differences between groups on the performance measure. An alpha level of .05 was set for all statistical tests.

Analysis of the posttest data revealed that self-reported completion of assigned reading was significantly related to performance, $F(2, 71) = 14.87$, $p < .001$. Subjects who indicated that they had read the assigned text ($n = 40$) performed significantly better on the posttest than those who indicated that they did not complete the reading ($n = 35$). The mean performance score of subjects who reported reading the text was 11.25 ($SD = 3.07$), whereas the mean performance score for those who reported that they did not read the text was 8.45 ($SD = 3.22$).

No statistically significant difference was found on the performance measure when the treatment groups were compared. The mean performance score for subjects using the game was 10.49 ($SD = 3.20$), and the mean performance score for those in the nongame group was 9.39 ($SD = 3.61$). In addition, a test of the interaction between the treatment and self-reported completion of reading assignment was not statistically significant, $F(2, 71) = 0.14$, $p > .05$.

Discussion

The major purpose of this study was to determine the effect of using an instructional game on student motivation and performance. The results of the study suggest that using an instructional game as a method of delivering practice did enhance the motivation of students in the four areas of attention, relevance, confidence, and satisfaction. However, the results show that using the instructional game to practice information did not contribute to enhanced performance when compared with a traditional method of practice. There are several possible explanations for the results found in this study.

In keeping with established ideas of the characteristics of a game, we used a game board that provided students with a visual representation of the information-processing model of learning and required players to be active participants. Keller (1987a) indicated that visual representations and active participation are two strategies that can increase student attention in an instructional setting.

Furthermore, use of the game may have contributed to the results found for attention, because of a novelty effect. Some researchers have reported that student motivation and interest fluctuate and decrease as the novelty effect of a game wears off (Dill, 1961; Greenlaw & Wyman, 1973), whereas others have reported that interest tends to persist over time in gaming settings (Dill & Doppelt, 1963). Although novelty may be a reason for increased attention in this study, instructional designers who are concerned with providing motivating practice to students should consider that explanation as positive. Motivation and attention can be increased when variability and novelty are used in the classroom (Brophy, 1987; Keller, 1983).

The results found in this study for the motivational factor of relevance are consistent with the theories proposed by gaming advocates. Both Abt (1968) and Rogers and Miller (1984) argued that students will not question the relevance of educational content when it is presented via an instructional game. In addition, instruction can be made relevant to students by designing materials that are responsive to their needs (Keller, 1983). Orbach (1979) indicated that games are excellent methods to motivate students with a high need for achievement, because a game can include an element of competition. Orbach (1979) also theorized that games can motivate students with a high need for affiliation when the game requires interaction among individuals and teams. The instructional game used in this study included a moderate level of competition and required students to interact cooperatively through the team approach.

The instructional game used in this study also provided circumstances for student-directed learning. As a motivational strategy, researchers have linked student-centered learning with increased confidence (Keller & Dodge, 1982). The finding that the game increased student confidence is consistent with theorists who have suggested that games can influence student efficacy (Abt, 1968) and with researchers who reported that students rate the task of gaming as less difficult than other instructional techniques (DeVries & Edwards, 1973).

The positive finding for satisfaction is also consistent with theory and research. Some scholars have indicated that instructional games contribute to motivation because they provide intrinsic reward and enjoyment (Coleman, 1968; Ernest, 1986; Rakes & Kutzman, 1982). Researchers have reported that instructional games lead to increases in student satisfaction (DeVries & Edwards, 1973; Strauss, 1986). The results of this study support theorists and researchers who have suggested that students enjoy the gaming approach in instruction.

Although our results did suggest that the instructional game had an effect on student motivation, the game used in this study did not have a significant impact on student performance. However, subjects who reported completing an assigned reading performed significantly better

May/June 1991 [Vol. 84(No. 5)]

and had more confidence about their performance than those who reported that they did not complete the reading. The results may have occurred because of the nature of the reading. Even though all the students were provided with necessary concepts and information in a lecture, the textbook, *Essentials of Learning for Instruction* (Gagne & Driscoll, 1988), provided readers with practice and feedback in addition to supplementing the lecture. The additional practice and feedback more than likely influenced both the performance and confidence of those who completed the assigned reading.

The findings of this study have some implications for the design of practice. Although many instructional design theorists have indicated that students should be provided with an opportunity to practice newly acquired skills and knowledge, most fail to address how to design practice that is motivational (Salisbury, Richards, & Klein, 1985). The results of this study suggest that instructional designers can provide students with a motivating practice alternative that is as effective as more traditional methods of practice by including a game into instruction. Although using the game to practice did not have an effect on immediate performance in this short-term study, motivating practice alternatives can possibly influence long-term performance because of increased student contact with materials that they find motivational. Future research should investigate the impact of gaming on long-term performance.

The current study also suggests that instructional designers should include reading assignments that provide additional practice in their instruction. The use of those types of readings will not only increase student performance, but also will lead to increases in student confidence about that performance.

As in our study, future research should integrate instructional games into a system to determine if the method has an impact on educational outcomes. Besides using a game as practice, research could be conducted to examine the effect of using a game to present other instructional events, such as stimulating recall of prior knowledge or as a review of learning. Researchers of instructional gaming should continue to investigate the effect of using a game on student motivation and should be specific in their operational definition of motivation. Implementation of our suggestions will assist us in determining how to design practice that is both effective and motivational.

REFERENCES

Abt, C. C. (1968). Games for learning. In S. S. Boocock & E. O. Schild (Eds.), *Simulation games in learning* (pp. 65–84). Beverly Hills, CA: Sage.

Allen, L. E., & Main, D. B. (1976). The effect of instructional gaming on absenteeism: The first step. *Journal for Research in Mathematics Education, 7*(2), 113–128.

Allington, R. L., & Strange, M. (1977). The problem with reading games. *The Reading Teacher, 31*, 272–274.

Andrews, M., & Thorpe, H. W. (1977). A critical analysis of instructional games. *Reading Improvement, 14*, 74–76.

Atkinson, F. D. (1977). Designing simulation/gaming activities: A systems approach. *Educational Technology, 17*(2), 38–43.

Boocock, S. S. (1968). From luxury item to learning tool: An overview of the theoretical literature on games. In S. S. Boocock and E. O. Schild (Eds.), *Simulation games in learning* (pp. 53–64). Beverly Hills, CA: Sage.

Boseman, F. G., & Schellenberger, R. E. (1974). Business gaming: An empirical appraisal. *Simulation & Games, 5*, 383–401.

Bright, G. W. (1980). Game moves as they relate to strategy and knowledge. *Journal of Experimental Education, 48*, 204–209.

Bright, G. W., Harvey, J. G., & Wheeler, M. M. (1979). Using games to retrain skills with basic multiplication facts. *Journal for Research in Mathematics Education, 10*, 103–110.

Brophy, J. (1987). Synthesis of research on strategies for motivating students to learn. *Educational Leadership, 45*(2), 40–48.

Clayton, M., & Rosenbloom, R. (1968). Goals and designs. In S. S. Boocock & E. O. Schild (Eds.), *Simulation games in learning* (pp. 85–92). Beverly Hills, CA: Sage.

Cohen, J. (1969). *Statistical power analysis for the behavioral sciences.* New York: Academic Press.

Coleman, J. S. (1968). Social processes and social simulation games. In S. S. Boocock & E. O. Schild (Eds.), *Simulation games in learning* (pp. 29–51). Beverly Hills, CA: Sage.

Dienes, Z. P. (1962). *An experimental study of mathematics learning.* New York: Hutchinson.

DeVries, D. L., & Edwards, K. L. (1973). Learning games and student teams: Their effects on classroom process. *American Educational Research Journal, 10*, 307–318.

DeVries, D. L., & Slavin, R. E. (1978). Teams-games-tournaments (TGT): Review of ten classroom experiments. *Journal of Research and Development in Education, 12*, 28–37.

Dill, W. R. (1961). The educational effects of management games. In W. R. Dill (Ed.), *Proceeding of the Conference on Business Games as Teaching Devices* (pp. 61–72). New Orleans, LA: Tulane University.

Dill, W. R., & Doppelt, N. (1963). The acquisition of experience in a complex management game. *Management Science, 10*, 30–46.

Ernest, P. (1986). Games: A rationale for their use in the teaching of mathematics in school. *Mathematics in School*, 2–5.

Fletcher, J. L. (1971). The effectiveness of simulation games as learning environments. *Simulation and Games, 2*, 259–286.

Friedlander, A. (1977). The Steeplechase. *Mathematics Teaching, 80*, 37–39.

Gagne, R. M., & Driscoll, M. P. (1988). *Essentialsl of learning for instruction* (2nd ed.). Englewood Cliffs, NJ: Prentice Hall.

Greenlaw, P. S., & Wyman, F. P. (1973). The teaching effectiveness of games in collegiate business courses. *Simulation & Games, 4*, 259–294.

Jacobs, R. L., & Baum, M. (1987). Simulation and games in training and development. *Simulation & Games, 18*, 385–394.

Keller, J. M. (1983). Motivational design of instruction. In C. M. Reigeluth (Ed.), *Instructional-design theories and models: An overview of their current status* (pp. 386–434). Hillsdale, NJ: Lawrence Erlbaum.

Keller, J. M. (1987a). Development and use of the ARCS model of instructional design. *Journal of Instructional Development, 10*(3), 2–10.

Keller, J. M. (1987b). *Instructional materials motivation scale (IMMS).* Unpublished manuscript. Florida State University, Tallahassee, FL.

Keller, J.M., & Dodge, B. (1982). *The ARCS model: Motivational strategies for instruction.* Unpublished manuscript. Syracuse University, Syracuse, NY.

Orbach, E. (1979). Simulation games and motivation for learning: A theoretical framework. *Simulation & Games, 10*, 3–40.

Pierfy, D. (1977). Comparative simulation game research: Stumbling blocks and stepping stones. *Simulation & Games, 8*, 255–269.

Raia, A. P. (1966). A study of the educational value of management games. *Journal of Business, 39*, 339–352.

Rakes, T. A., & Kutzman, S. K. (1982). The selection and use of reading games and activities. *Reading Horizons*, 67–70.

Reiser, R. A., & Gerlach, V. S. (1977). Research on simulation games in education: A critical analysis. *Educational Technology, 17*(12), 13–18.

Remus, W. E. (1981). Experimental designs for analyzing data on

Task 9 Example (*continued*)

games. *Simulation & Games, 12*, 3–14.

Rogers, P. J., & Miller, J. V. (1984). Playway mathematics: Theory, practice, and some results. *Educational Research, 26*, 200–207.

Salisbury, D. F., Richards, B. F., & Klein, J. D. (1986). Prescriptions for the design of practice activities for learning. *Journal of Instructional Development, 8*(4), 9–19.

Shubik, M. (1975). *The uses and methods of gaming.* New York: Elsevier.

Shubik, M. (1989). Gaming: Theory and practice, past and future. *Simulation & Games, 20*, 184–189.

Sleet, D. A. (1985). Application of a gaming strategy to improve nutrition education. *Simulation & Games, 16*, 63–70.

Stevens, J. (1986). *Applied multivariate statistics for the social sciences.* Hillsdale, NJ: Lawrence Erlbaum.

Stone, E. F. (1982). *Research design issues in studies assessing the effects of management education.* Paper presented at the National Academy of Management Conference, New York.

Straus, R. A. (1986). Simple games for teaching sociological perspectives. *Teaching Sociology, 14*, 119–128.

Wesson, C., Wilson, R., & Mandlebaum, L. H. (1988). Learning games for active student responding. *Teaching Exceptional Children*, 12–14.

Wolfe, J. (1985). The teaching effectiveness of games in collegiate business courses. *Simulation & Games, 16*, 251–288.

EFFECTS OF USING AN INSTRUCTIONAL GAME ON MOTIVATION AND PERFORMANCE

Self-Test for Task 9

Y = Yes
N = No
NA = Not applicable
?/X = Can't tell/Don't know

GENERAL EVALUATION CRITERIA

Introduction

CODE

Problem

Is there a statement of the problem? _____

Is the problem "researchable"? _____

Is background information on the problem presented? _____

Is the educational significance of the problem discussed? _____

Does the problem statement indicate the variables of interest
and the specific relationship between those variables which
was investigated? _____

When necessary, are variables directly or operationally defined? _____

Review of Related Literature

Is the review comprehensive? _____

Are all references cited relevant to the problem under
investigation? _____

Are most of the sources primary, i.e., are there only a few or
no secondary sources? _____

Have the references been critically analyzed and the results of
various studies compared and contrasted, i.e., is the review more
than a series of abstracts or annotations? _____

Is the review well organized? Does it logically flow in such a way
that the references least related to the problem are discussed first
and the most related references are discussed last? _____

Does the review conclude with a brief summary of the literature
and its implications for the problem investigated? _____

Do the implications discussed form an empirical or theoretical
rationale for the hypotheses which follow? _____

CODE

Hypotheses

Are specific questions to be answered listed or specific
hypotheses to be tested stated?   _____

Does each hypothesis state an expected relationship or
difference?   _____

If necessary, are variables directly or operationally defined?   _____

Is each hypothesis testable?   _____

Method

Subjects

Are the size and major characteristics of the population studied
described?   _____

If a sample was selected, is the method of selecting the sample
clearly described?   _____

Is the method of sample selection described one that is likely
to result in a representative, unbiased sample?   _____

Did the researcher avoid the use of volunteers?   _____

Are the size and major characteristics of the sample described?   _____

Does the sample size meet the suggested guidelines for minimum
sample size appropriate for the method of research represented?   _____

Instruments

Is a rationale given for the selection of the instruments
(or measurements) used?   _____

Is each instrument described in terms of purpose and content?   _____

Are the instruments appropriate for measuring the intended
variables?   _____

Is evidence presented that indicates that each instrument is
appropriate for the sample under study?   _____

Is instrument validity discussed and coefficients given if
appropriate?   _____

Is reliability discussed in terms of type and size of reliability
coefficients?   _____

If appropriate, are subtest reliabilities given?   _____

If an instrument was developed specifically for the study, are the
procedures involved in its development and validation described?   _____

If an instrument was developed specifically for the study,
are administration, scoring or tabulating, and interpretation
procedures fully described?   _____

CODE

Design and Procedure

Is the design appropriate for answering the questions or testing the hypotheses of the study?   _____

Are procedures described in sufficient detail to permit replication by another researcher?   _____

If a pilot study was conducted, are its execution and results described as well as its impact on the subsequent study?   _____

Are control procedures described?   _____

Did the researcher discuss or account for any potentially confounding variables that he or she was unable to control for?   _____

Results

Are appropriate descriptive statistics presented?   _____

Was the probability level, α, at which the results of the tests of significance were evaluated, specified in advance of data analysis?   _____

If parametric tests were used, is there evidence that the researcher avoided violating the required assumptions for parametric tests?   _____

Are the tests of significance described appropriate, given the hypotheses and design of the study?   _____

Was every hypothesis tested?   _____

Are the tests of significance interpreted using the appropriate degrees of freedom?   _____

Are the results clearly presented?   _____

Are the tables and figures (if any) well organized and easy to understand?   _____

Are the data in each table and figure described in the text?   _____

Discussion (Conclusions and Recommendations)

Is each result discussed in terms of the original hypothesis to which it relates?   _____

Is each result discussed in terms of its agreement or disagreement with previous results obtained by other researchers in other studies?   _____

Are generalizations consistent with the results?   _____

Are the possible effects of uncontrolled variables on the results discussed?   _____

Are theoretical and practical implications of the findings discussed?   _____

CODE

Are recommendations for future action made?   _____

Are the suggestions for future action based on practical
significance or on statistical significance only, i.e., has the
author avoided confusing practical and statistical significance?   _____

Are recommendations for future research made?   _____

Abstract (or Summary)

Is the problem restated?   _____

Are the number and type of subjects and instruments described?   _____

Is the design used identified?   _____

Are procedures described?   _____

Are the major results and conclusions restated?   _____

TYPE-SPECIFIC EVALUATION CRITERIA

Identify and diagram the experimental design used in this study:

Was an appropriate experimental design selected?   _____

Is a rationale for design selection given?   _____

Are sources of invalidity associated with the design
identified and discussed?   _____

Is the method of group formation described?   _____

Was the experimental group formed in the same way
as the control group?   _____

Were groups randomly formed and the use of existing
groups avoided?   _____

Were treatments randomly assigned to groups?   _____

Were critical extraneous variables identified?   _____

Were any control procedures applied to equate groups
on extraneous variables?   _____

Were possible reactive arrangements (e.g., the Hawthorne
effect) controlled for?   _____

APPENDIX A

Reference Tables

Table A.1

Ten Thousand Random Numbers

	00–04	05–09	10–14	15–19	20–24	25–29	30–34	35–39	40–44	45–49
00	54463	22662	65905	70639	79365	67382	29085	69831	47058	08186
01	15389	85205	18850	39226	42249	90669	96325	23248	60933	26927
02	85941	40756	82414	02015	13858	78030	16269	65978	01385	15345
03	61149	69440	11268	88218	58925	03638	52862	62733	33451	77455
04	05219	81619	81619	10651	67079	92511	59888	72095	83463	75577
05	41417	98326	87719	92294	46614	50948	64886	20002	97365	30976
06	28357	94070	20652	35774	16249	75019	21145	15217	47286	76305
07	17783	00015	10806	83091	91530	36466	39981	62481	49177	75779
08	40950	84820	29881	85966	62800	70326	84740	62660	77379	90279
09	82995	64157	66164	41180	10089	41757	78258	96488	88629	37231
10	96754	17676	55659	44105	47361	34833	86679	23930	53249	27083
11	34357	88040	53364	71726	45690	66334	60332	22554	90600	71113
12	06318	37403	49927	57715	50423	67372	63116	48888	21505	80182
13	62111	52820	07243	79931	89292	84767	85693	73947	22278	11551
14	47534	09243	67879	00544	23410	12740	02540	54440	32949	13491
15	98614	75993	84460	62846	59844	14922	49730	73443	48167	34770
16	24856	03648	44898	09351	98795	18644	39765	71058	90368	44104
17	96887	12479	80621	66223	86085	78285	02432	53342	42846	94771
18	90801	21472	42815	77408	37390	76766	52615	32141	30268	18106
19	55165	77312	83666	36028	28420	70219	81369	41943	47366	41067
20	75884	12952	84318	95108	72305	64620	91318	89872	45375	85436
21	16777	37116	58550	42958	21460	43910	01175	87894	81378	10620
22	46230	43877	80207	88877	89380	32992	91380	03164	98656	59337
23	42902	66892	46134	01432	94710	23474	20523	60137	60609	13119
24	81007	00333	39693	28039	10154	95425	39220	19774	31782	49037
25	68089	01122	51111	72373	06902	74373	96199	97017	41273	21546
26	20411	67081	89950	16944	93054	87687	96693	87236	77054	33848
27	58212	13160	06468	15718	82627	76999	05999	58680	96739	63700
28	70577	42866	24969	61210	76046	67699	42054	12696	93758	03283
29	94522	74358	71659	62038	79643	79169	44741	05437	39038	13163
30	42626	86819	85651	88678	17401	03252	99547	32404	17918	62880
31	16051	33763	57194	16752	54450	19031	58580	47629	54132	60631
32	08244	27647	33851	44705	94211	46716	11738	55784	95374	72655
33	59497	04392	09419	89964	51211	04894	72882	17805	21896	83864
34	97155	13428	40293	09985	58434	01412	69124	82171	59058	82859
35	98409	66162	95763	47420	20792	61527	20441	39435	11859	41567
36	45476	84882	65109	96597	25930	66790	65706	61203	53634	22557
37	89300	69700	50741	30329	11658	23166	05400	66669	48708	03887
38	50051	95137	91631	66315	91428	12275	24816	68091	71710	33258
39	31753	85178	31310	89642	98364	02306	24617	09609	83942	22716
40	79152	53829	77250	20190	56535	18760	69942	77448	33278	48805
41	44560	38750	83635	56540	64900	42912	13953	79149	18710	68618
42	68328	83378	63369	71381	39564	05615	42451	64559	97501	65747
43	46939	38689	58625	08342	30459	85863	20781	09284	26333	91777
44	83544	86141	15707	96256	23068	13782	08467	89469	93842	55349
45	91621	00881	04900	54224	46177	55309	17852	27491	89415	23466
46	91896	67126	04151	03795	59077	11848	12630	98375	53068	60142
47	55751	62515	22108	80830	02263	29303	37204	96926	30506	09808
48	85156	87689	95493	88842	00664	55017	55539	17771	69448	87530
49	07521	56898	12236	60277	39102	62315	12239	07105	11844	01117

Reprinted by permission from *Statistical Methods* by George W. Snedecor and William G. Cochran, sixth edition © 1967 by Iowa State University Press, p. 543–46.

Table A.1
(*continued*)

	50–54	55–59	60–64	65–69	70–74	75–79	80–84	85–89	90–94	95–99
00	59391	58030	52098	82718	87024	82848	04190	96574	90464	29065
01	99567	76364	77204	04615	27062	96621	43918	01896	83991	51141
02	10363	97518	51400	25670	98342	61891	27101	37855	06235	33316
03	96859	19558	64432	16706	99612	59798	32803	67708	15297	28612
04	11258	24591	36863	55368	31721	94335	34936	02566	80972	08188
05	95068	88628	35911	14530	33020	80428	33936	31855	34334	64865
06	54463	47237	73800	91017	36239	71824	83671	39892	60518	37092
07	16874	62677	57412	13215	31389	62233	80827	73917	82802	84420
08	92494	63157	76593	91316	03505	72389	96363	52887	01087	66091
09	15669	56689	35682	40844	53256	81872	35213	09840	34471	74441
10	99116	75486	84989	23476	52967	67104	39495	39100	17217	74073
11	15696	10703	65178	90637	63110	17622	53988	71087	84148	11670
12	97720	15369	51269	69620	03388	13699	33423	67453	43269	56720
13	11666	13841	71681	98000	35979	39719	81899	07449	47985	46967
14	71628	73130	78783	75691	41632	09847	61547	18707	85489	69944
15	40501	51089	99943	91843	41995	88931	73631	69361	05375	15417
16	22518	55576	98215	82068	10798	86211	36584	67466	69373	40054
17	75112	30485	62173	02132	14878	92879	22281	16783	86352	00077
18	80327	02671	98191	84342	90813	49268	94551	15496	20168	09271
19	60251	45548	02146	05597	48228	81366	34598	72856	66762	17002
20	57430	82270	10421	00540	43648	75888	66049	21511	47676	33444
21	73528	39559	34434	88586	54086	71693	43132	14414	79949	85193
22	25991	65959	70769	64721	86413	33475	42740	06175	82758	66248
23	78388	16638	09134	59980	63806	48472	39318	35434	24057	74739
24	12477	09965	96657	57994	59439	76330	24596	77515	09577	91871
25	83266	32883	42451	15579	38155	29793	40914	65990	16255	17777
26	76970	80876	10237	39515	79152	74798	39357	09054	73579	92359
27	37074	65198	44785	68624	98336	84481	97610	78735	46703	98265
28	83712	06514	30101	78295	54656	85417	43189	60048	72781	72606
29	20287	56862	69727	94443	64936	08366	27227	05158	50326	59566
30	74261	32592	86538	27041	65172	85532	07571	80609	39285	65340
31	64081	49863	08478	96001	18888	14810	70545	89755	59064	07210
32	05617	75818	47750	67814	29575	10526	66192	44464	27058	40467
33	26793	74951	95466	74307	13330	42664	85515	20632	05497	33625
34	65988	72850	48737	54719	52056	01596	03845	35067	03134	70322
35	27366	42271	44300	73399	21105	03280	73457	43093	05192	48657
36	56760	10909	98147	34736	33863	95256	12731	66598	50771	83665
37	72880	43338	93643	58904	59543	23943	11231	83268	65938	81581
38	77888	38100	03062	58103	47961	83841	25878	23746	55903	44115
39	28440	07819	21580	51459	47971	29882	13990	29226	23608	15873
40	63525	94441	77033	12147	51054	49955	58312	76923	96071	05813
41	47606	93410	16359	89033	89696	47231	64498	31776	05383	39902
42	52669	45030	96279	14709	52372	87832	02735	50803	72744	88208
43	16738	60159	07425	62369	07515	82721	37875	71153	21315	00132
44	59348	11695	45751	15865	74739	05572	32688	20271	65128	14551
45	12900	71775	29845	60774	94924	21810	38636	33717	67598	82521
46	75086	23537	49939	33595	13484	97588	28617	17979	70749	35234
47	99495	51534	29181	09993	38190	42553	68922	52125	91077	40197
48	26075	31671	45386	36583	93459	48599	52022	41330	60651	91321
49	13636	93596	23377	51133	95126	61496	42474	45141	46660	42338

Table A.1

(*continued*)

	00–04	05–09	10–14	15–19	20–24	25–29	30–34	35–39	40–44	45–49
50	64249	63664	39652	40646	97306	31741	07294	84149	46797	82487
51	26538	44249	04050	48174	65570	44072	40192	51153	11397	58212
52	05845	00512	78630	55328	18116	69296	91705	86224	29503	57071
53	74897	68373	67359	51014	33510	83048	17056	72506	82949	54600
54	20872	54570	35017	88132	25730	22626	86723	91691	13191	77212
55	31432	96156	89177	75541	81355	24480	77243	76690	42507	84362
56	66890	61505	01240	00660	05873	13568	76082	79172	57913	93448
57	41894	57790	79970	33106	86904	48119	52503	24130	72824	21627
58	11303	87118	81471	52936	08555	28420	49416	44448	04269	27029
59	54374	57325	16947	45356	78371	10563	97191	53798	12693	27928
60	64852	34421	61046	90849	13966	39810	42699	21753	76192	10508
61	16309	20384	09491	91588	97720	89846	30376	76970	23063	35894
62	42587	37065	24526	72602	57589	98131	37292	05967	26002	51945
63	40177	98590	97161	41682	84533	67588	62036	49967	01990	72308
64	82309	76128	93965	26743	24141	04838	40254	26065	07938	76236
65	79788	68243	59732	04257	27084	14743	17520	94501	55811	76099
66	40538	79000	89559	25026	42274	23489	34502	75508	06059	86682
67	64016	73598	18609	73150	62463	33102	45205	87440	96767	67042
68	49767	12691	17903	93871	99721	79109	09425	26904	07419	76013
69	76974	55108	29795	08404	82684	00497	51126	79935	57450	55671
70	23854	08480	85983	96025	50117	64610	99425	62291	86943	21541
71	68973	70551	25098	78033	98573	79848	31778	29555	61446	23037
72	36444	93600	65350	14971	25325	00427	52073	64280	18847	24768
73	03003	87800	07391	11594	21196	00781	32550	57158	58887	73041
74	17540	26188	36647	78386	04558	61463	57842	90382	77019	24210
75	38916	55809	47982	41968	69760	79422	80154	91486	19180	15100
76	64288	19843	69122	42502	48508	28820	59933	72998	99942	10515
77	86809	51564	38040	39418	49915	19000	58050	16899	79952	57849
78	99800	99566	14742	05028	30033	94889	55381	23656	75787	59223
79	92345	31890	95712	08279	91794	94068	49337	88674	35355	12267
80	90363	65162	32245	82279	79256	80834	06088	99462	56705	06118
81	64437	32242	48431	04835	39070	59702	31508	60935	22390	52246
82	91714	53662	28373	34333	55791	74758	51144	18827	10704	76803
83	20902	17646	31391	31459	33315	03444	55743	74701	58851	27427
84	12217	86007	70371	52281	14510	76094	96579	54853	78339	20839
85	45177	02863	42307	53571	22532	74921	17735	42201	80540	54721
86	28325	90814	08804	52746	47913	54577	47525	77705	95330	21866
87	29019	28776	56116	54791	64604	08815	46049	71186	34650	14994
88	84979	81353	56219	67062	26146	82567	33122	14124	46240	92973
89	50371	26347	48513	63915	11158	25563	91915	18431	92978	11591
90	53422	06825	69711	67950	64716	18003	49581	45378	99878	61130
91	67453	35651	89316	41620	32048	70225	47597	33137	31443	51445
92	07294	85353	74819	23445	68237	07202	99515	62282	53809	26685
93	79544	00302	45338	16015	66613	88968	14595	63836	77716	79596
94	64144	85442	82060	46471	24162	39500	87351	36637	42833	71875
95	90919	11883	58318	00042	52402	28210	34075	33272	00840	73268
96	06670	57353	86275	92276	77591	46924	60839	55437	03183	13191
97	36634	93976	52062	83678	41256	60948	18685	48992	19462	96062
98	75101	72891	85745	67106	26010	62107	60885	37503	55461	71213
99	05112	71222	72654	51583	05228	62056	57390	42746	39272	96659

Table A.1
(continued)

	50–54	55–59	60–64	65–69	70–74	75–79	80–84	85–89	90–94	95–99
50	32847	31282	03345	89593	69214	70381	78285	20054	91018	16742
51	16916	00041	30236	55023	14253	76582	12092	86533	92426	37655
52	66176	34037	21005	27137	03193	48970	64625	22394	39622	79085
53	46299	13335	12180	16861	38043	59292	62675	63631	37020	78195
54	22847	47839	45385	23289	47526	54098	45683	55849	51575	64689
55	41851	54160	92320	69936	34803	92479	33399	71160	64777	83378
56	28444	59497	91586	95917	68553	28639	06455	34174	11130	91994
57	47520	62378	98855	83174	13088	16561	68559	26679	06238	51254
58	34978	63271	13142	82681	05271	08822	06490	44984	49307	61617
59	37404	80416	69035	92980	49486	74378	75610	74976	70056	15478
60	32400	65482	52099	53676	74648	94148	65095	69597	52771	71551
61	89262	86332	51718	70663	11623	29834	79820	73002	84886	03591
62	86866	09127	98021	03871	27789	58444	44832	36505	40672	30180
63	90814	14833	08759	74645	05046	94056	99094	65091	32663	73040
64	19192	82756	20553	58446	55376	88914	75096	26119	83898	43816
65	77585	52593	56612	95766	10019	29531	73064	20953	53523	58136
66	23757	16364	05096	03192	62386	45389	85332	18877	55710	96459
67	45989	96257	23850	26216	23309	21526	07425	50254	19455	29315
68	92970	94243	07316	41467	64837	52406	25225	51553	31220	14032
69	74346	59596	40088	98176	17896	86900	20249	77753	19099	48885
70	87646	41309	27636	45153	29988	94770	07255	70908	05340	99751
71	50099	71038	45146	06146	55211	99429	43169	66259	99786	59180
72	10127	46900	64984	75348	04115	33624	68774	60013	35515	62556
73	67995	81977	18984	64091	02785	27762	42529	97144	80407	64524
74	26304	80217	84934	82657	69291	35397	98714	35104	08187	48109
75	81994	41070	56642	64091	31229	02595	13513	45148	78722	30144
76	59337	34662	79631	89403	65212	09975	06118	86197	58208	16162
77	51228	10937	62396	81460	47331	91403	95007	06047	16846	64809
78	31089	37995	29577	07828	42272	54016	21950	86192	99046	84864
79	38207	97938	93459	75174	79460	55436	57206	87644	21296	43393
80	88666	31142	09474	89712	63153	62333	42212	06140	42594	43671
81	53365	56134	67582	92557	89520	33452	05134	70628	27612	33738
82	89807	74530	38004	90102	11693	90257	05500	79920	62700	43325
83	18682	81038	85662	90915	91631	22223	91588	80774	07716	12548
84	63571	32579	63942	25371	09234	94592	98475	76884	37635	33608
85	68927	56492	67799	95398	77642	54913	91583	08421	81450	76229
86	56401	63186	39389	88798	31356	89235	97036	32341	33292	73757
87	24333	95603	02359	72942	46287	95382	08452	62862	97869	71775
88	17025	84202	95199	62272	06366	16175	97577	99304	41587	03686
89	02804	08253	52133	20224	68034	50865	57868	22343	55111	03607
90	08298	03879	20995	19850	73090	13191	18963	82244	78479	99121
91	59883	01785	82403	96062	03785	03488	12970	64896	38336	30030
92	46982	06682	62864	91837	74021	89094	39952	64158	79614	78235
93	31121	47266	07661	02051	67599	24471	69843	83696	71402	76287
94	97867	56641	63416	17577	30161	87320	37752	73276	48969	41915
95	57364	86746	08415	14621	49430	22311	15836	72492	49372	44103
96	09559	26263	69511	28064	75999	44540	13337	10918	79846	54809
97	53873	55571	00608	42661	91332	63956	74087	59008	47493	99581
98	35531	19162	86406	05299	77511	24311	57257	22826	77555	05941
99	28229	88629	25695	94932	30721	16197	78742	34974	97528	45447

Table A.2

Values of the Correlation Coefficient for Different Levels of Significance

df	p			
	.10	.05	.01	.001
1	.98769	.99692	.99988	.99999
2	.90000	.95000	.99000	.99900
3	.8054	.8783	.95873	.99116
4	.7293	.8114	.91720	.97406
5	.6694	.7545	.8745	.95074
6	.6215	.7067	.8343	.92493
7	.5822	.6664	.7977	.8982
8	.5494	.6319	.7646	.8721
9	.5214	.6021	.7348	.8471
10	.4973	.5760	.7079	.8233
11	.4762	.5529	.6835	.8010
12	.4575	.5324	.6614	.7800
13	.4409	.5139	.6411	.7603
14	.4259	.4973	.6226	.7420
15	.4124	.4821	.6055	.7246
16	.4000	.4683	.5897	.7084
17	.3887	.4555	.5751	.6932
18	.3783	.4438	.5614	.6787
19	.3687	.4329	.5487	.6652
20	.3598	.4227	.5368	.6524
25	.3233	.3809	.4869	.5974
30	.2960	.3494	.4487	.5541
35	.2746	.3246	.4182	.5189
40	.2573	.3044	.3932	.4896
45	.2428	.2875	.3721	.4648
50	.2306	.2732	.3541	.4433
60	.2108	.2500	.3248	.4078
70	.1954	.2319	.3017	.3799
80	.1829	.2172	.2830	.3568
90	.1726	.2050	.2673	.3375
100	.1638	.1946	.2540	.3211

Table A.2 is taken from Table VII of Fisher and Yates: *Statistical Tables for Biological, Agricultural and Medical Research,* published by Longman Group Ltd., London (previously published by Oliver and Boyd, Edinburgh), and by permission of the authors and publishers.

Table A.3
Standard Normal Curve Areas

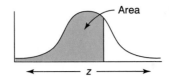

z	Area	z	Area	z	Area	z	Area
−3.00	.0013						
−2.99	.0014	−2.64	.0041	−2.29	.0110	−1.94	.0262
−2.98	.0014	−2.63	.0043	−2.28	.0113	−1.93	.0268
−2.97	.0015	−2.62	.0044	−2.27	.0116	−1.92	.0274
−2.96	.0015	−2.61	.0045	−2.26	.0119	−1.91	.0281
−2.95	.0016	−2.60	.0047	−2.25	.0122	−1.90	.0287
−2.94	.0016	−2.59	.0048	−2.24	.0125	−1.89	.0294
−2.93	.0017	−2.58	.0049	−2.23	.0129	−1.88	.0301
−2.92	.0018	−2.57	.0051	−2.22	.0132	−1.87	.0307
−2.91	.0018	−2.56	.0052	−2.21	.0136	−1.86	.0314
−2.90	.0019	−2.55	.0054	−2.20	.0139	−1.85	.0322
−2.89	.0019	−2.54	.0055	−2.19	.0143	−1.84	.0329
−2.88	.0020	−2.53	.0057	−2.18	.0146	−1.83	.0336
−2.87	.0021	−2.52	.0059	−2.17	.0150	−1.82	.0344
−2.86	.0021	−2.51	.0060	−2.16	.0154	−1.81	.0351
−2.85	.0022	−2.50	.0062	−2.15	.0158	−1.80	.0359
−2.84	.0023	−2.49	.0064	−2.14	.0162	−1.79	.0367
−2.83	.0023	−2.48	.0066	−2.13	.0166	−1.78	.0375
−2.82	.0024	−2.47	.0068	−2.12	.0170	−1.77	.0384
−2.81	.0025	−2.46	.0069	−2.11	.0174	−1.76	.0392
−2.80	.0026	−2.45	.0071	−2.10	.0179	−1.75	.0401
−2.79	.0026	−2.44	.0073	−2.09	.0183	−1.74	.0409
−2.78	.0027	−2.43	.0075	−2.08	.0188	−1.73	.0418
−2.77	.0028	−2.42	.0078	−2.07	.0192	−1.72	.0427
−2.76	.0029	−2.41	.0080	−2.06	.0197	−1.71	.0436
−2.75	.0030	−2.40	.0082	−2.05	.0202	−1.70	.0446
−2.74	.0031	−2.39	.0084	−2.04	.0207	−1.69	.0455
−2.73	.0032	−2.38	.0087	−2.03	.0212	−1.68	.0465
−2.72	.0033	−2.37	.0089	−2.02	.0217	−1.67	.0475
−2.71	.0034	−2.36	.0091	−2.01	.0222	−1.66	.0485
−2.70	.0035	−2.35	.0094	−2.00	.0228	−1.65	.0495
−2.69	.0036	−2.34	.0096	−1.99	.0233	−1.64	.0505
−2.68	.0037	−2.33	.0099	−1.98	.0239	−1.63	.0516
−2.67	.0038	−2.32	.0102	−1.97	.0244	−1.62	.0526
−2.66	.0039	−2.31	.0104	−1.96	.0250	−1.61	.0537
−2.65	.0040	−2.30	.0107	−1.95	.0256	−1.60	.0548

Table A.3

(*continued*)

z	Area	z	Area	z	Area	z	Area
−1.59	.0559	−1.19	.1170	−0.79	.2148	−0.39	.3483
−1.58	.0571	−1.18	.1190	−0.78	.2177	−0.38	.3520
−1.57	.0582	−1.17	.1210	−0.77	.2206	−0.37	.3557
−1.56	.0594	−1.16	.1230	−0.76	.2236	−0.36	.3594
−1.55	.0606	−1.15	.1251	−0.75	.2266	−0.35	.3632
−1.54	.0618	−1.14	.1271	−0.74	.2296	−0.34	.3669
−1.53	.0630	−1.13	.1292	−0.73	.2327	−0.33	.3707
−1.52	.0643	−1.12	.1314	−0.72	.2358	−0.32	.3745
−1.51	.0655	−1.11	.1335	−0.71	.2389	−0.31	.3783
−1.50	.0668	−1.10	.1357	−0.70	.2420	−0.30	.3821
−1.49	.0681	−1.09	.1379	−0.69	.2451	−0.29	.3859
−1.48	.0694	−1.08	.1401	−0.68	.2483	−0.28	.3897
−1.47	.0708	−1.07	.1423	−0.67	.2514	−0.27	.3936
−1.46	.0721	−1.06	.1446	−0.66	.2546	−0.26	.3974
−1.45	.0735	−1.05	.1469	−0.65	.2578	−0.25	.4013
−1.44	.0749	−1.04	.1492	−0.64	.2611	−0.24	.4052
−1.43	.0764	−1.03	.1515	−0.63	.2643	−0.23	.4090
−1.42	.0778	−1.02	.1539	−0.62	.2676	−0.22	.4129
−1.41	.0793	−1.01	.1562	−0.61	.2709	−0.21	.4168
−1.40	.0808	−1.00	.1587	−0.60	.2743	−0.20	.4207
−1.39	.0823	−0.99	.1611	−0.59	.2776	−0.19	.4247
−1.38	.0838	−0.98	.1635	−0.58	.2810	−0.18	.4286
−1.37	.0853	−0.97	.1660	−0.57	.2843	−0.17	.4325
−1.36	.0869	−0.96	.1685	−0.56	.2877	−0.16	.4364
−1.35	.0885	−0.95	.1711	−0.55	.2912	−0.15	.4404
−1.34	.0901	−0.94	.1736	−0.54	.2946	−0.14	.4443
−1.33	.0918	−0.93	.1762	−0.53	.2981	−0.13	.4483
−1.32	.0934	−0.92	.1788	−0.52	.3015	−0.12	.4522
−1.31	.0951	−0.91	.1814	−0.51	.3050	−0.11	.4562
−1.30	.0968	−0.90	.1841	−0.50	.3085	−0.10	.4602
−1.29	.0985	−0.89	.1867	−0.49	.3121	−0.09	.4641
−1.28	.1003	−0.88	.1894	−0.48	.3156	−0.08	.4681
−1.27	.1020	−0.87	.1922	−0.47	.3192	−0.07	.4721
−1.26	.1038	−0.86	.1949	−0.46	.3228	−0.06	.4761
−1.25	.1056	−0.85	.1977	−0.45	.3264	−0.05	.4801
−1.24	.1075	−0.84	.2005	−0.44	.3300	−0.04	.4840
−1.23	.1093	−0.83	.2033	−0.43	.3336	−0.03	.4880
−1.22	.1112	−0.82	.2061	−0.42	.3372	−0.02	.4920
−1.21	.1131	−0.81	.2090	−0.41	.3409	−0.01	.4960
−1.20	.1151	−0.80	.2119	−0.40	.3446	0.00	.5000

Table A.3
(*continued*)

z	Area	z	Area	z	Area	z	Area
0.01	.5040	0.41	.6591	0.81	.7910	1.21	.8869
0.02	.5080	0.42	.6628	0.82	.7939	1.22	.8888
0.03	.5120	0.43	.6664	0.83	.7967	1.23	.8907
0.04	.5160	0.44	.6700	0.84	.7995	1.24	.8925
0.05	.5199	0.45	.6736	0.85	.8023	1.25	.8944
0.06	.5239	0.46	.6772	0.86	.8051	1.26	.8962
0.07	.5279	0.47	.6808	0.87	.8078	1.27	.8980
0.08	.5319	0.48	.6844	0.88	.8106	1.28	.8997
0.09	.5359	0.49	.6879	0.89	.8133	1.29	.9015
0.10	.5398	0.50	.6915	0.90	.8159	1.30	.9032
0.11	.5438	0.51	.6950	0.91	.8186	1.31	.9049
0.12	.5478	0.52	.6985	0.92	.8212	1.32	.9066
0.13	.5517	0.53	.7019	0.93	.8238	1.33	.9082
0.14	.5557	0.54	.7054	0.94	.8264	1.34	.9099
0.15	.5596	0.55	.7088	0.95	.8289	1.35	.9115
0.16	.5636	0.56	.7123	0.96	.8315	1.36	.9131
0.17	.5675	0.57	.7157	0.97	.8340	1.37	.9147
0.18	.5714	0.58	.7190	0.98	.8365	1.38	.9162
0.19	.5753	0.59	.7224	0.99	.8389	1.39	.9177
0.20	.5793	0.60	.7257	1.00	.8413	1.40	.9192
0.21	.5832	0.61	.7291	1.01	.8438	1.41	.9207
0.22	.5871	0.62	.7324	1.02	.8461	1.42	.9222
0.23	.5910	0.63	.7357	1.03	.8485	1.43	.9236
0.24	.5948	0.64	.7389	1.04	.8508	1.44	.9251
0.25	.5987	0.65	.7422	1.05	.8531	1.45	.9265
0.26	.6026	0.66	.7454	1.06	.8554	1.46	.9279
0.27	.6064	0.67	.7486	1.07	.8577	1.47	.9292
0.28	.6103	0.68	.7517	1.08	.8599	1.48	.9306
0.29	.6141	0.69	.7549	1.09	.8621	1.49	.9319
0.30	.6179	0.70	.7580	1.10	.8643	1.50	.9332
0.31	.6217	0.71	.7611	1.11	.8665	1.51	.9345
0.32	.6255	0.72	.7642	1.12	.8686	1.52	.9357
0.33	.6293	0.73	.7673	1.13	.8708	1.53	.9370
0.34	.6331	0.74	.7704	1.14	.8729	1.54	.9382
0.35	.6368	0.75	.7734	1.15	.8749	1.55	.9394
0.36	.6406	0.76	.7764	1.16	.8770	1.56	.9406
0.37	.6443	0.77	.7794	1.17	.8790	1.57	.9418
0.38	.6480	0.78	.7823	1.18	.8810	1.58	.9429
0.39	.6517	0.79	.7852	1.19	.8830	1.59	.9441
0.40	.6554	0.80	.7881	1.20	.8849	1.60	.9452

Table A.3
(*continued*)

z	Area	z	Area	z	Area	z	Area
1.61	.9463	1.96	.9750	2.31	.9896	2.66	.9961
1.62	.9474	1.97	.9756	2.32	.9898	2.67	.9962
1.63	.9484	1.98	.9761	2.33	.9901	2.68	.9963
1.64	.9495	1.99	.9767	2.34	.9904	2.69	.9964
1.65	.9505	2.00	.9772	2.35	.9906	2.70	.9965
1.66	.9515	2.01	.9778	2.36	.9909	2.71	.9966
1.67	.9525	2.02	.9783	2.37	.9911	2.72	.9967
1.68	.9535	2.03	.9788	2.38	.9913	2.73	.9968
1.69	.9545	2.04	.9793	2.39	.9916	2.74	.9969
1.70	.9554	2.05	.9798	2.40	.9918	2.75	.9970
1.71	.9564	2.06	.9803	2.41	.9920	2.76	.9971
1.72	.9573	2.07	.9808	2.42	.9922	2.77	.9972
1.73	.9582	2.08	.9812	2.43	.9925	2.78	.9973
1.74	.9591	2.09	.9817	2.44	.9927	2.79	.9974
1.75	.9599	2.10	.9821	2.45	.9929	2.80	.9974
1.76	.9608	2.11	.9826	2.46	.9931	2.81	.9975
1.77	.9616	2.12	.9830	2.47	.9932	2.82	.9976
1.78	.9625	2.13	.9834	2.48	.9934	2.83	.9977
1.79	.9633	2.14	.9838	2.49	.9936	2.84	.9977
1.80	.9641	2.15	.9842	2.50	.9938	2.85	.9978
1.81	.9649	2.16	.9846	2.51	.9940	2.86	.9979
1.82	.9656	2.17	.9850	2.52	.9941	2.87	.9979
1.83	.9664	2.18	.9854	2.53	.9943	2.88	.9980
1.84	.9671	2.19	.9857	2.54	.9945	2.89	.9981
1.85	.9678	2.20	.9861	2.55	.9946	2.90	.9981
1.86	.9686	2.21	.9864	2.56	.9948	2.91	.9982
1.87	.9693	2.22	.9868	2.57	.9949	2.92	.9982
1.88	.9699	2.23	.9871	2.58	.9951	2.93	.9983
1.89	.9706	2.24	.9875	2.59	.9952	2.94	.9984
1.90	.9713	2.25	.9878	2.60	.9953	2.95	.9984
1.91	.9719	2.26	.9881	2.61	.9955	2.96	.9985
1.92	.9726	2.27	.9884	2.62	.9956	2.97	.9985
1.93	.9732	2.28	.9887	2.63	.9957	2.98	.9986
1.94	.9738	2.29	.9890	2.64	.9959	2.99	.9986
1.95	.9744	2.30	.9893	2.65	.9960	3.00	.9987

Table A.4

Distribution of t

| | | | *p* | |
df	.10	.05	.01	.001
1	6.314	12.706	63.657	636.619
2	2.920	4.303	9.925	31.598
3	2.353	3.182	5.841	12.924
4	2.132	2.776	4.604	8.610
5	2.015	2.571	4.032	6.869
6	1.943	2.447	3.707	5.959
7	1.895	2.365	3.499	5.408
8	1.860	2.306	3.355	5.041
9	1.833	2.262	3.250	4.781
10	1.812	2.228	3.169	4.587
11	1.796	2.201	3.106	4.437
12	1.782	2.179	3.055	4.318
13	1.771	2.160	3.012	4.221
14	1.761	2.145	2.977	4.140
15	1.753	2.131	2.947	4.073
16	1.746	2.120	2.921	4.015
17	1.740	2.110	2.898	3.965
18	1.734	2.101	2.878	3.922
19	1.729	2.093	2.861	3.883
20	1.725	2.086	2.845	3.850
21	1.721	2.080	2.831	3.819
22	1.717	2.074	2.819	3.792
23	1.714	2.069	2.807	3.767
24	1.711	2.064	2.797	3.745
25	1.708	2.060	2.787	3.725
26	1.706	2.056	2.779	3.707
27	1.703	2.052	2.771	3.690
28	1.701	2.048	2.763	3.674
29	1.699	2.045	2.756	3.659
30	1.697	2.042	2.750	3.646
40	1.684	2.021	2.704	3.551
60	1.671	2.000	2.660	3.460
120	1.658	1.980	2.617	3.373
∞	1.645	1.960	2.576	3.291

Table A.4 is taken from Table III of Fisher and Yates: *Statistical Tables for Biological, Agricultural and Medical Research,* published by Longman Group Ltd., London (previously published by Oliver and Boyd, Edinburgh), and by permission of the authors and publishers.

Table A.5

Distribution of F

<table>
<tr><td colspan="7" style="text-align:center">p = .10</td></tr>
<tr><td></td><td colspan="6" style="text-align:center">n_1^*</td></tr>
<tr><td>n_2^{**}</td><td>1</td><td>2</td><td>3</td><td>4</td><td>5</td><td>6</td></tr>
<tr><td>4</td><td>4.54</td><td>4.32</td><td>4.19</td><td>4.11</td><td>4.05</td><td>4.01</td></tr>
<tr><td>5</td><td>4.06</td><td>3.78</td><td>3.62</td><td>3.52</td><td>3.45</td><td>3.40</td></tr>
<tr><td>6</td><td>3.78</td><td>3.46</td><td>3.29</td><td>3.18</td><td>3.11</td><td>3.05</td></tr>
<tr><td>7</td><td>3.59</td><td>3.26</td><td>3.07</td><td>2.96</td><td>2.88</td><td>2.83</td></tr>
<tr><td>8</td><td>3.46</td><td>3.11</td><td>2.92</td><td>2.81</td><td>2.73</td><td>2.67</td></tr>
<tr><td>9</td><td>3.36</td><td>3.01</td><td>2.81</td><td>2.69</td><td>2.61</td><td>2.55</td></tr>
<tr><td>10</td><td>3.28</td><td>2.92</td><td>2.73</td><td>2.61</td><td>2.52</td><td>2.46</td></tr>
<tr><td>11</td><td>3.23</td><td>2.86</td><td>2.66</td><td>2.54</td><td>2.45</td><td>2.39</td></tr>
<tr><td>12</td><td>3.18</td><td>2.81</td><td>2.61</td><td>2.48</td><td>2.39</td><td>2.33</td></tr>
<tr><td>13</td><td>3.14</td><td>2.76</td><td>2.56</td><td>2.43</td><td>2.35</td><td>2.28</td></tr>
<tr><td>14</td><td>3.10</td><td>2.73</td><td>2.52</td><td>2.39</td><td>2.31</td><td>2.24</td></tr>
<tr><td>15</td><td>3.07</td><td>2.70</td><td>2.49</td><td>2.36</td><td>2.27</td><td>2.21</td></tr>
<tr><td>16</td><td>3.05</td><td>2.67</td><td>2.46</td><td>2.33</td><td>2.24</td><td>2.18</td></tr>
<tr><td>17</td><td>3.03</td><td>2.64</td><td>2.44</td><td>2.31</td><td>2.22</td><td>2.15</td></tr>
<tr><td>18</td><td>3.01</td><td>2.62</td><td>2.42</td><td>2.29</td><td>2.20</td><td>2.13</td></tr>
<tr><td>19</td><td>2.99</td><td>2.61</td><td>2.40</td><td>2.27</td><td>2.18</td><td>2.11</td></tr>
<tr><td>20</td><td>2.97</td><td>2.59</td><td>2.38</td><td>2.25</td><td>2.16</td><td>2.09</td></tr>
<tr><td>21</td><td>2.96</td><td>2.57</td><td>2.36</td><td>2.23</td><td>2.14</td><td>2.08</td></tr>
<tr><td>22</td><td>2.95</td><td>2.56</td><td>2.35</td><td>2.22</td><td>2.13</td><td>2.06</td></tr>
<tr><td>23</td><td>2.94</td><td>2.55</td><td>2.34</td><td>2.21</td><td>2.11</td><td>2.05</td></tr>
<tr><td>24</td><td>2.93</td><td>2.54</td><td>2.33</td><td>2.19</td><td>2.10</td><td>2.04</td></tr>
<tr><td>25</td><td>2.92</td><td>2.53</td><td>2.32</td><td>2.18</td><td>2.09</td><td>2.02</td></tr>
<tr><td>26</td><td>2.91</td><td>2.52</td><td>2.31</td><td>2.17</td><td>2.08</td><td>2.01</td></tr>
<tr><td>27</td><td>2.90</td><td>2.51</td><td>2.30</td><td>2.17</td><td>2.07</td><td>2.00</td></tr>
<tr><td>28</td><td>2.89</td><td>2.50</td><td>2.29</td><td>2.16</td><td>2.06</td><td>2.00</td></tr>
<tr><td>29</td><td>2.89</td><td>2.50</td><td>2.28</td><td>2.15</td><td>2.06</td><td>1.99</td></tr>
<tr><td>30</td><td>2.88</td><td>2.49</td><td>2.28</td><td>2.14</td><td>2.05</td><td>1.98</td></tr>
<tr><td>40</td><td>2.84</td><td>2.44</td><td>2.23</td><td>2.09</td><td>2.00</td><td>1.93</td></tr>
<tr><td>60</td><td>2.79</td><td>2.39</td><td>2.18</td><td>2.04</td><td>1.95</td><td>1.87</td></tr>
<tr><td>120</td><td>2.75</td><td>2.35</td><td>2.13</td><td>1.99</td><td>1.90</td><td>1.82</td></tr>
<tr><td>∞</td><td>2.71</td><td>2.30</td><td>2.08</td><td>1.94</td><td>1.85</td><td>1.77</td></tr>
</table>

$^*n_1$ = degrees of freedom for the mean square between
$^{**}n_2$ = degrees of freedom for the mean square within

Table A.5 is taken from Table V of Fisher and Yates: *Statistical Tables for Biological, Agricultural and Medical Research,* published by Longman Group Ltd., London (previously published by Oliver and Boyd, Edinburgh), and by permission of the authors and publishers.

Table A.5
(*continued*)

$p = .05$

	n_1*					
n_2**	1	2	3	4	5	6
4	7.71	6.94	6.59	6.39	6.26	6.16
5	6.61	5.79	5.41	5.19	5.05	4.95
6	5.99	5.14	4.76	4.53	4.39	4.28
7	5.59	4.74	4.35	4.12	3.97	3.87
8	5.32	4.46	4.07	3.84	3.69	3.58
9	5.12	4.26	3.86	3.63	3.48	3.37
10	4.96	4.10	3.71	3.48	3.33	3.22
11	4.84	3.98	3.59	3.36	3.20	3.09
12	4.75	3.88	3.49	3.26	3.11	3.00
13	4.67	3.80	3.41	3.18	3.02	2.92
14	4.60	3.74	3.34	3.11	2.96	2.85
15	4.54	3.68	3.29	3.06	2.90	2.79
16	4.49	3.63	3.24	3.01	2.85	2.74
17	4.45	3.59	3.20	2.96	2.81	2.70
18	4.41	3.55	3.16	2.93	2.77	2.66
19	4.38	3.52	3.13	2.90	2.74	2.63
20	4.35	3.49	3.10	2.87	2.71	2.60
21	4.32	3.47	3.07	2.84	2.68	2.57
22	4.30	3.44	3.05	2.82	2.66	2.55
23	4.28	3.42	3.03	2.80	2.64	2.53
24	4.26	3.40	3.01	2.78	2.62	2.51
25	4.24	3.38	2.99	2.76	2.60	2.49
26	4.22	3.37	2.98	2.74	2.59	2.47
27	4.21	3.35	2.96	2.73	2.57	2.46
28	4.20	3.34	2.95	2.71	2.56	2.44
29	4.18	3.33	2.93	2.70	2.54	2.43
30	4.17	3.32	2.92	2.69	2.53	2.42
40	4.08	3.23	2.84	2.61	2.45	2.34
60	4.00	3.15	2.76	2.52	2.37	2.25
120	3.92	3.07	2.68	2.45	2.29	2.17
∞	3.84	2.99	2.60	2.37	2.21	2.10

*n_1 = degrees of freedom for the mean square between
**n_2 = degrees of freedom for the mean square within

Table A.5
(*continued*)

$p = .01$

	n_1^*					
n_2^{**}	1	2	3	4	5	6
4	21.20	18.00	16.69	15.98	15.52	15.21
5	16.26	13.27	12.06	11.39	10.97	10.67
6	13.74	10.92	9.78	9.15	8.75	8.47
7	12.25	9.55	8.45	7.85	7.46	7.19
8	11.26	8.65	7.59	7.01	6.63	6.37
9	10.56	8.02	6.99	6.42	6.06	5.80
10	10.04	7.56	6.55	5.99	5.64	5.39
11	9.65	7.20	6.22	5.67	5.32	5.07
12	9.33	6.93	5.95	5.41	5.06	4.82
13	9.07	6.70	5.74	5.20	4.86	4.62
14	8.86	6.51	5.56	5.03	4.69	4.46
15	8.68	6.36	5.42	4.89	4.56	4.32
16	8.53	6.23	5.29	4.77	4.44	4.20
17	8.40	6.11	5.18	4.67	4.34	4.10
18	8.28	6.01	5.09	4.58	4.25	4.01
19	8.18	5.93	5.01	4.50	4.17	3.94
20	8.10	5.85	4.94	4.43	4.10	3.87
21	8.02	5.78	4.87	4.37	4.04	3.81
22	7.94	5.72	4.82	4.31	3.99	3.76
23	7.88	5.66	4.76	4.26	3.94	3.71
24	7.82	5.61	4.72	4.22	3.90	3.67
25	7.77	5.57	4.68	4.18	3.86	3.63
26	7.72	5.53	4.64	4.14	3.82	3.59
27	7.68	5.49	4.60	4.11	3.78	3.56
28	7.64	5.45	4.57	4.07	3.75	3.53
29	7.60	5.42	4.54	4.04	3.73	3.50
30	7.56	5.39	4.51	4.02	3.70	3.47
40	7.31	5.18	4.31	3.83	3.51	3.29
60	7.08	4.98	4.13	3.65	3.34	3.12
120	6.85	4.79	3.95	3.48	3.17	2.96
∞	6.64	4.60	3.78	3.32	3.02	2.80

$^*n_1$ = degrees of freedom for the mean square between
$^{**}n_2$ = degrees of freedom for the mean square within

Table A.5

(*continued*)

p = .001

n_2**	n_1* 1	2	3	4	5	6
4	74.14	61.25	56.18	53.44	51.71	50.53
5	47.18	37.12	33.20	31.09	29.75	28.84
6	35.51	27.00	23.70	21.92	20.81	20.03
7	29.25	21.69	18.77	17.19	16.21	15.52
8	25.42	18.49	15.83	14.39	13.49	12.86
9	22.86	16.39	13.90	12.56	11.71	11.13
10	21.04	14.91	12.55	11.28	10.48	9.92
11	19.69	13.81	11.56	10.35	9.58	9.05
12	18.64	12.97	10.80	9.63	8.89	8.38
13	17.81	12.31	10.21	9.07	8.35	7.86
14	17.14	11.78	9.73	8.62	7.92	7.43
15	16.59	11.34	9.34	8.25	7.57	7.09
16	16.12	10.97	9.00	7.94	7.27	6.81
17	15.72	10.66	8.73	7.68	7.02	6.56
18	15.38	10.39	8.49	7.46	6.81	6.35
19	15.08	10.16	8.28	7.26	6.62	6.18
20	14.82	9.95	8.10	7.10	6.46	6.02
21	14.59	9.77	7.94	6.95	6.32	5.88
22	14.38	9.61	7.80	6.81	6.19	5.76
23	14.19	9.47	7.67	6.69	6.08	5.65
24	14.03	9.34	7.55	6.59	5.98	5.55
25	13.88	9.22	7.45	6.49	5.88	5.46
26	13.74	9.12	7.36	6.41	5.80	5.38
27	13.61	9.02	7.27	6.33	5.73	5.31
28	13.50	8.93	7.19	6.25	5.66	5.24
29	13.39	8.85	7.12	6.19	5.59	5.18
30	13.29	8.77	7.05	6.12	5.53	5.12
40	12.61	8.25	6.60	5.70	5.13	4.73
60	11.97	7.76	6.17	5.31	4.76	4.37
120	11.38	7.32	5.79	4.95	4.42	4.04
∞	10.83	6.91	5.42	4.62	4.10	3.74

*n_1 = degrees of freedom for the mean square between
**n_2 = degrees of freedom for the mean square within

Tabel A.6
Distribution of X^2

df	.10	.05	.01	.001
		p		
1	2.706	3.841	6.635	10.827
2	4.605	5.991	9.210	13.815
3	6.251	7.815	11.345	16.266
4	7.779	9.488	13.277	18.467
5	9.236	11.070	15.086	20.515
6	10.645	12.592	16.812	22.457
7	12.017	14.067	18.475	24.322
8	13.362	15.507	20.090	26.125
9	14.684	16.919	21.666	27.877
10	15.987	18.307	23.209	29.588
11	17.275	19.675	24.725	31.264
12	18.549	21.026	26.217	32.909
13	19.812	22.362	27.688	34.528
14	21.064	23.685	29.141	36.123
15	22.307	24.996	30.578	37.697
16	23.542	26.296	32.000	39.252
17	24.769	27.587	33.409	40.790
18	25.989	28.869	34.805	42.312
19	27.204	30.144	36.191	43.820
20	28.412	31.410	37.566	45.315
21	29.615	32.671	38.932	46.797
22	30.813	33.924	40.289	48.268
23	32.007	35.172	41.638	49.728
24	33.196	36.415	42.980	51.179
25	34.382	37.652	44.314	52.620
26	35.563	38.885	45.642	54.052
27	36.741	40.113	46.963	55.476
28	37.916	41.337	48.278	56.893
29	39.087	42.557	49.588	58.302
30	40.256	43.773	50.892	59.703
32	42.585	46.194	53.486	62.487
34	44.903	48.602	56.061	65.247
36	47.212	50.999	58.619	67.985
38	49.513	53.384	61.162	70.703
40	51.805	55.759	63.691	73.402
42	54.090	58.124	66.206	76.084
44	56.369	60.481	68.710	78.750
46	58.641	62.830	71.201	81.400
48	60.907	65.171	73.683	84.037
50	63.167	67.505	76.154	86.661

Table A.6 is taken from Table IV of Fisher and Yates: *Statistical Tables for Biological, Agricultural and Medical Research,* published by Longman Group Ltd., London (previously published by Oliver and Boyd, Edinburgh), and by permission of the authors and publishers.

Glossary of Research-Related Terms

A-B design A single-subject design in which baseline measurements are repeatedly made until stability is presumably established, treatment is introduced, and an appropriate number of measurements are made during treatment.

A-B-A design A single-subject design in which baseline measurements are repeatedly made until stability is presumably established, treatment is introduced, and an appropriate number of measurements are made, and the treatment phase is followed by a second baseline phase.

A-B-A-B design A single-subject design in which baseline measurements are repeatedly made until stability is presumably established, treatment is introduced, and an appropriate number of measurements are made, and the treatment phase is followed by a second baseline phase, which is followed by a second treatment phase.

abstract A summary of a study, which appears at the beginning of the report and describes the most important aspects of the study, including major results and conclusions.

accessible population Refers to the population from which the researcher can realistically select subjects.

accidental sampling *See* convenience sampling.

achievement test An instrument that measures the current status of individuals with respect to proficiency in given areas of knowledge or skill.

additive designs Refers to variations of the A-B design which involve the addition of another phase or phases in which the experimental treatment is supplemented with another treatment.

alternating treatments design A variation of a multiple-baseline design which involves the relatively rapid alternation of treatments for a single subject.

analysis of covariance A statistical method of equating groups on one or more variables and for increasing the power of a statistical test; adjusts scores on a dependent variable for initial differences on some variable such as pretest performance or IQ.

applied research Research conducted for the purpose of applying, or testing, theory and evaluating its usefulness in solving problems.

aptitude test A measure of potential used to predict how well someone is likely to perform in a future situation.

artificial categories Categories which are operationally defined by the researcher.

assumption Any important "fact" presumed to be true but not actually verified; assumptions should be described in the procedures section of a research plan or report.

attenuation Refers to the principle that correlation coefficients tend to be lowered because less-than-perfectly reliable measures are used.

basic research Research conducted for the purpose of theory development or refinement.

case study The in-depth investigation of one "unit," e.g., individual, group, institution, organization, program or document.

causal-comparative research Research that attempts to determine the cause, or reason, for existing differences in the behavior or status of groups of individuals; also referred to as ex post facto research.

census survey Descriptive research that attempts to acquire data from each and every member of a population.

changing criterion design A variation of the A-B-A design in which the baseline phase is followed by successive treatment phases, each of which has a more stringent criterion for acceptable behavior level.

chi square A nonparametric test of significance appropriate when the data are in the form of frequency counts; it compares proportions actually observed in a study with proportions expected to see if they are significantly different.

clinical replication Refers to the development and application of a treatment package, composed of two or more interventions which have been found to be effective individually, designed for persons with complex behavior disorders.

cluster sampling Sampling in which intact groups, not individuals, are randomly selected.

coefficient alpha (α) *See* Cronbach's alpha.

common variance The variation in one variable that is attributable to its tendency to vary with another variable.

concurrent validity The degree to which the scores on a test are related to the scores on another, already established test administered at the same time, or to some other valid criterion available at the same time.

construct validity The degree to which a test measures an intended hypothetical construct, or nonobservable trait, which explains behavior.

contamination The situation that exists when the researcher's familiarity with the subjects affects the outcome of the study.

content analysis The systematic, quantitative description of the composition of the object of the study.

content validity The degree to which a test measures an intended content area; it is determined by expert judgment and requires both item validity and sampling validity.

control Efforts on the part of the researcher to remove the influence of any variable other than the independent variable that might affect performance on a dependent variable.

control group The group in a research study that either receives a different treatment than the experimental group or is treated as usual.

control variable A nonmanipulated variable, usually a physical or mental characteristic of the subjects (such as IQ).

convenience sampling The process of using as the sample whoever happens to be available, e.g., volunteers. (Also referred to as accidental sampling and haphazard sampling.)

correlational research Research that involves collecting data in order to determine whether, and to what degree, a relationship exists between two or more quantifiable variables.

correlation coefficient A decimal number between .00 and ± 1.00 that indicates the degree to which two variables are related.

counterbalanced design A quasi-experimental design in which all groups receive all treatments, each group receives the treatments in a different order, the number of groups equals the number of treatments, and all groups are posttested after each treatment.

criterion In a prediction study, the variable that is predicted.

criterion-related validity Validity which is determined by relating performance on a test to performance on another criterion; includes concurrent and predictive validity.

Cronbach's alpha (α) The general formula for estimating internal consistency based on a determination of how all items on a test relate to all other items and to the total test. (Also referred to as coefficient alpha and Cronbach's coefficient alpha.)

cross-validation Validation of a prediction equation with at least one group other than the group on which it was based; variables that are no longer found to be related to the criterion measure are removed from the equation.

curvilinear relationship A relationship in which increase in one variable is associated with a corresponding increase in another variable to a point, at which point further increase in the first variable is associated with a corresponding decrease in the other variable (or vice versa).

deductive hypothesis A hypothesis derived from theory which provides evidence which supports, expands, or contradicts the theory.

dependent variable The change or difference in behavior that occurs as a result of the independent variable; also referred to as the criterion variable, the effect, the outcome, or the posttest.

descriptive statistics Data analysis techniques enabling the researcher to meaningfully describe many scores with a small number of numerical indices.

developmental studies Studies concerned with behavior variables that differentiate children at different levels of age, growth, or maturation.

diagnostic test A type of achievement test yielding multiple scores for each area of achievement measured that facilitate identification of specific areas of deficiency.

differential selection of subjects Refers to the fact that groups may be different before a study even begins, and this initial difference may at least partially account for posttest differences.

direct replication Refers to the replication of a study by the same investigator, with the same subjects or with different subjects, in a specific setting.

ecological validity The degree to which results can be generalized to environments outside of the experimental setting.

educational research The formal, systematic application of the scientific method to the study of educational problems.

environmental variable A variable in the setting in which a study is conducted that might cause unwanted differences between groups (e.g., learning materials).

equivalent forms Two tests identical in every way except for the actual items included.

equivalent-forms reliability Indicates score variation that occurs from form to form of a test; also referred to as alternate-forms reliability.

ethnographic research *See* qualitative research.

evaluation The systematic process of collecting and analyzing data in order to make decisions.

experimental group The group in a research study that typically receives a new, or novel, treatment, a treatment under investigation.

experimental research Research in which at least one independent variable is manipulated, other relevant variables are controlled, and the effect on one or more dependent variables is observed.

experimenter bias A situation in which the researcher's expectations concerning the outcomes of the study actually contribute to producing various outcomes.

ex post facto research *See* causal-comparative research.

external criticism The scientific analysis of data to determine their authenticity.

external validity The degree to which results are generalizable, or applicable, to groups and environments outside of the experimental setting.

factorial analysis of variance The appropriate statistical analysis if a study is based on a factorial design and investigates two or more independent variables and the interactions between them; yields a separate *F* ratio for each independent variable and one for each interaction.

factorial design An experimental design that involves two or more dependent variables (at least one of which is manipulated) in order to study the effects of the variables individually and in interaction with each other.

fieldwork A qualitative research strategy that involves spending considerable time in the setting under study, immersing oneself in this setting, and collecting as much relevant information as possible as unobtrusively as possible.

follow-up study A study conducted to determine the status of a group of interest after some period of time.

generosity error The tendency to give an individual the benefit of the doubt whenever there is insufficient knowledge to make an objective judgment.

grounded theory Theory based on data collected in real-world settings which reflect what naturally occurred over an extended period of time.

halo effect The phenomenon whereby initial impressions concerning an individual (positive or negative) affect subsequent measurements.

haphazard sampling *See* convenience sampling.

hardcopy Refers to computer output that is printed out on paper.

hardware Refers to the actual equipment, the computer itself and related accessories such as printers.

Hawthorne effect A type of reactive arrangement resulting from the subjects' knowledge that they are involved in an experiment, or their feeling that they are in some way receiving "special" attention.

historical research The systematic collection and evaluation of data related to past occurrences in order to describe causes, effects, or trends of those events which may help to explain present events and anticipate future events.

history Any event which is not part of the experimental treatment but which may affect performance on the dependent variable.

hypothesis A tentative, reasonable, testable explanation for the occurrence of certain behaviors, phenomena, or events.

independent variable An activity or characteristic believed to make a difference with respect to some behavior; also referred to as the experimental variable, the cause, and the treatment.

inductive hypothesis A generalization based on observation.

inferential statistics Data analysis techniques for determining how likely it is that results based on a sample or samples are the same results that would have been obtained for an entire population.

instrumentation Unreliability in measuring instruments that may result in invalid assessment of subjects' performance.

interaction Refers to the situation in which different values of the independent variable are differentially effective depending upon the level of the control variable.

interjudge reliability The consistency of two (or more) independent scorers, raters, or observers.

internal criticism The scientific analysis of data to determine their accuracy which takes into consideration the knowledge and competence of the author, the time delay between the occurrence and recording of events, biased motives of the author, and consistency of the data.

internal validity The degree to which observed differences on the dependent variable are a direct result of manipulation of the independent variable, not some other variable.

interval scale A measurement scale that classifies and ranks subjects, is based upon predetermined equal intervals, but does not have a true zero point.

intervening variable A variable which intervenes between, or alters the relationship between, an independent variable and a dependent variable, which cannot be directly observed or controlled (e.g., anxiety) but which can be controlled for.

intrajudge reliability The consistency of the scoring, rating, or observing of an individual.

item validity The degree to which test items represent measurement in the intended content area.

John Henry effect The phenomenon whereby if for any reason members of a control group feel threatened or challenged by being in competition with an experimental group, they may outdo themselves and perform way beyond what would normally be expected.

judgment sampling The process of selecting a sample which is *believed* to be representative of a given population. (Also referred to as purposive sampling.)

Likert scale An instrument that asks an individual to respond to a series of statements by indicating whether she or he strongly agrees (SA), agrees (A), is undecided (U), disagrees (D), or strongly disagrees (SD) with each statement.

limitation An aspect of a study which the researcher knows may negatively affect the results or generalizability of the results, but over which he or she has no control.

linear relationship The situation in which an increase (or decrease) in one variable is associated with a corresponding increase (or decrease) in another variable.

logical validity Validity which is determined primarily through judgment; includes content validity.

matching A technique for equating groups on one or more variables, resulting in

each member of one group having a direct counterpart in another group.

maturation Physical or mental changes which occur within subjects over a period of time and which may affect their performance on a measure of the dependent variable.

mean The arithmetic average of a set of scores.

measures of central tendency Indices representing the average or typical score attained by a group of subjects.

measures of variability Indices indicating how spread out the scores are in a distribution.

median That point in a distribution above and below which are 50% of the scores.

menu-driven Refers to computer programs which allow the user to select desired analyses from a list, or menu, of options.

meta-analysis A statistical approach to summarizing the results of many studies which have investigated basically the same problem.

mode The score that is attained by more subjects in a group than any other score.

modem A device which permits telephone communication between two computers by converting computer language to audiotones.

mortality Refers to the fact that subjects who drop out of a study may share a characteristic such that their absence has a significant effect on the results of the study.

multiple-baseline design A single-subject design in which baseline data are collected on several behaviors for one subject or one behavior for several subjects and treatment is applied systematically over a period of time to each behavior (or each subject) one at a time until all behaviors (or subjects) are under treatment.

multiple comparisons Procedures used following application of analysis of variance to determine which means are significantly different from which other means.

multiple regression equation A prediction equation using two or more variables that individually predict a criterion to make a more accurate prediction.

multiple time-series design A variation of the time-series design that involves the addition of a control group to the basic design.

multiple-treatment interference Refers to the carry-over effects from an earlier treatment that make it difficult to assess the effectiveness of a later treatment.

naturalistic observation Observation in which the observer purposely controls or manipulates nothing, and in fact works very hard at not affecting the observed situation in any way.

negatively skewed distribution A distribution in which there are more extreme scores at the lower end than at the upper, or higher, end.

nominal scale The lowest level of measurement which classifies persons or objects into two or more categories; a person can only be in one category, and members of a category have a common set of characteristics.

nonequivalent control group design A quasi-experimental design involving at least two groups, both of which are pretested; one group receives the experimental treatment, and both groups are posttested.

nonparametric test A test of significance appropriate when the data represent an ordinal or nominal scale, when a parametric assumption has been greatly violated, or when the nature of the distribution is not known.

nonparticipant observation Observation in which the observer is not directly involved in the situation to be observed, i.e., the observer does not intentionally interact with or affect the object of the observation.

nonprobability sampling The process of selecting a sample using a technique which *does not* permit the researcher to specify the probability, or chance, that each member of a population has of being selected for the sample.

novelty effect A type of reactive arrangement resulting from increased interest, motivation, or participation on the part of subjects simply because they are doing something different.

null hypothesis States that there is no relationship (or difference) between variables and that any relationship found will be a chance relationship, the result of sampling error, not a true one.

observational research Descriptive research in which the desired data is obtained not by asking individuals for it but through such means as direct observation.

observer bias The phenomenon whereby an observer does not observe objectively and accurately, thus producing invalid observations.

observer effects The phenomenon whereby persons being observed behave atypically simply because they are being observed, thus producing invalid observations.

one-group pretest-posttest design A pre-experimental design involving one group which is pretested, exposed to a treatment, and posttested.

one-shot case study A pre-experimental design involving one group which is exposed to a treatment and then posttested.

operational definition One which defines concepts in terms of processes, or operations.

ordinal scale A measurement scale that classifies subjects and ranks them in terms of the degree to which they possess a characteristic of interest.

organismic variable A characteristic of a subject, or organism (e.g., sex), which cannot be directly controlled but which can be controlled for.

parameter A numerical index describing the behavior of a population.

parametric test A test of significance appropriate when the data represent an interval or ratio scale of measurement and other assumptions have been met.

participant observation Observation in which the observer actually becomes a part of, a participant in, the situation to be observed.

Pearson *r* A measure of correlation appropriate when the data represent either interval or ratio scales; it takes into account each and every score and produces a coefficient between .00 and ±1.00.

percentile rank A measure of relative position indicating the percentage of scores that fall at or below a given score.

pilot study A small-scale study conducted prior to the conducting of the actual study; the entire study is conducted, every procedure is followed, and the resulting data are analyzed——all according to the research plan.

placebo effect Refers to the discovery in medical research that any "medication" could make subjects feel better, even sugar and water.

population The group to which the researcher would like the results of a study to be generalizable.

positively skewed distribution A distribution in which there are more extreme scores at the upper, or higher, end than at the lower end.

posttest-only control group design A true experimental design involving at least two randomly formed groups; one group receives a new, or unusual, treatment and both groups are posttested.

prediction study An attempt to determine which of a number of variables are most highly related to a criterion variable, a complex variable to be predicted.

predictive validity The degree to which a test is able to predict how well an individual will do in a future situation.

predictor In a prediction study, the variable upon which the prediction is based.

pretest-postest control group design A true experimental design which involves at least two randomly formed groups; both groups are pretested, one group

receives a new, or unusual treatment, and both groups are posttested.

pretest sensitization *See* testing.

pretest-treatment interaction Refers to the fact that subjects may respond or react differently to a treatment because they have been pretested.

primary source Firsthand information such as the testimony of an eyewitness, an original document, a relic, or a description of a study written by the person who conducted it.

probability sampling The process of selecting a sample using a sampling technique which permits the researcher to specify the probability, or chance, that each member of a defined population has of being selected for the sample.

problem statement A statement which indicates the variables of interest to the researcher and the specific relationship between those variables which is to be, or was, investigated.

prospective causal-comparative research A variation of the basic approach to causal-comparative research which involves starting with the causes and investigating effects.

purposive sampling *See* judgment sampling.

qualitative approach The collection of extensive narrative data in order to gain insights into phenomena of interest.

qualitative research The collection of extensive narrative data on many variables over an extended period of time, in a naturalistic setting, in order to gain insights not possible using other types of research.

quantitative research The collection of numerical data in order to explain, predict and/or control phenomena of interest.

quartile deviation One-half of the difference between the upper quartile (the 75th percentile) and the lower quartile (the 25th percentile) in a distribution.

quota sampling The process of selecting a sample based on required, exact numbers, or quotas, of persons of varying characteristics.

random sampling The process of selecting a sample in such a way that all individuals in the defined population have an equal and independent chance of being selected for the sample.

range The difference between the highest and lowest score in a distribution.

rationale equivalence reliability An estimate of internal consistency based on a determination of how all items on a test relate to all other items and to the total test.

ratio scale The highest level of measurement that classifies subjects, ranks subjects, is based upon predetermined equal intervals, and has a true zero point.

reactive arrangements Threats to the external validity of a study associated with the way in which a study is conducted and the feelings and attitudes of the subjects involved.

readiness test A test administered prior to instruction or training in a specific area in order to determine whether and to what degree a student is ready for, or will profit from, instruction.

relationship study An attempt to gain insight into the variables, or factors, that are related to a complex variable such as academic achievement, motivation, and self-concept.

reliability The degree to which a test consistently measures whatever it measures.

replication Refers to when a study is done again; the second study may be a repetition of the original study, using different subjects, or it may represent an alternative approach to testing the same hypothesis.

research The formal, systematic application of the scientific method to the study of problems.

research hypothesis A statement of the expected relationship (or difference) between two variables.

research plan A detailed description of a proposed study designed to investigate a given problem.

response set The tendency of an observer to rate the majority of observees the same regardless of the observees' actual behavior.

retrospective causal-comparative research The basic approach to causal-comparative research which involves starting with effects and investigating causes.

review of literature The systematic identification, location, and analysis of documents containing information related to a research problem.

sample A number of individuals selected from a population for a study, preferably in such a way that they represent the larger group from which they were selected.

sample survey Research in which information about a population is inferred based on the responses of a sample selected from that population.

sampling The process of selecting a number of individuals (a sample) from a population, preferably in such a way that the individuals selected represent the larger group from which they were selected.

sampling bias Systematic sampling error; two major sources of sampling bias are the use of volunteers and the use of available groups.

sampling error Expected, chance variation in variables that occurs when a sample is selected from a population.

sampling validity The degree to which a test samples the total intended content area.

Scheffé test A conservative multiple comparison technique appropriate for making any and all possible comparisons involving a set of means.

secondary source Secondhand information, such as a brief description of a study written by someone other than the person who conducted it.

selection-maturation interaction Refers to the fact that if already formed groups are used in a study, one group may profit more (or less) from treatment or have an initial advantage (or disadvantage) because of maturation factors; selection may also interact with factors such as history and testing.

selection-treatment interaction Refers to the fact that if nonrepresentative groups are used in a study the results of the study may hold only for the groups involved and may not be representative of the treatment effect in the population.

self-report research Descriptive research in which information is solicited from individuals using, for example, questionnaires or interviews.

semantic differential scale An instrument that asks an individual to give a quantitative rating to the subject of the attitude scale on a number of bipolar adjectives such as good-bad, friendly-unfriendly, positive-negative.

shrinkage Refers to the tendency of a prediction equation to become less accurate when used with a different group, a group other than the one on which the equation was originally formulated.

simple analysis of variance (ANOVA) A parametric test of significance used to determine whether there is significant difference between or among two or more means at a selected probability level.

simulation observation Observation in which the researcher creates the situation to be observed and tells the subject what activities they are to engage in.

simultaneous replication Refers to when replication is done on a number of subjects with the same problem, at the same location, at the same time.

single-subject experimental designs Designs applied when the sample size is one; used to study the behavior change which an individual exhibits as a result of some intervention, or treatment.

single-variable designs A class of experimental designs involving only one independent variable (which is manipulated).

single variable rule An important principle of single-subject research which states that only one variable should be manipulated at a time.

skewed distribution A nonsymmetrical distribution in which there are more extreme scores at one end of the distribution than the other.

sociometric study A study that assesses and analyzes the interpersonal relationships within a group of individuals.

software Refers to the programs which give instructions to the computer concerning desired operations.

Solomon four-group design A true experimental design that involves random assignment of subjects to one of four groups; two groups are pretested, two are not; one of the pretested groups and one of the unpretested groups receive the experimental treatment, and all four groups are posttested.

Spearman rho A measure of correlation appropriate when the data for at least one of the variables are expressed as ranks; it produces a coefficient between .00 and ± 1.00.

specificity of variables Refers to the fact that a given study is conducted with a specific kind of subject, using specific measuring instruments, at a specific time, under a specific set of circumstances, factors that affect the generalizability of the results.

split-half reliability A type of reliability that is based on the internal consistency of a test and is estimated by dividing a test into two equivalent halves and correlating the scores on the two halves.

standard deviation The most stable measure of variability which takes into account each and every score in a distribution.

standard error of the mean The standard deviation of sample means which indicates by how much the sample means can be expected to differ if other samples from the same population are used.

standard error of measurement An estimate of how often one can expect errors of a given size in an individual's test score.

standard score A derived score that expresses how far a given raw score is from some reference point, typically the mean, in terms of standard deviation units.

stanines Standard scores that divide a distribution into nine parts.

static group comparison A pre-experimental design that involves at least two non-randomly formed groups; one receives a new, or unusual, treatment and both are posttested.

statistic A numerical index describing the behavior of a sample or samples.

statistical regression The tendency of subjects who score highest on a pretest to score lower on a posttest, and of subjects who score lowest on a pretest to score higher on a posttest.

statistical significance The conclusion that results are unlikely to have occurred by chance; the observed relationship or difference is probably a real one.

stratified sampling The process of selecting a sample in such a way that identified subgroups in the population are represented in the sample in the same proportion that they exist in the population or in equal proportion.

structured item A question and a list of alternative responses from which the responder selects; also referred to as a closed-form item.

subject variable A variable on which subjects in different groups in a study might differ, e.g., intelligence.

survey An attempt to collect data from members of a population in order to determine the current status of that population with respect to one or more variables.

systematic replication Refers to replication which follows direct replication, and which involves different investigators, behaviors, or settings.

systematic sampling Sampling in which individuals are selected from a list by taking every Kth name, where K equals the number of individuals on the list divided by the number of subjects desired for the sample.

***T* score** A standard score derived from a z score by multiplying the z score by 10 and adding 50.

***t* test for independent samples** A parametric test of significance used to determine whether there is a significant difference between the means of two independent samples at a selected probability level.

***t* test for nonindependent samples** A parametric test of significance used to determine whether there is a significant difference between the means of two matched, or nonindependent, samples at a selected probability level.

target population Refers to the population to which the researcher would ideally like to generalize results.

terminal A device for communicating with a computer which consists of a display screen and a keyboard.

test A means of measuring the knowledge, skill, feelings, intelligence, or aptitude of an individual or group.

testing A threat to experimental validity which refers to improved scores on a posttest which are a result of subjects having taken a pretest. (Also referred to as pretest-sensitization.)

test objectivity Refers to a situation in which an individual's score is the same, or essentially the same, regardless of who is doing the scoring.

test of significance A statistical test used to determine whether or not there is a significant difference between or among two or more means at a selected probability level.

test-retest reliability The degree to which scores on a test are consistent, or stable, over time.

time-series design A quasi-experimental design involving one group which is repeatedly pretested, exposed to an experimental treatment, and repeatedly posttested.

triangulation The use of multiple methods, data collection strategies, and/or data sources, in order to get a more complete picture and to cross-check information.

true categories Categories into which persons or objects naturally fall, independently of the research study.

Type I error The rejection by the researcher of a null hypothesis which is actually true.

Type II error The failure of a researcher to reject a null hypothesis which is really false.

unobtrusive measures Inanimate objects (such as school suspension lists) which can be observed in order to obtain desired information.

unstructured item A question giving the responder complete freedom of response.

validity The degree to which a test measures what it is intended to measure; a test is valid for a particular purpose for a particular group.

variable A concept that can assume any one of a range of values, e.g., intelligence, height, aptitude.

z score The most basic standard score that expresses how far a score is from a mean in terms of standard deviation.

Z score *See T* score.

APPENDIX C

Math Review

Reprinted by permission from *Statistics with a Sense of Humor: A Humorous Workbook and Guide to Study Skills* by Fred Pyrczak, Publisher, P.O. Box 39731, Los Angeles, CA 90039

Name: _____   Date: _____

Worksheet 1: MATH REVIEW: ORDER OF OPERATIONS

RIDDLE: Why did the bored man cut a hole in the carpet?

Directions: To find the answer to the riddle, write the answers to the problems on the lines.
The letter in the solution section beside the answer to the first problem is the first letter in the
answer to the riddle, the letter beside the answer to the second problem is the second letter,
and so on.

1. 5 x 10 + 6 x 2 = _____   10. 8/4 + (6)(0) = _____

2. 3 + 4 x 9 = _____   11. 169/(12 + 1) = _____

3. (9 + 28) x 6 = _____   12. (2 + 3 + 4)/3 = _____

4. 159 − 66 x 2 = _____   13. (2 + 18)/(9 − 5) = _____

5. 15 x 14 − 8 x 20 = _____   14. (1 + 5)(3) + (7)(2) = _____

6. 19 − 5 + 2 x 3 = _____   15. (9 + 9)(10 − 1)(2) = _____

7. 70 − 5 x 3 x 4 = _____   16. (15 − 4)(21/7)(63 − 59) =____

8. 6 + 8 x 1 x 5 = _____   17. (3)(1)(1) + (6/2)(9) = _____

9. 33/1 + 1 x 3 = _____

SOLUTION SECTION:

112(B)	62(T)	39(O)	10(H)	780(Y)	222(S)	3(O)
2(L)	63(A)	27(E)	177(Z)	186(X)	13(O)	5(R)
32(S)	50(E)	4,040(D)	20(T)	46(E)	30(W)	70(F)
132(O)	102(K)	36(F)	324(H)	187(B)	1(J)	48(I)

Write the answer to the riddle here, putting one letter on each line:

___ ___   ___ ___ ___   ___ ___ ___

___ ___ ___ ___ ___   ___ ___ ___ ___

Name: _____   Date: _____

Worksheet 2: MATH REVIEW: NEGATIVES

RIDDLE: What did the owner of the wreck of a car say about the noise it makes?

Directions: To find the answer to the riddle, write the answers to the problems on the lines. The word in the solution section beside the answer to the first problem is the first word in the answer to the riddle, the word beside the answer to the second problem is the second word, and so on.

1. $(-10)(-2)$ = _____   7. $19 + -3$ = _____   13. $(-15)(-33)$ = _____

2. $(-5)(47)$ = _____   8. $-28 + -28$ = _____   14. $(-11)(44)$ = _____

3. $(6)(-16)$ = _____   9. $-88 + 18$ = _____   15. $-2178/33$ = _____

4. $15/-3$ = _____   10. $15 - -15$ = _____   16. $188 + -99$ = _____

5. $-144/12$ = _____   11. $-29 - 14$ = _____   17. $-279 + -188$ = _____

6. $-169/-13$ = _____   12. $-30 - -29$ = _____   18. $-399 - 59$ = _____

SOLUTION SECTION:

-20(GARAGE)   235(TWO)   340(SKY)   20(THERE'S)   -96(ONE)

-235(ONLY)   96(ROAD)   -56(THAT)   -70(DOESN'T)   -1(SORT)

-458(HORN)   -467(THE)   5(IS)   -12(ON)   -5(THING)   13(MY)

-13(USE)   16(CAR)   12(BE)   30(MAKE)   0(FIX)   22(BUS)

495(OF)   -484(NOISE)   56(AN)   -66(AND)   70(TRANSPORTATION)

89(THAT'S)   -43(SOME)   -15(ALWAYS)   -59(HIGHWAY)

-495(MECHANIC)   66(BROKEN)   484(STRANDED)   467(FREEWAY)

Write the answer to the riddle here, putting one word on each line:

_____ _____ _____ _____ _____ _____

_____ _____ _____ _____ _____ _____

_____ _____ _____ _____ _____ _____

Name: _____   Date: _____

Worksheet 3: MATH REVIEW: ROUNDING

RIDDLE: What did the psychologist put on a sign in her office to make her patients pay?

Directions: To find the answer to the riddle, write the answers to the problems on the lines. The word in the solution beside the answer to the first problem is the first word in the answer to the riddle, the word beside the answer to the second problem is the second word, and so on.

Round as usual except when rounding off a number ending in a five (5). If the number immediately preceding a five is odd, round up. If the number immediately preceding a five is even, round down. Another way to state this principle is: "round to the nearest even number all numbers ending in 5." For example, 4.85 rounds to 4.8; 4.75 rounds to 4.8. Notice, however, that 4.851, which ends in a value greater than "5," rounds to 4.9.

1. Round 10.543 to the nearest hundredth: _____

2. Round 8.67 to the nearest tenth: _____

3. Round 8.4 to the nearest whole number: _____

4. Round 9.8452 to the nearest thousandth: _____

5. Round 15.839 to the nearest tenth: _____

6. Round 29.5 to the nearest whole number: _____

7. Round 15.86 to the nearest tenth: _____

8. Round 3.945 to the nearest hundredth: _____

9. Round 8.45 to the nearest tenth: _____

10. Round 10.555555 to the nearest hundredth: _____

SOLUTION SECTION:

29(CRAZY)   15.9(THE)   8.7(THE)   30(PAY)   3.95(AM)   8(AMNESIA)

10.56(ADVANCE) 8.4(IN) 8.5(ONLY) 3.94(PSYCHOLOGIST) 15.8(MUST)

9845(IS)   15.4(BILL)   9.85(HELPS)   9.846(NEVER)   10(LOVING)

9.845(PATIENTS) 9(LIFE) 10.54(ALL) 10.5(COUNSELING) 4(DISTURBED)

Write the answer to the riddle here, putting one word on each line:

_____   _____   _____   _____   _____   _____

_____   _____   _____   _____

Name: _____ Date: _____

Worksheet 4: MATH REVIEW: DECIMALS

RIDDLE: What did the bore do to help the party?

Directions: To find the answer to the riddle, write the answers to the problems on the lines. The letter in the solution section beside the answer to the first problem is the first letter in the answer to the riddle, the letter beside the answer to the second problem is the second letter, and so on.

    If an answer has more than two decimal places, round to two.

1. 0.02 multiplied by 1 = _____

2. 1.1 multiplied by 1.11 = _____

3. 5.999 multiplied by 0 = _____

4. 3.77 multiplied by 4.69 = _____

5. 12.4 divided into 169.38 = _____

6. 15.9 divided by 1 = _____

7. 12.1 plus 99.98 = _____

8. 3.11 plus 8.99 = _____

9. 18.3 subtracted from 25.46 = _____

10. 10.01 minus 8.873 = _____

SOLUTION SECTION:

1.22(E)	0.2(C)	0.14(X)	7.16(M)	71.6(D)	0(W)
6.00(K)	2.11(F)	0.02(H)	112.08(H)	101.19(P)
15.9(T)	1.59(B)	13.66(N)	1.21(J)	17.68(E)
1.366(G)	12.10(O)	0.177(R)	1.14(E)	1.111(S)

Write the answer to the riddle here, putting one letter on each line:

____ ____   ____ ____ ____ ____   ____ ____ ____ ____

Name: _____   Date: _____

Worksheet 5: MATH REVIEW: FRACTIONS AND DECIMALS

RIDDLE: Why should you respect the lily?

Directions: To find the answer to the riddle, write the answers to the problems on the lines. The word in the solution section beside the answer to the first problem is the first word in the answer to the riddle, the word beside the answer to the second problem is the second word, and so on. Express fractions in lowest terms.

1. 1/5 + 3/5 = _____   5. 2/3 x 2/3 = _____
2. 1/5 + 1/10 = _____   6. 2/5 x 4/7 = _____
3. 3/9 − 1/9 = _____   7. 2/9 divided by 1/9 = _____
4. 1 − 7/8 = _____   8. 5 divided into 2/3 = _____
9. What is the decimal equivalent of 1/2? = _____
10. What is the decimal equivalent of 3/4? = _____
11. What is the decimal equivalent of 2 and 2/3? = _____
12. What is the decimal equivalent of 2 and 3/4? = _____
13. What is the decimal equivalent of 2 and 1/10? = _____
14. What fraction corresponds to 0.2? = _____
15. What fraction corresponds to 0.11? = _____
16. What fraction corresponds to 0.555? = _____

SOLUTION SECTION:

4/5(NEVER)   2/5(SEE)   3/10(LOOK)   11/20(IS)   0.5(DAY)

0.55(FLOWERS)   2/3(FLORIST)   4/9(A)   2/9(DOWN)   2.1(LOOK)

1/5(DOWN)   11/100(ON)   2/35(CLEAN)   8/35(LILY)   1/8(ON)

2/81(HOPE)   2(BECAUSE)   2/15(ONE)   0.75(A)   2.67(LILY)

2.75(WILL)   111/200(YOU)   8/8(EASTER)   3 1/3(BEAUTIFUL)

Write the answer to the riddle here, putting one word on each line:

_____ _____ _____ _____ _____ _____ _____ _____

_____ _____ _____ _____ _____ _____ _____ _____

Name: _____   Date: _____

Worksheet 6: MATH REVIEW: ALGEBRAIC MANIPULATIONS

RIDDLE: When do actors and actresses get stage fright?

Directions: To find the answer to the riddle, write "T" for "true" or "F" for "false" on the line to the left of each statement. The word at the end of the first true statement is the first word in the answer to the riddle, the word at the end of the second true statement is the second word, and so on.

    All variables are distinct from one another; that is, no variable equals any other variable.

_____ 1. If $A = C/D$, then $C = (A)(D)$ (WHEN)

_____ 2. If $A = C/D$, then $D = C/A$ (THEY)

_____ 3. If $P/B = F$, then $P = F/B$ (GET)

_____ 4. If $X + Y = 10$, then $X = 10 - Y$ (SEE)

_____ 5. If $25 = A + B$, then $A = 25 - B$ (AN)

_____ 6. If $X + 25 = W$, then $X = W + 25$ (CURTAIN)

_____ 7. If $A = C - D$, then $D = C + A$ (APPLAUSE)

_____ 8. If $A - D = F$, then $A = F + D$ (EGG)

_____ 9. If $A = F - G - H$, then $F = A - G - H$ (STAGE)

_____ 10. If $(B)(C) = P$, then $B = P/C$ (OR)

_____ 11. If $Y = (B)(F)$, then $B = F/Y$ (SCRIPT)

_____ 12. If $X = (N)(B)(C)$, then $B = X/(N)(C)$ (A)

_____ 13. If $X + Y = B - C$, then $B = X + (Y)(C)$ (VOICE)

_____ 14 If $(B)(Y) = (X)(C)$, then $C = (B)(Y)/X$ (TOMATO)

Write in the answer to the riddle here, putting one word on each line:

_____   _____   _____   _____   _____   _____

_____   _____

CONCISE KEY

Worksheet 1: 1. 62, 2. 39, 3. 222, 4. 27, 5. 50, 6. 20, 7. 10, 8. 46, 9. 36, 10. 2, 11. 13, 12. 3, 13. 5, 14. 32, 15. 324, 16. 132, 17. 30   The answer to the riddle is: "To see the floor show."

Worksheet 2: 1. 20, 2. –235, 3. –96, 4. –5, 5. –12, 6. 13, 7. 16, 8. –56, 9. –70, 10. 30, 11. –43, 12. –1, 13. 495, 14. –484, 15. –66, 16. 89, 17. –467, 18. –458   The answer to the riddle is: "There's only one thing on my car that doesn't make some sort of noise and that's the horn."

Worksheet 3: 1. 10.54, 2. 8.7, 3. 8, 4. 9.845, 5. 15.8, 6. 30, 7. 15.9, 8. 3.94, 9. 8.4, 10. 10.56   The answer to the riddle is: "All the amnesia patients must pay the psychologist in advance."

Worksheet 4: 1. 0.02, 2. 1.22, 3. 0, 4. 17.68, 5. 13.66, 6. 15.9, 7. 112.08, 8. 12.10, 9. 7.16, 10. 1.14   The answer to the riddle is: "He went home."

Worksheet 5: 1. 4/5, 2. 3/10, 3. 2/9, 4. 1/8, 5. 4/9, 6. 8/35, 7. 2, 8. 2/15, 9. 0.5, 10. 0.75, 11. 2.67, 12. 2.75, 13. 2.1, 14. 1/5, 15. 11/100, 16. 111/200   The answer to the riddle is: "Never look down on a lily because one day a lily will look down on you."

Worksheet 6: 1. T, 2. T, 3. F, 4. T, 5. T, 6. F, 7. F, 8. T, 9. F, 10. T, 11. F, 12. T, 13. F, 14. T   The answer to the riddle is: "When they see an egg or a tomato."

STEP-BY-STEP KEY

WORKSHEET 1:

Order of operations: Do all work inside of parentheses first. Perform multiplication and division before performing addition and subtraction.

1. $5 \times 10 + 6 \times 2$
   $= 50 + 12$
   $= 62$

2. $3 + 4 \times 9$
   $= 3 + 36$
   $= 39$

3. $(9 + 28) \times 6$
   $= 37 \times 6$
   $= 222$

4. $159 - 66 \times 2$
   $= 159 - 132$
   $= 27$

5. $15 \times 14 - 8 \times 20$
   $= 210 - 160$
   $= 50$

6. $19 - 5 + 2 \times 3$
   $= 19 - 5 + 6$
   $= 14 + 6$
   $= 20$

7. $70 - 5 \times 3 \times 4$
   $= 70 - 15 \times 4$
   $= 70 - 60$
   $= 10$

8. $6 + 8 \times 1 \times 5$
   $= 6 + 8 \times 5$
   $= 6 + 40$
   $= 46$

9. $33/1 + 1 \times 3$
   $= 33 + 3$
   $= 36$

10. $8/4 + (6)(0)$
    $= 8/4 + 0$
    $= 2 + 0$
    $= 2$

11. $169/(12 + 1)$
    $= 169/13$
    $= 13$

12. $(2 + 3 + 4)/3$
    $= 9/3$
    $= 3$

13. $(2 + 18)/(9 - 5)$
    $= 20/4$
    $= 5$

14. $(1 + 5)(3) + (7)(2)$
    $= (6)(3) + (7)(2)$
    $= 18 + 14$
    $= 32$

15. $(9 + 9)(10 - 1)(2)$
    $= (18)(9)(2)$
    $= (162)(2)$
    $= 324$

16. $(15 - 4)(21/7)(63 - 59)$
    $= (11)(3)(4)$
    $= (33)(4)$
    $= 132$

17. $(3)(1)(1) + (6/2)(9)$
    $= 3 + (3)(9)$
    $= 3 + 27$
    $= 30$

WORKSHEET 2:

Rules for working with positive and negative numbers:

Multiplication:
When a negative number is multiplied by a positive number, the result is negative. When two negative numbers are multiplied, the result is positive.

1. $(-10)(-2) = 20$,   2. $(-5)(47) = -235$,   3. $(6)(-16) = -96$

Division:
When two numbers with the same sign are divided, the result is positive. When two numbers with opposite signs are divided, the result is negative.

4. $15/-3 = -5$,   5. $-144/12 = -12$,   6. $-169/-13 = 13$

Addition:
When numbers all have the same sign, add as usual. When numbers have different signs, first add all positive numbers together, then add all negative numbers together, and then subtract the negative sum from the positive sum.

7. $19 + -3 = 16$,   8. $-28 + -28 = -56$,   9. $-88 + 18 = -70$

Subtraction:
When subtracting negative numbers, change the sign of the number being subtracted and then add:

10. $15 - -15 = 30$,   11. $-29 - 14 = -43$,   12. $-30 - -29 = -1$

For items 13 through 18, follow the rules given above.

13. 495,   14. −484,   15. −66,   16. 89,   17. −467,   18. −458

WORKSHEET 3:

See the directions on Worksheet 3 for rules on rounding numbers that end in five (5).

1. Read 10.543 as 10.5(tenth's)4(hundredth's)3(thousandth's); therefore, to the nearest hundredth, 10.543 rounds to 10.54.

2. Read 8.67 as 8.6(tenth's)7(hundredth's); therefore, to the nearest tenth, 8.67 rounds to 8.7.

3. Read 8.4 as 8(whole number, one's place).4(tenth's); therefore, to the nearest whole number, 8.4 rounds to 8.

4. Read 9.8452 as 9.8(tenth's)4(hundredth's)5(thousandth's)2(ten thousandth's); therefore, to the nearest thousandth, 9.8452 rounds to 9.845.

5. 15.839, to the nearest tenth, rounds to 15.8.

6. Because 29.5 ends in 5, round to the nearest even number, which is 30.

7. 15.86 rounds to 15.9.

8. Because 3.945 ends in 5, round to the nearest even number, which is 3.94. (Notice that the "4" in the hundredth's place is even.)

9. Because 8.45 ends in 5, round to the nearest even number, which is 8.4. (Notice that the "4" in the tenth's place is even.)

10. Beyond the hundredth's place are four 5's. Therefore, at the point at which you are rounding, the number does not end in "5"; it ends in "5555," which is greater than 5. Therefore, 10.555555, to the nearest hundredth, rounds to 10.56.

WORKSHEET 4:

1. When multiplying, the answer has the total number of decimal places as the total number in the two multipliers. Since 0.02 x 1 has a total of two digits to the right of the decimal places, the answer is 0.02, which also has two digits to the right.

2. 1.1 x 1.11 has three digits to the right; therefore, the answer is 1.221, which rounds to 1.22.

3. Any number multiplied by zero equals zero.

4. (See explanation for item 1.) 3.77 x 4.69 = 17.6813 (four decimal places), which rounds to 17.68.

5. When dividing with a calculator, enter the numbers as shown. When dividing by hand, first move the decimal place in the divisor to the far right. (In this case, change 12.1 to 121.) Then, move the decimal place in 169.38 the same number of places to the right, changing 169.38 to 1693.8. Then divide as usual. The answer is 13.660 = 13.66.

6. (See explanation for item 5. Notice the difference between "divided into" and "divided by." This wording usually is not used in textbooks, but your instructor may use it in lectures.) The answer is 15.9. (Notice that division by one has no effect.)

7. Before adding, line up the decimal places one above the other and then add.

$$\begin{array}{r} 12.1 \\ +99.98 \\ \hline 112.08 \end{array}$$

8. (See explanation for item 7.) The answer is 12.10.

9. Before subtracting, line up the decimal places one above the other and then subtract.

$$\begin{array}{r} 25.46 \\ -18.3 \\ \hline 7.16 \end{array}$$

10. (See explanation for number 9. Notice the difference between "subtracted from" and "minus.")

$$\begin{array}{r} 10.01 \\ -8.873 \\ \hline 1.137 \end{array}$$, which rounds to 1.14

WORKSHEET 5:

(General note: For most beginning students, it is best to convert fractions to their decimal equivalents as soon as permitted under the rules of mathematics. For example, to convert $\frac{1}{5}$, divide 1 by 5, which yields 0.2. This is desirable since most calculators will not allow you to operate directly on fractions. In addition, it is conventional to report statistics with their decimal equivalents for fractional parts.

    Knowledge of fractions is important for understanding the meaning of certain statistics and for understanding their derivations, however.)

1. When adding fractions with a common denominator (same denominator), add the numerators and retain the common denominator. Thus, $\frac{1}{5} + \frac{3}{5} = \frac{4}{5}$.

2. When adding fractions with unlike denominators, first convert so that they both have the same denominator. In this case, by multiplying both the numerator and denominator of $\frac{1}{5}$ by 2, the equivalent fraction of $\frac{2}{10}$ is obtained. Then follow the instructions for item 1. Thus, $\frac{2}{10} + \frac{1}{10} = \frac{3}{10}$.

3. When subtracting fractions with a common denominator, subtract the numerators and retain the common denominator. Thus, $\frac{3}{9} - \frac{1}{9} = \frac{2}{9}$.

4. When subtracting a fraction from a whole number, first convert the whole number to a fractional equivalent with the same denominator. In this case, $1 = \frac{8}{8}$. Thus, $\frac{8}{8} - \frac{7}{8} = \frac{1}{8}$.

5. When multiplying fractions, multiply the numerators, then multiply the denominators. For example, $\frac{2}{3} \times \frac{2}{3} = \frac{4}{9}$.

6. (See the explanation for item number 5.) The answer is $\frac{8}{35}$.

7. To divide one fraction by another, invert the divisor (i.e., $\frac{1}{9}$ becomes $\frac{9}{1}$). Then multiply: $\frac{2}{9} \times \frac{9}{1} = \frac{18}{9}$. To simplify when the numerator is evenly divisible by the denominator, divide the denominator into the numerator: 18 divided by 9 = 2, which is the answer.

8. (See the explanation for item 7.) Note the difference in wording of items 7 and 8. In this case, 5 is the divisor; when inverted, it becomes $\frac{1}{5}$. Thus, $\frac{2}{3} \times \frac{1}{5} = \frac{2}{15}$.

9. To find the decimal equivalent of a fraction, divide the numerator by the denominator. In this case, divide 1 by 2, which yields an answer of 0.5.

10. (See the explanation for item 9.) The answer is 0.75.

11. To find the decimal equivalent of a mixed number (i.e., a whole number plus a fractional part), retain the whole number and convert the fractional part as described in the explanation for item 9. In this case, 2 and $\frac{2}{3}$ becomes 2 and .666, which rounds to 2.67.

12. (See the explanation for item 11.) The answer is 2.75.

13. (See the explanation for item 11.) The answer is 2.1.

14. Note that 0.2 is read as "two tenths." Therefore, it is equivalent to $\frac{2}{10}$. Since both the numerator and denominator are evenly divisible by 2, divide both by 2, which yields $\frac{1}{5}$, which is the answer expressed in lowest terms.

15. Note that 0.11 is read as "eleven one hundredths." Therefore, the answer is expressed as $\frac{11}{100}$.

16. Note that 0.555 is read as "five hundred fifty-five one thousandths." Therefore, it is equivalent to $\frac{555}{1000}$. Since 5 will divide evenly into both the numerator and denominator, simplify by division. This gives an answer of $\frac{111}{200}$.

WORKSHEET 6:

1. If $A = \frac{C}{D}$, then $C = (A)(D)$

   $A = \frac{C}{D}$

   $\frac{C}{D} = A$

   $(\frac{C}{D})(D) = (A)(D)$

   $C = (A)(D)$

   Therefore, the statement is true.

2. If $A = \frac{C}{D}$, then $D = \frac{C}{A}$

   $A = \frac{C}{D}$

   $(A)(D) = (\frac{C}{D})(D)$

   $(A)(D) = C$

   $\frac{(A)(D)}{A} = \frac{C}{A}$

   $D = \frac{C}{A}$

   Therefore, the statement is true.

3. If $\frac{P}{B} = F$, then $P = \frac{F}{B}$

   $\frac{P}{B} = F$

   $(\frac{P}{B})(B) = (F)(B)$

   $P = (F)(B)$

   Therefore, the statement is false.

4. If $X + Y = 10$, then $X = 10 - Y$

   $X + Y = 10$

   $X + Y - Y = 10 - Y$

   $X = 10 - Y$

   Therefore, the statement is true.

5. If $25 = A + B$, then $A = 25 - B$

   $25 = A + B$

   $A + B = 25$

   $A + B - B = 25 - B$

   $A = 25 - B$

   Therefore, the statement is true.

6. If $X + 25 = W$, then $X = W + 25$

   $X + 25 = W$

   $X + 25 - 25 = W - 25$

   $X = W - 25$

   Therefore, the statement is false.

7. If $A = C - D$, then $D = C + A$

   $A = C - D$

   $A + D = C - D + D$

   $A + D = C$

   $A + D - A = C - A$

   $D = C - A$

   Therefore, the statement is false.

8. If $A - D = F$, then $A = F + D$

   $A - D = F$

   $A - D + D = F + D$

   $A = F + D$

   Therefore, the statement is true.

9. If $A = F - G - H$, then
   $F = A - G - H$

   $A = F - G - H$

   $F - G - H = A$

   $F - G - H + G = A + G$

   $F - H = A + G$

   $F - H + H = A + G + H$

   $F = A + G + H$

   Therefore, the statement is false.

10. If $(B)(C) = P$, then $B = \frac{P}{C}$

    $(B)(C) = P$

    $\frac{(B)(C)}{C} = \frac{P}{C}$

    $B = \frac{P}{C}$

    Therefore, the statement is true.

11. If $Y = (B)(F)$, then $B = \frac{F}{Y}$

$Y = (B)(F)$

$(B)(F) = Y$

$\frac{(B)(F)}{F} = \frac{Y}{F}$

$B = \frac{Y}{F}$

Therefore, the statement is false.

12. If $X = (N)(B)(C)$, then $B = \frac{X}{(N)(C)}$

$X = (N)(B)(C)$

$(N)(B)(C) = X$

$\frac{(N)(B)(C)}{(N)(C)} = \frac{X}{(N)(C)}$

$B = \frac{X}{(N)(C)}$

Therefore, the statement is true.

13. If $X + Y = B - C$, then $B = X + (Y)(C)$

$X + Y = B - C$

$B - C = X + Y$

$B - C + C = X + Y + C$

$B = X + Y + C$

Therefore, the statement is false.

14. If $(B)(Y) = (X)(C)$, then $C = \frac{(B)(Y)}{X}$

$(B)(Y) = (X)(C)$

$(X)(C) = (B)(Y)$

$\frac{(X)(C)}{X} = \frac{(B)(Y)}{X}$

$C = \frac{(B)(Y)}{X}$

Therefore, the statement is true.

A P P E N D I X   D

Suggested Responses

Self-Test for Task 1-A   PART ONE

Motivational Effects on Test Scores of Elementary Students

The Problem The purpose of this study was to determine the effect of experimentally manipulated motivational conditions on elementary students' mathematical scores.

The Procedures Pairs of normal, heterogeneous classes at each grade level (3, 4, 6, 7 and 8) from each of 3 public schools were randomly chosen to participate; classes were selected for experimental and control conditions by a flip of a coin (i.e., one class of each pair became an experimental group and the other a control group). Form 7 of the Mathematics Concepts subtest of the Iowa Basic Skills (ITBS) test was the measuring instrument. Prior to taking the test, all students were given the instructions from the ITBS test manual. Experimental students were also read a brief motivational script on the importance of doing well. All participating teachers were trained to administer the test, and experimental teachers were given additional training regarding the script (e.g., read it exactly as it is written).

The Method of Analysis An analysis of variance was run (on test scores) to test the effects of the experimental and normal (control) conditions (as well as several other variables).

The Major Conclusion Students asked to try especially hard did considerably better than those who were given the usual standardized test instructions only.

Self-Test for Task 1-B

Type: Experimental

Reasons: A cause-effect relationship was investigated. The independent variable (cause), type of test instructions (motivational instructions versus usual instructions only), was manipulated. The researchers determined which students received motivational instructions and which students did not. The students' performance on the ITBS Mathematics Concepts subtest (the dependent variable, the effect) was compared.

Self-Test for Task 9   **PART NINE**

Effects of Using an Instructional Game on Motivation and Performance

GENERAL EVALUATION CRITERIA

Introduction

Problem   CODE

A statement? . . . .   Y
    Paragraph (//)7, sentence (S)1[1]
Researchable? . . . .   Y
Background information? . . . .   Y
    e.g. //2
Significance discussed? . . . .   Y
    e.g., //1
Variables and relationships discussed? . . . .   Y
Definitions? . . . .   Y
    e.g., //7, S3

Review of Related Literature
Comprehensive? . . . .   ?/X
    Appears to be
References relevant? . . . .   Y
Sources primary? . . . .   Y
Critical analysis? . . . .   Y
    e.g., //6
Well organized? . . . .   Y
Summary? . . . .   N
Rationale for hypotheses? . . . .   N

Hypotheses
Questions or hypotheses? . . . .   Y
    //7, S6 & 7
Expected differences stated? . . . .   Y
Variables defined? . . . .   Y
Testable? . . . .   Y

---

[1] //7 refers to paragraph 7 of the introduction section of the article. The introduction section ends where Method begins.

Method

Subjects CODE

Population described? . . . . Y&N
    Very briefly

Sample selection method described? . . . . NA

Selection method "good"? . . . . NA

Avoidance of volunteers? . . . . ?/X
    Hard to say; see //1, S2

Sample described? . . . . Y&N
    Size, yes; characteristics, no

Minimum sizes? . . . . Y
    $n^1 = 37$; $n^2 = 38$

Instruments

Rationale for selection? . . . . N

Instrument described? . . . . Y
    //6 & 7

Appropriate? . . . . Y

Evidence that it is appropriate for sample? . . . . N

Validity discussed? . . . . N

Reliability discussed? . . . . Y
    //6 & 7

Subtest reliabilities? . . . . Y
    //6

Procedures for development described? . . . . N
    Performance posttest not described

Administration, scoring, and interpretation procedures described? . . . . N

Design and Procedure

Design appropriate? . . . . Y

Procedures sufficiently detailed? . . . . Y

Pilot study described? . . . . NA

Control procedures described? . . . . Y
    e.g., //9

Confounding variables discussed? . . . . Y
    e.g., //10, S2

Results

Appropriate descriptive statistics? . . . . Y
    Table 1

Probability level specified in advance? . . . . Y
    e.g., //1

Parametric assumptions not violated? . . . . Y

Tests of significance appropriate? . . . . Y or ?/X

Every hypothesis tested? . . . . Y

Appropriate degrees of freedom? . . . . Y or ?/X

Results clearly presented? . . . . Y

Tables and figures well organized? . . . . Y

Data in each table and figure described? . . . . Y

Discussion (Conclusions and Recommendations)

	CODE
Results discussed in terms of hypothesis?	Y
Results discussed in terms of previous research?	Y
e.g., //3	
Generalizations consistent with results?	Y
e.g., //1	
Effects of uncontrolled variables discussed?	Y
e.g., //2	
Implications discussed?	Y
e.g., //7	
Recommendations for action?	Y
e.g., //8	
Suggestions based on practical significance?	Y
Effect sizes were presented under Results, //2, S4 & 5	
Recommendations for research?	Y
e.g., //9	

Abstract (or Summary)

Problem restated?	Y
Subjects and instruments described?	Y&N
Subjects briefly; instruments indirectly	
Design identified?	Y
Not named, but described	
Procedures?	Y
Results and conclusions?	Y

METHOD-SPECIFIC EVALUATION CRITERIA

Design used:
Basically a posttest-only control group design. The independent variable was type of practice.

$$R \qquad X_1 0 \qquad X_1 = \text{game}$$

$$R \qquad X_2 0 \qquad X_2 = \text{worksheet}$$

$$0 = \text{Motivation scale performance posttest}$$

Because of the inclusion of a second, unmanipulated independent variable, completion versus noncompletion of reading assignment, the design was a 2 x 2 factorial design, based on a posttest-only control group design.

Design appropriate?	Y
Design selection rationale?	N
Invalidity discussed?	N
But mortality was not a problem	
Group formation described?	Y
Random assignment	
Groups formed in same way?	Y
Groups randomly formed?	Y

	CODE
Treatments randomly assigned?	?/X
Extraneous variables described?	Y
e.g., //6, S3 – 5	
Groups equated?	N
Reactive arrangements controlled for?	N
But discussed, under Discussion, //2, S3 – 6	

AUTHOR INDEX